NATURE ᴛʀᴜꜱᴛ

Environmental law has failed us all. As ecosystems collapse across the globe and the climate crisis intensifies, environmental agencies worldwide use their authority to permit the very harm that they are supposed to prevent. Growing numbers of citizens now realize they must act before it is too late. This book exposes what is wrong with environmental law and offers transformational change based on the public trust doctrine. An ancient and enduring principle, the trust doctrine asserts public property rights to crucial resources. Its core logic compels government, as trustee, to protect natural inheritance such as air and water for all humanity. Propelled by populist impulses and democratic imperatives, the public trust surfaces at epic times in history as a manifest human right. But until now it has lacked the precision necessary for citizens, government employees, legislators, and judges to fully safeguard the natural resources we rely on for survival and prosperity. The Nature's Trust approach empowers citizens worldwide to protect their inalienable ecological rights for generations to come.

Mary Christina Wood is the Philip H. Knight Professor of Law and Faculty Director of the Environmental and Natural Resources Law Center at the University of Oregon School of Law. She has taught law for more than twenty years, specializing in property law, environmental law, and federal Indian law. She founded the school's top-ranked Environmental and Natural Resources Law Program and initiated several of the program's interdisciplinary research projects, including the Native Environmental Sovereignty Project and the Food Resiliency Project. She is the coauthor of a textbook on natural resources law and one on public trust law. She has also authored many articles and book chapters on the federal Indian trust obligation, wildlife law, and climate crisis.

Nature's Trust

ENVIRONMENTAL LAW FOR A
NEW ECOLOGICAL AGE

MARY CHRISTINA WOOD
University of Oregon School of Law

CAMBRIDGE
UNIVERSITY PRESS

CAMBRIDGE
UNIVERSITY PRESS

32 Avenue of the Americas, New York, NY 10013-2473, USA

Cambridge University Press is part of the University of Cambridge.

It furthers the University's mission by disseminating knowledge in the pursuit of education, learning, and research at the highest international levels of excellence.

www.cambridge.org
Information on this title: www.cambridge.org/9780521144117

First published 2014

Printed in the United States of America

A catalog record for this publication is available from the British Library.

Library of Congress Cataloging in Publication data
Wood, Mary Christina.
Nature's Trust : Environmental Law for a New Ecological Age / Mary Christina Wood, University of Oregon School of Law.
    pages cm
Includes bibliographical references and index.
ISBN 978-0-521-19513-3 (hardback) – ISBN 978-0-521-14411-7 (pbk.)
1. Environmental law – United States.   2. Conservation of natural resources – Law and legislation – United States.   3. Environmental law – Philosophy.   I. Title.
KF3775.W589   2013
344.7304′6–dc23   2013014274

ISBN 978-0-521-19513-3 Hardback
ISBN 978-0-521-14411-7 Paperback

*To Sage, Cam, and Nick
and all children of this world*

Contents

Preface

Drawn home over thousands of miles, by instinct honed over thousands of years, the fish circled together to shape loose sands into nests where they would lay their eggs. Clouds hung above them, darkly bruised with shades of winter. Hundreds of fins sliced through the water's surface, leaving soft riffles in the shallows. They were tired, but worked tirelessly, in the natal waters where they were born.

Within a few days these chum salmon would be corpses scattered along the tidelands, their descendants safely nestled in the ancient river cobble of the Columbia River. Their only legacy would be a continuous strand of life – here, and at no other place on Earth. These fish shunned other spawning grounds for one simple reason: they were not born there. What more perfect deed could they have to this land?[1]

I grew up watching these salmon at a place we called Wood's Landing, located on the Columbia River in the state of Washington. This spot had existed as an Indian fishing camp when Lewis and Clark floated by in dugout canoes on November 5, 1805. Nature thrived plentifully during that time. Salmon crowded by the hundreds into small creeks along the river to spawn. Meadows, wetlands, and red cedar groves provided rich cover for migratory birds and deer, which supplemented the Indians' fish diet. Squaw grasses gave sturdy raw material for nets and baskets. Stringy bark from cedar trees provided fiber for canoes, clothing, and huts. Camas root and thimbleberries proliferated.

Early in my childhood, I became aware that tribal life ran ancient in the region and that the non-Indians were newcomers. The Indian fishermen had left a clear imprint of their life at Wood's Landing. The high waters that work away at the riverbank every spring occasionally exposed stone "sinkers" that tribal people chiseled and used to weigh down fishing nets to capture the salmon coming up the stream. Years later, as I embarked on a career teaching environmental law, I held the memory of those ancient anchors embedded in the sediments at the place where I grew up.

As I began to focus my legal scholarship on Indian management of salmon, I realized that these sinkers gave clues to a remarkable story of environmental management. Tribes of the Columbia River perfected a system of harvest regulation that allowed return of 10 million–16 million fish a year to the basin. Oral history recounts that, even during times of food scarcity, Indian leaders exercised restraint so as not to diminish the species' capacity to support future runs. Under native stewardship, and even with concentrated human use, these populations were sustained for 10,000 years. Western environmental management fails to fathom such a time frame.

I began to think of tribal fishery management, having endured since time immemorial, as resembling a trust – guided by the interests of beneficiaries positioned several generations into the future. In Western property law, a trust bifurcates ownership between a trustee and a beneficiary. The trustee holds legal ownership and must manage the assets strictly for the advantage of the beneficiaries, who hold beneficial ownership. While the tribes would not have described their management in exact trust terminology, the old Indian proverb, "We do not inherit the Earth from our ancestors; we borrow it from our children," resonates as a trust in the deepest sense, both legally and culturally. To sustain a natural trust over many millennia, as the tribes of the Columbia River Basin did, requires extraordinary fiduciary stewardship. The "environmental law" emerging from tribal governance integrated the laws handed down by Nature itself.

But that is not the environmental law followed by industrialized society. Natural resources management changed radically when new sovereigns took control of the land. In the mid-1800s, the federal government forced the Columbia River tribes to relinquish most of their territory through treaties (though the tribes retained perpetual fishing rights on the lands they ceded). This huge property transfer positioned the newly created states of Washington and Oregon to control the salmon harvest. As novice governments, the states had no sovereign experience managing a natural resource. Presuming that the huge salmon runs remained inexhaustible, they allowed gluttonous harvest of the fishery by non-Indian commercial fishermen to serve a growing and insatiable global food market. Over just a few decades, these state trustees siphoned the abundance right out of the great salmon trust.

On the heels of this loss came a surge of industrialization and urbanization across the entire Pacific Northwest, affecting virtually every watershed used by salmon. Timber companies razed forests, pulp and paper mills polluted rivers, developers tore up wetlands, cities dumped sewage and toxins into waterways, and the federal government embarked on a dam-building frenzy, installing hydro facilities that posed death traps for salmon trying to migrate through the Columbia and Snake rivers. Those dams today kill more than 90 percent of the juveniles of some species.[2]

By 1995, the salmon's ecosystem had unraveled. The National Marine Fisheries Service declared that year, "Few examples of naturally functioning aquatic systems now remain in the Pacific Northwest."[3] Columbia River wild salmon runs dropped to about 2 percent of their historic levels. Some species passed into extinction. Tattered ecosystems imperiled coastal salmon stocks from California to Canada.

With the salmon trust bankrupt, the "interest" from this natural asset, as measured in fish harvest, diminished to nearly zero. In 1994, not enough salmon returned to the Columbia River to supply the tribal longhouses for their First Salmon feasts held in the spring to express reverence to the Creator for giving food to the people.[4] The crisis stood as a poignant illustration of an inescapable fact: the colonial trustees upon this land had devastated in a mere century what the native trustees had managed with fiduciary care for millennia.

The breathtaking failure could not be blamed on any lack of environmental law. Plenty of statutes exist, along with even more regulations implementing them. Untold hours and millions of dollars have been spent on legal processes under the Endangered Species Act (ESA) in the Columbia River Basin. Yet, even after two decades, litigation to save the salmon still drags on in the courts. To this day, environmental law has forced little improvement of basin conditions. The magnificent salmon, with their survival history of 5 million years on this planet, still swim in lethal waters toward extinction.

As a child growing up in the 1960s and 1970s, I witnessed part of this natural destruction from the banks of the Columbia River. My great-grandfather had purchased Wood's Landing in 1889 from a homesteader and had used the land for a small prune orchard. Until my middle-teen years, the area for many miles to the east and north still existed as farmland, as it had for the previous hundred years. For many generations, the fields, forests, and wetlands there had enticed children to explore, and I was no exception.

But children today will not have that opportunity, or anything close to it. Everything changed within a mere decade's time. In 1982, corporations constructed the enormous I-205 bridge over the Columbia River. It reaches like a dinosaur stretching over the river as if to devour the other side. Even before the ink dried on the final engineering plans for the bridge, land speculators from California bought all the farmland they could get their hands on, anticipating hordes of commuters traveling daily from Portland, Oregon, to new homes in Southwest Washington. Within only a few years, thousands of acres of farmland in Clark County, Washington, became wall-to-wall suburbia. The land speculators' quick fortunes bankrupted the county's natural assets.

Developers tore up cherished farms with abandon. Four-lane roads razed through fields even as vegetables pushed up through the soil. Bulldozers operated from dawn to dusk demolishing wetlands, creeks, forests, springs – anything that stood in the way of a developer's asphalt kingdom. Ripping up trees, tearing into soils, and bludgeoning delicate riparian areas, the giant machinery left no reminder of the ancient civilization that once existed there. McMansions sprouted everywhere, as far as the eye could see, separated only by strip malls pimpled with huge box stores and fast-food joints. Upstream from Wood's Landing, the lumber mill ran at peak capacity, spewing toxic air emissions that often hung stagnant over the entire area. Pollution froth floated across the salmon spawning grounds at Wood's Landing, all day, every day. This environmental annihilation continued incessantly, all with the blessing of federal, state, and local agencies. Permits issued from these jurisdictions like rows of falling dominoes.

In the mid-1990s, my academic attention inevitably turned to the regulatory system and its perpetual failures. The story of environmental ruin in the Columbia Basin was being repeated across the United States and in many other countries as well. Environmental laws had achieved some success. But the industrial machine moves fast, and its swath of wreckage far exceeds the isolated instances of protection. Across nearly all fronts of ecological assault, environmental law has failed in its basic purpose to safeguard natural resources.

The situation has worsened dramatically over the last two decades. Today's environmental losses boggle the mind and sicken the soul – everything from fisheries collapse to wetlands destruction, deforestation, pesticide contamination, ozone depletion, water pollution, air pollution, endangered species, overgrazing, nuclear waste disposal, ocean acidification, biodiversity crisis, and climate change. Much of this damage stays permanent. The agencies implementing the environmental laws have become perpetrators of legalized destruction, using permit provisions contained in nearly every statute to subvert the purposes Congress and state legislatures intended.

Serious endemic flaws exist across the system as a whole. The same forces that caused the Forest Service to cut nearly all of the public's ancient forest in the Pacific Northwest also prompted the U.S. Environmental Protection Agency to allow unacceptable levels of arsenic in drinking water. The same dynamics that moved city governments to issue permits for endless outbreaks of suburban sprawl caused water agencies to overappropriate rivers until many ran dry. The same pressures that drove the Corps of Engineers to allow wetlands destruction across the United States prompted the U.S. Fish and Wildlife Service to approve projects that pushed endangered species ever closer to extinction. These same forces now keep the U.S. Environmental Protection Agency from taking bold action to regulate carbon dioxide pollution as our planet heats to dangerous levels. Most worrisome, these dynamics persist at all levels of government. And they do not disappear with changes in political administrations – although some administrations produce far worse policy than others.

We ignore the colossal failures of environmental agencies at our peril. Over just the last few decades, government has engaged in a reckless gamble with ecology.

As James Gustave Speth wrote in his book A *Bridge at the Edge of the World*, if we continue business as usual, the world "won't be fit to live in" by mid-century.[5] *Won't be fit to live in.* The import of these words finds substantiation in countless scientific reports, as the introduction details. Time and opportunity now slip away too rapidly for incremental strategies to work. Scientists warn that only a narrow window of opportunity remains in which to address climate emergency and other environmental calamities before irrevocable tipping points forever change our planet.

Given this urgency, not enough time exists to rewrite all of environmental law. And we don't have to. The problem rarely resides in the individual laws themselves but rather in the paradigm that frames those laws. We can pass any new environmental law we want, no matter what it says, if it stays bounded by the frame in which we've operated for the last four decades, government will continue to impoverish natural resources until our society can no longer sustain itself. Environmental statutes passed to protect resources can fulfill their purpose only if the agencies act on behalf of the public they constitutionally serve. Environmental statutes do not declare a purpose of allowing rampant resource destruction, but we know from experience that they will accomplish precisely that result if the agencies stay captive to the industries they are supposed to regulate.

The political milieu in which government administers its laws matters greatly. The direction in which government chooses to devote its energy depends on whether leaders pursue the politics of scarcity or the politics of abundance. Politics of scarcity focus on creating legal mechanisms to allocate the benefits of an ever-declining natural resource. In other words, officials use the power of the state primarily to divide the last crumbs (allocating those to the most politically powerful individuals). These politics have led society to this perilous point in time. The politics of abundance, by contrast, reach persistently and undauntingly toward protecting and building natural wealth.

Management of the Columbia River salmon exemplifies the difference. When fish runs began to collapse in the late 1800s, the politics of scarcity took hold and have dominated environmental policy in the basin ever since. In the 1970s, the law focused on dividing the harvest of a fishery in freefall decline; ugly brawls broke out between fishermen locked in competition over the last fish. When regulation under the Endangered Species Act commenced in the early 1990s, instead of truly trying to rebuild the runs as the law requires, federal officials busied themselves with figuring how much death they could sanction without sending the species over the edge into extinction. Finding that magic line – between not enough death and too much death, not enough destruction and too much destruction, not enough risk and too much risk – describes the work of most environmental agencies today operating under the politics of scarcity.

Politics of scarcity inexorably hover over societies that sanctify unlimited indulgence. Simply put, these politics arise out of the difficulty of confronting greed. Developers, industrialists, and huge corporations exert relentless pressure on governmental officials to allow unconscionable exploit of natural resources that bring them enormous profit at the expense of the community. Their pressure, constantly applied, erodes the will on the part of state and federal officials to carry out the protective mandates of the law. Often it does not matter much what the law says; the politics will circumvent it. Every devastated watershed, every new mile of sprawl, every new clear cut, every new oil pipeline, and every blasted mountaintop reflects excessive indulgence condoned by the politics of scarcity.

Politics of abundance, by contrast, arise from an ethic of measured restraint. These politics reject unnecessary indulgence bound to satisfy only a few at grave expense to present and future generations. They focus not on dividing an ever-diminishing yield but on rebuilding a base of natural capital that will produce an increasing – and ultimately sustainable – yield in the future. Tribal leaders exercised politics of abundance to keep steady the fish runs in the Columbia River Basin for 10,000 years.[6] In today's world, the politics of abundance must begin with the denial of destructive permits and then turn to mammoth ecological restoration on all fronts.

Legal systems can support either the politics of scarcity or the politics of abundance, but Earth's natural systems can support only the latter. The politics of scarcity will manage human species survival in much the same way as it manages salmon survival – down to extinction. As Speth makes clear, society now teeters at the edge of an abyss. If we wish to endure on this planet, we must invoke all of the creativity and skill we can to build a "bridge across the abyss" to a new world. It will not happen on its own. We have to build it.

New paradigms plank the footings for such a bridge. Fortunately, many excellent books offer creative, well-grounded paradigm shifts in the areas of economics, business, industrial design, architecture, politics, religion, consumption, education, and culture. None, however, offer transformative shifts in environmental law. We simply cannot hope for ecological security if environmental agencies keep issuing permits for destruction as they have for the last forty years.

This book builds on an ancient and extant legal tradition to offer a legal paradigm called Nature's Trust, intended to catalyze a transformation of environmental law. The framework draws from principles of environmental obligation encompassed within the public trust doctrine. Dating back to Roman law, this doctrine stands as a pillar of ordered civilization to compel sovereign stewardship of crucial natural wealth. It characterizes the ecological endowment as a trust for present and future generations of citizens. Government, deriving its authority from the people as a whole, must act as a fiduciary to protect the natural resources held in trust from damage, as well as from dangerous privatization. Judicial decisions dating from the beginning of the United States voice this trust, and its principles manifest in the law of many other countries as well.

This venerable doctrine has been largely overlooked because of the proliferation of statutes across the legal landscape. Passed in the 1970s, these laws produced thousands of implementing regulations. Similarly to how an invasive plant species chokes out and conceals the presence of native vegetation, so these statutes and regulations obfuscate the public trust. Most agency regulators have never heard of the public trust and remain unaware of their fiduciary obligations to protect public ecological assets. Nevertheless, lawyers, citizens, judges, and regulators have commenced to unearth these principles and apply them to environmental controversies, because these principles *still exist in the law*. Embodying the politics of abundance, trust principles announce visionary precepts waiting at the periphery of an old, destructive regime.

People most vested in the current system will surely criticize trust aspirations as politically naïve, unrealistic, or overly optimistic. Has any true paradigm shift in history ever escaped such disparagement? Speth wisely asserts that if deep proposals seem "impractical, or politically naïve," or "radical or far-fetched" today, then wait until tomorrow. He writes, "In general, the world of practical affairs does not truly appreciate how much negative change is coming at us, nor how fast.... [W]e must look beyond the world of practical affairs to those who are thinking difficult and unconventional thoughts and proposing transformative change."[7]

In suggesting deep change for environmental law, this book roundly criticizes the present system. For anyone engrossed in perpetuating this system, the first part of the book may prove uncomfortable reading. For a law professor who has spent more than twenty years teaching this field, I assure you, it makes uncomfortable writing. My advice is to read on – but with hope and vision, not guilt or blame. We can only forge a promising and safe path if we first acknowledge the erratic dysfunction of environmental law, pinpoint where the legal sinkholes lie, and address a daunting set of problems with visionary aim and sincere purpose.

We simply cannot hope to turn the system around in time without the full commitment, participation, and (most of all) courage of the people working in the thousands of governmental agencies, legislatures, and judicial systems around the world. They sit as the present trustees of Earth's endowment, and, in the end, much of the needed transformation rests on their shoulders because they hold the levers of government. We need them to become the heroes of our day, and in large part, this book is written for them. But it likewise calls to the 7 billion beneficiaries of Nature's Trust presently living on Earth who depend on honest fiduciary management of natural resources by their governments. These beneficiaries hold the power of the people to exert timeless, populist rights against oppressive parties that pursue a perilous agenda of greed. And, for the countless future generations that will awake at their appointed time in the chain of life, this book seeks to carry out an everlasting covenant that places trust in their future.

We stand in an unthinkable moment in time – when food delivers poison, water runs toxic, species vanish, and global climate disaster threatens nearly all of Nature's Trust. But despite these alarming environmental conditions, democracy still allows us the freedom to rethink and redefine our place in the world according to Nature's Law. We still hold the liberty of moving from the politics of scarcity to the politics of abundance. That opportunity, however, will not linger for much longer. Actions taken by *this* generation of people already reverberate far into the future as ghostly echoes of an ill-considered past.

I write this book realizing that fate has delivered our generation into life at a pivotal moment. Our children and grandchildren have trust that we *will* claim this moment.

Acknowledgments

I had enormous help and support in writing this book. In many respects, *Nature's Trust* represents the aggregation of ideas drawn from the work of many colleagues, compiled into a framework that I hope will maximize the synergy of thought. While I cannot name everyone, special recognition goes to the writings and/or input of Zyg Plater, Eric Freyfogle, Gerald Torres, Keith Aoki (now deceased), Bill Rodgers, Pat McGinley, Charles Wilkinson, Michael M'Gonigle, Michael Blumm, Oliver Houck, Gus Speth, David Takacs, Burns Weston, David Bollier, Rena Steinzor, Tony Arnold, Tim Duane, Fred Cheever, Pat Parenteau, Edith Brown Weiss, Joel Mintz, Greg Munroe, and Mary Turnipseed. I owe thanks to Jan Laitos, who saw the potential of the trust idea from the beginning and connected me with Cambridge University Press. Special tribute goes to Joseph Sax, who wrote a landmark article on the public trust more than 40 years ago and later introduced me to the doctrine when I was a student in his water law course at Stanford Law School. I also express gratitude to Joseph Guth and Eric Freyfogle for their graciousness in allowing me to borrow the term "ecological age," which has appeared as a concept and term in their respective works.

My editor at Cambridge University Press, John Berger, saw the potential in this book from the beginning and has been tremendously supportive. I thank the full team at Cambridge University Press for doing a fantastic job in production.

My colleague, Heather Brinton, who directs the Environmental Law Program at University of Oregon School of Law, deserves special mention. She and I have had endless discussions over the years on every aspect of the trust doctrine. She is both a legal visionary and a stickler for detail. No one delves into an issue quite like Heather does, and I greatly value her insights.

I have benefited from discussions with many other thoughtful individuals on various aspects of the trust. Tom Bowerman gave me the idea of a frame change implicit in *Nature's Trust* and shared perspectives on the role of consumption, waste, and people's lifestyle choices in environmental destruction. Dune Lankard has been a constant reminder not only of the struggle of activists against huge corporate forces, but also of the great strides toward change that just one dedicated person can make in this world. Jim Hansen was very generous to share his time discussing climate science. Ted Strong gave me early insights years ago into the native trust approach and tribal management of salmon. John Davidson originated the concept of hazard resources as public trust assets. Others who offered ideas that informed the book include: Paul Vandevelder, Hal Darst, Jim McCarthy, Jaime Pinkham, Tim Ream, Tom Athanasiou, Dan Galpern, Charlie Tebbutt, Joe Guth, John De Graaf, Tuck Miller, Bear Brown, Jeff Ruch, Rick Piletz, and Kert Davies. Thanks goes to the many people who read parts of the manuscript, including Tom Waldo, Aaron Isherwood, Zach Klonoski, Nick Caleb, and Rance Shaw.

Countless friends and acquaintances in government agencies shared their insights over the twenty years I have taught environmental law. Suffice it to say, they are too numerous to mention here, but they all have my deep gratitude for their honest reflections on the state of environmental law and the pressures they face in state and federal environmental agencies.

Scores of attorneys are litigating public trust cases to protect our atmosphere against climate change. The world will be grateful for their enormous effort. I appreciate their generosity in taking time to talk with me about the public trust as I was writing this book. Thanks in particular goes to Andrea Rodgers, Elizabeth Brown, Tom Beers, Phil Gregory, John Melgren, Pete Frost, Tony Oposa, Sharon Duggan, Adam Abrams, Tanya Sanerib, and Greg Costello. Deserving particular mention is Julia Olson, who is coordinating the worldwide atmospheric trust litigation campaign (through Our Children's Trust) and whose perseverance and embrace of trust principles have inspired countless others. I have also learned much about the power of the trust concept to galvanize citizens from Kelly Mattheson, who produced (through her organization, WITNESS) a series of moving documentaries called *Stories of Trust* on the youth plaintiffs bringing public trust climate cases.

My school has provided tremendous support throughout this project; many thanks go to Dean Michael Moffitt and former dean Margie Paris. I am grateful for scholarship support provided through the Philip H. Knight Professorship. I also thank my many colleagues who shared useful information and ideas from their particular areas of expertise: Adell Amos, Barbara Aldave, Tim Hicks, Susan Gary, Garrett Epps, John Bonine, Dick Hildreth, Andrea Colles-Bjerre, Jim Mooney, Rob Illig, Ibrahim Gassama, Jim O'Fallon, and the late, beloved Svitlana Kravchenko. Jaye Barlous tracked down obscure sources, and Stephanie Midkiffe combed through newspapers for years on my behalf. Jill Forcier and Debbie Thurman deserve thanks for wonderful administrative support.

Dozens of law students – more than can be mentioned here – provided valuable assistance in both the research and editing process. Much of their inquiry into the trust has found its way into the pages of this book. Some are now lawyers working on public trust cases. Special recognition goes to Janie Morganson, Marianne Ober, Jamie Grifo, Zach Klonoski, John Brennan, Lynn Nickol, Drew Johnson, Jeff Gent, Maureen McGee, Sam Roberts, Adam Walters, Kelly Bauer, Alex Gavrillidis, Daniel Bartz, Bay Toft-Dupuy, Sam Chomper, Kenneth Safely, Chris Swensen, Kristopher Cahoon, Alex Gancayco, Orren Johnson, Seth Bichler, Charlotte Winkler, Amy Hicksted, Jilian Clearman, Meg Rowe, Conner Beckley, Christopher Cooney, Alexander Gancayco, Andrew Pollack, Andrew Welle, Jennifer Stallkemp, Kristen Thomas, Alek Wipperman, Zach Baker, and Zach Welcker.

Finally, I am most thankful for having a family that grounds me in all of my endeavors. My mother encouraged me all along until her death. She believed in this work and in this idea. My father instilled in me an appreciation of legacy and deep sense of intergenerational duty toward our descendants. I am grateful to my identical twin, Rebecca Wood, who, along with her four daughters, has fought to protect some of the natural places we love most. My sisters Ginny Burdick and Mardi Wood both gave me great encouragement. My brother Denny Burdick read the manuscript with enthusiasm. My sister-in-law, Sandy Wood, deserves heartfelt thanks for clipping articles for years. Several friends were graciously available to offer occasional advice on word choice and other details; that thanks goes to Catia, Kate, Charlie, Jennifer, Jim O., Jim I., Lynn, Lisa, Tom, and Ken.

The real inspiration for writing this book comes from our three sons, Sage, Cameron, and Nicholas. Throughout long stretches of research and writing, they brought me joy and never wavered in their support of this project. They reminded me often that this effort is to protect the future for all children.

Finally, my deepest gratitude goes to my husband, Joe, who gave me unbounded confidence and support in every stage of the project. There is not one idea in the book that Joe did not help me think through. He also poured over several drafts of each chapter and made astute edits throughout. Truthfully, some of the best phrases are from his pen. What meant the most, though, was Joe's abiding belief in this book's purpose to inspire a new ecological pathway for our world.

PART I

Environmental Law: Hospice for a Dying Planet

Introduction

"You Can't Negotiate with a Beetle"

You can't negotiate with a beetle. You are now dealing with natural law. And if you don't understand natural law, you will soon.

Oren Lyons

Oren Lyons's statement refers to 4 million acres of Canadian forest wiped out by beetles now thriving in warmer winter temperatures as a result of planetary heating. Lyons has a knack for putting environmental problems into terms that are hard to argue with. A member of the Onondaga Nation Council of Chiefs and professor of American studies, he emphasizes "natural law," a principle that has guided the indigenous approach to ecological management for thousands of years. As Lyons once put it in an interview:

> The thing that you have to understand about nature and natural law is, there's no mercy.... There's only law. And if you don't understand that law and you don't abide by that law, you will suffer the consequence. Whether you agree with it, understand it, comprehend it, it doesn't make any difference. You're going to suffer the consequence, and that's right where we're headed right now.[1]

THE NEW ECOLOGICAL AGE

The planet we inhabit seems suddenly and violently out of balance. The consequences of humanity's disregard for Nature's laws find glaring reflection through the prism of ocean life. Four hundred "dead zones" now murk the world's seas, collectively spanning tens of thousands of square miles. Off the coast of Oregon, a dead zone the size of Rhode Island resembles an underwater graveyard, with thousands of crab skeletons drifting in lifeless waters. In Moreton Bay, Australia, toxic fireweed can spread across the sea floor at a rate covering a football field every hour. When fishermen touch it, their skin breaks out into blistering welts, and their eyes burn and swell shut. Thousands of miles away on the Florida Gulf coast, a dreaded

3

red tide visits once a year and persists for months. Ocean breezes carry toxic wafts inland to waterfront communities, sending victims to the hospital with pneumonia, asthma, and bronchitis.[2]

Halfway between North America and Japan, the corpses of 200,000 dead albatross chicks speckle a rookery at Midway Atoll, their little gullets filled with plastic Legos, bottle caps, and Styrofoam balls that their parents plucked from the water and fed them. A garbage continent composed of plastic bottles, wrappers, and bags stretches twice the size of Texas in the Pacific Ocean.[3]

In New England, families that fished for generations have retired their boats because the oyster fishery has plummeted. Once providing a catch of millions of pounds of oysters a year, more than eight out of ten oyster reefs have vanished. Worldwide, nearly one-third of the sea fisheries have collapsed, and big fish populations have dropped 90 percent. Marine biologists project the complete loss of wild seafood just four decades from now: that would be the end of an entire food group that humans have relied on since time immemorial. Yet far out to sea, ocean fishing trawlers still scrape the bottom of the ocean in half-acre swaths. They haul in catches indiscriminately as if the marine life remained inexhaustible.[4]

All over the world, nitrogen and phosphorous compounds wash into the bays from septic tanks, farms, and sewers. Bulldozers chew up fragile wetlands along the coasts to create destination resorts and subdivisions. Every day, ocean water absorbs carbon dioxide emitted from industrial chimneys, coal-fired plants, and cars. Some ocean water has become so acidic from this pollution that the shells of sea creatures dissolve in it. Twenty percent of the coral reefs have disappeared, and the number could climb to 60 percent by 2030. Scientists warn of "potentially catastrophic consequences" for ocean life.[5]

Humans have toppled the oceans' chemical balance. Ancient forms of bacteria now thrive and proliferate, as if the seas have reverted to a primeval state. *Los Angeles Times* reporter Kenneth Weiss describes a "virulent pox" afflicting the world's oceans. In the words of one scientist, the seas now succumb to "the rise of slime," regressing to "a half-billion years ago when the oceans were ruled by jellyfish and bacteria."[6] As Oren Lyons would point out, you cannot negotiate with slime.

No one ever guaranteed that a lifestyle of colossal waste and resource consumption could continue indefinitely without consequences to our own species. But mass consumerism lulls people into assuming that good collateral exists behind a soaring ecological debt on the planet. Society seems mesmerized by an image of resilient Nature that cannot unravel before our very eyes. Even if it did unravel, leaders assure us, technology will develop in the nick of time to save civilization.

As part of the problem, industrialization has estranged people from their own survival. Many citizens live so detached from food production, water collection, and shelter provision that they remain oblivious to the basic connection between ecological health and human need. Neon indicators of environmental collapse attract little notice in mainstream society. Elizabeth Kolbert writes in *Field Notes from a Catastrophe*, "It may seem impossible to imagine that a technologically advanced society could choose, in essence, to destroy itself, but that is what we are now in the process of doing."[7]

Cascading calamities have prompted a body of "collapse scholarship." These writers no longer concern themselves with isolated problems such as a polluted river or a threatened species. Instead, they focus on a big picture that shows society now exhausting life-sustaining natural resources at a pace that threatens the future of civilization. James Speth inventories accumulating evidence in his book, *The Bridge at the Edge of the World*. Submitting that society faces a future of "catastrophes, breakdowns, and collapses," he asserts, "[W]e're headed toward a ruined planet." Jared Diamond carries a similar message in his book, *Collapse*. Observing no fewer than a dozen environmental time bombs with short fuses – crises relating to water, soil, toxics, overpopulation, deforestation, habitat destruction, overhunting, overfishing, introduction of nonnative species, climate change, energy shortages, and Earth's photosynthetic capacity – he notes, "If we solved 11 of the problems, but not the 12th, we would still be in trouble, whichever was the problem that remained unsolved. *We have to solve them all.*" This generation of humanity has clearly traveled into a new ecological era. As Bill McKibben submits in his book, *Eaarth*, it is as if humans now inhabit a different planet – one far less hospitable to our own survival.[8]

Presses are running at full speed to disseminate new ideas and transformative models to restructure society in a way that will allow humans to survive in the years ahead. It looms as a massive task. As Paul Hawken says in the film *The 11th Hour*, "There isn't one single thing that we make that doesn't require a complete re-make."[9] One would think that environmental law would lead visionary reform. Instead, environmental lawyers and regulators still do things very much the same way they did forty years ago. This book aims to bring environmental law face to face with the new ecological age unquestionably bearing down on us. It presents a transformative framework – Nature's Trust – to fundamentally redirect government's environmental policy from its present course of legalizing colossal damage to a project of epic restoration.

THE LEGAL MEMBRANE

Throughout most of human history, societies have governed their relationship to the environment through a series of customs, codes, and rules. Even during Justinian times, for example, the Roman Empire issued legal edicts on the taking of fish, the ownership of eroded soil, and the cultivation of bees.[10] No matter how simple or complex the rules may be, environmental law creates a legal membrane through which individuals act in relation to Nature. The efficacy of this law should be of utmost concern to citizens: any government that fails to protect its natural resources consigns its citizens to misery – and often death.

In *Collapse*, Jared Diamond studies why notably flourishing societies throughout history collapsed precipitously. These societies, he notes, often exhibited a characteristic mismatch between the society's consumption and the resources available. Less obvious is why the governing structure of the society sometimes allowed consumption to reach disastrous proportions grossly exceeding Nature's limits. Diamond attributes this in part to a conflict of interest between the short-term interests of the decision-making elite and the long-term interests of the society as a whole. As he describes, when members of the ruling elite pursue goals that become "good for themselves but bad for the rest of the group," they lead society on an unsustainable track, heading it toward collapse.[11] Today, the decision-making elite includes thousands of environmental agencies in nations across the world. Collectively, they rule over Earth's natural resources. Like the collapsed societies Diamond inventories, these officials now make decisions that are good for themselves but bad for society and future generations. Behind a veil of environmental law, their decisions push the entire world toward collapse.

Unique in the law, environmental regulation remains accountable to a supreme set of mandates – the laws of Nature, or Natural Law, as Oren Lyons and many indigenous leaders call it. Environmental law's primary function seeks to bring society into compliance with these natural laws, which, in the end, determine whether citizens prosper or perish. As Professor Richard Lazarus writes, "[E]cological catastrophe and human tragedy can occur when human laws fictionalize or otherwise ignore the laws of nature."[12] If environmental law, no matter how seemingly complex or sophisticated, becomes too detached from Nature's own laws, it will become irrelevant. If the hundreds of thousands of bureaucrats and legislators dispersed across the world today make decisions aimed to promote their own short-term interests as in the ruined societies Diamond describes, our collective future rests in dangerous hands.

The United States boasts the most elaborate environmental laws in the world. They exist as a convoluted morass of statutes, regulations, court decisions, and other legal instruments. Basic environmental law principles arose early in the country's history, but they morphed into statutory form only in the 1970s. This era gave rise to the Clean Water Act, the Clean Air Act, the Endangered Species Act, the National Environmental Policy Act, the Toxic Substances Control Act, the National Forest Management Act, and a multitude of others. Each statute spawned a cottage industry of lawyers and environmental consultants.[13]

Although directed at different problems, nearly all environmental statutes share one thing in common: they rely on agencies to carry out their mandates. Nature, in its entirety, has been partitioned among various bureaucracies – many thousands in all – spanning the federal, state, and local levels. Vast authority vests in these agencies to control or manage discrete parts of the environment. In the U.S., for example, state environmental agencies generally handle air and water pollution. Federal forests are the responsibility of the U.S. Forest Service. Endangered species fall to the U.S. Fish and Wildlife Service and the National Marine Fisheries Service. State water agencies issue water rights. Land use matters go to local agencies. The U.S. Environmental Protection Agency (EPA) regulates toxics and pesticides. Wetlands regulation is within the jurisdiction of the U.S. Army Corps of Engineers. And so on. These jurisdictional webs have vastly different reaches and regulatory strands, but they all reflect one thing: agencies are exerting tremendous dominion over Nature.

With few exceptions, statutes authorize agencies to issue permits to damage Nature. Such permit provisions form a common denominator to environmental and natural resource statutes, and a vast portion of the agencies' work today flows from them. Agencies regularly decide whether to permit harm to air, water, soils, forests, grasslands, wetlands, riparian areas, species, and other natural resources. The agencies enjoy tremendous discretion in making these decisions; in fact, agency discretion forms the crux of all modern environmental law. Such discretion rests on a presumption that agencies remain expert bodies that unfailingly exercise their judgment objectively, for the good of the public, and in accordance with protective statutory goals. That presumption now collides with reality.

Agency discretion drives the demise of Nature. For decades, environmental professionals working within this legal system have assumed it to be functional, and many other nations have modeled their environmental approach after the U.S. legal system. But the ancient membrane of law that supposedly functions as a system of community restraint now stretches tattered and pocked with holes. Our destruction of Nature threatens to create what scientists call a fundamentally "different planet."[4]

Two unavoidable questions loom large over environmental law. First, does this field of law work to keep society in compliance with Nature's own laws? Second, can it be effective in confronting the ecological challenges now coming at us with horrifying speed? These questions are of crucial importance not only for the United States but also for other nations confronting ravenous pressure to industrialize (as well as all other nations that must endure the planetary damage wrought by overconsuming nations). If the answer to either question is no, legal scholars must set their sights on a transformative legal paradigm.

Many litigators, scholars, and decision makers will claim that the environmental statutes work. They point to isolated successes in every statutory context. Rivers do not catch fire any more. Gasoline does not contain lead. The pesticide DDT no longer poisons eagles. Industries cleaned up their toxic mess at Love Canal. Influenced by these perceptions of success, when new problems come along, lawyers tend to turn to the old way of doing things. For example, lawyers responded initially to global warming by filing a petition to regulate carbon dioxide under the Clean Air Act.[15] Yet, well more than a decade after filing the petition, the federal government has still not acted to comprehensively control greenhouse gas pollution – even though scientists clearly warn of perilous planetary heating. Success, as we all know, remains relative. Over just the last few decades, industry has jumped from a white belt to a black belt in Earth-destroying capability, but the law has not changed. Despite entrenched presumptions that environmental law remains effective, the proof lies in the health of the ecosystems themselves. Society now violates Nature's laws not only at the level of species and individual ecosystems but also at the level of atmospheric function, ocean health, and biodiversity – a truly global level.

ECOLOGICAL BANKRUPTCY

Today's ecological losses reside in a different realm than the problems prompting passage of the environmental statutes forty years ago. When the Endangered Species Act was enacted, for example, overhunting and poaching were predominant threats to wildlife, and extinctions remained quite rare. Today, pollution, habitat loss, and climate change decimate wildlife. Imperiled species now show up ubiquitously, in nearly every kind of habitat system. Where one species struggles to survive, others usually do too, for when an ecosystem starts to unravel, its full weave of species frays.[16]

Historic problems of overharvest now stand utterly eclipsed by threats to the web of life itself. Today's major wildlife reports do not dwell so much on individual species. Instead, they talk about entire classes of life on Earth threatened. The International Union for Conservation of Nature (IUCN), which compiles data on the world's threatened species, estimates that more than a third (38 percent) of all species face possible extinction. Interpreting this statistic cannot be a matter of seeing a glass a third empty or two-thirds full. Because ecology embodies connectedness, 38 percent becomes the pull-engine on a death train. Leading conservation biologists now conclude that humanity has triggered the sixth mass extinction in Earth's history. As James Speth grimly reports, "The planet has not seen such a spasm of extinction in sixty-five million years, since the dinosaurs disappeared."[17]

Some characterize the sheer scale of this destruction by pointing out that humanity would need *two planets by 2030* to support its demand for goods and services. Society now exhausts resources at a breakneck pace. In the tropics, chainsaws have axed the rainforest at a rate of an acre every second, by some estimates. Half of the world's original forest has been obliterated (another 30 percent is degraded or fragmented). Half of the world's wetlands lay destroyed, and a third of the mangroves have disappeared.[18]

Despite its elaborate environmental laws, the United States has wiped out more than half (53 percent) of its wetlands and nearly all (90 percent) of its old-growth forests. At least 9,000 species face risk of extinction in the United States, according to the Council on Environmental Quality. Pollution fouls America, too; industry annually releases more than 4 billion pounds of toxic chemicals into waters, air, and soils. According to EPA, 95 percent of all Americans have an increased risk of lung cancer just from breathing toxins in outdoor air, and one in four Americans lives next to a toxic waste dump. Nearly half (44 percent) of all rivers and streams are unfit for fishing, recreation, and other public uses. Fish advisories for toxic contamination exist for about one out of every four rivers (24 percent). Mercury – a poison to humans – now shows up ubiquitously in fish.[19] Even babies are born polluted, harboring a cocktail of toxins in their bloodstreams.

This colossal damage to Earth had its genesis in the Industrial Revolution, but the real acceleration occurred during the modern era of environmental law. In the last thirty years, Earth's natural ecosystems have declined by 33 percent, and one-third of the planet's natural resources has been consumed. Has environmental law worked? If the health of the planet stands as any indicator, the answer must be clearly no. The law can claim small successes, but overall, destruction from industrial activity has far outpaced the ability of environmental law to protect resources. As political scientist Richard Andrews observes, environmental law has "only selectively, modestly, and temporarily held back" the larger forces responsible for resource collapse. Rather than safeguarding ecology, today's environmental law serves as the cane on which humanity leans as it walks the plank toward its own destruction.[20]

THE ILLUSION OF ENVIRONMENTAL LAW

U.S. agencies have turned environmental law inside out. Whereas Congress passed environmental statutes with the overriding goal of *protecting* the environment, the environmental agencies now use the statutes to legalize *destruction* of the environment. Under the Clean Air Act alone, nearly 15,000 permits (pending or in effect) allow the poisoning of American air sheds with harmful pollution, including highly toxic compounds. In just the seven years between 2001 and 2007, industries released 31.7 billion pounds of toxins into the environment in U.S. territory.[21] Other permits and regulatory loopholes allow harm to imperiled species, destruction of wetlands, leveling of forests, and gouging of landscapes. Granted, most permits carry mitigating conditions that lessen the damage that would otherwise occur, but the cumulative effect tallies inexorable, mounting losses. While undoubtedly some agencies remain loyal guardians of the public's natural assets, the bureaucratic mindset of most agencies today aligns all too closely with the industries they regulate.

Diamond's examination of collapsed societies shows that we should be wary of decision makers who make decisions to further their own short-term interests. The pursuit of self-interest by some agency heads surely rivals that of the ancient lords in *Collapse*. As Part I of this book shows, political appointees in agencies regularly hijack their administrative discretion to benefit their allied industries. Because political motives lie concealed behind a thick morass of complexity created by the agencies themselves, it remains exceedingly difficult to untangle corruption or misuse of office.[22]

To make matters worse, the judiciary has largely relinquished its role as an institutional check on environmental agencies, regularly invoking the administrative deference doctrine to give weight to agency decisions. The deference principle assumes that expert agencies act as unbiased decision makers, ever faithful to statutory goals. This approach insulates agency decisions from rigorous judicial examination of inappropriate political motivations that regularly influence the agencies. Through the deference doctrine, courts unwittingly create a judicial prop for an administrative facade that conceals political influence and, at times, outright corruption.[23]

For the most part, environmental law scholarship ignores these systemic problems. Most scholars confine their criticism to one statute's failure or one program's failure. The problem reaches much deeper and far beyond these isolated instances. Dysfunction permeates the entire structure of the administrative environmental state, both in the United States and in the many other nations that have replicated the U.S. environmental law system. Much like a manufacturer might put faulty and dangerous wiring in 100,000 separate products, the U.S. legal system has put out hundreds of thousands of regulations that no longer function as intended. Worse, they now operate in electrocution mode.

CLIMATE EMERGENCY AND THE BIG ADAPTATION

Even setting aside past failures, we should ask whether current environmental law can effectively confront the monumental challenges ahead. Planetary heating looms as a harbinger of death on a nearly unimaginable scale. In June 2007, a team of leading climate scientists warned that carbon dioxide and other greenhouse gas emissions have placed the Earth in "imminent peril" – literally on the verge of an irreversible tipping point that would impose catastrophic conditions on generations of humanity to come. Climate change from continued greenhouse gas pollution threatens to melt ice sheets over Greenland and at both poles, wipe out the coral reefs, turn the Amazon forest into savannah, and obliterate 40 percent to 70 percent of the world's species. Floods, hurricanes, killer heat waves, fires, disease, crop losses, food shortages, and droughts would arrive with unimaginable magnitude and regularity. Rising sea levels that inundate coastal areas worldwide would trigger desperate mass human migrations. In the words of the National Aeronautics and Space Administration (NASA) scientist James Hansen, society's continued carbon pollution will "transform the planet."[24]

Climate crisis presents nearly unfathomable urgency because of what scientists call "tipping points" – climate tripwires, so to speak. These thresholds, caused by human carbon pollution, trigger dangerous feedbacks capable of unraveling the planet's climate system. Once triggered, these viscous cycles continue despite any subsequent carbon reductions achieved by humanity. Such tipping points loom near. Some may be underway. Some may be intensifying. Vast areas of melting permafrost, for example, now release huge amounts of carbon dioxide and methane into the atmosphere. Melting polar ice caps intensify heating, because less ice remains to reflect heat away from Earth (what is known as the albedo effect). And the natural "sinks," such as oceans and forests, that historically absorbed society's carbon pollution have reached their limits. The oceans have turned acidic, and large swaths of forests (stressed from heat) are dying and then burning, releasing their stored carbon. In 2007, these and other alarming feedbacks caused scientists to warn that greenhouse gas (GHG) emissions put Earth "perilously close to dramatic climate change that *could run out of our control*, with great dangers for humans and other creatures."[25]

To put it starkly, we face a planetary emergency in which only a narrow window of time remains to act before tipping points foreclose all feasible options. Leading climate scientists believe the safety zone of carbon dioxide in the atmosphere lies below the level of 350 parts per million. Present levels have reached 400 parts per million, an amount not seen on Earth for at least 3 million years. The United Nations projects that humanity's aimless business as usual could heat the planet as much as 11 degrees Fahrenheit by the end of the century. To put that in perspective, all of the floods, fires, heat waves, melting, and weather disasters experienced thus far correlate with a mere 1.4-degree Fahrenheit rise (over preindustrial levels). Worse, even if all emissions ended tomorrow, the persisting carbon already in the atmosphere from 150 years of industrialization will still drive the planet's temperature to 3.6 degrees Fahrenheit over preindustrial levels by 2199.[26]

Against this horrific reality, climate crisis presents two monumental challenges, tagged in climate circles by the (rather uninspiring) terms *mitigation* and *adaptation*. *Mitigation* calls for slashing carbon emissions enough to prevent runaway heating. Dr. James Hansen and other leading scientists project that society must cut global carbon emissions on the order of 6 percent a year, beginning in 2013, to return the planet to a safety zone. This becomes a colossal undertaking, because fossil fuel powers nearly every aspect of modern industrial society. *Adaptation* means that society must figure out how to survive conditions it has never known. Thomas Friedman captures the twin tasks when he says: "Avoid the unmanageable and manage the unavoidable."[27]

The climate imperative necessitates protecting the remaining natural resources for two basic reasons. First, any effort to mitigate and thwart the tipping point must entail a drawdown of carbon pollution from the atmosphere. Extracting existing atmospheric CO_2 requires massive reforestation and soil sequestration to absorb carbon. Second, ecosystem protection (and restoration) will prove crucial for adapting to the climate heating that is already, unstoppably, underway. Many ecological systems will fail, and as they do, natural resources will become even more scarce. Worldwide, nations simply will not have all of the water, the species, the productive soils, and the forests inherited from past generations (around which they built their societies). Major rivers of the world already show significant loss of water due to climate change. Environmental law of the past geared its loose permissions toward conditions of the Industrial Age. But in a world under ecological siege, all remaining natural assets carry a premium for human survival and welfare. These stark understandings must connect law with the reality of our time.[28]

As Speth concludes: "[W]e now approach the fork ahead.... Beyond the fork, down either path, is the end of the world as we have known it. One path beyond the fork continues us on our current trajectory ... the abyss.... But there is the other path, and it leads to a bridge across the abyss."[29] Rather than launching a massive effort to build society's survival bridge across the abyss, government agencies persist in legalizing damage as if Nature had supernatural capacity to regenerate – indeed, as if the end were not already in sight. Agency reform stands urgent as never before. Yet many perceive deep change as remaining beyond political and practical possibility.

REALISM AND THE INEVITABILITY OF
TRANSFORMATIONAL CHANGE

Alex Steffen, author of *World Changing*, says: "We find ourselves facing two futures, one unthinkable and the other currently unimaginable." The severity and pervasiveness of administrative dysfunction means there can be no simple fix. All solutions will entail fresh dilemmas, complexities, and tradeoffs. But these cannot distract from imagining and implementing a different paradigm. Speth rightly argues that we need a "fresh conceptualization ... a new way of thinking." Many proposals still tinker around the edges of the same business-as-usual behavior that now drives the planet to catastrophe. As Steffen notes, "Faced with the need to reinvent the material basis of our civilization, we argue paper or plastic." He explains, "The magnitude of the crises we face, [and] the speed with which they are unfolding ... mean that the solutions we need to embrace are not going to be the same *sort of solutions* we're used to thinking of now."[30]

Steffen and others offer new operating principles of our society – concepts such as zero emissions, zero waste, living buildings, and green infrastructure. But an antiquated system of environmental regulation undermines these civilization-saving ideas. We cannot, on one hand, dare to imagine businesses eliminating pollution and waste, yet on the other hand give them permits to freely pollute. For the most part, environmental law lacks ideas truly calibrated to the magnitude of the problem and the pace of change. It offers only modest proposals for reform – a new regulation here, a new statute there. At this late date, tweaking the law becomes a fool's errand, having no more hope than throwing out a rescue rope that is too short. Instead, legal reform must reach beneath the individual statutes and regulations to address the level of dysfunction that propels this system of legalized damage.

A major source of administrative dysfunction arises from the vast discretion agencies enjoy – and the way they abuse it to serve private, corporate, and bureaucratic interests. As long as the decision-making frame presumes political discretion to allow damage, it matters little what new laws emerge, for they will develop the same bureaucratic sinkholes that consumed the 1970s laws. Only a transformative approach can address sources of legal decay. Moreover, a fundamental frame change in the field as a whole stands as the only practical response to an environmental bureaucracy that is now enormous. The legal machine churns out colossal damage on a *daily* basis by issuing (and reissuing) pollution permits at all jurisdictional levels. (In the course of just two months in 2009, for example, state agencies across 36 states reported 2,632 air and water pollution permits due for issuance or renewal.[31]) Additional, untold damage finds license through regulatory mechanisms such as wildlife "take" permits, wetlands permits, coastal zone permits, land use permits, mining, forestry, and grazing permits, water appropriation permits, and more. Efforts to push back this deluge cannot proceed on a permit-by-permit basis or even a program-by-program basis. Legal battles consume money, time, citizen input, and enormous human energy – inputs that dissipate quickly in the modern world. While an incremental approach might make sense if society had another three decades to accomplish it, climate crisis has annulled the luxury of time.

Unfortunately, however, even the most public-oriented staffers working within agencies tend to resist transformative change. They operate within highly restricted jurisdictional realms and work in isolated regulatory silos. The sheer complexity of environmental law draws them into consuming detail, burrowing them ever deeper into a malfunctioning system even as the need for change becomes all the more obvious to outside observers. Failing to see the big picture of ecological collapse, agency officials tend to approach problems all too narrowly.

Even those agency staffers who do recognize the ecological crisis often find themselves trapped by an entrenched institutional outlook – one that assumes that the political reality will never support deep change. But as Speth and others submit, the industrial paradigms producing that political reality are fast expiring. The status quo, if continued, will provoke ecological collapse, which in turn will dismantle the society's legal systems and their supporting paradigms. Diamond surmises that a res-olution to society's problems will appear, one way or another, within decades: "The only question is whether [the problems] will become resolved in pleasant ways of our own choice, or in unpleasant ways not of our choice, such as warfare, genocide, starvation, disease epidemics, and collapses of societies."[32]

In sum, the Earth defense effort requires an epochal project of rebuilding nat-ural wealth. Instead of incremental reform, the circumstances call out for a full paradigm shift that infuses all government decision making with restoration duty. Citizens worldwide must tap a wellspring of legal *obligation* to compel their govern-ments to tackle this challenge.

NATURE'S TRUST

This book develops a framework, Nature's Trust, to characterize government's ecological obligation in the modern ecological age. Nature's Trust draws forth an ancient and enduring legal principle known as the public trust doctrine. With roots extending back to early Roman law, the doctrine rests on a civic and judicial under-standing that some natural resources remain so vital to public welfare and human survival that they should not fall exclusively to private property ownership and con-trol. Under the public trust doctrine, natural resources such as waters, wildlife, and presumably air, remain common property belonging to the people as a whole. Such assets take the form of a perpetual trust for future generations. The public's lasting ownership interest in this trust vests in both present and future generations as legal beneficiaries.[33]

Public trust law demands that government act as a trustee in controlling and man-aging crucial natural assets. Held to strict fiduciary obligations, government must promote the interests of the citizen beneficiaries and ensure the sustained resource abundance necessary for society's endurance. The U.S. Supreme Court declared in *Geer v. Connecticut*: "[I]t is the duty of the legislature to enact such laws as will best preserve the subject of the trust, and secure its beneficial use in the future to the people of the state."[34] This duty arises as a limitation on government, an expectation that still smoulders in the popular sovereignty held by the people.

As a foundational property law principle, the trust doctrine imparts the original legal mechanism to ensure that government safeguards natural resources necessary for public welfare and survival. Long predating any statutory law, the reasoning of the public trust puts it on par with the highest liberties of citizens living in a free soci-ety. This public property right ranks so fundamental to citizens that some scholars describe it as a natural right or human right. As Professor Joseph Sax suggested more than four decades ago in a landmark article, the public trust responsibility under-pins democracy itself, demarcating a society of "citizens rather than of serfs."[35]

The American lodestar public trust opinion declaring the citizens' fundamental right to natural resources is *Illinois Central Railroad Co. v. Illinois* (*Illinois Central*). Announcing that the shoreline of Lake Michigan was held in public trust by the state of Michigan and could not be transferred to a private railroad corporation, the Supreme Court stated:

> [T]he decisions are numerous which declare that such property is held by the state, by virtue of its sovereignty, in trust for the public. The ownership of the navigable waters of the harbor, and of the lands under them, is a *subject of public concern to the whole people of the state*. The trust with which they are held, therefore, is governmental, and cannot be alienated.[36]

The essence of the doctrine requires trust management strictly for public benefit rather than for private exploit or political advantage. Simply stated, government trustees may not allocate rights to destroy what the people rightly own for themselves and for their posterity. Understood in this way, the trust imposes a fundamental constraint on governmental power. The *Geer* Court declared:

> [T]he power or control lodged in the State, resulting from this common ownership, is to be exercised, like all other powers of government, as a trust for the benefit of the people, and not as a prerogative for the advantage of the government as distinct from the people, or for the benefit of private individuals as distinguished from the public good.[37]

Although the public trust doctrine lies embedded in scores of U.S. judicial decisions decided over the past century, it has been all but lost in the administrative jungle that now chokes environmental law. Many modern-day bureaucrats and politicians no longer see themselves as trustees of public property and resources. They view their roles as those of political decision makers, vested with statutory discretion to allow damage to natural resources through the permit system. The present statutory system fails to impose a corresponding duty adequate to bridle this breathtaking power.

Revived in modern bureaucracy, the trust would introduce an old-but-new limitation on government acting through statutory law. The trust injects fiduciary duty into government action affecting the environment. Strict and enforceable standards of performance stay necessary to secure the implicit confidence reposed by citizens in the trustee, who exercises power over vital assets. Trustees, bound by exacting fiduciary obligations to protect the assets of the trust, must manage them prudently and restore damaged assets. The trustee must act in good faith and out of absolute loyalty to the citizen beneficiaries.

From an established public trust foundation, the Nature's Trust paradigm proposes an organizing framework responsive to the new ecological era. But to do so, it must push beyond current limitations associated with the public trust doctrine. While Sax's pioneering article suggested the trust as a cohesive paradigm for managing natural resources, much scholarship since has characterized the doctrine in an overly constrained manner. Law review articles tend to focus too much on a limited number of specific cases rather than on the bedrock fundamentals and the purposes animating the doctrine, both of which suggest broad potential to address modern crises. Some scholars express the public trust as a judicial tool, but they ignore the doctrine's fundamental applicability to the legislative and administrative branches of government. Many characterize the public trust as limited to water and wildlife, whereas the original rationale for the trust clearly extends to all natural resources needed by society. Some scholars assume the doctrine to be exclusively applicable to states, whereas its taproot lies in sovereign understandings that remain equally germane to the federal and local governments – both of which play key roles in today's environmental management. Much of the scholarship focuses on the public aspects of natural resource ownership without fully reconciling the doctrine with *private* property ownership – or explaining how ownership rules must adjust to a new era of natural scarcity and uncertainty. Few scholars have discussed in any detail how the trust might impart global obligations for planetary resources such as the oceans and atmosphere. And finally, the existing scholarship confines its characterization of the public trust to the legal sphere, whereas the trust also inspires as a political concept, an ethical mooring, a diplomatic framework, and an economic principle. This book builds on the public trust foundation to create a full paradigm shift in environmental law. Amid an ecological crisis, Nature's Trust principles instruct government to protect and restore the Earth endowment.

Part I of this book begins with a regulatory autopsy of environmental law, examining its many failure points. Chapter 1 provides a context for assessing legal dysfunction by recounting how President George W. Bush used high administrative offices to thwart carbon dioxide regulation under the Clean Air Act. Punctuating his administration's persistent regulatory obstruction to benefit the fossil fuel industry were clear warnings from the scientific community that government's failure to control carbon pollution would bring calamity to Earth's citizens. If any story shows the perils of agency politicization, this one does. Chapter 2 explores how administrative law now skews the balance of power among the three branches of government. Chapter 3 reveals the "politics of discretion," identifying portals through which industry influence gains entry to the administrative state. Chapter 4 lifts the veil on the political and industry maneuvering that persists behind a regulatory facade. Chapter 5 exposes a despotic administrative state resulting from a weakened judicial branch and a marginalized public.

Part II presents the Nature's Trust paradigm, which characterizes government's environmental duty as obligatory, inalienable, and fundamental to sovereignty itself. Chapter 6 describes an encompassing fiduciary limitation on the powers of government applicable on the federal, state, and local levels. Chapter 7 draws on the essential purposes of the trust to suggest that all natural assets, including air, atmosphere, oceans, rivers, wetlands, aquifers, forests, wildlife, and soils, comprise an "ecological *res*" that government must protect. Chapter 8 presents substantive standards of trust protection and restoration, and Chapter 9 discusses procedural duties incumbent on agency officials acting as trustees. Together, these two chapters characterize the trust obligation as an organic duty existing within the procedural edifice of statutory law, available to redirect agencies toward the task of rebuilding bankrupted natural assets. Chapter 10 outlines a property framework that organizes environmental obligations on a global scale. It positions multiple sovereigns as co-tenants of shared resources with mutual property-based obligations to prevent waste of common assets. Chapter 11 discusses how the judicial branch can enforce the people's trust through common law remedies using modern hybrid judicial/administrative tools.

Part III positions Nature' Trust within a broader social realm and weaves the trust approach with other transformative proposals that can guide society in a sustainable direction. Chapter 12 explores the moral and spiritual dimensions of the trust and suggests a powerful synergy between Nature's Trust and worldwide conservation faith movements. Chapter 13 describes how Nature's Trust principles reinforce contemporary initiatives toward natural capitalism. Chapter 14 explains the interface between private property rights and public property rights. It identifies the trust as an encumbrance on private title that has never been extinguished, an antecedent servitude that awakens even from long periods of dormancy to preserve natural infrastructure. Chapter 15 concludes the book by suggesting Nature's Trust as a paradigm capable of transcending cultures and national borders to catalyze citizen environmental democracy worldwide.

A POPULIST MANIFESTO

As this book will show, the legal dysfunction driving environmental law portends danger for all citizens. Far from protecting Nature, agencies now use their authority under environmental law to hospice a dying planet. Citizens of the world confront a monumental challenge: they must redirect the bureaucratic energy of their governments toward the epic task of rebuilding the assets in Nature's Trust. But transforming agencies requires a new way of thinking, a fresh characterization of normative values, and a robust set of legal footholds by which citizens can hold their government officials accountable. While no legal approach offers a panacea, the trust infuses existing environmental law and bureaucracy with a protective fiduciary purpose that can rise to modern ecological challenges. When taken to the global

level, the trust becomes a diplomatic framework from which international obligations emerge to protect the Earth endowment for all generations.

The sovereign trust obligation offers a catalyzing principle to citizens worldwide in
their common struggle to hold government accountable for protecting life-systems.
Nature's Trust and the primordial rights inculcating it create a populist manifesto
that surfaces at epic times through the generations of humanity. These principles
stand no less revolutionary for our time and our crises than the forcing of the Magna
Carta on the English monarchy in 1215 or Mahatma Gandhi's great Salt March to
the sea in 1930.[38] Resonating deeply and resolutely within the ancestral memory of
humanity, trust principles must now revive to stir a global assertion of citizenship in
defense of humanity and all future generations.

1

"You Are Doing a Great Job"

On January 17, 2007, world-renowned scientists stood with national evangelical leaders in Washington, D.C., to deliver an urgent call to action to President George W. Bush. This unprecedented alliance of science and religion had come together to warn that humans were destroying the community of life on which all living things on Earth depend. They declared, *"Business as usual cannot continue yet one more day."*[1]

Yet business as usual did continue, day after day, month after month, and year after year during a crucial window of opportunity to avert planetary heating when George W. Bush, a former oilman, sat as president of the United States. The climate politics of his administration reflect more than the ordinary corruption that weaves in and out of U.S. history like fraying threads on a flag. Instead, this saga shows a complete breakdown of environmental law amid a crisis so severe that the tenure of just one president could leave ecological wreckage. Bush's failure to uphold environmental law, and Obama's subsequent climate complacency, set the stage for virtually all of the themes in this book. More than any other story of regulatory failure, this one portrays the need for a transformative paradigm shift to hold government accountable for protecting the people's natural assets.

ENDANGERMENT ALL ALONG

The U.S. environmental bureaucracy has always had the capacity to mount an urgent atmospheric defense effort to curb climate heating – and to lead the rest of the world in doing so. Ample legal authority resides in the Clean Air Act (CAA), authorizing the U.S. Environmental Protection Agency (EPA) to force across-the-board carbon emissions reduction in nearly all sectors. As a preliminary step to regulation, however, EPA must determine that such carbon pollution could "reasonably be anticipated to *endanger public health or welfare.*" This determination, called an endangerment finding, triggers multiple statutory sections that can limit pollution sources. However, nothing can happen until EPA makes a formal endangerment finding.[2]

Such technical determinations create the fodder for environmental law. If EPA makes a formal finding of harm resulting from a particular activity, the harm is usually regulated. But when officials suppress science and resist making findings of harm, the statutory provisions sit idle and environmental law loses its firepower. In the climate context, without an endangerment finding from EPA, there can be no regulation under the statute's most potent provisions. Underlying and justifying this administrative system is a presumption that agencies will act as neutral seekers of the scientific truth and will regulate in the face of public harm. In many agencies today, that presumption has become a sham.

The EPA surely knew for well over two decades that carbon dioxide pollution could "endanger public health or welfare," the standard under the CAA. Congress drew attention to dangerous planetary heating in 1978 when it passed the National Climate Program Act. A subsequent report from the National Academy of Sciences (NAS) warned: "A wait-and-see policy may mean waiting until it is too late." But while Earth's climate clock ticked steadily down during the eight years George W. Bush held office (2001–2009), the president's former oil friends and political supporters called in their favors. Bush appointed agency heads throughout the federal bureaucracy who would serve his allied industries and stall carbon dioxide regulation. As the planet careened toward a dangerous climate tipping point, emissions soared. No regulation of carbon pollution occurred during the George W. Bush administration. At the end of Bush's second term as president, British writer George Monbiot charged: "His willful trashing of the Middle Climate – the interlude of benign temperatures which allowed human civilization to flourish – [is a crime] against humanity."[3]

THE EARLY WARNINGS

On June 23, 1988, a sweltering day in Washington, D.C., legislators and their staffers packed into a hot hearing room, sweat dripping from their foreheads. Their hand-made paper fans proved pathetic consolation for Nature's searing jurisdiction over the proceeding. In front of the Senate committee sat a renowned scientist, Dr. James Hansen, the director of the National Aeronautics and Space Administration's (NASA) Goddard Institute of Space Studies. He had come to present testimony on global warming.[4]

Sitting in the group of committee members was Senator Al Gore, who had organized the hearings. Gore's climate concern originated in a small undergraduate class he took from Professor Roger Revelle, a famous scientist who drew initial media attention to the planet's greenhouse effect. Revelle had displayed a graph to his class indicating that, even back in the 1960s, the concentration of carbon dioxide in the atmosphere was climbing at an alarming rate. Data at that time showed levels reaching 316 parts per million – exceeding the highest carbon dioxide concentration in history of 300 parts per million, as revealed in a 420,000-year-old ice core record.[5]

It seemed nearly certain that the American public would mobilize in response to the climate threat during that dreadful summer of 1988. An extraordinary heat wave had descended on the nation. The west suffered the driest summer on record. Lightning strikes exploded into wild forest infernos that scorched thousands of acres in Yellowstone National Park. A relentless drought left the southeastern United States parched. In the midwest, water levels dropped so low that barges could not navigate the Mississippi River. Crops withered across 40 percent of the nation's counties, costing $3.386 billion in disaster relief payments to farmers.[6]

Hansen crystallized the problem when he told the gathered senators, "The Earth is warmer in 1988 than at any time in the history of instrumental measurements. There is only a one percent chance of an accidental warming of this magnitude.... *The greenhouse effect has been detected, and it is changing our climate now.*"[7] The room fell silent.

Such a warning by the nation's top climate scientist should have kicked the environmental law system into overdrive. No new legislation was needed to solve this emergency. The CAA conferred ample authority to regulate carbon dioxide pollution. But political cross-tides often sweep statutory obligations out to sea, as discussed in Chapter 3. Industries exert power and influence behind closed agency doors to block regulation under the law. And yet, high-ranking officials know they must keep up a facade of bureaucratic legitimacy in the form of professed public benefit from their action – or inaction. An official cannot simply confess to the American public that he or she wants to ease regulation to return a political favor or to serve a few industry friends in hopes of gaining lucrative employment after leaving government. Above all, the industry's pollution must not be perceived to cause harm. Sometimes science risks blowing this facade by showing clear public risk from pollution. On those occasions, the science must be dealt with.

In 1989, as James Hansen was preparing another round of climate testimony to Congress, the White House Office of Management and Budget (OMB) interceded to change his written submission. The OMB's spin-doctoring followed a formula that officials would use repeatedly to mislead Congress and the American public on climate change. First, challenge the science or cast doubt on its conclusions. Second, blame global warming on Nature rather than on humans. Third, make clear that they will not mess with the economy.[8]

THE FOXES GUARDING THE GREENHOUSE

George W. Bush and Vice President Dick Cheney "came out of the oil patch," as Robert F. Kennedy Jr. puts it in his book, *Crimes Against Nature*. In a detailed exposé, Kennedy describes the president's environmental policy as one massive payback to the powerful industries that put him in office. In the 2000 election, energy interests contributed more than $48.3 million to Bush and the Republican Party, and then contributed another $58 million after President Bush took office. The money paid off in terms of inside influence over who would take the reins of the U.S. environmental law bureaucracy – and control the nation's vast natural resources. Kennedy reports that thirty-one out of forty-eight members of Bush's transition team had energy industry ties.[9]

When it came time to make agency appointments, Bush stacked nearly all of the highest government offices with industry operatives. Four cabinet secretaries, six key White House officials, and twenty other high-level appointments were, as Kennedy describes, "alumni of the industry and its allies." The lineup seemed to step beyond agency "capture," which occurs when industry pinch hitters find their way into official positions. It was more like corporate conquest of government.[10]

One of the most consequential decisions George W. Bush faced when he entered office was whether to regulate carbon dioxide and other greenhouse gases. In 1992, his father (President George H. W. Bush) signed the United Nations Framework Convention on Climate Change (UNFCCC) on behalf of the United States. In the agreement, 154 nations declared their collective aim to prevent "dangerous" human interference with Earth's climate system. Although the U.S. Senate unanimously ratified the UNFCCC, it contained no binding greenhouse gas reductions. A later global agreement, the 1997 Kyoto Protocol, contained binding emissions targets, but the U.S. Senate never ratified the treaty, so it carried no force in the United States. This left the CAA as the clearest avenue for controlling U.S. carbon dioxide pollution.[11]

When George W. Bush was still in the midst of his presidential campaign, running neck and neck against Vice President Al Gore, growing numbers of citizens became alarmed by evidence showing that carbon dioxide emissions were dangerously heating the planet. Not wanting Gore to sweep these votes, Bush made a clear campaign promise to regulate carbon dioxide. The promise raised political eyebrows because observers knew that regulating carbon dioxide would require Bush to turn his back on the very industries that were paying millions to put him in office – the coal, oil, gas, and automobile industries.[12]

A legal mechanism to force carbon dioxide regulation was already under way when Bush took office. In 1999, nineteen private organizations had petitioned EPA to control carbon dioxide emissions (and other greenhouse gases) from automobiles under the CAA. Bush appointed Christine Todd Whitman, former governor of New Jersey, as head of EPA. On January 23, 2001, EPA began formal public comment on the pending petition. Unbeknownst to Whitman, the process would matter little in the end.[13]

In late February, Whitman appeared on the political talk show *Crossfire* and reaffirmed Bush's commitment to regulate carbon dioxide. Her statement infuriated industry and spurred its right-wing think tank, the Competitive Enterprise Institute (CEI), to take action. The CEI had long acted as a mouthpiece for industry, including ExxonMobil, which funded it heavily. Myron Ebell, director of global warming policy for the CEI, responded to Whitman's statement by telling *The New York Times*, "This is a colossal mistake.... If they persist, there will be war." On March 1, 2001, Haley Barbour, former chair of the Republican National Committee and Bush's campaign strategist, fired off a letter to Vice President Cheney entitled, "Bush-Cheney Energy Policy and CO_2." Barbour, the future governor of Mississippi, was a powerful DC insider who had lobbied on behalf of the tobacco industry for years. He had acted on behalf of electric power companies when he wrote the letter to Cheney. As Kennedy describes, the president's major donors from the fossil fuel industry had enlisted Barbour to map out a Bush energy policy that would be "friendly to their interests."[14]

In his letter, Barbour wrote, "A moment of truth is arriving in the form of a decision whether this Administration's policy will be to regulate and/or tax CO_2 as a pollutant." Hinting that the very idea of regulation amounts to "eco-extremism," Barbour's memo set forth industry's no-regulation position – a position that would become U.S. policy, notwithstanding the 323 pages of the CAA.[15]

On March 13, 2001, the president made a sudden about-face from his earlier campaign promise and announced he would not regulate carbon dioxide. He attributed his turnaround to the "incomplete state of scientific knowledge" on global warming and the energy needs of the nation. But the real reason, later exposed by the *L.A. Times* and court documents, had to do with pressure exerted by the energy industry. Three days after Bush's announcement, former congressman Jack Kemp, serving as a Distinguished Fellow for the CEI, sent a letter to the U.S. Department of Energy secretary, Spencer Abraham. Applauding the administration for its new position on carbon dioxide regulation, Kemp credited the CEI for "giving the president intellectual support and political cover to 'do the right thing.'" A remarkable collusion between high-ranking public officials and corporate captains would then transpire to implement industry's antiregulatory agenda under the mantle of environmental law.[16]

The fossil fuel energy picture had begun to form in the first few days of Bush's administration as part of a clandestine process that ran parallel to the regulatory one initiated by the petition. Bush created a task force to develop a new template for energy policy. He put Vice President Cheney in charge and stacked it with people closely tied to the energy industry. Operating the official group in total secrecy, Cheney invited a parade of energy industry representatives to deliver regulatory wish lists. Kennedy wrote, "[The task force] behaved ... like a band of pirates divvying up the booty.... [T]he big energy companies all but held the pencil as the task force crafted its report." On May 17, 2001, Bush unveiled his energy task force's plan – "an orgy of industry plunder," Kennedy described, containing tax advantages, deregulation, and huge subsidies that would benefit "virtually every major polluter in the energy industry." A moment of truth had indeed arrived for energy policy, just as Barbour had said. During the George W. Bush presidency, the fossil fuel industry would enjoy a state of prolonged amnesty from environmental regulation.[17]

But while backdoor politics had settled the matter of carbon dioxide regulation, the legal process continued on its separate track. The public comment period for the carbon dioxide petition remained open until May 23, 2001, during which time EPA received 50,000 public comments. It would not be the first occasion, and certainly not the last, that a regulatory process offering strictly formal comment opportunities for the public proceeded simultaneously with industry's shoulder-to-shoulder politicking in agency backrooms – the former process largely oblivious to the latter.[18]

SUPPRESSING CLIMATE SCIENCE

Having made the political decision not to regulate carbon dioxide, the number one environmental challenge of the George W. Bush administration during the subsequent seven years was to suppress climate science. This became necessary for two reasons: first, to dampen rising public pressure to regulate carbon emissions; and second, to stifle evidence that would show endangerment from carbon pollution (which in turn could be used by the public in a lawsuit to force regulation under the CAA). Mounting climate evidence had the effect of loading the act's artillery of potential regulation and pointing it toward industry. An endangerment finding, which turned on climate science, was the regulatory trigger Bush most needed to avoid.

It would not be easy. The White House strategy became to shield industry from regulation for as long as possible by emphasizing scientific uncertainty over global warming. Early on, the White House searched for a trove of scientific doubt on climate change. On May 11, 2001, with less than two weeks to go before the close of the public comment period on the petition, the White House turned to the National Research Council (NRC), seeking assistance in identifying the "greatest certainties and uncertainties" in climate change science. The NRC returned a summary report three weeks later, on June 6, 2001. Its first two lines concluded, "Greenhouse gases are accumulating in Earth's atmosphere as a result of human activities, causing surface air temperatures and subsurface ocean temperatures to rise. *Temperatures are, in fact, rising.*"[19]

This could not have come as welcome language for the administration. The inside campaign quickly intensified, and during the full course of the Bush presidency, White House officials and agency heads doctored government reports, censored climate change scientists, and changed agency testimony to Congress. A congressional investigation would find:

> [T]he evidence before the Committee leads to one inescapable conclusion: the Bush Administration has engaged in a systematic effort to manipulate climate change science and mislead policymakers and the public about the dangers of global warming.... *The Bush Administration has acted as if the oil industry's communications plan were its mission statement.*[20]

Sooner or later, EPA would have to issue a technical finding stating whether carbon dioxide threatened to "endanger public health or welfare" under the CAA. But for two years and three months after the public comment period ended, the petition seeking carbon dioxide regulation languished in the agency. During this time, the fossil fuel industry engaged in an all-out "mystification" campaign to deny the reality of global warming and to discredit climate scientists who sounded the alarm about climate change, as Ross Gelbspan documented in his books, *Boiling Point* and *The Heat is On*. Every year of regulatory delay paid colossal profits to the fossil fuel industry – and continues to. As an internal document prepared by the American Petroleum Institute (API) in 1999 disclosed, "Climate is at the center of industry's business interests. Policies limiting carbon emissions reduce petroleum product use." Due to lack of regulation, the five biggest oil companies in the world reaped more than $1 trillion in profit in the first dozen years of the new millennium.[21]

Running the climate show on behalf of the oil industry was Phil Cooney, a lobbyist with API for fifteen years, who became the organization's "climate team leader." When Bush assumed the presidency, he appointed Cooney as chief of staff for the White House Council on Environmental Quality (CEQ) – the office that coordinates U.S. environmental policy. From his new government desk, Cooney continued to carry out the same climate disinformation campaign he helped establish at API.[22]

The industry strategy sought to "reposition global warming as theory (not fact)," as later revealed by internal documents prepared for industry in the early 1990s. To accomplish this, industry had to conjure uncertainty on the issue of climate change, despite overwhelming scientific consensus that carbon pollution caused global warming. As a detailed analysis by the Union of Concerned Scientists explains, the uncertainty strategy came directly from the tobacco industry's successful campaign to cast doubt in the minds of Americans about the dangers of smoking (even after the surgeon general's report linked smoking to lung cancer). Al Gore describes the techniques in *An Inconvenient Truth*: "They exaggerate minor uncertainties in order to pretend that the big conclusions are not a matter of consensus." George Monbiot observes, "They didn't have to win the argument to succeed, only to cause as much confusion as possible."[23]

To this end, industry think tanks recruited a handful of scientists to serve as climate skeptics and paid them to travel around the country to give speeches and press interviews that challenged the scientific consensus on human-caused climate change. As investigators discovered, ExxonMobil helped underwrite "the most sophisticated and most successful disinformation campaign" waged since the tobacco days. According to the Union of Concerned Scientists, between 1998 and 2005, ExxonMobil funneled $16 million "to a network of ideological and advocacy organizations that manufacture uncertainty on the issue." The Competitive Enterprise Institute (CEI) became particularly active.[24]

The industry strategy worked well. Gelbspan notes that the campaign "lulled people into a deep apathy about the crisis by persuading them that the issue of climate change is terminally stuck in scientific uncertainty. It is not." In fact, as the editor-in-chief of the prestigious journal *Science* explains, "Consensus as strong as the one that has developed around this topic is rare in science." In 2009, the stunning deceit came to light. Reporters gained documents from fourteen years earlier (1995) announcing the conclusion of industry's own scientists and technical experts that "the potential impact of human emissions of greenhouse gases such as CO_2 on climate *is well established and cannot be denied.*" Industry knew all along.[25]

The disinformation campaign maintains an active front within government itself. As the Union of Concerned Scientists reported in 2007, "ExxonMobil's cozy relationship with government officials ... enables the corporation to work behind the scenes to gain access to key decision makers. In some cases, the company's proxies have directly shaped the global warming message put forth by federal agencies." For the first several years of the George W. Bush administration, Phil Cooney served as a main operative from the inside, taking his pen to key government science reports and changing language so as to downplay the climate threat and stall regulation from EPA. A congressional investigation concluded that "White House edits to climate change documents mirror API's stated strategy on this issue."[26]

In May 2002, a key interagency report came out that sent industry and Cooney into a tailspin. The *U.S. Climate Action Report*, released by EPA (as required by previous international climate negotiations) underscored the threat of climate change and directly undermined Bush's antiregulatory stance. Jumping into action, Cooney turned to Myron Ebell, the global warming director at the CEI, for help in devising a strategy to discredit EPA and its unfavorable report. In response, Ebell sent a June 3, 2002 e-mail to Cooney discussing tactics for not only muting the *U.S.*

Climate Action Report, but also for getting rid of EPA's director, Christine Todd Whitman.[27]

Ebell began his e-mail to Cooney by saying, "Thanks for calling and asking for our help. I know you're in crisis mode.... I want to help you cool things down." But the first step, Ebell insisted, had to be taken by the administration. He advised Cooney: "[A]fter consulting with the team, I think that what we can do is limited until there is an official statement from the Administration repudiating the report ... and disavowing large parts of it." Ebell's strategy for dealing with the adverse report would be to blame EPA for "freelancing," as he called it. He suggested, "It seems to me that the folks at EPA are the obvious fall guys, and we would only hope that the fall guy (or gal) should be as high up as possible.... *Perhaps tomorrow we will call for Whitman to be fired.*"[28]

Bush issued the suggested statement the next day. He told the American people that the report was "put out by the bureaucracy" and that he had not shifted his stance on global warming policy. Cooney then drafted a letter to *The New York Times* in which he spun the problematic *Climate Action Report* in a way that *favored* Bush's no-action climate stance. Spinning is an old craft of politics, one used commonly for dealing with problematic scientific reports. Cooney had ample experience from his years at the API doctoring reports to emphasize uncertainty; as the congressional investigation found, "it was his job [at the API] to ensure that any governmental actions taken relating to climate change were consistent with the goals of the petroleum industry." In his draft letter to *The New York Times*, Cooney said that the *Climate Action Report* "reinforces" the "significant scientific uncertainties" surrounding global warming.[29]

As reporter Tim Dickinson recounts in an exposé, the *Climate Action Report* prompted a letter from Bill O'Keefe, Cooney's former boss at the API and a registered lobbyist for ExxonMobil, to Bush's chief of staff. In it, O'Keefe urged that all communications on climate science coming from the White House be better coordinated internally to maintain consistency (he suggested a task force), and to that end, he offered, "As you know, I am prepared and willing to help in any way I can." He faxed a copy of the letter to Cooney. A handwritten note at the bottom of the page read, "P.S. You are doing a great job."[30]

The White House disinformation campaign continued as the petition that sought regulation still languished in EPA. The congressional investigation found that Cooney and others at CEQ made 181 edits to a strategic plan for the U.S. Climate Change Science Program with the effect of "exaggerating or emphasizing scientific uncertainties related to global warming." They made 113 more edits that "deemphasized or diminished the importance of the human role in global warming." As Dickenson reports, after the 2002 fiasco with EPA's adverse report, "Cooney wielded a heavier pen when editing official reports on global warming. Not content obscuring science with uncertainty, he began to rewrite the science itself."[31]

In early 2003, EPA prepared the final drafts of a landmark *Report on the Environment*, the first ever national ecological picture. No one could have doubted the significance of the report's climate section, written by the very agency sitting on a petition to regulate carbon dioxide. The EPA would be hard-pressed to deny that petition if it found in its own report that carbon dioxide pollution caused dangerous global warming. On March 4, 2003, an OMB employee sent a heads-up e-mail to Cooney, saying, "Phil, I don't know whether you have reviewed the Climate Section of the EPA report, but I think you ... need to focus on it before this goes final. Even though this information is generally not new, I suspect this will generate negative press coverage."[32]

Cooney gave the section a hard edit, deleting clear statements like "Climate change has global consequences for human health and the environment" and injecting doubt instead. By the time he had completed his gloss-over, the climate section looked markedly different than what EPA had drafted. He put a cover sheet on the draft saying, "These changes must be made," and sent it back to EPA. Likewise, the OMB informed EPA, "no further changes may be made."[33]

A group of upset EPA staffers met to determine their course of action on May 6, 2003, and later prepared an internal memo outlining options. Clearly, the career staffers felt obliged to disseminate accurate climate information to the public, but they also warned EPA Director Christine Todd Whitman that any refusal to accept Cooney's changes would "antagonize the White House." Whitman opted to delete the five-page section entirely rather than issue a tampered report from her agency. Consequently, the final draft of EPA's "first-ever national picture of the U.S. environment" had no discussion of the biggest ecological threat facing the planet. Shortly thereafter, on May 21, 2003, Whitman announced her resignation.[34]

It had been four years since groups had filed the petition asking EPA to regulate carbon dioxide, and EPA had still taken no action. Whitman simply left the petition for her successor. Two months after she resigned, a killer heat wave gripped Europe, with scorching temperatures that lasted for weeks and left more than 70,000 people dead. Meanwhile, EPA had still not found "endangerment" from America's unregulated carbon dioxide pollution.[35]

EPA'S PETITION DENIAL

As of August 25, 2003, European officials were still struggling to deal with a mass of dead bodies. In Paris, refrigerated trucks and a warehouse had been set up to handle the overflow of unclaimed corpses. Seemingly oblivious to the aftermath of the climate tragedy, EPA officials issued a decision on August 28, 2003, denying the petition seeking regulation of carbon dioxide. United States' emissions accounted for nearly a third of the world's total, but the nation's top environmental agency had just made clear its refusal to control them.[36]

It had taken legal acrobatics to vault the CAA's clear mandate. Section 202 directs EPA to regulate emissions from new cars if the pollution *may reasonably be antici-pated to endanger public health or welfare.* Mounting evidence showing a strong link between carbon dioxide emissions and global warming made it increasingly difficult for EPA to worm out of this statutory obligation. But things moved fast after Whitman resigned. Cooney's boss at CEQ, James Connaughton (a former utility industry lobbyist), had injected himself directly into the process of preparing EPA's decision document, and key edits to the draft had come from his agency.[37]

From the outset, EPA's draft decision document had a glaring problem. Simply put, science did not support a no-regulation position. Flagging it, CEQ wrote, "Vulnerability: science." Other edits showed CEQ's spin strategy to deal with the shortcoming: first, filter all of the climate science presented by petitioners down to one report; then twist that report to assert scientific uncertainty; and finally, claim discretion not to regulate based on that uncertainty and additional policy concerns. As a later congressional investigation concluded, "CEQ apparently saw the science of global warming as an obstacle standing in the way of its desired result: the refusal to regulate."[38]

Officials chose to hone in on the 2001 National Research Council report as the touchstone science. (This was the report produced earlier in response to the White House's request). CEQ editors cherry-picked language from the report to paint a picture of uncertainty in climate science, seizing on one sentence stating that a causal link between greenhouse gases and climate change could not be "unequivo-cally" established. Actually, the NRC report contained many strong statements tying human carbon emissions to global warming, and these had appeared in the initial draft of EPA's decision document. If allowed to remain, such statements would have severely undermined EPA's petition denial. As to these, CEQ's edits read, "the above quotes are unnecessary and extremely harmful to the legal case being made in this document. This is not a survey of the science, but a legal argument." CEQ edits further instructed, "revise all science text in collaboration with [the Department of Justice]." By the final draft, the discussion of the NRC report had been substantially changed to conform to a deregulation stance. The manipulation provoked a group of leading climate scientists to later challenge EPA's decision as *amicus* parties in litigation, stating:

> EPA's use of selective quotations and its unbalanced treatment of uncertainty allowed it to draw conclusions that are *opposed to* the actual scientific conclusions of *Climate Change Science* [the NRC Report].... *EPA's denial of [the] petition to regulate was based on distortion and misrepresentation of the scientific findings of Climate Change Science.*[39]

As to the legal merits of the petition, EPA's decision document justified inaction on two grounds. First, the agency claimed it lacked authority to regulate because carbon dioxide is not an air pollutant under the CAA. This represented an about-face in agency position. In 1998, EPA's General Counsel had prepared a legal opinion stating plainly, "CO_2 emissions are within the scope of EPA's authority to regulate." Second, EPA concluded that, even if it had authority to regulate, it had *discretion* not to regulate. The claimed discretion to do nothing was quite predictable. Agency discretion nearly always favors industry as long as corporations have the political system wired at the highest levels of the bureaucracy. The final EPA document was signed by Jeffrey Holmstead, Assistant Administrator for Air and Regulation, who, before being appointed by Bush as the top regulator of air pollution in the country, worked as a leading lawyer-lobbyist for major utility companies.[40]

THE LEGAL CHALLENGE TO EPA'S DENIAL

After EPA issued its decision not to regulate, Massachusetts, joined by eleven other states, promptly brought litigation challenging it. These states, many of which sit along coastlines, were alarmed by the prospect of rising sea levels, diminished water supplies, flooding, drought, wildfires, and extreme damage to their natural resources and state property. Notably, the oil-drilling states of Louisiana and Mississippi did not join the challenge, even though they were then, and still are, sitting ducks for climate tragedy. Haley Barbour, the powerful Republican lobbyist who had issued the letter to Bush back in 2001 stating, "A moment of truth is arriving," became Mississippi's governor in 2004. Governor Barbour no doubt remained quite pleased that Bush's no-regulation policy – the one he had helped launch – had endured so well.[41]

The legal system moves at a snail's pace. It would take nearly two years after EPA's denial for the case, *Massachusetts v. EPA*, to be decided by the D.C. Court of Appeals. Meanwhile, scientific warnings carried increasing gravity. On January 10, 2005, Dr. Rajendra Pachauri, the chairman of the UN Intergovernmental Panel on Climate Change (IPCC), told an international conference of government leaders that the atmosphere had reached dangerous levels of carbon dioxide and that the world needed to make very deep cuts in emissions. He warned, "We have just a small window of opportunity and it is closing rather rapidly. There is not a moment to lose." He added, "We are risking the ability of the human race to survive."[42]

Over the ensuing months, word began to trickle to the press about the Bush administration's efforts to minimize threats of climate change to the American public. On June 8, 2005, *The New York Times* broke a story detailing Phil Cooney's interference into several key scientific reports. With supporting detail from multiple leaked internal drafts bearing Cooney's handwritten notes (as well as a divulging letter by whistle-blower Rick Piltz, a senior climate researcher whose agency's reports were edited by Cooney), reporter Andrew Revkin summarized Cooney's changes as creating "an air of doubt about findings that most climate experts say are robust." Two days after the *Times* article, Cooney resigned and immediately took a position with ExxonMobil. A White House spokeswoman said Cooney's timing to leave was merely coincidental. Commenting on his work with CEQ, she said, "Phil Cooney did a great job."[43]

A month after Cooney resigned, on July 15, 2005, the D.C. Court of Appeals issued its decision in *Massachusetts v. EPA*. It upheld EPA's petition denial, stating that EPA had properly exercised its discretion based on science and policy concerns. Raising issues of scientific uncertainty, the court made much of the statement in the NRC report that the link between greenhouse gas emissions and global warming could not be "unequivocally established." CEQ's spin job had worked like a charm. The White House's improper meddling with EPA's decision document would not come to light for another two and a half years and then only as a result of a congressional investigation. Once again, a court unknowingly gave deference to corruption.[44]

The next month, on August 29, 2005, a horrifying "moment of truth" arrived for Barbour's state of Mississippi. In the dead of night, at 2:00 AM, hurricane-force winds slammed the state's coastline. Over the course of 17 hours, Hurricane Katrina spun 11 tornadoes and created a 28-foot storm surge that obliterated many of Mississippi's coastal towns, leaving 238 people dead. In the neighboring state of Louisiana, storm-shocked communities recovered 1,079 bodies and suffered thousands of displaced residents. Climate scientist Michael MacCracken had warned in a 2004 affidavit prepared for the *Massachusetts v. EPA* litigation that climate change may increase the ferocity of hurricanes. In words that the Supreme Court would later call "eerily prescient," he stated that storm surges *could inundate New Orleans, significantly enhancing the risk to a major urban population.*" Katrina stormed in as one of fourteen hurricanes that year – an unprecedented record. Endangerment was manifest.[45]

The *Massachusetts v. EPA* case had been promptly appealed after the D.C. court's ruling, but the U.S. Supreme Court did not issue its opinion until April 2, 2007. As the case sat pending, the climate situation worsened. In February 2006, NASA scientist Jim Hansen alerted the press that NASA satellites showed the accelerated breakup of the Greenland ice sheet: "Twice as much ice is going into the sea as it was five years ago," he reported. The Bush administration tried to stop him from making the news public, but Hansen followed what he interpreted as the duties of his office and ignored their restrictions, warning the world, "Once a sheet starts to disintegrate, it can reach a tipping point beyond which breakup is explosively rapid."[46]

On February 2, 2007, two months before the Supreme Court handed down its *Massachusetts v. EPA* decision, the UN IPCC released a key climate report. Summarizing the conclusions of more than 600 authors and 620 expert reviewers from more than 40 countries, it said, "Warming of the climate system is *unequivocal*." The particular word choice threatened to pull the rug out from under the Bush administration's strategy for regulatory delay. EPA's decision document denying the petition to regulate had put nearly its full weight on one statement in the NRC climate report that said the link between greenhouse gases and climate change could not be "unequivocally" established. A leading UN report now telling the world that global warming was "unequivocal" could directly undercut EPA's position in front of the U.S. Supreme Court. The report unnerved industry. A right-wing, Exxon-funded Washington think tank, the American Enterprise Institute, jumped forward to offer scientists $10,000 awards (plus travel expenses and additional payments) to refute the IPCC report.[47]

On April 2, 2007, the Supreme Court finally issued its opinion in *Massachusetts v. EPA*, and it squarely held EPA's denial of the petition invalid. Addressing EPA's argument that it lacked authority to regulate carbon dioxide, the Court gave a litany of rebuttals: "We have little trouble concluding" that the Clean Air Act authorizes EPA to regulate carbon dioxide; "The statutory text forecloses EPA's reading" that "carbon dioxide is not an 'air pollutant'"; "The statute is unambiguous"; "EPA never identifies any action remotely suggesting that Congress meant to curtail its power to treat greenhouse gases as air pollutants"; and "We are moreover puzzled by EPA's roundabout argument." The EPA's first argument lay shredded.[48]

With equal derision, the Court rejected EPA's other argument – that EPA had discretion not to exercise its regulatory authority. Congress had not given EPA "roving license to ignore the statutory text," the Court scolded, but rather required the agency to exercise its judgment within "defined statutory limits." Noting that "EPA has refused to comply with this clear statutory command," the Court said, "[EPA] has offered a laundry list of reasons not to regulate [that] have nothing to do with whether greenhouse gas emissions contribute to climate change."[49]

Perhaps the most remarkable aspect of the case was not its outcome but rather the failure of everyone involved to call out the elephant in the room. The EPA's refusal to regulate stemmed from political collusion with industry at the highest levels of government, yet briefs in the case failed to mention the breakdown of the administrative system. Investigation into corruption already steamed under way in the U.S. House of Representatives. The House Committee on Oversight and Government Reform issued a report just eight months after the *Massachusetts v. EPA* opinion entitled, "Political Interference with Climate Change Science Under the Bush Administration," which fully documented the tainted EPA process. The Committee had held two hearings before the Supreme Court issued its decision. Fifteen months prior to the Supreme Court's opinion in *Massachusetts v. EPA*, Congress heard testimony by James Hansen on the administration's efforts to silence him and prevent him from having contacts with the press. Four months prior to the *Massachusetts v. EPA* opinion, the Union of Concerned Scientists released a statement, "Political Interference with Science," signed by more than 15,000 scientists from 50 states, including 52 Nobel Laureates, saying that the administration's actions compromised scientific integrity in decision making. Just a month prior to the *Massachusetts v. EPA* opinion, Hansen, back in front of Congress again, submitted testimony entitled "Political Interference with Climate Change Science," in which he stated, "In my more than three decades in government, I have never seen anything approaching the degree to which information flow from scientists to the public has been screened and controlled as it is now." The consequences of the political cover-up campaign, he made clear, could be ruinous:

> The effect of leaving the public confused about the reality of human-caused climate change is to delay actions.... [I]f we push the climate system hard enough it can obtain a momentum, it can pass tipping points, such that climate changes continue, out of our control.... [T]*here is the danger that we will create a different planet, one far outside the range that has existed in the course of human history.*[50]

Everyone knows what a gerbil cage looks like. The gerbil spends most of its time running in a wheel that spins around and around. No real progress occurs by spinning the wheel, but the gerbil stays occupied. Environmental law operates in much the same way. Lawyers, judges, and bureaucrats have very little sense of the urgency of the environmental crisis yet believe they are accomplishing a great deal as they spin through the statutory processes. Many legal scholars heralded the *Massachusetts v. EPA* decision as the first landmark climate opinion, but in actuality, it had little discernible effect on government's antiregulatory agenda.

The Supreme Court remanded the matter to the D.C. Circuit Court of Appeals for further proceedings, and that court, in turn, remanded half the claims to EPA and dismissed the other half. Basically, it returned the process to the same wheel-spinning agency that had violated the law in the first place. The Supreme Court had firmly stated that EPA must "ground its reasons for action or inaction in the statute." If the agency found endangerment from carbon dioxide pollution, it would have to regulate, under the clear terms of the statute. If the agency persisted in its refusal to find endangerment, it would have to give reasons based on science or another statutory basis, not politics. But no time frame bound this procedural remand to the agency. The delay tactics industry had used for years still paid off in soaring profits. Nearly two decades had passed since Hansen made his first testimony warning Congress about global warming, and eight years had passed since groups filed the endangerment petition asking EPA to regulate. Nature's clock ticked down, yet the legal system still posed no impediment to the dangerous pollution spewing from tailpipes and smoke stacks across America.[51]

THE CLIMATE WHIPSAW

Three weeks after the *Massachusetts v. EPA* decision, on April 27, 2007, James Hansen appeared before Congress again, this time to give testimony on the worsening climate crisis. The planet, he testified, was now in a state of emergency. The world must slash carbon emissions, he warned, because there could be no adaptation to continually rising sea levels caused by global warming. The "most critical action for saving the planet," he said, must be phasing out existing coal plants and preventing the construction of new ones because of their huge CO_2 emissions.[52]

Stopping big coal was like stopping a tidal wave. At the time, the United States was on a verge of a coal rush, and 151 new coal-fired plants were proposed nationwide. A halt to new coal-fired plants, however, remained feasible through the Clean Air Act. An endangerment finding would trigger regulation in several parts of the Act, including those affecting coal-fired plants. The Supreme Court had required EPA to consider the matter. Clearly, the future of coal hung in the balance of the agency's next move.[53]

By the summer of 2007, a torrent of science flooded the media, but it could not keep pace with the rapid ice melt on Earth. Satellite images of the polar ice sheets were unnerving scientists. They showed that the northern polar ice cap was shrinking nearly three times faster than the most *pessimistic* computer models predicted. At that rate, the summer sea ice could be gone by 2040.[54]

In July of that year, James Hansen and his colleagues published a scientific paper in Great Britain's most prestigious scientific journal that shattered the image of slow-moving climate change. The scientists had examined paleoclimate data in an effort to explore past climate conditions. Their analysis showed that a fast-feedback mechanism allows the planet to be "whipsawed between climate states," causing cataclysmic change within a relatively short period of time rather than across millennial time frames as many had assumed. One critical feedback, they said, results from the melting of the massive ice sheets at the poles. Because ice reflects heat and water absorbs heat, ice melting begets more melting – a phenomenon scientists call the "albedo effect." That alone could trigger a disastrous cycle. Hansen and his coauthors warned, "Recent greenhouse gas (GHG) emissions place the Earth *perilously close to dramatic climate change that could run out of our control*, with great danger for humans and other creatures." As to the vast reserves of fossil fuels remaining beneath the surface of the Earth – reserves that oil corporations remain bent on exploiting – the scientists said, "we, humanity, cannot release to the atmosphere all, or even most, fossil fuel CO_2. *To do so would guarantee dramatic climate change, yielding a different planet than the one on which civilization developed."*[55]

To prevent runaway heating, the scientists wrote, the amount of carbon dioxide in the atmosphere must not exceed 450 parts per million (ppm). At the time, the 450 ppm figure reflected general scientific consensus as to the danger point. Hansen had given Congress the same number in his testimony just three months earlier. The estimate, however, rested largely on the feedbacks, including the albedo effect at the poles. That situation stood anything but stable.[56]

"THE ARCTIC IS SCREAMING"

Despite the shocking ice melt, EPA remained silent as to the *Massachusetts v. EPA* remand sitting in the agency. The Clean Air Act seemed to have dropped off the table. Amid the vacuum of climate leadership, former vice president Al Gore took to the media to explain the extreme danger of carbon pollution to the public. He had kept a close watch on the Arctic situation as it unfolded during the summer of 2007. In an opinion editorial published on July 1, 2007 in *The New York Times*, he warned, "What is at risk of being destroyed is not the planet itself, but the conditions that have made it hospitable for human beings." Carbon dioxide levels, he pointed out, now approached 383 parts per million. "This is not a political issue. This is a moral issue, one that affects the survival of human civilization.... It is ... a planetary emergency," he implored.[57]

By September, news from the Arctic horrified observers. The ice sheet had now melted 20 percent below the previous record low in 2005. *"The Arctic Is Screaming,"* blared headlines nationwide, quoting Mark Serreze, a senior government scientist in Boulder, Colorado. Scientists around the world scrambled to revise their predictions based on the radical melt. Hansen and others warned that the Arctic ice sheet had reached or passed its own tipping point. Greenland ice was thawing dramatically too, adding up to 58 trillion gallons of water a year to the oceans, a rate more than double the prior decade's melting. Antarctica was no less worrisome: ice loss there had escalated by 59 percent over the prior decade. This deterioration was massive and abrupt, as evidenced by the sudden collapse in 2002 of an ice shelf the size of Rhode Island. Stable for the last 10,000 years, it disintegrated in three weeks.[58]

Breakdown of the planet's great ice masses would cause sea level rise, and some scientists began to doubt the IPCC's earlier models showing that such rise would be gradual. Two-thirds of the world's major cities lie in low-elevation coastal areas – cities like New York, London, and Tokyo. The "whipsaw effect" described by Hansen and his colleagues haunted many in the scientific community. Oregon State University researcher Ed Brook told reporters, "Everyone around the world could experience abrupt climate change in the future."[59]

Some scientists feared that this litany of bad news would cause people to give up and cease efforts to reduce carbon pollution. But as Hansen emphasized to the press, "It's not too late to stabilize climate." Repeatedly, he called for deep cuts in carbon emissions. The regulatory authority for mandatory reductions existed, as clearly affirmed by the Supreme Court in *Massachusetts v. EPA*. Hansen spoke adamantly when he told the press that he would not lose hope – because he has grandchildren.[60]

KANSAS ON THE GLOBE

By October 2007, more than six months had passed since the *Massachusetts v. EPA* decision. Obviously, industry operatives in the administration made sure that EPA would simply sit on the court's remand – ice sheet melt and tipping points notwithstanding. But when justice fails, citizens often turn to other tactics.

At 5:00 AM on October 8, 2007, thirty Greenpeace activists in Kent, England, broke a padlock at the Kingsnorth coal-fired plant – a plant that emitted nearly 20,000 metric tons of carbon dioxide a day into the atmosphere. They snuck inside and dispersed to the furnace, the conveyor belts, and the pump house, where they cut the electricity and successfully shut down the plant. They sought to call attention to the threat of runaway climate change as a result of new coal-fired plants. A pending permit, if approved, would allow the construction of a huge replacement coal plant at the site.[61]

While one man stayed on the ground and kept radio contact, one woman and the other four men of the group (which came to be known as the Kingsnorth Six) began a grueling scale of the 220-meter chimney. They climbed a narrow ladder between the four flues, hauling heavy bags that contained paint, ropes, food, and other supplies. "Imagine the most tired and in pain you've ever been in and multiply that by a million," one of them later described. In a physical feat that required nine hours in 120-degree temperatures and a miserable overnight stay at the top, they managed to paint "Gordon" – the name of the prime minister – down the front of the towering chimney. By all accounts, these were just ordinary people – but ones who risked their lives and liberty to stop coal. Police arrested them the next day and charged them with aggravated trespass and criminal damage. The trial would not occur for nearly a year, but it would draw the world's most prominent climate scientist, Dr. James Hansen, to their defense.

Ten days after the Kingsnorth action, in a boxy government building in Topeka, Kansas, Roderick Bremby, the Secretary of the Kansas Department of Health and Environment, mailed a letter. Addressed to the senior manager of Sunflower Electric Power Corporation, a company that sought a permit for a new coal-fired plant in Kansas, the letter noted the "deleterious impact of greenhouse gases on the environment in which we live." In stunning language that paralleled an endangerment finding, the letter continued, "emission of air pollution from the proposed coal fired plant, specifically carbon dioxide emissions, presents a *substantial endangerment to the health of persons or to the environment.*" It became the first-ever denial of a coal-fired plant permit based on the threat of global warming. When it hit the press, climate listserves around the planet buzzed with analysis. Of all surprises, Kansas had jumped in front of the federal EPA, which had not yet issued any endangerment finding on the federal level. The action drew the wrath of the coal industry, which ultimately spent $800,000 in an effort to get the Kansas legislature to overturn the decision. Twice the Kansas legislature passed bills allowing the plant to go forward, and twice Governor Kathleen Sebelius vetoed them.[62]

Days after the Kansas decision, on October 23, 2007, Congress took testimony on the impacts of climate change on health. The evidence would no doubt prove crucial to EPA's endangerment determination under the Clean Air Act, still lingering on remand before the agency. The testimony of Dr. Julie Gerberding, Director of the Center for Disease Control, would undoubtedly illuminate whether carbon dioxide pollution "endangers … public health or welfare" under the CAA. Analysts anticipated that strong testimony could set a nail in the coffin for the fossil fuel industries. But instead, the testimony seemed oddly tempered, at least in contrast to the myriad reports from the United Nations and scientists worldwide that warned of life-threatening consequences from climate change. Dr. Gerberding told Congress that climate change would have a "broad range of impacts on the health of Americans," but she revealed few details.[63]

Someone on the inside wasted no time in leaking an earlier version of her testimony to the press. It turned out this earlier version was twice the length of the final version submitted to Congress. A later discovery revealed that this initial version had been submitted to the White House for review. The White House deleted two crucial sections, "Climate Change Is a Public Health Concern," and "Climate Change Vulnerability." Defending the excisions, the White House said the testimony had not matched the science on global warming. The truth surfaced several months later when a senior advisor on climate change at EPA, Jason K. Burnett, resigned. In a letter to Congress, he explained in detail the White House's alteration of Gerberding's testimony. Vice President Cheney's office had forced her to delete the discussion about the consequences of climate change to public health out of concern that the testimony would establish "endangerment," making it harder to avoid regulating carbon dioxide.[64]

"THE STRAW ON THE CAMEL'S BACK"

On October 22, the day before Gerberding's muted testimony to Congress, Jim Hansen sat in a drab hearing room to testify before the Iowa Utilities Board, which considered a proposed permit for an Alliant Energy coal plant in Marshalltown, Iowa. The NASA climate scientist used every strategic forum possible in the legal system to get word out that global warming threatened the planet – and that society must phase out coal and switch to renewable energy to avoid crossing a catastrophic tipping point. He had appeared before Congress multiple times. He had written to prime ministers of other nations, governors of several states, and executives of coal companies. He had even gained the e-mails of every utility commissioner in every U.S. state and put them on his e-mail distribution list. For those who replied back requesting to be taken off the list, he would replace that person with the next person in line.[65]

This top scientist, gripped with urgency, told the Iowa commission, "the single most important action needed to decrease the present large planetary imbalance driving climate change is curtailment of CO_2 emissions from coal burning." His statement begged the question: How can just one coal-fired plant be of any significance? He explained, "Because of the danger of passing the ice sheet tipping point, even the emissions from one Iowa coal plant, with emissions of 5,900,000 tons of CO_2 per year and 297,000,000 over 50 years could be important as 'the straw on the camel's back.'"[66]

Scientists often speak in terms the public does not understand. But not Hansen. He continued, *"If we cannot stop the building of more coal-fired power plants, those coal trains will be death trains – no less gruesome than if they were boxcars headed to crematoria, loaded with uncountable irreplaceable species."* A robust set of scientific papers provided the technical basis for his astounding conclusion: every large proposed emitting coal-fired plant had to be stopped, and the old ones eventually bulldozed, in order to save the planet. If coal use continued according to business as usual, Hansen said, "a large fraction of the millions of species on Earth will be lost and it will be fair to assign a handful of those to [the Iowa plant]."[67]

"THIS IS THE DEFINING MOMENT"

On November 17, 2007, the UN IPCC issued its final Synthesis Report. The IPCC had just been named the recipient of the Nobel Peace Prize, along with Al Gore. The IPCC designed its synthesis report to focus the world on the upcoming climate negotiations that would take place in Bali, Indonesia, two weeks later. It warned of devastating climate impacts from continued greenhouse gas pollution – including sea level rise, submerged islands, and a 50 percent crop loss in Africa. Nearly one-third of the planet's species could go extinct, it projected.[68]

When the UN released the report, Rajendra Pachauri, head of the IPCC, met with the press. Even in the five years since the IPCC work had begun, he said, scientists have observed "much stronger trends in climate change," one of which was the record melting of polar ice during the summer of 2007. He warned that carbon reduction must start even earlier than previously thought: "If there's no action before 2012, that's too late."[69] He declared, "What we do in the next two to three years will determine our future. *This is the defining moment.*" At the same time, UN Secretary General Ban Ki-Moon urged the United States and China to take responsibility for their emissions: "Today the world's scientists have spoken, clearly and in one voice.... In Bali, I expect the world's policymakers to do the same." James Connaughton, chairman of the President's Council on Environmental Quality (CEQ), gave a press conference when the report came out. When asked how much warming the administration thought was acceptable, he responded, "We don't have a view on that."[70]

THE WORLD LOOKS TO BALI

From December 3 to 14, 2007, the world's leaders convened in Bali, Indonesia, to launch negotiations for a new global climate agreement. More than 200 scientists took the remarkable step of delivering a plea at Bali to take action to stabilize greenhouse gas concentrations at below 450 parts per million. This, they hoped, would limit global warming to 2°C above the preindustrial temperatures. The world had already warmed about .8°C, and there existed at least another .6°C in the pipeline from past emissions. Analyst Joseph Romm said, "No wonder scientists are getting desperate for action."[71]

The Executive Secretary of the UN climate body described Bali as "very much a make or break opportunity." Climate delegates from countries around the world all focused on getting the United States to commit to numerical goals for carbon reduction. No one could have hope of staving off a planetary catastrophe without the clear commitment of the United States to slash its carbon pollution.[72]

The remand in *Massachusetts v. EPA* created a slim opening for diplomatic pressure. If EPA came out with an endangerment finding before the Bali conference ended, the international community would know that the U.S. fossil fuel industry would have to be regulated under U.S. law. Climate thinkers in the United States dared to hope that the legal system would work as intended. Their anticipation seemed not entirely far-fetched. The EPA stood clearly charged by the highest court in the land to make a finding as to whether carbon dioxide pollution endangered public health and welfare. Legally, the White House could not make the determination. It must be a scientific, not political, finding under the clear terms of the statute and in accordance with the *Massachusetts v. EPA* ruling. The science certainly seemed to force an endangerment determination. That is, if the agency acted.

The remand had been sitting in the agency for eight months. Surely the career scientists and staffers at the agency had been working on the matter. If an endangerment finding came out during the Bali conference, the Bush negotiator would downplay it, but Gore could present it. He was scheduled to make an appearance near the end of the negotiations. He could tell the world, essentially, that although President Bush remained opposed to regulating carbon dioxide, the Supreme Court had forced regulation through the EPA. Negotiators could arrive at global targets for carbon reduction knowing that they would have some backing through U.S. environmental law. The EPA just had to issue an endangerment finding before the conference ended. Maybe the career staffers at the agency could pull it off.

On December 10, as the Bali conference met, Gore flew to Oslo, Norway, to accept his Nobel Peace Prize. His televised words reverberated in the conference rooms back at Bali and (undoubtedly) in the cramped staff offices of EPA. The former vice president said:

> We must act. The distinguished scientists ... have laid before us a choice.... We, the human species, are confronting a planetary emergency – a threat to the survival of our civilization that is gathering ominous and destructive potential even as we gather here. But there is hopeful news as well: we have the ability to solve this crisis and avoid the worst – though not all – of its consequences, if we act boldly, decisively and quickly.[73]

On the very same day, 15,000 geophysicists from around the world convened at the sprawling Moscone Center in San Francisco for their annual conference of the American Geophysical Union (AGU). At this distinguished gathering every year, the global climate picture gets updated. The ice meltdown from the summer consumed everyone's minds. Data was passed around the group as fast as gossip in a high school. The accelerating disintegration of the ice sheets at the north pole, in Greenland, and in West Antarctica likely meant that the scientists had aimed too high in estimating a safe atmospheric level of carbon dioxide. Rajendra Pachauri had said as much when he released the IPCC's report two weeks earlier.[74]

Early in the morning the next day, at 4:30 AM, Ross Gelbspan sent an e-mail to a climate listserve and later posted it on *Grist*. Gelbspan, the veteran Pulitzer Prize–winning reporter who had written the climate exposé, *Boiling Point*, had followed the climate crisis longer than most. Climate activists around the world woke up to his December 11 e-mail as they prepared to receive the day's news from Bali. They braced themselves. It came entitled, *Beyond the Point of No Return*, and read:

> We have failed to meet nature's deadline. In the next few years, this world will experience progressively more ominous and destabilizing changes. These will happen either incrementally – or in sudden, abrupt jumps.... There is no body of expertise – no authoritative answers – for this one. We are crossing a threshold into uncharted territory. And since there is no precedent to guide us, we are left with only our own hearts to consult, whatever courage we can muster, our

instinctive dedication to a human future – *and the intellectual integrity to look reality in the eye.*[75]

Things went sour in Bali that day. The U.S. negotiator flatly rejected mandatory greenhouse gas reductions, drawing the wrath of European leaders and other delegates. As the day drew on, emotions soared through the roof. Without regard to the Supreme Court remand in *Massachusetts v. EPA*, the Bush administration would stand for only voluntary reduction from U.S. industries. Climate negotiations reached an impasse.[76]

On December 13, Jim Hansen appeared before climate scientists in one packed room at the AGU conference in San Francisco. All wondered what he would make of the data now streaming in showing the collapse of the arctic ice sheet, the melting of Greenland, and the disintegration of ice shelves in West Antarctica. The scientists had professional interest in his conclusions, but it was the fact that they too had children and grandchildren that kept them at the edge of their seats.

Hansen presented his paper, *Earth's "Tipping Points" – How Close Are We?* He meticulously reviewed the ice breakup, presented modeling, and gave projected scenarios. The bombshell moment arrived when Hansen presented his bottom line: 350 ppm, not 450 ppm, likely represented the highest atmospheric concentration of carbon dioxide that could preserve the planet on which civilization developed. *The climate goal posts had just moved a mile.* The 450 ppm level had been the target that Hansen and most other scientists had offered over the prior several years. And 450 ppm had been the target that more than 200 scientists had called for in their plea to Bali delegates just weeks prior. But 450 sailed out the window now with the extraordinary meltdown of the Earth's ice masses over the summer of 2007. As Bill McKibben would write in a *Washington Post* article later that month, "[350 is] a number that may make what happened in Washington and Bali seem quaint and nearly irrelevant. It's the number that may define our future." Everyone in that AGU room knew that the atmospheric concentration of carbon dioxide was nearly 383 parts per million – and climbing fast. Levels had passed 350 ppm back in 1988 when George W. Bush's father was president. But Hansen left hope. With drastic carbon cuts, he said, the world could stave off disaster. We may not be beyond the point of no return. But, the scientists knew, the world clearly needed progress in Bali.[77]

Al Gore appeared in Bali that day, walking into a gathering of world delegates already on their feet. In his impassioned speech, Gore said he had been in touch with the scientists at the AGU conference. He conveyed the alarming news:

Just this week new evidence has been presented. I remember years ago listening to ... scientists ... express concern that some time towards the end of the 21st century we might ... [lose] the entire north polar ice cap. I remember only three years ago when they revised their estimates to say it could happen ... by 2050. I remember at the beginning of this year when I was shocked to hear them say along with others that it could happen in as little as 34 years and now, this week, they tell us it could completely disappear in as little as five to seven years....

For those who believed that this climate crisis was going to affect their grandchildren, and still said nothing, and were shaken a bit to hear that it would affect their children, and still said and did nothing, it is affecting us in the present generation, and it is up to us in this generation to solve this crisis.[78]

Gore had no formal authority to represent his country, but a Nobel Peace Prize mantled his words. Watching the emotional group of delegates, Gore must have sensed that many needed hope, vision, and leadership. Had EPA issued its endangerment finding before this crucial moment, Gore could have told the delegates that carbon dioxide pollution *would be regulated* in the United States, notwithstanding the president's recalcitrance, because the EPA held an obligation to carry out the law. However, EPA had issued nothing, absolutely nothing. Gore could only hope to keep the negotiations from unraveling entirely. He counseled the delegates to move forward, leave a placeholder for the United States in the agreements, and continue to hammer out a firm treaty with strict targets that could be adopted at the next climate conference scheduled for 2009 in Copenhagen, Denmark. Gore emphasized that those targets must take effect in 2010 rather than 2012 as previously contemplated. The IPCC's Rajendra Pachauri's statement made two weeks earlier hung over his words: "If there's no action by 2012, that's too late."[79]

After a protracted negotiation that brought tears, anger, boos, and desperation from many of the world's delegates, Bali produced a "road map" for future climate negotiations – but one with no signposts and no clear destination. Many doubted its usefulness. Only one party could claim resounding success: the negotiator for the Bush administration who had blocked any agreement that would define clear carbon cuts.[80]

The truth of what happened in the halls of EPA during the Bali Conference would come to light seven months later. On December 5, 2007, just two days after the Bali conference began, EPA Administrator Stephen Johnson had presented a proposed endangerment finding to the White House Office of Management and Budget. The twenty-eight-page document concluded that human carbon emissions, in fact, caused global warming. It detailed the enormous risk of harm from climate change, including exacerbated storms, flooding, heat waves, wildfires, drought, ecosystem damage, temperature extremes, rising sea levels, and a host of other damages. Most importantly, the document made a clear endangerment finding under the CAA. That one finding, had it been issued, would have triggered CAA regulation.[81]

Jason Burnett, Associate Deputy Administrator of EPA, had helped develop the endangerment finding in response to the *Massachusetts v. EPA* litigation. At 2:10

PM on December 5, he had sent the formal proposed endangerment finding as an e-mail attachment to the White House. According to an investigative report by the *Philadelphia Inquirer*, White House aides knew what the EPA finding would be. They also realized that if they opened the attachment, it would become public record. So, they never opened it. Instead, the White House called Administrator Johnson and instructed him to not issue the finding. Johnson complied with the request.

It must have been the case that many EPA officials inside the bureaucracy knew what had happened. The EPA task force in charge of producing the finding consisted of sixty to seventy people. But to all external observers, including many lawyers who had spent years on the case, the *Massachusetts v. EPA* remand still appeared in limbo. The Bali conference concluded without anyone outside of EPA realizing that the agency had in fact made the endangerment finding at a time when it could have been instrumental to international climate negotiations.

That revelation did not come to light until Jason Burnett resigned from his EPA post in June 2008 and disclosed to Congress the details regarding the White House's political interference with EPA. The next month, in July, the Senate Environment and Public Works Committee demanded to see the December 5 e-mail and the attachment containing the endangerment finding. The White House allowed three senators and their aides to view the document for a period of just three hours one evening; they were not allowed to copy it or take full notes. They viewed it under the supervision of White House aides.[82]

Nearly three years later, on February 8, 2011, a confidential letter came to light. It was from EPA Administrator Johnson to President Bush himself. Dated January 31, 2008 (a month after the Bali conference ended), the letter urged action to find endangerment, arguing:

[T]he Supreme Court's *Massachusetts v. EPA* decision still requires a response. That case combined with the latest science of climate change requires the Agency to propose a positive endangerment finding.... [T]he state of the latest climate change science does not permit a negative finding, nor does it permit a credible finding that we need to wait for more research.[83]

His appeal was in vain.

THE NO-ACTION REMAND

By June 1, 2008, the *Massachusetts v. EPA* remand still languished in EPA with no formal action. Late in the month, someone leaked a draft endangerment decision to the *Wall Street Journal*. The White House tried to prevent its publication, but the draft regulation appeared far and wide in media. According to the *Wall Street*

Journal, "The White House's Office of Management and Budget has asked EPA to delete sections of the document that say such emissions endanger public welfare, say how those gases could be regulated, and show an analysis of the cost of regulating greenhouse gases in the U.S. and other countries." Clearly, EPA staffers working on the draft had established a blueprint for an endangerment finding and subsequent regulation.[84]

On July 11, 2008, EPA released an iteration of the document called an "Advance Notice of Proposed Rule-Making." As a procedural action, it simply asked for public comment on carbon dioxide regulation. The measure seemed designed to stall actual regulation for several more months so that Bush could leave office without having to make an endangerment determination that would force him to regulate the industries that put him in office. Jason Burnett, the high-ranking EPA official who had worked on the endangerment remand after *Massachusetts v. EPA*, told a House Committee that senior EPA officials had met with representatives from the American Petroleum Institute, ExxonMobil, and other industry associations. The administration had told EPA to not move forward with regulation but instead to "emphasize the complexity of the challenge." The Advance Notice did exactly that. As the *Washington Post* summarized the situation: "To defer compliance with the Supreme Court's demand, the White House has walked a tortured policy path."[85]

With regulation effectively postponed as a result of the Advance Notice of Rule-Making, just days later, on July 17, EPA's Office of Research and Development released a peer-reviewed report entitled *Analyses of the Effects of Global Change on Human Health and Welfare and Human Systems*, in which it detailed the dangers to humans posed by climate change. The report found it "very likely" that increased deaths would result from hot weather alone. Seemingly a description of endangerment, the CAA's regulatory gate had already been closed by the Advance Notice of Rulemaking. With virtually no prospect of regulation during the Bush term, EPA soon thereafter issued a permit for a huge coal-fired plant at Desert Rock, Arizona, that would emit up to 10 million metric tons of carbon dioxide in the atmosphere a year. Jeffrey R. Holmstead, who just three years earlier had served as the highest EPA official for air pollution and who had signed EPA's denial of the petition to regulate, was the lawyer now in private practice who successfully sought the permit for the Desert Rock plant.[86]

THE KINGSNORTH TRIAL

Two months later, on September 3, 2008, Dr. James Hansen appeared in a British courtroom in Kent, England. He came there to testify on behalf of the Kingsnorth Six, the British citizens who had scaled the coal-fired plant at Kent a year earlier. The six hardly looked like criminals. Ordinary people with ordinary day jobs, they were terrified of jail. As their lawyer put it to the jury when introducing them, "[These are] the nicest defendants ever to be in a dock at a crown court and they are accused of trying to save the planet."[87]

The main defense that the barrister put forward on their behalf was a "lawful excuse" argument – that the six were justified in damaging property at the Kingsnorth power station to prevent even greater damage worldwide that would be wrought by climate change. It was roughly akin to the defense that excuses firefighters for breaking down a door to stop a fire. In the United States, this legal defense is called the "necessity defense." Could it be used to justify civil disobedience at a coal-fired plant that threatened the planet's atmosphere?[88]

The twelve jurors must have felt that they held the Earth in their hands as the world's most prominent climate scientist presented them with maps and charts, discussed tipping points, and explained the effects of runaway climate change on human life and property. He said that the 20,000 metric tons of carbon dioxide expelled into the atmosphere daily by the plant would result in up to 400 species on the planet going extinct. By shutting down the plant for even a day, the Kingsnorth Six would have helped prevent property damage on a far greater scale than they caused – damage stretching from the permafrost in Siberia, to the continental ice sheets, to the Yellow River in China, to the farms in sub-Saharan Africa, to the coast in Indonesia, to the slopes of Alaska, and indeed to England itself. Moving closer to the jury box, Hansen demonstrated how the jurors' own properties would be flooded by rising sea levels. The planet is in grave peril, he said: "Somebody needs to step forward and say there has to be a moratorium, draw a line in the sand and say no more coal-fired power stations."[89]

At the end of the ten-day trial, the jury fully acquitted the Kingsnorth Six. Two weeks after that, in New York City, Al Gore conveyed the urgency of climate action to an audience of hundreds of world leaders and chief executives at the Clinton Global Initiative meeting. Gore said he believed the "time has come" for young people to engage in civil disobedience to stop new coal-fired plants. Applause and cheers erupted throughout the room. In the first week of November, Australian protesters entered four separate coal plants and chained themselves to huge conveyor belts. The incidents forced shutdowns at each plant.[90]

On December 17, 2008, Hansen was back before the American Geophysical Union to deliver the prestigious Bjerknes Lecture. By then, the 350 ppm target had traveled around the world via the Internet, and scientists wanted to know what actions were needed to return the atmosphere to 350 ppm – and whether it even remained achievable. Hansen's prepared paper, "Target CO_2," called for a moratorium on coal-fired plants. The abstract read, "An initial 350 ppm CO_2 target may be achievable by phasing out coal use." But it also warned, "If the present overshoot of this target CO_2 is not brief, there is a possibility of seeding irreversible catastrophic effects."

Hansen's PowerPoint lineup consisted of sixty-nine complex graphs and charts, the sum of which provided a painful diagnosis of a planet in the throes of disaster. But at the tail end appeared a slide that seemed accidentally included. Brightening up the dark room, it was a picture of a toddler looking up with eyes widened to the wonders of the world. Hansen's voice softened as he told his audience of scientists:

> Jake is our newest grandchild, my son's first child. Jake has not done much of any-thing to cause global warming. He doesn't even walk yet. He crawls fast.... My par-ents lived about ninety years, so Jake will probably be around most of this century. He will live in the greenhouse world that we choose to create.[91]

THE COPENHAGEN COLLAPSE

In the end, George W. Bush left office without regulating carbon dioxide. The endangerment determination languished in the halls of EPA as President Obama took office. Eleven months later, on the first day of the next global climate confer-ence held (in December 2009) in Copenhagen, Denmark, EPA's new administra-tor, Lisa Jackson, finally issued the long-awaited endangerment finding under the CAA. A cynic might say the timing was just political show, as the finding itself did not result in regulation. The agency said it intended to give Congress a chance to act first.[92]

High hopes for a global climate agreement swirled at the opening of the Copenhagen conference, but by its second week no progress had been made, and the developing and industrialized nations remained in deadlock. Forty thousand people flooded the streets of Copenhagen in protest, and riots ensued. Within the conference halls, delegates from developing nations demanded a cap of 1.5°C heat-ing. Any greater warming, they maintained, would leave Africa lethally parched and the world's island states submerged. As the chief negotiator for a group of developing countries charged, the industrialized nations' proposed reparations fund of $10 bil-lion a year would not be enough "to buy the poor nations the coffins."[93]

Barack Obama appeared on the very last day. With mere hours remaining to form a global deal, many held their breath knowing that the president stood positioned to lead the world in confronting this crisis. But shortly into his remarks, all antici-pation evaporated. Speaking with a dispassionate tone, Obama offered reductions amounting to only 2 percent below 1990 levels by 2020 – a pathetic step in compari-son to the range required for any realistic hope of averting even 2°C of planetary heating, itself a target that Jim Hansen later called a "prescription for long-term disaster." The president had decided much earlier to punt the matter to Congress, and those cuts represented the most that the U.S. Senate could stomach after fos-sil fuel lobbyists had relentlessly scoured the bowels of Congress during the fall of 2009. It turned out that Obama had come to Copenhagen with empty pockets – no enacted legislation, no regulation, no effective judicial rulings, and no presidential will for leadership. After his Copenhagen appearance, nothing suggested to the world that Americans under this new president were any closer to taking responsibility for destroying the planet than they were under the president who had come out of the oil patch.[94]

The conference ended in chaos, with no agreement and no binding targets. Nations reconvened again for futile negotiations in Mexico City in 2010 and in South Africa in 2011. The feeble instrument emerging from the latter conference was called a "suicide pact" by Professor Pat Parenteau for its delay of binding emissions reductions until 2020.[95] Obama showed little personal interest in the climate crisis. Without U.S. commitments for emissions reduction, the international process predictably fizzled.

In Obama's first term, global carbon emissions soared by an unprecedented 6 percent (in 2010). The world saw disasters of biblical proportions: infernos raging in Russia, Colorado, and Australia; record-breaking heat waves in Texas; devastating floods in Pakistan and Bangkok; Superstorm Sandy in New York City. The year 2012 was the hottest year on record in the United States. While EPA took some steps, no comprehensive regulation of carbon dioxide had yet occurred when Obama ended his first term.[96]

But another legal strategy, called Atmospheric Trust Litigation, was well under way. In May 2011, youth from around the United States filed an unprecedented batch of lawsuits and petitions against the Obama administration and against every state government in America. This campaign focused on property rights – public property rights. Demanding government protection of their atmospheric trust under the public trust doctrine, and backed by over a dozen top scientist experts from around the world, the youth sought enforceable plans to lower carbon in every state according to a prescription developed by James Hansen and other leading climate scientists that year. The prescription set a numerical pathway to return the atmosphere to a safety zone of 350 ppm through 6 percent *annual* reduction of carbon dioxide emissions across the globe. As Dr. Hansen made clear in an *amicus* brief submitted in the federal lawsuit, time had run out, and the courts now held the last – and only – hope. Few attentive judges could read the famous scientist's brief without feeling the plight of youth worldwide on their shoulders. It declared, *"failure to act with all deliberate speed in the face of the clear scientific evidence of the danger functionally becomes a decision to eliminate the option of preserving a habitable climate system."*[97]

Only time will tell whether the coincidence of the George W. Bush presidency at a pivotal point in Earth's history will prove fatal for much of humanity and countless other species on the planet. British writer George Monbiot says, "If it is too late to prevent runaway climate change, the Bush team must carry much of the blame."[98]

But Obama's complacency now also stands to blame. With the climate window slamming shut, it matters little whether corruption or complacency stands in the way of an all-out atmospheric rescue.

At an even deeper level, the dysfunctional system of environmental law continues to perpetuate dangerous abuse of governmental authority. Despite its grand and complex facade, the present political paradigm invites corruption. The most elaborate environmental law system of the world cannot protect natural assets as long as there exists an alliance between industries and regulatory agencies. The next chapters show how that alliance plays out.

2

Modern Environmental Law: The Great Legal Experiment

In the middle of the night on August 30, 2004, a mining bulldozer, working in the dark, dislodged a huge rock. Gaining momentum as it went, the 1,000-pound boulder thundered down a mountain toward a small Appalachian town and smashed everything in its path. The boulder struck a house, where it crushed and killed a toddler, Jeremy Davidson, as he was sleeping peacefully in his bed. The tragedy punctuates a tyranny tightening over the region: Appalachian families are under siege by profit-crazed coal companies.[1]

Mining blasts continue relentlessly, day and night. Some occur within the town limits, some even next to people's homes. When the price of coal increases, the number of blasts skyrockets. On any given day, there can be thousands of explosions across Appalachia. The scale compares to war as "2,500 tons of explosives [are] detonated each day in West Virginia alone."[2]

To access the seams of coal buried deep underground, mining companies literally blow the tops off mountains. The ancient mountain peaks of Appalachia, gentle and picturesque, are disappearing fast. The coal companies have beheaded 500 mountains over the last 30 years. If they keep it up, Appalachia will appear an oddly buckled flatland, its forests razed and its landscape scarred with giant strip mines as far as the eye can see. As Robert F. Kennedy Jr. observed after a flyover: "[I] saw a sight that would sicken most Americans.... I saw the historic landscapes that gave America some of its most potent cultural legends ... the frontier hollows that cradled our democracy, the wilderness wellspring of our values, our virtues, our national character – all being leveled."[3]

After the civil war, carpetbaggers from the North moved down into the remote Appalachian Mountains. The newcomers saw coal seams snaking along the surface and recognized the hidden wealth. Southern Appalachia has suffered the plight of an abused colony ever since. For the first 100 years, the coal companies made it rich by accessing the "easy" seams located relatively close to the surface. They extracted coal by digging mines that extended underground. Today, the land base of the coal counties remains pocked with these invisible tombs of a past era.[4]

But the accessible seams of coal disappeared long ago. The remaining coal lies deep within the mountains. As mining practices morphed with the modern industrial age, the pick and shovel gave way to huge mountain-leveling backhoes, each equipped with a scoop that could hold twenty-six Ford Escorts, according to Kennedy's description. "Strip mining on steroids," one environmental attorney calls it. The machinery carves away at the blast-loosened mountaintop, causing hundreds of vertical feet of forest, rock, and soil covering the coal seams – the "overburden," as the coal companies describe these thick slices of Earth – to collapse into the valleys below, obliterating the streams that lace the watersheds. According to federal officials, 1,600 miles of Appalachian streams lie buried in valleys.[5]

Out of the exposed sediment leach heavy metals such as arsenic, selenium, and beryllium. The toxic slew oozes through the watershed, poisoning life in its path. Fish have been found dead in the mining drainage. Researchers predict serious health impacts to the human liver, kidney, spleen, bones, and digestive tract. Citizens anguish over a rash of health effects on their children. Outside one coal-processing plant, angry protesters hold up signs charging a "corporate child abuser." Communities across the coal counties of Tennessee, Kentucky, West Virginia, and Virginia frantically fight mountaintop removal. Diana Withen, a member of a small environmental group called Southern Appalachian Mountain Stewards, describes the mining area of Wise County, Virginia, as a ravaged moonscape: "I flew over it a couple of times. I couldn't even talk. How could this possibly be legal?" Indeed, that is the problem. The agencies use federal environmental law to legalize the blowing up of Appalachia and the poisoning of its watersheds.[6]

Permits for mountaintop removal fall under the purview of federal and state agencies implementing the Clean Water Act and the Surface Mining Control and Reclamation Act. Toss in review under the National Environmental Policy Act and the Endangered Species Act (ESA), and no less than five agencies jump into this legal thicket. Between 1985 and 2001, agencies approved 6,700 "valley fills" in central Appalachia, subjecting residents and property owners to what one observer called "waterboarding environmental policies." With few exceptions, all agencies fall in line with permits and oversight approvals to allow colossal, ongoing damage. Americans are often astonished to hear that environmental law permits such extraordinary harm when its very purpose was to prevent such harm. This contradiction now stands as the norm.[7]

Contrary to popular belief, environmental agencies often operate in a tight alliance with industry and private interests. Such agencies no longer represent public environmental values or defend public interests and needs, and it is necessary to debunk the myth that they do. This chapter explains how the legal reform emerging from the 1970s environmental movement changed the constitutional balance of environmental power over ecology and created a monster-sized bureaucracy that grew to legalize the destruction of Nature. While the discussion focuses on the U.S. experience, this history also holds lessons for the many other nations that adopted the U.S. approach to environmental law, thinking it a model of success.

EARTH DAY OPTIMISM

On April 22, 1970, on the first Earth Day, twenty million people across the United States took to the streets in protest. Citizens were fed up with water pollution, smog, clear-cutting, toxic waste dumps, strip-mining, nuclear proliferation, and the whole onslaught of environmental abuse. They demanded that government hold industry accountable.

In response, the U.S. Congress passed a bold suite of major federal environmental statutes. The Clean Air Act required a 90 percent reduction in car emissions of hydrocarbons and carbon monoxide by 1975. The Clean Water Act set a national goal to eliminate all pollution to navigable waters by 1985. The National Forest Management Act demanded sustainable management of the public forests and an end to wanton clear-cutting. The ESA called for recovery of imperiled species. Between 1969 and 1980, Congress passed eighteen environmental statutes. As Kennedy writes, Congress designed these laws to protect the people's ecological commons.[8] But statutes do not implement themselves: Congress authorizes agencies to carry out the mandates.

The U.S. Environmental Protection Agency (EPA) came into being at the end of 1970 to handle the bulk of pollution regulation. When it formed, the infant agency had just a $1.4 billion budget and 5,600 employees. The employees began with an enthusiastic and idealistic outlook – many joined because they wanted to save the world. Those were "the giddy days at EPA," as Dr. Devra Davis says in her book, *When Smoke Ran Like Water*.[9] With strong laws behind them, the new EPA officials felt emboldened to take on industry. The Clean Air Act, for example, required EPA to devise a standard for common air pollutants without delay. The task was Herculean and heroic at once.

Even four decades later, any criticism of the agencies and the legal regime born out of this environmental revolution risks alienating a good many people in the environmental community who revere the symbolism and momentum catalyzed by the widespread protests on Earth Day. Largely because the populism of the day reached unprecedented heights, its legal progeny gained almost untouchable status. Unfortunately, this all masked a botulism growing in the legal environment.

In actuality, as soon as the agencies created new regulations, industry started eroding them. William Ruckleshaus, the first head of EPA, described the duality of an idealistic agency bravado and cutthroat politics in those early days as comparable to running a 100-yard dash while simultaneously having an appendix taken out. Brutal tactics began at the outset. Under intense and sustained political pressure during the four decades since 1970, EPA and many other agencies fell captive to the industries they regulate. Few environmental law scholars pause to consider how 1970s reform and growth of agencies fundamentally restructured the delicate balance of power that underpins American environmental democracy – and how this now works massive harm on ecology. But as James Gustave Speth notes in *The Bridge at the Edge of the World*, "A great experiment has been conducted. The evidence is in." It is important to question the results.[10]

THE POWER SHIFT

The United States has three branches of government: legislative, executive, and judicial. Because the Founding Fathers stayed suspicious of consolidated authority, they crafted a system of checks and balances to ensure that no single branch would seize too much control over government. Today, however, the growth of the executive branch has squeezed out the other two branches in all environmental matters. This burgeoning administrative environmental state came to pass not so much by design or forethought, but by happenstance. Most Earth Day reformers reasonably believed that solutions would arrive in new statutes that would be implemented by agencies, but no one really anticipated how massive the resulting environmental bureaucracy would become. When the states started modeling their environmental approach after the federal system, and when local jurisdictions jumped into the regulatory ring, the agencies proliferated exponentially. Adding to the jurisdictional pile of federal, state, and local agencies, there now grows a massive, cross-purposing assemblage of regional agencies, task forces, and commissions trying to coordinate all of the other jurisdictions. As Speth observes, today's environmental bureaucracy presents "a huge and impenetrable regulatory and management apparatus."[11]

This hulking branch of government suffers from endemic problems, not the least of which remains agency capture. Although different agencies pursue disparate missions and regulatory objectives, they nevertheless tend to behave in much the same way. As Craig Collins concludes from a probing look across the major pollution programs in his book, *Toxic Loopholes*, "the seamy backstage drama of influence peddling, double-dealing, institutional corruption and public deception undermines our environmental laws."[12] When armed with statutory power to legalize pollution and resource destruction, this captured bureaucracy becomes a deadly force against Nature and the public itself. Owing to factors described in this and later chapters, the other two branches of government repeatedly fail to impose effective limits on agencies, despite a system of checks and balances carefully sewn through government by the Framers. The seams of democracy tore out a long time ago in environmental law.

The 1970s statutes siphoned power from one branch of government, the judiciary, and funneled it into another, the executive. Prior to this time, the courts played a fairly key role in environmental disputes. Some environmental statutes existed, of course, but judges often worked on a blank slate to resolve environmental problems. Their judicial craft entailed making common law (which simply means judge-made law). They borrowed doctrines of property law from England and applied them, with logic and reason, to the environmental circumstances of the new nation.[13]

We easily forget the role of the judicial system as it operated prior to the modern environmental era, but the common law set in place fundamental environmental principles. State judges fashioned entire bodies of water law, wildlife law, and mining law, for example. The Supreme Court penned the public trust doctrine in landmark cases such as *Illinois Central Railroad v. Illinois*, a decision that recognizes inalienable public property rights in crucial natural resources. Judges created principles to resolve environmental disputes between states, such as those involving air pollution and water allocation. For example, in *Georgia v. Tennessee Copper Co.*, the U.S. Supreme Court held that an industry located in one state would be liable for polluting the air of another state under nuisance law. These rules applied basic notions of justice, as formulated over the ages, to new circumstances as they arose.[14]

Before the modern environmental statutory era, judges resolved most environmental conflicts through nuisance law. Many of the old cases involved pollution disputes, such as those involving a factory that spewed toxic smoke over a community, or a pig farm that delivered a stench to neighbors across the fence. Nuisance doctrine allowed judges to balance private property rights with the economic interests of society. The test for private nuisance examines whether an activity causes "substantial harm" to property and whether such harm remains nevertheless justified by the "social utility" of the conduct. The nuisance inquiry is hardly pro-forma. This judicial exercise entails a searching look into the facts and law implicated under the circumstances, and the decision-making process trudges notoriously slow.[15]

When the industrial machine began to churn faster in the latter part of the twentieth century, it generated a manifold increase in ecological conflicts. Environmental problems swamped the ability of courts to keep up, and there surfaced a widespread belief that society needed a fixed and predictable set of rules to organize behavior. Accordingly, the judicial role began to give way to the regulatory state. Statutes and regulations started to proliferate across the legal landscape, particularly following the 1970s reform.[16] Nevertheless, the common law, while less frequently invoked today, still exists as an enduring source of law.

In large part, the environmental movement of the 1970s substituted executive-branch bureaucracy for judicial inquiry. Moreover, by including permit provisions in nearly every statute, Congress greased the wheels for industrial harm. Statutes streamlined what had been a careful fact-finding judicial inquiry into a ready-made agency response to environmental threats. Harried regulators flooded with permit applications could rubber-stamp generic conclusions into permit decisions. The "substantial harm" inquiry from the common law succumbed to a new mindset that held far less empathy for victims of environmental damage.

Pollution laws demonstrate this all too well. If a company puts the right technology device on its pollution-spewing plant and also meets the fixed standards established by regulation, the agencies assume that no harm bars a permit for damage. This does not mean, of course, that the plant will not foul public resources, or cause cancer in children, or ruin neighboring property – it just means that the plant has satisfied the minimal, generic standards of environmental regulation. These standards run an almost laughable gamut, from Best Available Technology to Best Available Control Technology, Best Available Control Measures, Best Demonstrated Available Technology, Best Available Technology Economically Achievable, Best Demonstrated Available Technology, and a mouthful of others.[17]

In addition to dispensing with the individualized "substantial harm" inquiry of nuisance law, regulatory streamlining also eliminated the inquiry into whether the harm could be justified by the "social utility" of the polluter's action. In nuisance cases, this test poses a hefty hurdle. A factory polluting a neighborhood would have to show a significant economic or social benefit to the community, as well as the lack of more benign alternatives, in order to justify the harm.[18] But in the mythology of modern-day regulation, nearly all industrial activity delivers a multitude of benefits to society – each to the same degree, regardless of the product purpose. A plant producing bubble gum, for example, receives no less favorable treatment for its discharges under the Clean Water Act than a plant producing a lifesaving medical device. While a reasonable person might presume that, in a time of scarcity, the natural assets should be allocated to the uses most essential to society, regulators typically do not think in such terms. The velvet gloves delivering permits to polluters are lined with unchallenged assumptions of benefit.

PARTITIONING NATURE THROUGH STATUTES

An old but true adage asserts that everything in Nature is connected – the land, water, wildlife, forests, air and atmosphere, soils, and oceans. But environmental law operates in defiance of ecology. It divides everything in Nature, allocates it among separate statutes, and parcels it out among an array of agencies. Charged with narrow mandates, agencies act within a multifarious and disjointed legal regime.

A sampling of major laws gives an idea of the absurd legal partitioning of Nature and the complexity it engenders. On the federal level, for example, there exist ten primary pollution statutes and several more secondary statutes. Call the big hitters the Clean Water Act, the Clean Air Act, the Safe Drinking Water Act, the Resource Conservation Recovery Act, the Comprehensive Environmental Response, Compensation, and Liability Act, the Toxic Substances Control Act, the Federal Insecticide, Fungicide, Rodenticide Act, the Oil Pollution Act, the Ocean Dumping Act, and the Occupational Safety and Health Act. For wildlife, Congress created the ESA, the Marine Mammal Protection Act, the Bald and Golden Eagle Protection Act, the Lacey Act, the Magnuson-Stevenson Fisheries Act, the Migratory Bird Treaty Act, the Wild Free-Roaming Horses and Burros Act, the Fish and Wildlife Coordination Act, and many more. For lands and waters, Congress passed the National Forest Management Act, the Federal Land Policy Management Act, the National Refuges Act, the Wilderness Act, the Surface Mining Control and Reclamation Act, the Parks Organic Act, and many others. The National Environmental Policy Act, the Administrative Procedure Act, and the Freedom of Information Act join any inventory as well because they provide the procedural game rules for agencies.

The preceding lists represent just a few slices of federal law, not nearly the whole environmental law regime. The laws then multiply on the state level. Nearly every state has a program to implement the major federal pollution laws, and most have water appropriation laws, wildlife laws, and forestry laws. On the local level, still more laws accumulate: land use laws, wetlands ordinances, tree ordinances, wildlife ordinances, open space ordinances, and so forth.

Four obvious institutional problems arise from this extreme fragmentation. First, the right hand of government often does not know what the left hand is doing, and agencies often work at cross-purposes. Second, public servants toiling within this tangled administrative jungle have little sense of the big picture. No one agency takes full responsibility for a natural asset. No cohesive force or legal doctrine moves these scattered agencies toward the imminent task of rebuilding Nature or leverages their bureaucratic strengths to meet unprecedented challenges ahead. Third, the regulations represent a Gordian knot to the outside world, too complex to sort through. The sheer length of the laws and regulations renders them largely inaccessible to the public. A volume containing the major federal pollution laws alone contains more than 2,000 pages, and regulations implementing the laws multiply exponentially. One court called the legal framework "mind-numbing."[19] But while this regulatory structure stands impenetrable for nearly all average people, it remains highly penetrable for industry-paid lobbyists and experts who make their money by figuring out the system and manipulating it to their advantage. And fourth, so many agencies work from different angles to manage interconnected resources that the resulting bureaucratic processes create a heavy drag on government's ability to solve environmental problems. Industry repeatedly exploits the bureaucratic inertia.

A microcosm of this regulatory mess manifests in the context of Columbia River Basin salmon protection. To protect the fish, environmental law must safeguard the species' full and remarkable life cycle from "gravel to gravel" – a journey that begins in the inland watersheds, proceeds out to the ocean, and returns to natal waters. Any significant weak link in its ecology will doom the species. Yet, different agencies exert control over different parts of the life cycle as the salmon encounter a gauntlet of harms. Professor Charles Wilkinson mapped the jurisdictional domain of salmon law and determined that a salmon trying to return from the ocean to its natal waters in the Lochsa River of Idaho would swim through seventeen separate jurisdictions, all of which try to coordinate with each other but without any obvious success to the species' recovery.[20]

An agency roll call in the Columbia River Basin displays the dizzying complexity now typical of environmental bureaucracy. The states of Oregon, Washington, and Idaho, as well as the fishing tribes, all set harvest quotas. The Pacific Fishery Management Council controls ocean harvest. The Bureau of Land Management oversees the rangeland that holds key riparian areas for salmon spawning. The Forest Service manages the timbered headwaters that support other vital spawning areas. The Army Corps of Engineers operates the Columbia River dams, which obstruct the salmon in their passage to and from the sea. The Northwest Power Planning Council churns out management plans for the federal hydro-system. The Federal Energy Regulatory Commission regulates yet another set of dams, ones privately operated. The Bureau of Reclamation controls a third set of dams that supply water to farmers. The state water agencies of Idaho, Washington, and Oregon appropriate the water from the rivers. The various cities and towns along the way oversee the land uses along the rivers and permit storm water pollution. The federal EPA and state agencies regulate the toxins, heavy metals, and pesticides that spill from industrial pipes, municipal sources, and nonpoint sources into the waterways. The Department of Energy supervises the radioactive groundwater entering the Columbia River from Hanford Nuclear Reservation (one of the most contaminated sites on the planet). The U.S. Fish and Wildlife Service manages the salmon hatcheries. The National Marine Fisheries Service and state wildlife agencies hold regulatory authority over a broad spectrum of actions harmful to the basin's species.[21]

All of these agencies exhibit different bureaucratic proclivities and missions. Many lock into political agendas set by the industries and interests they regulate. When agency rivalries obstruct the system, bureaucratic chaos sets into the basin and strangles salmon recovery progress at every turn. This colossal failure leaves a grim outlook for governmental action on climate change, as author Paul VanDevelder notes. He writes:

> If ever there were a story that foreshadowed the political and legal Waterloos that loom in seeking solutions to climate change, surely that cautionary tale is the one about the Columbia and Snake rivers' salmon and their imminent extinction.... The policy deadlock ... has flushed billions of taxpayer dollars out to sea over the last 15 years while doing very little to prevent 13 endangered salmon stocks from going extinct.... The Columbia-Snake corridor is the salmon's only option for survival, and [the courts are] probably their last hope.... If the law and science are unable to trump politics to save this fishery – a fishery that was the most productive in the world just two generations ago – how will we ever meet the towering challenges posed by global climate change?[22]

In retrospect, the splintered statutory scheme of environmental law was probably a bad idea. But these statutes exist on the books now. This structure, while hardly optimal, need not inevitably thwart environmental defense. If each agency provided peak protection to its jurisdictional resources, the collective array of agencies could form a formidable guard against environmental damage. Overlapping and redundant missions could install resilience in the system and strive toward fail-safe protection measures for communities and resources. Instead, nearly across the board, the agencies operate at the lowest level of regulatory vigilance. The contrast between this and the peak-protection approach is like the difference between chainmail and cheesecloth.

THE GREAT CONGRESSIONAL PUNT

Understandably, the millions of Americans who forced Congress to pass laws in the 1970s and ensuing decades claimed environmental victory for each law passed. Indeed, on their face, most of the statutes appear quite protective. Their beginning language typically prohibits the type of damage the statute is designed to prevent. But nearly all of the statutes have "outs" – escape hatches that allow precisely that damage. The Clean Water Act, for example, states a goal to "restore and maintain the chemical, physical, and biological integrity of the Nation's waters," yet gives the U.S. Army Corps of Engineers breathtaking authority to allow wetlands destruction, stating: "The Secretary may issue permits, after notice and opportunity for public hearings for the discharge of dredged or fill material into the navigable waters."[23] This sweeping language, as Chapter 3 shows, provides a legal lever that the Corps uses to allow obliteration of streams resulting from mountaintop removal.

The escape hatches in the various statutes usually take the form of permits, such as water pollution permits or air emission permits; these typically issue for five-year periods (sometimes longer), but they take other forms as well. Timber contracts memorialize the license to cut timber from public lands managed by the Forest Service. A plat approved by local land-use officials might reflect permission to pave over soils for a subdivision site. A "no jeopardy" opinion issued by the U.S. Fish and Wildlife Service gives a green light for damaging species listed as threatened or endangered under the ESA, or harming their habitat. In many statutes, a generic list of exemptions allows destructive activities. The particular form of the various regulatory loopholes may not be as important as their aggregate effect.[24]

On the face of it, one can easily understand the policy justification for these provisions: overly rigid prohibitions might not accommodate society's needs as circumstances change. But studies of legislative history reveal more than this general policy concern behind the exemptions and permit provisions. They show that industry lobbyists often insisted on these "outs" during an embattled legislative process. In many cases, the industry knew some regulation was inevitable and sought the broadest possible allowances to permit exactly the behavior (or close to it) that led to public demand for regulation in the first place. As Craig Collins explains:

> This ambush begins "in the womb," when these embryonic laws are still bills passing through Congress. Here, before they were born, even our most promising environmental bills were deformed and crippled by toxic loopholes created by politicians seeking to please the powerful polluting industries that lavish them with favors and fund their campaigns.

By securing permit provisions, industry gained a set of statutes that, in practice, act not so much as damage-preventing but damage-permitting. As Professor David Schoenbrod observes, Congress used these regulatory escape valves to punt the hard decisions to the agencies. He laments: "Delegation short-circuits [democracy] by allowing our elected lawmakers to hide behind unelected agency officials."[25]

The permit system strategy works well for industry as long as the agency uses its discretion to favor polluters rather than the public – which too frequently remains the case, as this book shows. But the *opposite assumption* implicitly underlies the vast grant of agency discretion. Discretion rests on the myth that the administrative process remains insulated from politics, does not submit to political capture, and yields decisions that result from expert judgment guided by the public interest. The modern environmental bureaucracy still draws its main justification from an unquestioned faith in agencies.[26]

Public forest management demonstrates the typical industry agenda carried out during the legislative process to create a statute that confers vast discretion to the implementing agency. The U.S. Forest Service manages the National Forests, which comprise 8.5 percent of the total land base of the United States. Owned by the public, these forests provide the headwaters for numerous rivers, support habitat for imperiled species, supply municipal drinking water for many cities, filter air pollution, and serve a crucial role in flood control, soil formation, climate control, and nutrient cycling.

Yet, despite this irreplaceable forest ecosystem value, more than fifty years ago, the Forest Service became a large-scale timber producer bent on "liquidating" the old-growth ancient forests in order to serve a ballooning private industry. In clear-cut after clear-cut, the Forest Service allowed logging companies to eradicate ancient forests and replace them with monoculture tree crops bearing little resemblance to, and providing few of the functions of, a real forest. Timber production surged far beyond sustainable levels. Industry also punched in enough logging roads to circle the globe fifteen times.[27]

Public outcry resulted in congressional hearings held in 1971, which drew condemning testimony against the Forest Service. Many members of the public called for a ban on clear-cutting. In 1973, a surprising court decision known as *Izaac Walton League v. Butz* gave them considerable ammunition. The court held that *existing* law (the Organic Act of 1897) already prohibited clear-cutting. The decision created the impetus for congressional action and spurred passage of the National Forest Management Act (NFMA) in 1976.[28]

NFMA was paraded as a reform to the Forest Service's management of public lands, but, in actuality, the "reform" simply institutionalized the discretion that the Forest Service and the timber industry sought. While heralded as a major victory for public forests, in fact NFMA amounted to a quiet victory for the timber industry, which had faced the prospect of an outright ban on clear-cutting as a result of the *Izaac Walton League* decision. Congress could have imposed a ban on clear-cutting in NFMA, but it did the opposite. It *repealed* the key provisions of the Organic Act that prevented clear-cutting and instead inserted a laundry list of standards into NFMA seemingly aimed at *restricting* the agency's clear-cutting. Under these new standards, the Forest Service could still allow clear-cuts, but not on steep slopes; the agency also had to protect the soils against erosion, ensure the diversity of wildlife species, meet aesthetic standards, replant denuded slopes, and not exceed the sustained yield of the forest.

As Professor Federico Cheever observes in his exhaustive study of NFMA, the enacted statute corresponded nearly exactly to what the Forest Service had asked for as a result of its continuing "institutional conversation" with Congress. An outright prohibition on clear-cutting could have been easily enforced by the public. Instead, NFMA's language pushed the discretion of the Forest Service into a more hidden, technical realm. As Cheever concludes, NFMA represented a resounding victory for Forest Service discretion.[29]

NFMA's standards proved wholly ineffective in curbing industry-dominated forest policy. Denuded slopes, massive soil erosion, habitat obliteration, and collapsing species populations all stand testament to the Forest Service's defiance of its statutory mandates – and the inability of the public to do much about it. As one exasperated court found in a Pacific Northwest forest case, the Forest Service and the Fish and Wildlife Service had engaged in a "remarkable series" of violations of environmental law, showing "deliberate and systematic refusal" to comply with NFMA's wildlife protections.[30]

In the Pacific Northwest, the Forest Service razed the ancient forests down to a few isolated remnants. By the time the courts finally put the brakes on logging through the Endangered Species Act, only about 10 percent of the ancient forest remained.[31] The story demonstrates how, by conferring broad discretion, Congress transferred breathtaking legal power to the Executive Branch to destroy natural resources belonging to the public – a public that believed NFMA would improve Forest Service behavior. Looking back, the Earth Day revolution brought forth a new environmental era, all right, but it would prove to be nothing close to what Americans wanted or expected from their government.

DEATH BY DISCRETION

One cannot wade just a little bit into any permitting provision of an environmental, natural resource, or land use statute. The permitting provisions can be intensely complicated, each representing a tangled array of regulatory practices, legal terminology, and court interpretations. But despite unique differences, similar patterns emerge during the permitting process, the primary one being that agencies typically use the permitting provisions to say "yes" to destructive proposals.

The rates of permit issuance show that many agency officials feel bound to approve applications for pollution or resource damage. Scholars offer telling examples. Professor Oliver Houck inventoried the number of times the U.S. Fish and Wildlife Service made jeopardy findings under Section 7 of the Endangered Species Act. A jeopardy finding effectively calls a halt to a proposed federal action because it indicates the Service's view that the action could threaten the survival of a species, which is prohibited by Section 7. Professor Houck found that jeopardy opinions were issued in less than 1 percent of the cases and concluded, "[T]he number of projects actually arrested by the ESA is nearly nonexistent." Similarly, a review of the U.S. Army Corps of Engineers wetlands permitting decisions under Section 404 of the Clean Water Act revealed that, out of 85,000 permits the Corps processes each year, it denies less than 0.3 percent of them.[32]

Even in the water pollution context, EPA has turned an intended phase-out of pollution into a discharge entitlement system. Section 101 of the Clean Water Act expressly states: "It is the national goal that the discharge of pollutants into the navigable waters be *eliminated* by 1985." The permit system Congress designed in Section 402 was intended as a transition tool to achieve the no-pollution goal by 1985 – hence its name, the National Pollution Discharge *Elimination* System. Permits were to last only five years, during which time industry was to move to a pollution-free state by employing new technology. Instead, EPA enshrined the permits and now routinely extends them administratively when the polluter completes an application for renewal. In an administrative maneuver that thoroughly subverts the statutory goal, the agency simply considers these permits to be "backlogged." In 2001, a national survey by U.S. Public Interest Research Group (PIRG) found that one out of every four facilities discharging under the Clean Water Act was operating under an expired permit.[33]

Considerable death and illness in the United States can be attributed to the agencies' rank failure to deny permits sought under environmental statutes. For example, the Clean Air Act supposedly protects Americans from air pollution, yet one EPA study counts as many as 50,000 deaths in the United States each year resulting from air pollution. According to EPA's consultants, air pollution from just 51 coal-fired power plants operating under the Clean Air Act shortens the lives of 5,500 Americans each year and "triggers between 107,000 and 170,000 asthma attacks per year."[34]

The airborne mercury from coal-fired plants delivers an additional fistful of health impacts to the American population. Settling in rivers and lakes far from the source of emission, airborne mercury concentrates in fish and subsequently enters the food chain. Eventually this neurotoxin accumulates at dangerous levels in the human body. If it settles in a pregnant mother, mercury can cause birth defects and stunted brain development. According to EPA's own estimates, 7 percent of women of childbearing age have blood mercury concentrations greater than what the agency considers safe, and more than 300,000 newborns each year may have increased risk of learning disabilities as a result of fetal exposure to methyl mercury. More than 50 percent of the mercury air pollution comes from coal-fired plants that EPA allows to operate under the Clean Air Act. Only in the waning days of 2011 did EPA finally issue a rule aimed to significantly decrease mercury emissions from coal-fired power plants. Twenty years in the making, the rule had been repeatedly stalled as a result of political interference from industry.[35]

Agencies cower before producers of toxic substances as well. The EPA reviews about 1,700 new compounds every year under the Toxic Substances Control Act, but allows 90 percent of them to enter the marketplace without restriction. A report by the U.S. Government Accountability Office concludes that EPA "lacks adequate scientific information on the toxicity of many chemicals that are or may be found in the environment" and that "EPA does not routinely assess the risks of the more than 83,000 commercial chemicals in use."[36]

Numerous pesticides remain unregulated (or underregulated) by EPA under the Federal Insecticide, Fungicide, and Rodenticide Act. For example, EPA allows the herbicide atrazine (banned in the European Union) despite its strongly suspected effect as an endocrine disrupter. Some studies suggest a link between this chemical and prostate cancer, birth defects, and infertility. Atrazine remains the most widely used weed killer in the United States and occurs in alarming concentrations across the Midwest. An estimated 33 million Americans unwittingly receive exposure to the chemical through their tap water.[37]

The regulatory situation under the Safe Drinking Water Act looks no different. A New York Times investigative report by Charles Duhigg showed that more than 20 percent of water treatment systems in the United States violated the Act within a five-year period. This means that more than 49 million people have consumed water with illegal amounts of contaminants such as radioactive substances, dangerous bacteria, arsenic, and a host of carcinogenic chemicals. According to the Times report, water contamination causes "millions of instances of illness within the United States each year." The dramatic surge in breast cancer and prostate cancer may be linked to polluted drinking water.[38]

Sewage sludge heaps onto a mounting pile of harms openly permitted by the environmental agencies. Euphemistically dubbed "biosolids" by EPA, sewage sludge is the leftover muck at municipal sewage plants after residential and industrial wastewater treatment. Industries discharge their toxic waste (often without pretreatment) to these plants, where it blends with sewage. This results in a highly hazardous sludge laced with up to 60,000 toxic substances – "an unpredictable mix of heavy metals, PCBs, dioxins, many synthetic chemicals and industrial solvents, radioactive waste, medicines, pesticides, asbestos, petroleum byproducts, bacteria, viruses and other hazardous residues," as Craig Collins describes. Each year, farmers spread millions of tons of this sewage sludge – free fertilizer – across thousands of acres of farm fields. This disposal serves municipalities who have no other cheap way to get rid of their hazardous waste. Investigators suspect that the sludge causes respiratory illness, infection, and even death. In Georgia, a high-profile lawsuit resulted in a federal judge ordering compensation for a farmer who lost hundreds of cows poisoned by sludge that contained levels of PCBs, arsenic, and toxic heavy metals at levels up to 2,500 times federal health standards. The Associated Press reported cow milk at a neighboring farm contained the chemical thallium (historically used as rat poison) at levels 120 times the concentration allowed by EPA for drinking water. Regardless, EPA still clings to its thirty-year policy of promoting the disposal of sewage sludge across America's farms. While this policy has been roundly challenged, the federal judge described EPA as taking "extraordinary steps to quash scientific dissent" that could undercut its biosolids program.[39]

These and other pollution horrors, many of which are compiled in Craig Collins's book, Toxic Loopholes, present an ominous pattern: for the most part, government does not work on behalf of its citizens to protect Nature. In fact, it does the opposite. Whether in the context of air, water, wildlife, soil, or any number of other resources, agencies use permit provisions and other loopholes to allow the very damage that the statues were enacted to prevent. The broad discretion Congress left in the statutes gives breathtaking power to the agencies, now dangerously used.

THE FALSE LURE OF MITIGATION

Across the board, agency program managers will defend even absurdly low permit denial rates by pointing out that nearly every permit has conditions attached to lessen the environmental damage. This is called "mitigation." It would be a lot worse, they contend, without the permit system. True, perhaps, but the mitigation rationale suffers three big problems. First, as the simple old saying goes, everything adds up. Even the most effective mitigation still allows mounting, cumulative damage – just less so than otherwise.

Second, mitigation often bears little relationship to the scale or even type of harm sought to be prevented by the statute in the first place. Typically, the agency negotiates mitigation measures with the permit applicant. During this process, regulatory rigor takes a vacation. The ESA context provides an example. When the U.S. Fish and Wildlife Service finds that a federal action could jeopardize the survival of a listed species, it will usually offer "Reasonable and Prudent Alternatives" (RPAs), which are mitigating conditions that allow the action to go forward. As the theory goes, if the applicant follows the RPAs, its action will not threaten the survival of the species. But Oliver Houck points out in his landmark study of ESA implementation that the RPAs may not contain measures adequate to protect the species. He concludes that the needs of the applicant, rather than the needs of the species, too often drive the process of arriving at RPAs. Professor Dan Rohlf concurs: "[T]he Services virtually always come up with a reasonable and prudent alternative that allows the action in question to proceed." The failure surfaces in the Columbia River salmon context, where one court found that a federal salmon plan, chock-full of mitigation-like conditions, "amounted to little more than an analytical sleight of hand." Houck concludes, "[T]here is no evidence that ... the Endangered Species Act is stopping the world. Indeed, there is little evidence that it is changing it very much at all."[40]

Third, mitigation conditions are notoriously hard to enforce. Many conditions that look great on paper stay on paper – they are never actually implemented. Agencies, particularly those that are not well funded, often fail to inspect ongoing operations for compliance with mitigation conditions. And courts sometimes hold that mitigating conditions simply cannot be enforced.[41] When not implemented, the mitigation measures amount to little more than regulatory placebos. For citizens who have relied on them, such conditions represent the ultimate agency bait and switch.

In light of this, one might ask whether we would be worse off without any environmental law. Probably. Environmental law may be a failure, but a "mitigated" failure at that. Presumably, it has slowed the pace of ecological demise. But that presumption only consoles until the endpoint of resource exhaustion, which now looms nearer than most could have fathomed when the permit system was designed. Asking, in retrospect, whether environmental law benefited the public during the interim becomes something of a moot point.

BANKRUPTING NATURE UNDER ENVIRONMENTAL LAW

This all presents an unavoidable question that the agencies nevertheless persistently avoid: Where will agencies draw the line against natural resource damage? Where lies the point at which they will deny permits? Generally, agencies treat this as a political, rather than legal, matter because they enjoy such broad discretion. The general pattern seems to be that agencies allow damage until the natural resource stands at the brink of collapse – or beyond. In short, they use their discretion under environmental law to bankrupt Nature.

The U.S. Fish and Wildlife Service's endangered species program reflects this. Congress clearly intended the ESA to achieve recovery of listed species, not push them closer to extinction. When a species becomes listed as "threatened" or "endangered," the statute requires the Service to create a recovery plan aimed at rebuilding populations. But in practice, with or without a recovery plan, the USFWS authorizes serial mortality hits to the species until it hovers just above the jeopardy threshold, which by definition lies just shy of extinction. Not at all surprisingly, the Service boasts recovery of only 26 species, whereas approximately 1,990 listed species languish on ESA deathbeds (and thousands more remain without any ESA protection at all).[42]

The same pattern recurs across nearly all agencies: they keep doling out permits until they sense that the next one will break the camel's back. The Forest Service allowed clear-cutting of the Pacific Northwest's ancient forests until less than 10 percent remained; water agencies in the West allocated rivers until many ran dry or at a seasonal trickle; state environmental agencies permitted so much pollution in waterways that fish from them could no longer be safely eaten; and cities allowed sprawl that gobbled up the most productive agrarian landscapes. The overall story takes its pages from Dr. Seuss's *The Lorax*.[43] In those instances where some resource remains, the permitting continues – as in Appalachia, where coal companies still devour mountaintops at breakneck speed. While the statutes expressed goals of clean air, pure water, and recovered species, the agencies substitute an entirely new focus: How much pollution and resource scarcity can we impose on communities, citizens, and children? The pervasive unwillingness of agencies to draw the line, no matter what statutory authority they call law, explains why society now reaches an ecological endpoint.

THE COMPLEXITY OF NOT SAYING NO

Law professors often tell their classes that the line between *prohibited* activity and *permitted* activity requires venturing onto a "slippery slope" iced with difficult distinctions. Asking agencies to draw a line around allowable damage to ecology enslaves them to a hopeless task. Nearly all agency regulatory energy goes into deciding how much environmental damage to permit – and then defending what often amounts to an indefensible decision. Once the agencies step out onto that slippery slope of issuing permits for environmental harm, it becomes nearly impossible for them to turn back unless they make a concerted decision to impose a moratorium or ban on the activity.

The belly fat of the whole environmental law system lies in its permitting process. The modern environmental bureaucracy generates mountains of studies, technical reports, environmental analysis, proposed rule-makings, and decision documents that prove useful only for destroying Nature. Water quality standards developed under the Clean Water Act demonstrate the tortured lengths to which agencies go in trying to rationalize their authorization of harm. Such standards ask, among other things, whether a particular body of water remains "fishable." To answer that question, the states and EPA have to examine the cancer risk that citizens bear from eating fish caught from public waters. To do this, agencies have to create assumptions about how much fish an average person eats. Quite some time ago, EPA established a national fish consumption standard of 17.5 grams per day. (For inquiring minds, that is about the amount of fish that easily fits on a cracker. Woe to the person who eats more.) Hundreds of pages prop up an analysis used to determine how much cancer risk falls to a person eating at this supposed average consumption rate. The risk analysis borders on the absurd, involving the oddest symbiosis of toxicology and the culinary arts. Inputs include the type of contaminant, where it resides within the fish, whether the fish has been filleted, skinned, or remains whole, how one cooks the fish (fried, steamed, baked, or broiled), what part of the fish one consumes, the body weight, sex, and age of the person eating it – everything short of the seasoning one might put on it (and that too may lie buried in some study). In short, EPA seemingly requires the public to use "Best Available Technology" in eating their catch of the day from polluted waters, but the agency never explains why it chooses to devote its vast resources and taxpayer money to study toxicity risk rather than study nontoxic alternatives that would markedly reduce public risk.[44]

The agencies' line-drawing exercise often proceeds without any compelling values steering their discretion. David Michaels explains EPA's approach to human toxic exposure in his book, *Doubt Is Their Product*. The EPA still frequently uses an aging model known as quantitative risk assessment to determine how much deadly pollution to allow. In decision after decision, EPA permits toxic pollution that carries a certain probability of causing cancer. These probabilities generally range from one in a million (10^{-6}) to one in 10,000 (10^{-4}). If EPA concludes a toxin will result in fewer cancer cases than its chosen probability goal, then it typically allows the pollution or chemical, deeming it an acceptable risk to society. To put it crassly, the agency selects how many innocent lives will likely be lost as a result of its regulatory action.[45]

But when we get right down to the basics of the matter, we cannot hope to make sense out of why EPA draws a line at 10^{-4}, 10^{-6}, or some other number. EPA spends a huge amount of public funding in its struggle to allow a risk of 10^{-4} or 10^{-6}, but no value difference exists between the two risk levels unless we want to count coffins. And nearly everyone in the pollution business knows this as a shell game; the real body burden of toxic chemicals likely remains far greater than what the agency discloses, because citizens get assaulted on a daily basis with any number of chemicals, each of which carries a risk factor. Despite this reality, EPA studies the chemicals one by one, assuming a simplicity found only in its regulatory dream world. As Dr. Thomas Burke, an epidemiologist at Johns Hopkins University, emphasized in a *New York Times* interview, EPA should study how these chemicals act in dangerous combinations.[46]

It does not take a PhD in toxicology to figure out that pervasive toxins in the environment contribute to soaring cancer rates in communities nationwide. Breast cancer rose 26 percent in just fifteen years from 1973 to 1988. Cancer now kills more American children between the ages of one and fourteen than any other disease. The American Cancer Society projects that about one out of two men and approximately one out of three women will fall victim to cancer in their lifetimes.[47] Yet EPA continues to regulate in the same way it has for the last forty years. The agency still assumes it ethical and appropriate to cause cancer to a modeled number of people in order to appease polluters.

The Occupational Safety and Health Administration (OSHA) displays the same proclivity when setting standards for workplace chemical exposure. David Michaels illustrates the problem in several case studies. When OSHA dealt with chromium 6, a deadly agent that causes lung cancer, it faced a choice of setting allowable exposure levels at 1 ug/m³ or 5 ug/m³. After intense pressure by the chrome industry, the agency chose the latter (less protective) standard, even though compelling studies justified far more protection. Under the less protective standard, OSHA calculated 10–45 lung cancer deaths per 1,000 workers over a lifetime of exposure. OSHA did not, of course, choose *which* workers would die, but OSHA settled on the number of how many were likely to die, in random sniper-style regulation. OSHA then granted the aerospace sector an extra lax standard, forcing those employees to dodge even more toxic bullets at their place of work.[48]

At the heart of this lies an uncomfortable truth: EPA's and OSHA's risk assessments make these agencies knowing participants in a highly discretionary chain of death.

Yet few within the bureaucracy question the agencies' approach to regulation. No honest discussion focuses on the human sacrifice implicit in these numbers. Continually choosing what they view as a reasonable amount of death over industry restriction, the agencies spend too little regulatory energy on eliminating harmful chemicals from the stream of commerce altogether. Against the impossibly slippery slope of risk assessment, one finds bans fairly straightforward. Bans free up an enormous amount of bureaucratic effort because they do not involve the consuming work of issuing new permits. Moreover, their enforcement is straightforward.

Part II of this book explains how a transformative shift away from chemicals and toxic pollution can be both cost-effective and feasible. Bringing forth a new protective paradigm, however, will not happen as long as those both within and outside the bureaucracy operate under a blind faith that the present system works. It does not. As this chapter explained, the agencies long ago grabbed the permit provisions of the statutes and ran away with them, using their legal authority to dole out damage until society began slamming into ecological end points. This mode of administrative implementation accomplishes a de facto repeal of the statutes that captured the public's imagination and hearts in the 1970s. Despite a cadre of hardworking and well-intentioned people in many agencies today, perversely, the very system intended to *restore* Nature actually *kills* Nature, while delivering a heavy dose of death and despair to innocent citizens. To move forward in any significant measure, we must fully understand the internal bureaucratic vulnerabilities that cause agencies to repeatedly exercise their discretion in subversion of the law. The next two chapters explain the dynamics that tempt agencies to favor corporations over the public.

3

The Politics of Discretion

Agency discretion operates as a pressure point in environmental law. It determines whether regulatory outcomes will serve the public or polluters. Industry knows that discretion sets an open season to lobby officials into bending the law to their favor. As Professor Houck warned in the Forest Service context, "[Discretion] throws [the] biologists, field managers, and forest rangers to the dogs.... [They] have no shield when the pressure comes on."[1]

After years of such pressure, an agency falls captive to the industry it regulates. At that point, government officials look at the industry in a different light – as a client the agency must serve. Discretion then becomes a legal conduit through which the agency delivers public resources directly into corporate hands. Houck put it bluntly as to the U.S. Forest Service: "The code words fool no one involved: more 'discretion' means that industry gets to cut more timber."[2]

The wrongful transfer of public resources to private interests in response to political pressure takes place behind a veil of legitimization provided by environmental law. Citizens rarely discover the influence of politics, and if they do, the solid proof usually arrives years after the wrongdoing takes place and decisions become final. Facts come to light through very limited avenues: from courageous whistle-blowers, persistent investigative journalists, dedicated public-interest lawyers (who sue the agency and gain documents through the discovery process), or as a result of formal investigations launched by congressional oversight committees, the Office of Inspector General, or the Government Accountability Office. In relation to the mass numbers of environmental permits that issue from state and federal agencies, these investigations are exceedingly rare.

Understanding the dynamics of agency discretion becomes a necessary predicate for holding government accountable to fiduciary standards, which is the thrust of a Nature's Trust approach. Nearly all agencies present a similar legal architecture despite differences in jurisdiction, legal authority, and mission. This chapter isolates three discretion portals through which politics or inappropriate bias can and often does enter into the process. These portals open at the stage of: (1) rule-making (2) technical determinations; and (3) enforcement choices. Reforming environmental law requires a strategy to address all three.

THE RULE-MAKING PORTAL

Agencies enact regulations to bring broad statutory directives to a more detailed level of implementation. The breathtaking ability of executive branch agencies to undermine laws at this stage escapes notice by the general public. Many assume that lawmaking culminates when the president or governor signs a bill passed by the legislature. But as noted in Chapter 2, legislatures regularly punt to agencies some of the most difficult decisions in a process called "delegation." Agencies carry the ball forward by promulgating regulations. Although the U.S. Constitution assigns the lawmaking role to the legislature, courts allow the legislature to delegate broad rule-making authority to agencies, as long as it sets discernible parameters for the agency to follow. In *Whitman v. American Trucking Associations*, the Supreme Court declared: "[W]e have 'almost never felt qualified to second-guess Congress regarding the permissible degree of policy judgment that can be left to those executing or applying the law.'"[3]

Operating in this almost unquestioned realm, rule-making through delegation presents a snake pit for democracy. It transfers difficult lawmaking choices from the legislators (who at least remain accountable to the public through elections) to agency officials who operate behind the scenes in obscure processes that often prove inaccessible to average citizens. Corporate powers find this lawmaking recipe delectable as they sink their forks into agency deliberations. As Craig Collins points out in *Toxic Loopholes*, the polluting industries develop an "illicit relationship" with agencies that pays off in weaker regulations. Well worth their investment of time and money, many notorious industry groups manipulate the rule-making process with the goal of either avoiding regulation altogether or delaying it for years or decades. One of the most stunning delay campaigns involved the regulation of lead. It took sixty years for EPA to ban this known neurotoxin from gasoline. For industry, every year of delay buys another year of profit from unregulated activity.[4]

At the rule-making stage, industry groups launch well-calculated power plays to advance their position. They hire agency lobbyists to resist adverse rule changes and push favorable rule changes through the process. As David Schoenbrod writes in *Power Without Responsibility*, even when a statute presents a clear objective, broad delegation to an agency provides an opening that allows industry to "pervert regulation to its own ends." Agencies often behave submissively to industry influence at this stage, watering down or sometimes completely subverting their statutory mandates through regulations. In an influential study of Endangered Species Act (ESA) implementation, for example, Professor Oliver Houck finds that the Department of Interior "substantially amended," through various regulatory sleights of hand, many of the ESA's firm requirements designed to prevent species extinction. He concludes: "Interior's regulations present a composite picture of an agency doing everything possible within law, and beyond, to limit the effect of protection under section 7(a)(2).... Interior has translated an act of mandatory requirements into concentric rings of discretion."[5]

Even a seemingly minor regulatory change can affect a vast amount of natural resources, because a regulation defines how a particular statute will be interpreted and administered across the land. The history of wetlands regulation under the Clean Water Act, for example, consists of intense interpretive wrangling over the scope of six key words that trigger a permit requirement under section 404(a): "*discharge* of *dredged* or *fill material* into the *navigable waters*." The regulatory construal of these terms carries high stakes, both for developers and for Nature. Interpreting "navigable waters" to exclude isolated wetlands, for example, excises tens of thousands of acres of wetlands from regulation, leaving them open for destruction. Excluding intermittent streams from the Clean Water Act's "navigable water" jurisdiction would remove from regulation 95 percent of the surface water in Arizona – in a state so parched that every drop counts. Interpreting "discharge" to exclude side-cast from bulldozing lets loose from the regulatory net a vast number of sensitive wetlands that developers gladly tear into. The definition of "fill material," as this section shows, determines whether or not mining companies can use pristine lakes as their waste dump sites.[6]

Because the discretion to make and change regulations always rests with the agencies, a flurry of lawmaking occurs every time a new administration (particularly one from a different political party) takes office. Presidents and governors regularly exploit their rule-making discretion to serve the interests that helped get them elected. Responding to such politics, environmental law wobbles pathetically. Perhaps no presidential administration in the history of modern environmental law has used delegated regulatory power more subversively than the George W. Bush administration. As Professor Pat Parenteau describes in an extensive midterm review:

> From day one, the Bush Administration has set about the task of systematically and unilaterally dismantling over thirty years of environmental and natural resources law.... [The administration] quarantined and then quietly put to sleep, scores of regulations issued by the previous administration – everything from arsenic in drinking water, to fuel efficiency standards, to snowmobiles in Yellowstone National Park. [This] has grown into a full-fledged ideological crusade to deregulate polluters, privatize public resources, limit public participation, manipulate science, and abdicate federal responsibility for tackling national and global environmental problems.[7]

Entire books now explain the George W. Bush anti-environmental regulatory agenda. The campaign straddled every agency having jurisdiction over ecology. In the air context, as Chapter 1 explained, EPA refused to regulate carbon dioxide even as the threat of global warming intensified to a perilous degree. The EPA also weakened previous rules from the Clinton administration regulating toxic mercury emissions from coal-fired plants. It used rule-making powers to excuse dinosaur power plants from pollution control requirements contained in the Clean Air Act (CAA) amendments, allowing thousands of factories and power plants nationwide to keep polluting indefinitely. The agency tried to ease the CAA rules restricting construction of new coal-fired plants near national parks and wilderness areas, a change that would have set the stage for at least two dozen new coal-fired plants to operate within 186 miles of national parks.[8]

In the forest context, the George W. Bush administration launched the "Healthy Forests Initiative" (Orwellian double-speak), which amounted to a set of industry-driven regulations allowing more logging of public forests. The initiative sawed through several long-standing regulations that gave public comment and appeal rights on timber sales, and it severely whittled down environmental protection requirements for major activities on national forests. The administration repealed the Clinton administration's "roadless rule," designed to protect the last remaining un-roaded areas of national forest from more road-building. On the regional level, the administration reversed protective policies for broad forest ecosystems such as those found in the Sierra Nevada and Pacific Northwest.[9]

In the Clean Water Act context, the Bush administration tried to increase the allowable amount of arsenic – a known poison and carcinogen – in public water systems. It tried to shrivel a broad spectrum of wetlands regulation. It cleared a regulatory barrier for mountaintop removal by defining mining waste as "fill" that could be permitted by the U.S. Army Corps of Engineers under its 404 program – a change discussed more later. The administration also scoured a Surface Mining Control and Reclamation Act (SMCRA) regulation, known as the stream buffer rule, which prohibited companies from dumping mining waste within 100 feet of significant streams (the change aimed to eliminate one of the last remaining legal obstacles to mountaintop removal). Across the environmental programs, long-standing regulatory protections toppled like pins to a full-strike bowling ball.[10]

This did not end until the hour Bush left office. In the waning days of his administration, Bush's agencies promulgated a series of "midnight regulations" – an eleventh-hour attempt to gut what remained of environmental law. One measure substantially loosened the ESA's requirement that federal agencies consult with the U.S. Fish and Wildlife Service (USFWS) to determine if their actions would send a species into extinction. Another tried to exempt certain hazardous farm emissions from reporting requirements. Another aimed to open 2 million acres of federal lands in the West to oil shale development. Yet another would have deregulated more than 100,000 tons of waste covered by the Resource Conservation and Recovery Act.[11]

The last chapters on some of these bureaucratic moves have yet to be written. President Obama's administration "froze" some of the midnight Bush regulations. Congress rejected others, such as the arsenic rule, in response to public outrage. Federal courts held others invalid. But some devastating ones, like the "fill rule" (explained later), still remain on the books. The vast majority of rule-makings, no matter which administration enacts them, escape challenge simply because the public lacks the enormous amount of time, energy, and expertise needed for litigation.[12]

The "fill rule," promulgated by the George W. Bush administration in 2002, illustrates how regulatory prestidigitation can thwart statutory intent altogether. That rule arises out of the Clean Water Act, which long ago announced the goal of protecting waters in their "fishable" and "swimmable" condition. Despite the Clean Water Act's clear legislative aim to safeguard clean waterways, the "fill rule" invites mining companies to use pristine lakes as dumping grounds for their toxic waste. It does so by exploiting a jurisdictional dichotomy within the statute. The Clean Water Act encompasses two main permit programs. Section 402 applies to the discharge of "pollutants" to waterways. Section 404 applies to the discharge of dredged or "fill material" to waterways. Section 402 and 404 can be thought of as two different statutory "rooms," so to speak. They are about as different as a bar and a church in terms of what they allow and who stays in charge.[13]

In charge of section 402 is EPA. This section requires polluters to comply with "effluent limitations" (limits on pollution). Back in 1982, EPA set forth an effluent limitation for froth-flotation gold mines that drew a hard regulatory line. It allowed "no discharge of process wastewater," based on the practical reasoning that no mining company should use a clean waterway as a waste treatment pond. A different agency, the U.S. Army Corps of Engineers, administers section 404 of the Act. In contrast to section 402, this section allows issuance of permits without direct pollution control standards. The Bush "fill rule," while complicated, essentially moved mining waste from one regulatory program to another by characterizing the waste as "fill" that would fall under section 404. The mining industry gladly snatches this regulatory dance card to shuffle from section 402 over to section 404, where it waltzes with a willing Corps of Engineers (a notoriously industry-friendly agency) to gain a permit for waste disposal that would have been out of reach in EPA's section 402 program. As Robert F. Kennedy Jr. observes, this one regulatory change probably amounts to the most significant weakening of the Clean Water Act in its entire history. As he puts it, "The Bush rule change created a loophole in the Clean Water Act big enough to drive a Dragline through."[14]

The ramifications of the "fill rule" stretch all the way to Alaska, where huge mining companies use toxic chemical processes and land-devouring equipment to extract bits of gold. In a case decided in June 2009, the U.S. Supreme Court upheld this application of the George W. Bush administration's "fill rule," finding valid a section 404 permit granted by the Corps of Engineers to a company called Coeur Alaska. The permit allows the company to transform a *publicly owned* 23-acre subalpine lake located in the Tongass National Forest into a mining waste-processing site. Coeur Alaska will dump 4.5 million tons of tailings into the water over the lifetime of the mine, raising the lake bottom 50 feet – essentially to its surface, as the lake was only 51 feet deep to begin with. The lake (rather, the hazardous waste pond) will receive treatment by a complex system of "reverse osmosis" to remove aluminum, suspended solids, and other pollutants before discharging into the stream below. The operation will destroy the entire resident population of lake fish and kill almost all of the other aquatic life as well, leaving ample uncertainty as to whether this public lake will ever be able to support aquatic life again.[15]

Make no mistake – this practice sullies the Clean Water Act, enacted to protect such waterways from pollution. As Chapter 2 explained, Congress specifically established a national policy to eliminate all pollution into the nation's navigable waters by 1985. The Senate Report stated that "[t]he use of any river, lake, stream or ocean as a waste treatment system is unacceptable." Subject to EPA's section 402 jurisdiction, the Coeur Alaska mine could not discharge into the lake. But by creating a detour around section 402, the "fill" rule allows the mining industry to completely undermine the primary objectives of the Clean Water Act. The Supreme Court upheld the rule on the basis of judicial deference given to the agencies (Chapter 5 takes up the matter of judicial deference). But as Justice Ginsberg scathed in dissent:

> The Court's reading ... strains credulity. A discharge of a pollutant, otherwise prohibited by firm statutory command, becomes lawful if it contains sufficient solid matter to raise the bottom of a water body, transformed into a waste disposal facility. *Whole categories of regulated industries can thereby gain immunity from a variety of pollution-control standards.* The loophole would swallow not only standards governing mining activities ... but also standards for dozens of other categories of regulated point sources.[16]

The "fill" rule also allows the mountaintop removal described in Chapter 2 because it permits coal companies to dump their "overburden" (the mountaintop, that is) into the valleys below, despite the fact that doing so obliterates streams and fills the valley with toxic material that should be prohibited under the pollution standards of section 402. (Moreover, the stream buffer rule, which should provide protection to waterways, remains in flux.) As Robert F. Kennedy Jr. traces the fill rule, it was a political payback by George W. Bush to the coal industry for contributing many millions of dollars to his campaign and to the Republican Party. Kennedy notes, "No industry had more highly placed sympathizers in the Bush camp than King

Coal." Industry pressure to pass a coal-friendly rule came as a result of a 2001 lawsuit brought against the Corps of Engineers for allowing the dumping of mountaintops into streams under section 404 of the Clean Water Act. The lawsuit threw the Corps' regulatory practice into question (and raised a cloud of issues over 27 pending valley fills that would have destroyed 6 miles of stream). It brought a quick response by the Bush administration to promulgate a final fill rule that would clearly allow the practice.[17]

As Kennedy describes, Steven Griles pushed through the fill rule. Appointed by Bush as the second-highest official in the Department of Interior, Griles was formerly the senior vice president for a Virginia-based coal company and D.C. lobbyist for the National Mining Association and major coal companies. Prior to the rule change, Kennedy reports, Griles appeared at a conference of the West Virginia Coal Association. There, he vowed that the George W. Bush administration would "fix the federal rules very soon" to allow dumping of mountaintop waste in the valleys. Later embroiled in charges of ethical violations, Griles resigned and was sentenced to prison for illegal conduct related to another scandal. His legacy in the form of the fill rule, however, still remains as a legal basis for industry to destroy public resources.[18]

THE TECHNICAL DECISION PORTAL

Subversive regulations such as those described in the previous section can skewer statutory mandates. However, the bulk of agency work lies not in devising broad regulations but in *applying* the regulations to specific circumstances. Inevitably, an agency must make technical determinations to assess whether, in fact, a damaging proposal meets the standards of law as detailed in the regulations. Here, where the rubber meets the road, the bureaucratic machine steamrolls over Nature. Agency technical decisions approve colossal natural loss in the form of chemical registrations, pollution permits, timber sales, mining plan approvals, water appropriations, no-jeopardy opinions, land use approvals, and a gamut of other mechanisms. If the process of rule-making described earlier seems obscure to the public, this stage of agency work operates at a nearly invisible level and draws far less public scrutiny. A rule changing the definition of "fill" under the Clean Water Act will stir the wrath of major environmental groups, but a developer's obliteration of a wetland pursuant to a permit may attract no public attention at all. The universe of involved citizens contracts measurably at the stage of ground-altering activity.

At this stage in the process, some agencies use technical discretion as free rein to contravene statutory intent. While the public may assume agencies implement regulations in a formulaic, objective fashion requiring very little judgment, in fact agency behavior can be highly politicized and even corrupt. A host of scientific and technical presumptions flow into permit and other approval decisions, and the agencies commonly invoke their vast discretion to choose assumptions that ease the burden on politically powerful permit applicants. Like any equation, the input determines the output. Recall the Clean Water Act's water quality standards, which (as Chapter 2 explained) aim to protect waters in "fishable" condition. As a result of pollution allowed by state agencies, fish from public waters harbor in their flesh an array of highly toxic compounds such as mercury, cadmium, pesticides, and dioxin. The higher the public's fish consumption, the less pollution the agencies can allow in order to meet the Clean Water Act's standard of "fishable" waters. One way an agency can ease up on polluters is to assume that people eat very little fish. In other words, average fish consumption forms an input to the "objective" process of issuing a permit that must calibrate to water quality standards. As Chapter 2 noted, EPA's national fish consumption standard (adopted by more than a dozen states) is 17.5 grams per day. By comparison, a six-ounce can of tuna (not including the water or oil) holds 142 grams of fish, about eight times this assumed consumption amount. The standard begs the question: Do eight people generally share one can of tuna? Fish consumption standards can involve some "interesting guesswork," Professor Catherine O'Neill notes in a comprehensive study of the matter.[19]

Jeff Ruch, Executive Director of Public Employees for Environmental Responsibility (PEER), explains that, in the context of issuing guidance under the Endangered Species Act, agencies engage in technical manipulations that "on their face appear neutral but are, in fact, designed to skew scientific results." Agencies routinely massage assumptions or cherry-pick ones favorable to industry in order to allow damaging action to proceed. As just one example, Ruch points to a genetics policy issued by USFWS Southwest Regional Director Dale Hall in 2005 that had the effect of precluding agency biologists from considering the vulnerability of individual species populations (as differentiated from the species as a whole) in making certain ESA decisions. Such an obscure policy would draw snores from the public, but it carried enormous ramifications for ESA regulation – as intended. Ruch explains that the policy would allow the USFWS to declare an entire wildlife species secure simply based on the status of a single population, even one held in captivity. He points out, "This means the agency could pronounce [a] species recovered even if a majority of populations were on the brink of extinction." With its impartial veneer, the new policy was likely timed to block the ESA listing (and recovery plans) of particular species in Hall's Southwest region that would have precluded development. Hall later became director of the USFWS.[20]

Subtle judgments often play a key role in technical determinations, and make them greatly susceptible to manipulation. As Professor Holly Doremus explains, the cloak of agency science hides many nonscientific choices. An obvious example arises from the Service's determination under the ESA as to whether a proposed federal action will "jeopardize" the survival of a species. Section 7 requires the Service to base its judgment solely on the "best scientific and commercial data available." Yet, a crucial element of the jeopardy evaluation involves deciding on an acceptable risk to the species. "Jeopardy" could be defined as a 20 percent risk of extinction, a 50 percent risk of extinction, a 90 percent risk, or any other percentage of risk, and no regulation exists to guide the Service's choice of risk in making a jeopardy determination. A similar risk dilemma embeds in technical decisions as to whether an activity poses unreasonable risk of human injury or death (from exposure to chemicals and pollution). These hidden risk quotients enable agencies to adjust their decisions to political factors and then disguise the manipulation with a complicated technical finding. Doremus observes this pattern (albeit varying in degree) across the political spectrum, stating, "The Clinton administration used this discretion to roughly calibrate [ESA] listing activity based on the level of political opposition. The Bush administration has exploited it to avoid listing species at all."[21]

The technical realm remains highly susceptible to inappropriate influence simply because complexity shrouds the decisions and renders agencies less accountable to the public. Unless an agency insider leaks information, no red flags alert the public to the possibility of corruptive influence at this crucial stage. Instead, the public labors in formal comment processes and public hearings under the impression that the agency will make its technical decision on purely _technical_ grounds – an impression agency leaders try their hardest to maintain. Of course, upstream of this agency process flows the agency science on which technical decisions are based. It too remains politicized – a matter taken up in Chapter 4.

Likely because of its highly technical nature, the ESA has proven a notorious magnet for political influence into on-the-ground decisions. Back in 1989, at the peak of the timber wars in the Pacific Northwest, the General Accounting Office found that political factors tainted the U.S. Fish and Wildlife Service's decision not to list the northern spotted owl – a listing that would have slammed the breaks on clear-cutting ancient forest across the region. During the George W. Bush administration, political factors again skewed the process. This time, the spotlight turned to hundreds of ESA decisions rendered suspect because of the inappropriate influence by Julie MacDonald, Deputy Assistant Secretary for Fish and Wildlife and Parks. The Office of Inspector General (OIG) found that MacDonald was "heavily involved" with editing and reshaping reports from field scientists on endangered species, even though she had no formal educational background in the natural sciences. According to one high official, MacDonald repeatedly insisted that field biologists revise their scientific findings to "fit what she wanted." MacDonald resigned on May 1, 2007 amid a firestorm of ethical complaints.[22]

ESA regulation in the Klamath Basin provides another example of politics sauntering through agency doors at the technical stage. In 2002, the National Marine

Fisheries Service and the USFWS gave a green light to a ten-year plan offered by the Bureau of Reclamation to withdraw massive amounts of water from a river that supports imperiled fish. A *Washington Post* investigation found that Vice President Dick Cheney, who wanted to curry political favor with the farmers in the region, became substantially involved with the ESA's highly technical "no-jeopardy" determination. Michael Kelly, a biologist who led the ESA review of the ten-year plan, resigned in protest and charged that technical recommendations were altered as a result of political intervention in the scientific study process. Months after the biological opinion issued allowing massive water withdrawals, 77,000 dead salmon showed up in the Klamath Basin – the biggest fish kill the West had ever seen. In later litigation, a federal magistrate found evidence that "improper political pressure led an agency to ignore its own scientists and implement a plan which jeopardizes a threatened species and violates federal law." The Ninth Circuit found the Bureau's decade-long plan patently in violation of the ESA. The court observed that, by the plan's ninth year, "all the water in the world" could not save the fish, for there would be "none left to protect."[23]

At an extreme, the disregard for civic duty and ethics can permeate the day-to-day work of an agency. The Minerals Management Service (MMS) became a poster child of corruption when a two-year investigation by the U.S. Department of Interior Inspector General found "'a culture of ethical failure' and an agency rife with conflicts of interest." The investigation revealed that, between 2002 through 2006, nineteen workers at the Service's royalty collection office in Denver – nearly a third of the office – had sex with, used drugs with, and accepted gifts and expensive trips from the very energy company representatives that they were supposed to deal with at arm's length in administering the public's oil assets. A subsequent congressional report concluded that the MMS neglected to collect millions of dollars in oil royalties owed to the public. One U.S. senator acknowledged, "the oil industry holds shocking sway over the administration and even key federal employees."[24]

THE ENFORCEMENT PORTAL

The third discretion portal involves enforcement. Professor Peter Yeager once explained the key role of enforcement in any legal regime:

> [E]nforcement is the centerpiece of regulation, the visible hand of the state reaching into society to correct wrongs.... [B]oth symbolically and practically, enforcement is a capstone, a final indicator of the state's seriousness of purpose and a key determinant of the permeability of the barrier between compliance and lawlessness.[25]

Weak enforcement drains the law of its potency. Yet discretion subverts environmental law at this stage as well. Just as a police officer has latitude to look the other way from a jaywalker, the agencies enjoy tremendous discretion as to how they conduct inspections and whether to prosecute violations. All too often, discretion pulls the plug on enforcement action. To be sure, many legitimate factors sway an agency not to enforce in particular circumstances. Agencies struggle with endemic problems such as perpetual underfunding and statutory limitations that constrain their authority. It some cases, lack of firm evidence justifies not prosecuting. Nevertheless, in many regulatory programs, weak enforcement results directly from the violator's political influence over the agency. Craig Collins summarizes the influence of political factors in EPA's enforcement of major pollution laws, describing a record that remains "shamefully defective."[26]

Inspection marks the first point of enforcement. An entire regulatory program can lose credibility as a result of an agency's notorious failure to inspect facilities frequently. As David Michaels points out in his study of the Occupational Safety and Health Administration (OSHA), that agency has only enough inspectors to visit a regulated work place once every 133 years. Inspection duties for pollution law compliance falls primarily to the state, and while efforts vary considerably, Collins describes state inspection programs as "notoriously underfunded and apathetic." When inspections do occur, they often follow a friendly "heads up" call from the regulator – which plummets the chances of discovering illegal practices.[27]

Prosecution of violators marks the second point of enforcement. Here, the political pressure intensifies. A well-known example arises from the New Source Review (NSR) cases handled by the George W. Bush administration. The CAA amendments of 1977 required about 1,500 old "grandfathered" polluting plants to comply with a strict set of pollution control standards as they expanded or made upgrades. This was called the "New Source Review" requirement. In the mid-1990s, EPA began an NSR enforcement campaign against the utility industry when its investigation revealed that 70 percent of coal-fired electricity-generating stations operated in violation of these NSR requirements. In 1999, EPA referred nine lawsuits to the U.S. Department of Justice for prosecution against large electric utility companies. The lawsuits targeted a total of fifty-one power plants that together accounted for 40 percent of the megawattage generated in the United States. The prosecutions held huge stakes for public health. Robert Kennedy Jr. surmises that "every year thousands of citizens in each state die prematurely of respiratory illnesses that can be linked to polluted air from grandfathered plants."[28]

However, as Professor Joel Mintz reports in a comprehensive article, the utility industry devised a "massive political lobbying strategy to derail the suits and avoid liability."[29] It contributed so copiously to Bush's campaign that a number of the main utility industry lawyers and lobbyists gained status as Bush "pioneers" for individually raising more than $100,000 in political contributions. According to Mintz, these Bush pioneers included executives from the very same electric companies that were either already defendants in NSR litigation brought by government or under active investigation by EPA's enforcement staff. Collectively, the coal plant operators donated the largest sum given by any single industry to Bush's 2000 campaign.

Political payback began with Cheney's energy task force, described in Chapter 1. Out of a process that involved multiple backdoor meetings with industry and behind-the-scenes lobbying of the White House by some of the most powerful individuals in the Republican Party (one of whom later became chair of Bush's reelection campaign), the "NSR rule rollback" emerged as a strategy to pull the rug out from under the pending prosecutions. A new NSR rule promulgated by the Bush administration essentially raised the threshold for triggering the pollution control standards. As Mintz explains, the threshold levitated so high as to make it "almost inconceivable that NSR standards would ever apply to actual electric-generating stations in particular cases." Suddenly, even the dirtiest plants were operating legally. One high-ranking EPA official said frankly in an interview, "[T]he goal of NSR reform was to prevent any enforcement case from going forward." When the regulatory requirements lifted, the lawsuits evaporated. The EPA's chief enforcement officer, Eric Schaeffer, resigned in protest and later said in an interview with Kennedy, "With the Bush administration, whether or not environmental laws are enforced depends on who you know.... If you've got a good lobbyist, you can just buy your way out of trouble."[30]

Enforcement failures extend well beyond these high-profile cases. They occur systematically in many programs. For example, Collins reports that 41 percent of U.S. oil refineries and one-third of iron and steel plants violate the CAA in significant ways, according to EPA's own figures. He also notes that many of the biggest industrial polluters, including fossil fuel corporations and auto companies, "openly violate the CAA on a daily basis, on a massive scale, year after year," without penalty. Summarizing multiple enforcement failures, Collins concludes that for the biggest corporate polluters in the United States, "getting off the hook for violating clean air laws is just part of doing business."[31]

The same story plays out in the Clean Water Act context. US PIRG reports that nearly 30 percent (1,798) of facilities surveyed (between 2000 and 2001) across the United States were in significant noncompliance with the terms of their water pollution permit, and that both EPA and state agencies "failed to properly pursue and punish polluters." A more recent investigation conducted by Charles Duhigg for *The New York Times* showed that the number of facilities violating the Clean Water Act increased more than 16 percent from 2004 to 2007. Through the Freedom of Information Act, the *Times* gained hundreds of thousands of water pollution records and compiled them into a database. It revealed that over a five-year period, 23,000 companies violated water pollution laws, some multiple times, totaling more than 500,000 violations. In many instances, the polluters reported their violations to the regulators under statutory reporting requirements, but with no consequence. According to the *Times* research, fewer than 3 percent of the Clean Water Act violations resulted in fines or other action by regulators. Across more than thirty states, federal regulators sat aware of enforcement deficiencies but took no action. As the *Times* reports, "[Agency officials] describe a regulatory system – at EPA and among state agencies – that in many ways simply does not work."[32]

The New York Times conducted another investigative report on EPA's enforcement of the Safe Drinking Water Act. In that context, the *Times* found that 20 percent of the water treatment systems in the United States violated the law, delivering contaminated water to potentially more than 49 million people. Nevertheless, EPA and state officials fined or punished fewer than 6 percent of the violators. In virtually hundreds of cases, illegal pollution continued for years.[33]

Political pressure emerges as a major culprit in this systemic enforcement failure. As one official interviewed by the *Times* put it, "[agency staff] had been pressured by industry-friendly politicians to drop continuing pollution investigations." Another said, "'The same people who told us to ignore Safe Drinking Water Act violations are still running the divisions. . . . There's no accountability, and so nothing's going to change.'" As a case study, the *Times* focused on environmental violations by coal companies in West Virginia. Over a period of five years in one 8-mile radius, coal companies injected 1.9 billion gallons of toxic coal slurry and sludge from their mining operations into the ground and dumped millions of gallons more into open lagoons. Pollution reports submitted by the companies to regulators showed that 93 percent of the waste contained toxins such as arsenic, lead, chromium, beryllium, or nickel at illegal concentrations, with some surpassing legal limits by 1,000 percent. The same types of chemicals appeared in the tap water of nearby residents, and medical officials noted "unusually high rates of health problems" in the community (30 of 100 residents interviewed as part of litigation, for example, underwent gallbladder removal surgery).[34]

Despite flagrant violations of environmental law, state officials never fined the companies for their illegal actions. One former West Virginia official disclosed in a *Times* interview that he was fired from his position for taking aggressive enforcement measures; others in the agency feared retribution: "Everyone was terrified of doing their job," one said. A federal regulator in another *Times* interview said that his "hands [were] tied. . . . Everyone knew polluters were getting away with murder. But these polluters are some of the biggest campaign contributors in town, so no one really cared if they were dumping poisons into streams."[35]

Politics drives enforcement failure across other states as well. Commentator Steve Duin portrays the Oregon Department of Environmental Quality (DEQ) as caught in a state of "'regulatory captivity' – operating at the pleasure of the industries it regulates." Pointing out serial instances of state enforcement failure stemming from industry pressure, Duin describes the agency as an "emasculated, isolated, compromised disaster." In fact, many (if not most) states suffer from lack of political will to enforce strict environmental requirements. As Collins explains, states tend to be "even more heavily swayed" than federal officials by industry lobbying power and campaign contributions.[36]

Ongoing, systematic enforcement failures create a regulatory milieu where tolerated lawlessness becomes the norm, and staffers come to accept the circumstance with varying degree of resignation. As one federal district court judge wrote in a West Virginia mountaintop removal case after finding that state and federal officials repeatedly ignored mining companies' violations of federal law:

> [T]he direct consequences of the agency's decade-long delay [are] thousands of acres of un-reclaimed strip-mined land, untreated polluted water, and millions (potentially billions) of dollars of State liabilities. The indirect results, however, may be more damaging: *a climate of lawlessness*, which creates a pervasive impression that continued disregard for federal law and statutory requirements goes unpunished, or possibly unnoticed. Agency warnings have no more effect than a wink and a nod, a deadline is just an arbitrary date on the calendar and, once passed, not to be mentioned again. Financial benefits accrue to the owners and operators who were not required to incur the statutory burden and costs attendant to surface mining; political benefits accrue to the state executive and legislators who escape accountability while the mining industry gets a free pass. Why should the state actors do otherwise when the federal regulatory enforcers' findings, requirements, and warnings remain toothless and without effect?[37]

WAITING FOR POLITICAL WINDS TO TURN

In sum, the politics of discretion allows power and influence to enter agency portals at all three major decision-making junctures: rule-making, technical decisions, and enforcement. This intrusion moves agencies to manipulate law to industry's advantage – so much so that agencies regularly shield or legalize the very damage their authorizing statutes were designed to prevent.

Political manipulation of discretionary decision making has proved to be the bane of environmental law for decades. But environmental advocates have never confronted the problem in a transformative way. Why? Because they hold out hope that, once political winds shift, discretion will work in their favor. History mocks such reasoning time and time again.

Even when political winds shift back to a more nature-friendly administration, the all-consuming work of bandaging hemorrhages inflicted by the prior administration can hopelessly sap bureaucratic energy and leave little for the important task of forging new policies. Moreover, a slash-and-burn expedition through environmental regulations during just one presidential or gubernatorial term can leave a charred natural landscape for generations to come. Pollution accumulates in rivers, species slip into extinction, mines contaminate entire watersheds, and toxins implant cancer time bombs in the population. During every corrupt administration, incalculable natural losses accrue to society with devastating effects on communities, families, and children. Tolerating agency abuse of discretion until the environmentalists win the next election will never move Nature to the positive side of the ledger sheet.

Moreover, history shows that industry pressure on agencies continues no matter what administration takes office. While extraordinary corruption fueled the environmental rampage of the George W. Bush administration, other administrations too have used their delegated power to subvert the clear goals that Congress set forth in the environmental statutes. The stories of James Watt, Ann Gorsuch, and Rita Lavelle during the Reagan administration, for example, illustrate an era marked by unseemly regulatory favors to industry. And it would be a mistake to assume that corrupt exercise of discretion occurs only in Republican administrations. Even the so-called environmentally friendly Democratic administrations cower before industry. The Clinton administration became known for indulging political interests. At least eight high-stakes ESA conflicts drew inappropriate intervention by high-ranking political officials in the Department of Interior to reverse the technical findings of agency scientists. As PEER's executive director, Jeff Ruch, noted in congressional testimony, "The ESA has been plagued by politics since its inception.... The principle difference [between the Clinton and George W. Bush administrations] is that what was an occasional event during the Clinton administration is now a daily occurrence [in the George W. Bush administration]. [P]olitical intervention has become a matter of routine." And the Obama administration also has capitulated on crucial environmental matters in response to political pressure. In 2011, for example, President Obama tabled a smog regulation that EPA had been working on for years, a move widely reported as aiming to appease industry. Most serious of all, as Chapter 1 explains, Obama waffled on carbon dioxide regulation even as the window of opportunity to prevent climate catastrophe was fast closing.[38]

Industry's capture of agencies remains a long-standing institutional problem. The EPA, for example, shows a propensity for politicization that spans several administrations. As Professor Michael Blumm points out, the agency has, for decades, ignored the Clean Water Act's primary goal of phasing out pollution. He explains:

> Often, when the goal of a comprehensive approach to clean water conflicted with administrative convenience or received political wisdom, EPA compromised that goal.... [C]ompromises came under Republican as well as Democratic administrations, so crass politics does not help to explain the results. Instead, it seems more likely that the explanation lies in a maturing bureaucracy more interested in self-preservation than in championing the environmental goals established in

its authorizing legislation.... The upshot is that after thirty years the nation's water pollution control effort is half-baked.[39]

OSHA presents another example of an agency falling captive to the industry it supposedly regulates and remaining that way through multiple administrations. While the agency's mission is to reduce workplace hazards, David Michaels documents long-standing agency capitulation that leaves workers vulnerable to serious workplace exposure to lead, benzene, vinyl chloride, chromium 6, diacetyl, beryllium, and a host of other harmful chemicals. Summarizing numerous in-depth case studies in his book, *Doubt is Their Product*, Michaels concludes:

> [T]he agency has pretty much stopped working.... Workers wait for OSHA at their peril. It is as simple as that. New workplace health standards are rare, and it makes little difference whether the White House is in Democratic or Republican hands. In the last ten years OSHA has issued workplace standards for a total of two new chemicals. Two. [T]he agency enforces permissible exposure limits for fewer than two hundred of the approximately three thousand chemicals [that are high-volume]. Of these OSHA standards, all but a handful were borrowed whole from the voluntary levels established by industry consensus groups.... Many are now hopelessly, dangerously out of date; new science has had no impact on these regulations. Because OSHA has been so beaten down by the opponents of regulation, it has virtually given up on developing new regulations or strengthening outdated ones.[40]

In sum, discretion breeds dysfunction across environmental agencies. Any strategy of waiting for political winds to turn in Nature's favor only reinforces the problem, because polluting industries benefit from *any* delay – for them, it translates into profits. The situation calls for a fresh infusion of legal obligation into agency decision making. But to have any hope of reforming the administrative process, we must understand the precise dynamics that infect decision making within agencies. The next chapter takes up that subject.

4

Behind the Grand Façade

Call it obvious: big money rides on many environmental and land-use decisions, and industries have strong incentives to defeat regulation at every possible turn. Doing so becomes an inextricable part of corporate business – it is called regulatory affairs. As Chapter 3 explained, industry groups mount aggressive antiregulatory campaigns directed at the executive branch of government, which holds permitting authority under environmental statutes.

An antiregulatory campaign works like a well-oiled machine, each part creating powerful torque. As this chapter explains, industry leaders prevail upon state governors as well as the president to place their loyalists in the highest ranks of agencies. They deploy public-relations campaigns to calm the public about the harm caused by their toxic chemicals and harmful practices. They hire and dispatch paid "experts" to produce skewed studies disguised as objective "science," which portray minimal risk from their industrial practices. They even create professional-looking journals in which to publish the drummed-up science. And moving upstream to the headwaters of the science that threatens to expose their harm, they attack legitimate, credentialed scientists through lawsuits and relentless criticism, seeking to damage their credibility and careers through harassment campaigns that can persist for years.[1]

As troublesome as electoral campaign financing has become, industry's broadscale antiregulatory campaigns directed at agencies are even more disconcerting because they remain so hidden from the public eye. Citizens generally know about the dangers of campaign financing, but they remain largely oblivious to the corporate campaigns waged every day against regulatory agencies.

Industry groups use a now-predictable set of tactics across nearly all contexts of environmental and natural resources regulation.[2] The following discussion describes these tactics as well as the dysfunction they create in environmental law. Inevitably, as Chapter 3 explained, industry's political influence within agencies flows through the channels of administrative discretion accorded by statutes. While this chapter focuses on the U.S. environmental bureaucracy, the same general dynamics operate in many other countries as well. Only by exposing these sources of bureaucratic dysfunction in environmental law can there be any hope of instilling a fiduciary obligation that protects the public interest.

THE POLITICAL OPERATIVES

Within every agency, employees fall into two general ranks. The highest officers sit as political appointees, and the lower staff members remain "career employees." A marked difference exists between the two. The career employees persevere through various political administrations and enjoy a degree of civil-service protection. Their jobs should not evaporate when a new administration takes office. Forming the agency backbone, career employees hold considerable expertise accumulated over time.

The political appointees, in contrast, arrive as newcomers who bring strong political agendas to the agency. Not surprisingly, they tend to reflect the party orientation of the person who appointed them – the president at the federal level or the governor at the state level. To a certain extent, the political biases they carry probably contribute to the diversity of approaches shaping the executive branch over time. Certainly, many political chiefs – indeed the majority in some administrations – remain ethical and civic-minded champions of the public good. However, some high appointees join the agencies already beholden to particular corporations or interests, especially those that helped put their boss (the president or governor) in office. As Professor Richard Lazarus observes, political chiefs, whether at the federal, state, or local level, show a responsiveness "to the same kinds of shorter-term political pressures applied to the legislative branch."[3] When agency heads feel politically indebted to a specific faction of the private sector, they act not so much as political chiefs as political *operatives* and may steer the agency in corrupt directions.

Typically, political operatives come from the private industrial sector and oversee the very regulatory programs that they spent their former careers fighting. While perhaps all administrations harbor some of these individuals, the George W. Bush administration touted the most obvious slate in recent history. As Robert F. Kennedy Jr. remarked at the time, "virtually all the principal environmental agencies are being operated by lobbyists from the very businesses they're supposed to regulate."[4]

A few examples typify the role. James Connaughton, chairman of the President's Council on Environmental Quality (CEQ) from 2001 to 2009, was a former lobbyist for industrial polluters. As head of the CEQ, he undermined the regulation of carbon dioxide in the face of global warming. After leaving government, he became executive vice president of Constellation Energy, where he oversaw government and public affairs for environmental policy.[5]

Steven Griles, a former lobbyist for the oil, gas, and other energy industries, became the second-highest official of the Department of the Interior (DOI). As the Associated Press described, Griles earned a reputation as the "go-to broker" in George W. Bush's program to lease out vast oil, gas, and coal reserves across federal lands in the West. Embroiled in charges that he used his office to benefit former clients, the DOI's Inspector General described Griles's misdeeds as exemplifying "institutional failure." Even though Griles was not found guilty of specific ethical violations relating to the land-management charges, he later went to jail on other violations involving the Abramoff lobbying scandal.[6]

Jeffrey Holmstead was appointed as head of the Environmental Protection Agency's (EPA's) Office of Air and Radiation and took command of the agency's regulation of coal-fired plants. Formerly a lobbyist with the law firm of Latham & Watkins, he had represented electric utilities with coal-fired plants that opposed air-pollution regulation. After leaving office in 2005, Holmstead joined the law firm of Bracewell & Giuliani and became the lawyer for a huge coal-fired plant proposed for New Mexico – a plant in need of a permit from the office he had just left.

Gale Norton, formerly a senior lawyer with the Mountain States Legal Foundation (a conservative nonprofit organization associated with the wise-use movement that promotes extractive industry uses of public lands), became secretary of the DOI, a position that gave her control over oil and gas leasing on public lands. Norton resigned in 2006 and took a job later that year with Royal Dutch Shell Company, providing legal support for their oil-shale development. Two months prior to her resignation from the DOI, her department awarded three leases to a Shell subsidiary on public lands in Colorado that were potentially worth hundreds of billions of dollars. The timing brought Norton a criminal investigation that ended without prosecution.[7]

Plenty of other high-level appointees also fit the bill of a political operative. Mark Rey left a long career as one of the Pacific Northwest's main timber industry lawyers to take the reins of the U.S. Forest Service. Phil Cooney, former oil industry lobbyist, became head of the CEQ. Linda Fisher, former lobbyist for the chemical giant Monsanto Corporation, became second-in-command at EPA.[8]

Such individuals typically bring three characteristics to the job. First, they show a strong loyalty to their former clients and a profound disloyalty to the public. Second, they have deep familiarity with, and resentment toward, the regulatory framework that consumed their prior careers. Third, they know how to transform the law in subtle ways – with surgical skill. When political operatives permeate the lower ranks of power (such as the deputy-secretary and assistant-administrator positions), the impact turns acute. As reporter Bruce Barcott explains in an exposé of the George W. Bush administration in *The New York Times Magazine*, "These second-tier appointees knew exactly which rules and regulations to change because they had been trying to change them, on behalf of their industries, for years." Regulatory subversion can prove as effective as a legislative repeal, but does not draw the outside scrutiny that legislative action would. Kennedy Jr. uses the term "stealth tactics."[9]

Political operatives pull the levers of the bureaucracy to push through regulatory, technical, or enforcement changes that will favor the industries to which they remain loyal. Rey, for example, forged new forest management rules that benefited the timber industry. Griles orchestrated the "fill rule" and stream buffer rules (discussed in Chapter 3) that eased regulation of the mining industry. Holmstead accomplished a rollback of air pollution rules pushed by the utility industry.[10]

When a particular industry has well-placed political operatives working within an agency, industry takes a hand in regulating itself. Industry lawyers deliver actual drafts of the regulations they seek into extended bureaucratic hands. It is an old trick. The public assumes that the particular regulation aims to protect the environment, while actually the regulation offers the very loopholes industry needs to continue polluting the public's resources. Because the details can be complex to sort through, the public rarely figures out the truth of the matter. One set of rules emerging from the George W. Bush administration, for example, was the Clean Air Mercury Rule, which allowed a significant increase in toxic mercury pollution. The proposed rule contained an approach mirrored in memos to federal officials from Latham & Watkins, Holmstead's old law firm, to federal officials.[11]

THE POLITICIZATION OF SCIENCE WITHIN BUREAUCRACIES

With political operatives installed at the highest bureaucratic levels, agencies exhibit a dangerous propensity to politicize the science behind agency decisions. As Chapter 1 explained, science provides the foundation for nearly all decision making under environmental and natural resource statutes. The core legitimacy of the administrative state rests on the assumption that this science remains "pure" and untainted by bias. While many agency career staff hold faithful to these principles, all too often the objective science they produce becomes a dartboard for inside politics.

Several books devote in-depth treatment to the problem of politicized science within agencies. Additionally, the Union of Concerned Scientists (UCS) maintains an ongoing scientific integrity program in which it analyzes administrative abuse of science. An open letter signed by more than 15,000 agency scientists urges decision makers to restore scientific integrity to the administrative process. While the Obama administration took preliminary steps to develop scientific-integrity procedures within agencies, a progress report by the UCS indicates that many critical steps remain in limbo. The discussion that follows briefly describes three patterns of political interference that occur with disturbing regularity. As Chapter 9 discusses, a fiduciary framework of decision making would characterize all three as violating the government's trust obligation that is owed to the public.[12]

Alteration of Reports and Testimony. Political operatives repeatedly take aim at scientific reports and congressional testimony prepared by career staff that may undercut an administration's political positions. Notorious abuses occurred during the George W. Bush administration in the context of climate policy. As discussed in Chapter 1, the Office of Management and Budget (OMB) and the CEQ scrubbed key scientific reports and testimony in order to downplay the threat of global warming. In a 2007 UCS survey of climate scientists working in seven federal agencies, 73 percent of the respondents perceived "inappropriate interference" with climate science research during the previous five years.[13]

The interference reaches well beyond hot-button climate reports. In another UCS survey, 24 percent of scientists in the National Marine Fisheries Service (NMFS) and 20 percent of scientists in the U.S. Fish and Wildlife Service (USFWS) reported being directed to "inappropriately exclude or alter technical information" from scientific documents. In a survey of EPA scientists, 18 percent said they had experienced frequent or occasional edits during review of documents to "change the meaning of scientific findings." One high-profile example investigated by the EPA's Office of Inspector General involved the regulation of mercury emissions from coal-fired plants. In the process of preparing a proposed rule, EPA senior management instructed staffers to manipulate technical and scientific analysis in order to keep costs down for the electric utility industry.[14]

Suppression of Speech. Political operatives also try to thwart government scientists from conveying damaging conclusions to the press, public, or the broader scientific community. This interference strikes at a mainstay of environmental democracy – access to the press. In a report called *Freedom to Speak?* the UCS documents interference within multiple federal agencies. While some agency supervisors allow their staff scientists open communication with the press, others impose various policies designed to achieve "message control." In those agencies, many scientists interviewed felt "intimidated and unable to speak freely." A well-known example lies in the attempt of the National Aeronautics and Space Administration (NASA) (through its Office of Public Affairs) to silence Dr. Jim Hansen, the agency's chief climate scientist. According to NASA's inspector general, the office undertook "unilateral actions in editing or downgrading press releases or denying media access on a known controversial topic."[15]

Political Interference with Scientific Determinations. Finally, political operatives tend to interfere with the technical decisions made by agency professional staff. At this stage, the agency chiefs put pressure on personnel they supervise to make permit decisions in favor of their allied industries. UCS surveys conducted between 2005 and 2008 show this type of interference with alarming frequency. In one survey,

43 percent of the responding scientists at EPA knew of "many or some" cases in which political appointees meddled inappropriately in scientific decisions. Similarly, 42 percent of the EPA respondents knew of "many or some" cases in which commercial interests "inappropriately induced the reversal or withdrawal of EPA scientific conclusions or decisions through political intervention." The UCS described an agency "under siege" from political interference.[16]

Surveys of the USFWS and NMFS revealed the same pattern. Of the USFWS respondents whose work dealt with endangered species, 44 percent reported being directed to "refrain from making jeopardy or other findings that are protective of species." More than half of all NMFS respondents (53 percent) knew of cases where commercial interests "inappropriately induced the reversal or withdrawal of scientific conclusions or decisions through political intervention." In one poll, 70 percent of responding staff scientists from various agencies (and 89 percent of scientist managers in the USFWS) knew of cases in which political appointees "injected themselves" into agency determinations. In the Minerals Management Service (MMS), the agency with authority over deepwater oil drilling (the kind that triggered the British Petroleum Deep Water Horizon disaster), *The New York Times* reported (in 2010) that current and former agency scientists experienced regular pressure by agency officials "to change the findings of their internal studies if they predicted that an accident was likely to occur or if wildlife might be harmed."[17]

In his book, *Undermining Science*, Seth Shulman notes an "unprecedented level of political interference and manipulation" in agency scientific processes from George W. Bush political appointees. But while unprecedented at the time, the dynamics persist to varying degrees. A 2010 UCS survey of scientists at the Food and Drug Administration (FDA) and the U.S. Department of Agriculture – the agencies responsible for food safety in the United States – showed reports of political interference by 34 percent of respondents. One agency scientist said, "Food safety has succumbed to the higher priority of global corporate profits." In a completely separate context, allegations of political interference tainted the State Department's handling of the controversial Keystone Pipeline decision in 2011, triggering an investigation by the Office of Inspector General. Regardless of the administration holding power, political operatives can make illicit maneuvers that flout the very premise of agency neutrality.[18]

THE POLITICS OF SELF-INTEREST

As a very basic matter, politicized decision making within agencies happens because self-interest infects the process. Bias can be present on an individual level (affecting decisions made by agency staffers) or on an institutional level (resulting from budget pressures, for example). On the individual level, self-interest forms around the nearly ubiquitous desire to maintain one's employment. This factor alone confers enormous power to political chiefs: they have the ability to fire subordinates. In highly captured agencies, the interest in job security may rise to an institutionalized, but unstated, de facto criterion in a multitude of regulatory decisions. Jeff Ruch, executive director of Public Employees for Environmental Responsibility (PEER), summarized the problem in testimony to Congress: "In the federal civil service, scientists risk their jobs and their careers if they are courageous enough to deliver accurate but politically inconvenient findings." The chilling effect from this can sweep broadly. In a UCS survey of scientists working for the USFWS, 42 percent of the respondents said they could not openly express in public their concerns about the biological needs of species and habitats without fear of retaliation.[19]

When used as a political club, firing power forces agency rank-and-file employees into submission, and public servants become passive accomplices to the institutional subversion of environmental law. Scant legal protection exists for a government scientist who jeopardizes his or her job out of commitment to scientific integrity. The Whistleblower Protection Act protects only a limited realm of action, such as an employee's disclosure of wrongdoing that presents an outright violation of a law or a threat to public health or safety. Moreover, a 2006 Supreme Court case, *Garcetti v. Ceballos*, held that public servants have no First Amendment rights when acting in their employment role. The government, in essence, owns their speech. That decision all but strangles the ability of government scientists to make honest disclosures in their official capacity about the work of their agencies.[20]

Apart from outright retribution for practicing scientific integrity, there comes another bias affecting agency decisions – the employees' own interest in career advancement. Officials who seek more lucrative private-sector jobs encounter prospective employers on a daily basis in their agency work. Industry shows eagerness to hire government workers who know the system and can influence the friends they leave behind at the agencies. Wishing to keep such job prospects open, some agency staffers have the incentive to avoid making decisions (such as permit denials) that would blacklist them in the industry they aspire to join.

Moving to the broader level of institutional bias, agency budget sources can create conflicts of interest that undermine environmental requirements. As Professor Fred Cheever writes in reference to Forest Service decisions, "Deep Throat told us to 'follow the money.'" The National Forest Management Act (NFMA) requires the agency to follow principles of sustained yield in planning timber harvest on public lands, but internal pressure mounts to "get the cut out" even when that means pushing beyond the limits of the law. This pressure stems from Congress's fiscal policy allowing the Forest Service to keep a percentage of receipts from its timber sales – receipts that keep the office lights on and the agency positions staffed. The conflict of interest has drawn the attention of a few judges at the federal level.

A panel of Sixth Circuit judges observed, "[T]hese biases undermine even the facial neutrality of the National Forest Management Act." More recently, Ninth Circuit Judge Noonan called out Forest Service bias in a case challenging timber sales. The agency had proposed such sales as a funding source for its fire prevention activities. Judge Noonan charged:

> The financial incentive of the Forest Service in implementing the forest plan is as operative, as tangible, and as troublesome as it would be if ... the agency was the paid accomplice of the loggers.... [T]he the decision-makers are influenced by the monetary reward to their agency, a reward to be paid by a successful bidder as part of the agency's plan.... *Can an agency which has announced its strong financial interest in the outcome proceed objectively?* Could an umpire call balls and strikes objectively if he were paid for the strikes he called?[21]

On both the state and federal levels, individual legislators flex their budget appropriations muscle to intimidate agencies into easing the regulatory burden for corporations that funded their campaigns. As Lazarus explains, congressional control over agency funding gives individual legislators leverage to micromanage executive branch activity in furtherance of "narrow, short-term interests of their constituents." When this happens, industry's legislative campaign contributions land an extra punch in another branch of government. Jackie Dingfelder, Oregon state representative, described the problem with respect to the state's Department of Environmental Quality (DEQ): "[If the agency] did something industry and the Legislature didn't like, they would get slapped down by their budget being cut.... It intimidated DEQ and held them hostage to some extent." Such inappropriate legislative interference spans a number of federal agencies. In a UCS survey, a majority of responding scientists working at the USFWS, as well as more than 40 percent of respondents at the NMFS, said they knew of inappropriate interventions by members of Congress (or in some cases local political officeholders) into agency decisions. When legislators overstep their boundaries and try to influence the execution of the law – a function that the Constitution assigns to the executive branch of government – they eviscerate the separation of powers underlying American constitutional democracy.[22]

BULLYING WITHIN THE FEDERAL FAMILY

In the federal government, pressure also flows from the Department of Justice (DOJ) and the OMB to undermine the goals of environmental statutes. The DOJ serves as the government's central law enforcement agency and provides a litigation team in cases arising under federal environmental statutes. The OMB reviews and approves (or disapproves) all regulations from other agencies before they become final. These agencies sometimes act as henchmen for the White House, thwarting regulatory or enforcement initiatives that could upset corporate allies of the president or his party.

The Department of Justice

The DOJ represents the United States in all litigation before the courts. Because it decides whether to take an enforcement case or let it pass, the DOJ holds tremendous power to shape environmental law. As Chapter 3 explained, the broad success of any pollution or natural resource program rests on its enforcement. When the DOJ refuses to enforce violations in court, it deprives the agency of the benefit of its most hard-hitting compliance tool. The George W. Bush DOJ gained a reputation for looking the other way when polluters violated the law, as demonstrated by its questionable handling of the prosecutions against coal-fired plants and oil companies.

Apart from its enforcement discretion, the DOJ also decides the United States' posture in other litigation, such as citizen environmental lawsuits brought against federal agencies and contests over water rights. In this role, the DOJ often finds itself mired in conflicts of interest resulting from the fact that it represents agencies with diametrically opposed positions in the same case. In environmental litigation arising over fish habitat requirements in the Klamath Basin, for example, four different federal agencies take positions on water policies – some pushing for water to remain in the river, others advocating for drawing water out of the river for farmers. Serving as the government's mouthpiece in court, the DOJ chooses which agency position to represent and, once the choice is made, effectively muzzles the others. Strict professional ethical standards generally prohibit attorneys from representing clients with conflicting interests, exactly for the reason that such conflicts tempt the attorney to push one client's interest under the rug to benefit the other client's interest. The DOJ, however, has never viewed agency conflicts of interest as an ethical problem. It clings to the idea that the executive branch has only one voice in court, and that differences between the agencies should be resolved outside of court through intervention by the White House. This situation only aggravates the extraordinary politicization of environmental law.[23]

Even beyond these internal tangles, the DOJ has, at notable times, used its position to cross into dark ethical territory. During the George W. Bush administration, the DOJ pursued a perverse "sue and settle" strategy that allowed extractive industries and other corporate interests to gain more access to public assets. As Professor Michael Blumm explains:

> The pattern resembled a Trojan Horse: the government would [allegedly] invite litigation from the industry; then, once a case was filed in a forum picked by the

industry, the government would agree to a settlement that would give the industry all that it could have hoped for in the litigation, undermining environmental protection in the process. All this was accomplished behind closed doors.

Through such "sweetheart settlements," the DOJ unraveled protections for endangered species, reversed a snowmobile ban in the Yellowstone National Park, and blocked the Clinton roadless rule that protected remaining old-growth forests from further road building. As Blumm puts it, "In this manner, the Bush Administration revolutionized public land policy without having to seek legislation or public comment." These examples all point to the DOJ's degenerative role in environmental democracy. With troubling regularity, the DOJ acts as a legal squire for the president, using its office in ways to undermine the public interest.[24]

Office of Management and Budget

OMB oversees agency budgets, a function that gives it tremendous power over all agencies within the executive branch. In many respects, OMB behaves as the bully in the house. As Devra Davis notes, "For a federal official, a summons to OMB, no matter what the stripes of the administration, resembles nothing so much as a trip to the woodshed. OMB remains the cop at the door with respect to which agencies get how much money, when they get it, and for what." In 1980, Congress gave OMB more leverage through the Paperwork Reduction Act. Despite its innocuous title, that statute created within the OMB the Office of Information and Regulatory Affairs (OIRA), assigning it the duty of broadly supervising the federal rule-making process. Under this authority, OIRA reviews all federal regulations even before they reach the stage of formal proposal, and again before they become final.[25]

This role of OMB and OIRA lurks unfamiliar to Americans who see only the exterior facade of the regulatory process. The Administrative Procedure Act (APA) requires agencies to notify citizens of proposed rules, provide opportunity for public comment, and publish final rules. But behind this seemingly straightforward statutory process lies a veritable maze of internal decision-making steps. At crucial junctures OIRA exercises review and approval authority over agencies' proposed regulations – with no external check on its discretion. When OIRA blocks necessary and justifiable regulations, as it often does, it throws a dangerous wrench into the intended implementation of statutes. Regulations become outdated when industry churns out new chemicals, destructive processes, and more dangerous types of pollution. To carry out their statutory missions, environmental agencies must respond by updating their regulations or creating new ones altogether. Even after career staffers manage to navigate strong political cross-currents within their agency to produce a responsive regulation, OIRA often capsizes the boat. As one Bush II-era EPA scientist described in a UCS survey, "Currently, [the White House

Office of Management and Budget] is allowed to force or make changes as they want, and [EPA actions] are held hostage until this happens." Robert Kennedy Jr. elaborates:

> Practically unknown outside the Beltway, OIRA's power is unmatched among federal agencies.... Federal departments and agencies develop these new regulations through an open process, guided by expert advice and mandatory public comment. Typically this takes six or seven years. Then, at the end of this highly democratic process, these regulations disappear into OIRA – only to emerge dramatically altered or not at all.... Its decisions can profoundly affect the nation's health, safety, and environmental safeguards – unimpeded by public debate or accountability.[26]

On paper, OIRA's internal review aims to coordinate regulatory policy and ensure consistency with presidential priorities. In practice, however, OIRA exploits its leverage over agencies to act as a political gatekeeper. It has often suppressed regulatory initiatives that the president did not find politically palatable – regardless of statutory mandates prompting the regulations. Robert Kennedy Jr. describes OIRA during the period when Dr. John Graham, a long-reputed friend of big industry, served as its administrator. In his capacity as government's regulatory czar, Graham enjoyed extraordinary power over virtually every new rule affecting the environment, public health, and workplace safety. As Robert Kennedy Jr. describes, OIRA simply did industry's bidding: "Like some deadly spider, John Graham sits in his secretive office and spins a dangerous web, weaving backroom deals with industry lobbyists and making a mockery of democratic government." The UCS reports that, pursuant to Graham's invitation, industry created a list of seventy-six regulations they wanted changed.[27]

Presidential directives passed over the years make it easier for OIRA to block regulation coming out of environmental agencies. President Reagan issued an executive order (E.O. 12291) requiring agencies to engage in cost-benefit analysis for all of their regulations. Within just a few months, OIRA rejected dozens of rules on this basis. In 1993, President Clinton signed Executive Order 12866, providing that irresolvable conflicts between agency heads and OMB shall be decided ultimately by the president. This throws many agency decisions directly into the lion's den of White House politics. In 2007, President George W. Bush issued yet another executive order (E.O. 13422) requiring each agency to identify the "specific market failure" that necessitated its proposed rule. The change, giving OIRA yet another basis on which to reject an agency rule, has made OIRA "more powerful and ideologically driven," observes reporter Osha Gray Davidson.[28]

Perhaps most significant, Congress passed the Data Quality Act (DQA) in 2003, which gave OMB a role in assuring the "quality" of data that agencies use in making decisions. The purpose seems innocuous – after all, how can anyone argue with the goal of producing good information? But as David Michaels explains:

> [Industry's] goal has always been to stall and, they hope, to stop agencies' attempts to actually issue regulations that protect the environment and public health. The DQA now gives them an official means with which to kill or alter government documents that serve as the scientific basis for the action.... It takes no great imagination to understand how industry can use the DQA to challenge in piecemeal fashion the quality of individual scientific studies. Their aim is to discredit and dismantle the body of evidence that an agency reviews in considering action and regulation.... The potential for mischief posed by the DQA is practically unlimited. For industry, it is a boon beyond calculation.[29]

Big industry (particularly the tobacco sector) had a heavy hand in pushing the DQA, which passed as an appropriation rider with no debate, hearings, or legislative history. Now industry groups essentially use this act as an administrative spin wheel to trap and stall out the regulatory process altogether. They continually generate studies showing no harm from their actions. Every new study, no matter how biased, provides a basis for a new DQA challenge against agency science.

OIRA, itself a high-voltage political agency, ironically stands charged with ensuring that the environmental rule-making process remains grounded in objective, quality science – but the agency lacks an adequate scientific staff. OIRA has an "all-you-can-meet" policy that corporations readily exploit, interacting with OIRA five times more frequently than do public interest groups, according to the Center for Progressive Reform. Through its DQA leverage, OIRA continually returns regulations back to the agency, sending agency environmental staff on a fool's errand time and time again. OIRA wields its breathtaking power over the regulatory process in near-total secrecy. Reporter Osha Gray Davidson writes, "With little or no oversight by Congress, the media, or the public, OIRA could allow a proposed rule to move ahead or kill it on the spot." Robert Kennedy Jr. observes, "OIRA may be the most antidemocratic institution in government."[30]

INDUSTRY CORRUPTION OF SCIENCE:
MANUFACTURING DOUBT

Outside the agencies, forces constantly undermine the body of scientific research that should supply much of the rational basis for government decisions. Industry groups have a tremendous amount at stake in the development of science even before it ever reaches the administrative process. As Professors Wendy Wagner and Rena Steinzor observe in their book, *Rescuing Science from Politics*, "The more emphasis that regulators place on science, the greater the affected parties' incentives to do what they can to control its content and production." These incentives manifest in perfidious ways. Industry groups move upstream of the regulatory process to infiltrate the very forums that produce, critique, and verify scientific information. When they achieve success, distorted science flows into the agency decision-making process as an effluent stream of uncertainty. There it dilutes the compelling science that would otherwise provide an impetus for agencies to protect public health and the environment. This industry manipulation of science is nothing new. It has persisted for decades – for as long as the petroleum industry resisted the regulation of lead in gasoline, and for as long as the tobacco industry has fought the regulation of cigarettes. This subject, too, now consumes entire books. In *Merchants of Doubt*, Naomi Oreskes and Erik Conway provide one case study after another with riveting detail as to the tactics repeatedly used to skew science. The original strategy was hatched from the tobacco industry (David Michaels calls it "Big Tobacco's Playbook"), and other regulated industries continue to deploy it in the very same way.[31]

The basic strategy requires the manufacture of doubt. Industry groups find multiple ways to attack a scientific consensus that their chemicals, products, and practices cause harm to the public health and ecology. Their strategy now seems as obvious to analysts as a first-quarter fake, but it continues to work exactly as intended in the public policy realm. As long as doubt persists in the public's mind, public pressure for regulation simmers at a low level. And as long as doubt obscures the body of science that agencies rely on in making regulatory decisions, delay carries the day – sometimes for years on end.[32]

An infamous internal memo written by a cigarette company executive presented the "manufacturing doubt" strategy. It said: "Doubt is our product since it is the best means of competing with the 'body of fact' that exists in the minds of the general public. It is also the means of establishing a controversy." Industry think tanks have become experts at manufacturing doubt, and they receive literally millions of dollars from corporate members to keep uncertainty afloat in the regulatory process. In his book, *Climate Cover-Up*, James Hoggan exposes the fossil fuel industry's relentless efforts to conjure doubt so as to confuse the public about climate change – even in face of scientific consensus finding human-caused global warming "unequivocal." He calls industry's campaign a "story of deceit, of poisoning public judgment – of an anti-democratic attack on our political structures and a strategic undermining of the journalistic watchdogs who keep our social institutions honest." It is Big Tobacco's Playbook, page for page. A well-known political strategy document submitted by political consultant Frank Luntz to Republican leaders in 2002 recommends instilling doubt as a means of diffusing regulatory momentum to address greenhouse gas pollution. He wrote:

Voters believe that there is *no consensus* about global warming within the scientific community. Should the public come to believe that the scientific issues are settled, their views about global warming will change accordingly. Therefore, *you need to continue to make the lack of scientific certainty a primary issue in the debate....* There is still a window of opportunity to challenge the science.[33]

Even as the Senate was debating climate cap and trade legislation in 2009 and many Republican Senators had come to recognize climate as a real threat, Oklahoma's Senator Inhofe (heavily funded by the energy industry) exclaimed in protest against the bill, "Science is not settled! Everyone knows it's not settled!" Ridiculed as the last "flat-earther" by *Washington Post* columnist Dana Milbank, Senator Inhofe stayed on message with the Luntz memo, calling climate change the "greatest hoax ever perpetrated on the American people."[34] The actual hoax worked supremely well to idle government agencies in face of the greatest ecological threat humanity has ever faced. As several books now document, industry relies on three primary methods to manufacture doubt.

Generating Bogus Studies and Calling Them "Sound Science." Industry-funded groups hire consultants to write reports challenging the science that exposes harm resulting from their products or practices. As Michaels describes, these "authoritative-looking" reports summarize "the friendly science commissioned by the companies themselves." Such reports aim their message at legislators, the press, and the public. These scientific facsimiles lack credentialed authors or rigorous peer review, but, by displaying a scientific-looking format and cover page, they might easily fool congress members and their staff who often look no deeper than the executive summary. As Devra Davis recounts, the tactic of drumming up uncertainty through industry reports worked marvelously in a protracted industry campaign resisting regulation of lead in gasoline. Of course, as most Americans know by now, lead works horrors on the developing brains of children. Industry finally lost the battle, but it profited six decades from regulatory delay while children's health suffered incalculably.[35]

The EPA further enables this industry manipulation when it enters into joint research ventures with corporations. The American Chemical Council has become EPA's "main research partner," according to PEER. The Government Accountability Office has warned that EPA lacks safeguards to evaluate, much less manage, potential conflicts of interests in such industry research grants. In the dark subterranean world of regulatory process, these joint venture reports worm their way into agency science and decision making. A well-known example arises from EPA's use of an industry-funded risk assessment in creating a regulation for formaldehyde emissions (a chemical commonly used in household building products and furniture). As discovered by the *L.A. Times*, the rule exempted certain wood-processing plants from regulatory requirements despite studies by both the National Institute of Occupational Safety and Health and the National Cancer Institute that suggested links between formaldehyde exposure and human leukemia. The industry study that EPA relied on had offered an exposure standard nearly 10,000 times weaker than EPA's prior standards for formaldehyde exposure.[36]

Phony Peer Review. The traditional scientific method relies on the core element of peer review. In this process, independent experts rigorously question the assumptions, data, methodology, and conclusions of a study in an effort to advance the common search for truth. Most scientific studies, no matter who conducts them, depend on publication in peer-reviewed journals as a means of gaining credibility in the field. This becomes quite a challenge for industry-concocted studies that could wither under objective expert scrutiny. To respond to this hurdle, Michaels explains, industry sets up a collection of its own "captured journals." Describing them as "vanity journals that present themselves to the unwary as independent sources of information and science," Michaels notes that the peer reviewers "are carefully chosen, like-minded corporate consultants sitting in friendly judgment on studies that are exquisitely structured to influence a regulatory proceeding or court case." Such journals offer the facial imprinter of "peer review," even though, if judged by scientific rigor, they should enjoy no more credibility than a kangaroo court.[37]

Industry groups take their manipulation of peer review one step further by engaging experts or faux-experts to launch vicious "peer review" counter-attacks on scientists whose studies threaten to expose harm from the industry's chemicals, pollutants, and practices. Again, the simple aim is to conjure up uncertainty amid a field of credible science. Naomi Oreskes and Erik Conway describe the pattern as "fighting facts, and merchandizing doubt." A small cadre of industry-loyal "scientists" tries to turn science inside out by branding the peer-reviewed, credible science as "junk science" while trumpeting corporate-driven, biased science as "sound science." "Orwellian indeed," as Michaels says; their all-out denigration of independent scientists whose studies do not serve the corporate agenda amounts to, in his words, "[p]erhaps the sleaziest behavior of all."[38]

The practice can reach egregious levels. Industry scientists often harass and condemn scientists whose work runs adverse to their interests. Industry lawyers threaten lawsuits, complain to the scientists' superiors, and lodge scientific misconduct complaints with the agencies funding the scientists. As Professors Wagner and Steinzor describe, scientists on the front lines of the nation's most pressing disputes feel like "hunted prey." Orchestrated assaults on scientists now occur so commonly that some commentators fear a threat to the whole scientific enterprise. Even if the integrity of science survives, this tactic now sows so much confusion that legislators, citizens, and agency officials who lack time to scrutinize assumptions and data find it increasingly difficult to know which body of "science" remains valid.[39]

The Public Deception Campaigns. Industry public relations firms carry the "manufacturing doubt" strategy a step further by deploying various tactics to mislead the public. Public relations experts adroitly present a new burden of proof when their industry's pollution draws blame for harming people or ecology. They promote the idea that science must be "certain" about the risks to health and environment before regulation against their industry can be justified. As David Michaels notes, society does not need, and certainly cannot obtain, proof beyond a reasonable doubt to protect the public from toxic industry practices. He writes, "Our regulatory systems call for using the best evidence available at the present time. Waiting for absolute certainty is a recipe for failure: People will die ... if we wait for absolute proof."[40]

The shifted burden of proof feeds right into stories produced by unwary journalists who seek to present "both sides," not knowing that one side may be superficial, fraudulent, and rejected by the broader scientific community. In his book, *Boiling Point*, which chronicles the press coverage of global warming, journalist Ross Gelbspan notes that American journalists gave undue attention to the industry's denial of global warming even though it flatly contradicted the solid scientific consensus. As Gelbspan describes, the fossil fuel industry's disinformation strategy involved recruiting "hired guns [and] a tiny handful of industry-funded 'greenhouse skeptics,' most of whom are laughingstocks in the scientific community." Handsomely paid – more than $1 million over ten years – to tour the country, they conjured doubts about the science "in order to preempt any public demand for action." Their success was striking. As Gelbspan notes, polls show tremendous confusion among Americans about whether humans cause global warming through massive carbon dioxide pollution. Gelbspan concludes: "The industry-funded campaign goes far beyond traditional public relations spin. It basically amounts to the privatization of truth."[41]

THE GRAND FAÇADE

The preceding discussion shows how industry pursues an aggressive and unseemly agenda to influence regulatory agencies. Politically primed bureaucracies respond to such industry pressure by repeatedly subverting the law through decisions made on the basis of politics rather than law or science. Some agencies show more political repellency than others, but not enough of them exist to sustain the tired old myth of agency neutrality, and certainly not enough exist to dismiss grave concerns over widespread corruption of today's bureaucracy.

But the more politicized an agency becomes, the more vested its officials become in perpetuating the myth that they run a neutral, objective institution. They cannot afford to have their behavior seen by the outside world as "political" in the sense of favoring one interest over another for reasons falling well outside their statutory authority. They also do not want to risk their agency's actions being overturned by a court under the Administrative Procedure Act on the basis that they are biased or "arbitrary or capricious" – which could describe any decision that

fails to be a strict output of statutorily defined factors, background common law, or
constitutional law.

In short, agencies need a "cover" for the politics that drive many of their decisions.
In this vein, Professor Holly Doremus explains an agency propensity to "scientize"
decisions in order to cast them with a sense of legitimacy. As she writes:

> Science is a politically appealing justification because it promises objective, rational
> decisions [and] decisions free of the corrupting influences of politics and money.
> Science-based decisions are far less likely to appear tied to the interests of a narrow
> special-interest group than decisions openly based on economics.[42]

Across many agencies, officials use science as a facade to justify the agency's political favoritism. Professor Wagner calls this the "science charade," explaining that it
permeates agency decision making throughout the regulatory process. An agency
may use science to camouflage decisions made as a result of hard-knuckle politics,
or it may use science to hide value judgments embedded in some environmental
decisions. Doremus explains that when "a cloak of science" conceals judgments,
"highly specialized knowledge and a sizeable investment of time may be needed to
unpack scientized decisions."[43]

COMPLEXITY, TECHNO-JARGON, EUPHEMISMS – AND AGENCY SPIN

Bureaucratic acronyms and techno-jargon give a ready-made veil to ongoing politi-
cal manipulation, operating to ward off oversight from judges, journalists, envi-
ronmental groups, and citizens. Every environmental agency uses dozens or even
hundreds of acronyms that blather an alphabetic mix meaningless to the public.
Clean Air Act regulations, for example, display the acronyms BACT, BART, MACT,
RACT, SIP, NSPS, NSR, CEMS, HAPS, LAER, NESHAPS, PPM, NAAQS, PSD,
TAMS, VOC, and dozens of others. Regulations under the Resource Conservation
Recovery Act use UST, TSDF, TCLP, SQG, MCL, LQG, HSWA, CAMU, CAS,
CESQG, and many more.[44] Encasing agency decisions in an impenetrable vocabu-
lary, this mumbo jumbo goes far in shielding bureaucrats from outside scrutiny.

Agencies persistently use euphemisms and comfort language to cause further public deception. Skilled agency public relations officers spin language in press releases
and other documents in ways designed to lull the public into complacency. The
George W. Bush administration, for example, cast radical rollbacks of regulatory
protection in terms that sounded rather benign, even reformist. The gutting of many
Clean Air Act protections occurred under the "Clear Skies Initiative." The "Healthy
Forests Initiative," another name with a feel-good ring to it, accomplished a tear-
through of the environmental analysis and public process. Presenting a host of such

case studies, Seth Shulman found a "concerted campaign to deceive the American public on a breathtaking array of issues." Professor Christine Klein describes the same strategy in the George W. Bush's "midnight regulations" (discussed in Chapter 3). She notes that these dismantled environmental protections using a "consistent set of code words – language so bureaucratic and malleable that it is nearly impossible for the casual reader to discern the core purpose or likely consequence of the regulations." As she describes:

> One regulation, which was intended to "clarify" existing regulations and to "streamline the permitting process," allows coal mining activities to be conducted near perennial or intermittent streams, potentially allowing over 1000 miles of Appalachian streams to be filled with the debris from mountaintops.... [Another] regulation passed under the auspices of "reduc[ing] reporting burdens on America's farms" exempts farmers from an obligation to report certain hazardous air emissions from animal waste, potentially applying to feedlots that generate more raw waste than an entire city.[45]

Yet the deceit campaign originated long prior to the George W. Bush administration. A history of double-speak has marked the Forest Service's approach to public affairs for decades, for example. In the aftermath of the intense logging wars of the 1980s, the agency shunned any use of the word "cut" or "harvest" or "log" in nearly all of its timber sale documents. Still today, it delicately presents clear cuts to the public as "treatments," bringing to mind something other than ecological ravage. Professor Oliver Houck penned a *Field Guide to Important Euphemisms in Environmental Law* several years ago, in which he quipped:

> One of the reasons environmental law is difficult is that it can be so embarrassing. It is one thing to say that you picked up a speeding ticket or had to pay back taxes. It is another to admit that you are using the Hudson River for a sewer or that you cut loose fourteen hundred tons of toxins over Los Angeles last year. The result is the rise of a new vocabulary to soften the blow. Just as military experts talk of collateral damage to describe the impact of weapons gone awry, so virtually every agency and industry that whacks the environment has developed its own language of damage control ... a set of euphemisms intended to blur the effects of strip mining, channel dredging, clearcutting, waste dumping and other dark features we would like to imagine were otherwise.[46]

AGGREGATING THE DYSFUNCTION

As this chapter explained, industry groups and agencies use an assortment of tactics to bend regulations to allow destructive proposals. The tactical success of such groups manifests in polluted water supplies, toxic air emissions, contaminated fish, toppled mountain ranges, exterminated species, soaring cancer rates, suburban sprawl, ocean dead zones, and an atmosphere primed for runaway climate heating. For the most part, however, the public remains oblivious to the political manipulation and deception that now serves as standard practice in environmental law.

The systematic warping of agency decisions to favor industry over the public interest threatens democracy itself. The next chapter explores how the executive branch amasses almost unilateral power in the environmental realm – to the point of failed constitutional checks and balances, diminished public oversight, and accelerated environmental damage. As Chapter 5 shows, the aggrandized power of the executive branch creates an administrative tyranny over Nature.

5

The Administrative Tyranny over Nature

In the waning days of the George W. Bush administration, Tim DeChristopher, an economics student from the University of Utah, showed up at a Bureau of Land Management (BLM) auction to protest the sale of 166 oil and gas leases across spectacular public lands near two national parks, Arches Park and Canyonlands Park. Pushed through without the environmental review required by law, the BLM was offering several leases that day for a thief's price of $2.25 per acre. When the process commenced, DeChristopher formed the idea to pose as an authentic bidder to drive up the prices. He raised a bidding paddle.

DeChristopher made significant headway – bidding $1.7 million on 22,000 acres – before being discovered. The auction ended in confusion, and federal officials promptly arrested him for disrupting a federal auction. He was sent to federal prison for two years. His audacity, however, saved some of the most glorious lands in Utah by buying time and drawing national attention to the BLM's shocking management practices. A judge subsequently blocked several of the leases, and the Department of the Interior later withdrew others.[1]

Despite the fact that DeChristopher protected priceless public property – property leased illegally in violation of environmental requirements – the Department of Justice, through its U.S. Attorney's office in Utah, refused to drop the prosecution. Federal officials decided to use the case to deter others from acting outside of environmental law's formalistic processes. Such processes, as this chapter explains, often keep citizens at bay while government delivers the public's assets to industry.

As we have seen, environmental law is not what it appears. Agencies at the local, state, and federal levels have turned the statutes into a broad-scale permitting system that allows colossal damage. Politicized agencies repeatedly serve industrial and development interests at the expense of the public. Time and again, science provides an impenetrable cover-up for decisions that sabotage statutory purposes. Despite its original goals, environmental law now institutionalizes a marriage of power and wealth behind the veil of bureaucratic formality.

In his book, *The Assault on Reason*, former Vice-President Al Gore warns: "If wealth can be easily exchanged for power, then the concentration of either can double the corrupting potential of both. Freedom's helix then spirals downward."[2] In the United States, the Founding Fathers tried to guard against such corruption by creating a unique constitutional architecture that established substantial checks against aggrandized power. This chapter explains why those checks have failed.

THE BULWARKS OF AMERICAN DEMOCRACY

American democracy provides two main bulwarks against corruption. The first involves the structure of the government itself. The second, discussed later, relies on the citizenry. With respect to the first, a three-branch system of government disperses authority to prevent unilateral amassment of power – the kind that invites tyranny. The legislature makes the laws, the executive (the president and administrative agencies) implements the laws, and the judiciary interprets and enforces the laws. The separation-of-powers principle anchors this design. It requires each branch to perform only its designated function and prohibits each from invading the province of the other two. Professor Bruce Ackerman notes that these principles function as a "complex machine which encourages each official to question the extent to which other constitutional officials are successfully representing the People's true political wishes." When appropriate balance between the branches exists, it yields "a whole more 'representative' than any of its constituent parts."[3]

As this chapter shows, however, the checks and balances over executive environmental agencies have largely disintegrated. The legislature and courts function as feeble players, providing only minimal restraints on agency power. Some of this may be an unintended consequence of environmental law's complexity, which triggers a hands-off reaction in many who encounter it, including judges and legislators. Much may be attributable, however, to the modern "imperial Presidency." In his book, *Takeover*, reporter Charlie Savage exposes a deliberate strategy (originating with the George W. Bush administration) to aggrandize presidential power. The modern presidential role, Savage concludes, reflects a rank departure from constitutional expectations:

> American-style constitutional democracy – the Founders' vision of using checks and balances to prevent the concentration of government power – is being transformed. No matter whether the issue is national security or domestic policy, the bottom line is that the extraordinary power of the American government is being consolidated, and the limits are evaporating on what the small number of people atop the executive branch can do with that authority.

Expansion of executive power erodes the most fundamental underpinnings of democracy, and the trend remains difficult to reverse. As Savage points out, "The accretion of presidential power, history has shown, often acts like a one-way ratchet: It can be increased far more easily than it can be reduced."[4]

The second main protection against government corruption resides with the public. At its best, democracy rests on the consent of the governed. When the public objects to government policies or senses corruption, it can reclaim power through elections. Abraham Lincoln referred to this as the "strongest bulwark of any government." But, as Gore explains, citizens can wield their democratic power only through civic engagement. Unfortunately, citizenship has waned. Describing a "wholesale alienation" of Americans from the democratic process, Gore asserts: "In contemporary America, we have created a wealthy society with tens of millions of incredibly talented and resourceful individuals who play virtually no role whatsoever as citizens." This, he notes, triggers a public spiral away from democracy: "[T]he more Americans who disconnect from the democratic process, the less legitimate it becomes."[5]

Environmental justice, democracy, and sustainability stand a meager chance of fruition in the face of a dispassionate citizenry. Yet it may be little wonder that citizens have become so detached from crucial environmental decisions. As Chapter 4 explained, agencies create formidable moats of complexity around the executive fortress that they inhabit. A public that feels disengaged, disenfranchised, and duped by government officials has little motivation to engage in the formalistic processes set up by the agencies themselves. At such point, civil disobedience by catalysts such as Tim DeChristopher becomes the last, and often most effective, measure. The discussion in the next section explores the breakdown of these two mainstays of democracy (checks and balances, and a watchful citizenry), explaining how their demise allows nearly unfettered environmental power to accumulate in the executive branch, at both the federal and state levels.

A DYSFUNCTIONAL AND DISREPUTABLE LEGISLATURE

Democracy hinges on a strong Congress that represents the people. Vested with law-making authority by the voting citizens, Congress remains duty-bound to enact environmental laws to protect public resources and public health. An active Congress in the 1970s passed a slate of bold new environmental laws, but Congress's role plummeted in the ensuing years. Environmental crises such as climate change, mass extinctions, the dying of oceans, and others described at the outset of this book worsen in the face of colossal legislative neglect. Professor Richard Lazarus characterizes the phenomenon as "congressional descent," stating that "[b]etween 1970 and the early part of the twenty-first century, Congress's ability to serve a constructive role in the ongoing process of environmental lawmaking has virtually disappeared.... Now, Congress passes almost no coherent, comprehensive environmental legislation and displays no ability to deliberate openly and systematically in response to changing circumstances and new information." The problem extends well beyond the environmental realm. Gore notes: "The most serious – and most surprising – failure of checks and balances in the last several years has been the abdication by Congress of its role as a coequal branch of government."[6]

Rather than address environmental problems by passing statutes as a deliberative body, individual legislators seize power by pushing appropriation riders. These are substantive laws tacked onto appropriations packages that fund government operations. Not at all problem-solving in nature, riders often represent subversive legislative moves. They act as sneaker waves of environmental law, coming up suddenly at the whim of an appropriations committee chairman and washing out major portions of environmental statutes for the period of time the rider has effect (usually one year). Riders do not proceed through the standard legislative committees that generate environmental statutes, nor do they usually involve hearings, floor debates, or any other type of thoughtful process. Their authors bury them in thick appropriations bills, hiding some so well that even their legislative colleagues may not know about them. Lazarus criticizes riders as "the kind of ad hoc, incoherent lawmaking resulting from closed-door appropriations deal-making that is of questionable efficacy for any area of law, but especially for environmental law because of its widespread distributional consequences."[7]

The task of locating riders subsumed in a voluminous appropriations package is like looking for a needle in a haystack. To legislators who use riders, their appeal begins with their unique agility in escaping democratic processes. Flying under the public radar, many riders "would never pass muster on their own merits," Lazarus notes.[8] Riders also have a certain "over the barrel" quality to them. To reject a rider, the president must veto an entire appropriations package, and with it the funding needed to keep the executive branch (or part of it) operating. Adding to this, many riders silence the third branch of government by restricting or eliminating judicial review. At every turn, riders flaunt the system of checks and balances and defy the open, deliberative processes fundamental to U.S. democracy. Yet they have become an entrenched feature of congressional environmental policy.[9]

Riders might be well justified where emergencies necessitate rapid action to protect vital resources against irrevocable damage – in essence, to maintain the status quo while Congress deliberates a long-term solution. But instead, most riders aim to *block* environmental protection. Politicians usually launch these legislative missiles to relieve a favored industry from regulation it finds onerous. They can destroy an environmental program in calculated measure. One rider, for example, prevented the listing of species under the Endangered Species Act. The use of riders surged measurably during the Clinton administration, as they became the tool of choice for legislators to undermine President Clinton's pro-environment initiatives. Between 1998 and

2000, for example, Congress passed 143 anti-environment riders running the gamut from mining to forestry, endangered species, water pollution, and much more.[10]

The 1995 Salvage Logging Rider, arguably one of the most destructive anti-environment riders ever passed, waived all restrictions on timber harvest nationwide and quashed judicial review of timber sales. Timber-funded senators conjured the rider to resurrect timber sales that the Forest Service had previously cancelled because of the extraordinary environmental damage they would cause. The "Lawless Logging Rider," as many called it, sat atop an appropriations package that President Clinton found impossible to reject – it provided relief to the Oklahoma City bombing victims.[11]

Through clever drafting, a legislator can target an agency program in the executive branch with drone-like precision. One rider, for example, withdrew funding from a particular forestry official who managed timber sales. As Lazarus describes, "The rider's aim was no less than to shut down the operations of one specific federal official." Another defunded the Fish Passage Center (FPC), the scientific agency that provides fish population data used in environmental lawsuits challenging the Columbia River hydropower system. Without funding for the FPC, the flow of data would dry up; without the data, the lawsuits would lose their key factual thrust against the hydropower industry. Idaho's former senator Larry Craig crafted the rider. A longtime recipient of campaign contributions from the electric utility industry, Craig drew the title of "legislator of the year" by the National Hydropower Association in 2002.[12]

Even beyond the rampant use of riders and a long-standing failure to legislate coherently on environmental matters, Congress also abdicates its oversight duty to ensure that agencies carry out the environmental laws they administer. Traditionally, this oversight role served as a vital check on the executive branch, particularly in the environmental realm where Congress delegates vast discretion to federal agencies. In the early days after the statutes were passed, Congress held regular oversight hearings to monitor the agencies' implementation of statutes. This watchdog role fell away during those years of the George W. Bush presidency when Republicans held a majority in both houses. While oversight hearings recommenced when the Democrats regained control of Congress, they now tend to focus on individual instances of alleged corruption rather than on system failure across the field.[13]

Lazarus concludes: "What is currently missing from the lawmaking equation is congressional capacity." A feeble Congress endangers democracy by removing a significant governing branch from the equation of checks and balances necessary to prevent despotic government. Several congressional culture problems, including the demise of bipartisanship and deliberative democracy, stand largely to blame for this legislative dysfunction. But beneath it all lies the campaign financing system. Powerful interests give money to individual legislators in the expectation of delivered legislative goods – producing, as Gore observes, "an atmosphere conducive to pervasive institutionalized corruption." The Supreme Court's 2010 *Citizens United* decision gave corporations even more free reign to buy political offices through unrestricted campaign contributions. Environmental stability cannot come about if corporate money continues to poison the wellsprings of democracy. Until true campaign financing reform is achieved, legislative subversion of environmental law on behalf of industry will likely undermine all other reforms. The trust paradigm discussed in Chapter 9 would challenge campaign finance conflicts of interests as a violation of the duty of loyalty to citizens.[14]

THE DIMINISHED JUDICIAL BRANCH

The judiciary once served as a powerful institutional arbitrator of environmental disputes. As Chapter 2 explained, courts treated many natural-resource conflicts as matters of property law falling squarely within their traditional province. But this judicial role diminished when the administrative state burgeoned in the twentieth century. Roscoe Pound, a renowned "dean" of American jurisprudence, wrote with chagrin in the 1950s about this state of affairs even before the surge of modern statutory environmental law, stating, "The tendency has been to give to administrative agencies of every kind wide and undifferentiated powers [and] on the part of the agencies to exercise powers of policy making and of adjudication to the verge of, if not beyond, the limits of our constitutional polity."[15]

Despite the modern conservative movement deprecating "activist courts," the tripartite system of constitutional government requires a robust judiciary to enforce the law and vindicate the core rights of citizens. Pound emphasized the crucial role of judicial enforcement over agencies:

> [A]ll exercise of the power of politically organized society calls for checks.... That checks are peculiarly needed with respect to administrative adjudication is made clear by certain general and persistent tendencies of administrative agencies, [to] give effect to policies beyond or even at variance with the statutes.... [A] *dominant administration, not checked by law applied by an independent judiciary, means a mere preachment bill of rights.*[16]

The judiciary has made a dramatic retreat in the field of environmental law over the last few decades. As the following discussion shows, four overriding factors, all relating to the statutory character of modern law, contribute to its diminished role.

Closing the Gates: The Standing Doctrine

To begin with, the judiciary shows a growing propensity to keep environmental cases out of court using a doctrine known as standing, which limits the parties that can pursue a claim. The doctrine requires (among other things) that the party bringing the suit show an "injury in fact" that reflects a personal stake in the outcome of the controversy. Deriving from the Constitution's Article III, which gives power to the courts to review only "cases" and "controversies," the standing rule has a compelling justification. Only parties suffering actual harm are likely to pursue their claims aggressively, thereby assuring the "concrete adverseness" which necessarily sharpens the issues for litigation.[17]

In the environmental realm, however, standing takes on a new dimension. Citizen plaintiffs sue for harm to ecology, a situation markedly different from traditional harms related to personal or economic injury. Congress deliberately included in many environmental statutes "citizen suit provisions" that allow citizens to sue polluters and the government. Fully aware that government enforcement alone would be deficient, Congress intended these suits to supplement government enforcement efforts. In the 1990s, however, the Supreme Court markedly tightened the standing requirements for such citizen suits. As Professor Lisa Kloppenberg notes in her book, *Playing It Safe*, "Instead of ruling on the merits of environmental controversies, the Court aggressively developed constitutional law to make it harder for environmentalists to bring such disputes to federal courts." She explains it as a clear "avoidance" strategy designed to "sidestep" ruling on environmental issues, writing, "Generally, the standing barrier is a one-way proposition that disadvantages plaintiffs.... In environmental cases, the barrier is often deployed against environmentalist plaintiffs, but not against plaintiffs charging that environmental protection harms their rights." The upshot of an overly restrictive standing doctrine, as Kloppenberg explains, is to alter the balance of powers "because the judiciary no longer serves as a check on agency action." Kloppenberg concludes that the Supreme Court's avoidance stance has made environmental law ineffectual to deal with modern environmental problems.[18]

Narrow (Often Procedural) Statutory Grounds

A second factor diminishing the role of the judiciary concerns the exceedingly narrow scope of the claims courts typically resolve. Lawyers now mold nearly all cases around confined statutory language rather than broad precepts of property rights under common law approaches. In large part, this penchant for statutory claims reflects law schools' curricular emphasis on statutory environmental law, much to the exclusion of common law. Lawyers emerging from law schools gravitate to the familiar statutes when strategizing ways to stop environmentally harmful action. But these statutory claims rarely bring a broad focus to the ecological harm at issue. As Chapter 2 explained, statutes divide environmental jurisdiction among a multitude of agencies. Statutory requirements run exceedingly narrow, each aimed at a particular facet of agency resource management. And most statutory requirements are procedural, not substantive, involving questions such as whether an agency complied with a required time frame in promulgating a rule, or analyzed the environmental effects of a proposal, or properly issued a plan, and so forth.

Of course, statutory lawsuits often prove vital in blocking damaging proposals. But not surprisingly, judicial opinions tend to mirror the statutory minutia that forms the basis of the lawsuits. By navigating the exceedingly narrow statutory gullies of environmental law, judges rarely address the deeper problems of institutional mismanagement of an entire ecological resource, much less the political corruption of the decision-making process. As a result, a mounting pile of inconsequential judicial opinions now clutters the field of environmental law. Some long-standing conflicts, such as those involving regional old-growth forests and endangered species, have collectively generated hundreds of judicial rulings without resolving the most basic conflicts surrounding resource management. As later chapters show, public trust cases can focus courts on the macro level of resource management and on the procedural duty of loyalty owed to the public. Such common law cases require (as they always have) judges to craft principles imbued with fundamental notions of justice.

The Judicial Deference Syndrome

The administrative deference doctrine presents a third limitation on the judiciary. Courts invoke the doctrine to give weight to agency decisions instead of fully exercising their independent judgment over a disputed matter. Good reasons exist for granting some degree of deference to agencies, but too much deference applied unmindful of the context undercuts the independent review function of courts. The administrative deference doctrine regularly appears in two separate contexts.

In the first context, courts apply what has become known as "Chevron deference" (named for the case, *Chevron, U.S.A., Inc. v. Nat. Resources Def. Council, Inc.*, that announced the principle). This amounts to legal deference toward an agency's interpretation of the statute it administers. If a court finds statutory language ambiguous and the agency's interpretation reasonable, it will generally defer to the agency's rule and uphold it. The approach finds some justification in the fact that agencies gain substantial experience administering a program over the years and, more so than judges, understand the practical and policy constraints that should inform statutory interpretation. The rationale breaks down, however, when an agency's interpretation of its statute arises out of political pressure – not an infrequent occurrence, as previous chapters explained. Given that agencies not only gain experience but also succumb to industry capture over the course of several decades, the *Chevron* approach lacks sophistication.[19]

The second context in which deference plays a role involves an agency's techni-cal decision making. On the face of it, the rationale for deference here seems per-fectly compelling. Agencies amass enormous scientific expertise over the course of administering a program. The deference principle abides confidence in nonbiased administrative expertise and portrays courts as no match for agencies in the scientific and technical realm. As one commentator writes:

> The proliferation of administrative agencies emerging from the New Deal reflected a faith that modern social and economic problems required an expert's attention. Those who rationalized the New Deal's regulatory initiatives regarded expertise and specialization as the particular strengths of the administrative process. That expertise was not shared by judges, since it springs only from that continuity of interest, that ability and desire to devote fifty-two weeks a year, year after year, to a particular problem.... [A] month of experience will be worth a year of hearings.[20]

As previous chapters show, however, the assumption of neutral agency decision makers often proves a sham. Political influence and bias regularly infect technical decisions, rendering the basic premise of automatic deference questionable at best.

The deference doctrine steers courts away from examining political motivations or conflicts of interest that may have inappropriately shaped the agencies' scientific conclusions. Invoking the deference principle, judges become notably reticent to second-guess the agencies, so much so that they allow officials to escape scrutiny for their most disingenuous actions – political decisions intentionally masked as neutral technical findings. In such circumstances, deference can virtually insulate political corruption from judicial review. The deference principle stands out as an oddity in the law, forming a marked contrast to the nonadministrative realm of trial practice (involving disputes between private parties) where courts routinely – and aggressively – examine expert opinions for bias and credibility. The "battle of the experts" characteristic of nonadministrative litigation would become a spectacle if judges accorded blind deference to one side's experts, ignoring elements of bias and credentials that prove so important to weighing opposing opinions.[21]

Used too broadly, this deference doctrine diminishes the role of the judiciary while aggrandizing the role of the executive branch and its multifarious agencies. Perhaps more than any other factor, the deference doctrine compromises the constitutional checks and balances. Yet only a few judges have squarely recognized the problem. In a 1997 case, the chief judge for the Sixth Circuit noted significant potential for "bias and abuse" in the Forest Service planning process and stated: "We would be abdicating our constitutional role were we simply to 'rubber stamp' this complex agency decision."[22] But this gem of judicial wisdom gained scant attention in the law academy and the judicial branch, and was quickly forgotten. The deference doctrine all but immunizes politicized agency action across the field. It relegates the judicial branch to something of a constitutional imposter in environmental law – a branch that purports to, but actually does not, carry out its assigned role in a checks-and-balances system of government. As Chapter 11 explains, the trust doctrine urges a far less deferential role for courts.

The Ineffectual Remedy

Insufficient remedies compound the other three factors limiting the judiciary. Owing to the process-oriented nature of the cases coming before them, judges focus their remedies on required procedural corrections rather than on substantive protections for the affected resource. More often than not, a court simply remands the case back to the agency when it finds the law violated. Rarely do courts provide firm side-walls to the remand or oversee it in any fashion. Not at all surprisingly, on remand, the agencies often march to the same political tune that produced the illegality in the first place. The remand remedy creates a procedural spinning wheel in which the various parties continually expend tremendous amounts of energy, time, and money while achieving little in the way of actual resolution of their long-standing disputes.[23]

Endless reruns occur, for example, in the context of Endangered Species Act litigation. An initial lawsuit may challenge the Fish and Wildlife Service's failure to list a species; a remand forces the Service to reconsider its decision. After listing, a lawsuit might be filed against another agency for failure to consult on an action affecting the species, resulting in a remand ordering consultation. Then there may be a challenge to a no-jeopardy decision resulting from the ordered consultation, resulting in a remand back to the agency to reinitiate consultation. Serial court challenges to the consultation process might ensue.

Arguably, on one level, the remand remedy appropriately respects the separation of powers between the courts and the agencies. The courts, for example, cannot make a listing decision, or a jeopardy determination, so they remand to the agency to do so. On another level, however, the remand becomes superficial in those cases where the real problem lies in the agency's politicized decision making and its entrenched institutional recalcitrance in following the law. Constant court challenges and remands rarely strike at the heart of this problem. Courts are capable of exercising far more aggressive oversight of the remand process, but this level of judicial engagement remains a rarity.[24] Most courts offer only procedural remedies in face of statutory violations and consider the case off their docket after remanding it back to the offending agency. As Chapter 11 explains, the remedy for trust violations holds more force.

All of these factors combine to wither the judicial function in environmental law to the point that, while the courts remain prominent in the most visible national disputes, the judiciary has become fairly ineffectual in actually curbing agency wrongdoing. Some of the most contentious natural resources litigation in the country still continues after a quarter-century without resolving the basic underlying issues that cause government delinquency. Exceptions exist, of course, but in the big picture of environmental law, a self-enfeebled modern judiciary no longer carries its constitutional weight in maintaining the balance of power contemplated by the Founding Fathers.[25]

THE REMOTE PUBLIC

Ultimately, the voting public represents a last bastion against a tyrannical power grab by one branch of government. But the citizenry now fails as well in protecting ecology and public health. Generally speaking, the problem is not a lack of opportunity for citizen participation. While some notable gaps still exist, the majority of situations offer plenty of process – if anything, too much, as explained later. But daunting logistical hurdles now stand in the way of meaningful citizen involvement.

Two federal statutes provide processes for public information and citizen input into regulatory decision making. The Administrative Procedure Act (APA) requires all federal agencies to publicize their proposed rules. The National Environmental Policy Act (NEPA) allows the public to comment on federal actions affecting the environment. These public processes in NEPA and the APA still operate as originally designed, but several factors cause citizens to forfeit their opportunities. One problem involves the tendency of citizens to ignore the prospect of environmental harm until too late in the legal process. Visible harm and actual injury strikes the greatest jolt to the public's sensibilities. But by the time the bulldozers and chainsaws start up – just when a citizen's foggy awareness ripens into pointed outrage – the agencies have long since granted the necessary permits. Public notice and opportunity for comment occur far in advance of actual harm at a time when the proposal is just that – a proposal. Citizens remain complacent at that stage because they logically assume that their government, with its huge assortment of environmental agencies and permitting requirements, will protect the public and natural resources from harm.[26]

Time presents another significant barrier to citizen participation. Making use of a public process, or lobbying the legislature, or even understanding the issue can devour an enormous amount of personal time. To put the matter in perspective, one environmental impact statement alone may require hundreds of pages of reading, with several hundred more pages of technical appendices. The sheer complexity generated by the agencies through the morass of acronyms and technical jargon described in Chapter 4 makes this difficult and tedious reading. With environmental management fragmented among several agencies (and with each agency having its own numerous processes), the myriad of public participation opportunities can drain and wear down even the most motivated citizenry. Moreover, citizen activists must devote considerable time to garnering interest and support in the community. Grassroots campaigns, while often effective, can prove exhausting. As many studies show, personal time in the United States has plummeted since the 1970s (when NEPA was enacted), and economic distress factors force many to work overtime or take on more than one job. This time scarcity sets entirely new game rules for civic involvement. Paul Loeb, a longtime analyst of citizen movements, observes: "[E]ndless work makes it harder to be an active citizen."[27]

If citizens had unlimited time to avail themselves of seemingly endless processes, perhaps current modes of environmental democracy could function. But when one considers the pace of industrial change and the fact that a citizen might face an onslaught of proposals affecting his or her living environment at any given time (on the local, state, and federal levels), the burden of citizen vigilance becomes more than a full-time job – with no allocated time or pay. On this playing field of process, industry easily outmatches the public. As David Schoenbrod explains in his book, *Power Without Responsibility*, because the industries have "concentrated" interests in regulation, they devote the resources necessary to gaining favorable permit approvals. They pay lobbyists, consultants, and lawyers to game the process at every turn.[28] Citizens who struggle to squeeze in time from a busy workday to show up at a meeting will often find paid industry representatives already sitting there.

To imagine that such a system could work well in the face of modern circumstances is little more than a fantasy. Yet agencies routinely indulge this chimera in a way that prejudices the public. If people fail to show up en masse at a hearing or fail to comment on a proposal, decision makers deem the public silence as an indication of noninterest or general acquiescence on the issue. For all practical purposes, then, the public faces an unspoken default penalty – somewhat like a party to litigation who does not show up at a trial. While public processes remain a vital component of democracy, they scream out for practical reform to reflect these modern pitfalls.

But there lies an even more fundamental problem as well. The fact remains that, despite all of these existing public comment processes, nothing forces agencies to heed public opinion. When government agencies become beholden to industry, citizens find it not worth the price of postage to ask the agency for resource protection. The NEPA rules affirmatively require agencies to respond to public comments, but captured agencies treat this as a meaningless chore. NEPA officers sort through public comments, cubbyhole them into categories, then develop a set of generic responses to each category. President George W. Bush demonstrated just how futile public comment might be when, in the waning months of office, he dropped a bombshell by proposing a rule that would have greatly restricted the consultation procedures under the Endangered Species Act. (While the administration characterized the rule as a "narrow change," many analysts thought it to be the biggest change in endangered species rules since 1986.) A swift outcry from the environmental community brought 200,000 public comments on the proposed rule. Bound by NEPA's mandate to respond to all of these comments in a short time frame so that the rule could take effect before Bush left office, the Department of Interior hired a team of fifteen people to serve as comment reviewers. With only 32 hours in which to review the comments before the deadline expired, the team had to review an average of 6,250 comments every hour (around 7 comments every minute per team member). Obviously, the administration could not have considered, even superficially, the totality of public comment within such a crammed time frame. That the sham was even attempted shows the disregard some agencies have for democratic ideals. Even with longer time frames, nothing forces agencies to take seriously the public comments they receive; quite often, agencies pursue their proposed action even in face of substantial public opposition. Fully captured agencies use the public processes set up by environmental statutes as faux-processes to maintain the facade that they care to hear about citizen concerns.[29]

ENVIRONMENTAL GROUPS: MIDDLEMEN OF DEMOCRACY

Citizen environmental democracy now falls primarily to the foster care of advocacy groups who present an institutionalized face of public concern. Whether these organizations inject a heroic thumb in the failed dike of environmental law or unwittingly enable the demise of environmentalism continues to be debated. To a certain extent, they may do both. In light of the limitations described earlier, the public truly needs the structure, resources, and expertise of environmental groups to maintain any degree of vigilance over today's flood of complex environmental issues. In that respect, environmental groups act as a government watchdog and the public's seeing-eye dog at once. They play a crucial role in alerting their members to ecological threats and explaining governmental decision-making processes. They help members participate in the comment process, usually by offering prepared "canned" comments that allow citizens to submit an approximation of their opinions with a click of the e-mail button. Many undertake community education programs and inform the press. Some groups take the extra step of litigating.

Mainstream environmental groups, however, tend to operate in ways that perpetuate, rather than challenge, the very dysfunction that grips the environmental system as a whole. Ironically, their magnificent success in streamlining public comment on environmental issues also amounts to one of their main downfalls. The large groups have become institutional brokers of environmental democracy, peddling environmentalism of a ready-made sort. Citizens overwhelmingly purchase their democratic participation through these groups instead of dedicating the countless hours required for more direct participation. While surely a necessary response to modern time pressures, citizen democracy loses its vitality when citizens resort to the services of middlemen in voicing environmental concern. Regulators and legislators easily recognize the "virtual constituency" that generates thousands of one-click e-mail messages on controversial issues. They dismiss these by one-click actions of their own. By contrast, hostile citizens who march in the streets, chain themselves to trees, or show up in the agency offices remain difficult to ignore. While some environmental groups facilitate face-to-face contact between citizens and government officials, not enough groups treat democracy-building as part of their mission.

At another level, large environmental groups rarely challenge (openly at least) the dysfunction that infects nearly the entire system of natural resource governance. Environmental groups that have become establishment players tend to work within the bureaucracy and assume its functionality. By playing it safe within the rules of the game set down by the agencies, these groups miss opportunities to target systemic causes – such as money-driven politics, bureaucratic discretion, and judicial passivity – that perpetuate environmental harm on a daily basis. As Ross Gelbspan wrote, quoting one journalist, "'These groups are running around trying to put out all these fires, but nobody's going after the pyromaniac.'"[30]

As a related matter, the large environmental groups draw criticism for their failure to push the political paradigm into pioneering territory. As Gelbspan notes, mainstream groups generally show "minimalist goals" and fall into a pattern of "relentless accommodation." Defined by what is "politically acceptable," the environmentalist agenda often finds itself seriously detached from Nature's own requirements. This, Gelbspan observes, works deadly aspirations for the planet. He explains in the context of climate crisis:

> Several of the country's leading national environmental groups are promoting limits for future atmospheric carbon levels that are the best they think they can negotiate. Although those carbon levels may be politically realistic, they would likely be climatically catastrophic.... Activists compromise. Nature does not.[31]

Finally, too many mainstream groups tend to drain ecological issues of all passion and populist force. In their alerts and advocacy statements, the environmental representatives speak very much as the bureaucrats do, sterilizing their discourse so much that they miss conveying the violence done to Nature and human communities. Much like the bureaucrats, these environmental groups tend to frame all manner of transgressions as procedural harms – the failure to consult, the failure to produce a plan, the failure to explore alternatives under NEPA, the failure to enact a regulation. Such droning advocacy sedates the citizens to the gross injustice and outright perils arising from much of government's environmental decision making.

As Gelbspan says in *Boiling Point*, "What is missing from virtually all these groups is an expression of the rage they all feel."[32]

Can we blame these professional environmental advocates? They do not wish to be perceived as zealots and lose credibility. They work within the system as they find it, and their one-issue successes lend some confidence to their tedious style. But in their aim to be conventional, they burrow down into the catacombs dug by the bureaucracies they challenge – and in doing so, lead their membership through dense tunnels of techno-speak without illuminating the fundamental values that produced the environmental laws in the first place. The public disengages more with every passing year. Similar points spark from Michael Shellenberger and Ted Nordhaus's controversial essay, "The Death of Environmentalism," which explores the loss of political momentum in the environmental movement. The authors criticize mainstream environmental groups for their failure to form a long-term societal vision and galvanize broad support around deeply held human values. The authors write that such groups focus obsessively on "technical policy fixes," that is, "proposals that provide neither the popular inspiration nor the political alliances the community needs to deal with the problem."[33]

By avoiding a discourse of values, the environmental movement leaves a dangerous vacuum that the conservative far right fills with astonishing ease. Conservative groups relentlessly promote private property rights and individual (antigovernmental) libertarian values – rhetoric that many Americans find intoxicating. Their property rights talk hoists an extreme corporate agenda that causes colossal harm to natural resources and communities, yet draws no counter-questioning by the environmental groups at the most fundamental level. Working overtime to defend imperiled landscapes and species against massive harm, environmental groups rarely pause to challenge the concept of unfettered private property rights (and corporate power) used irresponsibly and dangerously.

Long-standing *public property rights* could serve as a magnetic counterweight to market fundamentalism. Such public rights support natural abundance, community stability, economic prosperity, child welfare, human health, personal fulfillment, and national security – all strongly shared societal values. But these public property rights have yet to be tapped by environmental groups in a way that will energize the public. Chapter 12 suggests the trust principle as a legal repository for these deeply rooted values.

NEPA'S DISAPPOINTMENT: BUREAUCRACY'S INTERNAL CONSCIENCE FAILS

The prior discussion focused on the two primary linchpins of democracy: an active citizenry and separate but equally powerful branches of government. With both in decline, the executive branch now asserts unprecedented control over Nature. But there exists another possible check on this power: NEPA, which Congress designed as a tool to inform the internal conscience of the government. A landmark environmental statute, it expresses the "continuing responsibility of the Federal Government to ... assure for all Americans safe, healthful, productive, and esthetically and culturally pleasing surroundings" and to attain beneficial use of the environment *"without degradation, risk to health or safety, or other undesirable and unintended consequences."*[34] To this end, NEPA requires federal agencies to study the environmental effects of their proposed decisions before taking action. Many other countries have NEPA-like statutes that similarly require government to assess environmental effects of proposed agency decisions.

Coupled with the statute's clarion call for environmental protection, NEPA procedures should operate as an auto-brake on damaging decisions, even without a scintilla of public involvement. Congress assumed better environmental results would come about when agencies became aware of the environmental impact of their proposed actions. Unfortunately, a contrary temperament prevails today: agencies repeatedly turn away from NEPA's original purposes. While NEPA calls upon agencies to first objectively study the environmental consequences of their proposed actions and then make a reasoned decision based on that information, agencies often predetermine their preferred course of action and use NEPA processes to rationalize what they have already decided. Rather than providing an internal decision-making tool, NEPA often amounts to a cover-up tool.

One of the most spurious yet common agency practices allows private consultants, selected by the project proponent itself, to take charge of the NEPA process, even though doing so entails obvious conflicts of interest and invites corruption. In a *New York Times* interview, Professor John Echeverria called this pervasive practice "NEPA's dirty little secret," noting, "What's normal is deplorable."[35] The Keystone XL Pipeline, conceived to transport oil from the dirty tar sands of Alberta, Canada, 1,700 miles to refineries on the Gulf of Mexico, presents a prime example of how an industry-friendly NEPA consultant can pave the way for an environmentally devastating proposal. The State Department held permitting authority over the proposal, and with it the responsibility to comply with NEPA. As *The New York Times* reported, the State Department contracted out its NEPA duties to a private consultant chosen through a bidding process managed by TransCanada – the pipeline developer! TransCanada selected Cardno Entrix as its top choice from a list of three candidates. The State Department then selected Cardno Entrix in the face of what most people outside of Washington D.C. might call a clear conflict of interest: the company had openly listed TransCanada as a "major client." With the approval of the State Department, TransCanada paid Cardno Entrix for review of its proposed pipeline. According to *The New York Times*, Cardno Entrix also helped organize the required public hearings – a NEPA charade in full swing. Cardno Entrix's environmental analysis ultimately found that the pipeline would have only "limited adverse environmental impacts." Tempered language, to be sure: NASA scientist James Hansen declared that the pipeline would amount to "game over" for the planet's climate system because of the huge amounts of greenhouse gas emissions from the dirty oil it would transport. Reporters discovered that a primary lobbyist for TransCanada had close ties to Hillary Clinton, head of the State Department, having served as a top staffperson in her 2008 presidential campaign. The State Department's Office of the Inspector General investigated the NEPA process shrouding the pipeline but found no improprieties because the practices were so common among federal agencies – perhaps the strongest sign that NEPA biases have become institutionalized as normative standards of conduct.[36]

Without a doubt, widespread agency disregard of NEPA traces to the Supreme Court's unwillingness to find any substantive environmental mandate in the statute despite Congress's forceful language. In *Vermont Yankee Nuclear Power Corp. v. Natural Resources Defense Council*, Justice Rehnquist declared: "NEPA does set forth significant substantive goals for the Nation, but its mandate to the agencies is essentially procedural." In other words, agencies may destroy the environment as long as they follow the correct procedures in doing so. Nearly all scholars agree that Rehnquist's dismissive opinion demoted NEPA to a paperwork chore. Describing NEPA as a "process-monger," Professor William Rodgers asserts:

> Process, without more, is fundamentally a toothless exercise, committed only to the perfection of forms. No amount of process, other than by leaps of faith, can make the environment demonstrably cleaner, healthier, or more diverse.... [E]ach loss presages the next temporary win, and each win gives way to the next provisional loss.[37]

Despite its lack of substance under current Supreme Court precedent, NEPA remains notorious for achieving delay. Citizens bringing NEPA challenges against agency proposals will often buy enough time to mount a successful grassroots campaign against the proposed action. But these environmental successes should not be confused with the intended effect of NEPA. Neither should they distract attention from the internal conscience of the agencies, which NEPA was supposed to enlighten.

LEGAL REQUIREMENTS FOR SAVING THE PLANET

To summarize, through the various manipulations described earlier in the chapter, the executive branch now conducts its environmental operations as a de facto unitary government with little check or balance from Congress or the courts, and with only minimal restraint from the citizenry. As a result, something close to an administrative tyranny now rules over the public's natural resources. Legalizing ecological demise at nearly every turn with mounting injury to planetary systems, government creates unprecedented risk for humanity's future.

Supreme urgency lies in the task of remaking environmental law. In view of climate crisis and a looming atmospheric "tipping point," society likely has only a narrow window of time remaining to steer legal institutions in a safe direction. Incremental measures will not achieve the goal; the exigencies of our time require transformative change. To this end, several criteria anchor an encompassing approach.

First, legal reform must produce a firm, abiding obligation to protect *and restore* natural resources. Government must rechannel its expertise and revenues away from its current occupation of destroying resources to the mission of rebuilding natural abundance. Second, the political discretion model of administrative law must yield to strict fiduciary restraints on governmental actors. Each governmental agency must answer to an enforceable ecological duty that runs organic to government as a whole, binding every agency. Third, agencies must create new processes to engage citizens meaningfully in environmental issues and policy. The old notify-permit-destroy cycle of environmental law cannot continue.

Fourth, a new legal formulation of environmental responsibility must comport with ecological reality. Nature's laws must determine the parameters and obligations of government action affecting the environment. Fifth, legal approaches within the United States should be consistent with, and link into, global obligations toward trans-boundary resources such as the atmosphere, oceans, migratory wildlife, and international waterways. Finally, a truly game-changing legal framework must activate other realms of society in pursuit of a new and encompassing vision. A synergistic relationship between law, economics, politics, and ethics must materialize rapidly. To this end, law should reflect a strong moral imperative, dovetail with fresh equitable economic approaches, and revive the fundamental underpinnings of democracy.

THE VESSELS OF DEMOCRACY AND STATE

Part II of the book develops the public trust approach as a transformative paradigm shift for environmental law and explains its potential in meeting the criteria listed in the preceding section. But before turning to this new paradigm, it is worth pausing to consider whether modern governmental bodies, now substantially decayed as a result of institutional corruption, can even provide a sound vessel to carry forward principles of environmental democracy and justice. Professor Michael M'Gonigle, for example, casts doubt on whether the modern industrial state can ever achieve environmental ends. Highlighting the inherent contradiction between the state's "essential commitment to capital accumulation" on one hand and its "variable commitment to democratic legitimation" on the other, M'Gonigle identifies a troubling dualism: modern political power depends on making citizens happy in their economic lives, which many leaders take as a mandate to perpetuate industrial capitalism.[38] Yet the state has a duty to regulate the harms flowing from this massively destructive consumptive enterprise. As M'Gonigle submits, industrial capitalism lies at the core of the environmental crisis, yet the state relies on industrial capitalism to sustain its own political survival. Therein lies the stark contradiction between government's own political need and its duty to citizens. Illustrating this inherent "contradiction of the state" in the context of the 2009 Copenhagen climate talks, M'Gonigle writes:

> Everyone is lobbying state representatives like mad to save us. But the state is, in fact, the greatest global liquidator of them all. Not Exxon or Cargill or CocaCola – but every single government at Copenhagen. Ever since the modern state took shape, governments have aided and abetted, subsidized and [licensed], sold off and profited from resource destruction. This liquidation makes economic growth possible – and meaningful environmental regulation impossible.... The dependency of the state [itself] on this liquidation is near total.... *When the Titanic dining room runs out of dessert, we passengers don't like it.*[39]

M'Gonigle's observation begs the question of whether government can sever its own umbilical cord to corporate-controlled industrial capitalism and, if not, whether any corrections within the legal system will do any good.

An increasing number of visionaries posit that the only solution lies in moving society to a more sustainable economic model, one that meets the needs of citizens while protecting ecological health. A renaissance of economic thinking focuses on replacing industrial capitalism with more benign approaches (discussed in Chapter 13). While, as Professor Oliver Houck notes, "their share of the intellectual landscape remains unfortunately small," the current momentum of ideas may prove unstoppable.[40] The challenge of legal reformers will be to develop a transformational legal paradigm that can work in synergy with, and thereby leverage, these innovations in economic thinking.

Many submit that the most promising ground for economic innovation and sustainability lies at the local level, where governments better understand citizen needs and face more immediately the damage and poisons flung from profit-driven industries. Local governments hold the primary infrastructure that supports citizens' security and comfort. Given a few more natural catastrophes in the new ecological age, these basic interests of citizens may well prove formidable counterweights to the forces of growth and consumption that still drive political choices today. It remains an open question whether the federal government will remain too rigid and captured by big industry to actually advance sustainable economic models, but the point may soon be moot. Many solid thinkers acknowledge the possibility of dramatic transference of power brought on not by any statutory reform, but by practical exigencies set down by Nature's own laws – cataclysmic ecological change bringing serial disasters and financial chaos that the federal government cannot readily absorb, causing centralized governance to greatly weaken. As M'Gonigle points out, many respected critics of the present system believe that "systemic rebuilding awaits catastrophe."[41]

In a power shift triggered by ecological upheaval, localized institutions with proximity to survival resources could ascend as the dominant governing institutions of society. Any forward-looking, transformative legal approach, then, ought to develop with these potentialities in mind so that its principles stand as compelling at the local level as at the state, regional and federal levels – and not only in the United States, but in nations throughout the world. The next section of this book advances Nature's Trust as a legal paradigm suited for the New Ecological Age.

PART II

The People's Natural Trust

6

The Inalienable Attribute of Sovereignty

Nature's Trust presents the antithesis of the discretion model that has bred corruption and cover-up in many environmental agencies. It draws from the ancient yet enduring public trust principle, which safeguards crucial natural resources as common property of all citizens. The doctrine holds government, as trustee of ecological assets, to a quintessential duty of protection. As the Supreme Court emphasized in *Geer v. Connecticut*: "[I]t is the duty of the legislature to enact such laws as will best preserve the subject of the trust, and secure its beneficial use in the future to the people of the state."[1]

Infused with expectations of democracy, Nature's Trust repositions all players in their relationship to ecology. It conceives of government officials as public trustees rather than as arbitrary political actors, and it bears no tolerance toward disloyal public servants. It presents Nature as the trust *res*, a priceless endowment comprised of tangible and quantifiable assets, instead of a vague "environment" with amorphous value. The citizens stand as beneficiaries holding a clear public property interest in these natural resources, rather than as weakened political constituents with increasingly desperate environmental appeals to bring to their public officials. The approach views polluters as marauders of trust assets rather than as "stakeholders" controlling the political sphere. As Professor Joseph Sax observed more than four decades ago, the public trust demarcates a society of "citizens rather than of serfs."[2] At this point in history when ecology comes under siege by large corporations and government acts as their accomplice in irrevocable resource loss, the trust demands massive rebuilding and restitution of the people's rightful natural wealth.

POPULAR SOVEREIGNTY AND THE PUBLIC TRUST

The public trust doctrine speaks to one of the most essential purposes of government: protecting crucial natural assets for the survival and welfare of citizens. The doctrine has germinated in countless forms of government through the ages. Professor

Gerald Torres describes the trust as "the law's DNA." Professor Charles Wilkinson writes: "The real headwaters of the public trust doctrine ... arise in rivulets from all reaches of the basin that holds the societies of the world." With concepts reflected in indigenous systems, the trust also finds expression in such venerable codes as the Roman Institutes of Justinian (535 AD) and the Magna Carta of England. The doctrine surfaces in hundreds of court decisions in the United States. In *Geer*, the Supreme Court found the trust apparent "through all vicissitudes of governmental authority." Many nations (as far flung as the Philippines, India, and South Africa) embrace the doctrine as a central principle in their legal systems.[3]

The true origins of the trust reach far deeper than any one nation's legal system, for the trust ascribes most anciently to natural law – "the law which natural reason appoints for all mankind." The core purpose of the public trust lies in protecting the citizens' unyielding interest in their own survival (and that of their children). As Peter Brown writes in his book, *Restoring the Public Trust*, "[T]he trustee's fundamental duty is to preserve humanity." In his *Second Treatise of Government*, John Locke wrote that the "Fundamental, Sacred, and unalterable Law of *Self-Preservation*" forms the very basis of society and creates a fiduciary obligation on the part of government to protect this human right. If so, the people's interest in the ecology essential for their survival and well-being limits their government's ability to destroy it. The Philippines Supreme Court announced this primordial principle in *Oposa v. Factoran* when it halted logging of that country's last remaining ancient forest. The *Oposa* Court declared, "[E]very generation has a responsibility to the next to preserve that rhythm and harmony for the full enjoyment of a balanced and healthful ecology.... [This] belongs to a different category of rights [than civil and political rights] altogether for *it concerns nothing less than self-preservation and self-perpetuation ... the advancement of which may even be said to predate all governments and constitutions*."[4]

Natural law kept certain resources available for common use in support of the people's survival and welfare. As the *Institutes of Justinian* declared: "By the law of nature these things are common to mankind – the air, running water, the sea, and consequently the shores of the sea." This common ownership evolved into a trust concept that limits government's ability to privatize resources. As the U.S. Supreme Court announced in *Geer*, "the ownership is that of the people in their united sovereignty." Left under exclusive private dominion, key ecological assets could be consumed to the detriment of all, causing chaos and societal collapse. The trust protects against disastrous consumption of the commonwealth by securing a perpetual public *property right* in crucial natural resources. As the U.S. Supreme Court held in the landmark public trust case, *Illinois Central Railroad v. Illinois*, the state legislature cannot, "consistently with the principles of the law of nature and the constitution of a well-ordered society," make an absolute grant of the shoreline and waters of Lake

Michigan to a private railroad, thereby "'divesting all the citizens of their common right.'" The Court emphasized, "'It would be a grievance which never could be long borne by a free people.'"[5]

Courts resoundingly emphasize that government's duty to protect commonwealth runs not only to present citizens, but also to future generations as beneficiaries of the trust. The beneficiary class cannot be severed between the present and future citizens, because future generations continually materialize through birth into the present generation. Moreover, the immediate beneficial interest of present citizens inherently embodies future concerns, because all living citizens hold a direct stake in the remainder of their own life spans, and most also have concrete and discernible interests in the life spans of children to whom they bear close attachment and/or parental duty. Recognizing property rights in the unborn, the trust presents the most forceful existing legal construct to protect the interests of future generations.[6]

The trust mediates a basic accommodation between private property and public needs. Explained in greater detail in Chapter 14, private use and enjoyment of trust property by individuals and corporations remains at all times subject to an antecedent encumbrance in favor of the public in order to maintain the ecological stability necessary for society to thrive. As the Supreme Court declared in the 1907 case, *Georgia v. Tennessee Copper Company*: "[T]he state has an interest independent of and behind the titles of its citizens, in all the earth and air within its domain."[7]

A government's trust duty requires administering the natural endowment strictly on behalf of the people, rather than to favor singular interests. The *Geer* Court emphasized in the context of wildlife: "[T]he power or control lodged in the state, resulting from this common ownership, is to be exercised, like all other powers of government, *as a trust for the benefit of the people*, and not as a prerogative for the advantage of the government as distinct from the people, or for the benefit of private individuals as distinguished from the public good." This rule, after all, animates the long-standing political philosophy that deems government legitimate only if it acts for "the common good," as Jean Jacques Rousseau famously wrote in *The Social Contract*. Public fiduciary duty runs quite opposite to the permissive style of administrative discretion that now dominates statutory law, whereby government agencies issue innumerable permits and licenses that collectively drive the people's ecological trust into bankruptcy. As a property-based counterweight to discretion, the trust enshrines the citizens' right to demand government protection of the endowment, for their "common good."[8]

Within the broad formulation of government, the public trust exists wholly distinct from the police power, even though both originate from the same wellspring of sovereignty and both comprise attributes of government. The police power represents government's legislative authority to promote public health and welfare (thus producing the statutory law that now dominates today's legal system). This police power can reach the full spectrum of public concerns, including matters relating to crime, family, morals, health, and business. In contrast to the police power, the public trust emerges from the property realm and can limit the scope of government action. A sovereign property interest arises from government's control over a particular territory (just as private title to property comes from an individual's association with a particular parcel). The trust defines the character of this sovereign property ownership, recognizing rights held perpetually by the people. Weaving together two civic strands of power and obligation, the trust embodies: (1) the people's delegation of authority to their government to control and manage resources; and (2) the people's assertion, through a fiduciary obligation, of limits on that authority to ensure that it functions to benefit the public rather than special interests (who may have greater sway over the legislative process).[9]

The trust emerges twin-born with democracy. When government derives its power from the people, the sovereign's property interests necessarily amount to a trust. An oligarchy or dictatorship, in contrast, rejects the balance between public and private property rights, instead aiming its power to serve select ruling interests at the expense of citizens. Justice Paul Finn of Australia describes the fiduciary duty of government as inevitable when a nation's political convictions embrace the "inexorable logic of popular sovereignty." He states:

> If the powers of government belong to and are derived from the people, can the donees of those powers under our constitutional arrangements properly be characterized in terms other than that they are the trustees, the fiduciaries, of those powers for the people? Though separated by more than two centuries, our answer should be that of the American colonists after the Revolution.... The institutions of government, the officers and agencies of government, exist for the people, to serve the interests of the people, and, as such, are accountable to the people.... Sovereignty and trust probably are best seen as expressions of intrinsic qualities of our democracy.[10]

As Peter Brown explains, the original archetype of American democracy took shape around a general fiduciary obligation toward the citizens as a whole. This fiduciary concept infuses sovereign duties ranging far beyond the property realm. Locke's *Second Treatise of Government*, a philosophical manifesto that forged many democratic ideals, declared a core principle that fiduciary obligation formed an inherent constraint on governmental power – and that the people shall serve in constant judgment of their government's performance. As Brown surmises (quoting Locke): "The government conforms to the terms of the trust when it discharges its duties 'to be directed to no other end but the peace, safety, and public good of the people.'"[11]

A fiduciary conception of government tills the fields of democracy. Arising from the government's fiduciary duty is the public trust, a limitation on the sovereign's power over natural assets. Any government deriving its authority from the people never gains delegated authority to manage resources in a way that would jeopardize present or future generations or compromise crucial public needs. To suppose otherwise imputes a gross irrationality on the part of the people. As Brown notes, Locke's *Second Treatise* elaborates the circumstances justifying citizens to "legitimately rebel because the executive or legislator has violated the terms of the trust." Legislators and agencies acting in repudiation of trust principles do so illegitimately outside the sphere of authority granted to them. That government officials now do so regularly demonstrates how far modern bureaucracy has strayed from its purpose – and how far citizens have wandered from their vigil over democracy. As Brown observes, while the trust remains a vibrant part of the law and political tradition in the United States, it has "disappeared from the political arena." Citizens of the United States and other Western democracies now face a dangerous transference of power from the people to corporations, and considerable political introspection will prove necessary to set democracy back on track. The progression of the body politic toward an undaunted democratic destiny finds a bright beacon in the public trust principle.[12]

CONSTITUTIONAL COMMONWEALTH: "OF THE PEOPLE, BY THE PEOPLE, FOR THE PEOPLE"

Properly understood, the public trust stands as a fundamental attribute of sovereignty – a constitutive principle that government cannot shed.[13] As a federal district court explained: "The trust is of such a nature that it can be held only by the sovereign, and can only be destroyed by the destruction of the sovereign." Along with the distinct police power, the trust forms the sovereign architecture around which the Constitution and all other laws meld. Professor Torres describes the trust as the slate on which "all constitutions and laws are written." It cannot be repudiated, abridged, or surrendered by any legislature. As the Supreme Court declared in *Illinois Central*: "The state can no more abdicate its trust over property in which the whole people are interested ... than it can abdicate its police powers in the administration of government and the preservation of the peace.... Every legislature must, at the time of its existence, exercise the power of the state in the execution of the trust devolved upon it." When properly recognized as an attribute of sovereignty, the trust holds constitutional magnitude and achieves doctrinal supremacy over contrary laws. (Constitutional commands give courts power to overturn legislative action, while judge-made common law alone does not carry such trump force.)[14]

As Professor John Davidson explains, the trust's core concern for future generations lodged deeply in the original thinking that created the United States' constitutional democracy. The Founding Fathers thought carefully about the sovereign legacy they would design to carry the nation into the distant future. They formed a governmental structure aimed to "secure the Blessings of Liberty to ourselves and our Posterity." The inclusion of "Posterity," which means descendants and future generations, underscores an inalienable duty engrained in government itself as part of its constituted purpose: to govern for the *endurance* of the nation, and thus for the benefit of future generations as well as present ones. As the influential political philosopher Edmund Burke wrote, "Society is indeed a contract ... a partnership not only between those who are living, but between those who are living, those who are dead, and those who are to be born." This intergenerational bond between citizens proves necessary for any concept of enduring nationhood, for without concern for "Posterity," the nation would aspire to a mere temporary state. The same holds true for other nations. As the India Supreme Court declared in a 2010 public trust decision, *Reliance Natural Resources v. Reliance Industries Ltd.*:

> The concept of people as a nation does not include just the living; it includes those who are unborn and waiting to be instantiated. Conservation of resources, especially scarce ones, is both a matter of efficient use to alleviate the suffering of the living and also of ensuring that such use does not lead to diminishment of the prospects of their use by future generations.[15]

A rich assemblage of correspondence by Thomas Jefferson reflects deeply on matters of equity and rights between generations. By the law of Nature, Jefferson surmised, one generation could not bind another with natural debt. In an 1816 letter to John Taylor, he wrote of "every generation coming equally, by the laws of the Creator of the world, to the free possession of the earth He made for their subsistence, unencumbered by their predecessors, who, like them, were but tenants for life." Similarly, Jefferson's 1789 letter to James Madison described "fundamental principles" of every government that centered on the concept of usufruct (which means the right to use another's property for a limited time without damaging or diminishing it):

> I set out on this ground, which I suppose to be self evident, *"that the earth belongs in usufruct to the living"*: that the dead have neither powers nor rights over it.... [T]he present generation of men ... have the same rights over the soil on which they were produced, as the preceding generations had. They derive these rights not from their predecessors, but from nature.... [B]etween society and society, or generation and generation, there is no municipal obligation, no umpire but the law of nature. [B]y the law of nature, one generation is to another as one independent nation to another.[16]

This generational sovereignty sets bounds on legislative power in the American democracy. A well-established constitutional principle known as the *reserved powers doctrine* limits the ability of any one legislature to take action that will bind a future legislature in any crucial sphere of government concern. In an illuminating article, Professor Douglas Grant locates the constitutional underpinning of the public trust in this doctrine. As he explains, a present legislature cannot relinquish "essential attributes of sovereign power" that come implicitly reserved to the legislature in perpetuity. The Supreme Court declared the reserved power doctrine in *Newton v. Commissioners*: "Every succeeding legislature possesses the same jurisdiction and power with respect to them as its predecessors.... It is vital to the public welfare that each one should be able at all times to do whatever the varying circumstances and present exigencies touching the subject involved may require." The public trust applies this principle in the context of natural resources. Alienating resources that remain crucial to society would amount to relinquishing essential sovereign powers in violation of the Constitution's reserved powers doctrine. The public trust principle thus holds such resources in trust, placing their free alienation beyond the power of the legislature.[17]

The U.S. Supreme Court drew on the doctrine in the landmark *Illinois Central Railroad* case to hold that the Illinois legislature could not grant the shore of Lake Michigan to a railroad company. The shoreline, Justice Field stated, invoked chief sovereign interests as a "subject of concern to the whole people." Privatizing the shoreline would tie the hands of future legislatures that would have no less need of it to support public welfare. Justice Field quoted a prior case that described navigable waterways as "natural highways," the obstruction of which "would be very likely to end in materially crippling, if not destroying" the public's right to navigation. In a celebrated passage, Field declared:

> A grant of all the lands under the navigable waters of a state has never been adjudged to be within the legislative power.... Surely an act of the legislature transferring the title to its submerged lands ... would be repudiated, without hesitation, as a gross perversion of the trust over the property under which it is held.... *It would not be listened to that the control and management of the harbor of that great city – a subject of concern to the whole people of the state – should thus be placed elsewhere than in the state itself....* The legislature could not give away nor sell the discretion of its successors.... The legislation which may be needed one day for the harbor may be different from the legislation that may be required at another day.[18]

This and other landmark decisions hold that ownership of crucial resources must remain in the reserved sovereignty of the people and off limits to legislative alienation in order to protect future generations. A contrary result, Justice Field admonished, "would place every harbor in the country at the mercy of a majority of the legislature of the state in which the harbor is situated." A distrust of the legislative branch animates these cases, for the courts recognize that each legislative body consists of individuals, seated for finite terms, who may be tempted to purloin public property through legislative acts to serve their political allies. The trust not only sets limits on the legislative power to privatize or damage natural resources, but also enables courts to enforce that limitation through something akin to a judicial veto that invalidates the conveyance. In this manner, the public trust relies on courts to prevent any one set of legislators from wielding so much power as to cripple future legislatures in meeting the ecological needs of society.

Characterizing the trust as an attribute of sovereignty bores down to legal bedrock. Accordingly, it needs no specific mention in the Constitution to hold paramount legal force. As one court declared in the context of the police power (the other attribute of sovereignty): "Because the police power is *inherent in the sovereignty of each state*, that power is not dependent for its existence or inalienability upon the written constitution or the positive law." This too explains why the trust doctrine emerges in other countries despite differences in constitutional language. The Philippines Supreme Court in *Oposa* emphasized:

> [T]hese basic rights need not even be written in the Constitution for they are assumed to exist from the inception of humankind. If they are now explicitly mentioned ... it is because of the well-founded fear of its framers that unless [these rights] are mandated as state policies by the Constitution itself ... the day would not be too far when all else would be lost not only for the present generation, but also for those to come – *generations which stand to inherit nothing but parched earth incapable of sustaining life*.[19]

Several nations, as well as some states in the United States, have taken the step of expressly announcing the public trust in their constitutions or statutes. Such explicit reference does not suggest previous doctrinal truancy, but rather reflects a legislative urge to codify the principle. In Hawaii, for example, the public trust doctrine received its first judicial pronouncement in a 1973 decision by the Hawaiian Supreme Court. Five years later, in 1978, the state added an express public trust provision to its constitution, which declared: "All public natural resources are held in trust by the State for the benefit of the people." In its landmark *Waiāhole Ditch* decision, the Hawaiian Supreme Court made clear that the public trust doctrine exists independently of such legislative expression, because it represents "an inherent attribute of sovereign authority that the government 'ought not, and ergo ... cannot surrender.'"[20]

Some academics, however, take issue with what they view as an expansive historical interpretation of the trust. Professor Jim Huffman charges that courts and scholars have created a "mythological history of the doctrine." Such academic musings could continue endlessly, but society can no longer afford them. The trust remains a well-recognized and fundamental government duty that carries urgent importance in modern times. Citizens face environmental devastation as a result of the very malfeasance and recalcitrance on the part of government that the trust emerged to prevent. Professor Grant's analysis, arguably the most rigorous constitutional inquiry to date, offers a resolute constitutional framework within which to position the American trust, by characterizing the principle as a limit on government implicit in the reserved powers doctrine. The origins of the trust suggest a principle organic to government itself; the trust presents a cogent duality with the constitutional reserved power doctrine; numerous courts describe the trust as an "attribute of sovereignty;" and the logic of the public trust harmonizes with the political tradition of democracy. Given all this, the doctrine holds legitimacy in carrying the consummate constitutional force necessary to curb legislative and executive abuse of fiduciary obligation. As a group of leading environmental scholars declared in an *amicus* brief submitted in atmospheric trust litigation (seeking government control of carbon pollution), the public trust stands as "a fundamental attribute of sovereignty embedded in the Constitution itself, applicable to both the federal and state governments."[21]

THE CO-TRUSTEES OF FEDERALISM

Throughout the first two centuries of U.S. history, the public trust primarily focused on the states. Few cases involved the federal government, and for an understandable reason: until the 1970s, the federal role in natural resources remained minimal in comparison to that of the states. Only in the 1970s, when Congress could no longer ignore the colossal failure of states to conserve their natural resources, did Congress intervene to pass environmental statutes. As Part I of the book explained, the new statutes conferred an astounding amount of federal power over the nation's natural resources. Remarkably, some courts and scholars conclude that this power remains unfettered by any trust obligation to the people. From the historical domination of states in public trust cases, they mistakenly assume that the trust applies only to the states. For example, in a 2012 Supreme Court case, *PPL Montana v. Montana*, the Court casually referred to the trust as a "state law" doctrine. Because the case itself did not pose the question of whether a federal trust principle exists, the opinion lacked any analysis of the matter. But however unmindful the reference, the description of the trust as a state law doctrine, even as dictum, poses the risk that lower courts will simply parrot its language.[22]

Repudiating the existence of a federal public trust obligation would leave the federal government with a frightening degree of control over the people's environmental assets with no corresponding check of fiduciary obligation. Such open-ended power that leaves the citizens impotent would demolish basic assumptions of democracy – and gape as an anomaly in the United States' legal system. Congress itself has explicitly recognized a federal trust duty in the National Environmental Policy Act (NEPA), which declares a national duty to "fulfill the responsibilities of each generation as trustee of the environment for succeeding generations."[23]

In retrospect, the analytical misstep seemingly occurred when scholars began to associate the trust exclusively with state ownership of streambeds along navigable waterways. Because the streambeds prove vital to sovereignty, courts throughout history have found their ownership vested in the states, which act as primary sovereigns. Moreover, courts uniformly held that such sovereign ownership took the form of a trust, limiting the ability of states to grant streambeds away to private parties. Scholars assumed that because the trust applied to states, it amounted to a state law doctrine. But the next step – that there is no federal trust – does not logically follow. The settled applicability of the trust to states in no way forecloses its application to the federal government, for nothing suggests that the trust must be exclusive to one sovereign. In fact, the case law shows otherwise. The Supreme Court has continually emphasized federal interests in streambeds and submerged lands, describing a supreme federal "navigational servitude" to protect the public's need of unimpeded navigation on waterways. Although not explicitly labeled a public trust interest, the servitude operates in the same way, defeating private property interests that interfere with public needs. Properly understood, these streambed cases extend as a branch of a much larger jurisprudential tree that sends its roots into the composition of sovereignty itself. A growing number of modern scholars now point out that the trust, aptly recognized as an attribute of sovereignty, must necessarily apply to *both* the federal and state sovereigns. As Mary Turnipseed and several coauthors explain:

> [A] dual trusteeship of U.S. public trust resources follows this co-sovereign system; and, it is in this context that a federal public trust doctrine is best located. If state public trust duties accompany the sovereign authority of state governments to govern, then it follows that a federal public trust burden also conveys with the sovereign authority of the federal government to govern.[24]

While binding both federal and state governments, the trust nevertheless operates differently for each, because it must reflect the constitutional constraints that encumber each sovereign. The trust functions within the distinctive federal and state spheres defined by the Constitution. The most considered explanation of this relationship comes from a federal case, *U.S. v. 1.58 Acres of Land*, involving conflicting sovereign interests in the shoreline of Massachusetts. Affirming both federal and state trust interests in the property and shaping each to the constitutional framework, the federal district court characterized the state legislature as a "co-trustee" with Congress and declared, "Since the trust impressed upon this property is governmental and administered jointly by the state and federal governments by virtue of their sovereignty, neither sovereign may alienate this land free and clear of the public trust.... [N]either government has the power to destroy the trust or to destroy the other sovereign." As the court explained, each sovereign administers the trust to carry out its constitutional role: "This formulation recognizes the division of sovereignty between the state and federal governments." Congress must administer the trust "in its capacity as trustee of the jus publicum" to protect national public interests (pursuant to federal power delegated by the Constitution), while the states must administer the trust "in their capacity as co-trustee of the jus publicum" so as to protect public interests that relate to uniquely state prerogatives.[25]

A foundational line of cases shows that the Supreme Court has always presupposed the existence of a federal trust in management of public lands. The Court in *Light v. United States* declared, for example: "All the public lands of the nation are held in trust for the people of the whole country." While it also said, "it is not for the courts to say how that trust shall be administered. That is for Congress to determine," such deference concerns the right of Congress to judge between competing public uses and does not at all sanction private use that destroys public assets – something occurring with regularity today. The Supreme Court has consistently required that government manage the people's lands for *public* purposes, stating, in *U. S. v. Trinidad Coal*, for example, "In the matter of disposing of the vacant coal lands of the United States, the government should not be regarded as occupying the attitude of a mere seller of real estate for its market value.... They were held in trust for all the people."[26]

Supreme Court case law regarding the coastline further recognizes federal trust obligations. In *Alabama v. Texas*, Justice Reed wrote: "The United States holds resources and territory in trust for its citizens in one sense, but not in the sense that a private trustee holds a *cestui que trust*. The responsibility of Congress is to utilize the assets that come into its hands as sovereign in the way that it decides is best for the future of the Nation." And Justice Douglas explained:

> [W]e are dealing here with incidents of national sovereignty. The marginal sea is not an oil well; it is more than a mass of water; it is a protective belt for the entire Nation over which the United States must exercise exclusive and paramount authority. *The authority over it can no more be abdicated than any of the other great powers of the Federal Government. It is to be exercised for the benefit of the whole....* Could Congress cede the great Columbia River or the mighty Mississippi to a State or a power company? I should think not. For they are arteries of commerce that attach to the national sovereignty and remain there until and unless the Constitution is changed. What is true of a great river would seem to be even more obviously true of the marginal sea.[27]

Several clear doctrinal landmarks emerge from this jurisprudence, as summarized by the federal district court in *1.58 Acres of Land*. First, both the federal government and states hold trust interests in property within their jurisdictions as necessary to promote public welfare. Second, both federal and state trust obligations arise as attributes of sovereignty; each government manages public trust assets to carry out its constitutional function. Third, their respective government interests synchronize by characterizing the federal and state governments as "co-trustee[s]." The presence of multiple co-trustees mirrors standard trust law, imposing on each trustee the responsibility for carrying out trust purposes. However, in the case of the American trust, the federal power clearly ranks supreme where it conflicts directly with state interests; this primacy emanates from the Constitution's Supremacy Clause.[28]

Under the Constitution, states hold general sovereign power on behalf of the people. They also carry out traditional trustee functions over natural resources within their borders. But the federal trust interest remains omnipresent, albeit dormant at times. Intuitively, four different (but common) situations activate the federal trust: (1) where circumstances involve trans-boundary interstate assets (such as an interstate rivers, lakes, underground aquifers, migratory wildlife, the air, and atmosphere); (2) where state trustees utterly fail to discharge their fiduciary duties to protect assets within their jurisdiction; (3) where national exigencies demand federal involvement, such as those involving national security, commerce among states, broad ecological or public health threats, or natural disasters; and (4) where disputes arise over resources shared with other nations or tribal sovereigns (such as oceans, fisheries, atmosphere, and the like). The worsening climate crisis, notably, represents all four circumstances converging at once into a national and planetary emergency that calls forth the federal public trust obligation in no uncertain terms.

TRIBES AS TRUSTEES (AGAIN)

The paradigm of trust obligation, at least in the United States, also positions the tribes in the sovereign fiduciary framework. As the original governments across the land, tribes possess inherent sovereignty pre-existing the federal government or any state. In a Nature's Trust approach, these native nations take their rightful place as co-trustees of shared ecological assets along with the states and the federal government. In many cases, tribal ancestral memory traces back thousands of years in managing a local landscape according to indigenous "natural law," as the term is still used in Indian Country. The Navajo Nation (the Diné), for one, explains "natural law" to include "the duty and responsibility of the Diné to protect and preserve the beauty of the natural world for future generations." These governments with the most uninterrupted and intimate knowledge of local ecosystems and landscapes may prove crucial to restoring ecological wealth.[29]

The art of managing resources for natural abundance stands out as a recognized hallmark of traditional native sovereignty. While it stands true that some tribes today conduct resource management in a manner indistinguishable from industrial corporations, there still remains, in many other tribes, a vibrant and strong traditional lineage of place-based, sustainable ecological governance – indeed so enduring and compelling that society ignores it at its peril. The Seventh Generation principle, observed by appointing a tribal statesman to represent future generations at council meetings, epitomizes the Native obligation to safeguard the interests of beneficiaries in distant generations. It finds reflection today in several modern tribal codes and policy statements. This sovereign mandate essentially centers on a trust concept that, broadly speaking, shows a close parallel to the ancient public trust principle.[30]

A tribal trusteeship springs from the pre-colonial native sovereign control over natural resources and endures along with the continuing sovereign stature of tribes. If positioned as modern co-trustees with the states and federal government, tribes can bring to bear their ecological expertise and indigenous world-view to restore ecology located beyond reservation boundaries.[31] The retained sovereign property rights of tribes provide at least five footholds for doing so. First, reserved treaty rights to off-reservation resources (fisheries, wildlife, and waters) position tribes as co-tenants of such resources. They remain co-owners, in effect, along with the states. As co-tenant trustees, tribes have legal standing to enjoin states from diminishing the shared assets. The federal district court of Washington, for example, held that the Stevens treaties of the Pacific Northwest carry an implied right of environmental protection that tribes can assert to protect fish habitat off the reservation. Second, the tribal trustees remain the recognized beneficiaries of a federal Indian trust obligation. Arising as a sovereign covenant from the vast cessions of Indian territory, this federal trust duty (distinct from the federal public trust duty) promises protection of Indian lands and resources on and off the reservation. Courts emphasize that this trust imposes the "most exacting fiduciary standards" on the federal government when dealing with Indian property. The Indian trust obligation legally infuses all federal agencies with a duty of protection that stands independent from statutory environmental requirements. Third, as recognized sovereigns, the tribes have the ability to form land trusts and hold conservation easements across private lands in ceded territory. A tribal conservation trust movement using private property tools shows promising momentum. Fourth, the sovereign status of tribes positions them to engage in governmental partnerships with state or federal agencies aimed towards co-management and restoration across their ceded territories. Already through such arrangements, tribes have called back wolves to the Idaho wilderness, returned salmon to the Umatilla Basin, and re-established cui-ui fish in Nevada's Pyramid Lake, among other remarkable feats. And finally, tribal sovereigns can create programs under federal environmental statutes and enact strict pollution standards that, in some cases, may restrict upstream dischargers outside the reservation.[32]

For many tribes, the urgency of ecosystem degradation now hastens the task of reclaiming environmental sovereignty. On a land base that still writhes under the exploitative impulses of the majority society, modern corporations (like the colonialists who preceded them) devour natural resources in Indian Country with hardly a check from environmental law. If the present statutory framework of environmental law continues to monopolize decision making, tribes will find themselves increasingly marginalized, asserting claims appearing ever more antiquated against the spreading malignancies of industrial capitalism. Yet to forge a meaningful role in environmental policy, tribes must ride the jagged boundaries between native vision and a colonial industrialized worldview. A Nature's Trust framework positions tribes to resurrect their historic trusteeship (along with the ancestral ecological values and traditional knowledge that imbue it) using modern legal venues. And however ironic it may seem, a tribal partnership in restoring ecology now stands every bit as momentous for the rest of America as it does for Native America. As the renowned Indian law scholar Rennard Strickland writes, "History suggests that if mankind is to survive, the next five hundred years must be rooted in the pre-Columbian ethic of the Native American.... The continuation of the past, the conqueror's exploitation of the earth, can mean only one thing. No one, Indian or non-Indian, will survive."[33]

THE TRIPARTITE STRUCTURE OF PUBLIC TRUST

To summarize, the previous discussion situates the federal government, states, and tribes as the three sovereign co-trustees in the Nature's Trust paradigm and suggests how this framework could operate within the U.S. (and presumably in other countries with indigenous nations as well). A remaining matter concerns the balance of power between the three branches of government on both the state and federal levels. As Chapter 5 explained, America's tripartite system now totters under an over-bearing federal executive branch that wields almost unchecked power in environmental law. While agencies use their statutory authority to permit colossal environmental destruction, Congress and state legislatures loiter passively on the sidelines, and the judicial branch deferentially approves agency decisions that flaunt statutory goals to serve special interests. Nature's Trust invigorates all three branches of government, holding each to a constitutional fiduciary duty to protect the people's natural endowment. In so doing, the trust braces the Founder's system of checks and balances, which remains essential to prevent despotic control by any one branch. While Chapters 8 and 9 describe in more detail the fiduciary duties of each branch, this section briefly sketches their respective roles within the Nature's Trust framework.

A long line of cases make clear that legislatures lead as trustees of the public's natural assets, pursuant to their constitutionally-appointed function of making the law. Properly recognized as trustees, federal and state legislatures remain bound by traditional fiduciary duties. The trust expectation exposes four glaring breaches of legislative fiduciary duty – ones utterly condoned by today's politics. First, by extending agencies nearly carte-blanche authority to permit damage to the environment, Congress has abandoned its core trust duty to ensure the productivity and health of the trust. While a trustee may delegate administration of the trust to an agent, it may not surrender essential trustee functions. But as Chapter 5 explained, Congress no longer maintains effective oversight of environmental agencies. Second, a trustee must take action where trust assets stand imperiled. The Wisconsin Supreme Court stated: "The trust reposed in the state is not a passive trust; it is active.... [T]he trust ... requires the lawmaking body to act in all cases where action is necessary, not only to preserve the trust, but to promote it." Trust duties demand that Congress and state legislatures actively address the pending catastrophic climate "tipping point" as well as other immediate environmental disasters. Third, a trustee must exercise prudence in managing the trust, defined by courts as reasonable care, skill, and caution. As Chapter 5 explained, Congress no longer engages in careful deliberation over environmental policy. Instead, legislative action often takes the form of destructive appropriation riders that slide through with negligible debate, reflection, or substantiation. Fourth, and perhaps most importantly, a trustee bears a strict duty of loyalty in administering trust assets. In the case of a public trust, loyalty must flow exclusively to the general public – the present and future beneficiaries of the trust – and not to singular moneyed interests. The opposite approach prevails in Congress today as lawmakers trade legislative outcomes (however concealed or indirect) for campaign contributions by corporations and the wealthy. The duty of loyalty would scatter a good many lobbyists feasting in the dark on under-the-table political deals made in Congress and the state legislatures. These ongoing legislative breaches of trust are examined in greater depth in Chapters 8 and 9. Chapter 11 analyzes how the courts might enforce these fiduciary duties without invading the prerogatives of the legislative branch.[34]

Turning to the executive branch, the environmental agencies (on both the federal and state levels) perform as agents of the trustee, specifically empowered (by Congress and the state legislatures respectively) to manage and administer the public trust. Recognizing that these agencies stand uniquely as trustee-agents towards public property, Nature's Trust assigns special obligations to them within the broader realm of administrative law. Specifically, their conduct must meet strict fiduciary standards of asset protection, restoration, and the duties of loyalty and prudence, among others. In other words, agency management of the public's irreplaceable trust assets must answer to a gold standard of fiduciary care.

Finally, the judicial branch remains the ultimate guardian of the public trust, having had two centuries of experience in crafting the contours of this sovereign obligation. Of course, debate swirls around the appropriate role of the judiciary in the U.S. constitutional system. Those perceiving an activist judiciary will criticize any court intervention to protect vital natural resources. A primary judicial function, however, has always been to ensure that legislative enactments comport with constitutional expectations. Recognized as a constitutional doctrine, the public trust empowers courts to invalidate executive and legislative acts that violate the public's property rights in natural resources. As one federal court declared: "The very purpose of the public trust doctrine is to police the legislature's disposition of public lands." Another stated: "The check and balance of judicial review provides a level of protection against improvident dissipation of an irreplaceable res." Professor Joseph Sax explains that active judicial enforcement of the public trust remains essential to protect society's stability. In face of modern environmental damage so destabilizing as to provoke social, biological and economic crisis, the judicial role becomes ever more paramount.[35]

AN ENCOMPASSING APPROACH

This chapter presented the public trust as a natural right sanctified through the social compact – a basic human right to lasting ecological resources for survival and well-being. Holding government accountable to inalienable fiduciary duties towards the people, the trust reflects the most ancient understandings of popular sovereignty and remains capable of assertion against any government purporting to gain its power directly from its citizens. While the trust travels the spectrum from overt to subtle recognition in legal systems world-wide, it forms a core expectation of democracy everywhere. As such, it galvanizes political interest among citizens even as it sets in place a straightforward legal framework for government decision making.

At a time when agencies across the planet use statutory environmental law to eradicate Earth's remaining resources, a shift back to the trust concept carries unprecedented urgency – particularly to curb the atmospheric pollution that can ignite runaway climate heating. In contrast to the highly technical, incremental, and discretionary framework of modern statutory law, the trust explains the duties of government – and appraises the performance of its officers – through a prism of long-standing, inherent, and deeply understood public property rights. Nature's Trust neither hinges on, nor plays hostage to, environmental statutes and regulations. Instead, it grows from a legally enduring principle having roots in judicially formulated doctrine preceding the modern system of statutory law. A broad return to trust precepts represents a natural progression in the cycle of legal thought rotating through successive eras of civilization.

As an organic dimension of sovereignty, the trust obligation arguably infuses governments worldwide with fiduciary duty. This universal trust concept assumes paramount importance today, because all conventional international treaty processes have proved ineffectual in addressing planetary ecological crises. The trust alone seemingly offers a penultimate obligation with an encompassing global reach. Chapter 10, for example, suggests how a global climate trust concept can find enforcement through atmospheric trust litigation to prevent states, cities, and national governments across the planet from leaving orphan shares of deadly pollution on the doorsteps of Earth.

But even in its highest aspirations, Nature's Trust cannot supplant present-day environmental law. Rather, it provides a fiduciary frame that gives meaning to environmental law and invigorates it – unseating corruptible political discretion and installing in its place firm property-based obligations to manage natural resources for the long-term security of citizens. The procedural edifice of statutory law gives structure and order to the trust obligation as carried out though modern governmental agencies and institutions. Later chapters explore how to meaningfully apply the trust within this statutory framework.

Some prefatory comments and caveats give context to ensuing chapters. First, the public trust does not offer a panacea. Government, if anything, remains a work in progress requiring constant adjustment. There will always be tendencies on the part of those in power to serve special narrow interests rather than the public interest. Inoculating governmental decision makers against selfish urges innate to human nature largely defines the democratic struggle itself. Nature's Trust offers a paradigm that refocuses citizen attention on the problem, but only constant citizen vigilance will keep government corruption at bay. Second, the implementation of Nature's Trust principles will require substantial work – in some cases, revisions of legal doctrines or regulations, and judicial enforcement. This book cannot hope to delve into every angle of that undertaking. It provides a framework of fiduciary obligation, but lawyers, judges, agency officials, legislators, and citizens will furnish the principles specific and appropriate to their various legal institutions and environmental contexts. Third, the corporate moneyed interests that have long benefited from the status quo will undoubtedly try to dismiss Nature's Trust as not representing "the law" by pointing out that government does not currently adhere to trust principles. It is true that government has systematically violated its trust obligation, and for a very long time. The simple response is this: no law should be defined by its violation.

The most daunting road block to a Nature's Trust paradigm may well arise from those who would naturally be its most ardent advocates but who find themselves so demoralized by the overwhelming corporate influence on government that they find any transformative approach unimaginable. However, history teaches a hopeful lessen. Through the ages, nations have evolved and re-birthed their legal norms, often dramatically. In the United States, some of the most monumental societal shifts have emerged in the context of property law, the source of the public trust doctrine. A mere two centuries ago, American property law recognized and protected a right to hold human beings as slaves. Today, it is inconceivable to think of the law sanctioning such an egregious violation of basic human rights. As society progresses in its understanding of Nature and the relationship of ecology to the human right of survival, the public will become ever less tolerant of government's environmental oppression. The unstoppable assertion of public liberty may again find its most powerful venue in property law.

Today's citizens sit snared in a deadly ecological trap set by a government-industry alliance acting through statutory environmental law. Government's ongoing failure to heed its sovereign trust obligation now manifests epochal – in Earth's melting ice masses, dying oceans, species extinctions, devastated crops, parching droughts, super-storms, and killer heat waves. Citizens coalescing in sheer democratic impulse against these atrocities stand ready to assert their natural rights to the constitutional commonwealth as beneficiaries of the ancient public trust. As Peter Brown observes, the trust theory arises not so much as a new idea but rather as "the rediscovery of an old one that has been lost to our political consciousness."[36] Just as in the past, the trust now rises as a universal call for people agitated by the exhaustion and collapse of resources sanctioned by those in power. In the most basic sense, Nature's Trust aims towards the emancipation of Humanity from the environmental tyranny tightening around communities throughout the world.

7

The Ecological *Res*

In times of extreme drought, will a parched community be able to assert public rights to a scarce water supply? Or instead, will a profiteering corporation monopolize the water and charge citizens exorbitant rates to sustain their very survival? Will the law treat water as a commodity or a protected life source? These questions loom as corporations make swift maneuvers across the globe to privatize water. Maude Barlow observes in her book, *Blue Covenant*: "[T]he world is moving toward a corporate-controlled freshwater cartel, with private companies, backed by governments and global institutions, making fundamental decisions about who has access to water and under what conditions."[1] The public's right to waters hinges on the matter taken up in this chapter: the scope of resources protected under of the public trust. Identifying trust assets begins the process of casting a net of fiduciary obligation over government trustees and setting boundaries on private exploits of crucial resources.

The trust *res* consists of assets held in the trust, designed to serve the trust's purpose and requiring protection so as to meet that purpose when the time comes. Private trusts hold financial assets like stocks and bonds. The *res* of Nature's Trust consists of ecological assets, natural wealth that must sustain all foreseeable future generations of humanity. It amounts to humanity's survival account – the only one it has. Government trustees must protect trust resources for the benefit of present and future generations, allowing their privatization only in limited circumstances. Cleaving any category of natural resource from the trust endowment leaves it open to destruction for profit, with seemingly no end. As the Supreme Court of India remarked in recognizing a public trust in natural gas reserves: "Historically, and all across the globe, predatory forms of capitalism seem to organize themselves, first and foremost, around the extractive industries that seek to exploit the vast, but exhaustible, natural resources. Water, forests, minerals and oil – they are all being privatized; and not yet satisfied, the voices that speak for predatory capitalism seek more."[2]

As first elaborated by the old cases, the antebellum scope of the *res* extends to submerged lands and overlying waters along navigable waterways. Additional natural resources have found their way into the ambit of the *res* through various court decisions, but in slow and incremental fashion.³ In defining the *res*, this chapter departs from the piecemeal approach that characterizes most public trust jurisprudence and scholarship. It presents instead a holistic conception of the *res* encompassing all natural assets and ecology – a Nature's Trust. In so doing, it brings the public trust doctrine into alignment with Nature's own laws and resurrects the original doctrine with the range necessary to carry out its purposes not only for this generation, but also for those to come. While this chapter identifies the assets in the people's trust, it leaves for Chapter 8 the matter of defining sovereign responsibilities toward those assets.

THE ESSENTIAL TRUST PURPOSE

The trust works a decidedly utilitarian task. Courts look squarely to the needs of the public in defining the scope of the trust endowment. The essential framework for defining trust assets organizes around a test of "public concern" as set forth in *Illinois Central* (discussed in Chapter 6). The 1892 case involved the legislative convey-ance of Chicago's waterfront to a private railroad company. At the time of the case, lakebeds served a vital role for fishing, navigation, and commerce, three primary occupations of a burgeoning society. Because of these public needs, the Court held that the legislature had no power to put the lakebed into private hands – it was an inalienable part of the people's sovereign trust, "freed from the obstruction or interference of private parties." Explaining that the trust arises "necessarily from the public character of the property," the Court declared: "The ownership of the navigable waters of the harbor and of the lands under them is a *subject of public concern to the whole people of the state.*" This historic passage reverberates through all of public trust law. Where a natural resource is a "subject of public concern to the whole people," it warrants protection as an asset in the people's trust. Professor Charles Wilkinson explains: "The public trust doctrine is rooted in the precept that some resources are so central to the well-being of the community that they must be protected by distinctive, judge-made principles."⁴

Courts must constantly refresh their understanding of "public concern" in order to determine the appropriate scope of the trust. To not do so would render the doc-trine irrelevant to the imperatives of society, leaving courts hostile to the very citi-zens who vest government with sovereign authority to define "property." As Thomas Jefferson once remarked:

> [L]aws and institutions must go hand in hand with the progress of the human mind. As that becomes more developed, more enlightened, as new discoveries are made, new truths discovered and manners and opinions change, with the change of circumstances, institutions must advance also to keep pace with the

times. We might as well require a man to wear still the coat which fitted him when a boy, as civilized society to remain ever under the regimen of their barbarous ancestors.[5]

In the face of looming environmental calamities to which the political branches have not responded, the judiciary's ability to modernize the public trust could prove crucial to the welfare of future generations. Public trust jurisprudence already shows inherent capacity and inclination to expand to meet modern concerns. As the New Jersey Supreme Court observed: "[W]e perceive the public trust doctrine not to be 'fixed or static,' but one to 'be molded and extended to meet changing conditions and needs of the public it was created to benefit.'"[6]

The doctrine's ability to adjust to change derives from its common law character. Common law simply amounts to judge-made law. Most often, common law surrenders to statutory law where the two conflict, but not in the case of the public trust doctrine, which (as Chapter 6 explained) deals with inalienable restraints on the legislature. Reflecting the constitutional character of an attribute of sovereignty, judicial iterations of the public trust amount to rare constitutive common law. As Chapter 11 further elaborates, the public trust jurisprudence harbors a judicial "veto" when the legislature has transgressed its fiduciary obligations.[7]

The common law characteristically shows fidelity to deep jurisprudential principles while maintaining its capacity to adapt to new circumstances. It does so by tapping a wellspring of justice, logic, equity, and reasonableness – currents of thought that keep the basic doctrines from dissolving as they encounter radical change in society. As the Oregon Supreme Court stated long ago:

> The very essence of the common law is flexibility and adaptability.... If the common law should become ... crystallized ... it would cease to be the common law of history, and would be an inelastic and arbitrary [c]ode.... [O]ne of the established principles of the common law ... [is] that precedents must yield to the reason of different or modified conditions.[8]

Cut from this cloth of common law, the public trust steadfastly remains the law of change. Responding to advances in scientific understanding and society's emerging requirements, many courts have readily expanded their conception of the trust *res*. As the Supreme Court of Hawaii emphasized, "the 'purposes' or 'uses' of the public trust have evolved with changing public values and needs." Whereas the original cases highlighted the overriding public needs of fishing, navigation, and commerce (still known as the "traditional" interests protected by the doctrine), various courts now recognize modern imperatives such as biodiversity, wildlife habitat, aesthetics, and recreation. These cases continue to underscore essential sovereign functions. In finding, for example, that recreation amounts to a public trust interest, the Supreme Court of New Jersey reasoned that "'[h]ealth, recreation and sports are encompassed in and intimately related to the general welfare of a well-balanced state.'" Protecting a slate of modern concerns, the doctrine reaches, in many states, well beyond its traditional scope to assets such as groundwater, wetlands, dry sand beaches, parks, and non-navigable waterways. In these cases, the trust *res* and the societal interests it serves remain inextricably connected, as the conjoined twins of public trust law. When one takes a step forward, so does the other.[9]

THE TRADITIONAL SCOPE

While many courts prudently modernize the public trust, some courts remain loathe to extend the trust *res* beyond its historic footprint. These courts have kept their analytical legs so planted in the submerged lands that they refuse to recognize *any* modern public interests; their antiquated approach has the twins of public trust law still fishing for their sustenance from submerged lands.[10] This kind of time warp slows the law's response to the crises pounding at humanity's door in a new age that demands aggressive ecological recovery. When the public trust detaches from modern needs, it unmoors from its original purpose of protecting society.

Simply because most trust cases from the past involved submerged lands, some scholars and judges assume the doctrine's reach remains limited to those areas. However, if one dives to the conceptual depths of the public trust doctrine, one finds the central purposes of the trust not at all streambed-dependent. Fundamentally, the trust protects both the natural infrastructure essential to societal welfare and the public's right to use such ecological wealth. In both cases, it guards against monopolistic exploitation and possession of resources. The Supreme Court's attention to submerged lands in *Illinois Central* reflected society's core interests *at that time* – fishing, navigation, and commerce. But the governing rationale of *Illinois Central* was not limited to streambeds – rather, it tied discernibly to crucial societal interests. The Court made clear that traditional public trust resources, such as navigable waters and soils under them, exist as part of a broader category of property imbued with the public trust. Justice Field declared: "So with trusts connected with public property, *or property of a special character*, like lands under navigable waters, they cannot be placed entirely beyond the direction and control of the State." If streambeds amounted to the sole resource on the face of the Earth needed by human beings, then, indeed, the doctrine would justifiably find its limits at water's edge. But the reality is far more daunting: humans need all of ecology. Fishing, navigation, and commerce insufficiently define the exigencies of modern society. Pressing needs today include groundwater protection, biodiversity, climate stability, healthy forests, productive soils, and flood control – among many other concerns unfathomable to nineteenth-century judges.[11]

The timidity of some courts to step even gingerly over the high water mark may be best explained by a practical observation. Courts and scholars limit the scope of the trust *res* out of a reluctance to tread heavily on private property interests. As the geographic scope of the trust expands, more dilemmas inevitably arise, particularly those lingering at the interface of public interests and private property use. Should the trust encompass the full ecology of Nature, government officials must act in a fiduciary capacity with respect to all decisions having environmental consequences, and private property owners must comport with trust standards as well. Because the *res* forms the analytical point of entry for the entire doctrine, commentators pushing an expansive private property rights agenda urge an exceedingly narrow scope of trust assets.[12]

But protecting a full ecological *res* does not bar all forms of privatization. It does mean that natural resources cannot be privatized to an extent that allows singular interests to destroy the public's natural commonwealth. As Professor Gerald Torres observes, private interests may use the wealth of the nation, but their use finds limits in the "material requirements of the culture to reproduce itself into the future." The public trust, as Professor Michael Blumm has emphasized, fundamentally represents an accommodation between public and private property rights. It invokes long-standing tools of property law to maintain the people's reserved sovereign interest in natural assets crucial to society, wherever located.[13]

Those who portray the doctrine as characteristically water-based seem to seek assurances that it will not reach over the fence to protect resources on upland private property. These thinkers approach the legal terrain much as a surveyor would, with an eye toward containing the doctrine within clear physical boundaries so that it will not encroach into people's private lots. Unfortunately, surveyor lines cannot fully define the relationship between the public trust and private property rights. As conservation biologist Reed Noss observes, "If we are really interested in maintaining ecological processes and the services they provide to human society, then conservation must be extended to entire landscapes or regional ecosystems.... Ecosystems do not respect property and jurisdictional lines."[14] Much of the trust doctrine concerns the proper *accommodation* between private property owners' use of land and society's remaining interest in such land. To ignore this aspect deprives the doctrine of its greatest strength and most pressing challenge.

Hefty precedent already recognizes non-water-based trust interests. The 1896 Supreme Court case, *Geer v. Connecticut*, established a public trust over wildlife, or *ferae naturae*, wherever located.[15] The traditional analysis, by placing its anchor in streambeds, offers no explanation for this already fully recognized trust over wildlife. When the trust applies to *ferae naturae*, its protection swims, flies, leaps, and slithers without hesitation across private boundaries. Chapter 14 takes up the matter of identifying the appropriate uses of private property consistent with the public trust.

JUDICIAL CROSSROADS

Public trust jurisprudence in the United States has progressed in an ad hoc fashion, each state developing its own set of rules to define which assets fall within the trust *res*. In 1988, the Supreme Court in *Phillips Petroleum* seemingly extended an open bid for states to do just that when it declared: "[I]t has been long established that the individual States have the authority to define the limits of the lands held in public trust and to recognize private rights in such lands as they see fit."[16] The ruling endorsed a disarray of approaches, resulting in a different form of the doctrine in each of the fifty states. Rather than addressing society's urgent interest in restoring ecological stability, most courts step forward hesitatingly, pulling one resource at a time into the *res*.

The tentativeness of courts to venture into new terrain and waters becomes evident in decisions concerning groundwater, a resource of unquestionable importance to society. While the Supreme Court of Hawaii has unequivocally recognized groundwater as a trust asset, some other courts exclude it from the trust out of apparent apathy to public need, and the remaining states have not addressed the matter. Against this sketchy legal backdrop, bottled water companies suck springs dry across the United States, and industries contaminate aquifers with shocking amounts of toxic chemicals, causing untold death and illness to citizens. In the same way, air and atmosphere receive staggering amounts of pollution simply because judicial treatment remains scant.[17]

In this vacuous judicial theater, the natural resources auditioning for the trust appear on stage in painfully slow order. And yet a full cast waits behind the curtains, brilliantly choreographed according to Nature's laws. The problem here is one of timing. The traditional approach of defining the trust *res* state by state, asset by asset, may not save the playhouse before it burns down. Even if all natural assets that remain unquestionably crucial to society ultimately receive protection in the courts, the lapse of protection in the meanwhile hazards irrevocable loss. Industries will exploit judicial silence to their advantage.

The judiciary thus finds itself at a crossroads. Despite 200 years of experience with the trust doctrine, many courts still cling to a superficial analysis that turns on categorical designation of resources as within or outside of the trust. Judges now face a monumentally new task – devising legal rules that address the collapse of ecology. Just as nineteenth-century courts were pressed to remodel ancient trust principles inherited from English common law to fit the new American democracy, so must modern courts, confronted by climate exigencies, now coax and urge the essential trust principle through a transition of epic importance today. As the *Arnold v. Mundy* court famously declared in 1821 in percipient words that still ring true, the trust involves key questions "momentous in their nature, as well as in their magnitude."[18]

The reserved nineteenth-century judicial approach laboriously focused on individual assets in the *res* out of a limited understanding of ecology. It will inevitably mature into an all-encompassing approach to reflect the modern grasp of ecology – and the modern collapse of ecology. The "public concern" test emanating from *Illinois Central* should reconceive the value of natural resources in view of surging population pressure, pollution, and resource depletion. To do anything less leaves the trust, as Jefferson might have said, to wear a coat too small for today's swelling girth of environmental problems. Recognizing ecological functions of paramount concern, courts should make a judicial leap from submerged lands to a full *ecological res*. The step is but one in a progression from the public trust doctrine to a Nature's Trust framework.

THE ECOLOGICAL *RES*

Nature's Trust defines the *res* in a holistic fashion, embracing ecosystems and all of their component parts. Compelled, ironically, by both advances in scientific understanding as well as the gaping hole of remaining scientific uncertainty, Nature's Trust brings the law much closer to how ecology actually works. Rather than promote highly variable recognition of trust resources between jurisdictions, this approach accepts that environmental processes operate completely independent of doctrinal idiosyncrasies. Groundwater is groundwater, whether located in New Jersey or Idaho or Australia. Air is air, whether located in Pennsylvania, California, or Brazil. Both amount to trust assets because they perform crucial functions in support of human existence. This approach does not erase the sovereign's latitude conferred by the Supreme Court in *Phillips Petroleum*. It simply redirects state autonomy to a different focus: applying the fiduciary obligation. As fleshed out in Chapter 8, each sovereign faces unique circumstances in administering the trust. Every body politic will exhibit different public needs, perhaps diverging even more as societies become more localized in their efforts to brace against unprecedented environmental conditions. The particularized task of administering the trust, carried out within the firm sidewalls of fiduciary obligation, falls to each sovereign uniquely, requiring the latitude emphasized in *Phillips Petroleum*.

Scientific Understanding

Unlike the traditional approach, the Nature's Trust framework finds its definitional core in scientific understanding of ecology. The essential support for human life derives from complex interactions among a multitude of biological and physical features, not any one of which can be excised from the system without grave consequence. As the Ecological Society of America explains: "Ecosystems include physical and chemical components, such as soils, water, and nutrients that support the organisms living within them. These organisms may range from large animals and plants to microscopic bacteria. *Ecosystems include the interactions among all organisms in a given habitat.*"[19]

Nature's interconnected operations necessitate a holistic approach to land management. Many simple solutions that epitomized the past now lay widely criticized as inadequate. As conservation biologist Reed Noss notes in the context of species protection:

> Conservation is not as simple today as in the past. One hundred years ago it seemed that if we could just stop the plume hunters from shooting egrets to decorate ladies' hats, and if we could only save a few areas of spectacular scenery in national parks, we were doing well. Somewhat later it became apparent that we had to protect many kinds of habitats – wetlands, grasslands, deserts, forests of all kinds – to save wildlife.[20]

Unfortunately, most courts have not kept pace with advanced understanding of ecology. Even though the discipline of conservation biology now spans several decades and ecology courses appear at every level of education, the judiciary has not taken adequate strides to infuse this science into its doctrinal formulas. This inattentiveness to ecological reality, in part, explains a persistent judicial proclivity to atomize the trust *res* into various assets, excluding many from the ambit of trust protection despite their essential contribution to ecology. As legal scholar Robert Keiter observes: "[T]he current legal system – based as it is upon politically defined boundaries, private property rights, a consumptive ethic, and single-resource management – runs counter to basic precepts of biodiversity conservation."[21]

Some courts have pioneered an integrated, scientifically sound approach at the frontiers of public trust law. The Supreme Court of Hawaii declared in *Waiāhole Ditch* that the public trust *res* includes both groundwater and water – indeed, "all water resources without exception or distinction," reasoning, "Modern science and technology have discredited the surface-ground dichotomy." It emphasized that the trust demands "maintenance of ecological balance." Similarly, the Supreme Court of California said in *Marks v. Whitney* that the trust protects "lands in their natural state, so that they may serve as ecological units for scientific study, as open space, and as environments which provide food and habitat for birds and marine life."[22]

In a 1972 case, *Just v. Marionette County*, the Wisconsin Supreme Court accorded public trust protection to wetlands, emphasizing the "interrelationship of the wetlands, the swamps and the natural environment of shorelands to the purity of the water." Holding that the land must be preserved in its natural state, the court declared: "swamps and wetlands serve a vital role in nature, *are part of the balance of nature* and are essential to the purity of the water in our lakes and streams. Swamps and wetlands *are a necessary part of the ecological creation.*" And in a case arising in the Philippines, *Oposa v. Factoran*, the Supreme Court enjoined logging of ancient forest, recognizing its vital role in agricultural and soil productivity, wildlife habitat, water supply, and climate regulation. The court framed its decision around the citizens' constitutional right to a "balanced and healthful ecology," sustained by the "rhythm and harmony of nature." Taking a full ecological approach, the court made clear: "Nature means the created world in its entirety."[23]

These kernels of judicial reasoning show an emerging judicial understanding of the integral and synergistic role of all natural resources in ecosystem relationships. The key concept alluded to by all four courts centers on *ecological balance*, which requires the full functioning of all parts of the ecosystem in synchrony. The *res*, when properly conceived, contains the relevant ecosystem as a whole. A contrary approach (categorically excluding certain natural resources from the protective ambit of the trust) defies ecological reality, as pointed out long ago by Aldo Leopold when he wrote:

Conservation is a state of harmony between men and land. By land is meant all of the things on, over, or in the earth. Harmony with land is like harmony with a friend; you cannot cherish his right hand and chop off his left. That is to say, you cannot love game and hate predators; you cannot conserve the waters and waste the ranges; you cannot build the forest and mine the farm. The land is one organism. Its parts, like our own parts, compete with each other and co-operate with each other. The competitions are as much a part of the inner workings as the co-operations. You can regulate them – cautiously – but not abolish them.... For the biotic community to survive, its internal processes must balance.[24]

Ecosystem Services as a "Public Concern"

As noted at the outset, the interests served by the trust and the assets included in the trust *res* remain inextricably connected. Recognition of whole Nature as the trust *res* logically follows from the inclusion of "ecosystem services" within the realm of societal interests protected by the trust. As defined by scientists, such services amount to "the myriad life support functions [that] ecosystems provide and *without which human civilizations could not thrive.*" Examples of such services include climate regulation, provision of water, flood risk reduction, waste decomposition, food production, storm buffering, plant pollination, dispersion of seeds, water purification, flood water absorption, ground water recharge, erosion control, regulation of disease, medicinal production, aesthetic and recreational services, nutrient recycling, animal habitat, biodiversity maintenance, pest control, and a myriad of others. Full inventories of these ecological services appear in comprehensive reports, including the UN 2004 Millennium Ecosystem Assessment. Natural infrastructure provides these services to society often at much lower cost and a higher level of effectiveness than human-made infrastructure. One leading report places a global worth of $30 trillion per year for seventeen major ecosystem services. But these vital services hinge on *ecosystem function*, which results from the synergistic interactions of the plants, animals, and other organisms in the ecosystem. As Reed Noss explains, "Disruption of the characteristic processes of any ecosystem will likely lead to biotic impoverishment."[25]

Recognizing ecosystem service as a primary "public concern" pursuant to *Illinois Central* brings the full ecology of Nature within the protective ambit of the public trust *res*. Law scholars J. B. Ruhl and James Salzman point out that the emphasis on "natural capital" and the ecosystem services it provides fits well within the utilitarian approach of public trust law and the doctrine's "traditional sensibilities."[26] As noted, some courts (such as those in California, Hawaii, and Wisconsin) already recognize biodiversity and the "natural state" of ecology as interests served by the trust. This framework embraces the value of ecosystem services derived from assets *wherever they lie*. Climate balance, a keystone ecosystem service, depends on the atmosphere, which envelops the entire planet. Although considerable judicial distance lies between the streambeds (the doctrine's traditional focus) and the vast atmosphere, judges must make the leap of recognizing the atmosphere as a public trust asset to retain any meaning in the doctrine at all, since climate serves as the functional hinge for all life sources on Earth. Only by extending trust protection to the full ecological *res* will judges adhere to their own original precedent that coalesces around society's most basic needs.

Along with protecting those resources necessary to meet the *needs* of society, the trust must also provide a check on privatization of *hazard resources*, a term Professor John Davidson coined to describe resources that, when exploited with current technology, risk devastating ecological consequences. Oil accessed through deep-sea drilling, natural gas pulled through the "fracking" process, coal burned for energy, and uranium extracted for use in nuclear power plants are examples of resources in which society maintains a strong public interest in view of the hazards they pose to current and future generations. Rather than allow government to relinquish power over these resources through full privatization, Davidson argues that government must instead maintain its sovereign check over their use by treating these as trust resources. Invoking fable images, Davidson explains that the public trust not only protects the "nest in which the goose lays the golden egg," but in its hazard trust aspect, must also protect society from "the dragon that lies beneath the castle, capable of laying waste to the kingdom."[27]

The Police Power's Concomitant Reach

There should be nothing surprising about the public trust doctrine reaching to all facets of ecology. In fact, the police power, geared toward protecting public health and safety, touches on nearly every conceivable part of Nature. The ambit of the police power finds evidence in thousands of pages of environmental law that deal variously with forests, wetlands, beaches, soils, wildlife, air, minerals, and waters in all forms. These statutes show that the public has a demonstrable interest spanning the entire scope of ecology. They also indicate that almost every ecosystem proves to be "a subject of public concern to the whole people," the test put forth in *Illinois Central*. But recall that the statutes, while enacted to protect these resources, have been commandeered to permit massive, irrevocable destruction of Nature. The public trust's duty of protection provides a counterweight to that statutory power. The challenge remains for courts to forthrightly align the geographical scope of the public trust obligation with the scope of government's police power in natural resources law.[28]

One Texas court has already signaled this direction. In a key atmospheric trust litigation case, the Texas Commission on Environmental Quality had argued that the trust applied only to water. Judge Gisela Triana disagreed, holding that the public trust not only includes atmosphere but "all natural resources of the State." Just days later, Judge Sarah Singleton of the New Mexico district court allowed a similar atmospheric trust suit to go forward (denying the state's motion to dismiss it). Many statutory iterations of the public trust already reflect a holistic approach by bundling all natural resources into the trust *res*. For example, the federal Comprehensive Environmental Response, Compensation, and Liability Act (CERCLA) authorizes sovereign trustees to recover natural resource damages for injury to "land, fish, wildlife, biota, air, water, ground water, drinking water supplies, and other such resources." Similarly, Hawaii's constitutional enactment of the public trust states: "All public natural resources are held in trust by the State for the benefit of the people." Pennsylvania's constitution declares a "Public Estate," proclaiming: "Pennsylvania's public natural resources are the common property of all the people, including generations yet to come. As trustee of these resources, the Commonwealth shall conserve and maintain them for the benefit of all the people." The same approach appears in local ordinances sprouting in environmentally oppressed areas such as the coal regions of Pennsylvania. An ordinance enacted by Packer Township, in Pennsylvania, for example, declares the right of "natural communities and ecosystems" to "exist and flourish." This integrated approach now has a global foothold as well. Ecuador enacted a constitutional provision establishing Nature's "right to integral respect for its existence and for the maintenance and regeneration of its life cycles, structure, functions and evolutionary processes." Bolivia followed suit in

2011. India constitutionally enshrined its public trust doctrine to include all natural resources. In a broad survey of public trust law in other countries, Professor Michael Blumm and R. D. Guthrie conclude that many legal systems apply the trust doctrine to embrace protection for all natural resources, not just navigable waterways. Notably, as Western societies move toward a holistic approach in protecting Nature, they gravitate to the indigenous management model. Traditional native communities, some of the most sustainable societies in the world, incorporate in both their cultural worldview and legal outlook the awareness of, and abidance for, the interconnectedness of all ecology.[29]

A Reserved Power Rationale

A compelling justification for recognizing an ecological *res* emanates directly from the landmark *Illinois Central* case. As explained in Chapter 6, the Court protected the shoreline of Lake Michigan in order to preserve legislative ability to provide for public needs in the future. Under the reserved powers doctrine, no legislature can take action to tie the hands of future legislatures in meeting essential sovereign purposes. The privatization of crucial resources, which could result in their destruction or monopolization, clearly handicaps the ability of future legislatures to meet public needs. As the *Illinois Central* Court stated:

> The legislature could not give away nor sell the discretion of its successors in respect to matters, the government of which, from the very nature of things, must vary with varying circumstances. *The legislation which may be needed one day for the harbor may be different from the legislation that may be required at another day.*[30]

This statement underscores the fact that some natural wealth remains irreplaceable, not fungible. When a species goes extinct, it cannot be resurrected. When a toxic pollutant contaminates an aquifer, no ready replacement exists. When loggers raze an old-growth forest, another will not evolve for hundreds or thousands of years, if ever. If the world passes the climate tipping point, there will be no reprieve. While other aspects of civil life lend themselves to correction through economic or social reform, transgressions of Nature's laws cannot be easily, if ever, rectified. The collapse of the natural infrastructure would drastically narrow any legislative options to protect society's survival and welfare into the future. The heart of the constitutional reserved power doctrine, as applied in *Illinois Central*, lies not in protecting streambeds, but in safeguarding all natural wealth necessary to meet public needs in the future.

This rationale requires fierce protection of ecosystems, the function of which may not be fully understood even by the best biologists living today. As Aldo Leopold wrote, "Only those who know the most about [ecology] can appreciate how little we know about it. The last word in ignorance is the man who says of an animal or plant: 'What good is it?'" In a similar vein, Supreme Court Justice William O. Douglas urged protection of Nature for the uncertain potential it holds in meeting human needs. In a famous case, *Sierra Club v. Morton*, he wrote:

> A teaspoon of living earth contains 5 million bacteria, 20 million fungi, one million protozoa, and 200,000 algae. No living human can predict what vital miracles may be locked in this dab of life, this stupendous reservoir of genetic materials that have evolved continuously since the dawn of the earth. For example, molds have existed on earth for about 2 billion years. But only in this century did we unlock the secret of the penicillins, tetracyclines, and other antibiotics from the lowly molds, and thus fashion the most powerful and effective medicines ever discovered by man.... When a species is gone, it is gone forever, Nature's genetic chain, billions of years in the making, is broken for all time.[31]

Contemporary science embraces such uncertainty. As Reed Noss frankly admits, "'Ecosystems are not only more complex than we think, but more complex than we can think.'... Humility demands that we prefer erring on the side of preservation to erring on the side of development." Protecting the full ecological *res* as a part of the public trust amounts to the best hedge against uncertainty. It is an institutionalized precautionary approach against squandering priceless and irreplaceable assets out of sheer ignorance of their present and future value. Aldo Leopold famously declared:

> If the land mechanism as a whole is good, then every part is good, whether we understand it or not. If the biota, in the course of aeons, has built something we like but do not understand, then who but a fool would discard seemingly useless parts? To keep every cog and wheel is the first precaution of intelligent tinkering.[32]

Protecting Options on a Heating Planet

Climate crisis brings this caution, and the reserved powers rationale, to the forefront of public trust jurisprudence. Scientists estimate unavoidable global temperature increase as a result of the past and present greenhouse gas pollution already lingering in the atmosphere. The U.S. Climate Impacts Report issued in 2009 projects that society's business-as-usual course would cause 2–11.5 degrees Fahrenheit heating by 2100. Climate upheaval will hurl new threats to society on a scale unimaginable to those sitting in government office today. Rising sea levels, forest loss, species extinctions, searing heat waves, diminished waters, superstorms, raging wildfires, desertification, spread of disease, massive flooding, and many other disasters will test humanity's ability to survive. The Climate Impacts Report warns: "[S]ociety won't be adapting to a new steady state but rather to a rapidly moving target ... outside the range to which society has adapted in the past." As author Ross Gelbspan asserts, climate crisis presents "a civilizational issue."[33]

Analysts fully expect that, as climate-ravaged locales on Earth become inhospitable to human habitation, mass migrations of climate refugees will occur, triggering global outbreaks of war. A report issued by the Center for a New American Security describes: "*No precedent exists for a disaster of this magnitude – one that affects entire civilizations in multiple ways simultaneously.*" This and a multitude of other reports project that the current trajectory of carbon dioxide pollution will trigger planetary heating on a scale that will send civilization into interminable distress. A string of legal conclusions must follow: (1) ongoing atmospheric pollution allowed by current legislatures will almost certainly cripple the ability of future legislatures to carry out sovereign functions; (2) the reserved powers principle requires protecting the atmosphere as part of the trust *res* in order to preserve even a modicum of legislative capacity in providing for the needs of future citizens; and (3) climate circumstances also require recognizing all remaining natural infrastructure as part of the trust *res*, because in face of the ecological upheaval that society has already set irrevocably in motion, all resources now carry a premium of societal value. In light of these conclusions, any judicial approach that still shackles the trust analysis to streambeds will prove increasingly marginal. As the Philippines Supreme Court warned in the *Oposa* case, prevailing policies of exploitation threaten to leave "nothing but parched earth incapable of sustaining life."[34]

A FACTOR-BASED APPROACH TO DEFINING THE *RES*

Despite compelling reasons for treating all natural assets as part of the trust, some courts will undoubtedly cling to the established judicial practice of evaluating each asset in isolation to determine whether it merits trust protection. In this regard, the key test emerging from *Illinois Central* remains that of "public concern." But "public concern" amounts to a broad notion that requires distillation into clearly enumerated factors to guide courts. This section briefly assembles reasoning from landmark public trust opinions to identify six different factors that courts use to sweep an asset into the people's trust. This factor-applying analysis leads, on a different path, to the same endpoint as the ecological *res* analysis earlier in the chapter.

All of the factors find grounding in a concept illuminated by Professor Joseph Sax. As he recognized long ago, the core of the trust rationale lies in the "reasonable expectations" of society, which are not limited to private title ownership. Sax observed: "The central idea of the public trust is preventing the destabilizing disappointment of expectations held in common but without formal recognition such as title." The essential inquiry, he said, identifies the trustee's obligation "with an eye toward insulating those expectations that support social, economic and ecological systems from avoidable destabilization and disruption."[35]

From this central idea spring six factors, which might be summarized as: (1) public need; (2) scarcity; (3) customary use and reasonable expectation; (4) unique and irreplaceable common heritage; (5) suitability for common use; and (6) ancillary function. Although these factors overlap in some measure, they nevertheless merit separate iteration. A given case may turn on the applicability of just one factor in isolation or on several factors operating in combination. Applying these factors, it becomes apparent that virtually all categories of natural resources merit protection as assets in the trust – air and atmosphere, surface waters, groundwater, dry sand beaches, wildlife, fisheries, plant life, wetlands, soils, minerals and energy sources, forests, grasslands, and public lands.

Public Need. This factor considers whether the resource meets a public need. Public need formed the crux of the *Illinois Central* decision, which recognized fishing, commerce, and navigation as paramount requirements of society at the time. In *Marks v. Whitney*, the California Supreme Court emphasized "changing public needs" as the core inquiry in a trust case. The New Jersey Supreme Court declared dry sand beaches as encumbered by a public trust easement, noting that the public's need for recreation was "'intimately related to the general welfare of a well-balanced state.'" Some public trust decisions frame public need as a need to *prevent harm* to the public. In finding the public trust applicable to wetlands, for example, the Wisconsin Supreme Court noted the need to "prevent a harm from the change in the natural character of the citizens' property." Public needs run the spectrum from immediate survival needs, such as food and water and safety from storms, to underlying ecological needs that prove necessary to support life on Earth, such as biodiversity and climate regulation, both recognized by some modern courts as public trust interests. Courts also recognize certain public needs that rank more tangential but nevertheless promote the general welfare, such as aesthetics and recreation. More broadly, Professor Torres defines the scope of the *res* by noting the state's basic fiduciary obligation to facilitate "cultural self-perpetuation through time." The public trust, he submits, protects those assets "essential to culture itself."[36]

A comprehensive study conducted as part of the Millennium Ecosystem Assessment shows that virtually all categories of natural resources meet one or more of these basic public needs, and most meet several at once. The rivers are, as Justice Holmes recognized long ago, "a necessity of life." Groundwater ranks equally supreme, providing about half of the drinking water of the United States (and nearly all of the drinking water for farm communities). Recognizing this crucial role of water, South Africa legally enshrined a public trust right to all water. The air and atmospheric health count as essential to human survival – and to all facets of civilization. Fish and wildlife provide food and biodiversity in support of all of life on

Earth. Even the bees demonstrate irreplaceable worth by pollinating crops (valued at $15 billion in the United States annually). Dryland soils prove indispensable both for food production and for providing carbon sinks to absorb greenhouse gas pollution from the atmosphere. The wetlands and coastal areas establish essential storm barriers and provide pollution filtration, in addition to habitat for fish and wildlife. The forests provide crucial carbon sequestration, water storage, wood production, and wildlife habitat. Nearly all public parks, dry sand beaches, waterways, and many wetlands serve recreational needs. The traditional "streambed-only" formulation of the public trust excludes most of these resources – a clear mark of its shortfall.[37]

Scarcity. The second factor asks whether the resource remains scarce in relation to the ecological and public demand for it. The Supreme Court of Hawaii recognized restricted supply relative to burgeoning needs when it extended trust protection to all water resources in the state. The Philippines Supreme Court in *Oposa v. Factoran* enjoined logging out of alarm over the vanishing forests in that country. Scarcity was also a key factor driving the India Supreme Court's assertion of a public trust over natural gas reserves. Describing the "acute scarcity of natural gas in India," the Court observed that diminishing supplies justifies governmental intervention to force conservation so as to promote societal needs and intergenerational equities that private markets ignore.[38]

Many natural resources are doomed to scarcity in a climate-stricken future. Water ranks foremost among them. UN scientists predict that more than 3 billion people will lack access to clean water by 2080 as a result of climate change. As to wildlife and plant life, scientists estimate that climate change threatens 20–30 percent of all species on Earth. They describe the present world as in the throes of the Sixth Extinction. Terry Glavin explains this period of mass extinction as "comparable to only five cataclysms that have occurred over the past 440 million years." Even apart from climate-induced collapse, many resources are already scarce. Ancient forests, wetlands, and grasslands now cover only a fraction of their historic range. Soils and air, while not "scarce" in quantity, remain rare in their unpolluted condition. Readily accessible oil supplies become increasingly scarce, causing analysts to warn of societal crash triggered by "peak oil."[39]

Customary Use, Enjoyment, and Reasonable Expectation. The third factor asks whether the public customarily uses or enjoys the natural asset to the extent of having reasonable expectations of its continued existence and abundance. This factor most closely parallels Professor Sax's emphasis (explained earlier). In the judicial context, this factor already finds precise elaboration regarding dry sand beaches. The Oregon Supreme Court drew on the doctrine of custom (best described as a branch of the overall public trust) to affirm public access rights across private property. Recognized since the days of old English law, the principle protects uninterrupted public use of land extending back for as long as "the memory of man runneth not to the contrary." As the Oregon court noted, "[F]rom the time of the earliest settlement to the present day, the general public has assumed that the dry-sand area was part of the public beach."[40]

Particularly when applied more generously than formal English common law (which requires custom back to time immemorial), this factor draws several natural resources into the trust ambit. Customary, long-standing use by the public characterizes air, surface water, and wildlife. Public lands such as national and state parks, refuges, monuments, and forest lands – all specifically designated in public ownership – accrue customary use and enjoyment over time, which gives rise to reasonable expectations justifying their protection as trust assets. Ultimately, however, this factor cannot be trimmed down to areas of public access. In the most basic sense, it safeguards the public's continued expectation in ecological conditions that support human survival, comfort, and dignity.

Unique and Irreplaceable Common Heritage. A fourth factor considers whether particular lands or resources boast such unique or irreplaceable characteristics that they fall within the people's "common heritage." This factor describes community sentiments of entitlement and just inheritance. An influential article by Professor Harrison Dunning suggests that the public trust embodies "a fundamental notion of how government is to operate with regard to common heritage natural resources." The Supreme Court of California emphasized this factor when it observed in its leading public trust opinion involving Mono Lake that streams, lakes, marshlands, and tidelands all make up the state's "common heritage." The Supreme Court of New Jersey classified the state's dry sand beaches in this way too, stating, "Beaches are a unique resource and are irreplaceable." In the same vein, a Nevada Supreme Court Justice passionately argued that Lake Walker warrants recognition as a trust asset, reasoning, "The public expects this unique natural resource to be preserved and for all of us to always be able to marvel at this massive glittering body of water lying majestically in the midst of a dry mountainous desert."[41]

Common heritage assets become admired by the community over a period of time, whether purely for their aesthetics or for a combination of values. This factor alone describes most rivers. As Justice Oliver Wendell Holmes expressed, "A river is more than an amenity, it is a treasure." The Supreme Court of California described Mono Lake as "a scenic and ecological treasure of national significance" in conferring trust protection. The portrayal could equally apply to Yellowstone National Park, the Florida Everglades, the Grand Canyon, the Columbia River Gorge, the Pacific Northwest old-growth forests, the Appalachian mountaintops, and many other national parks, monuments, and scenic areas. As Professor Charles Wilkinson observed, "The increasing use of trust language in public lands cases indicates an awareness that the special values of the federal lands, like other resources on which the trust has been impressed, have been gradually but indelibly imprinted on our national consciousness." Just as important, a local wetland or an ancient grandfather tree, while unknown outside of the community, may become a vital part of that locality's natural heritage.[42]

Suitability for Common Use. A fifth factor examines natural suitability for common use. Roman law classified key resources as "res communes" owned by all. As far back as 535 A.D., the Institutes of Justinian declared: "By the law of nature these things are common to mankind – the air, running water, the sea and consequently the shores of the sea." This factor weighed heavily in the *Illinois Central* decision that extended trust protection to Lake Michigan's shoreline; the Court noted its value for fishing, navigation, and commerce – common uses in which the "whole people are interested." And several decisions have found rivers as "natural highway[s] for transportation." The suitability for common use holds reverse logic as well: the unsuitability for private use. As the Oregon Supreme Court pointed out in affirming public property rights in dry sand beaches, the sand area "is unstable in its seaward boundaries, unsafe during winter storms, and for the most part unfit for the construction of permanent structures." By the same reasoning, air and atmosphere are *only* suitable for common use because of their incapability of being captured or bounded.[43]

Ancillary Function. A final factor asks whether the asset serves an "ancillary" function to an already recognized public trust asset. Perceptive courts understand the futility of protecting certain trust assets without extending trust protection to their supporting ecology as well. The Supreme Court of New Jersey invoked this reasoning when it extended the public trust doctrine upland from its traditional realm below the high water mark. Public trust rights to access the dry sand were found "ancillary to the public's right to enjoy the tidal lands." The court explained: "Reasonable enjoyment of the foreshore and the sea cannot be realized unless some enjoyment of the dry sand area is also allowed. The complete pleasure of swimming must be accompanied by intermittent periods of rest and relaxation beyond the water's edge." Likewise, the Supreme Court of California extended the public trust doctrine to non-navigable waterways that had a clear hydrological connection with traditional navigable waters. By all logic, the "ancillary function" factor should confer trust status to forested slopes adjoining streambeds, as slope stability directly impacts the health of the stream below. Similarly, habitat of any form plays an ancillary role in protecting wildlife, a classic trust asset (known as *ferae naturae*). The atmosphere merits public trust protection for its pivotal role in climate regulation, which in turn affects virtually all traditionally recognized public trust assets (streambeds, navigable waters, fish, and wildlife). And so on.[44]

A full application of these factors to Nature's assets would easily consume a separate book, but even the brief synopsis in this chapter indicates that all classic categories of natural resources warrant inclusion in the trust *res*. Whether courts take this more laborious approach of applying distinguishing factors to individual resource classes, or adopt the encompassing approach that recognizes a full ecological *res* to comport with modern scientific understanding, both analytical paths suggest the same unremarkable conclusion: humans need all of Nature. The distinct web of life, with all of its innumerable strands, meets *Illinois Central*'s "public concern" benchmark for public trust protection.

THE COMMONS DISTINGUISHED

A final matter remains in positioning the trust *res* in relation to what has become widely known as the commons. An emerging field of commons thinking and activism advances paradigms to manage common resources in a manner that generally eschews state control. The commons approach is often urged for assets, both natural and human-made, that bear significant importance to society, such as historic places or objects, educational systems, the Internet, scientific and medical information, literary and artistic works, and natural resources. A growing movement treats all, equally, as the commons.[45] The commons terminology can be confusing, because, on the legal level, natural resources held in trust remain distinguishable from the commons. A trust encompasses a firm and definite fiduciary obligation under the law, attached to bounded public property, and having specific beneficiaries. It arises as a distinct, formal, legal limitation on government officers. While its purpose allows communal use and benefit for a class of citizens, it should not be confused with "the commons," which can refer to a broader ambit of public goods or benefits, managed outside of any state regime.

But although natural resources subject to the public trust cannot accurately be termed the commons in a strict legal sense, much can be gained by positioning the trust within the broader commons movement. The term "commons" holds galvanizing popular force when used broadly on the less formal and more generic level; it strikes a chord for citizens yearning to free their communities from the state's environmental oppression and corruption. A growing commons movement in the United States signals public expectations in certain resources and spaces. The public aims of this movement, in this sense, run opposite to one of Garrett Hardin's identified solutions to what he called the "tragedy of the commons," namely, *privatization* of the commons. Some have argued that the failure to allocate private property rights in a commons results in overexploitation of the resource. As David Bollier explains, the commons movement represents "dissatisfaction with [this] standard market narrative" and "alarm at the market's tendency to regard everything as a commodity for sale." As such, the commons represents "a third force in political life, always struggling to express its interests over and against those of the market and the state."[46]

The commons approach has recently gained considerable practical and theoretical appeal as a paradigm shift that breaks away from the disastrous state/ market model. This can be attributed in large part to a visionary book, *Green Governance*, in which Burns H. Weston and David Bollier fuse commons thinking with human rights imperatives to arrive at a distinctive platform of ecological governance. Their liberating proposal escapes the dominant, repressive "State/ Market duopoly" which has proved "incapable of meeting human needs in ecologically responsible, socially equitable ways." Joining other thinkers in saying that "new forms of governance are needed," they draw on the commons philosophy and worldview (iterated as a "social and moral economy") to present an alternative paradigm to central governing state institutions. Managed outside of, and independent of, state institutions, a commons embraces "the self-determined norms, practices, and traditions that commoners themselves devise for nurturing and protecting their shared resources."[47]

Important to this paradigm is what the authors call "Vernacular Law." Distinguished from formal state law, Vernacular Law "originates in the informal, unofficial zones of society and is a source of moral legitimacy and power in its own right." Circulating in a culture of the commons, it consists of "informal, socially negotiated values, principles, and rules that a given community develops" to manage resources – indeed, a "cultural ballast that gives a commons stability and self-confidence, even in the absence of formal law." These community norms can represent the very same values and customs underlying the public trust, as Chapter 12 describes; they give the trust vibrancy and support citizens in their irrepressible impulse for asserting public rights. As Weston and Bollier explain:

> [T]he public trust may be seen as having shared origins with the Vernacular Law of the Commons, which is philosophically linked also to natural law and human rights. The public trust doctrine is an instrument of State power; the Commons asserts its own moral and political authority as Vernacular Law, independent of the State. Both the public trust doctrine and the Vernacular Law of the Commons have solid grounding in natural law, which today expresses itself, relative to the natural environment especially, in terms of what today we call human rights law.[48]

While Weston and Bollier make clear that the public trust doctrine and the commons paradigm are not one and the same, they point to a powerful symbiosis between the two, noting that the public trust provides "a venerable principle of State Law that can reinforce the commons by recognizing the importance of commonly held use rights," and in that sense can be "an antidote to the 'tragedy of the commons' by requiring the State to uphold its responsibilities to protect resources that belong to the citizenry at large." As they describe (with credit to commons scholar Peter Barnes), "the trust is a familiar legal form that can serve as a template for designing new sorts of commons institutions." Put another way, "the trust is to the Commons as the corporation is to the marketplace."⁴⁹

The Vernacular Law of the commons holds compelling appeal in describing natural resources because it draws from a community-minded culture taking shape in many varied societal contexts. Bollier notes that commoners think of natural resources as the "inherited elements of nature," belonging to everyone as the "common heritage of mankind." As he describes, "The commons is one way to assert a 'particularizing language' declaring that natural resources are 'not for sale.'"⁵⁰

Nevertheless, there remains considerable potential for confusion when characterizing natural assets as the "commons," because doing so impliedly brings Nature's gifts into a broad umbrella extending far beyond the environment. For purposes of the public trust in its *legal iteration*, great care should be taken to distinguish natural resources from human-created resources. The latter resources, which include historic objects, art, artifacts, and the Internet, cannot be properly "public trust assets." Although a few courts have accorded public trust protection to historic objects, and some scholars have urged inclusion of cultural heritage in the trust corpus, the effort misses the fundamental and obvious demarcation between human-created resources and humanity's natural inheritance, as elaborated below. This does not imply that human-created assets do not warrant strong protection; they most certainly do for their unquestionable importance to community identity and history. But guardianship over these societal treasures can be a matter of the duty owed by government to its citizens pursuant to its general fiduciary obligation, as described in Chapter 6.⁵¹

Because the public trust invokes a potent legal tool, particularly in view of emerging recognition of its constitutional force, it should apply to natural objects only – those subject to the "laws of Nature," which ultimately govern human survival and crucial aspects of societal welfare. The public trust doctrine risks losing a key part of its rationale if stretched beyond the natural realm. Cultural and historic objects can be fundamentally distinguished from natural assets on at least four grounds. First, they are not Nature-made and have no direct interaction or symbiosis with natural assets. They are not part of the web of life and do not fit within any conception of the ecological *res*. Second, the values provided by human-created resources fall into a category of public benefit altogether different from the ecosystem service values provided by natural resources. Although both human-made and natural resources contribute to public needs and even reflect "public concern," only natural resources – which include even the "lowly mold," as recognized by Justice Douglas – protect a core, primitive interest in enabling overall human survival. Third, there exists no baseline against which to assess the abundance of human-created resources and form fiduciary standards for their management. The baseline for Nature's gifts finds reference in the originating wealth in Earth's Endowment.

An endangered species, for example, has a historic range and population. A work of art, by contrast, forms part of an ever-expanding body of human creation. Finally, human-created resources and natural resources have been treated separately under the law since Roman times. The Institutes of Justinian, for example, found that "[t]hings sacred, religious and holy" were the property of no one and subject to divine law, but the Code distinguished those from natural resources such as air, running water, the sea and the shores of the sea, all of which remain "common to mankind." In sum, while the commons movement establishes valuable linkages between various natural and human-created resources in search of a common ethical underpinning as to their management, the grouping should not extend to the more exact and bounded public trust doctrine of the legal sphere that remains justifiably and traditionally restricted to natural bounty.[52]

To summarize this chapter, Nature's Trust demonstrates a seemingly inevitable progression of the public trust doctrine toward a holistic approach that recognizes the people's interests in all resources sustaining ecological balance – which is to say, all natural resources. Confining the doctrine to the "traditional" approach, which holds its anchor in streambeds, would render the doctrine a relic in the modern era of ecological collapse. If, indeed, the body of public trust law aims to protect society and safeguard the natural infrastructure necessary for the citizens' survival and prosperity, courts can no longer tether it to artificial categories defined by courts two centuries ago. Nature's Trust recognizes a full ecological *res*. Ecological integrity, rather than navigability, forms its talisman.

This encompassing approach obviates the question of whether any particular asset – a wetland, a forest, a species, a soil bank, and so forth – falls within the trust. Because all constituent parts of Nature connect inextricably in their performance of vital ecosystem services, they remain, quite simply, all part of Nature's Trust. But this does not mean that everything natural warrants equal levels of protection. Making a conceptual leap to a full ecological *res* puts far greater force of impact on the next question, namely what standards of protection apply. Chapter 8 takes up that matter.

8

Fiduciary Standards of Protection and Restoration

If government allowed corporations to raid the Social Security Fund, American citizens would rise up in arms over the theft of "their" property. Yet under current environmental law, corporations do just that. Aided by the government, mega-corporations seize astonishing amounts of property belonging to the citizens in common. This looting creates razed forests, toxic watersheds, ocean dead zones, suburban sprawl, decapitated mountains, ocean oil geysers, vanished species, and climate crisis. While this wreaks havoc for countless citizens, it provokes only dim outcry from the public, because the political frame surrounding environmental law conceals the public property character of these resources and thus obscures the sovereign's obligation in managing them. The political realm depicts Nature as an amorphous milieu, not really owned by anyone, that corporations can lawfully plunder with government's blessing, bestowed through permits. Environmental law might house a den of thieves, but the public perceives no theft. By contrast, a trust framework characterizes natural assets as the public's inherited natural wealth that, with decisive justice, should pass down through the generations of citizens. It imposes an unwavering fiduciary obligation on government trustees to safeguard the commonwealth. This chapter brings definition to that obligation.

POLITICS AS "REALITY": THE CONTROLLING FRAME OF ENVIRONMENTAL LAW

Social frames influence people's perception of reality. The current social frame legitimizes environmental oppression of human beings and their fellow species by casting resource disputes as, essentially, political contests. The only property rights recognized by this frame are private ones. When the public ends up on the losing side of the contest, the frame applauds the protection of private property rights (and, tangentially, economic interests) with little or no acknowledgment of the public property rights and human rights trammeled in the process.

This frame perpetuates a decision-making arena that remains masterfully rigged in favor of industry. As earlier chapters explained, state and federal elected leaders draw on the environmental regulatory process to generate political paybacks for their industry supporters. Within a receptive political milieu, big corporations retain a full envoy of lobbyists, lawyers, consultants, and public relations agents to muscle agencies to their advantage. The public fights as a lightweight in this arena, outboxed by the corporations nearly every time. Minority populations and low-income communities face nearly impossible political handicaps. Many live surrounded by industrial waste dumps and chemical-spewing plants – modern death camps to those who fall victim to cancer from the toxic exposure – but the political frame ruling environmental law readily legitimizes the horror of it all.[1]

As Part I of this book explained, bureaucracies become enfeebled by corporate manipulations until fully captured by the very industries they regulate. When that happens, corruption takes on an institutionalized form, and agencies deploy the full force of law against the public interest. Well-intentioned government employees working within the agencies may fail to see this progression; it creeps up incrementally, and the outer shell of law shows no indication.

When the public staggers on the losing side of the environmental contests, government agencies explain their failure to carry out the law on the basis of "political reality." This "political reality" characterizes the public loss as legitimate, even as it repudiates statutory purposes. A familiar set of excuses is heard daily in the halls of agencies and legislatures: "We could not get a climate bill passed; the political support just wasn't there"; "We can't bring an enforcement action against that company – heads would roll"; "Public resistance to government is too great; we regulated as much as we could." Such laments continue as if the law no longer mattered. This "political reality" becomes a self-serving truism defined and perpetuated by those in power. And it works astonishingly well in bringing lower-ranked agency staffers on board with the corporate political agenda of the agency, often despite their deep reservations and best intentions to the contrary. The "political reality" also delivers a potent tranquilizer to the public – after all, who will argue with reality? The political frame leads to public demoralization, political submission, and citizen passivity.

Operating within this political frame, government agencies have squandered the public's natural wealth, leaving a pittance for humanity's posterity. Today's environmental crisis impels changing the frame. As George Lakoff writes, "Reframing is changing the way the public sees the world. It is changing what counts as common sense."[2] This book reframes Nature as a legal trust encompassing property belonging to the citizens – an irreplaceable *res* to rebuild and sustain through all generations. A trust frame centers on fiduciary obligation rather than political discretion. Trustees remain duty-bound to protect the assets of the trust – in spite of the "political reality." As a matter of property law, strict fiduciary standards require protection regardless of whether the public has any political clout or even shows any interest in the matter. The trust provides a different lens through which to view and assess the legitimacy of government outcomes. It returns us to an ancient and animating vernacular, one that empowers citizens to protect their public *property* rights. Moreover, as a legal tool, it activates the courts to enforce protection of public assets, a matter further explored in Chapter 11.

The trustee's fiduciary obligation consists of both substantive and procedural standards. Designed to restrain and channel the trustee's power over the assets (the *res*), the trust compels the trustee to act wholly and uncompromisingly in favor of the beneficiaries' interests. This chapter illuminates six substantive fiduciary obligations in administering Nature's Trust. The next chapter delineates procedural duties incumbent upon public trustees. Procedural and substantive duties connect integrally. Procedural duties set forth strict protocol designed to keep the eyes of officials on their substantive trust obligations and steer administrative loyalty unwaveringly toward the public, largely by prohibiting flirtations that could give rise to conflicts of interests. In the end, however, substantive duties, rather than procedural ones, determine the destiny of the planet and humanity's future.

The six substantive fiduciary duties require a public trustee to: (1) protect the *res*; (2) conserve the natural inheritance of future generations (the duty against waste); (3) maximize the societal value of natural resources; (4) restore the trust *res* where it has been damaged; (5) recover natural resource damages from third parties that have injured public trust assets; and (6) refrain from alienating (that is, privatizing) the trust except in limited circumstances. These essential parameters of fiduciary obligation derive from modern court decisions as well as venerable principles of private trust law. If citizen beneficiaries and courts hold public officials accountable to these obligations, environmental management will aim toward replenishment, rather than depletion, of the natural commonwealth – and the people's interests, rather than corporate interests, will rank supreme in ecological decision making. Viewed in aggregate, these obligations present a necessary paradigm shift for environmental law.

THE FIDUCIARY DUTY OF PROTECTION

At the heart of trust law rests a fundamental fiduciary duty to protect the assets of the trust from damage. As one leading treatise explains: "The trustee ... is obligated to the beneficiary to do all acts necessary for the preservation of the trust *res* which would be performed by a reasonably prudent man employing his own like property for purposes similar to those of the trust." Scores of public trust cases emphasize this duty of protection, stating that the trustees must prevent "substantial impairment" to the trust. Enforcing the duty of asset protection must be the first step in arresting devastation to the people's natural endowment.[3]

Because individual natural assets exist as part of a larger system, the government's fiduciary duty requires protecting the ecological *res* as a whole – a macro approach that the statutes, with their myopic focus, utterly miss. Thus, the fiduciary duty to protect waters and fish becomes also a duty to protect *air* from toxic mercury pollution that spews from coal-fired plants, falls into the lakes, and accumulates in fish tissue. A duty to protect groundwater becomes a concomitant duty to protect *soils* from toxic fertilizers and pesticides that migrate into the aquifers. A duty to protect wildlife evokes, at the same time, a duty to protect the *forests* in which they live. In defining this duty of protection, asset health forms the key driver, as the fiduciary obligation must always find its reference in Nature's own mandates. As is the case with any trust, courts must rely on experts with relevant expertise to determine whether a trustee meets fiduciary duties. Political litmus tests and perceived political "realities" have no relevance to asset health and thus occupy no legitimate place in judging fiduciary performance.

The sovereign trust imposes an active, not passive, duty of protection. Under well-established principles of trust law, a trustee may not sit idle and allow the trust property to "fall into ruin on his watch." A leading treatise explains that a trustee faces liability for damages if he "should have known of danger to the trust, could have protected the trust, but did not do so." This active vigilance finds reflection in another ancient tenant of trust law that prohibits "permissive waste" or "decay" of property brought on by the trustee's failure to exercise ordinary care for the protection of the estate.[4]

Government's do-nothing climate policy epitomizes the breach of this fiduciary duty. As Burns Weston and Tracy Bach assert, business as usual "now appears an irreversible experiment with the only atmosphere humans have." But other examples, such as the 2010 British Petroleum oil disaster in the Gulf of Mexico, also show a breathtaking abdication of responsibility. The U.S. Minerals Management Service (MMS) stands charged with the trust responsibility to administer public oil resources and protect the oceans from associated damage. For years, it shunned its supervisory role and extended nearly carte blanche latitude to the oil companies to embark on treacherous drilling operations more than a mile beneath the ocean floor. Government oversight was so nonexistent that, when the 2010 blowout happened, high officials floundered incompetent to address it. They had only meager technological expertise and information at their disposal because they had left the operations completely in industry hands. As President Obama frankly admitted, the MMS had long issued permits "based on little more than assurances of safety from the oil companies." Powerless to command any emergency effort to stop the gusher, officials depended on a response by the very company that had caused the disaster in the first place. As the admiral of the U.S. Coast Guard was forced to admit, "They have the eyes and ears that are down there.... They are necessarily the modality by which this is going to get solved."[5]

Understanding government's fiduciary obligation as an active, not passive, duty runs crucial to environmental reform. The active duty requires both legislatures and agencies to respond to threats before they transpire into calamity. Severe environmental syndromes – including climate instability, biodiversity collapse, ocean acidification, and water depletion – now advance at a pace heretofore unimagined, yet agencies and legislatures sit stunningly idle. Regardless of the social and economic priorities occupying the headlines, the active trust duty demands that legislators and agency officials be constantly attentive to natural resource imperatives. As the Hawaii Supreme Court emphasized in the water context, government may not act as a "mere 'umpire passively calling balls and strikes for adversaries appearing before it,' but instead must take the initiative in considering, protecting, and advancing public rights in the resources at every stage of the planning and decision-making process."[6]

PROTECTING POSTERITY'S PROPERTY: OUR CHILDREN'S TRUST

The public trust consistently points toward the interests of posterity. As the Hawaiian Supreme Court and other courts have emphasized, "The beneficiaries of the public trust are not just present generations but those to come." More than two decades ago, Professor Edith Brown Weiss described the concept of a "planetary trust" to infuse principles of intergenerational equity into the management of natural resources.[7] This forward-looking duty comes with an obvious dilemma: How should society divide natural resources between the present and the future? The inquiry must distinguish between the renewable resources, which, if managed correctly, provide ongoing services, and the nonrenewable resources, which amount to a finite trove.

The Renewable Resources

The renewable resources in Nature's Trust bear analogy to financial assets. In the financial world, a capital asset produces income (or "yield") in the form of interest, dividends, rents, and the like. In a perpetual financial trust, this yield distributes to present beneficiaries, while the capital portion of the account remains conserved for future beneficiaries so that they may likewise receive a yield (income) during their lifetimes. If the trustee wrongly invades the capital portion of the account, the yield declines and diminishes the return to future beneficiaries.[8]

Natural assets have "capital" and "yield" as well. Broadly speaking, the yield consists of ecological services, and the capital consists of the physical and biological systems producing such services. For example, the natural capital supporting a fishery includes the rivers, ocean, gravel beds, and a base population of fish to spawn and perpetuate the species. Present beneficiaries can take a certain "yield" of fish produced by this natural capital without compromising the long-term productivity of the asset. However, if the trustee allows the beneficiaries to overharvest the fish or pollute and obstruct the rivers, the natural capital of the ecological account will plunge, and the yield will return fewer fish in subsequent years. Just as in the financial context, the capital determines the yield.[9]

The Columbia River Basin salmon collapse demonstrates what happens when government trustees invade the capital portion of the account. Prior to non-Indian settlement, tribal sovereigns managed the salmon asset as a perpetual endowment, harvesting only the amount of fish that would not diminish the species' replenishing capacity. Under such management, the salmon trust provided returns of 10–16 million fish a year for 10,000 years. State and federal trustees have run the asset into bankruptcy within just the last century and a half by allowing the eradication of natural capital across the entire basin – from dams, clear-cuts, pollution, paved-over wetlands, and overharvest of fish. Only scant numbers of fish now return from what was once the world's largest commercial fishery. The same impoverishment replays across the wildlife trust. Three to five billion passenger pigeons once darkened the skies of America in flocks that could stretch a mile and take several hours to pass. Thirty million bison once roamed the Great Plains in massive herds, some 25 miles wide and 50 miles long. Like the salmon, colonialists annihilated these within a century. The Earth Endowment once held an amount of wealth that can scarcely be imagined today.[10]

In a perpetual trust, the present beneficiaries can claim only the yield, or income, of the trust asset. The legal doctrine speaking most directly to this limit is the age-old waste principle, which stands as a jealous guardian of future interests. Well-appointed to protect the public trust against generational theft, the rule prohibits trustees from raiding the trust inheritance and withering the wealth available to future beneficiaries. Illegal waste of property has been described as the "consumption of things belonging to the inheritance," and a "spoil or destruction [of] corporeal hereditaments." The waste rule limits the consumptive rights of a life-tenant (the present property owner who owns the property only for his lifetime, at the end of which the property passes to the "remainderman"). Generally, the life-tenant may consume only the "usufruct" of property – that is, the natural products of the land, otherwise called "profits," that can replenish of their own accord. The life-tenant may not purloin the capital portion of the account; in other words, he may pick the fruit, but he may not chop down the tree that bears the fruit. As one court stated, remaindermen stand entitled to receive the "identical estate" that the present holder had without "permanent injury to it."[11]

Courts can readily apply this duty against waste to the public's natural trust. As the Hawaiian Supreme Court emphasized, "The check and balance of judicial review provides a level of protection against improvident disposition of an irreplaceable res." To carry out the waste rule, courts describe the life-tenant as a "quasi-trustee" for the remainderman. The same description runs apt for the generations of humanity. Each living generation exists as a class comprised of Earth's life-tenants, assuming the duties of quasi-trustee for future "remainder" generations and bound by a lasting obligation to prevent waste to their ecological inheritance. The Philippines Supreme Court declared this principle when it halted forest harvesting in the *Oposa* case, stating: "Each generation has a responsibility to the next to preserve that rhythm and harmony [of Nature] for the full enjoyment of a balanced and healthful ecology." This legal doctrine presents a powerful counterweight to an importunate political tendency of government officials to overindulge the living generation (people who vote and make campaign contributions) and swindle future citizens (who have no political clout at all).[12]

Derived from common law, the rule against waste adapts to changing times. As one court made clear, the rule incorporates "such reasonable modifications as may be demanded by the growth of civilization and varying conditions." In England, an island of scarce resources, the waste doctrine proved quite rigid. It prohibited, for example, the current holder of property from converting meadow for farmland or cutting timber beyond that necessary for ordinary household use. In the context of early America, a frontier that seemed to offer limitless bounty, the doctrine eased considerably. Courts allowed some waste-like actions if they felt these would improve the property inherited by a future holder. For example, they regularly countenanced the clearing of timber to make land fit for cultivation. But while this made sense during an era of ecological abundance, the doctrine must again transform in response to extreme natural scarcity. The planet's current conditions approximate historic England far more than the American continent at the turn of the nineteenth century. Against the backdrop of climate change, surging population levels, and collapsing resources, the doctrine must prove a great deal more exacting than when it first landed on the shores of America.[13]

The suite of U.S. pollution laws enacted in the 1970s signaled this transition. The National Environmental Policy Act recognized the "profound impact" of humans stemming from population growth, urbanization, industrialization, and resource exploitation. In passing environmental legislation, Congress's chief intent focused on sustaining natural wealth for future generations. This meant closing the gates on natural destruction, retaining the ecological abundance that existed at the time, and restoring ecology where that could be achieved. The environmental laws that were enacted demarcated a crucial boundary between natural capital and yield. All shared the trenchant prohibition against waste. The Clean Water Act, for example, declared a national goal of restoring the "integrity of the Nation's waters." The National Forest Management Act imposed a principle of "sustained yield" in timber harvest. The Federal Land Policy and Management Act carried the same principle to other vast tracts of federal land. The Marine Mammal Protection Act required conserving marine species at "optimum sustainable" populations. Scores of other statutes reflect this disposition. The permit provisions in such laws were not intended to siphon priceless natural capital from the account of future generations, but rather to allocate only the profits of Nature among users of the present generation.[14]

Nearly all agencies, however, regularly issue pollution and extraction permits that transgress the crucial boundary between natural capital and yield. They allow corporations to blow off mountaintops, obliterate streams, suck wells dry, raze huge swaths of forest, dump billions of tons of toxins in waters and soils, spew carbon pollution into the air, bulldoze and pave over wetlands, exterminate species, and produce cancer-causing chemicals that trigger health impacts persisting through multiple generations of human offspring. Today's permit systems rob the remainder generations of their natural entitlement and, in so doing, repudiate the duty to prevent waste to the assets. A trustee may not invite a raid on the trust he manages. The whole permit system cries out for an overhaul.

A Nature's Trust approach would restructure permit systems to allocate only the *interest* portion of renewable resources to the present generation. This concept does not hold any novelty: all of the so-called sustainability efforts aim toward this bottom line. However, such efforts lack the sound legal structure offered by the trust that compels restraint. Though strict, the trust is not Draconian. Trustees may appropriately allow non-harmful asset uses when consistent with the duty of protection. For example, some amount of water can be withdrawn from a stream without impacting the riparian and hydrological functioning of the system as a whole. A portion of a healthy fishery can be harvested without compromising populations in the future. Certain trees can be cut without impairing overall forest functions. Some nontoxic pollution can be absorbed in a waterway and assimilated by the biological, physical, and chemical processes that are constantly at work. And too, trustees may allow damage to existing trust uses if necessary for clear public benefit, as described below.[15]

But the vast amount of resource use and pollution legalized today and in the past extends far beyond these limits, often triggering a spiral of irrevocable loss. A watershed contaminated with massive toxic mining waste becomes "dead," unable to support any life at all for stretches of miles, like the Red River in New Mexico or the Alamosa River in Colorado. A species with only remnant populations vanishes into extinction, like the passenger pigeon, some species of Columbia River salmon, and a multitude of others. A mountain in ancient Appalachia, blown up, can never be resurrected. A landscape poisoned with radioactive waste remains lethal for tens of thousands of years, adding to a number of "sacrifice zones" on the planet. These examples represent the complete dissolution of a trust asset, with not a fragment remaining from which to rebuild abundance. Yet this same behavior represents business as usual under modern environmental law. The aggregate result of insti-tutionalizing this breach of duty will be what scientists describe as a "transformed planet" that future generations stand to inherit.[16]

Allowing such damage out of loyalty to political supporters incriminates trustees beyond the pale. Citizens would recognize this conduct as corruption in other con-texts, but the permit system shrouds even outrageous decisions in a veil of legality. Citizens have not assembled the legal arguments by which to hold their officials accountable, nor have they clarified the moral injustice that would sharpen their outrage. As long as they, and their environmental lawyers, structure their challenges within the same frame that government officials use to legalize this massive plun-dering, agencies will remain largely unaccountable to the very citizens who entrust them with authority.

The Nonrenewable Resources

Some public trust resources are nonrenewable. These have no reoccurring "prof-its" that can be used without invading the principal of the trust. In fact, the very use of these public trust resources exhausts the capital of the account. Examples include oil, gas, minerals, coal, and fossilized sources of groundwater. With respect to these, government allows capricious use of such resources without regard to saving a reserve for the future – again, antithetical to the trustee's duty of prudent management.

Peak oil provides the best example of this folly. Experts warn of the approaching end to cheap oil supplies. The easy reserves have been spent, leaving only those that require far more energy, technology, and treacherous operations to develop. Moreover, extreme ecological peril mounts with further use of oil. Burning the remaining reserves would push the Earth past looming climate tipping points and "beyond the point of no return," Dr. James Hansen warns in his book, *Storms of My Grandchildren*. He describes the result as a "devastated, sweltering Earth purged of life." Yet as Tom Friedman explains in his book, *Hot, Flat, and Crowded*, govern-ment has not responded to these dangers; instead it continues to enable oil addic-tion by posturing that oil supplies are "largely inexhaustible, inexpensive, politically benign, and … climatically benign as well."[17]

Modern natural resources law offers no set of factors to guide the prudent dis-pensation of oil reserves in light of both the scarcity of the resource and the perils associated with its continued use. Rather than fashion a logical way of prioritizing oil uses, oil politics still drives production as if no pitfalls existed. Just two years after the BP oil spill, for example, the Obama administration opened millions of acres to oil exploration and approved more than 400 permits to push drill rigs into ever more treacherous waters and deeper into the Earth's crust – even as climate-related tragedies mounted worldwide. The public trust demands rational policy in face of both scarcity and danger in using a natural resource. Recognizing this, the Supreme Court of India, for example, has declared a public trust over all of the nation's natural gas supplies, so as to balance current and future consumption needs.[18]

The question remains: How should such finite, nonrenewable resources be managed in light of the trust obligation to provide for the welfare of *both* present and future citizens? On its face, the waste doctrine described earlier would seem to prohibit *any* use of a nonrenewable resource, because doing so diminishes the inheritance available to future generations. However, that approach would deprive all beneficiaries of any benefit from the trust.

Three principles might inform a rational approach. First, private trust law requires that receipts from sale of mineral resources go into an account and be treated as principle rather than as income that present beneficiaries may consume. In this manner, the mineral assets convert to cash, but the benefit continues in perpetuity for future generations. Professor Weiss persuasively argues that society should invest such money into research and development of benign alternative sources, such as wind, solar, and geothermal, to meet public energy needs.[19]

Second, because the future needs for a nonrenewable resource remain inherently uncertain, prudent rationing – or budgeting – should be the norm of any allocation scheme. Since the dawn of civilization, humanity has metered its use of scarce resources as a strategy to sustain communities. As Professor Weiss concludes, "Certainly trustees should be forbidden to use up all known reserves of a given resource when no substitutes are available." Notably, the rationing strategy also works when a generally renewable resource, such as water, takes on nonrenewable features as a result of climate heating or other conditions. Water restrictions have become commonplace to manage scarce water supplies in drought-stricken cities worldwide, including in the United States.[20]

A form of rationing presents the most obvious response to the prospect of peak oil and climate danger; government should meter use of this problematic resource during a transition period aimed to aggressively develop nonnuclear renewable energy sources. Many politicians shudder to think of tightening the belt on their constituents' oil consumption, but climate disasters clearly demonstrate the rationing scenario as the lesser of two evils. History provides ample instances of oil production and consumption abruptly curtailed by government. The Oil Crisis of 1973 prompted forms of gas rationing. In World War II, the government rationed gas to citizens and limited the pleasure driving of nonessential vehicles. And in 1909, President Taft issued an emergency proclamation that swiftly ended private oil exploration on federal lands – just days after being alerted that oil companies were depleting reserves so quickly that the national supply would be drained within a few months, after which "the Government will be obliged to repurchase the very oil that it has practically given away." Whether a resource originates as nonrenewable (like oil and gas) or whether it becomes partially nonrenewable as a result of changing climate conditions (like water), the trustee's fiduciary obligation should require metering use of the scarce resource. Government must also prevent corporate monopolies to assure citizens equitable access to the resource during a time when transition to an alternative source can occur with all deliberate speed.[21]

A third principle seems obvious but warrants iteration. Use of nonrenewable resources should not cause ancillary damage to other valuable public trust assets. For example, if oil drilling cannot be safely conducted without harm to the oceans, it should not occur. Similarly, coal, oil, and gas production should be quickly phased out, as their emissions load the atmosphere with dangerous carbon dioxide. Use of these resources creates significant unavoidable damage that violates government's fiduciary responsibility to protect Nature's capital.

MAXIMIZING SOCIETAL VALUE OF TRUST ASSETS

The prior discussion explained how the doctrine of waste mediates resource use between present and future generations. For renewable resources, present generations must generally confine their use to the "interest" portion of the asset – the usufruct, or the income, so to speak. But what if that quotient is not enough to satisfy the demands of present users? Water, for example, presents a zero-sum game between competing users, because demand for water often exceeds availability. Similarly, what about nonrenewable resources that must be meted out over time? Natural resource laws do not satisfactorily address how to allocate valuable assets in a way that best serves society. Governments tend to allocate scarce resources on the basis of political power, or historical practice, or in haphazard fashion according to who arrives first in line at the permitting office. Oddly enough, few commentators have suggested any decision-making matrix to prioritize uses in a world of scarcity, even though that task remains ever more unavoidable as time progresses.

Leading cases demand that government trustees manage trust resources to "maximize their social and economic benefits to the people."[22] Three core precepts derived from existing precedent give content to this rule: (1) there can be no squander of the asset; (2) the asset must be used for its highest public purpose; and (3) trustees may not allocate public resources primarily to serve private purposes. These principles manifest most clearly in decisions governing the allocation of increasingly scarce water supplies.

Waste Not, Want Not: The Rule Against Squandering Valuable Resources

The first principle dates back to time immemorial in nearly all societies. It reflects abhorrence toward squandering valuable materials – the kind of waste that our grandparents despised. One leading treatise defines the ancient waste doctrine as prohibiting the "employment of resources prodigally or without any considerable return or effect." The prohibition also appears in international law: the World Charter for Nature provides, "Natural resources shall not be wasted."[23]

Professor Weiss notes that this sort of waste arises from inefficient resource extraction, of which rampant examples exist. Leaky irrigation ditches lose sizable amounts of water en route to farmers. Deep-sea fishing vessels drag huge nets indiscriminately across the ocean floor, killing many millions of tons of "bycatch" fish that are rejected each year. Clear-cutting harvest methods butcher entire forest landscapes, eradicating biodiversity and harming soils, to access certain trees that could be harvested moderately through selective harvest practices. Industrial open-pit mining gouges enormous swaths of land, leaving giant piles of toxic tailings and sending poisons into the watersheds. All reflect a society not practicing prudent and rational use of natural resources. But because industrial capitalism removes its production process from consumers, the general public has little idea of this gargantuan waste. Environmental permit systems institutionalize resource squander by utterly ignoring the basic question of whether the proposed use will be wasteful or its end product even useful.[24]

Allowing inefficient use (waste) of a trust asset contravenes the fiduciary trust duty to maximize its value. This duty of prudent management finds clearest expression in the allocation of water. Many water codes directly prohibit waste of water, and permit writers generally have authority to deny a proposed water use on that basis alone.[25] In practice, however, they rarely do. To meet the exigencies of resource scarcity, environmental law must internalize the waste prohibition as a fundamental tenant of trust management extending to all resources.

This approach should prohibit not only direct squander of resources but, just as important, the *collateral* squander of resources, which occurs when the pursuit of one resource destroys the natural capital of ancillary resources or entire ecosystems – without societal costs, benefits, and alternatives justifying the damage. Collateral squander occurs, for example, in Appalachian coal mining, where companies destroy mountains and streams to get coal. This type of squander also surfaces in nearly every pollution context – evident, for example, when a mill discharges toxins into a public waterway, or a coal-fired plant spews mercury pollution into the air and carbon dioxide into the atmosphere, or when a farmer applies pesticides that leach into drinking water wells.

The waste prohibition directs a necessary focus to alternative technologies and production methods. Often, even minimal inquiry can topple the legitimacy of longtime fouling practices. In Appalachia, for example, community groups point out that some of the very mountaintops slated for obliteration in pursuit of coal could support wind turbines to produce significant amounts of renewable energy into the far distant future. Coal River Mountain in West Virginia demonstrates the potential. Located in an area of Appalachia described by longtime residents as "almost heaven," this forested mountain rises more than 3,000 feet and may offer enough potential wind power to provide energy for 70,000 homes *perpetually*. Yet Massey Energy Company announced plans to blast out Coal River Mountain pursuant to state permits. The choice between destroying a mountain for a finite supply of dirty coal or using its hallowed reaches for a perpetual wind supply wholly escapes environmental law and its narrow permit provisions. A Nature's Trust approach would demand inquisition of colossal waste and force alternatives to the devastating practices that typify natural resources management today.[26]

The Highest and Best Societal Use

Competing demands for a resource nearly always exist. Cases dealing with water allocation make clear that trustees must achieve the "highest and best use" of public resources so as to maximize their value to society. The current environmental regulatory system, however, ignores the value (or non-value) of a resource use. It issues permits to pollute with no inquiry as to whether any public purpose justifies the harm. This approach cannot prove functional in times of ecological scarcity. Trustees will have to rethink allocation and management schemes to prioritize various uses in order to ensure that the most urgent needs of society stand first in line. In its leading public trust opinion, the Hawaii Supreme Court called for "rigorous and affirmative" public interest review in face of inadequate water supplies.[27]

Existing water law offers a model to draw from in creating a hierarchy of uses for public trust assets. Most states accord supreme ranking to domestic uses, and particularly drinking water uses, suggesting survival support as the highest "public use." The Hawaii Supreme Court also recognized in-stream water conservation as a paramount use necessary for ecological function; this departs from an outdated and rightly discarded view that only consumptive uses (ones that draw water out of the stream) can be "beneficial."[28]

A trust focus on the public benefits of resource use should extend beyond water to the full realm of natural resource management. This, however, requires debunking a powerful myth about the capitalistic endeavor and mass production, namely that markets will determine social value and that all products, no matter what their purpose, create social benefit (and so much so that they all deserve a permit to pollute the public's commonwealth). Not unlike Dr. Seuss's story of the Once-ler in *The Lorax* who cut down the magnificent Truffula trees to produce massive amounts of unnecessary thneeds – destroying the waters, forest, air, fish, and wildlife in the process – billions of marginally useful products now flood today's market and leave ravaged ecosystems at their site of production. Few question whether their value justifies eradicating trust resources that support human survival. Corporate marketing campaigns banish the curiosity by elevating all manner of merchandise and junk to an exalted commercial position. When plucking products off store shelves, consumers generally lack the full suite of information necessary to make decisions regarding sensible use of their public trust assets. Instead, they rely on government to manage their air, waters, wildlife, soils, and other resources prudently so as not to squander these valuable assets for trivial purposes. But environmental law, as we have seen, obviates this logical presumed care by erasing social utility from the administrative equation altogether. The frontiers of public trust law must necessarily search for the "highest and best" use of the trust resource.

Such a test logically demands a trustee to consider alternatives to proposals that damage or consume public trust assets. Alternatives analysis has always formed a central part of rational decision making, but for the most part, modern environmental law ignores it at the final decision stage. While the National Environmental Policy Act (NEPA) requires agencies to engage in a pre-decisional search for alternatives, it does nothing to *force* government to choose an environmentally benign alternative (as Chapter 5 explained). In fact, the propensity of most agencies remains to choose resource-damaging actions that serve their political allies.

Many polluting uses of air, water, and soil would find little or no justification under a trust approach. Usually, a corporation pollutes these valuable assets simply to capitalize on a free repository for waste disposal – hardly a use of public property for maximum societal value. In the Clean Water Act, Congress made it quite clear that the highest and best uses of the nation's rivers were for fishing, swimming, and drinking water purposes.[29] Rivers can accommodate a multitude of such benign co-uses by huge populations. Pollution, on the other hand, amounts to de facto privatization of a public resource by making it unfit for the public purposes to which it is naturally suited. It narrows the myriad of possible uses to one that leaves unclaimed harm.

An inquiry into alternatives can often reveal benign substitute processes that would protect the public resource. Many leading observers submit that a new industrial revolution could nearly eliminate waste and pollution from production processes, a matter taken up in Chapter 13. The Environmental Protection Agency (EPA), however, still clings to an outdated permitting approach that focuses on treatment technologies for the toxins and pollutants used by industry. As Craig Collins notes in *Toxic Loopholes*, "Laws that target end-of-the-pipe releases ... are extremely costly and complex to oversee, hard to obey, easy to defy and do not sufficiently protect people or the environment. Instead of preventing pollution in the first place, this approach generates an onerous regulatory regime with few actual benefits to show for it."[30]

The same antiquated approach permeates chemical regulation. As Chapter 2 explained, agencies use expensive risk assessments to justify certain levels of "safe" chemical exposure that they deem acceptable for the public. Such assessments leave considerable risk borne by communities. Public health professor Joel Tickner criticizes the approach as "quantifying and analyzing problems rather than trying to solve or prevent them." Contending that the money spent in expensive risk assessments would be much better applied to eliminating chemicals in the first place, he notes that while "a typical two-year cancer bioassay for a single chemical may cost several million dollars, currently the entire federal government budget for green chemistry – the design of safer and cleaner chemicals – is about the same." Agencies continue to treat toxic technologies and chemicals as "inevitable."[31]

The more effective and often cost-saving alternative seeks to minimize toxins at the outset. To this end, Collins urges a revamp of the regulatory system based on principles of toxic source reduction and zero waste. The challenge becomes particularly urgent for Persistent, Bioaccumulative Toxins (PBTs). These chemicals – called the "worst of the worst" by the Washington Department of Ecology – persist for many decades (or much longer) in the environment and accumulate up the food chain, becoming ever more toxic as they concentrate in animals and humans. PBTs have become ubiquitous. They poison babies prior to birth and create a toxic legacy for even their grandchildren. Studies expose many instances of senseless exposure that could have been prevented simply by revamping an outdated production process. For example, the chlorine bleaching process (still used by some pulp and paper mills) emits dioxin, a highly dangerous PBT that lodges in river sediments, bioaccumulates in fish, and then poses a significant cancer risk to those humans who eat the fish – all damage wrought for the purpose of *white* toilet paper and other paper products. While a Total Chlorine Free (TCF) bleaching method presents a feasible non-dioxin alternative, it is not universally used. "[T]he spigot remains wide open" for too many PBTs, as the Washington Toxics Coalition charges. Its pioneering report, *Visualizing Zero*, proposes a comprehensive regulatory strategy to end PBT contamination. The approach illustrates what could become a cutting edge of public trust analysis – forcing a production alternatives inquiry as part of the trustee's duty to maximize the value of the public's trust assets.[32]

The Scrutiny of Private Use

Leading cases set forth a third fiduciary principle that limits the use of public assets for private gain. The principle assumes that when private parties use public trust resources for singular purposes, they do not necessarily maximize value to the public as the trust requires. As the Supreme Court in *Geer v. Connecticut* said, the trust is "for the benefit of the people, and not ... for the benefit of private individuals as distinguished from the public good." Carrying forth this basic tenet the Supreme Court of Hawaii declared:

> While ... the public trust may allow grants of private interests in trust resources under certain circumstances, they in no way establish private commercial use as

among the public purposes protected by the trust.... Although its purpose has evolved over time, the public trust has never been understood to safeguard rights of exclusive use for private commercial gain. Such an interpretation, indeed, eviscerates the trust's basic purpose of reserving the resource for use and access by the general public without preference or restriction.[33]

The public trust does not establish a blanket prohibition against private use of public resources, but it does require trustees to allocate resources entirely out of consideration for public good rather than to serve private ends. Thus the motivations, monetary gain, and pecuniary interests of the private user cannot factor into the decision. The trust frame consequently inverts many of the arguments private entrepreneurs make in their appeals to government permit writers. Characteristically trying to pressure officials into allowing their proposals, applicants emphasize their expected economic losses should the permits not issue. Their appeals carry traction in a political frame in which the specter of profits often commandeers agency decisions. Changing the frame makes a difference. Viewed through the trust lens, the applicant's projected profits stand not only irrelevant but flatly inappropriate for consideration by the public trustee.

Nevertheless, private applicants often style their arguments at least superficially to meet the public purpose test by promising to bring jobs and tax revenues to the community. But in the typical circumstance, this "economic boost" argument blurs far too amorphous to form a valid premise for a trust decision. Applicants rarely provide legal assurances to back up their ambitious jobs-and-taxes rhetoric, so nothing prevents a bait and switch after the permit issues. Some modern public trust cases take the sensible approach of simply dismissing claims of jobs and tax revenues because they dither too remote and uncertain to offer any real grounding for a trust allocation decision. In the landmark *Mono Lake* case, the California Supreme Court said that basing public trust decisions on claims of general economic benefit would "in practical effect ... impose no restrictions on the state's ability to allocate trust property." Drawing from its tideland trust precedent, it asserted that "no one could contend that the state could grant tidelands free of the trust merely because the grant served some public purpose, such as increasing tax revenues, or because the grantee might put the property to a commercial use."[34]

In similar fashion, the Hawaii Supreme Court rejected an argument that public trust principles protect "private use of resources for economic development." Instead, it subjected private uses to a *"higher level* of scrutiny," stating that "[t]he burden ultimately lies with those seeking or approving such uses to justify them in light of the purposes protected by the trust."[35] This test actually aims to harness private enterprise to promote the public good – a long-standing objective of public economic policy. It contrasts notably with the current political discretion framework, which regularly promotes private schemes that harm the public good.

Following a trust approach, government must not allow use of public assets to serve exclusively private purposes. Private use must be justified by a tangible public purpose and need. But the system of allocating scarce resources has not always followed these rules. For example, states have doled out Western water largely on the first-come-first-served basis, favoring early uses regardless of whether they actually served public purposes. Public trust cases accordingly make clear that state water agencies hold a duty to review formerly granted appropriation permits and revoke them when public purposes demand. As the Hawaii court admonished, "The continuing authority of the state over its water resources precludes any grant or assertion of vested rights to use water to the detriment of public trust purposes." Logically, the same approach should govern all natural resource permits.[36]

PHASING OUT AND RETIRING PERMITS

Meeting these fiduciary obligations will require agencies to significantly curtail new pollution permits as well as design a process to retire many existing permits. Observing the crucial boundary between natural capital and yield, permits must confine pollution, extraction, and use of natural resources to the scope of what Nature can readily assimilate without substantial impairment to the *res*. While many agency staffers today undoubtedly think of the permit system as a permanent fixture of environmental law, Congress expressly regarded it as a transition tool, evidenced most clearly in the language of the Clean Water Act (CWA), which established the National Pollution Discharge Elimination System. The CWA's opening provision declared that permits to pollute waterways were not to be issued after 1985. As the Senate Report accompanying the legislation explained, "[T]his legislation would clearly establish that no one has the right to pollute – that pollution continues because of technological limits, not because of any inherent rights to use the nation's waterways for the purpose of disposing of wastes." Even decades later, EPA and state agencies still roundly ignore this express no-pollution goal. Nevertheless, because permits do not confer a permanent right to pollute, an agency can retire them without encroaching on private property rights.[37]

Ending pollution and resource damage would parallel a turning point in public lands policy that occurred more than 100 years ago, when Congress abruptly ended frenzied disposition and privatization of public lands and required retention of public lands for public purposes. Implemented through a number of statutes, this steadfast retention policy secured the federal areas that collectively make up a third of the nation's land base today, including the national forests, parks, refuges, and monuments. In quite similar fashion, the environmental legislation of the 1970s signaled a retention era for *ecology* in its abundant form. The agencies dawdle four decades late in administering this policy direction.[38]

In large part, the agencies' delay in phasing out pollution can be explained by their fear of political backlash. Fouling industries fiercely protest any agency action to stop pollution, often charging that it works unfairness for them. But corporate objections must be taken in context. It will always seem unfair to draw the line now rather than later, and fairness arguments never get easier. And of course, many corporations have unclean hands; their pollution has often harmed those who gain the least from their activities. Fairness to society, rather than fairness to corporations, becomes the more pressing matter. Manifestly, pollution must end at some point or humans will be left with, in the words of the Philippines Supreme Court, "a parched earth incapable of supporting life."[39] Polluting industries that poison public resources no longer function as the essential plough horses of the economy, but instead trudge as dinosaurs of a bygone era. The structured phase-out of pollution permits will clear a path for new clean businesses that can promote economic prosperity without causing peril to ecology, as Chapter 13 explains in greater detail.

Of course, any no-pollution policy must come to terms with the role of individuals (as distinguished from industries). Overpopulation magnifies even minute forms of damage into colossal problems. Prescription drugs flushed down the toilet en masse cause great harm to aquatic life. Thousands of wood-burning household stoves emitting particulates in an area can send asthmatic children to the hospital. Emissions from automobiles pollute the atmosphere with carbon dioxide. As millions of miniscule contributions overwhelm ecosystems, overpopulation has become an overarching environmental policy issue. While equitable solutions lie beyond the scope of this book, societies must recognize the need for bringing population into balance with resources and regulate micro-pollution until the world population declines to sustainable levels.

But abating the harm from industries and individuals marks only a beginning point, perhaps an illusory one at that. In a world of scant and tenuously functioning ecological resources, agencies cannot hope to meet their fiduciary obligations simply by putting the brakes on massive harm. They must create programs to rebuild the public assets damaged over the past several decades. The next section engages the fiduciary duty to restore damaged assets.

THE DUTY OF RESTORATION

Trust law requires the trustee to restore lost wealth in the *res* resulting from a breach of trust or third-party damage. This basic principle seeks to return the beneficiaries to their rightful position. Several environmental laws reflect a restoration duty as well. The Endangered Species Act, for example, calls for recovering imperiled species. The Clean Water Act announces the goal of restoring the nation's waters. The Comprehensive Environmental Response, Cleanup, Liability Act and parts of the

Resource Conservation Recovery Act promote the cleanup of hazardous waste – a form of land restoration. Though long ignored, the duty to restore the natural trust rests firmly embedded in the law as a sovereign fiduciary obligation.[40]

The urgency of climate crisis and other planetary threats compels an about-face in the bureaucratic emphasis of administrative trustees: as agencies retire permits to pollute, they must redirect the massive funding of permit programs into restoration efforts. Such a change would leverage the taxpayers' money in a shift to create natural wealth rather than fund natural loss. Multilateral restoration efforts already drive cleanup of the Hudson River, the removal of large dams in the Klamath Basin, the restoration of the Great Lakes, and a host of other endeavors. An agency shift from permitting damage to restoring ecosystems significantly recasts government's role in local communities – from an oppressive adversary whose policies threaten the fundamental health and well-being of residents to a local partner reviving natural infrastructure for the common benefit of all.

The real issue becomes not where to draw the line against further resource damage – that line was passed long ago – but where to draw the line on ambitious restoration goals. What is the fiduciary restoration imperative owed to present and future citizens? Should one contemplate, for example, the restoration of New York City? And how does one reconcile less-than-full restoration with the strict fiduciary obligation that requires making the beneficiaries whole again? The answer must lie in "reasonableness," a ubiquitous standard that appears across nearly all legal contexts. Dismantling thriving cities or necessary built infrastructure would impose clear harm to humans and would not serve the basic trust purpose of protecting human survival and welfare – therefore, it would not be reasonable or feasible. Some scenarios of restoration stay impossible on that basis alone.[41]

But the context in which "reasonableness" operates can rapidly change. For example, scientists warn of significant sea level rise by the end of the century. A rise of just 1 meter threatens 145 million people who live along coastlines, many in huge metropolises. Long before Superstorm Sandy struck in 2012, the New York Museum of Modern Art solicited engineering designs to prepare New York City for a sea level rise of 2 feet or more. One of the leading proposals would create buffers of wetlands and marsh around the city, cultivate oyster farms (which once flourished in the area), and establish permeable coastlines outside the city. The design envisions rebuilding streets in low-lying areas to allow the high tide in, as well as ripping up pavement and installing vegetation in its place to absorb water. Battery Park would essentially turn back into a wetland. Beyond its creative practicality, the design shows that trustees must think well beyond past conventions in confronting the realities now upon us in a strikingly new ecological age.[42]

A pathbreaking textbook edited by F. Stuart Chapin, III and colleagues points the way toward restoration through an approach known as "resilience-based ecosystem stewardship." The strategy grows out of three underlying premises. First, realistic restoration goals must hit a moving target and calibrate to a "trajectory of change" rather than to historic conditions. The foundational "steady state" assumption that characteristically guided scientists in the past has cracked. Assuming that Nature evolved slowly, scientists used to design their ecosystem recovery goals to restore historic conditions or at least protect remaining ecological function. But as the authors explain, "It is no longer possible to manage systems so that they will remain the same as in the recent past." Planetary heating, for example, will push entire habitat ranges into new climate zones. Second, a new vision must center on a concept of "resilience." Resilience-based planning seeks to protect ecological linchpins that hold together natural systems, an objective the authors deem "crucial to the future of humanity and the Earth System." While past recovery goals focused on individual assets, attention must now shift to "whole ecosystems that provide a suite of ecosystem services rather than a single resource such as fish or trees." Management must sustain the "*functional* properties of systems that are important to society, and to do so under conditions where the system itself is constantly changing." Third, a new focus on basic human needs and survival must drive future restoration efforts. While past recovery efforts generally ignored human needs, climate disruption creates an altogether new imperative. As the authors emphasize, "We must understand the world, region, or community as a *social-ecological system*."[43]

The fundamental transition from steady-state management to a resilience-recovery strategy presents a parallel challenge for environmental law: moving from a regulatory regime that drives ecological harm to a paradigm of legal obligation focused on protecting and recovering Earth's basic life systems. As explained in Chapter 7, the trust doctrine adapts to the ever-evolving circumstances of society. Much in kinship with "resilience based ecosystem stewardship," Nature's Trust urges a holistic reorientation that shifts the focus from individual assets to the full "ecological *res*" and the suite of life support services it provides.

Trust principles prioritize atmospheric recovery as the most urgent environmental imperative on the planet, for if Earth crosses a tipping point into runaway heating, no amount of resilience-based ecosystem stewardship can save the conditions needed for human survival. Recovery entails drawing down atmospheric greenhouse gas levels as rapidly as possible to achieve climate equilibrium. Leading scientists have developed a prescription calling for massive reforestation and soil measures to draw down 100 gigatons of carbon dioxide from the atmosphere over time. This must, of course, happen simultaneously with aggressive phase-out of carbon emissions, reaching a 6 percent annual reduction beginning in 2013. As Dr. Jim Hansen has warned, "[D]elay in undertaking sharp reductions in emissions will undermine any realistic chance of preserving a habitable climate system."[44] Chapter 10 further discusses this global atmospheric trust duty and the atmospheric trust litigation brought by youth to enforce it.

RECOUPING NATURAL RESOURCE DAMAGES

Restoring the depleted ecological trust requires massive funds. Trustees have an affirmative obligation to recoup monetary damages against third parties that harm or destroy trust assets. This duty helps ensure that the beneficiaries will be made whole for loss or damage of their property. In the public trust context, the duty demands recovery of natural resource damages (NRDs).

This duty lodges in both the common law and statutes. Damages provided by statutes address the full array of assets in the trust, including air, wildlife, fish, soils, waters, and other natural resources. In the United States, a detailed methodology developed by the Department of Interior assigns a monetary value to these assets as a basis for calculating damages. Statutes designate the federal government, states, and tribes as sovereign trustees able to assert NRD claims. Using these legal authorities, trustees have recovered damages for harm from oil spills and mining.[45]

But overall, government trustees remain delinquent as to this duty as well. While private trustees have the well-settled authority and *duty* to seek damages against third parties that caused harm to the trust *res*, attempts to recover the public's natural resource damages have been notably few. Though at least one state supreme court has underscored a government obligation to recoup NRDs, little attention has focused on whether citizen beneficiaries can hold their government trustees liable for failure to seek natural resource damages. Trust logic assumes they should be able to. As one treatise explains, all property owners have a right "to have third persons refrain from injuring or appropriating the subject of [the] property right." Recognizing the danger of recalcitrant trustees, private trust law allows beneficiaries to sue an indolent trustee who neglects to bring a suit for damage to trust property (and a beneficiary may even sue the third-party wrongdoer where the trustee fails to do so, as long as the suit also names the trustee as a defendant).[46]

One complication to NRD recovery, however, emerges from federal statutory provisions that immunize polluters from liability for actions authorized by federal permits. When granting a permit, federal law essentially gives the damaging activity a shield from liability, regardless of how devastating the consequences to the people's trust. From the polluters' perspective, the rule can be justified as a matter of fairness: the government should not issue a permit and then sue for subsequent damage allowed by it. But from the trust perspective, the rule makes little sense when so many permits have been issued in contravention of the fiduciary duty to protect the trust in the first place. It is one matter to let polluters harm and destroy assets in the trust; it is yet another to let them do it for free. In theory, the "polluter pays" principle should require compensation for all damage to the trust, permitted or not. Canada has adopted that principle in its environmental law.[47]

Even current law does not apply the permit shield where the pollution falls outside the parameters of the permit. Moreover, tribes may sue for damage allowed by permit if the federal government violated its trust obligation toward them in issuing the permit, which seems to be frequently the case. One of the most compelling natural resource damage claims would compensate for harm wrought by greenhouse gas polluters. Depending on judicial interpretation of the permit shield, one can imagine entire industry sectors forced to pay compensation for their damage to Nature's Trust.[48]

ALIENATING THE TRUST

A final substantive duty within the bundle of fiduciary obligations deals with "alienating" property from the public trust – that is, conveying public trust land or resources into private ownership. While Chapter 14 deals extensively with this and other aspects of the private/public interface of property law, this section summarizes some general points. To begin with, the *sine qua non* of public trust law guards against the privatization of public trust assets. This in no way denigrates private ownership, which creates a cherished realm of privacy, security, and enrichment. Much property can be held under private title without any impact on public interests. But courts have long recognized that parcels vital to society should remain in public ownership.

Historic cases iterate public trust principles that determine when submersible trust lands may be conveyed into private ownership. The Supreme Court inaugurated this doctrinal lineage in *Illinois Central* when it held that the state of Illinois violated the public trust by transferring the shoreline of Lake Michigan to a private railroad company. The Court stated, "The harbor of Chicago is of immense value to the people of the state of Illinois ... and the idea that its legislature can deprive the state of control over its bed and waters, and place the same in the hands of a private corporation ... is a proposition that cannot be defended."[49]

The *Illinois Central* Court delineated a two-part test in which alienation of land from the trust to private parties can be appropriate: (1) where trustees make the grant in aid of navigation, commerce, or other trust purposes; and (2) where the grant does not cause "substantial impairment" to the public interest in the lands and waters remaining. Some modern courts have added yet another element, finding a public trust violation when the "primary purpose" of a legislative grant is to benefit a private interest. The judicial approach can be quite strict. As the Illinois federal district court declared in *Lake Michigan*, "[A]ny attempt by the state to relinquish its power over a public resource should be invalidated under the doctrine."[50] The legality of alienating valuable trust assets becomes ever more indefensible as society's needs escalate in relation to an natural trust already grossly diminished.

This chapter summarized the substantive fiduciary obligations that infuse government with duties aimed to protect the people's trust from despoliation. Of course, the history of natural resource management in the United States (as well as in many other nations) has largely been a story of trust violations that have left the trust bankrupt, or nearly so. In the private financial world, bankruptcies bring on corporate reorganizations and restructurings. Having pushed Nature's Trust into the equivalent condition, environmental agencies now require a full, supervised overhaul. Remaining assets demand jealous protection by public trustees because they provide the last base from which to build a vital restoration effort needed to sustain life on Earth. Flexibility for communities and economies must be found not in schemes to further degrade resources, but rather in the genius of social innovations that can increase efficiency, reduce waste, and help society adjust to extreme ecological scarcity. The next chapter takes the fiduciary obligation a step further by analyzing its procedural requirements.

9

From Bureaucrats to Trustees

The current political frame controlling environmental law turns many government officials into pawns of moneyed power, as prior chapters explained. The frame allows vast and amorphous discretion that proves highly susceptible to corruption; it bends too often to the influence of profiteering industries. Behind the facade of law, such discretion repeatedly dupes the citizens while permitting corporations to pillage the public commonwealth. In contrast, the fiduciary role stands exacting and rigorous, wrapped in time-tested procedural duties. Justice Benjamin Cardozo once said: "A trustee is held to something stricter than the morals of the market place. Not honesty alone, but the punctilio of an honor the most sensitive."[1] Fiduciary duties require the trustee to act strictly on behalf of the public beneficiaries.

Steadfast and unbending loyalty to the beneficiaries remains the essence of any trust. It has always been recognized that a trustee holds tremendous power over the assets and that without strict procedural duties, he might abuse that power to serve his own self-interest. The fiduciary duty thus places clear boundaries on what the trustee can and cannot do. As Justice Cardozo explained, "Many forms of conduct permissible in a workaday world for those acting at arm's length, are forbidden to those bound by fiduciary ties.... Only thus has the level of conduct for fiduciaries been kept at a level higher than that trodden by the crowd."[2]

This chapter delves into the procedural duties that should bind government trustees in managing Nature's Trust. Long before the modern administrative state, commentators punctuated the fiduciary duties of public servants with the well-worn phrase: "When a man assumes a public trust, he should consider himself as public property." Imported from private trust law, procedural duties work to ensure that government's awesome control over the people's natural assets advances the interests of the citizenry rather than singular private interests. While all government officers take an oath of office to uphold the public interest, the fiduciary duty of loyalty rises as an elevated duty incumbent on those officials managing *public trust property*. These apply both to legislators (as primary trustees) and their agents (agency officials). Fiduciary expectations raise the bar for any public official. Author Peter Brown notes: "[T]he trustee model ... could transform our politics. It would give elected officials a renewed sense of mission. It would give citizens a fresh reason to expect integrity from their government."[3]

Procedurally, a trustee has five main duties: (1) maintain uncompromised loyalty to the beneficiaries; (2) adequately supervise agents; (3) exercise good faith and reasonable skill in managing the assets; (4) use caution in managing the assets; and (5) furnish information to the beneficiaries regarding trust management and asset health. These duties run to government as a whole, adapted to the legislatures and agencies each uniquely as the following discussion explains. Existing ethical codes incorporate some of these duties, but they do not reach far enough or deep enough. Moreover, their free-standing nature fails to impart a legal frame that raises a "punctilio of an honor" associated with public office.

LEAD US NOT INTO TEMPTATION: THE DUTY OF UNDIVIDED LOYALTY

Justice Cardozo described an "unbending and inveterate" judicial tradition of enforcing fiduciary standards. Courts strictly enforce the duty of undivided loyalty so as to deter personal self-interest from influencing trust management decisions. As George T. Bogert explains, self-interested trust management would be "highly dangerous" given the degree of control a trustee has over property. Accordingly, courts require the trustees to avoid all conflicts of interest so as to eliminate even the *possibility* for any temptation to enter into decisions concerning the trust. Thus a court will invalidate a trust transaction tainted by a conflict of interest regardless of whether the trustee acted in good faith or whether the transaction was, or was not, actually detrimental to the beneficiaries. This approach banishes not only self-interested conduct but also conduct motivated to enrich a third person. As one commentator explains the judicial reasoning behind these rigorous rules:

> [H]uman nature will cause any person to favor his or her personal interests over the interests of another, and it is this assumption of disloyalty that gives rise to the strict prohibitions of trustee conflicts of interest.... [A]s the beneficiary is assumed to be on the losing end of any conflict with the fiduciary's personal interests, loyalty can be preserved only if the relationship is stripped of the possibility of such conflicts. *The duty of loyalty is, therefore, not the duty to resist temptation but to eliminate temptation, as the former is assumed to be impossible.* The trustee is at the pinnacle of fiduciary duty and is held to the highest standards.... [T]he trustee's duty of loyalty will be paramount and unforgiving, at least one hundred percent.[4]

The Supreme Court brought this expectation of loyalty into the public trust context when it declared in *Geer v. Connecticut*: "[T]he power ... is to be exercised, like all other powers of government, as a trust for the benefit of the people, and not as a prerogative for the advantage of the government as distinct from the people."[5] When government trustees use their offices to favor anyone other than the beneficiary public, they breach the duty of loyalty. This remains true whether the benefit accrues to a third-party industry applicant, the bureaucracy, or the official herself. The trust aims to remove public natural assets from the inherent vulnerability of "political" decisions that tend to favor influential parties over the public.

A New View of "Stakeholders"

Part I of this book demonstrated how agencies routinely ignore their duty of loyalty. Agencies habitually make decisions to serve their own bureaucratic interests or those of third parties – often private industry. Professor Gerald Torres describes the implicit danger this holds for natural resource management: "The essence of government corruption is to use the power of the state to convert public assets for personal gain." Taken to an extreme, the flaunting of loyalty can lead to an agency displaying dangerous institutional disregard for civic duty and ethics. For example, a sordid relationship between the Mineral Management Service (MMS) and the oil industry (described in Chapter 3) led the Office of Inspector General to describe a "culture of ethical failure" and an agency "rife with conflicts of interest." Even exposure of such extraordinary transgressions, however, does nothing to shatter the political paradigm that excuses daily breaches of loyalty. Even though agencies sometimes remove officials engaged in blatant corruption, these measures become swallowed up by the same political paradigm that continues to devour the trust.[6]

Agency public relations offices spend a great deal of effort seeking to validate the existing paradigm – and thereby suppress any duty of loyalty – in the public's mind. Constant reference to private industry groups as "stakeholders" in agency decisions casts industry as a proper cohort of government. Even the biggest polluters and land mutilators have gained honored status with agencies: they receive agency awards for good corporate behavior, sit on government advisory groups, and enjoy special outreach by agency officials when a proposed regulation affects their industry. As Chapter 1 revealed, some of the highest government officials enjoy a perfidious coziness with industry executives.

The very notion of industry "stakeholder" refutes the trust approach, which more properly views polluters as marauders of the trust. The primary fiduciary duty to protect the *res* for the beneficiaries requires trustees to maintain a scrupulous, ever-distant, and suspicious demeanor toward parties that could damage the trust. The duty of loyalty demands that a trustee "refrain from placing himself in a position where his personal interest or that of a third person does or may conflict with the interest of the beneficiaries."[7] This rule should provoke considerable wariness toward any collaboration with plunderers of the trust through "stakeholder" partnerships. While industry has a right to engage public processes just as citizens do, the practices of captured agencies trespass appropriate boundaries of fiduciary behavior, as earlier chapters explained. The discussion now turns to strategies for instilling a duty of loyalty in both Congress and agencies.

Congress: Political Contributions and Legislative Horse-Trading

The political frame puts legislative responsibility up "for sale." Congressional officials regularly accept campaign contributions from industries that expect favorable treatment from their decisions. Evaluated against the trust duty, a legislator's acceptance of such campaign contributions amounts to a palpable breach of loyalty because it engenders obvious self-interest: if the legislator does not use her lawmaking position to offer paybacks to the industries that supported her, the money will dry up in the next campaign. The incentive for self-dealing – exactly the kind of temptation that the trust abhors – could hardly be more blatant. It should not be surprising that legislators funded by the timber industry push laws to clear-cut public lands, that those funded by the coal industry obstruct mining reform, that those funded by big agribusiness vote against pesticide regulation, and so on. Popular culture understands this all too well. The problem is not that this corruption goes unrecognized, but that it has become institutionalized. Seemingly resigned to it, citizens remain unaware of any other paradigm that would yield a higher standard of ethical behavior from their government. Worse, the U.S. Supreme Court's 2010 decision in *Citizens United* allows corporations to make massive donations to political campaigns – a holding that surely pounds another nail in the coffin of democracy.[8]

The public trust paradigm contemplates a fundamentally different approach, at least in the realm of natural resources management. As Chapter 6 noted, when legislators preside over natural resource decisions, they sit not merely as elected officials but as trustees of public property. In this capacity, they remain bound by the strict duty of loyalty toward the beneficiaries – namely, to present and future citizens, not special interests. This heightened standard of ethical behavior and loyalty finds justification in the fact that future generations hold legal property rights under the trust yet enjoy no political voting power in the legislative process. The duty of loyalty would prohibit a legislator from voting on a particular resource issue if he or she accepted significant campaign contributions from an industry that had a tangible stake in the outcome of that issue. The duty of loyalty frontally challenges and delegitimizes precisely the political behavior that now regularly subverts the public interest.

This duty also prohibits legislative "vote trading" on environmental matters. Legislators often cast a particular vote on one issue in order to gain a vote from a colleague on a completely unrelated issue. This pervasive vote trading proves poisonous for public policy making because it causes legislators to cast their votes in ways motivated by reasons quite apart from the merits of the proposal at hand. As a per se matter, a legislator who trades a vote on a natural resource issue in order to influence the outcome of a wholly unrelated issue does not make a decision on behalf of the beneficiaries' best interest in the immediate issue and thereby violates the duty of loyalty owed to the public.

Actualizing the duty of loyalty in natural resource lawmaking requires much thought and undoubtedly new processes. The challenge becomes more difficult because legislators have little incentive to upset the political cart that peddles their jobs. Apart from public campaign financing, a more immediate method for curbing undue influence and corruption might arise from disclosure and recusal principles. At the very least, these should apply to members of committees that regularly deal with natural resources so as to ensure the highest standard of public fiduciary care.

A substantial body of law already imposes reasonable rules of recusal for the elected judiciary, which holds itself to strict prohibitions against conflict of interest. These could readily be adapted for legislators who receive contributions from corporations, as the rules strike at the same target in both contexts: conflicts of interest that could infect decision making with bias. In a case involving the coal giant, Massey Corporation, the Supreme Court laid out the bare-minimum constitutional parameters of required due process, presenting a test that dovetails with the loyalty test in the trust context: "The Court asks not whether the judge is actually, subjectively biased, but whether the average judge in his position is 'likely' to be neutral, or whether there is an unconstitutional 'potential for bias.'" Not all contributions to judicial campaigns pose a concern; some remain "too remote and insubstantial to violate constitutional constraints." The analysis must focus on "the contribution's relative size in comparison to the total amount of money contributed to the campaign, the total amount spent in the election, and the apparent effect such contribution had on the outcome of the election." The analysis does not ask whether direct corruption (actual vote buying that involves monetary exchange) occurred. Instead, even a "serious, objective risk of actual bias" requires recusal. In *Massey*, the Court had no trouble finding circumstances that offended constitutional due process guarantees. There, the president of Massey Coal Corporation, Don Blankenship, had played a pivotal role in getting Judge Benjamin elected to the West Virginia Supreme Court of Appeals at the very time that an appeal from a hefty judgment against his company was pending. The Supreme Court determined: "Though not a bribe or criminal influence, Justice Benjamin would nevertheless feel a debt of gratitude to Blankenship for his extraordinary efforts to get him elected." A similar standard should require legislative recusal on natural resource decisions. In addition, another, more basic ethical rule for judicial conduct should govern legislative trustee functions as well: the general requirement to "avoid impropriety and the appearance of impropriety."[9]

By providing a new frame through which to evaluate government, the trust may help sharpen citizens' intuitive understandings about what elected officials should and should not be doing. Using the trust frame, populist outrage over *Citizens United* could force institutional change. Apart from citizen demands, however, the judiciary should invalidate legislative action that violates the trust duty of loyalty (this seemingly converges with constitutional concepts of due process as well). When a court finds a breach of loyalty, it should order a legislative remand and send the matter back to the legislature to reconsider it with protections against bias in the next round. Professor Torres notes that a legislative remand provides an appropriate remedy in public trust cases where statutes violate the fiduciary duty. Professor Sax also highlights the remedy in breach-of-trust cases. Such remand does not overstep the proper judicial role, because the court does not decide *what* the law should be, but only that the lawmaking process comport with sidewalls of fiduciary obligation that protect public assets against self-interest and corruption on the part of the trustees.[10]

The Administrative Duty of Loyalty

Applying the duty of loyalty to the administrative branch would seem less problematic than applying it to the congressional branch if only because the former does not run directly off campaign contributions. But in many respects, the challenge of eliminating disloyal behavior in the executive branch stands more difficult, because improper pressures bear in subtle ways. As Part I of this book explained, a multitude of laws already impress a duty of public loyalty. A regulation setting forth ethical obligations of public servants begins by stating: "Public service is a public trust. Each employee has a responsibility to the United States Government and its citizens to place loyalty to the Constitution, laws and ethical principles above private gain." The regulation limits a plethora of behaviors, such as deciding matters in which an employee has a financial interest, accepting gifts as part of his or her employment, and even seeking new positions with entities that could be subject to regulation by the employee's agency. But despite these anti-corruption protections, the political frame in which most agencies operate today breeds a culture of temptation. Trust law, as noted, aims to "keep all trustees *out of temptation*." Public trust law, then, must create a new institutional culture that rejects commonly practiced, but nevertheless wrongful, behavior – not unlike past campaigns aimed to eradicate sexual harassment or discrimination in the workplace.[11]

The effort entails ferreting out the sources of political pressure on agency personnel, staff scientists, and regulatory decision makers. Measures will vary from agency to agency. Various watchdog groups have offered general administrative tools to address three basic goals: (1) eliminate the temptation for self-interested behavior; (2) uncover breaches of loyalty where they occur and establish appropriate penalties for breaches; and (3) invalidate any decision infected by politicized decision making. The General Accounting Office (GAO) and Offices of Inspector General also stand positioned to make overall institutional reform recommendations.

ELIMINATING TEMPTATION

Reform efforts to eliminate temptation must focus on the portals of discretion through which political players try to influence agency decisions, as described in Chapter 3. Sometimes overhaul of the basic structure of an entire agency becomes necessary to eliminate an institutional conflict of interest. For example, the BP oil calamity prompted Interior Secretary Salazar to restructure the Minerals Management Service (MMS), an agency that had long wallowed in corruption as a result of enmeshment with the oil industry. Conflicts of interest were deeply embedded in MMS's bureaucratic structure. Not only was the agency responsible for environmental oversight of drilling operations, but it was also the oil industry's close partner in maximizing revenues from public oil reserves. When the drive for profits dominated environmental oversight functions, the agency waived key safety and study requirements, including ones for the Deepwater Horizon rig responsible for the BP oil spill in 2010. Even as oil still spewed from the ocean floor, Salazar rightly decided to split the agency so as to sever its environmental policing function from its royalty collection and leasing function. But the correction, woefully overdue, should not have required catastrophe to materialize. Proactive restructuring should be the goal for many agencies. For example, much like the MMS, the U.S. Forest Service struggles with its own internal conflict of interest, one that continually pressures staffers to compromise environmental concerns in a perpetual push to "get the cut out" (as Chapter 4 explained).[12]

Scrubbing bias from trust-managing agencies also requires closing the revolving door of government that allows employees to readily move from regulating agencies to regulated industries. As Chapter 4 explained, a transfer of personnel between corporations and the agencies that regulate them creates a milieu in which political operatives use their agency positions to make policies or rule changes that benefit the industries they left – and often hope to rejoin. As author Craig Collins writes in *Toxic Loopholes*, "Common sense and the long, sordid record of corporate malfeasance clearly demonstrate that the fox cannot be trusted to guard the henhouse."[13]

Government ethics rules currently set a two-year period prohibiting high officials from representing private interests before their former agencies.[14] But two years represents a relatively brief time frame on a regulatory horizon that, for any given matter, can easily straddle a decade. Moreover, the rule can only be enforced criminally, which necessitates a lawsuit filed by the U.S. Department of Justice – a rare occurrence for an agency that itself proves highly politicized. A much stronger set of rules is needed to insulate government from polluter influence.

Ultimately, however, employees will honor their duty of loyalty only when they find that violating fiduciary obligations cannot be worth the risk of punishment. Under private trust law, trustees remain personally liable for damages caused by their breach of trust, and in some cases may even be criminally liable. Agencies need strict and predictable personnel standards, backed by a strong enforcement regime, to protect against tainted decision making. Apart from penalties or termination for the trustee who breaches the duty of loyalty, consequences should also accrue to regulated industries that inappropriately try to influence agencies. In private trust law, a person who "aids a trustee to commit a breach of trust" may be liable for such action.[15] The line between appropriate participation in public process and inappropriate influence behind the scenes requires clear demarcation. Just as ethical rules govern lobbying in the legislative sphere, so must rules in the administrative sphere hinder third-party accomplices to fiduciary breaches.

Reporting and Disclosure Requirements for All Employees

Supreme Court Justice Louis Brandeis famously said: "Sunlight is said to be the best of disinfectants."[16] He meant that full public disclosure of the decision-making process helps prevent corruption. The logic traces back to the bulwarks of American democracy discussed in Chapter 5. The Founding Fathers expected citizens to act as vigilant watchdogs over their government. Since then, however, much has changed both in government and among citizens. Ordinary citizens find the complexity of environmental regulation daunting and no longer engage their government as the founders envisioned.

Within the agencies, many of the most important decisions concerning public trust property rarely see the light of day. While the requirements of the Administrative Procedure Act and the Freedom of Information Act require public disclosure of information, the results have proven not nearly sufficient. Agencies regularly close their shutters to public scrutiny by creating red tape, onerous copying costs, thoroughly redacted documents, and overinclusive responses that leave citizens with boxes of unnecessary information to sort through. Many citizens simply give up. Presently, much of the most incriminating information on breach of loyalty comes to light only through agency leaks, congressional committee investigations, GAO investigations, judicial subpoenas, or press investigations – years after a decision is set in stone and works harm. Public interest reform must aim to deliver timely information to the citizens *before* the agency makes its final decision – and also equip citizens with better tools for using the information productively. The discussion that follows suggests three broad parameters to accomplish this.

First, the public should have greater access to those crucial agency documents that reveal the actual process of decision making – documents often deemed "internal." A sequence of drafts marked up by supervisors can illuminate, as little else can, politicized decision making. Second, automatic public disclosure requirements must encompass all external and internal contacts made in the course of decision making. Intense, face-to-face lobbying occurs in the back halls of some agencies, hidden from the public like a secret poker game over a pot of public trust assets. Disclosing the players remains a basic step towards reform. Third, the scientific and technical staff within agencies must be bound by an ethical duty to report transgressions of public loyalty, and be fully protected from retribution when they do so. Agency staff represent a rich source of information on trust performance, but many work amid a culture of cover-up, not disclosure. Some agencies even subject their scientists and technical staff to gag orders, requiring them to gain preapproval to speak or write on matters pertaining to their job functions. Moreover, when agency staffers blow the whistle on government breaches, they often face serious personal retribution (in the form of job loss or forced transfer). Protections provided by the Whistleblower Protection Act have proven demonstrably inadequate.[17]

Of course, open disclosure of agency decision making will do little good if the citizens themselves lack the ability to process and act on the information. Citizens need crucial information presented in a clear and concise form. They also require independent expertise to interpret highly technical and complex information relevant to an agency's decision. Finally, citizens need a legal means of presenting breaches of fiduciary obligation both within the agencies and in the court system. While citizens sometimes have the option to sue agencies under federal statutory provisions through citizen suits, these suits often traverse barren legal terrain because they present only narrow grounds (as discussed in Chapter 5), tangle plaintiffs in procedural complexity, and often miss the mark on the duty of loyalty altogether. Such realities call for an innovative regime of beneficiary trust enforcement in the courts, for without a rigorous judicial role, a "trust" is really not a trust, but rather unchecked dominion.

Voiding Decisions That Violate the Duty of Loyalty

In private trust law, a court will set aside a decision stained by breach of loyalty even if a trustee held good faith in making it. The same result should obtain in the administrative public trust context. Instead, courts take the opposite approach – giving blind deference to agency technical decisions, as Chapter 5 explained. Rarely do judges explore agency decisions for bias or politicized interventions that violate the duty of public loyalty. Environmental attorneys can be partly to blame for perpetuating this deference model because they continue to narrowly frame their cases around statutory violations and often ignore the elephant in the room – the breach of loyalty that perpetuates the very statutory failure they challenge. As an example, the *Massachusetts v. EPA* litigation aimed to force EPA regulation of greenhouse gases (detailed in Chapter 1) never delved into matters regarding inappropriate influence from the White House, alteration of scientific reports, suppression of scientific testimony, and outright collusion with industry – all procedural transgressions that breached the duty of loyalty to the public and caused EPA (for years) to abdicate its responsibility. The agency's long-standing failure to implement the Court's *Massachusetts* ruling should not have been surprising, as the case simply returned the regulatory process to the same political forces that gave rise to the litigation in the first place.[18]

Courts should establish a threshold inquiry that explores the integrity of the decision-making process. Where the process itself violates the duty of loyalty, courts can set aside the agency decision as they would in the private trust context and remand it back to the agency with explicit instructions that protect the procedural integrity of administrative decisions from bias or undue influence during reconsideration. Or, courts can heighten their supervision over the agency process as described in Chapter 11.

THE LEGISLATIVE TRUSTEE'S DUTY WHEN DELEGATING TO AGENCIES AND CO-TRUSTEES

As noted in Chapter 5, Congress and state legislatures bear much responsibility for the failure of environmental law because of their abysmal record in supervising agencies. After delegating enormous power and discretion to the executive branch, the legislatures have taken nearly a hands-off stance toward environmental problems, ignoring even wholesale failure to carry out statutory goals. On the few occasions where egregious agency corruption comes to light, a legislative body may conduct oversight hearings, but only rarely do these lead to systemic reform.

Legislatures may properly delegate management authority to executive branch agencies, but they remain trustees all the same. As one treatise explains, trustees require agents, both for the time and the expertise they can devote to matters of trust administration, but trustees may not abdicate their own responsibilities toward the beneficiaries.[19] The trustee-agent dichotomy fits the constitutional legislative-executive relationship as a hand in a glove: it rationalizes the separation of powers between the branches and illuminates the distinct role of legislatures (as primary trustees) to make the law and of agencies (as agents of the trustees) to carry out the law.

But the legislature-trustee's subsequent neglect in overseeing trust management offends a basic trust law principle. As one leading treatise describes, "A trustee owes his beneficiary the duty of using reasonable care in employing, instructing and supervising [an] ... agent to whom he legally delegates the use of a trust power." To this end, the trustee must properly "supervise and check the performance of the work delegated."[20] Instead, Congress and many state legislatures simply ignore their environmental oversight duties. The danger, of course, becomes that the agents will abuse their delegated authority and manage the trust assets either incompetently or to promote their own self-interest – which describes much of today's environmental management. The perils of unsupervised delegation and un-scrutinized deference engender serious concerns in both trust law and constitutional law.

A second, but different, delegation problem relates to the legislature's use of appropriation riders. A legislative body comprises many co-trustees, namely the individual legislators. Under trust law, each trustee bears the personal responsibility to ensure proper administration of the trust according to its purposes. As one treatise explains, "A co-trustee owes a duty to be active in the performance of the trust. If he turns over to a fellow trustee important trust functions he is guilty of an illegal attempt at delegation." This duty helps ensure that all co-trustees act honestly and efficiently: "It is the duty of one trustee to protect the trust estate from any misfeasance by his co-trustee." Yet some legislators ignore this basic obligation. Frequently, a small group of individual legislators will co-opt environmental lawmaking through the backdoor process of appropriations riders, as Chapter 5 explained. These legislators spearhead riders to gain favorable regulatory exemptions for the industries that fund their campaigns, in clear breach of their fiduciary duty of loyalty. Typically, other legislators – the co-trustees – have little involvement in these riders, perhaps even unaware that they lay buried deeply within the appropriations package. Yet by voting on the package without delving into the substance or procedural bias of the riders embedded within, these other legislators overlook their basic duty to monitor co-trustees for blatant breaches of fiduciary duty.[21]

While these trust violations may be obvious, the solutions can seem obscure. Certainly on the political level, changing the frame to illuminate duties impressed on legislators when legislating marks a step forward. But legislative shortcomings in agency oversight evade judicial correction, because the institutional deficiencies draw out over long time frames, and judicial cases must focus on discrete controversies. However, in regard to appropriations riders that threaten crucial natural resources, the trust approach offers potentially new grounds for judicial scrutiny of these undemocratic measures. Courts may feasibly examine appropriation riders to determine whether they emerge from a process of diligent, nonbiased decision making in which a majority of legislators participate – and overturn those that do not for violating the duty against illegal delegation to co-trustees. The U.S. Supreme Court has rarely examined the constitutionality of riders, although they remain decidedly different from bills that proceed through the normal deliberative legislative processes. Where a court finds breach of the procedural fiduciary duty, it can remand the rider back to the legislature with explicit instructions to comport with the public trust on the next round of consideration.

THE DUTY OF GOOD FAITH AND REASONABLE SKILL

Trust law further imposes basic standards of competence in asset management. As one court summarized, trustees must "act in good faith and employ such vigilance, sagacity, diligence and prudence" as people would in managing their own affairs. If the trustee has greater skill than an ordinary person, trust law obligates the trustee to use that skill when managing the trust. As trustees, these duties logically apply to federal and state environmental agencies, most of which hold a high level of expertise in their scientific and technical staff. Environmental statutes reflect this fiduciary obligation by setting forth scientific standards for environmental management.[22]

But the current political framework encourages many agencies to ignore their duty of good faith and diligence, in two ways. First, agencies regularly fail to develop or use the information they need to manage public trust assets prudently. The National Environmental Policy Act (NEPA) requires agencies to explore impacts and alternatives, but as Part I of this book pointed out, many agency personnel resent the NEPA process and do not use the statute as intended. Often, they make political decisions first and use NEPA's process to provide a post hoc rationale. Or they allow consultants for the private applicant – the party with the most bias in the matter – to perform the environmental analysis, festering NEPA with self-interest. Agencies also exempt some extremely hazardous activities from NEPA analysis altogether by using "categorical exemptions." The MMS, for example, waived standard environmental review for the catastrophic Deep Horizon drilling operation. Overall, MMS grants between 250 and 400 environmental waivers a year for Gulf of Mexico projects – arguably in gross disregard of the trustee's fiduciary duty to exercise diligence in managing ocean trust assets.[23]

Second, some agencies will suppress or distort existing information needed to properly manage trust assets, as detailed in Chapter 4. When agency officials distort science, they not only violate their duty to manage public assets prudently and in good faith, but they also fail in their duty to apply specialized expertise and skill in asset management. A key report issued by the Union of Concerned Scientists reveals nine patterns of malfeasance in this regard: (1) falsifying data and results; (2) selectively editing documents to create false uncertainty; (3) tampering with scientific protocol; (4) intimidating and/or coercing scientists; (5) censoring scientists; (6) hiding and/or delaying release of scientific findings; (7) disregarding legally required science; (8) condoning conflicts of interest; and (9) corrupting scientific advisory panels.[24] Apart from abusing the information process in these ways, agencies sometimes simply ignore sound information altogether and make decisions based on political factors wholly extraneous to proper trust management goals, as Part I described. Collectively, these behaviors careen the administrative state away from its duties of good faith, skill, and prudence.

A plethora of reports offered by groups such as the Union of Concerned Scientists, the Government Accountability Project, Public Employees for Environmental Responsibility, the Center for Science in the Public Interest, the Center for Progressive Reform, and others suggest reform measures tailored to restoring scientific integrity within the agencies – measures that would also go far in addressing the duty of loyalty discussed above. These measures include: (1) strengthening whistle-blowing protections for scientists; (2) requiring disclosure of industry ties and contacts in government-funded science; (3) eliminating conflicts of interest among members of scientific advisory boards; (4) ensuring robust, unbiased scientific input into federal policymaking; (5) protecting the freedom of scientists to communicate with the media and the public; (6) revealing political interference with scientific documents before they become subject to political review; (7) disclosing a record of all meetings between agency staff and outside entities on proposed regulations or decisions; and (8) preventing the Office of Management and Budget from subverting the scientific work in the agencies. These reforms, all reinforced by more specific recommendations, would hasten compliance with the full suite of procedural duties that should mantle trust management decisions.[25]

FIDUCIARY CAUTION IN ECOLOGICAL CRISIS: THE PRECAUTIONARY APPROACH

A trustee must exercise reasonable caution in managing the trust assets. In the case of a financial *res*, for example, a trustee may not invest funds in "speculative or hazardous ventures" and must avoid new ventures of which he has little knowledge.[26] This rule aims to preserve the corpus of the trust. High-risk management, even if bearing the prospect of high yields, places the assets in peril. For an ecological trust, the consequences of high-risk management may be deadly and irrevocable – causing acidified oceans, runaway climate heating, extinct species, and soaring cancer rates. But despite this, agencies routinely throw caution to the wind.

The problem lies in the agencies' treatment of uncertainty: they treat it exactly backward. Uncertainty should hinder, not advance, hazardous proposals. Yet agencies regularly allow perilous action to proceed in the face of uncertain harm. The treatment of toxic chemicals demonstrates their approach. Little information exists on the health effects of the 70,000 industrial chemicals in commerce today, yet EPA allows industry to spew thousands of new chemicals into the environment, most untested and unregulated. The EPA gives its go-ahead based on studies permeated with uncertainty as to "safe" levels of toxic exposure. Joel Tickner, a national expert in risk assessments, warns that the soaring production of these substances presents "a large-scale experiment" on human and ecosystem health.[27]

Some industry exploits, like the deep-sea oil drilling allowed by MMS, cross into a zone of risk well beyond the limits of any cautionary or prudent management. MMS permitted BP to puncture the ocean floor and drill deep into the Earth's crust in an area known for the presence of dangerous methane hydrates. Prior to the BP oil calamity, MMS had never even studied a worst-case explosion scenario. It had considered spills of only 4,600 barrels of oil, whereas BP's well discharged in excess of 4.9 million barrels. Even after the BP catastrophe, MMS continued to issue environmental waivers for perilous projects in the Gulf. The agency's management typifies exactly the behavior that the trust aims to avoid – investment in "speculative or hazardous ventures." Operating in a similar vacuum of uncertainty, other environmental agencies allow earth-maiming ventures, genetic modification of seeds, nuclear energy production, and broad use of chemical poisons. At staggering cost, these agencies use NEPA documents and risk assessments to mislead the public into thinking that they safeguard public health and protect the environment when in fact they repeatedly allow corporations to roll the ecological dice with public assets. Rather than instill prudence and caution in agencies, the present system institutionalizes reckless behavior.[28]

The trustee's duty to act prudently suggests agencies should adopt the "precautionary approach," which requires erring on the side of caution where uncertainty exists. As one textbook explains, the principle demands "anticipatory actions" to avoid environmental harm *before* it occurs. In a lodestar opinion, *Ethyl Corp v. EPA*, the D.C. Circuit embraced the precautionary approach when upholding EPA's authority to regulate lead in gasoline in face of scientific uncertainty, noting a "special judicial interest in favor of protection of the health and welfare of people, even in areas where certainty does not exist." The Hawaii Supreme Court followed *Ethyl Corp*'s precautionary approach in managing public trust water assets, stating in its landmark *Waiāhole Ditch* case:

> Where scientific evidence is preliminary and not yet conclusive regarding the management of fresh water resources which are part of the public trust, it is prudent to adopt "precautionary principles" in protecting the resource. That is, where there are present or potential threats of serious damage, lack of full scientific certainty should not be a basis for postponing effective measures to prevent environmental degradation.... [W]here uncertainty exists, a trustee's duty to protect the resource mitigates in favor of choosing presumptions that also protect the resource.

The court further reasoned (quoting *Ethyl Corp.*): "'Petitioners suggest that anything less than certainty, that any speculation, is irresponsible. But when statutes seek to avoid environmental catastrophe, can preventative, albeit uncertain, decisions legitimately be so labeled?'"[29]

The precautionary approach already appears in the law of the European Union, described by one expert as a "general customary rule." The Ecuador Constitution makes the precautionary principle a centerpiece of government obligation, declaring: "The State will apply precaution and restriction measures in all the activities that can lead to the extinction of species, the destruction of the ecosystems or the permanent alteration of the natural cycles." The principle inhabits international law as well. The 1992 Rio Declaration of the United Nations Conference on Environment and Development states:

> In order to protect the environment, the precautionary approach shall be widely applied by States according to their capabilities. Where there are threats of serious or irreversible damage, lack of full scientific certainty shall not be used as a reason for postponing cost-effective measures to prevent environmental degradation.[30]

Logically, the greater and more irreversible the possible damage, the more caution should apply to a given situation. The precautionary principle finds its apex in the context of climate-altering actions such as the release of greenhouse gases. The United Nations Framework Convention on Climate Change (to which the United States is a party) declares: "The Parties should take precautionary measures to anticipate, prevent or minimize the causes of climate change and mitigate its adverse effects. Where there are threats of serious or irreversible damage, lack of full scientific certainty should not be used as a reason for postponing such measures." As leading climate scientists emphasized in a landmark report issued just prior to the Copenhagen climate negotiations in 2009:

> Delay in action risks irreversible damage.... The risk of transgressing critical thresholds ("tipping points") increases strongly with ongoing climate change. Thus waiting for higher levels of scientific certainty could mean that some tipping points will be crossed before they are recognized.[31]

Yet the present political frame constructed and controlled by industry leaders and their public relations firms warps caution into an errant behavior. They persistently maintain that regulation carrying any significant economic cost (including foiled expectations of profits) should not occur until the harm from their activities has been conclusively established. It is an age-old trick (first conceived by the tobacco industry) of twisting scientific uncertainty to their advantage. David Michaels calls it a "classic uncertainty campaign" (as described in Chapter 4).[32] The fact remains that irreversible damage – including human illness and death – often occurs before scientists firmly establish harm from the industry's activity. Even so, industry propaganda remains powerfully alluring to citizens who may not understand the lethal risks associated with, for example, toxic pollution, but who remain in constant fright of the economic decline that industry has convinced them may follow in the wake of regulation. For all of its triumphs, industrialism has disconnected entire generations of people from their environment and dulled their sense of personal risk associated with ecological harm.

The precautionary approach protects the status quo until proven safeguards come into being. As a legal doctrine, it offers a control device for a regulatory engine that now drives high-speed destruction of the planet. This fiduciary duty of prudence and caution must bind all government trustees, because environmental threats from industry now come too rapid and numerous for responsible evaluation within the constraints of current regulatory time frames. Agencies can best implement the approach by halting new permits through moratoria and by suspending permits that allow ultrahazardous activity. Leading environmental thinkers offer specific suggestions for reform that run the gamut of regulatory contexts.[33]

FURNISHING INFORMATION TO THE BENEFICIARIES: THE TRUST ACCOUNTING

As a final procedural duty, the trustee must disclose to the beneficiaries all matters pertaining to the health of the trust. This disclosure, called an "accounting," provides the process by which beneficiaries may ensure proper management of their assets. In the financial context, the scope of an accounting includes all information "in which the beneficiary has a legitimate concern."[34] This requires, at the very least, a clear and concise statement of the nature and value of the trust *res*, a summary of profits and expenses, and the amount and location of any balance. A natural asset accounting would parallel this kind of wealth assessment, using various indicia that reflect the health of the asset: species populations, pollution levels, river flows, forest age classes, and the like.

U.S. environmental law already provides many reporting requirements that assess overall resource health. The Endangered Species Act (ESA), for example, requires the U.S. Fish and Wildlife Service to regularly evaluate the condition of listed species. The Global Change Research Act of 1990 requires periodic assessments of climate. The Emergency Planning and Community Right to Know Act requires EPA to make public the toxic emissions and discharges reported by industries. A crucial difference exists, however, between such statutorily required reports and trust accountings: the latter must specifically enable the beneficiaries to check on the management of their trust property. This means the information must be readily accessible and delivered to the beneficiaries, understandable by private citizens, and formatted to provide a basis for enforcement against the trustee. To put it in familiar terms, a natural accounting is like a bank statement for the ecological *res.*[35]

Carbon accountings, for example, can become a particularly crucial tool in face of climate crisis. Modern modeling can quantify a carbon footprint on virtually any jurisdictional scale. An accounting would establish a baseline of carbon pollution emitted within a particular jurisdiction (local, state, or federal) and track pollution reduction over time. Courts can require use of climate accountings to enforce government's fiduciary obligation to protect the atmosphere according to the prescription set by scientists which, as Chapter 8 explained, calls for 6 percent annual emissions reductions.[36]

Government trustees have largely eschewed their duty to provide clear accountings to citizen beneficiaries. Many agencies do not conduct systematic or regular surveys of the resources they manage. Those that do may not make them fully and readily available to the public. And, as earlier chapters explained, some agencies wage all-out public deception campaigns to cover up extensive damage and threats to public property. When an agency actively distorts the health of an environmental asset, the situation resembles a banker cooking the books on a personal savings account.

Many agency Web sites that initially held promise as repositories for accessible public information have instead devolved into public relations displays. Rather than provide straightforward and forthright summaries of the natural account under their management, agencies clutter their home pages with feel-good stories about environmental projects, voluntary environmental opportunities, tool kits for classrooms, popular topics, press releases, forms, and all manner of miscellaneous information – distractions from the big picture of asset health that citizen beneficiaries need to know about to enforce their property rights to the public trust. As Chapter 5 pointed out, the public generally lacks the time and resources to monitor government trustees. Statutes such as NEPA and the Freedom of Information Act, while geared to providing information, now prove too laborious and costly for average citizens due to the sheer complexity of environmental problems. Amidst an industrial onslaught of environmental damage, agencies must devise new methods to disseminate information in accessible and digestible fashion. But even more, environmental problems of grave magnitude and consequence demand a step beyond providing information. These problems require the involvement of focused citizen-beneficiary advisory groups – administrative juries of sorts – that offer stipends for service and have scientific consultants and other resources necessary to undertake vigilant supervision of government trust management.

A NEW SENSE OF AGENCY MISSION

As this book has explained, vast administrative discretion currently steers agencies toward favoring singular moneyed interests over the public. Infusing both the substantive and procedural fiduciary duties (described in this and the last chapter) into agency decision making requires institutional overhaul, though not necessarily statutory reform. Agency officials must change the agency's entire mindset to carry out substantive duties of protection and restoration and adhere scrupulously to the procedural duties of loyalty, diligence, good faith, caution, and accounting. This means doing business in a dramatically different way. The question remains: How do these duties weave their way into the institutional and cultural fabric of an agency?

Many legal and administrative management strategies can turn the ship. Executive orders from the president, or secretarial orders from department chiefs, can clearly set forth the fiduciary obligation. A host of internal measures – such as listed fiduciary procedures, employee trainings in trust responsibility, systems of accountability and review, employee performance standards and appraisals, bonuses and pay raises tied to fiduciary performance, and greater whistle-blower protection – would advance a trust paradigm in administrative law.

But as suggested in Chapter 8, agencies also need to develop responsive legal approaches that will enable them to deny permits for damaging action and to suspend and ultimately revoke many existing permits. While agency officials typically beg out of these duties by lamenting their lack of legal authority, often the authority for denying permits already exists but has not been tapped for a very long time. Most statutes and regulations have boilerplate provisions allowing agencies to respond to nuisances or imminent threats to the environment or human health. These provisions can often provide an ample reservoir of authority to protect public assets. Where no explicit authority exists, the implied powers of government to respond to the threat of damage can be strong. When President Taft decided to halt oil and gas development on federal lands in order to protect supplies needed for national defense, the Supreme Court upheld his action, saying:

> These rules or laws for the disposal of public land are necessarily general in their nature. Emergencies may occur, or conditions may so change as to require that the agent in charge should, in the public interest, withhold the land from sale.... The power of the Executive, as agent in charge, to retain that property from sale, need not necessarily be expressed in writing.[37]

To this end, an emergency moratorium (such as the one President Obama issued immediately after the BP Gulf oil spill) may offer the most effective means of securing immediate stability while legal analysis explores longer-term solutions that necessitate statutory or regulatory reform.

Ultimately, the challenge of transforming agencies and their officials from bureaucrats to trustees looms larger than isolated questions of legal authority. The project requires ending the tyranny of administrative discretion in environmental law. As Chapter 5 pointed out, the combination of consolidated power in the agencies and a corporate viselike grip on the executive branch has reached dangerous proportions and continues without any meaningful redress by the other two branches of government. As this book has maintained, minor tweaks in the system of environmental law will do little good; they will likely drown in the torrents of dysfunction now flowing through agencies at every level of government. An institutional overhaul geared toward reining in administrative discretion and rechanneling agencies toward the public good will require revitalizing the balance of power among the three branches of government and creating a new system of checks and balances within the agencies themselves. Chapter 11 takes up the subject of restoring the judicial branch's constitutional role in environmental policy.

The goal of infusing agencies with trust duties greatly challenges the bureaucratic status quo, because the institutional culture in most agencies recognizes the political paradigm as its reality. Like any institutional culture, people mold their careers to it. As individuals tunnel down into the statutes they administer, they become more narrowly focused on the minutia of their daily work and more keenly aware of the internal political forces that dictate their decisions. A passionate sense of public duty – precisely what prompts many public servants to enter government in the first place – can wane over time. At the end of the day, many agency employees sincerely believe they are doing the right thing, which might make the effort to bring about internal change even harder.

Certainly reform efforts need to institutionalize predictable, punitive consequences for agency violations of fiduciary duties owed to the public. Ultimately, however, punitive systems will only go so far. A very personal challenge must ultimately find its way into the hearts of those public servants who have the sense that agencies have not behaved as they should have, that agencies have been serving some powers other than the public, that their own personal actions, if not illegal, do not fulfill the spirit of the public oath they took – and that their time in history proves so pivotal that they must become the change agents within their institutions, daunting and personally risky as that prospect may be. Agency reforms will fail if agents of change remain unprotected in their courageous action. They must be nurtured in their sense of public mission and championed by the broader community they serve. This becomes possible by dismantling the oppressive frame of politicized discretion and setting in its place a new frame that views government officials as trustees of priceless ecological assets owned by the public, managed for citizens of both this generation and all to come. The table that follows depicts this paradigm shift.

Components	Political Model	Trust Model
Congress/state legislatures	Politicians	Trustees
Agency staffers	Politicized bureaucrats	Agents of the trustees
Citizens	Political constituents	Trust beneficiaries
Natural resources	Diffused, intangible parts of the environment	Quantifiable, valuable assets
Government decision-making	Political discretion	Fiduciary obligation
Polluting industries	Stakeholders	Trust despoilers

This transformation holds unique potential because of its versatility across jurisdictions. The trust offers a full paradigm shift for any environmental or land management agency on the local, state, regional, national, or international level. Essential fiduciary concepts thus provide a mutual basis for cross-jurisdictional cooperation and responsibility in managing shared assets that transcend state and national boundaries. Chapter 10 explores this aspect further and offers Nature's Trust as a platform for creating new approaches to global ecological responsibility.

10

Beyond Borders: Shared Ecology and the Duties of Sovereign Co-Tenant Trustees

All humankind shares the Earth Endowment, but legal institutions have never devised a rational way to conserve natural bounty for the collective advancement and security of humanity. Global ecological problems arise within an international context that presumes complete national autonomy within borders. This nation-state model may operate well for many social and economic concerns, but it fails to adequately order ecological rights. Boundary-based governance perpetuates a fictional and obsolete assumption that all of ecology can be carved up and divided among sovereigns. The approach runs anathema to Nature's own laws, which thread a complex web of life from resources that remain inextricably connected and interdependent across borders. Nations depart from these natural laws at their individual and collective peril.

The boundary approach creates two obvious problems. First, some planetary resources – like oceans and the atmosphere – cannot be divided. These indivisible assets tempt a free-for-all and race-to-exploit behavior among nations. Dying oceans, overfished marine stocks, and the polluted atmosphere signify the colossal failure of nations to organize respective ecological obligations into one coherent global framework. As to bounded assets, the focus on territorial sovereignty fails to characterize any duties flowing to nations and citizens located outside domestic national borders. Accordingly, transborder harm proliferates. Emissions from coal-fired plants in China contaminate fish swimming in the Great Lakes of the United States. Greenhouse gas pollution from the United States contributes (through planetary heating) to rising sea levels that will drown island nations and parch much of Africa. Radioactive fallout from Japan's 2011 Fukushima nuclear plant disaster persists in the United States and other countries. By making a sovereign jigsaw puzzle out of ecology, national boundaries allow perpetrators of trans-boundary harm to escape legal accountability. The problem has always been one of externalities: economic benefits accrue to the polluter and citizens of one nation, while significant costs of such pollution fall to citizens of other nations.[1]

For most of human history, the flaws inherent in boundary-based governance remained tolerable. Because rudimentary technology limited the human capacity to effectuate harm, damage usually stayed localized. But that has changed. Over the last few decades, a dangerous concoction of corporate ambition and super-technology has elevated human annihilative ingenuity to the planetary level. The ability of multinational corporations to inflict global harm now far outpaces the capacity of current legal arrangements to formulate and impose responsibility on them. The resulting ecological calamities make one thing quite obvious: environmental law can no longer stumble along in a fantasy world organized by boundaries alone. As Susan Buck writes in her book, *The Global Commons*, "The entire issue of transboundary resources and pollution makes it clear that absolute sovereignty is an idea whose time has passed." Society must now conceptualize and implement constructs of shared sovereign responsibility capable of transcending jurisdictional borders. To be adequate, this collective responsibility must calibrate directly to Nature's own "planetary boundaries" – requirements for a functioning planet. As the legal commentator Blackstone recognized long ago, "Th[e] law of nature ... is of course superior in obligation to every other. It is binding over all the globe in all countries, and at all times: no human laws are of any validity, if contrary to this."[2]

This chapter advances the public trust framework to create a model of international environmental obligation. A growing number of legal and policy thinkers urge the application of public trust principles to unprecedented problems of global ecology. As international law scholar Peter Sand wrote in a pioneering article: "A transfer of the public trust concept from the national to the global level is conceivable, feasible, and tolerable."[3] There remains, however, the task of extrapolating general trust principles into a more precise logical construct that can organize and enforce ecological duties among the nation-states.

Nature's Trust characterizes global environmental syndromes as matters of property law in which a set of discernable rules can promote a common, civilized plan of asset protection – even in a world governed by multiple sovereigns with fragmented jurisdiction over the planet. The trust framework finds its premise in the principle that all nations stand as sovereign trustees of natural resources, as Chapter 6 described. The approach arranges these sovereign trust interests into a co-tenancy property framework encompassing the entire Earth Endowment. Packaging problems of planetary ecology in these property terms enables domestic courts of various nations to summon clear and enforceable fiduciary standards to hold political leaders accountable for global ecological duties. The trust-based model cannot be, of course, a panacea for the world's environmental problems. But as a strategy, it diversifies the legal avenues available to citizens to address grave global problems that elude conventional approaches. As a predicate to describing the trust approach, the following section first addresses the pitfalls of traditional international governance models.

THE FAILED INTERNATIONAL DIPLOMACY MODEL

Nearly always, world leaders punt global ecological problems to the realm of international negotiation – a forum aimed toward producing a treaty among nations. While the treaty process has worked somewhat well for environmental problems of a singular nature (such as international whaling and chlorofluorocarbon [CFC] pollution threatening the ozone layer), it does not come close to adequately addressing many of the complex and unfathomably urgent problems of today's world, such as climate crisis, ocean acidification, biodiversity loss, and others. These failures beg fresh introspection into the effectiveness of international legal approaches in the modern ecological age.

Four endemic problems beleaguer the negotiated treaty approach to international trans-boundary problems. First, no normative sense of obligation anchors diplomatic treaty talks. Instead, national representatives merely *negotiate* responsibility according to their political interests. This negotiation process can be vulnerable to capture by the very industries that cause the global damage in the first place. When industry influence carries over to the international realm, treaty negotiations sink to a lowest common denominator of what the politics will allow instead of reaching toward consummate solutions. For example, international climate talks organize around the amount of carbon emissions reduction politicians feel comfortable committing to rather than the amount needed to recover atmospheric equilibrium. During the 2010 Copenhagen negotiations, a UN analysis showed that the totality of various national pledges, even if actually fulfilled, would still not prevent a disastrous 3°C temperature rise.[4] Averting climate disaster presents a matter of carbon math, not carbon politics.

Second, the negotiated framework model creates a negative ripple effect when one country's abdication of responsibility becomes an excuse for all other nations to avoid responsibility. In the world of international diplomacy, failure breeds more failure. Again, an example rises out of the climate context. For years, political leaders in the United States have told American citizens that the United States cannot commit to carbon dioxide emissions reductions until China gives a similar commitment – something China steadfastly refuses to do. Chinese leaders, in turn, refuse to commit to firm reductions until the United States gives a firm commitment – which the United States steadfastly refuses to do. This "not me first" mentality creates a deadly game of chicken between the two biggest polluters on the planet, and international treaty processes lack any means of breaking the stalemate. Worse, the international impasse sabotages domestic reform efforts, because political leaders insist that they cannot settle on national targets absent a full international agreement allocating responsibility. This becomes a self-perpetuating cycle of inaction that can last for years as planetary threats grow increasingly grave.[5]

Third, the negotiated framework model may prove too unwieldy to deliver any decisive allocations of international responsibility in times of crisis. International agreements entail several time-consuming stages. Nations come forth with various proposals. They send such proposals back and forth, and modify them. They finally accept or reject them as a community of sovereigns. The sheer number of negotiating parties and the complexity of the issues may overwhelm a system that had its genesis in another era. The 2009 Copenhagen climate negotiations, for example, involved more than 100 nations; nearly 100,000 activists attended to influence the diplomats. The press described the talks as "in serious disarray" and "chaotic from the start." The talks ended in failure, without any clear commitments, and serial diplomatic failures have ensued ever since. As the report from the UN Brundtland Commission aptly observed twenty-five years ago, modern legal regimes stand "rapidly outdistanced by the accelerating pace and expanding scale of impacts" on the environment.[6]

Finally, negotiated treaties rely on domestic implementation, which in turn depends on Congress ratifying the treaties and the agencies implementing them. Where domestic policy remains unsettled, the negotiation of international agreements may put the cart before the horse. The 1997 Kyoto Protocol on greenhouse gas emissions illustrates the problem. Even though Vice President Gore signed the agreement on behalf of the United States, President Clinton never submitted it to Congress for ratification, thus leaving the world's largest polluter-nation unfettered by its obligations. And even if national legislatures ratify a treaty, an international agreement will fail if not supported by robust and committed administrative agencies operating within the signatory nations. As this book has pointed out, corporations now exert dangerous influence over both the legislatures that must chose whether or not to ratify the treaties and the agencies that must implement those that are ratified. Richard J. Barnet and John Cavanagh warn in their book, *Global Dreams*, that multinational corporations have "outgrown political institutions at the local, national, and supranational levels." This leaves the world with "an authority crisis without precedent in modern times."[7]

Too many treaty promises succumb to administrative sabotage long after the spotlight and glamour of international diplomacy has faded. Rampant failure in domestic enforcement among signatory nations can, in practicality, nullify treaties. Because there exists no global "superpower" with jurisdiction over nations, no mechanism holds nations to their treaty promises. In this sense, international "law" is not really law at all.

Ignoring these obvious shortcomings, many thinkers assume that the traditional model of international diplomacy will surely work next time. But given its inherent problems, the prospect remains doubtful. The situation demands a more diversified legal strategy. Public trust principles stand positioned to not only infuse international negotiations with clearer global duties, but more importantly, provide a basis for asserting global obligations in *domestic venues*. By aiming toward a conception of global ecological property law, the Nature's Trust approach develops principles of reciprocal responsibility toward planetary resources. Citizens can assert these principles to hold their leaders accountable in whatever domestic judicial or legislative processes may be available. In other words, principles of global responsibility need not await iteration through international negotiation: they can derive from normative duties incumbent on owners of shared property. The "liability now" emphasis of Nature's Trust aims to fill (at least partially) a dangerous vacuum of international responsibility that now gapes wide in the wake of treaty negotiation failure.

THE GLOBAL SOVEREIGN CO-TENANCY

The Nature's Trust approach builds on a "planetary trust" concept established by Professor Edith Brown Weiss several decades ago in her landmark work, *In Fairness to Future Generations*. She described an intergenerational trust for the Earth and suggested: "The dual role of each generation as trustee of the planet for present and future generations and as beneficiary of the planetary legacy imposes certain obligations upon each generation and gives it certain rights."[8] Nature's Trust provides a sovereign structure for this concept by describing nations as bound together in property relationships toward the planet they share.

The premise of this approach recognizes that sovereigns do, in fact, assert property rights within their territorial boundaries. As one court expressed long ago, "Everything susceptible of property is considered as belonging to the nation that possesses the country, and as forming the entire mass of its wealth." U.S. courts have consistently found that states and tribes may assert shared property rights in fisheries, wildlife, and water passing through their borders. As Justice O'Connor once observed, "each sovereign whose territory temporarily shelters [migratory] wildlife has a legitimate and protectable interest in that wildlife."[9]

These sovereign property interests take the form of a public trust. As noted in Chapter 6, public property ownership of crucial resources dates back to Roman law, a doctrinal wellspring of legal systems worldwide. The premise of public trust responsibility has global reach, transcending different legal systems and cultures. Ved Nanda and William Ris observe: "The principles of public trust are such that they can be understood and embraced by most countries of the world." Professor Michael Blumm describes the doctrine as evolving towards a "general principle of international law." A remarkably fluid precept, the trust has manifold origins, shows varied iterations, and proliferates across the globe through multiple routes. Many nations have enacted constitutional provisions that codify the trust precept. By necessity, the doctrine has adapted to new sovereign circumstances as nations have changed their governing character. At times in various countries, the public trust doctrine has rested in dormancy, and then has been resurrected to fit new circumstances. The doctrine comes to life through the efforts of lawyers, judges, citizens, and legislators who recognize its universal force in compelling governmental obedience to a covenant owed to both present and future generations of citizens.[10]

Sovereign trust interests held by the various nations operate in combination to create a duty-based platform for global ecological responsibility. As Patricia W. Birnie and colleagues observe, "[T]he most convincing characterization [of international environmental law] is no longer that of neighborly relations, but of environmental trusteeship, with ... concern for community interests at a global level, not merely those of states *inter se*." Where two or more sovereigns hold trust rights in a resource, these logically arrange into what property law would call a co-tenancy. A co-tenancy describes joint ownership by two or more parties, each holding a right to possession. U.S. courts have applied this co-tenancy construct to describe the relationship of states and tribes in the context of fisheries. In landmark U.S. Indian treaty fishing rights litigation, the Ninth Circuit characterized tribal and state sovereigns as analogous to "co-tenants," each having rights in a shared salmon fishery migrating between their borders. A similar, and complimentary, concept lies in the characterization of "co-trustees," which describes two or more trustees having shared authority over a trust *res*, or assets. Like the co-tenancy principle, this concept also materializes on the sovereign level. In *United States v. 1.58 Acres of Land*, a federal district court described the federal government and the state of Massachusetts as "co-trustees" of submerged public trust lands in Boston Harbor. The fusion of co-tenant and co-trustee status binds nations in a *co-tenant trustee* relationship vis-à-vis shared planetary resources. Because both co-trustees and co-tenants owe duties to one another respecting their shared property, this co-tenant trustee relationship gives rise to shared sovereign obligations toward global trust property.[11]

Under common law, both the co-trustee and co-tenancy relationships impose a duty against waste, or derogation, of the common asset. As one leading treatise makes clear, co-trustees hold their powers jointly, and "all must unite in their exercise." Co-trustees also have duties to take action against other co-trustees to protect the estate for the beneficiaries. Similarly, co-tenants share the obligation not to waste the common asset to which both stand equally entitled, and courts have declared this duty applicable to sovereign trustees. In the treaty fishing litigation, the Ninth Circuit explained:

> Cotenants stand in a fiduciary relationship one to the other. Each has the right to full enjoyment of the property, but must use it as a reasonable property owner. A cotenant is liable for waste if he destroys the property or abuses it so as to permanently impair its value.... By analogy, neither the treaty Indians nor the state on behalf of its citizens may permit the subject matter of these treaties to be destroyed.[12]

These property principles illuminate international obligations. As *co-tenant trustees* of one integral Earth Endowment, all countries share intrinsic, reciprocal duties to protect planetary assets. By considering such assets in their functional ecological entirety rather than as fragmented resources existing within national territorial boundaries – a disjointed and failed jurisdictional approach – the trust broadens the scope of interests to which each sovereign stands accountable to encompass present and future members of humankind. As Peter Sand observes, "The essence of transnational environmental trusteeship ... is the democratic *accountability* of states for their management of trust resources in the interest of the beneficiaries – the world's 'peoples.'"[13] At the same time, of course, any international trust concept must acknowledge legitimate sovereign territorial prerogatives and autonomy.

The Nature's Trust framework takes the following four-step approach to establishing and enforcing international ecological duties: it (1) characterizes planetary trust assets; (2) identifies co-tenant sovereign trustees of such assets according to their assertion of territorial interests in, or dominion over, the assets; (3) defines universal fiduciary obligations aimed to protect the ecological integrity of planetary assets; and (4) searches for domestic forums within the legal systems of each sovereign co-tenant trustee to hold leaders accountable for carrying out such fiduciary obligations. As discussed later, the approach scales up and down the jurisdictional ladder: not only can it define multiple nations' responsibilities toward an asset, but it can also define respective state and tribal responsibilities toward shared assets within a nation as well.

IDENTIFYING PLANETARY PROPERTY AND ITS TRUSTEES

The difference between domestic trust assets and global trust assets pertains to the scale of interest in the asset: global resources evoke planetary concern held by humanity as a whole. These trust assets can be identified pursuant to the same factors that prove useful in characterizing domestic public trust assets (as discussed in Chapter 7), namely: (1) public need; (2) scarcity; (3) customary use and reasonable expectation; (4) unique and irreplaceable common heritage; (5) suitability for common use; and (6) ancillary function. In addition, the global trust should reach resources carrying ultrahazardous potential. From these factors emerge four types of planetary trust assets described below. Notably, international law instruments express stewardship obligations over many of these resources, although they fall short in establishing enforceable obligations for their protection.

Earth Structures and Systems. The first category comprises the planetary structure and circulatory systems that interact to support all life on Earth. The structure includes, for example, the deep-sea bed and the core of the Earth. The circulatory systems include the oceans and atmosphere. All rank supreme in terms of global "public need," one of the factors courts use to identify a trust asset. The oceans and atmosphere, moreover, remain suitable only for common use, another identifying factor. As far back as Roman times, the Justinian Code declared air and oceans as "common to mankind." The U.S. Supreme Court has said of the high seas, "The Pacific Ocean belongs to no one nation, but is the common property of all," and Justice Black once wrote, "Ocean waters are the highways of the world. They are no less such because they happen to lap the shores of different nations that border them." Various international treaties express global trust interests in these resources. The United Nations Convention on the Law of the Sea (UNCLOS) declares the seabed and ocean resources to be the "common heritage of mankind," imposing on nations the duty of conservation and the duty to prevent "unnecessary waste." The United Nations Framework Convention on Climate Change (UNFCCC) calls on nations to "protect the climate system for the benefit of present and future generations of humankind." Considerable commentary already suggests an international trust concept in the context of oceans and atmosphere.[14]

Living Resource Hereditaments. The second category consists of Earth's living resources that carry planetary importance in their totality. They include, for example, species biodiversity and the pool of genetic plant material, both crucial for sustaining humanity's food supply and the web of life. Here again, international treaties signal these resources as planetary trust assets. The 2001 FAO International Treaty on Plant Genetic Resources for Food and Agriculture declares a responsibility to past and future generations to conserve the world's diversity of plant genetic resources for food and agriculture. The 1992 Convention on Biological Diversity (CBD) affirms that "the conservation of biological diversity is a common concern of humankind," and that "States are responsible for conserving their biological diversity." Other living resource hereditaments include major forests, such as the Amazon, the rainforests of Indonesia, and the Pacific Northwest's ancient forest, for example. Such living resources fulfill global public need by providing crucial ecological functions (including the absorption of carbon dioxide pollution) to maintain life on Earth. Resources such as individual wildlife species may be thought of as planetary assets because of their scarcity or because they make up the "unique and irreplaceable" common heritage of humankind, both relevant factors for identifying public trust assets. The tigers in Siberia, the giraffes in Africa, the elephants in Indonesia, the plankton in the seas – as well as other glorious, indispensable, or irreplaceable species that make up Earth's animal kingdom – evoke worldwide interest and concern.[15]

Planetary Fixtures. A third category of global trust resource includes extraordinary planetary formations and fixtures, such as the Great Barrier Reefs of Australia, the Waterton-Glacier International Peace Park that straddles the United States and Canada, and the Galapagos Islands falling under the sovereignty of Ecuador. The

World Heritage Convention designates these and hundreds of other spectacular natural sites as World Heritage Sites – sites that make up the "unique and irreplaceable" common heritage of humankind and hold "outstanding universal value" for present and future generations of humanity. Clear global interests arise in their management despite the fact that many such places fall within the territorial boundaries of just one nation. Currently more than 900 designated cultural and natural world heritage sites exist across 157 countries.[16]

Global Hazard Resources. A fourth trust category reaches to the dangerous materials of Nature. As Professor John Davidson urges, fiduciary concepts should not only protect vital and irreplaceable assets, but should also limit the ability of governments to engage in ecological ultrahazardous activity (discussed in Chapter 7). In a similar vein, Professor Edith Brown Weiss underscores a global duty to future generations to prevent disasters. On a planetary level, the concern applies to hazards that carry potential to damage or destroy the Earth's living systems. A ghastly example of this prospect lies in Japan's nuclear reactors at Fukushima, which scientific observers warn could contaminate much of the northern hemisphere if another major seismic event rattles the unstable reactor #4 and ignites a fire that reaches the seven pools of high-level radioactive waste stored onsite. The international trust responsibility demands proactive, precautionary action in face of such global hazards. In a famous advisory opinion issued by the International Court of Justice in 1996, Judge Christopher Weeramantry announced "the principle of trusteeship of earth resources" with respect to the proliferation of nuclear weapons, a situation bearing danger similar to the operation of nuclear power plants. The distant transportability, long-term persistence, and lethal consequences of radioactive contamination all create a scale of global interest that far outweighs parochial concerns, most of which typically focus on local jobs and the availability of regional energy supplies.[17]

The global hazard category extends well beyond nuclear power activity to all actions holding potential to cause large-scale irrevocable planetary damage, such as deep-sea drilling that imperils ocean resources, fossil fuel production that damages climate systems, and risky geoengineering attempts to mitigate planetary heating. A potential breach of trust toward global beneficiaries occurs not only when government allows ultrahazardous activity, but also when agencies confer power to private corporations to use or manage these hazard resources. As became evident with BP's operation of deep-sea oil drilling and Tokyo Electric's management of nuclear power plants, privatizing hazard resources can bring disaster. Corporations are incentivized to compromise costly safety measures in order to maximize their profits. The global trust aims to prevent such privatization.

After characterizing a planetary trust resource, the next step involves identifying the nations situated as co-tenant trustees of the asset. Generally speaking, the sovereigns that assert dominion and control over, or gain direct beneficial use of, the asset hold recognized property rights to it. All global trust resources can be situated along a continuum of national dominion. At one end, nations assert clear and exclusive dominion over purely domestic resources. Here the possessory interests run most acute. Examples of such domestic trust assets include a forest, a mineral deposit, a shoreline, or an underground aquifer located entirely within national boundaries. (Professor Sand rightly argues that some of these domestic resources exist as a matter of global common concern notwithstanding the fact that they fall squarely within a nation's territorial boundaries.)[18] At the other end of the continuum, nations assert non-possessory interests in those resources that are not capable of possession but provide mutual societal benefit, like oceans, atmosphere, and space. In the middle of the continuum, nations assert shared possessory interests in trans-boundary resources of a transitory nature, such as a migratory species of wildlife. Some assets, like international waterways, straddle the categories: the submerged beds fix clearly within national borders, but the water remains transitory, running between borders.

Regardless of where the asset falls on this continuum, the sovereign trustees that stand positioned to manage the resource become identifiable from the territorial dominion or beneficial interests they claim. A few examples demonstrate the concept. The United States and Canada serve as co-tenant sovereign trustees of the Great Lakes trust. Eight co-tenant sovereign trustees manage the Amazon Forest trust: Brazil, Bolivia, Peru, Ecuador, Columbia, Venezuela, Guyana, and Suriname. Within the United States, multiple state and tribal sovereign trustees oversee the Columbia River trust; Canada acts as a co-trustee of that trust with the United States on the international level. Eight states hold the Ogallala Aquifer in co-tenant trusteeship: Colorado, Kansas, Nebraska, New Mexico, Oklahoma, South Dakota, Texas, and Wyoming. All nations on Earth share the atmospheric trust and the oceans trust as co-tenant sovereign trustees.

A trust paradigm does not disturb nations' assertions of beneficial interests in global assets, but it does broaden the *duties* of each sovereign trustee with respect to the asset as a whole. By recognizing co-tenancy sovereign interests in planetary assets, the analysis enlarges the group of beneficiary interests that a nation must account for in asserting control over such assets, no matter where they fall on the continuum of possession and dominion. In their use and management, each co-tenant trustee of a shared planetary asset bears a duty toward all of the beneficiaries of the joint trust – that is, the present and future global citizenry. Likewise, apart from this duty toward citizens worldwide, a government owes a parallel fiduciary duty to protect the *planetary interests* of its own citizens in maintaining the functionality of global ecology.

The principle works in a rather straightforward manner with respect to obviously shared resources like the oceans, atmosphere, or a migrating fishery. Co-tenant duties to maintain the asset apply to all sovereign co-trustees of that asset, and these duties stand capable of enforcement by the citizen beneficiaries of each sovereign, as illustrated in the context of Atmospheric Trust Litigation, discussed later. But what about assets that fall on the other end of the continuum – the purely domestic resources (with planetary importance), as well as those that straddle categories? As to these, Sand argues, the sovereign must still act as a fiduciary managing a public trust. Yet traditional law has never analyzed the bundle of sovereign property interests in a way that fully recognizes obligations flowing to those outside the sovereign's borders. Where possessory use seems exclusive, the law must find a basis for inherent property obligations owed to the broader world.[19]

A global trust construct may draw useful analogies from property law, which offers many arrangements that vest owners with full possession yet impose obligations toward external interests. Owners of a condominium, for example, enjoy full and exclusive possession of their single unit, but that unit is of part of a larger structure (including the building's exterior walls and its roof) owned in common with other unit owners. All owners share a duty not to damage or waste the supporting structure. The very same logic extends, for example, to the deep sea bed of the planet. While nations may assert exclusive possession over their shoreline zones, the deep sea bed itself functions, in essence, as the floor of the planet. All nations have a co-tenancy interest in it, even though particular nations may exercise exclusive possessory rights over parts of it – their territorial "units," so to speak. An ensemble of duties flowing from this co-tenancy relationship limits the action any one nation can take in managing its possessory interests. While the economic interests of local citizens may support oil drilling, for instance, the planetary interests of those same citizens and the interests of co-tenant nations in the ocean floor flatly contravene dangerous deep-sea drilling that threatens the oceans and living systems.

DEFINING AND ENFORCING A FIDUCIARY OBLIGATION TOWARD PLANETARY ASSETS

Once a natural resource becomes identified as a planetary trust asset, legal principles evaluate its management according to measures of *asset health* and *functionality*, as explained in Chapter 8. Nature's own laws, scientifically interpreted, set the parameters. By applying scientifically defined planetary prescriptions as fiduciary obligations, the trust formulation creates a uniform and principled approach to global ecological responsibility. It offers beneficiaries concrete, science-based descriptions of government obligation, divesting leaders of their presumed prerogative to take only that action urged by their own political ambition.

Global fiduciary obligations flow to two separate classes of interests. First, each trustee government bears a fiduciary duty to its own citizens as well as citizens of the world to protect their planetary inheritance. Second, each nation owes a duty to all other nations, arising from the sovereign co-tenancy relationship, to prevent waste to common global assets. These two duties merge into a uniform obligation of asset protection. The mere existence of such duties, however, does not ensure they will be carried out. Citizens must explore opportunities to press the fiduciary obligation in their own legal systems. While such systems vary greatly between nations, this discussion offers five common approaches.

First and foremost, citizens should pursue enforcement of global trust obligations against their own governments in domestic courts. It is well settled that beneficiaries may sue the trustee to protect their property.[20] Recognizing that planetary fiduciary duties encumber sovereign management of a joint trust asset, judges need not shunt all ecological questions of global significance to the international political realm. Citizen beneficiaries that bring suit represent not only their own interests as members of the sovereign public, but also assert broader global interests in their capacity as world citizens, thus making the fiduciary duty a matter of domestic law and obligation. This duty provides the basis for a judicial remedy that can impose discrete and actionable baselines, benchmarks, and goals calibrated to scientific prescriptions for asset health, as the discussion below shows.

Second, the trust positions subnational sovereigns to assert property-based rights both in domestic courts and in legislative venues. In the United States, for example, states and tribes may bring suit (so far as allowed by principles of sovereign immunity) as co-tenants of common resources against other states, tribes, or the federal government for waste to the joint assets. As the Ninth Circuit court said in a treaty fishing case, "A court will enjoin the commission of waste." Apart from litigation, positioning domestic sovereigns as co-tenants of shared ecology in policy realms may help disassemble power-based relationships that have suppressed many native nations and states from protecting resources beyond their jurisdictional reach and may strengthen a sovereign pluralism that leads to more diverse approaches to ecological management.[21]

Third, the trust framework offers a fresh model for domestic legislative reform. By reframing global ecological problems (such as climate crisis) in terms of property rights, citizens can present a logical conception of global ecological responsibility for the domestic agenda. Science-based prescriptions for global asset protection provide benchmarks of fiduciary obligation and legislative accountability. In terms of time and money spent, domestic advocacy may prove more productive for citizens than attending international treaty negotiations, where they wield minimal political power.

Fourth, the trust provides a basis for national governments and subnational sovereigns (such as tribes and states) to seek natural resource damage actions against corporations that have polluted planetary resources. Global ecological crises require huge amounts of money for restoration measures. Strangely, the current realm of international diplomacy altogether ignores polluters, overlooking both their colossal culpability in causing the harm and their deep-pocket ability to finance mitigation through natural resource damages. While multinational corporations hold the lion's share of aggregate global wealth, they have rarely been sent the bill for their damage to planetary property. As Chapter 8 explained, federal, tribal, and state trustees stand positioned to collect natural resource damages for harm to trust property. An immediately obvious global campaign would focus on the fossil fuel corporations to fund massive reforestation and soil sequestration needed to draw down carbon dioxide from the atmosphere. Another would target the nuclear corporations to fund the dismantlement of dangerous plants and encasement of radioactive waste they have generated. Of course, weighty challenges exist in the collection of natural resource damages. The international community of nations will have to devise a fair way of allocating money damages gained by any one nation-trustee for harm to a shared asset. Moreover, domestic courts issuing damage judgments in one country might have to rely on courts in another country for enforcing those judgments. In 2009, for example, a court in Ecuador ordered Chevron Corporation to pay $27 billion for polluting the country's rainforest, but collection of the judgment depends on courts in other countries having jurisdiction over the company's assets.[22]

Finally, the Nature's Trust framework may give rise to new international governance regimes that operate like actual trusts. Just as land trusts came into being to manage private lands in accordance with trust principles, other innovations could occur on the international scale, perhaps using the UN structure. New trust institutions could honor nation-state autonomy while offering a more organized and principled framework for assigning global ecological obligations. To be at all effective, however, they must link into domestic enforcement mechanisms – which further underscores the importance of the judicial branch, a matter taken up in the next chapter.

Ultimately, the trust offers a transformative shift in how citizens and their leaders may think about ecology on the planetary level. With any paradigm shift comes innumerable new approaches, not confined to any one branch of government or any one nation. The striking commonality of the trust concept in legal systems worldwide creates possibilities for international, orchestrated strategies of domestic litigation and legislative reform to force protection of planetary assets. The discussion that follows explores one such movement already well under way, Atmospheric Trust Litigation (ATL).

ATMOSPHERIC TRUST LITIGATION

Urgency drives the ATL campaign to protect the planet's climate. The concentration of CO_2 in the atmosphere has reached a level not seen on Earth for at least 3 million years, and scientists warn that the business-as-usual (BAU) approach could "loc[k] in climate change at a scale that would profoundly and adversely affect all of human civilization and all of the world's major ecosystems." Dr. James Hansen, head of NASA's Goddard Institute for Space Studies, expressed the situation in an *amicus* science brief submitted in an ATL case brought against the U.S. government:

> [U]nabated fossil fuel emissions continue to drive the Earth increasingly out of energy balance. Unless action is undertaken without further delay ... Earth's climate system will be pressed toward and past points of no return.... [D]elay in undertaking sharp reductions in emissions will undermine any realistic chance of preserving a habitable climate system.[23]

Like other problems of global magnitude, climate crisis demands broad system-changing solutions. ATL presents a macro-scope litigation approach to climate crisis focused on the atmosphere as a single asset in its entirety. It characterizes all nations on Earth as co-tenant sovereign trustees of that atmosphere, bound together in a property-based framework of corollary and mutual responsibilities. As trustees, all nations owe a primary fiduciary obligation toward their citizen beneficiaries to restore atmospheric health. In addition, as nations joined in co-tenancy, each has a duty to the others to prevent waste of the common asset. ATL seeks to accomplish through decentralized domestic litigation, in countries across the globe, what has thus far eluded the international diplomatic treaty-making process: concrete requirements for emissions reduction.[24]

A Planetary Prescription for Climate

The UNFCCC declared a universal responsibility to avoid "dangerous anthropogenic interference" – a standard that expresses a guiding international principle for defining the atmospheric fiduciary obligation. Scientific prescriptions must form the yardstick for quantifying this obligation. Leading climate scientists warn that the planet needs to return to an atmospheric CO_2 concentration of approximately 350 ppm to avoid a climate point of no return. Mapping a glide path of global emissions reduction to achieve that target presents a scientific task requiring calculations about the rate of greenhouse gas absorption from the remaining natural sinks on Earth, the energy balance in the atmosphere, and a myriad of other technical issues.[25]

In May 2011, Dr. Hansen joined with other leading scientists across the world to issue a pathbreaking paper setting forth a trajectory of global carbon emissions reduction aiming to return the atmosphere to equilibrium at 350 ppm by the end of the century. It requires an *annual* 6 percent global decline in carbon dioxide emissions, beginning in 2013. This reduction amounts to "what is minimally needed to avert truly dangerous climate change and preserve the physical status quo of a habitable climate system," Dr. Hansen explains. Additionally, the prescription calls for extracting roughly 100 gigatons of CO_2 from the atmosphere through reforestation and improved soil practices in agriculture. As other analysts note, an "Emergency Pathway" to 350 ppm will require a level of societal mobilization "with few if any peacetime precedents."[26]

The start date for global carbon emissions reduction proves crucial. Delay pushes the planet perilously closer to unknown climate tipping points that may erupt into runaway heating. Scientists also stress that delay "drastically increases" both the speed at which emissions must be cut and the amount of emissions reduction required. Had the world commenced this effort back in 2005, the projected rate of reduction would have been only 3.5 percent per year to achieve 350 ppm by 2100 (in contrast to the 6 percent now required). If humanity waits too long to bend the rising curve of emissions, the slope of necessary emissions reduction becomes so steep a descent that it becomes impossible to achieve, consigning youth and future generations to a climate system careening out of equilibrium. To put it another way, the only feasible remaining pathways show a starting point of *now*. Courts stand as crucial players in this carbon reduction because they have the power to order swift and decisive relief during this narrow remaining window of opportunity.[27]

The global trajectory of 6 percent annual carbon emissions reduction represents the atmospheric fiduciary obligation shared by all co-trustee sovereigns on Earth. Of course, this scientifically prescribed pathway of carbon reduction does not reflect an absolutist no-waste approach; that would require halting virtually all carbon emissions tomorrow, which would prove impossible. Judicial approaches, by their very nature, involve equitable balancing of interests to avoid draconian results. That aside, the deadly consequences to humanity from further delay in emissions reduction should move courts to embrace the most aggressive feasible pathways.

An Organic Obligation: The Inexcusability of Orphan Shares

Having set a global trajectory projected to restore atmospheric equilibrium, the next step becomes imposing responsibility on the various sovereign co-tenants of the world to achieve it. Never before has the law faced an environmental problem of this complexity and magnitude. Nevertheless, societies have allocated environmental responsibility for millennia, and the underlying precepts stay remarkably fixed even as the context changes. They emerge from natural law notions of justice shared worldwide.

Because all sovereigns participate through their industries and societies in the pollution of the atmosphere, a legal framework of carbon responsibility must operate on the macro level to provide a principled, organic duty for every sovereign on Earth. In order for global carbon pollution to ultimately reach near-zero – which climate scientists deem necessary to restore atmospheric equilibrium – all nations must accede to a carbon reduction imperative. This premise runs precisely opposite to the operating assumption driving current climate negotiations – that national leaders enjoy discretion whether or not to assume climate responsibility. Even one nation's failure to take responsibility leaves an "orphan share" of pollution that creates a fatal deficit in the overall necessary reduction.[28]

Characterizing the atmosphere as one integral trust asset imbues each nation with inherent legal obligations to protect it. Under the co-tenancy model of property law, no nation can simply "opt out" of responsibility or disclaim a fiduciary duty toward an asset it shares as property with other nations. While diplomats in international treaty negotiations continue to shirk climate responsibility by saying that they should not act until other countries act, the judicial system should respond differently (in a property frame) on the basis that shared *rights* give rise to shared *responsibilities*. A court's lack of jurisdiction over other nation-trustees does not defeat its jurisdiction over the fiduciary actors in its own nation. Courts regularly deal with incremental parts of larger problems and render meaningful relief, although their remedy fails to solve the problem in its entirety. As the U.S. Supreme Court once proclaimed in an equal protection case, "It is no requirement of equal protection that all evils of the same genus be eradicated or none at all." The Court took the same view when it underscored U.S. climate responsibility in *Massachusetts v. EPA*, stating, "Nor is it dispositive that developing countries such as China and India are poised to increase greenhouse gas emissions substantially over the next century: A reduction in domestic emissions would slow the pace of global emissions increases, no matter what happens elsewhere." In other words, courts may certainly impose a fiduciary obligation on the sovereign actors under their jurisdiction despite their lack of authority over every other sovereign on Earth.[29]

Nevertheless, there remains a significant challenge conceptualizing each nation's obligation. In diplomacy venues, developing nations claim a continued right to pollute in order to achieve the standard of living that Western economies have enjoyed. They seem to plead an "opt-out" of the shared duty to protect the common asset. The waste doctrine of property law, however, elevates conservation duty over economic ambition. Emphasizing conservation as a supreme, organic encumbrance on any sovereign right, the U.S. Supreme Court once declared in the Pacific Northwest treaty fishing litigation:

> We do not imply that these fishing rights persist down to the very last steelhead in the river. Rights can be controlled by the need to conserve a species; and the time may come when the life of a steelhead is so precarious in a particular stream that all fishing should be banned until the species regains assurance of survival.

The same conservation logic gains even greater force when applied to the atmosphere, because climate equilibrium sustains all life on Earth. It makes no sense to pursue a higher standard of living if doing so threatens the human ability to survive. In the industrialized world too, no amount of jobs creation justifies disastrous fossil fuel emissions. As the UNFCCC plainly states, nations have a right to "*sustainable* development," meaning that no nation has a right to pursue economic development that irrevocably harms the atmosphere.[30]

The Waste Doctrine Applied Differentially to Carbon Reduction

The most straightforward way of accomplishing necessary global carbon reduction imposes an across-the-board mandate on all countries to reduce their own emissions by the 6 percent that scientists prescribed for the planet. This allocation would ensure that the carbon reduction "adds up" to the required amount because, if each and every piece of the global pollution "pie" reduces by a fixed amount, the global pie as a whole will shrink by the same amount. However, differences between countries defeat any such simple approach. Some countries have only minimal per capita carbon emissions, and asking them to shoulder the same proportionate burden as the countries with much larger amounts would not only be patently unfair but impractical as well, because such reduction may jeopardize their ability to provide for citizens' basic living requirements. Moreover, some countries (like the United States and other industrialized nations) have contributed vastly greater amounts of historic pollution than other nations and should bear more responsibility.

But while these challenges greatly complicate the task of allocating international liability for carbon reduction, the task itself can be avoided only at grave peril to humanity's collective future. Recognizing the many disparities among countries, the UNFCCC called for "common but differentiated responsibilities" in reducing carbon emissions. While treaty negotiations have utterly failed to translate that concept into a global scheme of carbon reduction, judges stand better positioned to do so. Judges are not new to the task of formulating principled factors and arranging them into a coherent liability scheme. They regularly allocate liability among multiple players in complex natural settings and do so with the public interest in mind. For example, in hazardous waste contexts, courts routinely impose responsibility on dozens or even hundreds of parties for cleaning up a contaminated site. They allocate scarce water supplies among hundreds or even thousands of competing claimants in river basins. No liability scheme will be perfect, but the judicial tradition allows for arriving at rough approximations of justice rather than precise formulations that could hopelessly drag out the process. As one famous treatise on equity observed, "Courts of Justice aim at practical good and general convenience rather than at theoretical perfection." Courts stand positioned to enforce carbon reduction in their own countries by adjusting the 6 percent global prescription to a time frame responsive to the individual circumstances of each nation. The 6 percent represents a global marker that serves as a departing point for quantifying the government's fiduciary obligation.[31]

Several factors become relevant to the judicial task of arriving at a nation-specific trajectory. First is the country's global share of carbon emissions. The top ten polluters account for roughly two-thirds of the world's total carbon pollution, with the United States and China as the top two polluting nations in the world (each has about a 20 percent share). Judges in those countries should impose particularly aggressive time frames for carbon reduction, because orphan shares of pollution from either country could plunge the planet into full catastrophe. The second factor focuses on historical emissions. Like a hazardous waste cleanup, those parties that dumped larger quantities of pollution should bear more responsibility. As to this, certainly, the United States shoulders a colossal share of liability, followed by other industrialized nations. A third factor points to the country's "per capita emissions," the amount of carbon dioxide emitted on average by each person in a particular country. This varies widely. The average American produces nearly 17.22 metric tons of carbon dioxide emissions a year, while the average Indian produces only about 1.64 metric tons. (Both nations stand among the top five polluters of the planet, reflecting a huge population disparity between the two). Countries with the high per capita rates show excessive consumption and ample capacity for dramatic reductions, both of which justify a steep trajectory of carbon reduction.[32]

A fourth factor examines the purpose behind the carbon emissions, because this plays a prominent role in allocating any scarce natural resource. Emphasizing that the atmosphere has little remaining "space" for carbon pollution before crossing irrevocable climate thresholds, some scientists speak in terms of a global "budget" for the world's carbon emissions. Viewed this way, the available "space" for remaining carbon pollution amounts to a scarce resource in itself. Just as judges currently allocate rights in rivers with too little water to meet competing demands, so must courts prioritize multiple calls on the atmosphere. As the damaging activity becomes more excessive relative to the basic needs of the general population, it becomes less tolerable from an equity and waste standpoint. Not unlike curtailing nonessential "luxury uses" of water in times of scarcity, so might courts impose a steep trajectory of reduction on luxury carbon emissions. The English government endorsed this approach for a period of time when it rejected new airport runways near London that would serve "binge flying" – that is, "jetting off to weekend homes in Spain and bachelor parties in Prague."[33]

Much of the work configuring an international liability scheme for carbon reduction has already been accomplished in a leading analysis called the *Greenhouse Development Rights Framework* (GDRF), prepared by the Stockholm Environment

Institute and EcoEquity. The GDRF presents an objective framework of responsibility based on the UNFCCC's "common but differentiated" standard. The analysis takes into account both historic emissions since 1990 and a nation's financial standing to carry out carbon reduction without threatening the most basic needs of its population. Using these two factors, the GDRF creates an index to show each country's logical share of the global "ecological debt." From there, it delineates individualized carbon reduction trajectories for each nation. Most important, the pathways are designed to calibrate to, *and collectively meet,* a planetary trajectory for necessary carbon reduction. The approach therefore offers a global distribution scheme of carbon reduction informed by logical factors that can effectuate the UNFCCC's standard of "common but differentiated responsibilities." Moreover, the trajectories adjust to change, both demographic and atmospheric. The GDRF positions domestic courts to assign sovereign fiduciary responsibility to their nations as part of a macro, uniform approach to global carbon reduction calibrated to meet planetary requirements.[34]

The Judicial Role

Though climate crisis invokes complex science and policy concerns, the urgency in carbon reduction requires a decisive and straightforward approach that can be accomplished through atmospheric trust decrees emanating from courts worldwide. Two causes of action, available to different classes of parties, aim to enforce this atmospheric fiduciary obligation. First, citizen beneficiaries can bring suit against their governmental trustees for failing to protect their atmospheric trust. In the United States, youth citizens have brought ATL lawsuits against eleven states as well as the federal government, and administrative petitions are pending in the remaining states. Second, a sovereign trustee may bring an action against a co-tenant trustee for committing waste to common property. This becomes most feasible on the domestic level (as in a suit by one state against another, or by tribes against the federal government), but other, less enforceable venues may arise in international courts. Waste and breach-of-trust claims find grounding within the same basic property framework, both linking to the scientific prescription of carbon reduction as the expression of sovereign duty. As with any claim, litigants must navigate a myriad of procedural barriers.[35]

Atmospheric trust litigation seeks a remedy that provides the macro relief necessary to effectuate the sovereign's share of global emissions reduction. The remedy finds its sidewalls in a declaratory judgment iterating the principles of law – which alone can greatly clarify government climate responsibility worldwide. Injunctive relief, however, remains necessary to force government action. ATL cases call for government trustees to develop an enforceable plan for reducing carbon emissions in accordance with the 6 percent prescription. Courts are not positioned to tell the trustees *how* to accomplish the carbon reduction – that remains the job of the trustees – but courts can help ensure that adequate reductions actually occur. Government trustees must report emissions reduction progress to the court in regular intervals, through carbon accountings. Because carbon reduction requires steady progress over many decades, a court must invoke ongoing jurisdiction (not unusual for cases that require protracted remedies against government institutions). The judicial role in ATL stands much the same as in other litigation that requires broad remedial plans and continuing oversight – such as cases against recalcitrant managers of school districts and prisons – a matter taken up in the next chapter. In sum, by offering a uniform remedy linked to the global climate prescription, the trust principle provides a basis for orchestrated, yet independent, lawsuits worldwide to protect common atmospheric property.[36]

The ATL Hatch

The atmospheric trust strategy hatched in the form of unprecedented petitions and litigation initiated by youth across the United States during the first week of May 2011. A sixteen-year-old named Alec Loorz brought a climate lawsuit in federal court against the Obama administration. Alec had formed the organization *Kids v. Global Warming* when he was twelve years old. Amassing climate warnings from scientists, his complaint declared: "Americans and the world as a whole face impending catastrophe." John Thiebes, a twenty-three-year-old farmer, brought a climate lawsuit in the Supreme Court of Montana. He and other young petitioners described disappearing glaciers, water scarcity, and the increased occurrences of wildfire threatening Montana. Jaime Lynn Butler, a ten-year-old member of the Navajo Nation, sued the governor of Arizona. Her complaint explained the severe water shortages from climate change impacting her family's work in agriculture. Sixteen-year-old Akilah Sanders-Reed sued the governor of New Mexico, recounting the dried-up streams and diminished water supplies for the farmers that supply her food. Nelson Kanuk, a sixteen-year-old Alaska native living in the remote village of Kipnuk, sued the state of Alaska; his complaint depicted the massive flooding of his village caused by rising sea levels, melting ice, and warmer temperatures – all of which will force his family to move from their home in just a matter of years. Fifteen-year-old Kelsey Juliana and eleven-year-old Olivia Cherniak sued the governor of Oregon. Their complaint listed climate effects projected for Oregon by mid-century, including extreme weather events, intensified wildfires, rising sea levels, and a 50 percent loss in snowpack, which directly threatens the region's water supplies. These stories, along with those of dozens of other youth plaintiffs and petitioners, fused into a legal campaign of extraordinary magnitude.

It had never happened before in the history of law: a simultaneous *hatch* of legal actions. Young people launched legal processes in every U.S. state. Internationally, an ATL lawsuit was filed in Ukraine, and plans for ATL suits in other countries began taking shape as well. Coordinated by the nonprofit organization, Our Children's Trust, the suits and petitions all declared a sovereign trust duty to protect the atmosphere needed by the youth and future generations for their long-term survival. They demanded judicially enforceable Climate Recovery Plans from government trustees to reduce carbon emissions by at least 6 percent annually, beginning in 2013, following the scientific prescription formulated by Dr. James Hansen and other scientists. These plans would be backed up by annual carbon accountings to show compliance with the prescription. More than a dozen renowned scientists and experts submitted declarations in support of the litigation.[37]

During the week of the "hatch," thousands of youth took to the streets in more than 125 marches held in cities across the United States and in countries throughout the world, from Kuwait to Nepal, to Pakistan, to Bangladesh. Wherever they marched, young arms lifted signs stating: "*iMatter. Our Future Matters.*" The youth met with the press. They appeared on talk shows. They met with elected officials. They gave talks to schools. Wire services provided national coverage, and blogs began to buzz with news of the "inconvenient lawsuits." Video documentaries featuring individual youth plaintiffs ensued. Produced by the nonprofit organization, WITNESS, the documentaries showed in film festivals around the world, and film awards began to stream in.[38]

As state agencies denied ATL petitions, more lawsuits followed. Youth brought suit in Iowa. Texas too. Then Kansas. And Uganda. As the lowest trial court judges dismissed suits, the youth raised appeals in higher courts. More lawsuits – many more – were in the making, revealed Julia Olson, the lawyer-strategist and mother of two who founded Our Children's Trust and coordinated the ATL campaign. Within just a year, the cadre of pro bono ATL attorneys representing youth had grown to more than forty lawyers dispersed around the United States; lawyers in other countries began preparing for an international hatch of lawsuits as well.

The stakes remain unfathomably high for young people. By late 2011, the International Energy Agency's chief economist, Fatih Birol, reported that emissions rates were soaring toward an 11°F heating scenario by century's end. He said: "[E]verybody, even school children, knows this will have catastrophic implications for all of us." No scientist gives assurance that the projected heating will be survivable on any broad scale. In fact, many flatly say these temperatures would prove calamitous for the human race. Yet the executive and legislative branches in the United States and in many other countries still do little or nothing to curb the greenhouse gas pollution. Dr. James Hansen minced no words when he said in his *amicus* brief supporting the atmospheric trust litigation: "[F]ailure to act with all deliberate speed in the face of the clear scientific evidence of the danger functionally becomes a decision to *eliminate the option of preserving a habitable climate system.*"[39]

Worldwide, young people might feel as if they are locked in a heating greenhouse, their leaders poised to throw out the keys. Courts stand as a last resort – but a resort nonetheless.

11

Nature's Justice: The Role of the Courts

The cornerstone of any trust lies in judicial enforcement. If fiduciary obligations become unenforceable in court, a trustee can exert untrammeled power over the beneficiaries' property and use that power to advance his own singular interests. Judge Learned Hand once stated that courts must have the ability to enforce fiduciary obligations, or what claimed to be a trust would amount to no more than a "precatory admonition."[1] Yet, by nearly all appearances, environmental law has degenerated into this. Government trustees today enjoy nearly unchecked control over Nature without the concomitant restraint and enforcement that a public trust demands.

As Chapter 5 presented, the modern statutory era of environmental law in the United States postured courts in a way that caused them to retreat from their meaningful role. Courts today render decisions under statutory law that rank fairly insignificant in the broad scheme of mounting ecological threats. Time and again, they fail to penetrate the systemic dysfunction that causes agencies to subvert statutory goals. The Nature's Trust paradigm revives the constitutionally appointed role of courts as a coequal third branch of government positioned to enforce sovereign legal obligations toward the public's natural assets. While this chapter principally focuses on the role of courts in the United States, the basic analysis carries relevance elsewhere as well. An active judiciary remains the cornerstone of trust protection in any country.

THE JUDICIAL ROLE IN ENVIRONMENTAL DEMOCRACY

Debate never stops over the proper role of courts in a democracy. Without retreading that ground, this chapter focuses on the court's apposite role in environmental law. Today's courts sit in a diminutive position, issuing narrow judgments on procedural and technical minutiae ensconced in voluminous statutes and regulations. The regulatory muddle stands so omnipotent over professional time and energy that it becomes easy to forget that, for most of the nation's history, courts sculpted fundamental principles of sovereign duty toward ecology through judge-made common law. In many ways, this historic role represented the pinnacle of environmental judging in America.

Courts crafted common law using doctrines derived from England. Adapting these principles to the blank slate of new America, celebrated judges wrote towering opinions such as *Illinois Central* that portrayed a righteous conception of popular justice. Their legal strokes emerged from a canvass of common sense as these courts molded the common law to unprecedented circumstances. Justice Holmes reflected the judicial demeanor when he famously wrote that the law must answer to "[t]he felt necessities of the time."[2] Formulating universal axioms, courts played a leading role in defining the ecological rights and responsibilities of citizens in a fast-growing nation.

As Chapter 2 explained, a rapid transformation in law and legal institutions occurred with the New Deal (1930s) and magnified in the 1970s with the enactment of environmental statutes. Agencies and regulations proliferated across the American legal landscape. The agencies became the new tribunals of justice, supplanting much of the judicial role with administrative regulation and adjudication. This sharp growth of agencies winnowed the judiciary to a mere twig of its original branch of government. While there have been perennial moments during post–New Deal history where the courts have played a truly transformative role in American society – most notably during the civil rights era – modern environmental law lacks such punctuation.[3]

Certainly good reasons existed for enacting environmental statutes. Case-by-case resolution of conflict in the court system could not keep pace with industry's infliction of damage on resources and ecosystems. The nation needed uniform and comprehensive standards, along with an administrative framework to implement them – and the statutes promised that. But after the legislatures passed the statutes, lawyers premised the vast majority of their court claims on statutory or regulatory violations, which afforded more precise, and seemingly more enforceable, mandates than common law. As Chapter 5 explained, courts assume a very different posture in cases arising under statutory law.

Statutory claims come to court as regulatory mazes that agencies create out of underlying environmental disputes. Courts do not give fresh scrutiny to these cases as they would to those arising under common law. Instead, litigation centers around the "administrative record" created by the agency itself, containing the evidence and conclusions gained from the regulatory process. Burying environmental harm in a tangle of technical complexity and regulatory jargon (sometimes extending over thousands of pages), the administrative record can conceal even the most egregious wrongs committed by polluters upon the public.

By limiting their review of environmental cases to this administrative record, judges give agencies the first crack at characterizing the dispute. Moreover, judges give deference to the agencies, assuming them to be neutral institutions endowed with superior technical expertise. Whereas this deferent posture may have originated as a judicial choice, it eventually became a practical reality as a result of the complexity of many regulatory cases. As a result of their deferential posture, today's courts uphold many agency decisions that work grave environmental harm. They jettison many important cases on procedural grounds. They issue remedies that remand illegal agency actions to the same flawed process that produced the litigation in the first place. While some exceptional judges manage to cut through the administrative veneer to get at the heart of an issue and render meaningful remedies, they remain few in number.

Today's opinions present a dull contrast to their historic predecessors. As judges burrow down into complex and procedure-laden regulations, their writings often emerge technical and narrow in concentration, bland in justice, overstuffed with process, and lacking any moral tone. Characteristically brittle, they ossify an area of law that demands agility as society confronts eclipsing environmental threats. Despite massive time and resources, it stands painfully clear how little modern environmental litigation has accomplished. Statutory cases often last for years, sometimes even decades. They proliferate in scores of opinions and rulings that accumulate into entire subfields of law, but they rarely resolve the real conflict. Statutory claims tend to focus on the procedural failings of an agency, because attorneys find those easier to prove than shortfalls in substantive protection. The remedy sought for such violations is also procedural, usually forcing another study, another finding, another public comment period, or another agency process. Interminable litigation over some of America's most celebrated resources – such as Alaska's old growth forests, the Appalachia Mountains, and the Colorado River – yields an avalanche of procedural determinations with little in the way of durable protection.

In hindsight, the rise of the administrative state and concomitant judicial descent happened without adequate thought or precaution for the future of constitutional democracy, which relies appreciably on an even balance of power allocated between the three branches of government. Roscoe Pound, former Dean of Harvard Law School and a renowned legal scholar, early on expressed much trepidation over what he viewed as a new "administrative absolutism." In 1942, he warned, "Once established, an absolute bureaucracy will not be easy to dethrone."[4]

Today's ecological crises demand judicial intervention to rein in runaway agencies, arrest the siphoning of natural wealth belonging to the public, and re-anchor environmental law to its original moorings of justice, public interest, and community morality. Public trust claims hold the potential to summon dormant judicial capacity in ways that statutory claims tend not to. First, public trust claims can be macro in scope. They seek to hold agencies – perhaps a multitude of them – to their fiduciary responsibilities of protecting assets in their integral entirety. Statutory violations, by contrast, typically engender only micro claims directed at just one agency and just one type of violation. Judicial remedies for these fail to solve problems that have reached systemic levels of dysfunction. Second, trust claims seek to hold public officials accountable to *substantive* fiduciary obligations, not just procedural formalities. Substantive fiduciary performance looks to actual protection of the asset, regardless of whether government followed correct procedures in resource management. Third, trust claims can assert a duty of loyalty to the public. This subjects to challenge the politicized or self-interested decision making that often takes place behind the furtive curtains of administrative discretion. Fourth, trust claims stand independent of agency process and do not rest on an administrative record. Accordingly, they invite examination of a wider range of evidence as to agency behavior and environmental conditions. Fifth, a trust claim should not trigger blanket deference to agency technical decisions. Courts repeatedly underscore the judicial role in keeping trustees accountable.[5] And finally, a trust claim can invoke more potent judicial power in reviewing legislative action. While most environmental statutory claims merely engage questions of statutory *implementation*, a trust claim (so fashioned) can challenge the statute itself as a violation of legislative *fiduciary duty*. These differences, discussed more fully later in the chapter, revive aspects of historic judging.

Not everyone views an invigorated judiciary as a good thing. Particularly resistant will be those corporate interests currently benefiting from a weak court system that defers to the captured political branches of government. As Dean Roscoe Pound said decades ago, "Not a little ... denunciation of judges proceeds from those who do not wish the law to operate equally and exactly but wish to see it warped in their favor and resent judicial resistance to pressure under which administrative officials would yield." As he emphasized, a "constitutional legal polity" requires institutional checks. In a more perfect government where the political branches truly represent and serve the public's interest, judicial intervention would not be needed. But at a time when industry influence largely commands both legislatures and agencies, the court's role becomes crucial. As Professor Joseph Sax observed in his seminal article on the public trust:

> [S]elf-interested and powerful minorities often have an undue influence on the public resource decisions of legislative and administrative bodies and cause those bodies to ignore broadly based public interests. Thus, the function which the courts must perform, and have been performing, is to promote equality of political power for a disorganized and diffuse majority by remanding appropriate cases to the legislature after public opinion has been aroused.

Sax characterized the public trust doctrine as "a medium for democratization," a tool courts invoke to "mend perceived imperfections in the legislative and administrative process." As he wrote, "In the ideal world, legislatures are the most representative and responsive public agencies; and to the extent that judicial intervention moves legislatures toward that ideal, the citizenry is well served."[6]

Some commentators bristle at the strong judicial posture embraced by a public trust approach. Professor Jim Huffman wrote: "[Professor Sax's] central thesis is that democracy sometimes does not work.... Unanswered is the question of why the judiciary, an elitist institution with few democratic credentials, should be in a position to second-guess the actions of a legislature and its administrators." But an elitist portrait of the judiciary (which brings to mind nine justices sitting on the U.S. Supreme Court) does not fully characterize this branch of government. While the Supreme Court sits as the highest federal court, it decides very few cases. Judicial power in the United States disperses across thousands of judges collectively at the federal, state, tribal, and municipal levels, sitting in trial, appellate, and supreme courts. Moreover, many state court judges do, in fact, sit for election (although federal judges do not). Huffman's criticism also seems to rest on a tenuous assumption: that the legislatures are fairly elected and that the agencies carry out the laws in loyal manner. As prior chapters explained, that idealism increasingly diverges from reality. Corporate interests finance campaigns, and legislators regularly use their offices to support legislation directly benefiting their campaign donors. Judges at least operate under strict ethical standards designed to prevent bias that might stem from campaign contributions or other conflicts of interest. (Of course these rules fail at times, and an elected judiciary stands corruptible in ways that do not plague a tenured judiciary). As to agencies, Professor Sandi Zellmer and others point out that they have become a de facto "fourth branch of government," without being elected by the public.[7]

Critics of a robust judiciary rarely confront the main takeaway lesson of fifth-grade civics class – that the U.S. Constitutional system rests on three, not two, branches of government. The basic checks and balances inherent in a three-branch system create a crucial tension in government that remains vital for preventing any one branch from seizing tyrannical power. Like a bow string losing force when not taut, democracy loses its essential vitality when the legal and political tension between the branches turns flaccid. The point stands equally true in other countries as well. As Justice Velasco, a Justice of the Supreme Court of the Philippines wrote: "Surely, it is not judicial activism when courts carry out their constitutionally assigned function of judicial review.... [I]t becomes the primordial duty of the judiciary to compel the executive to perform its lawful functions."[8]

The discussion that follows describes a judicial role of enforcing fiduciary obligations toward Nature's Trust. Chapters 8 and 9 offered a set of duties applicable to both legislatures (as primary trustees) and agencies (as agents of the trustee). Courts have accumulated vast experience in applying the full set of fiduciary obligations to private trustees. Adapting these to the public realm yields a fiduciary framework in which courts may meaningfully review agency and legislative action. Such judicial review, of course, must bear comity to the different position of agencies and legislatures in the constitutional structure.[9]

JUDICIAL REVIEW OF AGENCY ACTION: THE DEFERENCE DOCTRINE

Nearly all environmental law cases now come to court as challenges to agency action. The court's review typically asks whether the agencies complied with statutory law. Congress gave agencies vast discretion in implementing broad directives, yet as prior chapters explained, agencies often exploit this discretion to serve politically powerful interests. Within this context, the public trust steers agency discretion toward meeting fiduciary duties owed to the public and future beneficiaries. In that way, the trust operates as an interstitial set of obligations – not contravening statutory mandates, but augmenting them.

To hold agencies accountable under the public trust, courts must reevaluate their use of the agency deference doctrine, which presently operates as a suit of armor for agency decisions of a technical and scientific nature (which describes most environmental decisions). Reasoning that such matters fall within agency expertise and that courts lack technical capacity, courts fail to look deeply into the political factors that tend to inappropriately predetermine a regulatory outcome. Given that agencies often mask political and biased decisions behind a thick veneer of complicated science, the deference doctrine repeatedly sets a judicial stage on which, Sara Clark notes, the courts act as "complicit player[s] in the science charade." Professor Wendy Wagner explains: "By insisting on technical justifications on the one hand, and pledging not to scrutinize the accuracy of the technical explanations on the other, the courts not only fail to prevent the science charade, they make it almost obligatory."[10]

Extreme deference works an aberration in the law. The very purpose of courts aims to discern truth in actions challenged by lawsuits. When a court plays hands-off in deference to one of the parties, a crucial element of the judicial process falls away. In the private trust context, courts enforce fiduciary duties with rigor. They root out bias and demand loyalty to the beneficiaries. They insist on asset protection. They prohibit speculative and risky management. In complex tort cases, as well, courts take a meaningful look at all evidence presented, no matter how daunting the technical material. Yet the deference doctrine of environmental law somehow escapes question by judges and lawyers despite its untoward effect of giving the agencies extraordinary cover in litigation challenging their technical decisions.

As a practical reality, judicial deference leaves agencies nearly unsupervised. Long ago, Roscoe Pound called for judicial counterweights to ensure that bureaucrats "in reality *and not in pretense* apply the standard committed to them." Similarly, Justice William O. Douglas warned of "oppressive" agencies and said, "[t]here must be some check on them." Suspicion toward agencies rarely finds its way into modern judicial opinions, though there are some exceptions. In *Sierra Club v. Espy*, a 1994 case challenging the Forest Service's clear-cut logging program, a federal district judge in Texas described the potential of "excessively self-aggrandized, run-amok executive agencies" to frustrate and subvert statutory law. The judge noted: "Judicial refusals to enjoin such violations abdicate, for one thing, the courts' affirmative role in the Constitution's system of checks and balances."[11]

Judges certainly could reshape the deference doctrine into a more searching approach that better reflects the modern administrative age. Nature's Trust urges the kind of deference developed in the realm of private trust law. Commonly, express trusts confer some discretion to the trustee in order to secure the advantage of the trustee's "wisdom and guidance" on behalf of the beneficiary, but courts do not allow such discretion to overcome the fundamental duties of a trustee. As Justice Cardozo once said, even the broadest conferral of discretion does not mean that it can be "recklessly or willfully abused." Trustees, he noted, subject themselves to "obligations of fidelity and diligence that attach to the office of trustee."[12]

The duty of loyalty remains particularly fundamental to the trust. In the private context, courts enforce the duty of loyalty rigorously, often voiding transactions found in breach of it. Yet, as Chapter 5 explained, courts turn a blind eye to conflicts of interest and bias in the agency context. Only recently has any judge overtly recognized the potential for abuse and offered a logical remedy. In a 2008 case, *Sierra Forest Legacy v. Rey* (discussed briefly in Chapter 4), an environmental group challenged a Forest Service decision to allow logging in the Sierra Nevada region so as to bring in revenue to the agency to fund its fuel reduction program for the same area. While the majority opinion stayed safely within the narrow confines of statutory law to enjoin the logging, Judge Noonan wrote a concurring opinion that struck at the heart of the matter. Pointing out that the Forest Service's harvest scheme would bring in money to fund the agency, he noted the obvious bias that compromised the agency's impartiality, finding the circumstance "as troublesome as it would be if instead of an impartial agency decision the agency was the paid accomplice of the loggers." Judge Noonan would have "vitiate[d] entirely" the ultimate decisions, deeming them irreparably infected and thus invalid – a result squarely in accordance with trust law's approach of voiding decisions made from a conflict of interest. Judge Noonan's reasoning should send long-overdue tremors of logic through the bedrock assumptions underlying current environmental law. As more judges come to question the neutrality of agency decisions, an awakening to the failings of the deference doctrine may be inevitable. Once courts push aside automatic deference, as they really must in a public trust case, a full suite of fiduciary obligations comes into focus.[13]

Trustees must adhere to a panoply of duties, all vitally important to the beneficiaries. If any one of these duties cannot be enforceable in court, it ceases to be a trust duty. Broadly speaking, the duties divide into substantive ones and procedural ones, as inventoried and explained in Chapters 8 and 9, respectively. The procedural duties ensure that the trustee eliminates potential for bias, maintains loyalty to the beneficiaries, exercises due diligence, and manages assets with utmost prudence and caution. When an agency violates these, the court should normally vacate the offending agency decision, as Judge Noonan suggested in the *Sierra Forest Legacy* case.

Substantive duties, such as the duty of asset protection, tend to be deeply enmeshed in technical circumstances and therefore more difficult for courts to grapple with. Here, courts must rework the deference principle so as to determine whether the agency action truly protects the natural asset to the fullest extent feasible. Inevitably, courts will often have to consider alternate formulations submitted by scientists outside of the agency. The plaintiffs – the parties suing the government trustee – usually provide these experts. For example, in a trust suit challenging river management, an agency may contend that imperiled fish will survive a 30 percent water level decline (to serve irrigators), whereas an independent scientist may conclude that the fish cannot survive more than a 20 percent decline. This "battle of the experts" remains standard fare in nearly every kind of lawsuit outside of administrative law, but the deference doctrine stifles it in environmental law, where it may be needed most. In order to evaluate whether the agency meets the fiduciary duty of protection, the court must determine which science – the agency's or the beneficiaries' – stands most credible.

Judges are hardly new to the task of choosing between conflicting experts. They have developed rigorous methods of reviewing science in cases not involving government agencies and can readily invoke those approaches to evaluate the management of public trust assets. In the 1993 case, *Daubert v. Merrell Dow Pharmaceuticals*, the U.S. Supreme Court called on courts to carefully assess the credibility of scientific evidence in private cases that turn on scientific proof. Courts invoke a variety of tools to gain the expertise necessary to evaluate scientific evidence. They often use court-appointed experts, technical advisors, and special masters to resolve difficult scientific questions in toxic torts and product liability cases. The judiciary's deep engagement with science in a post-*Daubert* world seemingly deflates the primary rationale courts still use to justify agency deference: that judges remain ill-equipped to scrutinize the merits of science. Bringing to bear the same technical resources that they use in cases between private parties, courts stand positioned to judge whether an agency's program protects the functionality of natural resources. While judges may not relish sorting through environmental science, the words of the Ninth Circuit panel in the *Daubert* remand resonate equally for public trust cases: "[W]e take a deep breath and proceed with this heady task."[14]

REVIEW OF CONGRESSIONAL ACTION: JUDICIAL CHECKS AND VETOES

Courts find themselves in a very different posture when reviewing legislative action (as opposed to agency action) because of the legislature's constitutional role in making laws. State and federal legislators stand as the ultimate public trustees (whereas agencies act as agents of these trustees). In order for the public trust rights of citizen beneficiaries to be enforceable – which, by definition, they must be in order to amount to a trust – the judiciary must have the power to override the legislature on crucial occasions where the trustee fails to meet its fiduciary obligation. As explained in Chapter 6, whereas judicial common law generally yields to legislative enactments (a statute will typically "preempt," or trump, the common law), a different situation exists with the public trust. Professor Harrison Dunning wrote an extensive article in which he observes that some courts have found the doctrine "immune from legislative abolition," treating it as "more than a conventional notion of the common law." As he explains these judicial results, the public trust doctrine constrains legislatures because it exists as "an implied state constitutional doctrine, on[e] that springs from a fundamental notion of how government is to operate with regard to common heritage natural resources." Judicial pronouncements of a constitutional nature carry superior force over legislative statutes. The public trust, as an attribute of sovereignty, falls into that hallowed realm, because no government can disclaim it, as prior chapters explained. The U.S. Supreme Court declared in the landmark *Illinois Central* case: "The state can no more abdicate its trust over property in which the whole people are interested ... than it can abdicate its police powers in the administration of government and the preservation of the peace." In Arizona, modern courts have twice struck legislative attempts to restrict the trust.[15]

As the federal district court of Illinois described in one case, the judicial purpose remains "to police" the legislature's disposition of the public trust. Doing so, however, means that courts must survey the boundary between deference and control and decide what posture becomes appropriate for a given case. On one hand, they must exercise that degree of scrutiny and power over the legislature necessary to meaningfully enforce citizen beneficiaries' rights. On the other hand, courts sometimes wisely refuse to invade the prerogatives of legislative bodies that citizens vote into office. Emerging from these opposing objectives come two options that could be called a judicial "veto" and a judicial "check." In the veto instance, the court overrides the legislature's decision entirely. For example, in *Lake Michigan Federation v. United States Army Corps of Engineers*, the Illinois federal court invalidated the legislature's conveyance of shoreline trust property to a private college, rejecting any deference to the legislature and explaining, "If courts were to rubber stamp legislative decisions ... the doctrine would have no teeth. The legislature would have unfettered discretion to breach the public trust as long as it was able to articulate some gain to the public." But in the judicial check scenario, the court shows deference by remanding the case for further reconsideration and proceedings in the legislature. As Professor Joseph Sax explained the legislative remand:

> The closer a court can come to thrusting decision making upon a truly representative body – such as by requiring a legislature to determine an issue openly and explicitly – the less a court will involve itself in the merits of a controversy.... [E]ven those courts which are the most active and interventionist in the public trust area are not interested in displacing legislative bodies as the final authorities in setting resource policies.[16]

Public trust case law reflects both approaches. The Supreme Court's decisions in *Illinois Central* and *Lake Michigan* manifestly underscore the veto authority by finding legislative conveyances of property invalid. But often, courts express deference to the legislature to balance public interests in resource management. As the California Supreme Court said in *Marks v. Whitney*, "It is a political question, within the wisdom and power of the Legislature, acting within the scope of its duties as trustee, to determine whether public trust uses should be modified or extinguished."[17]

Professor Douglas Grant provides a reasonable basis for choosing between a judicial veto and a judicial check through legislative remand. A remand becomes appropriate, he argues, "[w]here a legislative ... grant of a trust resource causes harm that is fully reparable reasonably quickly." This seems an appropriate remedy, for example, when the issue involves conflict over various present beneficial uses of the public asset, none of which would cause irrevocable harm. But where the harm becomes "irreparable or is not reparable within a reasonable time," Grant contends, the circumstances warrant a judicial veto. This approach finds a firm anchor within trust law's prohibition against waste. A trustee may not allow an asset to be destroyed or impaired to the extent that it deprives beneficiaries of their future entitlement. Grant ties the authority for the judicial veto back to the basic constitutional restriction on legislative action expressed by the reserved powers doctrine (discussed in Chapter 6). As the Court in *Illinois Central* emphasized, one legislature may not bind a successor legislature in matters crucial to sovereignty. Grant notes:

> When the environmental harm is likely to be objectionable to a future legislature but not reparable by it within a reasonable time, there is a sense in which the future

legislature's police power discretion over the resource will have been destroyed by the earlier legislature's grant if that grant is allowed to stand.[18]

Apart from the court's role in reviewing substantive duties of legislative trustees, judicial scrutiny should also extend to the procedural fiduciary duties, the duty of loyalty ranking high among them. A judicial check in the form of a legislative remand becomes appropriate when invalidating legislation on loyalty grounds. In that instance, courts do not substitute their judgment for that of the legislature, but allow the legislature to eliminate personal conflicts of interest in the second round of decision making. Judges may find this approach quite novel, as they may have rarely scrutinized legislative enactments for taint of bias. But as Chapter 9 suggested, courts should enforce these duties against legislators exercising power over natural resources because in that realm they act not only as political representatives, but as trustees of public property. Courts that would certainly punish a legislator who succumbed to outright bribery are quite capable of recognizing more nuanced transgressions of this duty of loyalty that ripple through campaign finance arrangements and other conflicts of interest.

THE MODERN TRUST REMEDY

The protection of Nature's Trust ultimately requires courts to perforate the legal dysfunction that drives society toward ecological collapse. To reassume their constitutionally appointed role, judges must find ways of creating effective relief for environmental transgressions caused by agencies and legislatures. Structuring relief remains one of the most challenging aspects of trust enforcement because, in many cases, harm results from agency or legislative *inaction* rather than action. For example, climate crisis worsens when state and federal governments fail to regulate greenhouse gas pollution. And nuclear power plants sit as ticking time bombs when government fails to remove and secure the unsafe radioactive waste they hold.

The Supreme Court of Washington recognized this inherent distinction between forcing government action and halting it. In the education funding context, it stated:

> The vast majority of constitutional provisions ... are framed as negative restrictions on government action. With respect to those rights, the role of the court is to police the outer limits of government power.... This approach ultimately provides the wrong lens for analyzing positive constitutional rights, where the court is concerned not with whether the State has done too much, but with whether the State has done enough. *Positive constitutional rights do not restrain government action; they require it.*

Describing the right to education as a "positive right," the court observed that these rights require the court to take "a more active stance in ensuring that the State complies with its affirmative constitutional duty." This designation of positive rights runs equally cogent in illuminating citizen-beneficiaries' deeply rooted public trust expectations: they lodge in government's *affirmative duties* of asset protection and restoration.[19]

Certainly, the enforcement of positive rights can test the limits of judicial restraint, as the Washington Supreme Court readily acknowledged. But judges in the United States hold tremendous authority and discretion under their equitable powers to structure remedies that will address the harm. Invoking a judicial tool called an injunction, a court may enjoin (that is, forbid) harmful action and also compel affirmative action. This allows courts to back up their proclamations with orders that achieve results. As one treatise explains, an injunction provides "an ancient and familiar tool of equity ... used whenever the circumstances warrant." Where harm to positive rights results from a derelict agency failing to take action where it should, a court must sometimes take over aspects of that agency's functions at least temporarily. Courts achieve this through a "structural injunction" described as "an order by which a court takes control of a public institution."[20]

Institutional judicial remedies can aim prospectively, sweep broadly, and respond to a myriad of scientific and management challenges. While such judicial intervention surpasses the traditional role of courts, the severe breakdown of agencies has spurred it in a number of different contexts. The desegregation cases of the 1950s and 1960s displayed the most notorious judicial administrative role as courts undertook detailed management of entire school bussing systems. But an ensemble of other U.S. cases dealing with prison overcrowding, treaty fishing rights, dam operations, school funding, and land use issues also exemplifies judicial vigor and innovation in addressing bureaucratic delinquency. U.S. courts have also developed management capacity in the corporate context when supervising bankruptcy reorganizations and providing compensation for class action tort victims (a task that requires elaborate systems for locating and notifying victims, evaluating the basis for individual claims, and processing the claims).[21] In all of these contexts, courts recognize that they must gain administrative capacity of some sort in order to give effect to their legal rulings.

The discussion that follows briefly showcases five U.S. cases as well as one case from the Philippines to demonstrate remedy tools that will prove useful in litigation to enforce Nature's Trust. Three notable circumstances prompted vigorous judicial intervention in all of these cases: (1) systemic collapse of an administrative system charged with achieving a particular goal for society (i.e., prison management, education, pollution control, fair land use, protection of treaty rights, and species conservation); (2) a threat of irreparable harm to life, health, welfare, or property rights; and (3) persistent agency and/or legislative delay in solving the problem after repeated opportunities to do so. In all of these cases, the judicial posture initially showed measured restraint typical of the judicial temperament, but as the crises worsened and became more urgent, the courts moved to a more interventionist, problem-solving stance. The discussion begins with a brief summary of these cases to provide a backdrop for more extensive discussion of the tools used in fashioning meaningful remedies.

The Mount Laurel Land Use Litigation (1974–1983)

This litigation was brought against the City of Mt. Laurel, New Jersey, for its discriminatory zoning laws that caused a severe shortage in affordable housing.[22] Concluding that housing, along with food, amounts to one of the "most basic human needs," the New Jersey Supreme Court held that each town in the state held a state constitutional duty to provide a "fair share" of affordable housing. In the first stage of the litigation, the court directed the city to pass new land use regulations to carry out its housing responsibility, explaining, "Courts do not build housing .... The municipality should first have full opportunity to itself act without judicial supervision."[23]

Eight years later, in *Mount Laurel II*, the court reviewed the ordinance resulting from that effort and found it defective. Expressing disdain at the city's recalcitrance, the court declared the need to put some judicial steel into the process and created a detailed remedy structure that envisioned judicial supervision of land use planning in the state. It explained: "In the absence of executive or legislative action to satisfy the constitutional obligation underlying *Mount Laurel*, the judiciary has no choice but to enforce it itself." Recognizing that any remedy would require "firm judicial management," the court devised detailed methods of developing land use criteria – statewide – under judicial supervision. Commandeering the traditional state and city land use processes, Chief Justice Wilentz explained:

> As we said at the outset, while we have always preferred legislative to judicial action in this field, we shall continue - until the Legislature acts - to do our best to uphold the constitutional obligation that underlies the *Mount Laurel* doctrine. That is our duty. We may not build houses, but we do enforce the Constitution.[24]

The Columbia River Salmon Litigation (1991–Present)

This litigation challenged the National Marine Fisheries Service's (NMFS) implementation of the Endangered Species Act (ESA) as it applies to the imperiled salmon in the Columbia River.[25] The ESA requires federal agencies to avoid action likely to "jeopardize" the survival of listed species. To this end, it charges NFMS with producing a "biological opinion" that determines whether a proposed federal action poses jeopardy to the species. During the initial eleven years of ESA litigation over Columbia River salmon, NMFS rendered four biological opinions under the ESA that basically affirmed status quo hydro-operations – which proved lethal to fish. After repeated judicial remands to NFMS that yielded no measurable improvement to salmon, salmon stocks were still in severe decline. In 2005, after NMFS submitted yet another deficient biological opinion to the federal district court of Oregon, Judge James Redden lamented that "[t]he entire remand time was lost and wasted." Detailing a "pattern of earlier failures" by NMFS, Judge Redden sharpened the court's role by ordering a hefty "spill" of water over the dams to assist juvenile salmon migrating to the sea. In addition, he threatened to force the issue of dam removal. Warning that he would "run the river" if the government failed to protect the salmon, the judge declared:

> I recognize [NMFS] alone is charged with the responsibility of drafting a valid biological opinion. So far, they have not succeeded. Courts do defer to administrative agencies, and they should, and I have. Experience, however, shows that the court should, and sometimes must, be more than a passive participant in the remand process.... The government's inaction appears to some parties to be a strategy intended to avoid making hard choices and offending those who favor the *status quo*. Without real action from the Action Agencies, the result will be the loss of the wild salmon.[26]

The California Prison Litigation (1990–Present)

California's overcrowded prison system has been the subject of litigation for more than two decades. The state's failure to provide adequate medical and mental health care has resulted in death for undeserving prisoners: "As of mid-2005, a California inmate was dying needlessly died *every six or seven days*," a court found. That year, Governor Arnold Schwarzenegger issued an Emergency Declaration stating that the state's prisons have become places "'of extreme peril'" to the inmates. In 2007, the state's independent oversight agency reported, "California's correctional system is in a tailspin."[27]

Two class action lawsuits established constitutional violations resulting from prison conditions. As time passed without satisfactory response from the state, two federal district courts handling the separate suits asserted increasing control over the situation. At first the judges issued narrow orders requiring California to develop and implement remedial plans to improve prison medical and mental health care. Those, however, utterly failed, leading one of the judges to explain: "The problem of a highly dysfunctional, largely decrepit, overly bureaucratic, and politically driven prison system ... is too far gone to be corrected by conventional methods." Months later, he concluded: "By all accounts, the California prison medical care system is broken beyond repair." Explaining that the court had given the state "every reasonable opportunity to bring its prison medical system up to constitutional standards," the judge asserted, "death is virtually guaranteed in the absence of drastic action."[28]

Both judges stepped up their remedial measures. One appointed a special master to supervise more than seventy orders issued by the court. The other appointed a Receiver to take over aspects of the prison system, explaining:

> [I]t is not a measure that the Court has sought, nor is it one the Court relishes. Rather, the Court is simply at the end of the road with nowhere else to turn. Indeed, it would be fair to say that the Receivership is being imposed on the Court, rather than on the State, for it is the State's abdication of responsibility that has led to the current crisis.[29]

Ultimately, even those measures failed because of grossly overcrowded prison conditions (some prisons approached 300 percent of their intended capacity). Finally, at the request of both district court judges, a special three-judge panel convened. Finding California's prisons "bursting at the seams" and concluding that "no relief besides a prisoner release order can bring the California prison system into constitutional compliance," it issued a detailed prison release order for up to 40,000 inmates (in conformance with standards provided by relevant federal law), declaring:

> We recognize the gravity of the population reduction order we issue herein, and we do not intervene in matters of prison population lightly. Nonetheless, when federal court intervention becomes the only means by which to enforce rights guaranteed by the Constitution, federal courts are obligated to act.... California's prisoners ... can wait no longer.

The U.S. Supreme Court upheld the order on appeal, explaining that "breadth and flexibility are inherent in equitable remedies." The Court concluded: "This extensive and ongoing constitutional violation requires a remedy, and a remedy will not be achieved without a reduction in overcrowding."[30]

Pacific Northwest Treaty Rights Litigation (1969–Present)
In this litigation, the federal government (in its capacity as trustee for Indian tribes) sued the states of Washington and Oregon to enforce treaty fishing rights against discriminatory state regulation.[31] The treaty rights date back to the mid-1800s when the tribes ceded nearly all of their aboriginal lands to the federal government but retained, in explicit treaty provisions, their right to fish in perpetuity at "usual and accustomed areas" off the reservation. For a culture that has relied on the region's abundant salmon over thousands of years, these treaty rights amount to fundamental civil rights. During the 1800s and early 1900s, however, demands on the region's salmon fishery grew exponentially, and the states began enacting fishing restrictions. When tribal fishers attempted to exercise treaty fishing rights, state officials arrested them. By the 1970s, these arrests flared into violent conflicts between game wardens and Indian fishermen. As Charles Wilkinson describes:

There were scores of raids … ugly, heartrending brawls. In time, the banks of the Nisqually merged with the schoolhouse steps of Little Rock, the bridge at Selma, and the back of the bus in Montgomery.… As with all the blood struggles of minority people for freedom the world over, a sorrow, a poignancy shared the air with the tear gas.[32]

In Washington state, federal district court judge George H. Boldt issued a landmark opinion (famously known as the "Boldt opinion") dividing the harvest of salmon between states and tribes in equal shares. A case with parallel circumstances in Oregon (*Sohappy v. Smith*) had been decided by federal district court judge Robert C. Belloni in 1969; he imposed roughly the same division of fish under a "fair share" equitable allocation. Judge Belloni convinced the states and tribes to enter into a negotiated fish harvest management plan to implement the remedy. But in Washington, tensions erupted from the Boldt opinion. Across the region, bumper stickers bore the slogans, "Slice Belloni, Screw Boldt." Defiant state officials refused to take necessary regulatory measures to allow tribal fishers half of the harvest, and several state court rulings openly repudiated the federal judge's orders. The U.S. Supreme Court later quoted the Ninth Circuit in saying, "'Except for some desegregation cases … the district court has faced the most concerted official and private efforts to frustrate a decree of a federal court witnessed in this century.'" The breakdown in state enforcement led Judge Boldt to issue a series of detailed orders directly managing fish harvest – orders that positioned the court, essentially, as a "perpetual fishmaster" on the river. As Fronda Woods describes:

> Finally, Judge Boldt gave up on the state fisheries agencies. On August 31, 1977, he assumed direct control of the fisheries. For the next two years, fisheries in Puget Sound and Washington coastal waters were managed and policed through federal court orders and federal marshals. Fishermen who violated the orders found themselves facing criminal contempt citations.

On appeal, the U.S. Supreme Court resoundingly upheld the district court's actions, stating:

> The state's extraordinary machinations in resisting [Judge Boldt's] decree have forced the district court to take over a large share of the management of the state's fishery in order to enforce its decrees.… [The litigants] offered the court no reasonable choice.… [T]he District Court may assume direct supervision of the fisheries if state recalcitrance or state-law barriers should be continued.[33]

Washington State Education Litigation (1975–Present)

This line of litigation originated in 1975, when the Seattle school district sued the state of Washington for failing to provide ample funds for education as required by Article IX of the state's constitution.[34] The Washington State Supreme Court found the education system's shortcomings unconstitutional, holding that the constitution imposed an "affirmative duty" to provide sufficient funding for educating all children within its borders. The court deferred any substantive remedy in deference to ongoing legislative reforms. A second lawsuit ensued, producing a trial court ruling that outlined a detailed enforcement plan. Nevertheless, over the next thirty years, the education system remained seriously underfunded. By 2007, "massive underfunding" of the school system meant that 46 school districts (serving 17,000 students) had no money for textbooks or technology. That year, citizens sued individually and on behalf of their children, alleging that the education system still did not pass constitutional muster.

On appeal, the Washington Supreme Court again found the system unconstitutional. Explaining its own role in the system, it stated:

> [The constitution] contemplates a sharing of powers and responsibilities among all three branches of government.... "[I]t is emphatically the province and duty of the judicial department to say what the law is ... even when that interpretation serves as a check on the activities of another branch...." [The constitution presents] a mandate, not to a single branch of government, but to the entire state. We will not abdicate our judicial role.[35]

While the state argued that any judicial remedy should await fruition of the legislative reforms already under way, the court found that approach too deferential. It opted instead for a legislative remand with continuing jurisdiction in the courts to oversee progress, explaining:

> This court cannot idly stand by as the legislature makes unfulfilled promises for reform. We therefore reject as a viable remedy the State's invitation for the court simply to defer to the legislature's implementation of [a reform statute].... A better way forward is for the judiciary to retain jurisdiction over this case to monitor implementation of the reforms ... and more generally, the State's compliance with its paramount duty. This option strikes the appropriate balance between deferring to the legislature to determine the precise means for discharging its [constitutional] duty, while also recognizing this court's constitutional obligation.[36]

The Manila Bay Litigation (1999–Present)
In this litigation, fourteen young citizens of the Philippines brought suit against twelve different agencies and departments for neglecting to protect Manila Bay, which once supported abundant marine life, a thriving fishing industry, and spectacular water recreation.[37] By 1995, the Bay was heavily polluted with sewage, garbage, heavy metals, chemicals, pathogens, leachates, and other contaminants (some deadly) that discharged into six major tributary rivers and the Bay itself. Despite multiple explicit legal mandates to protect and restore the Bay, environmental agencies had wholly failed to do so. Justice Prebitero J. Velasco of the Supreme Court of

the Philippines described the Bay as a "slowly dying expanse." The youth plaintiffs asked the Court to order officials to restore the Bay's waters to a level suitable for swimming, skin-diving, and other forms of contact recreation as provided by law.[38]

In 2009, Justice Velasco penned a unanimous Supreme Court opinion forcing the cleanup of the entire Bay. This same court had issued the *Oposa v. Factoran* decision decades earlier that halted logging of the country's last remaining old growth. That decision had declared that the right to a balanced and healthful ecology "need not even be written in the Constitution for [it is] assumed to exist from the inception of humankind." Equating the two cases, the Supreme Court called the cleanup of Manila Bay "an issue of transcendental importance with intergenerational implications." While (predictably) the government defendants sought cover under a mantle of discretion, the Court painstakingly inventoried statutory duties and sharply criticized the agencies for their "cavalier attitude" toward the environmental pollution. Justice Velasco outlined an encompassing and aggressive remedy structure that essentially seated the Supreme Court of the Philippines in the position of overseeing the cleanup of Manila Bay under its continuing jurisdiction. As in the *Oposa* case, the Court emphasized the public trust as the crucible of obligation, declaring:

> Even assuming the absence of a categorical legal provision specifically prodding petitioners to clean up the bay, [the agencies] cannot escape their obligation to future generations of Filipinos to keep the waters of the Manila Bay clean and clear as humanly as possible. Anything less would be a betrayal of the trust reposed in them.[39]

In all of the aforementioned cases, judges faced politicization of the other two branches of government (particularly the agencies) and official behavior that infringed on the citizens' crucial human rights or interests. While exercising as much restraint as due caution would permit given the irrevocable harm presented, the judges in these cases assembled far-reaching remedies to address the institutional dysfunction. As a practical matter, the courts usurped aspects of the agencies' function or discretion to some extent. In every one of the cases, they braved a political firestorm in order to carry out their appointed role. Ultimately, what provoked their hard-hitting remedies was a realization that active judicial intervention remained necessary to right egregious action or inaction by government officials operating behind a massive edifice of discretion.

Forging New Judicial Models: Institutional Litigation and the Structural Injunction

The judicial rulings described in the preceding section ascend to the systemic level to address wholesale government failure. In the United States, for example, they extended across an entire fish conservation program, a prison system, a land use scheme, an educational funding system, and a fish harvest regime. In the most far-reaching judicial sweep of all, the Philippines Supreme Court's order covered the full Manila Bay tributary basin of 17,000 square kilometers and extended to a dozen agencies. These institutional remedies hold the legitimacy of affirmation by the highest supreme courts on the federal and state levels.

Rarely do environmental problems have one isolated cause that can be fixed by holding just one agency accountable. Statutory law splinters management of trust assets among a multitude of agencies, all of which must be held accountable in order to protect that asset. As in the cases above, courts must innovate systems-wide, macro-scale remedies in order to address mismanagement on the systemic level. An effective trust remedy achieves three criteria: (1) it holds government officials accountable for performing fiduciary duties; (2) it ensures actual protection and restoration of natural resources; and (3) it respects the constitutional role of the other branches.

The sheer complexity of meaningful judicial remedies can be difficult for today's judges. But in a tipping-point world, effective relief depends on close supervision or even usurpation of those aspects of the administrative system that have gone terribly awry. The old "defer to the agencies" justice no longer suffices in face of severe agency recalcitrance. As in the cases mentioned earlier, sometimes courts can effectively protect the citizen rights only by providing a surrogate judicial-administrative process. The discussion that follows spotlights innovations from those cases discussed to suggest features of structural injunctions for institutional public trust litigation.

Declaratory Judgment: Sidewalls and Benchmarks

The foundation for a Nature's Trust remedy lies in the declaratory judgment, which precisely describes government's obligations. In *Manila Bay*, for example, the Supreme Court of the Philippines expressed a duty to clean up, rehabilitate, and protect the waters. In the treaty fishing cases, the court declared a tribal treaty right to a "fair share" of the salmon fishery. In *Mt. Laurel*, the various cities had to provide a "fair share" of affordable housing needed in the region. Such parameters create the framework for a more detailed remedy by forming the sidewalls of expected behavior beyond which the parties cannot deviate without judicial retribution. In a public trust case, a court must declare the trustees' fiduciary obligations toward the beneficiaries. This alone can transform the paradigm of government behavior from unfettered discretion to exacting obligation.

Often, the obligation must be quantified to have any practical effect. The treaty fishing cases, for example, imposed variations of a 50–50 allocation. The California prison cases resulted in an order to reduce populations to 137.5 percent of the buildings' design capacity. The *Mount Laurel* fair housing standard used formulas calibrated to an urban population. The ESA salmon case turned on complex population and reproduction parameters. In public trust cases, the precise standard must reflect the functional needs of the resource. For example, in atmospheric trust litigation, scientists prescribed a minimum of 6 percent annual carbon emissions reduction to restore atmospheric equilibrium at 350 parts per million, as Chapter 10 explained. Such specific parameters become the sidewalls to any remedy.

Of course, settling on a number that perfectly quantifies a legal obligation conjures an impossible task. But courts show comfortable resignation to that reality, often noting that their broad power of equity gives generous latitude for estimation, approximation, and adjustment. For example, in the prison case, the three-judge panel candidly admitted that prison population reduction does not present "an exact science," and even one of the experts admitted that "there's nothing magical" about any specific population percentage relative to the design capacity of the prison. Ultimately, the panel considered two targets (one submitted by the plaintiffs – 130 percent, and one by the wardens – 145 percent) and settled on a percentage goal that landed dead center between the two: 137.5 percent of design capacity. In the treaty cases, too, courts repeatedly emphasized that "precise mathematical equality" in allocating the fish between states and tribes remained impossible to achieve but unnecessary for the judicial remedy.[40]

Along with judicial sidewalls, an equally important component of the judicial declaration in public trust cases will be a series of goals tied to specific timeframes. "Benchmarks," as decision makers call them, arise out of a court's practical recognition that agencies will tend to procrastinate indefinitely. The three-judge prison panel ordered a series of six-month "population reduction benchmarks" to bring the current population in thirty-three California prisons to the 137.5 percent of design capacity within two years. The Philippines Supreme Court ordered the Metropolitan Municipal Development Authority to construct and bring to full operation a sanitary landfill within one year of the decision. A court may add stinging judicial admonitions as well. As the *Manila* court scolded, "Time is of the essence.... The era of delays, procrastination, and *ad hoc* measures is over."[41]

Sometimes courts cannot feasibly specify remedial measures at the stage of declaratory relief. Developing measures may require further scientific analysis or more data. In order to prevent vexing technical issues from clouding the basic task of defining the fiduciary obligation, courts can bifurcate public trust cases into a "liability" stage and a "remedy" stage. This has been the approach in past treaty litigation. The liability stage allows the court to declare legal obligations, while the remedy stage demands a more innovative judicial role to administer and enforce those duties.[42]

Defining Remedial Details: Measured Judicial Supervision

Like the cases featured earlier in the chapter, many public trust cases have their genesis in long-standing and severe agency neglect of duty. Remedying this some-times requires judges to grab the agency wheel and steer it back on course – similar to what a bankruptcy judge does with a terribly managed company. When dealing with a recalcitrant or inept agency, it does little good for judges to issue sweeping declarations of law and then remand the matter back to the agency only to have derelict officials deliver a dead letter months or years later. Using innovation and practical sense, judges can invoke their inherent equitable authorities to create the outcome that the agency would have created itself had it carried out its fiduciary obligations to the citizens. The remedy institutional litigation aims to create, under the auspices of the court, is a free-standing administrative function to undertake remedial planning, decision-making, and/or other agency tasks, for as long as (but no longer than) necessary. Modulating some of their conventional judicial strategies to meet the practical challenges of the modern administrative setting, courts man-aging institutional cases drill down into deep levels of complexity that may have pre-viously deterred courts and vitiated meaningful relief. As one of the most effective tools, a court may appoint a special master to handle complex factual issues, make determinations on reoccurring matters arising within the case, and recommend how the court should rule in particular circumstances. Courts commonly use special masters to administer structural injunctions; they did so in the California prison liti-gation, the Mt. Laurel case, and the Washington and Oregon treaty fishing cases, for example. Ultimately, the decisions and plans of action resulting from a hybrid judi-cial/administrative effort become bundled in a judicial order that provides enforce-ment capability under penalty of contempt of court.

The foundation for any judicial action-forcing remedy involves two tasks: creating a plan of measureable steps and providing oversight to ensure proper execution of the plan. Sometimes, an adequate plan already exists and simply needs implementation and enforcement. In the Manila Bay case, for example, the Department of Environment and Natural Resources (DENR) had developed a comprehensive cleanup plan for Manila Bay, but it lacked authority over the many other agencies that had jurisdiction over other aspects of the problem. Given that virtually all of these agencies stood as defendants in the Manila Bay lawsuit, the Supreme Court simply ordered that the DENR plan be carried out. It designated the DENR as the lead agency and charged it with the duty of making sure the other agencies fulfilled their regulatory roles. Leaving little to chance (or worse, discretion), the Court outlined ambitious tasks falling to each of the dozen agencies, which included the Coast Guard, a fisheries agency, the water and sewer agency, the municipal waste treatment agency, the Department of Agriculture, a public works agency, the port authority, the Department of Health, the

Department of Education, the Department of Budget and Management, and a federal agency that supervised all local governments. Specific duties included building landfills, demolishing illegal structures in beach zones, and prosecuting violations of environmental laws. The Court even tasked the Department of Education to integrate lessons on pollution prevention in all levels of the curricula.[43]

This encompassing order, in effect, took a problem that had been fractured among a dozen agency jurisdictions and unified the responsibility into one comprehensive, mandatory framework that dispelled nearly all discretion. Because the Court fashioned its order to enforce the entire DENR plan, agencies would risk retribution if they failed to carry out their duties. This approach essentially gave judicial force to a comprehensive, macro-level plan that, prior to the litigation, gnawed toothlessly. As Justice Velasco later commented about the opinion:

> The Court tried to address all possible causes, whether direct or contributory, to the pollution and decay of the bay.... [All of the Court's] directives ... were deemed necessary for a holistic and long-term solution.... [T]he ruling ordered any and all government agencies whose official functions and statutory duties have a connection, *however remote*, to the cleaning and rehabilitation of the Manila Bay to spare no effort, at the implied risk of contempt of court, to perform these functions and duties so as to achieve the desired purpose.[44]

One aspect of the Court's approach deserves special mention. Much of the Manila Bay crisis resulted from agencies simply not enforcing the law against thousands of land occupants and factories that continually and illegally dumped raw sewage and waste from illegal structures into receiving waterways. As Chapter 3 explained, environmental agencies chronically claim discretion whether or not to *enforce* the law. Recognizing the perils of lax enforcement (which basically yields the same results as having no law at all), the Philippines Supreme Court made clear that enforcement did not fall to discretion but had always remained a matter of *duty* – "ministerial duty." It thus invoked its mandamus authority against the agencies – a potent judicial remedy where the Court directly compels an official to carry out a legal duty. The Court declared that statutory directives "would not be set to naught by administrative inaction or indifference." The mandamus approach seared enforcement discretion to a char. By 2010, the agency that had turned a blind eye to enforcement for years was ordering demolition of illegal beach structures – even some ancillary to multimillion-dollar resorts. The mandamus remedy essentially injected a trust obligation into statutory law and transformed enforcement *discretion* into enforcement *obligation*. The same approach would revolutionize U.S. environmental law.[45]

The Philippines remedy worked off of an existing plan. But sometimes there exists no adequate plan conveniently waiting for judicial implementation. In that case, the court must force the agencies to create a plan within a specified time frame and then order the agency to carry out the plan (upon court approval). In the California prison case, the three-judge panel ordered the state to develop a prison population reduction plan. When it came back with an inadequate plan, the panel ordered the state to go back to the drawing board. The second plan passed judicial muster, and the panel ordered the state to achieve the plan's benchmarks for population reduction. In the ESA salmon case, Judge Redden required NMFS to create an adequate recovery plan for salmon. In a move that veered outside of the traditional ESA remedy, he forced NMFS to consult with the treaty tribes (the co-tenant sovereign trustees of the fishery) in developing their plan.[46]

Sometimes courts take over the task of developing a plan, especially if it would be a waste of time to leave the matter to recalcitrant agencies. To do this, the judge might create a new planning body or authorize a special master to serve as an instrumentality of the court. For example, the *Mount Laurel* court needed to ensure that municipalities would rewrite their zoning ordinances to comply with their constitutional duty to provide "fair housing." It designated three trial judges to supervise this process across the state. The court ordered the cities to devise land use ordinances, but if they failed, the governing judge could appoint a special master to help craft a zoning ordinance that met constitutional mandates. As Justice Wienezt described the special master, "[h]e or she is an expert, a negotiator, a mediator, and a catalyst – a person who will help the municipality select from the innumerable combinations of actions that could satisfy the constitutional obligation." At the end of the process, the master would provide an opinion to the court as to whether the ordinance was constitutionally adequate. If the ordinance did not suffice, the trial court could issue a series of direct orders aimed at land use in the city; these could suspend aspects of existing land use plans and enjoin projects. Recognizing the innovative aspects of its remedy structure, the court said: "Indeed the history of Chancery is as much a history of remedy as it is of obligation. The process of remedial development has not yet been frozen."[47]

In the Washington treaty fishing case, Judge Boldt encountered such state resistance to his ruling that he created his own administrative planning and enforcement process to assure the tribes a fair share of the fish harvest. Through a number of court orders, he required the state and tribes to consult with each other to estimate fish run sizes and harvestable numbers of fish. He established a Fisheries Advisory Board to consider questions of a technical nature, and he appointed a Fisheries Science and Management Expert to both assist the court and facilitate state and tribal cooperation. He appointed a U.S. Magistrate to act as Special Master to oversee the case and resolve questions that could be addressed without court involvement. Under this judicial regime, federal marshals policed and enforced fisheries harvest; violation of court orders constituted contempt of court.[48]

Courts may also arrive at a remedial plan to implement the liability rulings by coaxing the parties into a settlement. If the parties can agree on management parameters, these details can be wrapped into a consent decree that carries the ongoing force of a court order. Judge Belloni's treaty fishing case took this approach. The State of Oregon and the treaty tribes entered into the Columbia River Fish Management Plan (CRFMP) – a model of judicial administration that gained nationwide acclaim. The CRFMP set forth detailed management criteria for each fishery, established technical and policy committees, and created a dispute resolution process that involved the court only as a last resort. The court appointed a scientific advisor to serve as the eyes and ears for the judge on scientific matters and to help ensure the scientific integrity of the process. By allowing the sovereign parties to identify points of agreement and work out the details of a remedy using their own administrative and scientific expertise, the consent decree process relieves courts of the burden of devising a remedy to fit complex circumstances – a task that often exceeds judicial bandwidth in terms of resources, capacity, and expertise.[49]

Ultimately, the most aggressive judicial remedy comes in the form of a receivership, a regular tool used by bankruptcy judges for mismanaged corporations. In administrative cases, the court appoints a receiver to take over some or all agency functions. For example, in one of the California prison cases, the court stripped the failed prison supervisor of his oversight duties and transferred them to the court-appointed receiver with direction to "provide leadership and executive management of the California prison medical health care delivery system." Removal and replacement of a trustee also provides a standard remedy in the context of private trust lawsuits where a trustee has violated his duty of loyalty or engaged in gross mismanagement.[50]

In some cases, the appropriate remedy requires legislation rather than administrative action. In this instance, a legislative remand becomes the most suitable remedy. In the Washington education case, for example, the court remanded the matter to the legislature, noting its suitability for resolving "difficult policy questions inherent in forming the details of an education system." Yet, the court emphasized it would enforce the constitutional sidewalls of legislative duty, stating, "While the Legislature must *act* pursuant to the constitutional mandate to discharge its duty, the general authority to select the *means* of discharging that duty should be left to the Legislature." The court retained jurisdiction to ensure adequate and timely legislative progress, noting various options to facilitate its oversight (such as use of a special master, appointment of some "oversight entity," a remand to the trial court, or retention of the matter in its own court).[51]

Judicial Backstops and Punitive Measures

An institutional judicial remedy nearly always involves ongoing court jurisdiction to oversee the remedy to fruition. The court simply leaves the case open so that parties can challenge aspects of it without bringing an entirely new lawsuit. The courts retained ongoing jurisdiction in all of the cases featured in this chapter. Typically the judges require periodic reports to the court (at regular intervals of three or six months, for example) to ensure that the government meets benchmarks of the injunction in timely fashion.[52]

If agency foot-dragging continues despite the quasi-administrative judicial remedy, courts will often provide partial relief through targeted orders. These could be thought of as "backstops" because they come in as a last resort. Usually tailored as narrowly as possible, these orders nevertheless respond to the urgency of the situation. In the prison cases, the backstop after years of litigation (in two cases) became a population reduction order that released thousands of prisoners. In the *Mount Laurel* case, the Supreme Court authorized a "builder's remedy" whereby the trial court would issue a building permit to a developer with a low-cost housing project (as long as the cities did not present overriding environmental concerns to the contrary). The backstop relief in the Columbia River ESA litigation amounted to a court-ordered spill of water through the dams. An even more far-reaching remedy shadowed the case: "[I]f all else fails," the court admonished, the government would have to consider breaching four major Snake River dams.[53]

Of course the ultimate enforcement tool becomes punitive action personally directed to the lead bureaucrats charged with carrying out the legal duty. Called "contempt of court," a refusal to carry out judicial orders can result in jail time for the officials charged. Without such pain of personal enforcement, bureaucratic inertia can continue indefinitely under agency heads repudiating their public duties. All of the remedial orders against agencies in the cases described in this chapter came backed by threat of contempt of court. The threat frequently surfaces in other cases as well. In 2008, for example, a federal judge threatened U.S. Department of Agriculture Undersecretary Mark Rey with contempt of court for the agency's refusal to complete environmental analysis regarding the use of fire retardant that kills fish. (The judge also threatened to ground a fleet of air tankers that sprayed the chemical retardant). In litigation over the administration of Indian trust funds, a court held the Secretary of the U.S. Department of Interior under serial contempt orders for failing to produce an adequate accounting; these contempt orders lasted for years through different administrations (but did not result in jail time).[54]

Tackling Barriers: Budget Constraints and Law Reform

In nearly all cases of agency failure, bureaucratic officials plead two excuses time and again: lack of funding and lack of authority. While some judges seem at a loss to evaluate these excuses, others tackle them head on. Such courts seem to bite deeper into the root causes of institutional failure to hold the agency heads accountable.

Regarding funding, administrators typically believe they lack enough money for the work tasked to their agency. If courts yielded to that argument, they would create a permanent detour around legal obligations. Astute judges use the excuse as an invitation to take a hard look at the books and ask three questions: (1) What does it cost to comply with the judgment? (2) Does the agency budget contain enough money to cover the cost? (3) If there is not enough money, have the agency officials made efforts to acquire additional funding? In the Manila Bay case, the federal budget agency was actually a named defendant. The Philippines Supreme Court ordered that agency to consider incorporating an adequate budget for the bay cleanup in the General Appropriations Act. In the Washington education case, the Washington Supreme Court found that the legislature must provide "dependable and regular tax sources," which did not include levy dollars that remain temporary and "wholly dependent upon the whim of the electorate." In the California prison case, the court required the state to work with the counties to calculate the additional county costs associated with release of prisoners (such as costs of rehabilitation and job training) and specify how much of the prison budget savings (from a reduced inmate population) could be redistributed to the counties. In a case (not discussed in this chapter) involving the U.S. Fish and Wildlife Service's failure to designate a critical habitat under the ESA, the judge examined the agency's overall budget in depth and found significant expenditures on projects other than the legally required action. Criticizing the budget allocations, the court determined: "This is not an acceptable way of setting priorities, nor does it establish anything but unwillingness to comply with this court's order."[55]

Aside from budget constraints, many agencies complain that the legal regime in which they operate limits their authority. Some judges vault this hurdle by asking the agencies to specify with precision any existing legal barriers and to describe the efforts made to remove the obstacle (such as seeking legislative or regulatory reform). For example, in one of the California prison cases, the district judge invited the state to "present it with a series of proposed orders so that the Court could help empower them to overcome some of their bureaucratic hurdles on their own." Similarly, the three-judge panel ordered the state to notify the court if waivers of state law became necessary.[56]

NATURE'S JUDGES

This book has suggested that courts remain both well situated and fully obligated to prevent environmental agencies from mismanaging public trust assets into a state of bankruptcy – a situation that threatens human life, welfare, and, ultimately, civilization itself. History awaits courageous and extraordinary judges who will revive the judiciary's role in environmental law. They will be Nature's judges – who, like the judges described earlier in the chapter, summon their ancient and fundamental powers of equity to vindicate the rights of citizens against officials veering dangerously astray of their legal obligations. While respecting the careful constitutional allocation of authority between the three branches of government, these judges will not yield to tired bureaucratic excuses for entrenched institutional failure. As Alexander Hamilton wrote long ago in the Federalist Papers, federal courts remain obligated to enforce rights guaranteed by the Constitution: "Without this, all the reservations of particular rights or privileges would amount to nothing."[57]

Unfortunately, many of today's judges show distaste and fatigue at the prospect of managing the complex details of a meaningful remedy. They may hastily dismiss trust claims on procedural grounds, or characterize the trust issue as a political question committed to the other branches of government. This, indeed, has been the result of some (but not all) of the lowest-court rulings in Atmospheric Trust Litigation (described in Chapter 10).[58] When judges suggest that the task of carbon regulation should be left to the agencies or legislature, they remind everyone but themselves that, *of course* these branches vested with duty and expertise should act – but they have not, and their indolence will surely continue absent judicial enforcement. While the court's function cannot be to do the work of the agencies or legislatures, it is decidedly the court's appointed role to force these branches to do their work. A reluctant and passive judiciary denigrates democracy, surely. But even worse for today's youth, abdication of judicial responsibility leaves unchecked carbon dioxide pollution and global warming that threatens their future survival. The Washington Supreme Court struck a proper posture in its education case when it said:

> [T]he remedy question proves elusive ... [due to] the delicate balancing of powers and responsibilities among coordinate branches of government. This court is appropriately sensitive to the legislature's role in reforming and funding education, and we must proceed cautiously. At the same time, the constitution requires the judiciary to determine compliance with [its provisions].... What we have learned from experience is that this court cannot stand on the sidelines and hope the State meets its constitutional mandate to amply fund education.... While we recognize that the issue is complex and no option may prove wholly satisfactory, this is not a reason for the judiciary to throw up its hands and offer no remedy at all. Ultimately, it is our responsibility to hold the State accountable to meet its constitutional duty.... This court intends to remain vigilant.[59]

Arriving at judicial public trust remedies for captured agencies and legislatures will not be easy, but judges routinely adjudicate difficult cases and often show enormous dedication and innovation in doing so. Judge Boldt's detailed orders implementing the remedy in Washington's treaty fishing case, for example, consumed 120 printed pages in the case reporter. Today's environmental crises hold unparalleled stakes for humanity and will require unprecedented commitment on the part of judges. But as

Justice O'Connor wrote in a complex treaty fishing case, "the difficulty of providing equitable relief has never provided an excuse for shirking the duty imposed on us by the Constitution."[60]

In June 2012, a team of twenty-two scientists published an article in the prestigious journal, *Nature*, warning that humans are now causing "state shifts" in biological systems – "planetary-scale critical transition[s] ... with the potential to transform Earth rapidly and irreversibly into a state unknown in human experience."[61] As society confronts unprecedented change, courts must cross unexplored terrain with time-tested purpose and modern agility. Where constitutional rights infuse the common law – as in the public trust – the judicial role must realize its highest capabilities to protect the needs of citizens against indolent agencies. Courts have always gathered the shifting sands of time onto the scales of justice, and they are called do so again. If there remains a habitable planet at the end of the century, it may be because extraordinary jurists across the world rose to their constitutional duties and vindicated the rights of the people as beneficiaries of Nature's Trust – in solidarity with great legal thinkers that came before them, and in heroism to the ages. Always, judicial relief must find grounding in the broader context of society's moral understandings, a matter taken up in the next chapter.

PART III

The Public Trust and the Great Transition

12

Nature's Trust and the Heart of Humanity

When a legal framework is severed from the moral pulse of humanity, it staggers as a moribund hulk of admonition. At worst it can become the instrument of tyrants. As Ronald D. Dworkin emphasizes, "Moral principle is the foundation of law."[1] Law must tap the deepest moral understandings of humanity not only to maintain credibility and respect in society at large, but also to inspire citizens to participate in democracy. When the citizens lose sight of the purposes served by law, they cease to engage their own government. Democracy degenerates from there into a faux-democracy in which the citizens assume they have power but actually do not.

This chapter picks up a theme from Part I that environmental law has lost much of its citizen support. The discussion begins by suggesting why statutory environmental law fails to inspire ecological protection. It then explores how the Nature's Trust paradigm shift can galvanize citizens by harnessing the power of moral thinking around the public trust, a doctrine that retrieves essential human wisdom deposited by the ancients.

PROCESS WITHOUT PRINCIPLE

As explained in Chapter 5, environmental law long ago strayed from the populist movement that gave rise to its hopeful inception. The law has become self-strangulating in its complexity. Iterated in hundreds of thousands of pages of regulations and spoken in a foreign tongue of acronyms, environmental law now forms a kingdom ruled by elite specialist lawyers, government bureaucrats, and highly paid corporate lobbyists. When average citizens try to defend their communities from environmental destruction – no matter how heart-wrenching or permanent the harm, and regardless of how short-sighted and narrow the private motive propelling it – they find themselves pulled into a regulatory processor that dices up the moral force of their position. The system regularly spews permissions that revolt the reasonable mind. Citizens who express their moral position in public hearings

or legislative processes commonly stand rebuked by their own governmental officials on the basis that their statements fall irrelevant. The message becomes: stick to
the law, even if we've made it too complex for you to understand. Operating within
a regulatory framework that seems morally vacant and beyond the reach of popular understanding, the environmental movement has careened away from its most
important political base.[2]

Because of this unmooring, the legal system now sanctions Nature's annihilation – as in the bombing of Appalachia, where a corporate quest for coal has already
scalped 500 mountain peaks, buried or polluted nearly 2,000 miles of streams, and
forced families to abandon homes that held their ancestors. The rampage continues
there and elsewhere because today's bureaucratic processes scour from the conversation all that can be intuitively understood and morally compelled. In administrative hearings, corporations and agency officials impose a fully controlled narrative
that leaves no room for the basic objections – such as outcries against the eradication
of American heritage and the purging of human communities that have lived in
the quiet hollows of ancient Appalachia for generations. Within the vocabulary of
environmental law, actions that might well be described as crimes against humanity, relentless assaults against the community, theft against future generations, or
even reckless endangerment of innocent children all succumb to the terminology
of an antiseptic regulatory system. Consequently, many citizens no longer see the
moral force of environmental law, nor summon it in their everyday interactions and
struggles. Egregious harms become defined as permissible and legitimate – indeed,
fully legalized – exploits. So dehumanizing is the regulatory techno-jargon, and so
capable of casting a mind-numbing pall over the hazards of environmental damage, that society's most destructive inclinations now gain acceptance as if they were
normal.[3]

One would think that environmental law would coalesce broad communities
around the goal of environmental protection. Society's interest in an enduring natural trust – one that provides a lasting array of both corporeal and intangible benefits – nearly always dwarfs the corporate interest that exploits it to ruin. Ecological
health implicates, ever less remotely, the survival interests of all humankind. As
John F. Kennedy declared, "[O]ur most basic common link is that we all inhabit
this small planet. We all breathe the same air. We all cherish our children's future.
And we are all mortal."[4]

But instead of enjoying broad civic agreement on essential resource protection,
society finds itself constantly whipsawed by environmental disputes. As Indian law
scholar Rennard Strickland warns, "Civilization faces a crisis of the spirit, a great
conflict in basic human values." If nothing else, this state of affairs pays wicked
tribute to a grand manipulation of public sentiment by industry's "public relations"
firms, described in Chapter 4. If citizens yearn for a deeper, principled truth, then

environmental statutes must regain their moral grounding or they will continue to serve the very marauders that their makers designed them to protect against.[5]

To be at all durable, the law must hinge on durable values, ones focused around community protection rather than corporate profit. Focusing on public welfare and survival, the trust champions core human rights and calls to engrained human inclinations. Many courts and commentators attribute the origins of the trust to "natural law" – not the iteration offered by theologians, but rather an amalgamation of legal principle, moral edict, social ethic, and custom that reflects the shared reasoning of humankind across all cultures, religions, and nations. Drawing on natural law, the public trust creates space for religious and moral synergy with environmental law.[6]

The trust concept echoes throughout the indigenous world, in the voices of traditional native leaders who continue to express a spiritual responsibility to future generations and other species. One proverb exhorting, "we do not inherit the earth from our forefathers, we borrow it from our children," captures the concept of both a legal trust and a sacred trust intertwined as a covenant running through the generations. In some sense, industrial society's modern struggle with Nature could be characterized as a turbulent cultural journey toward the same cove of ecological balance that has held anchor for indigenous societies over millennia – and humanity's own survival may well depend on reaching the harbor in time.

THE MORAL COMPASS OF NATURE'S TRUST

A trust construct intertwines multiple moral understandings, including: (1) an ethic toward future generations; (2) an affirmation of public rights to natural assets; (3) a condemnation of waste; and (4) a duty to other living creatures. Together, these can illuminate a more sustainable course for society. As the following discussion explains, the first three values infused American culture prior to the modern environmental era. The fourth ranks as a feature of indigenous society and marks a natural and current progression of Western society. These moral precepts reach not only to the foundations of human experience but are reflected, to varying degrees, in religious thinking. By drawing on these values, the Nature's Trust approach revives an imperative nearly silenced by the din of industrialization.

The Covenant Between Generations

An impelling human impulse has always urged protection of natural legacy and wealth for the coming generations. Perhaps, as Kathleen Dean Moore and Michael P. Nelson suggest in *Moral Ground*, this serves as a "driving force of evolution," a primordial instinct to protect one's young. As the renowned scientist E.O. Wilson writes in *The Creation*, "If there is any moral precept shared by people of all beliefs, it is that we owe ourselves and future generations a beautiful, rich, and healthful environment." Human rights scholar Burns Weston sums it up this way:

> [I]t is the rare person who will deny this intergenerational responsibility in principle.... Somewhere deep inside, all of us know that life is an energetic concurrence of the past, present, and future; that we are a temporary part of it; and that, whatever our past failings, we must reach beyond our egoistic selves to ensure its continuity with fairness to today's children and communities of the future.[7]

For centuries, Western political discourse gave resolute expression to this cultural inclination. The eighteenth-century philosopher Edmund Burke, for example, spoke of "the great primeval contract of eternal society," describing a partnership "not only between those who are living, but between those who are living, those who are dead, and those who are to be born." He contended that living persons did not have the right to "commit waste on the inheritance, by destroying at their pleasure the whole original fabric of their society; hazarding to leave to those who come after them, a ruin instead of an habitation."[8]

Thomas Jefferson also proclaimed a moral duty to future generations. Expressing a view of generational sovereignty that prohibited the diminution of natural wealth, he famously declared in a letter to James Madison in 1789: "I set out on this ground which I suppose to be self evident, 'that the earth belongs in usufruct to the living.'" Jefferson explained the entitlement of "every generation coming equally, by the laws of the Creator of the world, to the free possession of the earth He made for their subsistence, unencumbered by their predecessors, who, like them, were but tenants for life."[9]

By the end of the nineteenth century, the trust principle pressed so indelibly on the American political conscience that U.S. officials asserted it in a dispute over seal hunting brought before an international tribunal of arbitration. Condemning the overconsumption of Earth's resources, America's legal brief stated:

> The earth was designed as the permanent abode of man through ceaseless generations. Each generation, as it appears upon the scene, is entitled only to use the fair inheritance. It is against the law of nature that any waste should be committed to the disadvantage of the succeeding tenants.... That one generation may not only consume or destroy the annual increase of the products of the earth, but the stock also, thus leaving an inadequate provision for the multitude of successors which it brings into life, is a notion so repugnant to reason as scarcely to need formal refutation.[10]

Theodore Roosevelt took the same moral stance in political speeches made in the early twentieth century. Speaking at the rim of the Grand Canyon in 1903, Roosevelt declared:

> We have gotten past the stage, my fellow citizens, when we are to be pardoned if we treat any part of our country as something to be skinned for two or three years

for the use of the present generation, whether it is the forest, the water, the scenery. Whatever it is, handle it so that your children's children will get the benefit of it.[11]

Roosevelt recognized that the anticipatory nature of any democracy engenders hope of its own endurance and therefore creates duties toward future generations. His celebrated passages wove conservation into the very fabric of American democracy:

> The "greatest good of the greatest number" applies to the number within the womb of time, compared to which those now alive form but an insignificant fraction. Our duty to the whole, including the unborn generations, bids us to restrain an unprincipled present-day minority from wasting the heritage of these unborn generations. The movement for the conservation of all our natural resources [is] essentially democratic in spirit, purpose, and method.[12]

The duty toward future generations finds powerful expression across multiple faiths as today's religious leaders assert it in their appeal to save the Earth from ecological crisis. In an interfaith gathering held in Greenland in 2007, a coalition of Muslim, Buddhist, Hindu, Jewish, Christian, and Shinto leaders implored citizens to leave the planet "in all its wisdom and beauty to the generations to come." Pope Benedict XVI urged a "greater sense of intergenerational solidarity" and declared a "grave duty to hand the earth on to future generations in such a condition that they too can worthily inhabit it." Proverbs 13:22 advises: "A good man leaves an inheritance to his children's children."[13]

But environmental bureaucracy now drives society on a deviant track. While decades have passed since Edith Brown Weiss advanced the notion of "intergenerational equity" as an emergent legal principle, today's agencies still pay only lip service to that responsibility. In practice, their combined actions legalize, through permit systems, massive generational theft, as the first part of this book explained. Moore and Nelson contend that society's continued infliction of environmental damage in face of copious information pointing to a devastating ecological future amounts to "a moral abomination ... a deliberate theft, a preventable child abuse."[14]

The trust approach provides tangible legal backing to the concept of intergenerational equity. It remains the only environmental doctrine to do so, characterizing natural legacy as a *property endowment*. Scores of public trust cases declare that future generations are legal beneficiaries with entitlement to the *res* of the public trust. This enduring property right forms a fundamental limit on government. As one justice of the Massachusetts Supreme Court said in a tidelands case, "[T]he public trust doctrine stands as a covenant between the people of the Commonwealth and their government, a covenant to safeguard our tidelands *for all generations* for the use of the people." Government, as an enduring social institution, remains uniquely capable of carrying out intergenerational duties. As the Mississippi Supreme Court said in a school funding trust case from the turn of the century, "Decades count for little, so far as time even is concerned, in the earthly immortality of a state."[15]

Professor John Davidson describes the public trust doctrine as protecting two distinct dimensions of the natural resource commons: the "*intra*-generational commons" and the "*inter*-generational commons." As he points out, recent cases have focused on the *intra*-generational commons by preventing action that could diminish present-day public use. The *inter*-generational trust stands rooted in fundamental constitutional delineations of legislative capacity. As Chapter 6 explained, the reserved powers doctrine prevents legislatures from taking action to deprive later legislatures of the crucial resources they will need to fulfill the sovereign requirements of the people. Such action would encroach on the reserved powers of future legislatures, which stand on equal sovereign footing with present ones. As the landmark *Illinois Central* case declared in finding the Illinois legislature could not sell the shoreline of Lake Michigan, "The legislature could not give away nor sell the discretion of its successors in respect to matters, the government of which, from the very nature of things, must vary with varying circumstances." Davidson's emphasis on this "temporal dimension" of the *inter*-generational trust to protect future legislatures and the successor generations of citizens they represent finds clear reflection in cases such as *Lamprey v. Metcalf,* which said: "To hand over all these lakes to private ownership ... would be a *great wrong upon the public for all time,* the extent of which cannot, perhaps, be now even anticipated." In the analogous school trust realm, the Mississippi Supreme Court held that the public school fund must "endure always as a perpetual trust, for the recurring generations of children in this commonwealth, and not as the source of a fund intended to benefit the children of any particular decades." The intergenerational trust concept buttresses environmental law with strong crossbeams of moral understanding that recognizes the rights of future humanity.[16]

The Commonwealth Ethic – Thou Shalt Not Steal

The other dimension of the trust, with its *intra*-generational focus, protects property rights held in common by present citizens to crucial natural resources. This aspect reinforces a societal value that could be termed "the commonwealth ethic." For centuries legal commentators have said that natural law designates certain resources as common to all humankind and not susceptible to private ownership – these include the air, the running water, the sea, and wildlife. As this book has reasoned, such public rights must extend across the full tapestry of Nature to support the ecosystems sustaining life on the planet. The ecological web comprises a "commonwealth" itself – public assets in constant interaction to support life, welfare, and community prosperity.

The ancient idea that the community as a whole shares Nature's gifts lodges deeply in indigenous society, which rejects many notions of private property in favor of communal stewardship arrangements. In the United States, too, early polit-ical conceptions of "commonwealth" formed a central part of the identity of states. Even today, Massachusetts, Kentucky, Pennsylvania, and Virginia still bear the "commonwealth" title. An ecological "commons" movement now gains momen-tum worldwide by tapping into long-held beliefs affirming community rights in resources.[17]

Similar to the other trust values, the commonwealth ethic draws profound paral-lels with interfaith religious beliefs, which view the Earth as a sacred endowment created for the benefit of all humanity. Pope Benedict XVI describes the environ-ment as "God's gift to all people" and declares that "[t]he goods of creation belong to humanity as a whole." A consortium of evangelical pastors and leading scientists explain "creation" as "a gift, a sacred trust from the hands of the Creator." In the Hebrew tradition, the Book of Leviticus declares a limit on privatization: "And the land shall not be sold in perpetuity; for the land is mine: for ye are strangers and sojourners with me."[18]

This all-encompassing reverent view of Creation elevates the discussion of envi-ronmental policy well above private property boundaries. When dealing with moral and religious understandings, desecration of the "sacred trust," regardless of whether or not the act occurs within private property boundaries, defiles God's Creation. If all of humanity (not just a powerful minority) came entitled to benefit from God's endowment, then vandalizing Creation flaunts the cardinal principle, "Thou shalt not steal." Ecumenical Patriarch Bartholomew I has written: "[W]e proclaim the sanctity of all life, the entire creation being God's and reflecting His continuing will that life abound.... [T]o commit a crime against the natural world is a sin."[19]

The public trust doctrine works as a legal sentinel, walking in step with both religious Creation Care and engrained social ethics to protect community rights to commonwealth against reckless profiteers. As Chapter 14 describes in more detail, courts invoke the doctrine to prevent privatization of crucial resources needed by the people. Modern environmental law runs at cross-purposes to this commonwealth principle by readily handing out permits to pollute and destroy vital resources – de facto privatization. One of the most dangerous trends toward privatizing the com-monwealth lies in a global campaign waged by corporations to commodify drinking water supplies, a matter taken up in Chapter 14. The public trust acts as a last bastion of law to counter this privatization on a global scale. Recognizing its role of vindi-cating basic human rights, Maude Barlow and Tony Clarke urge new global water "ethic" premised on trust principles:

> Water must be declared and understood for all time to be the common property of all. In a world where everything is being privatized, citizens must establish clear perimeters around those areas that are sacred to life and necessary for the survival of the planet. Simply, governments must declare that water belongs to the earth and

all species and is a fundamental human right. No one has the right to appropriate it for profit. *Water must be declared a public trust.*[20]

Waste Not, Want Not

Another core principle of public trust law (explained in Chapter 8) compels using resources to their highest and most beneficial public use, and rejecting waste. One finds this imperative indelibly impressed on traditional native societies. "Indigenous thinking," as native scholar Winona LaDuke describes, holds that "you always take only what you need and you leave the rest." To do otherwise, she explains, would violate natural law.[21] Lying at the core of sustainable thinking, the waste injunction stands as a reasonable arbitrator between temperance and greed.

Religions across the world shun waste. As Roger Gottlieb notes in his book, *A Greener Faith*, Jewish Talmudic laws prohibit personal waste: "Those who waste, warned the Talmud, are on their way to idol worship, because wasting indicates a profound loss of self-control." Many Christian denominations also reject waste. Pope Benedict XVI issued a strong pronouncement in 2010 when he challenged "prevailing models of consumption" and called for "profound cultural renewal" toward a lifestyle "marked by sobriety." The Catholic Social Justice and Ecology Secretariat has drawn attention to "the implications of greed and over-consumption ... [and] the incredible generation of waste." In Buddhist teachings, the desire to possess and consume lies at the core of human misery; Gottlieb notes that Buddhist theology poses a "direct negation of the consumerist compulsions of twenty-first-century market society." Islam likewise scorns waste. The Honorable Christopher G. Weeramantry, a former justice on the International Court of Justice and an internationally renowned legal scholar, describes Islam as "adamant that resources should be utilized only to the extent of necessities and a luxurious life with extravagance should be avoided." He explains: "A creation which is so valuable and designed with such a high purpose must be respected, and wastefulness in its use is not a sign of due respect." Perhaps the most famous pronouncement against waste comes from Mahatma Gandhi, a Hindu, who admonished: "Live simply so that others may simply live."[22]

Despite widespread religious prohibition, waste infests Western consumer-driven economies. This was not always the case – even in America, where people now produce prodigious quantities of waste without blinking an eye at the moral ramifications of doing so. During World War II, people conserved many items so as to support the troops, who required massive amounts of food and necessities. Waste was considered unpatriotic, un-American. Goods such as aluminum, meat, gas, sugar, coffee, and other basics queued in short supply and were rationed. Children collected foil gum wrappers to send to the military for metal recycling. Household cooks collected waste fats from frying to send to rendering plants for the production of explosives. The U.S. government propagated a strong anti-waste ethic, issuing posters that declared, for example: "Food is a Weapon: Don't Waste It." As one account describes, "consumers were deluged with government sponsored messages urging them to avoid waste."[23]

But within just a few decades after World War II ended, the waste that had been resoundingly and deeply regarded as a personal disgrace and threat to national security had become a hallmark of U.S. culture. Inebriating consumers with material desire, America's economy vomits 250 million tons of garbage a year. In 2009, Annie Leonard drew attention to the consumption syndrome through her successful cartoon production, *The Story of Stuff*, which shows mass production from its inception to its throwaway end. Documentary producer John de Graaf also challenges modern consumerism, depicting it as a contagious epidemic which he calls *Affluenza*. The disorder has now spread viral across the globe, afflicting cultures that once strongly embraced an anti-waste ethic.[24]

Whether any consumer sobriety survives to hearten a cultural transformation remains to be seen. If it does, the trust doctrine's prohibition against waste can realign ecological resource management with revived cultural scruples. Some indicators point to a resurgence of the no-waste culture, such as a Voluntary Simplicity movement that now gains adherents worldwide. Staggering individual debt and economic collapse has undoubtedly prompted some consumer spending temperance. But aside from these distress factors, positive motivations also rise from widespread claims of a more fulfilling, healthier lifestyle associated with frugality.[25]

Earth Jurisprudence and Natural Beneficiaries

A fourth value embraced by the public trust concerns the right of Nature to exist and flourish. The great conservation writer, Aldo Leopold, surmised that society trudged on an evolutionary journey toward realizing what he called a "land ethic." This ethic enlarges the recognized community to which humans owe responsibility to include the land, air, waters, plants, and animals – in short, all of Nature. While this land ethic has not yet permeated industrial society, it has always ranked central to indigenous society. As the Navajo Nation expresses its natural law, "All creation, from Mother Earth and Father Sky to the animals, those who live in water, those who fly and plant life have their own laws, and have rights and freedom to exist." Gottlieb finds strands of the ethic in general religious thinking as well, stating, "[t]he environment has rights, deserves compassion, and can suffer (is 'cruciform').... Distinguishing between ourselves and nature reflects a self-centered arrogance that will make spiritual growth impossible."[26]

Several global initiatives now accord rights to Nature. Ecuador's amended constitution declares: "Natural communities and ecosystems possess the unalienable right to exist, flourish and evolve within Ecuador." Bolivia has enacted a similar provision in its constitution. "Rights of Nature" ordinances have been proposed or adopted in about two dozen U.S. cities spanning Pennsylvania, New Hampshire, Virginia, Washington, and Maine. On an international level, the approach finds reflection in a 1982 UN Resolution, *The World Charter for Nature*, which states: "Every form of life is unique [and] warranting respect regardless of its worth to man."[27]

U.S. Supreme Court Justice William O. Douglas broached the concept of Nature's rights in U.S. law when he argued in his famous *Sierra Club v. Morton* dissent that natural resources should have standing in court to sue for their own preservation. Noting that other inanimate objects, such as ships and corporations, had legal personality to sue in their own right, he reasoned, "So it should be as respects valleys, alpine meadows, rivers, lakes, estuaries, beaches, ridges, groves of trees, swampland, or even air that feels the destructive pressures of modern technology and modern life."[28] But his view has not yet taken hold in the U.S. legal system. While environmental groups have standing to sue to protect natural resources, they usually frame their claims around procedural violations, as explained in prior chapters. This approach remains flaccid: tolerance of procedurally correct damage sails leagues away from outright recognition that Nature itself has rights.

Nevertheless, ecological attitudes show signs of shifting, even within the law. A new theoretical approach called Earth Jurisprudence urges a Western legal ethic to sustain diversity of the natural world. Inspired by the vision of Thomas Berry (a Catholic priest moved by principles of deep ecology), Earth Jurisprudence directly confronts the human supremacy that drives most environmental policy. As Sister Patricia Siemen points out, Earth Jurisprudence accords rights to Nature and its components, "not as objects useful to humans, nor as a means to something desirable for humankind, but as subjects, as ends in themselves." Professor Judith Koons describes Earth as the "center of the moral community" and explains, "In this Earth ethic, the role of humanity changes 'from conqueror of the land-community to plain member and citizen of it.'" In a globalized world locked in conflict over planetary resources, Earth Jurisprudence may bridge a deep moral gulf between indigenous and industrialized nations regarding humanity's relationship with Nature.[29]

Even though environmental law currently fails to recognize the rights of Nature, ecological norms can shift quickly in democracies. In *Wild Law*, Cormac Cullinan observes that the slavery abolition movement came about rapidly when people questioned the morality of holding human slaves as property. Cullinan suggests that the destruction of Nature destines toward a similar result.[30] The loss of remarkable natural features and wildlife across the planet may hasten this moral awakening, as a growing number of citizens mourn the Arctic polar bears, the Siberian tigers, the Himalayan mountain glaciers, the coral reefs, and the Amazon rainforest. Moore and Nelson observe the emergence of a "new ethical awareness" in society and explain: "[W]hile humans and human interests certainly matter, they are not the only things that matter. A moral life will also honor the interests – and the beauty and mystery – of all the Earth."[31]

Environmental reform proposals should reserve political, cultural, and legal space for these values, still nascent in the West. At first glance, it may seem as if the public trust doctrine runs counter to a moral progression recognizing the rights of Nature, because the doctrine identifies natural resources as assets in the trust to be used for the benefit of humankind. Some environmental philosophers might surmise that an anthropocentric view of Nature ought to be annulled altogether. Realistically, the law is unlikely to deviate from its human-centered perspective anytime soon. However, even within the anthropocentric perspective, the law can certainly recognize humans as reliant for their very survival on the health of Nature and its biodiversity. Characterizing Earth as a full community of balance, the holistic conception of an ecological *res* within Nature's Trust synchronizes with Earth Jurisprudence. Humans, as beneficiaries of Nature's Trust, remain ecologically inseparable from the broader community of species; therefore, protection of the *res* in its full integrity naturally flows from the beneficiaries' rights.

Some eco-jurisprudentialists may nevertheless object to the public trust doctrine for its anchoring in property law, as they may construe property ownership to imply hegemony. But history shows otherwise. All but the most nomadic of human societies have developed property law systems to minimize human conflict over resource use. Some of the most sustainable indigenous communities, in fact, lived under highly advanced and enduring property regimes. The difference between Western and traditional indigenous systems is not that one has property law and the other does not, but rather that their property classifications justify fundamentally different results. The Western legal tradition allows exploitation on the theory that natural resources can be fully privatized – altered, destroyed, used, and sold at the whim of the owner. Indigenous property systems treat ecological resources as intrinsically communal, intergenerational, and spiritually imbued with obligation. If Western law were to emulate indigenous systems, the analogues would be found in tenancies in common, shared easements and profits, leaseholds, life estates, future interests, and trusts, rather than the fee simple absolute title taken by many to allow dominion over ecology. As explained further in Chapter 14, Nature's Trust expresses a fiduciary construct of private property ownership to prevent environmentally injurious uses. Similar to the indigenous approach, this fiduciary restraint shows concern for the long-term survival of the community.

In summary, the moral compass of Nature's Trust displays directional points oriented to four essential understandings of humanity: the duty to future generations, the right to commonwealth, the admonition against waste, and the rights of Nature to exist and flourish. In substantial measure, these four values derive from a community's survival intelligence. That they flourished in a premodern age marked by close human dependence on Nature is not surprising. That they became suppressed during a period of human history when technology divorced people from their natural environment is equally not surprising. That such values would find resurgence in a world gripped by extreme scarcity as a result of overconsumption seems almost to be expected. The trust holds the salt of the Earth and empowers the wisdom humans have always known.

AWAKENING ENVIRONMENTAL DEMOCRACY

A vibrant environmental law framework must not only present a strong moral imperative, but must also provide a common-sense narrative that will encourage citizens to participate in their government – and, when necessary, wrest back the reins of democracy. To this end, it must accomplish the following: (1) explain the citizens' role in democracy in such a way that empowers them to demand protection of Nature rather than discouraging them from doing so; (2) explain the legitimacy and proper function of government (particularly as to regulating actions that destroy the environment); (3) provide a linkage between citizen advocacy and individual responsibilities (for example, consumption choices); and (4) express a principled foundation of responsibility around which other major institutions, such as churches and schools, can also coalesce. As the following discussion explains, a public trust narrative can advance all four objectives.

Citizen Beneficiaries

Within a political framework, citizens must press for environmental protection by lobbying Congress, state legislatures, and state and federal agencies. The success of this lobbying effort depends in large part on the political clout the citizen holds – which, in turn, may correlate with wealth. Citizen groups with meager resources sometimes become marginalized, while wealthy interests pull the political levers they oiled with campaign contributions (a situation exacerbated by the U.S. Supreme Court's ruling in *Citizens United*, which removed limits on corporate campaign contributions).[32] Within the political system, moreover, children and future generations lack power: these classes have no vote even though they stand to lose the most from irreparable environmental harm. A disenfranchised, apathetic citizenry now lies in the ditches of modern political life (which may explain why the large advocacy groups have been unable to mobilize a new environmental movement).

The public trust can inspire a narrative that imbues citizens with a firmer sense of legal standing toward their government. In addition to recognizing their status as political constituents, the trust identifies citizens as beneficiaries holding a *public property right* to crucial natural assets – in equal measure as members of a living class. This common property right postures citizens to monitor the commonwealth and empowers them to demand enforcement of their collective trust. Such property rights stand fundamentally distinguishable from the citizens' political rights as constituents. Within the trust paradigm, a government's legal duties also flow to children and future citizens, both recognized as beneficiary classes. No trust duties flow to corporations as institutional creatures formed by the state through incorporation law (they lack beneficiary status, as explained in the next chapter). As a property law obligation, the fiduciary duty to protect the trust remains steadfast whether officials are lobbied or not, and whether the public shows up at hearings or not. In this way the trust paradigm exerts an equalizing force that *purchased democracy* does not.

Seeped in moral implication, the trust can arm citizens with more powerful rhetorical devices to challenge government's environmental mismanagement. Statutes, as Chapter 4 explained, permit all manner of harms as disguised by acronyms and techno-jargon. Within the statutory system, a mother protesting a toxic facility near her children's school, for example, might find herself having to speak in terms of ARARs, MCLs, NESHAPs, SIPs, MACT, BDCT, and BACT.[33] Few incoherencies impede democracy more than the utter lack of accessible language by which citizens can hold their government officials accountable. The trust requires no translation.

Unfortunately, environmental organizations have rarely used the public trust as a focal point for grassroots mobilization. Instead they rely almost exclusively on statutory law. However, a water trust case in Hawaii demonstrates the doctrine's potential to galvanize a citizen base. That litigation involved Native Hawaiians, family farmers, and local community groups that formed a coalition to assert public trust rights to water previously diverted to serve large sugar plantations. Their legal effort culminated in a stunningly successful Hawaii Supreme Court opinion that declared a public trust over all surface and groundwater in the state, as described in earlier chapters. Two lawyers representing the coalition reported that the public trust doctrine "energized the community with a sense of higher purpose." It also offered a morally grounded dialect of environmental obligation in a battle that spilled into a broad public arena: "The trust has given the [coalition] a cause with a powerful message: they are fighting not for 'their' water, but for water belonging to all, including generations unborn."[34]

Government's Legitimacy

The trust approach also legitimizes government's function of regulating private enterprise at a time when multinationals amass more wealth and control more of the world's natural resources than ever before. Understanding government's proper role in the marketplace remains crucial for a citizenry to adequately chaperone government's courtship of industry. Amid a growing political identity crisis, fiduciary trust duties help characterize the basic relationship between government, citizens, and corporations.

This relationship has long been the subject of an ideological agenda aiming to remove restraints on industry, as Peter Brown explains in his book, *Restoring the Public Trust*. Beginning with the Reagan presidency, an extreme libertarian approach aspired to redefine the sphere of the state, professing that the free market could allocate resources more efficiently than could government and achieve greater production, economic growth, and rising income for workers. Such a shift, however, refutes government's classic purpose to protect public rights from potentially harmful private actors. It has drawn sharp criticism for leading to the repeal of laws that had protected society from unscrupulous business operators. As John Perkins describes in his book, *Hoodwinked*, the "less government is good government" era was marked by "greed, an obsession with materialism, excessive debt … the formation of huge conglomerates, and ultimately the type of corruption symbolized by Enron, Bernard Madoff, and the debacle on Wall Street." Moreover, U.S. corporations waged a global campaign to spread a "messianic belief in privatization and profits" to persuade governments of other countries to open up valuable natural resources for their exploit.[35]

Market extremists sold their political philosophy to the public in value-laden terms that underscored personal liberty. As Brown explains, an unregulated free market seemed a "genuine alternative to coercion." The same drumbeat still reverberates in political life today, spilling over to the environmental realm. Manipulative messaging can obscure even the most atrocious harm to individuals, workers, families, children, and communities, inflicted by profiteers let off the regulatory leash. Brown warns, "Unless a *public philosophy* is set out, articulated, and promoted … we can expect nothing more than the continued destruction of our society and the biosphere."[36]

For decades, the free-market rhetoric continued without a counterveiling political narrative defining the legitimacy of government and the state-market relationship. Brown explains: "While the Right was investing millions of dollars in articulating a philosophically coherent approach to policy – and spelling out *and selling* the programs that followed from it – the Left was making no comparable effort.… Liberal intellectuals themselves had given up on the job of providing an overarching, but concrete, political vision." The Left had no dearth of think tanks, but liberal groups eschewed discussion of values, preferring to maintain an objective veneer as if values did not matter. Market extremists took advantage of the vacuum to assert a highly questionable moral foundation as unquestionable. This antigovernment agenda continues today through verbal fistfuls of cost-benefit analysis, private property rights, and incessant talk of growth, all designed to damage government's role in protecting core public values such as health, safety, and ecological abundance.[37]

The public trust advances a counternarrative to this by asserting the populist foundation of government legitimacy. As Brown notes, "This ancient idea – that the government is a trust, that those who govern are trustees – is what most of us already believe." The people's sovereignty creates government's duty to protect the commonwealth. The duality of sovereign power and fiduciary obligation to restrain private market actors from wrongly appropriating or destroying public assets forms a pillar in the foyer of legitimate government. The Supreme Court of India, for example, directly underscored this role when it declared a public trust over that country's natural gas. In language that flips the free-market philosophy on its head, the Court explained that *the people* confer power to the state to ensure equitable and non-harmful use of their common natural resources. It warned that industry-state collusions lead to the "evisceration of the [government's] moral authority." Emphasizing that strong state institutions remain necessary to manage natural resources and that government must "always be watchful that [corporations] do not take over the essential functions of the State," the Court's statements underscore a commonality among citizens worldwide: no matter what the national context, government's retreat from environmental responsibility affronts the people's reserved sovereignty and their individual liberty to live free of ecological harm.[38]

The Citizen as an Ethical Actor

Beyond providing a narrative of government legitimacy, the trust also suggests a platform of individual responsibility to protect ecology. Serious detachment exists today between the aspirations of environmental policy and individual conduct. While pollution remains conceptually bad – so much so that hundreds of thousands of pages of statutes and regulations aim to prevent it – individuals engage daily in a throwaway culture that condones pollution and waste as a matter of convenience. The individual's role remains that of consumer, not an ethical citizen duty-bound to community or generational needs. Environmental policy reform proposals usually give scant attention to the underlying individual choices that drive natural destruction.

The public trust doctrine positions the citizen in a richer moral context by emphasizing generational obligation – analogous to the well-known indigenous duty to the Seventh Generation. In her book, *In Fairness to Future Generations*, Edith Brown Weiss characterizes the present generation as "trustee" for future generations. The responsibility falling to a generation derivatively falls to all individuals within it. This trust worldview thereby recognizes an additional individual role: a person identifies not simply as a citizen of State X, or a consumer of Brand Z, but also as an accountable member of a particular generation that holds duties towards the next. Peter Brown explains:

> When we see ourselves as members of a community that stretches backward and forward in time, we can see that we ourselves are stewards of land and the diversity and productivity of the earth generally.... We work in cooperation with government in the discharge of these sacred duties to our children and our children's children.

At a time when philosophers and ethicists call for the "greatest exercise of the moral imagination that the world has ever seen" to put society on a sustainable track, it becomes crucial to align legal principle with ethical personal conduct adequate to match humanity's predicaments. A public trust effectuates a moral obligation that follows the lineage of humanity as it comes to life in present generations.[39]

But with an exclusive focus on government trustees, U.S. public trust cases have not gone so far as to characterize the *individual* as imbued with fiduciary obligation. Nevertheless, the individual-trustee concept may prove a natural progression as the doctrine develops. Professor Craig Anthony Arnold suggests a fiduciary duty assumed individually and shared by the public as a whole. Writing about the water trust, he explains, "While each of us is a beneficiary of the government's ownership ... of water, each of us also profoundly affects how the government's responsibility for water is effectuated.... We are co-beneficiaries but we are also co-trustees or co-managers."[40]

Leading court opinions in other countries explicitly define an individual trust duty. In the *Oposa* case, the Philippines Supreme Court declared that "every generation has a responsibility to the next to preserve that rhythm and harmony for the full enjoyment of a balanced and healthful ecology." The Court found that "the minors' assertion of their right to a sound environment constitutes, at the same time, the performance of their obligation to ensure the protection of that right for the generations to come." The India Supreme Court set forth the same concept in one of its landmark trust opinions, stating: "The Public Trust Doctrine is a tool for exerting long-established public rights over short-term public rights and private gain. Today, every person exercising his or her right to use the air, water, or land and associated natural ecosystems has the obligation to secure for the rest of us the right to live or otherwise use that same resource or property for the long term and enjoyment by future generations." The Court underscored an individual duty to not "impair or diminish the people's rights and the people's long term interest in that property or resource."[41]

Religious Environmentalism and Nature's Trust

With its analogue in religious and ethical thought, the trust doctrine also holds unique potential to unite churches, schools, and communities behind a massive

environmental restoration effort. This discussion focuses on the potential for reli-
gious-legal synergy within the trust frame. Law and religion justifiably stand on two
sides of a formal partition because of the constitutional separation of church and
state, but this severance does not prevent faith communities from supporting legal
objectives that advance their values. As Roger Gottlieb suggests, religion offers "profound contributions" to make in response to the environmental crisis.[42] One could
easily surmise that the colossal challenge of shifting entire societies toward sustainability within an urgent time frame cannot be accomplished *without* the full commitment of religious institutions.

Religion has not always allied with environmentalism. Gottlieb readily acknowledges that some Christian religious teachings have long propounded interpretations
of the Bible that emphasize full human dominion over Nature. All too often, dominion has meant destruction. But as he explains, modern eco-theologians now question these old interpretations and provide alternative readings of ancient religious
texts that emphasize the stewardship aspects of the Bible. He concludes: "Blanket
condemnation of religion as *the* source of environmental problems would leave
many people with a painful and ultimately untenable choice between environmentalism and faith. Religious environmentalists deny the necessity of such a choice."
And in fact, some environmental leaders today emphasize that environmental concerns reside at the heart of their religious interests. As the Reverend Canon Sally
G. Bingham says describing multiple faith teachings in her book, *Love God, Heal
Earth*, "It is a direct violation of our faiths to stand by and let our home, our neighbor's home, the gift of the Creator, perish. This is the realm of religion, no doubt
about it."[43]

That is certainly not to say that all faith leaders promote environmental protection.
Some extremist religious factions condemn environmentalism. In his climate book,
Down to the Wire, David Orr describes an "unholy alliance" between a branch of
Christian fundamentalists, the fossil fuel industry, and other big polluters. But these
factions, while quite vocal, are marginalized by highly visible faith leaders who voice
reverence for divine Creation. They include Roman Catholic Pope Benedict XVI,
Islamic leader Fazlun Khalid, Rabbi Warren Stone, Ecumenical Greek Orthodox
Patriarch Bartholomew I, the Dalai Lama of Tibet, Episcopal priest Sally Bingham,
and Evangelical leader Richard Cizik, among many others.[44]

Alliances from diverse faith traditions increasingly form to influence government
environmental policy. Some produce resolutions, such as ones issued by interfaith
coalitions opposing mountaintop removal in Appalachia. Some engage in civil disobedience to defend Creation, such as the priests, ministers, and rabbis who, in 2001,
knelt in prayer in front of the U.S. Department of Energy headquarters to protest
Bush's policy proposal to drill in the Arctic National Wildlife Refuge (those arrested
spent Easter Holy Week behind bars). Some participate in litigation as *amicus*

curiae, such as an interfaith coalition supporting an Atmospheric Trust Litigation case in front of the Washington Supreme Court. Asserting a human right to climate stability through the public trust doctrine, one of the coalition members expressed, "[A]ll of creation – including the atmosphere – is a sacred trust that humanity and its institutions have a responsibility to protect."[45]

A striking environmental partnership has formed between scientists and the religious community, prompted in no small measure by a book written by a renowned Harvard conservation biologist, E. O. Wilson. In *The Creation: An Appeal to Save Life On Earth*, Wilson invoked his own Baptist upbringing to suggest an alliance between scientists and religious leaders on what he saw as their common ground. The emerging faith-science partnership presents a powerful duality: scientists study and report the harm to Nature, while religious leaders offer a righteous path in response. In 2007, twenty-eight renowned scientists and evangelical leaders gathered together in Washington D.C. to issue an "Urgent Call to Action" to protect Creation.[46]

Religion offers multifaceted contributions to the environmental movement of the new millennium. Passionate preachers and spiritual leaders can activate entire congregations behind policy agendas in a way that impersonal e-mail appeals from advocacy groups may not be able to. Moreover, Gottlieb contends that, because the present ecological crisis reflects fundamentally a crisis of spiritualism, religion stands uniquely positioned to prompt change in personal attitudes and behavior. Today's problems, he points out, cannot be resolved by political, economic, or technological fixes alone, as they manifest a "profound and wide-ranging failing of virtually every aspect of modern society."

The moral vision of religion, Gottlieb suggests, can urge a fundamental shift in basic values from overconsumption to a simple, needs-based lifestyle – both by rejecting the former as unethical and by embracing the latter as spiritual. Perhaps singularly, religion can inspire personal change despite cognitive recognition that individual action counts little in relation to the problem as a whole. Gottlieb writes: "The willingness to resist requires a kind of faith that one's actions make a difference, even if it is hard to see what that difference is. We [find God in] ... a faith that reflects a passionate choice rather than a reasoned account of current social forces and trends." As a practical matter, too, religious communities offer a welcoming annex in which families and individuals can practice new lifestyles, some of them communally supported; church kitchens and gardens can build support for local, organic food; congregations can aggregate their individual change to produce significant cumulative results on a path of carbon reduction. Finally, as Gottlieb points out, religion can overcome the personal hopelessness that shadows daunting, global ecological predicaments. Religious life, he asserts, equips a believer to deal with the full range of human emotions that inevitably pour forth in the wake of environmental collapse – a range that will doubtless include shame, despair, fear, grief, anger, and denial. He writes: "[I]t is the job of religion to lend a hand precisely when things seem darkest."47

Religion and law can find powerful synergy on behalf of ecological protection when secular leaders voice a legal mandate recognized also as a spiritual command by all major religions. Remarkably, the world's major religions appear to observe a sacred trusteeship that, in faith terms, mirrors the legal iteration of the public trust. Perhaps this commonality should not be surprising, given that the public trust traces back to natural law that remains deeply infused with religious, spiritual, and moral tradition springing from the basic intuition of humankind.

In legal terms, a trustee holds the property of another with the obligation to protect it and use it for that person's benefit. The trust imbues power with responsibility. Many modern religious leaders and scholars of diverse faiths highlight with notable clarity a parallel trusteeship that springs from God's divine bequest of Creation to humanity. The conferral of power to human beings remains intrinsically and spiritually bridled by stewardship obligation. This understanding finds adherents even within the Christian tradition, which engendered some of the most emphatic interpretations regarding human "domination" over Nature. As Rev. Sally Bingham proclaims, "Dominion isn't exploit and plunder; dominion is care, compassion and concern." Similarly, in a Creation Address, Pope Benedict XVI declared that God's grant of "dominion" to humankind came entrusted with strong stewardship obligations. He explained:

> [T]he true meaning of God's original command, as the Book of Genesis clearly shows, was not a simple conferral of authority, but rather a summons to responsibility.... Biblical Revelation made us see that nature is a gift of the Creator, who gave it an inbuilt order and enabled man to draw from it the principles needed to "till it and keep it" [cf. Gen. 2:15]. Everything that exists belongs to God, who has *entrusted it to man*, albeit not for his arbitrary use.... Man thus has a duty to exercise responsible stewardship over creation, to care for it and to cultivate it.48

The sacred trust conferred upon humanity remains a consistent theme in other major religions as well, invoked to explain a holy bond between God, humankind, and Creation. A Jewish prayer, for example, iterates God's command to Adam: "This is the last world I shall make. I place it in your hands: hold it in trust." Justice Weeramantry points to a similar trusteeship paradigm operating in Islam, Buddhism, and Hinduism religions. In a series of essays, he describes Islamic notions of trust:

> [A] reason why, in Islam, humans are expected to protect the environment is that no other creature is able to perform this task. Humans are the only beings that God has "entrusted" with the responsibility of looking after the earth.... It is impermissible in Islam to abuse one's rights as khalifa (agents or trustees), because the notion

of acting in "good faith" underpins Islamic law. *The planet was inherited by all humankind and all its posterity from generation to generation.... Each generation is only the trustee.*

In *Islam and Ecology: A Bestowed Trust*, Richard C. Foltz writes: "the vice regency of God (*khilāfa*) made human beings ... custodians of the entire natural world. Human beings exist ... by virtue of a trust that they have taken upon themselves in pre-eternity." Islamic faith leader Dr. Hamid Mavani explains:

> From the Islamic perspective, all that is on the earth was created to serve humanity and human beings were delegated to make use of the resources as the deputy and vice-regent of God. Human being is a trustee and will be asked to respond to how he/she executed his stewardship of the earth on the Day of Reckoning.[49]

As Justice Weeramantry describes Buddhist environmentalism, it too involves "principles of trusteeship." Justice Weeramantry recounts a story of a monk preaching to the king of Sri Lanka as the king hunted in the royal forest: "The monk's sermon included a reminder to the King that although he was the King of the country, he was not the owner but the trustee of the land on which he was hunting." The Buddhist leader, His Holiness the Dalai Lama, also presents religious instruction heavily infused with obligations to future generations, which is the hallmark of a trust.[50]

A modern survey of Hinduism highlights the trust as well, as described by the great leader Gandhi: "All land belongs to God and has been given to humans in trusteeship. All should have what they need – nobody should own more." Justice Weeramantry describes the trusteeship of earth resources in his essay on Hinduism:

> The assets of nature are there for humans to use for their sustenance and development. But the assets of nature are held in trust.... Trusteeship of resources is based on the philosophy that the wealth of nature provided by God is provided for humanity in general and not for this generation or that. The long term vision of Hinduism reaches through to thousands of generations and all eternity. It is totally incompatible with this notion that any one generation has the right to diminish or extinguish the resources that nature provides. *Indeed this would almost amount to sacrilege and also to theft from future generations of their rightful inheritance.*[51]

Characterizing any religious tenet can carry the danger of oversimplification. But the preceding descriptions suggest a common point of light in human faiths: a *sacred trust* giving rise to holy covenants of obligation that inure to the benefit of future generations and to all of Creation. A legal paradigm premised on the trust concept falls gracefully – and uniquely – into this processional of religious teachings. When law's injunctions mirror religious and moral instruction, society gains a powerful symbiosis and alignment – a renewed steadiness in purpose. Judges, who hold the power of the pen, can once again breathe life into the law by expressing this unassailable moral foundation. By contrast, when secular majority society lacks the heartfelt connection and purpose of eternal commitment to the chain of human life and other species, statutory commands catch the winds of greed that seem to blow incessantly through the living generations on Earth. The next chapter explores how modern economic forces drive a propensity to waste and destroy Nature's resources.

In summary, Nature's Trust encompasses a paradigm. Not simply a legal premise for the protection of ecology, its moral and religious voice speaks to fundamental purposes underlying environmental law that have long since been lost in the modern world. The trust protects future generations, secures the commonwealth for the public, promotes the highest non-wasteful uses of resources, and underscores the right of Nature to exist and flourish. Trust-imbued words of rightful inheritance can be spoken anywhere in the world, for the trust covenant rests in the hearts of all humanity.

Aligned with religious trust convictions, the public trust of law holds whispers of epochal resonation as it stirs humanity to confront the crisis of ecology. Nature's Trust sounds a clarion call in mosques, temples, churches, synagogues, and prayer lodges all over the world to save Creation. This call echoes in the blasted hollows of Appalachia, in the cancer alleys of industrial corridors, on the banks of rivers that now carry only ghost-fish, and at the base of immortal mountains weeping their last glaciers into the sea. It summons people of faith everywhere to rise up and defend the holy sanctuary of Earth.

13

Using Earth's Interest, Not Its Principal

In May 2010, citizens across the world watched in horror as a geyser at the bottom of the sea gushed millions of gallons of oil into the Gulf of Mexico. After puncturing the ocean's floor, BP had no way to hold back the hemorrhage. Yet, when President Obama responded by imposing an emergency moratorium against deep-sea oil drilling, Louisiana Governor Bobby Jindal drew his political daggers and accused the president of stealing 6,000 jobs away from Louisiana workers. He complained that the moratorium's impact on drilling jobs compounded the "huge economic losses" inflicted on the state's seafood and tourism industry from the spill.[1]

Louisiana citizens should have choked on the governor's whopping contradiction, but instead they swallowed it whole. In the Gulf Coast region, politicians demand – in the same breath – pristine beaches, abundant shellfish, teeming marine life, and an industry that, with just one blowout, can slime the waters and murk the sands with millions of gallons of toxic petroleum. As the old saying goes, you can't have your cake and eat it too. But like so many Americans, Louisianans become easily roused by fighting talk that focuses on the economy. Just weeks after Governor Jindal's tirade, the Louisiana fervor erupted into a "Rally for Economic Survival" at which time the governor declared, "We're in the middle of a war to defend our way of life.... [L]et our people work."[2]

If any story demonstrates manipulative use of economic rhetoric to agitate the public against sensible environmental protection, this one does. The tale repeats time and again across the contexts of logging, mining, pollution, and land development. When environmental advocates invoke the law to halt ruinous actions, their success only fuels the "jobs versus environment" simplification of what remains a far more complex problem. Environmental regulation has long been the whipping boy for an economy that caters to destructive corporations.

Making matters worse, the current environmental regulatory system lacks an economic approach that offers hope of prosperity consistent with ecological protection. Though aiming to control harm inflicted by the industrial economy, environmental statutes nevertheless perpetuate that same economy by authorizing permits to pollute and destroy. Moreover, environmental advocates remain largely in denial as to the scope of economic change required to prevent environmental calamity. In a provocative essay, *Capitalism vs. The Climate*, Naomi Klein criticizes professional environmentalists for perpetuating the idea that the climate crisis can be addressed by individual action such as buying green products, changing light-bulbs, and using hybrid cars. Rather than offering shopping advice or market-based solutions, she says, environmental policy thinkers must confront the scale of deep change needed – "a radically new conception of realism, as well as a very different understanding of limits."[3]

At long last, environmentalists have both the opportunity and imperative to expose the perils of status quo economics and set forth a practical vision of prosperous, ecologically based economies. A robust and progressive body of literature begins this task by pointing to the same exit route for economic collapse and environmental chaos. In *Climate Capitalism*, for example, Hunter Lovins and Boyd Cohen assert that climate change results from a "crisis of capitalism" and submit that these "twin threats, to the climate and to the economy, are linked in both cause and cure."[4] This chapter draws from such literature to develop the economic contours of a Nature's Trust paradigm.

An economic appraisal of the Earth Endowment includes wealth that comes in the form of oceans, rivers, forests, aquifers, fish, wildlife, atmosphere, soils, seeds, wetlands, tidelands, grasslands, glaciers, mountains, minerals, and all other natural resources – assets that many now call "natural capital." These provide the infrastructure and services that support every manner of human activity, including all businesses on Earth. The business-as-usual (BAU) economy devours this wealth. As Juliet Schor explains in her book, *Plentitude*, the market "cannibalize[s] its very conditions of existence." In *Bridge at the Edge of the World*, James Gustave Speth asserts that capitalism will leave a world not "fit to live in" by mid-century. As Burns H. Weston and David Bollier write in *Green Governance*, the market-state has led society "over the not-so-long run, [to] a dead end – literally." As others point out, sustaining humanity at current economic and population growth scenarios would require the equivalent of another planet by 2030.[5]

But despite neon indicators of ecological collapse, most traditional economists still huddle beneath umbrella assumptions that become ever more drenched by reality. Even in the wake of the 2008 U.S. economic collapse, these thinkers urged conventional fixes. Schor observes, "The main conversation was about how to put more money into people's hands and how to get them back to buying cars, any cars; building more houses [and] accumulating more stuff.... As the world was hurtling toward an ecological precipice of unfathomable dimensions, the macroeconomic conversation was basically about how to get there faster." A growing number of realists recognize that an obese economy will collapse from its own weight. Lovins and Cohen conclude: "Business as usual will not endure, and it would be a recipe for disaster if it did."[6]

This chapter focuses primarily on assumptions driving the U.S. economy, not only because this economy produces a lion's share of the world's pollution, but also because it has engendered a dangerous form of capitalism that now wreaks havoc on ecosystems worldwide. This economy may be destined for transformative change due to its own dysfunction: it no longer provides nearly the prosperity or stability it once did. Instead, it delivers crushing job losses, soaring personal debt, a mind-boggling flow of imported oil (at grave risk to world security), jobs outsourced to foreign countries, a national savings rate of zero, oppressive working hours, a staggering percentage of home foreclosures, a financial system veering on the brink of collapse, and an income disparity that now careens far out of any defensible realm. As many observe, the disastrous effects of such economic realities lace together to form a scheme that advantages the ultra-wealthy while hurling increasingly intolerable circumstances at average workers and their families. Economic change becomes inevitable, Speth submits, because "[a] system that cannot deliver the well-being of people and nature is in deep trouble."[7]

The 2008 economic collapse sharpens the edge to such conversations. Speth reports a rising movement against modern capitalism "stronger than many imagine," and Schor asserts that the basic assumptions of capitalism have been hoisted "up for discussion." These thinkers rock the boat of conventional economics, which has insisted for decades that society will benefit as long as huge corporations float on their riches – postulating that a rising tide lifts all ships. For a long time, such seductive assurances allowed the corporate empire to amass dangerous power. But the economic wreckage of 2008 caused many smart people to wonder if something had gone wrong with the system steering the economy. The mothership of modern capitalism – namely the unregulated "free market" long promoted by libertarian conservatives – has sprung major leaks. There seems no getting around the fact that, in addition to causing colossal ecological damage, modern corporate enterprise leaves millions of families and individuals drowning in the swells of poverty.[8]

Of course, these criticisms amount to blasphemy for conventional economists who have long peddled capitalism as nothing short of gospel. Those who exploit status quo conditions cling to an ultra-narrow presentation of economic choice. Their often bullying rhetoric intimates that anyone who challenges capitalism must be a communist or a state socialist. But as Speth notes, far more expansive and hopeful possibilities exist than the corporate capitalists would have the downtrodden believe. There are many forms of capitalism, he points out. The challenge becomes not to eradicate capitalism altogether, but rather, as John Perkins observes in his book,

Hoodwinked, to rein in its "predatory mutant" form. Progressive thinkers like Perkins and Speth suggest recalibrating the relationship between government and the corporations to safeguard public values while still protecting private entrepreneurship and innovation. Speth identifies the challenge as bringing about "a nonsocialist system" that can "take us beyond capitalism as we know it today."[9]

Klein points out that climate stability, the most pressing of all environmental challenges, cannot be achieved in the present capitalist system. When conservative free-market voices assert that climate action would fundamentally undermine our present economic system, she says, they are correct: "Responding to climate change requires that we break every rule in the free-market playbook and that we do so with great urgency." Arriving at new adaptive economic systems, Klein says, will require "shredding the free market ideology that has dominated the global economy for more than three decades." This, she contends, remains a hopeful prospect in light of the inequalities and social failures of the present state-market system, failures that now prompt citizens worldwide to rise up against their nations' elites in demand of economic justice and the end of corruption. As Klein concludes, "Climate change doesn't conflict with demands for a new kind of economy. Rather, it adds to them an existential imperative."[10]

And in fact, an economic renaissance now glimmers in the shadows of industrial capitalism as a growing cadre of visionaries offer ideas for a more productive, equitable, and sustainable economy. These thinkers dare to ask: "What's the economy for, anyway?" Lovins queries: "Is the point of the economy to enrich the 20 percent of the population that owns 80 percent of global wealth, at the cost of misery for the rest?" Innovative ideas abound under titles of "green governance," "plentitude," "climate capitalism," "the right relationship," "transition," "power down," "post-industrial economy," "the Earth community," a "new home front," and many others. While branching into multiple variants, these approaches all bundle core values into a new economic worldview. They envision human dignity, non-tangible forms of wealth, community resilience, and ecological abundance – enduring societal concerns residing at the core of a Nature's Trust paradigm, as described in Chapter 12.[11]

Drawing from this economic literature, the discussion that follows compiles a critique of several entrenched assumptions driving the BAU economy. Specifically, these relate to: (1) economic accounting; (2) the role of fossil fuels; (3) unlimited growth; (4) waste and pollution; (5) consumers and their consumption; and (6) the role of corporations. Obsolete assumptions from all six areas form flying buttresses in an economic architecture many now think teeters on the brink of collapse. This chapter explores these six areas in search of new premises that can provide the footings for a stable economic structure – one that observes Nature's own limits in accordance with a trust paradigm.

BALANCING EARTH'S BUDGET

The first set of assumptions concerns accounting systems. The Industrial Revolution and its aftermath brought the Earth Endowment – the fund we all rely on for food, water, shelter, and our very survival – to the verge of bankruptcy. Conventional accounting deserves much of the blame for this state of affairs for employing an artificial definition of wealth fabricated by economists long ago. Put simply, conventional accounting ignores the appropriation of ecological wealth. The system allows private capitalists to destroy assets belonging to the public without paying any price. As Paul Hawken, Amory Lovins, and L. Hunter Lovins describe in their landmark work, *Natural Capitalism*, "'[I]ndustrial capitalism' ... liquidates its capital and calls it income. It neglects to assign any value to the largest stocks of capital it employs – the natural resources and living systems." Accordingly, it also fails to account for the staggering costs of environmental loss. Juliet Schor explains:

> The canonical models used by the mainstream are addressed to what happens within markets, rather than to economic dynamics more broadly. Because air, water, and many natural resources are neither owned nor priced, the effects of economic activity on their health and functioning do not fall within the purview of the standard treatments.... [M]ost economists have practiced their craft as if nature did not exist.[12]

The industrial complex ballooned under this system. It freely appropriated valuable assets held in trust for the people and converted them into products from which it made profits. As corporate captains gobbled up the world's natural capital, their own financial accounts swelled in profligate excess. Such massive ecological theft could not have continued without the tight collusion of government and industry. But also perpetuating it was a Western view that deemed Nature amorphous and lacking in value. Money doesn't grow on trees, so the saying goes.

Within this conventional paradigm, gross domestic product (GDP) has become the conventional keystone indicator of economic health. As Lovins and Cohen explain, "We are expected to be happy when [it] grows, and worried when it falls." In their book, *What's the Economy For Anyway*, John de Graaf and David Batker lament GDP's imperial rein over other indicators: "Fattening King GDP is more important to most of our leaders than reducing unemployment, controlling inflation, stabilizing interest rates, reducing debt or paying attention to a host of lesser economic dukes, barons, or other measures." A growing number of economists and world leaders have come to question GDP as an appropriate economic indicator. Lovins and Cohen blame the BAU economy for bringing the world "to the edge of a crumbling cliff," and one high-level commission established by French President Nicolas Sarkozy concluded that leaders relying on GDP act as pilots "steering a course without a reliable compass."[13]

The problem lies in GDP's false portrayal of wealth and its masking of massive ecological impoverishment. Operating within its own wonderland, it tallies the flow of money from business transactions in a way that wholly ignores environmental costs. As Juliet Schor explains, GDP remains "decoupled from" pollution, raw materials depletion, and environmental impact. It accordingly fails to account for the huge "drawdowns" from the Earth Endowment that industry takes without payment. Lovins and Cohen borrow the term "cheater capitalism" to describe the problem. When politicians present this economics shell game to the public, citizens are led to believe their government's policies create more wealth than is actually the case, so they give support to resource-depleting policies. The wealth picture changes dramatically when analysts incorporate the costs of environmental degradation. As one example highlighted by Schor shows, the U.S. electric power industry's $22.2 billion in earnings would flip over to a $28.2 billion net loss if experts accounted for harms and liabilities from three major pollutants emitted by the industry.[14]

Conventional economics considers such environmental costs as "external" to the market and call them "externalities" for that reason. But "externalities" often just indicate that the casualties fall elsewhere – shoved onto the shoulders of innocents who gain little or nothing from industry's exploit. The communities living in the blasted region of Appalachia become "externalities." The families with toxic water running through their taps because of nearby natural gas drilling remain "externalities." The hairless children lying in cancer wards as a result of chemical exposure die as "externalities."[15]

Economic realists insist on a full ecological accounting showing *both* the wealth created and the costs imposed by BAU. This would reveal, for example, up to $12 billion in toxic waste cleanup costs resulting from the mining industry's practices over the past ten years. It would show billions of *annual costs* in health-related harm caused by pollution emitted by the fossil fuel industry. It would recognize hundreds of billions of dollars in weather-related damages in the United States projected to result from climate change. BAU economics shows none of this. Its false accounting creates a vicious cycle because it warps the market signals and induces consumers to make environmentally damaging choices. As Schor explains, activities or goods that harm the environment carry too low a price in BAU accounting: "As a result, the market generates too many plastics, toxic chemicals, and fossil fuel-dependent trips."[16]

Certainly mainstream society has not come to appreciate the costs of climate change brought on by BAU. Even a purely economic calculation (ignoring human tragedies) yields astounding costs of adaptation approaching $1.5 trillion *every year*. The costs of Hurricane Katrina alone soared to $100 billion. Climate disaster, according to the British government's Stern Review, could consume up to 20 percent or more of the world's GDP – yet proactive measures taken now to reduce greenhouse gas emissions would cost only 1–2 percent of the GDP. Ultimately, climate crisis presents a significant business problem, for as Dr. Rajendra Pachauri, chairman of the UN Intergovernmental Panel on Climate Change (IPCC), stated in no uncertain terms, "We are risking the ability of the human race to survive."[17] As the new saying goes, *There is nothing worse for business than the end of civilization.*

The "natural capitalism" approach would redesign the economic structure to harmonize with government's sovereign duty to protect the assets held in public trust. It demands a long-overdue balancing of the ledger sheet to mitigate the world's ecological deficit. This requires internalizing the costs of ecological damage and reorienting business strategies so as to make profits from Earth's interest rather than its principle. To this end, Lovins and Cohen advocate "full cost accounting" (to include externalities and environmental harm) as an inherent requirement of a "true free market." Similarly, Speth advances the "polluter pays" principle (currently, polluters obtain the right to pollute for free). This would require despoilers to pay for the damages they cause, at a pricing "discouragingly, forbiddingly high." As he acknowledges, the standard may often preclude a particular discharge, impact, or product. This approach aligns with public trust principles, which would demand the phase-out of most pollution permits and charge natural resource damages for harm to public assets.[18]

Along with these changes, economic policy must also transform the public subsidy program, which further skews the "free market." Across the world, subsidies of environmentally and economically destructive enterprises run about $850 billion, or nearly 2.5 percent of the world's economy. Indirect subsidies of the U.S. fossil fuel industry alone totaled about $120 billion in 2005. In 2011, the Obama administration proposed adding $36 billion in subsidies for the nuclear industry to underwrite new reactor construction, even though the waste from the old reactors continues to pose immense threats with no feasible disposal strategy in sight. Through its subsidy policy, the trustee actually pays third parties to appropriate and destroy the natural wealth that the trustee remains obligated to protect.[19]

Those who rationalize such subsidies argue that they promote sectors of the economy that serve public values. But actually, many subsidies flow from political favors and make no policy sense – which is why critics call them "perverse." Policy must ultimately come to terms with the inevitable expiration of destructive industries in a new ecological age. A trust approach would end financial support of the fossil fuel and nuclear industries and shift investment to three parallel tracks. The first would finance society's switch to renewable energy, a measure that would both reduce planet-scale threats (radioactive contamination and climate crisis) and achieve energy cost savings over the long term. Currently, solar, wind, and other safe renewable industries gain just 1 percent of the amount of subsidies handed to the fossil fuel industry. The second track must fund investment into infrastructure – such as new roads, dikes, flood control systems, and much more – that will allow society to adapt to increasingly chaotic climate conditions. As Bill McKibben describes this necessary infrastructure overhaul, "The list goes on endlessly, one place after another, one billion after another." This adaptation must include huge amounts of public funding for decommissioning, cleaning up, or moving dangerous facilities (such as nuclear power plants, chemical plants, and petroleum refineries) that sit in the zone of sea level rise and storm surge. And the third track requires investment toward ecological restoration. Natural capital produces dividends in the form of ecosystem services worth many trillions of dollars annually. As Gretchen Daily concludes in her book, *Nature's Services*, "safeguarding ecosystem services represents one of the wisest economic investments society could make."[20]

THE END OF FOSSIL FUELS

A second BAU assumption destined for collapse concerns cheap fossil fuels – that their availability will last indefinitely. Reliance on fossil fuels grows ever more tenuous in the face of urgent warnings of diminishing oil supplies and escalating prices. As reviewed in prior chapters, "peak oil" does not mean that Earth's oil reserves suddenly vanish. Rather, it means that the cost of extracting remaining supplies becomes prohibitively expensive. Under peak oil scenarios, Lovins and Cohen surmise, "The global economy grinds to a halt."[21]

Any concoction of possible events – including political instability in oil-producing countries, soaring demand for oil in the Middle East and Asia, interrupted domestic oil supplies, terrorist attacks, and hurricane or extreme weather events – could trigger an oil crisis. Lovins and Cohen warn: "This could happen. Tomorrow." Because of society's wholesale dependence on oil for food, transportation, and energy, spikes in oil prices become "life-and-death issues for billions" worldwide.[22]

Conventional economics utterly ignores these latent perils of fossil fuel dependence; like the other industrial assumptions discussed in this chapter, this too must surrender to new thinking. But there remains a peak oil paradox: a transition to clean energy must prove *more rapid* than the rate at which existing supplies will deplete, because emissions from burning the remaining fossil fuels would be catastrophic to Earth's climate system. The atmosphere provides currency for virtually all of life's transactions. Climate scientists such as Dr. James Hansen have made clear that releasing all, or even most, of the remaining fossil fuel CO_2 into the atmosphere would "guarantee dramatic climate change, yielding a different planet than the one on which civilization developed."[23]

The extraordinary ecological imperative to protect the atmosphere (by ending the oil economy) aligns with other inexorable societal forces, not the least of which are security concerns. As a distinguished board of retired admirals and generals commissioned by the CNA Corporation has warned, the United States' current energy posture presents a "serious and urgent threat" to national security. A report issued by the Center for a New American Security (CNAS) similarly declares that growing world demand for petroleum poses "major geostrategic risks." Quite obviously, oil dependence embroils the United States in war and requires continued military presence in the Persian Gulf: "America's thirst for oil leaves little choice," the CNA board points out. The United States tripled its imported oil from the early 1980s to 2009, and Americans now burn through 344 million gallons of gasoline *per day* on average.[24]

Global oil dependence places world security in the hands of volatile petro-dictators that gain ever more leverage as oil supplies run scarce. The U.S. economy gulps 25 percent of the world's total production of oil but controls less than 3 percent of the supply. Columnist Tom Friedman points out in *Hot, Flat, and Crowded* the absurdity of the United States funding both sides of the war on terror, "We are financing the U.S. Army, Navy, Air Force, and Marine Corps with our tax dollars, and we are indirectly financing, with our energy purchases, al-Qaeda, Hamas, Hezbollah, and Islamic Jihad...." He adds, "I cannot think of anything more stupid." The security outlook becomes more ominous over the long term. CNAS projects that by 2085, the last reserves of oil will likely be held by some of the most hostile and volatile nations: Venezuela, Iran, Iraq, Kuwait, and the United Arab Emirates.[25]

Peak oil also threatens to ground even the U.S. military. CNAS warns that the petroleum needed to operate weapons and transportation systems may not remain affordable or reliably available even three decades hence. Already, costs have climbed to a nearly prohibitive level of $400 per gallon (including convoy protection). Reliance on fossil fuel creates an Achilles heel for fighting and logistical forces, requiring an "extraordinary commitment" of combat resources (armored vehicles, helicopters, and fixed-wing fighter aircraft) to protect fuel lines.[26]

Beyond dangerous dependence on oil, military advisors warn of grave disruption of world security caused by climate change resulting from continued fossil fuel emissions. The CNA board explains:

> Unlike most conventional security threats that involve a single entity acting in specific ways at different points in time, climate change has the potential to result in multiple chronic conditions, occurring globally within the same time frame.... Because climate change also has the potential to create natural and humanitarian disasters on a scale far beyond those we see today, its consequences will likely foster political instability where societal demands exceed the capacity of governments to cope.[27]

Similar alerts jump from the pages of a world security report coauthored by a former head of the CIA, a former Chief of Staff, and a former Deputy Assistant Secretary of Defense, published by the Center for Strategic and International Studies. Describing a scenario of a 2.6C° average increase in global temperature by 2040, they state: "Massive nonlinear events in the global environment give rise to massive nonlinear social events.... *[N]ations around the world will be overwhelmed by the scale of change....* The social consequences range from increased religious fervor to outright chaos."[28]

These factors converge to place the United States in a "dangerous and untenable position," the CNA report concludes. Whether the energy transition can occur in time to prevent environmental catastrophe and economic collapse from peak oil remains to be seen. In an ambitious call, CNAS urges the Department of Defense to switch from fossil fuels to alternative energy by 2040. In *Apollo's Fire*, Congressmen Jay Inslee (now governor of Washington) and Bracken Hendricks envision a national renewable energy project on the scale of President Kennedy's original space mission.[29]

Several proposals already exist for developing renewable forms of energy such as wind, solar, and biofuels to eliminate carbon dioxide emissions. In *Carbon-Free, Nuclear-Free*, Dr. Arjun Makhijani presents a detailed plan for the United States to reach zero carbon emissions by 2050 and phase out nuclear power at the same time. In *Plan B 4.0*, Lester Brown explains a strategy of reducing carbon emissions 80 percent below 2009 levels by 2020 (without resorting to additional nuclear power). On a local level, mayors now declare pace-setting renewable energy goals; San Francisco aims to have 100 percent renewable power by 2020. There are also momentum gains in converting present waste streams to energy. Lovins and Cohen recount a multitude of go-getter companies now making fuel out of unconventional sources such as dirty diapers, pond scum, slaughterhouse waste, and leftover cooking grease. Many predict a significant economic boost and multiplied job opportunities resulting from a broad-scale energy transition.[30]

Such optimism aside, however, Richard Heinberg offers a sobering reflection on the energy transition. When calculating the significant investment of fossil fuel necessary to create a new clean energy infrastructure (such as windmills and solar panels), he finds "no clear practical scenario" by which today's conventional energy sources can be replaced by alternative energy sources at a level sufficient to sustain industrial society at its present consumptive scale. A reality check rings out in Heinberg's oft-quoted statement, "The party's over." As he elaborates:

> [W]e are living today at the end of the period of greatest material abundance in human history – an abundance based on temporary sources of cheap energy that made all else possible. Now that the most important of those sources are entering their inevitable sunset phase, we are at the beginning of a period of overall economic contraction.

Heinberg points out that society can realistically achieve transition only by scaling back on the excesses of modern life. Some call this "powering down." But this does not portend a doomsday scenario. It suggests, rather, a return to more modest living with localized systems of production, less waste and frivolous consumption, and more community cohesion. It also suggests that other flying buttresses of the existing economic structure must be replaced by new assumptions. These are taken up in the sections that follow.[31]

FROM GROWTH TO STABILITY

One such assumption concerns economic growth. Richard Heinberg laments: "During the past few decades, growth has become virtually the sole index of national economic well-being. When an economy grows, jobs appear, investments yield high returns, and everyone is happy. When the economy stops growing, financial bloodletting and general misery ensue." Yet unrestrained growth has brought environmental calamity. Polluted waterways, depleted fish stocks, toxic air sheds, extinct species, denuded forests, and countless other indicators show a natural trust teetering on the edge of bankruptcy. Ignoring these falling stocks of Nature, mainstream economists continue to frolic in a fantasy of their own making – a reality-defying world in which the juggernaut economy operates completely unconstrained by natural limits. When the growth frenzy received a hard challenge back in 1972 from the best-selling book, *The Limits to Growth*, business interests mounted a vicious campaign against it. As Richard Heinberg notes, challenges to growth were "heretical at the time."[32]

Over the ensuing decades, growth continued to be the overriding standard by which millions throughout the industrialized world defined their own prosperity. Clive Hamilton observes: "[The] obsession with growth appears to be a fetish – that is, an inanimate object worshipped for its apparent magical powers."[33] As citizens of industrialized countries became increasingly dependent on paychecks issued by corporations, wages became the primary proxy for food, water, medicine, and shelter. Human survival intelligence faded, and self-sufficiency withered through participation in an external market, with the result that chaotic economic growth took on the characteristics of a lifeline. For a society caught in the throes of economic oppression and insecurity, the prospect of curbing economic growth understandably riles deep hostility.

But the growth lifeline is now coming unfastened from Nature's own life sources. As Heinberg explains, "At some point in time, humanity's ever increasing resource consumption will meet the very real limits of a planet with finite natural resources." The economy now devours natural resources at a pace that puts citizens and future generations in peril. For decades, environmental lawyers and government regulators have simply assumed that their legal tools remained adequate to achieve environmental protection. But Speth and others surmise that environmental law cannot function in a political economy that drives relentless growth and treats legitimate challenges to it as profane. As Canadian law professor Michael M'Gonigle points out, the failure of environmental law lies in its implicit acceptance of growth-driven political and economic practices that have "fatally bracketed what [the] law is able to achieve." Speth submits: "Today's politics will never deliver environmental sustainability."[34]

Many bright thinkers now challenge the premise of an economy that bloats the present market far outside of the planet's ecological belts. As John de Graaf explains, "[E]very economy, from household to planet level, has physical boundaries and thresholds where costs eventually surpass benefits.... Macroeconomics needs a when-to-stop rule." Speth urges a "healthy skepticism of growth-mania and a redefinition of what society should be striving to grow." Lovins and Cohen write: "[I]nfinite growth in physical stuff in a finite world is the ideology of a cancer cell, and a violation of the operating rules of the planet on which we all live." Herman Daly points out: "[T]he macro-economy becomes an absurdity if its scale is structurally required to grow beyond the biophysical limits of the Earth."[35] These thinkers all urge a dose of realism.

The 2008 economic collapse may have at least partially evaporated the growth potion from the cauldron of conventional economics. Juliet Schor suggests that growth is not only unnecessary for a healthy economy but can be economically destructive as well. She attributes massive business failures to economic growth forced by "financialization" of the U.S. economy. Noting that Wall Street lenders muscled American business into a grow-or-die situation, she explains: "When companies borrow money, or become highly leveraged, they need bigger profits, because they have to use them not only to improve productivity, but also to pay off their bankers." Such finance-mandated expansion, she concludes, has "decimated and bankrupted many once-healthy companies." A new economy, Schor asserts, need not be slave to growth: "It's time to become far more discriminating, and reframe the debate to figure out what needs to grow and what needs to shrink." If not shackled by over-indebtedness, small businesses might operate successfully at relatively the same size for years – for them, the "growth imperative" disappears.[36]

A great deal of scholarship defines the characteristics of a "post growth society," as Speth calls it. In contrast to the growth paradigm that flatly ignored environmental parameters, this economic system observes Nature's boundaries first and foremost. Herman Daly pioneered the paradigm shift in his now classic book, *Toward a Steady State Economy*, published in 1973, in which he posited that human economies must exist in an approximately steady state so as not to exceed natural limits. As he elaborated in 2008:

> [A] steady-state economy is not a failed growth economy. [It] is not designed to grow.... [It is] an economy with constant population and constant stock of capital, maintained by a low rate of throughput that is within the regenerative and assimilative capacities of the ecosystem.[37]

A steady-state economy steps into alignment with the core purpose of Nature's Trust – to protect society's natural capital for present and future generations. A multitude of new books offering different strategies for achieving a steady-state economy share many common elements. They include: (1) a rapid transition away from fossil fuels; (2) an increase in "intensive growth" (greater efficiency in the use of natural capital); (3) reduced production and consumption of nonessential material goods; (4) reduced working hours and increased leisure time; (5) a reconfiguration of financial systems; (6) ecological pricing and tax reform; (7) an increase in small, diversified businesses; (8) re-localized economies and curbed global markets; (9) policy measures to reduce income disparity; (10) an investment in public infrastructure to allow sustainable living; (11) restoration of ecosystems; (12) a transition from industrialized agriculture to labor-intensive organic, sustainable farming; and (13) population stabilization and gradual decline. These measures, along with many other proposals, aim to enhance human well-being, protect economic stability, and reduce financial inequality. They offer hope for the millions left stranded by the growth economy.[38]

ELIMINATING WASTE AND POLLUTION

Waste and pollution present two more flying buttresses of the failed industrial economy. Environmental law has legitimized both, allowing agencies to give permits to pollute and allocate scarce natural resources to industries without regard to public need or benefit. These behaviors offend core standards of trust responsibility, as Chapter 8 explained. Waste fails to put assets to their highest and best societal use. Pollution both damages trust assets and commits waste by using precious resources (such as soils, waterways, and air sheds) for dumping grounds rather than for higher and sustainable uses such as food production, species habitat, and general human life support. As Chapter 8 concluded, government bears a fiduciary responsibility to protect Nature's Trust by phasing out pollution permits and disallowing the appropriation of public resources for wasteful ends. Both steps remain necessary in order for society to adapt to extreme resource scarcity.

Like endless growth, waste and pollution have escaped rigorous social challenge until recently. Citizens have tolerated these ills as inevitable by-products of economic prosperity. But are they inevitable? Might they simply represent the repercussions of a corporate strategy to maximize profits without paying the costs? Until recently, the idea of revamping environmental law to phase out waste and pollution would have seemed idealistic and unachievable. But a growing number of professionals working in the fields of industrial design, green architecture, business, and urban transportation now envision an economy – a "natural capitalism" – fully in alignment with the requirements of Nature's Trust.

As Lovins and Cohen describe, natural capitalism's first principle calls for increasing efficiency in the use of natural assets. In today's business world, "eco-efficiency" often boosts profit margins. As they point out, DuPont Corporation saves $2.2 billion a year through measures to reduce waste. Ford Motor Company expects to save $1 million each year by shutting off unused computers. Wal-Mart saves $25 million each year by limiting truck idling and has saved $11 billion in just two years with a waste reduction program. Enormous opportunities exist for improving energy efficiency. One estimate projects that the U.S. economy wastes 87 percent of the energy it consumes. Researchers at Cambridge University calculated that the world could reduce its energy demand 85 percent by using existing technology and retrofitting.[39]

But despite its win-win appeal, reducing waste does not become an end-all solution. As Juliet Schor notes, efficiencies sometimes cause an unintended "rebound" effect. As prices drop through efficiency gains, people consume more – a result that cancels out the environmental gain. Moreover, efficiencies never solve the ultimate problem of pollution. As William McDonough and Michael Braungart point out in their pathbreaking book, *Cradle to Cradle*, "eco-efficiency only works to make the old, destructive system a bit less so." They conclude: "Relying on eco-efficiency to save the environment will in fact achieve the opposite; it will let industry finish off everything, quietly, persistently, and completely."[40]

Recycling offers another strategy, but it too has problems. Recycling extends the use of some product materials, but the process creates significant carbon emissions during the transportation, breakdown of material, and production of new materials. On that basis alone, it remains a far cry from an ultimate solution to climate crisis. Moreover, as McDonough and Braungart point out, "recycling" actually entails a process of *"downcycling"* – a transformation that reduces the quality and usefulness of the material over time. Typical downcycled products receive additional chemicals to make them suitable for other products. Downcycled plastic, for example, often contains more chemicals than original plastic.[41]

McDonough and Braungart present an optimistic design shift based on a "cradle-to-cradle" principle that, mimicking Nature itself, wastes nothing. As the authors explain, this approach means to "design things – products, packaging, and systems – from the very beginning on the understanding that waste does not exist." In a cradle-to-cradle system, every product becomes a beneficial input for another product, without the degrading and carbon-intensive process of recycling. They elaborate, "Products can be composed either of materials that biodegrade and become food for *biological cycles*, or of technical materials that stay in closed-loop *technical cycles*, in which they continually circulate as valuable nutrients for industry." This design shift, which Lovins and Cohen highlight as a second core principle of natural capitalism, manifests in concepts such as the "circular economy" and "biomimicry." Many examples of biomimicry design already exist: styrofoam made from orange peels; cement made from seawater and carbon dioxide waste (similar to the way coral reefs were formed); biodegradable plastic made largely from CO_2; batteries made from viruses (mimicking how the red abalone makes its shell); and living roofs that provide a food supply atop a building. McDonough and Braungart envision the cradle-to-cradle design approach as creating "a world of abundance, not one of limits, pollution, and waste."[42]

But today's industrial manufacturing, they point out, perpetuates an "outdated and unintelligent design" that originated in the 1800s with the birth of the Industrial Revolution. Early industrialists conceived techniques to mass-produce with specific goals calibrated toward a burgeoning market. Assuming endless resource abundance, products were made without regard to the natural system of which they were a part, and with the intention that they would be disposed of in a "grave" (typically a landfill or incinerator) at the end of their useful life. This "cradle-to-grave" design remains in place today, with a linear focus on delivering a product to a customer "quickly and cheaply without considering much else."[43]

Current environmental regulations cater to this obsolete design approach by imposing end-of-the-pipe limitations to reduce, dilute, treat, or otherwise manage pollution. As McDonough and Braungart point out, this regulatory system misses opportunities for redesigning processes altogether to eliminate toxins in the first place. As they state, "[U]ltimately a regulation is a signal of design failure. In fact, it is what we call a *license to harm*: a permit issued by a government to an industry so that it may dispense sickness, destruction, and death at an 'acceptable' rate." They assert, "[G]ood design can require no regulation at all."[44]

A "cradle-to-cradle" design portends an end to the dumping, burning, and burying of waste – an end to pollution itself. The concept becomes key for bringing the economy into alignment with a Nature's Trust paradigm. As prior chapters of this book explained, environmental agencies spend nearly all of their resources and technical expertise on a task that, in the end, remains both futile and perilous to human beings: drawing an impossible line between "unsafe" and "safe" levels of pollution. In the shift to a closed-loop, cradle-to-cradle economy, agencies would redirect resources and expertise to the task of banning toxins, phasing out pollution, recovering ecosystems, and creating infrastructure to help communities adapt to the realities of a heating planet.

THE END OF ENDLESS CONSUMPTION: CONSUMERS
BECOMING PRODUCERS

Consumption represents yet another crumbling pillar of the failed economy. In today's globalized, industrialized world, complex webs of commerce stretch across the planet to link producers, suppliers, transporters, middlemen, distributers, marketers, and consumers. The average individual depends on an increasingly chaotic global market for buying food, clothing, medicine, transportation, and information tools. Such mass global consumption creates environmental havoc, soaring carbon emissions, and a wasteful garbage culture. Within this market, for example, Americans use 1.14 million brown paper bags every hour, 15 million sheets of office paper every five minutes, 106,000 aluminum cans every thirty seconds, and 2 million plastic beverage bottles every five minutes. Extolling the benefits of global mass production, conventional economists fail to question the deeper ramifications of this throwaway lifestyle.[45]

In order to envision a sustainable economy in alignment with Nature's Trust principles, one must reimagine the role of the consumer and contemplate an end to overconsumption. A wealth of new scholarship now questions whether frenzied consumption actually delivers happiness and well-being to citizens. Analysts in this emerging field methodically unpack the concept of happiness into its component parts. As John de Graaf and David Batker write, "None of [them] conclude that the economic route to happiness consists of endlessly widening the superhighway of accumulation." In fact, research indicates that wealth and accumulation beyond a certain point does not yield commensurate happiness. Speth sums it up this way: "[T]here are diminishing returns to consumption as one moves from meeting basic needs to consumer satiation." Recognizing the mounting costs – environmental, social, and economic – of mass consumption, he concludes, "In the United States we are beyond the point where we should have stopped." Americans may already sense that. As Speth reports results from one U.S. survey, 81 percent of the respondents said Americans remain too focused on shopping and spending, and 88 percent said that American society has become too materialistic.[46]

Many authors point to leisure time as a crucial component of overall happiness and note that Americans have compromised time wealth for material wealth. The average American workday has increased substantially, with annual work time now exceeding that of some European countries by more than a month and a half. Schor concludes: "Millions of Americans have lost control over the basic rhythm of their daily lives. They work too much, eat too quickly, socialize too little, drive and sit in traffic for too many hours, don't get enough sleep, and feel harried too much of the time.... [A]s a culture we have a shared experience of temporal impoverishment." Similarly, Italian author Stefano Bartolini describes Americans as "oppressed by *time-squeeze, time-pressure, time-poverty.*" In his book, *Manifesto for Happiness*, he describes how the American dream of consumption has become a cultural nightmare. Advising that America presents an "example [of] ... what must not be done," Bartolini points out that the United States ranks worst in the entire Western world for trends in happiness indicators, the result of a "profound and decades-long social crisis."[47]

A lifestyle shift becomes imperative to both economic renewal and ecological recovery. Juliet Schor describes such a transformation in *Plentitude*. Observing that the BAU market economy will offer less and less job security to the average person, she recommends a "shift out of the market, cutting losses by diversifying." Noting that most people's "dominant asset" consists of their time (labor hours), she advocates a personal and household embrace of "self-provisioning" as a means of providing for food, shelter, and clothing on a more ecologically sustainable basis. Changing the very nature of consumption, she explains, can produce more time wealth for citizens:

> [O]ver the past three decades, Americans have been transferring an increasing frac-
> tion of their time into market activity. Households have put more hours into paid
> labor and reduced time spent in home production. They're compensating in part
> by purchasing more goods and services, and buying them at later stages of process-
> ing (e.g. more prepared foods).... It's time to reclaim hours, build skills, invest
> in people, save more, and perfect the art of self-provisioning.... The more self-
> provisioning one can do, the less income one has to earn to reproduce a standard
> of living.[48]

The *Plentitude* model reaches back to a time not so long ago when Americans spent a good deal more of their hours growing and preparing food and meeting their other basic needs. During World War II, for example, households commonly ate from backyard "Victory Gardens," which collectively produced 40 percent of the nation's vegetables. The *Plentitude* model envisions increased home food production as well as resurgent, local markets comprised of small community-based merchants – a tran-sition also endorsed by David Korten in his call to relocate the economy from Wall Street to Main Street. These visions simultaneously aim toward higher personal sat-isfaction, economic efficiency, household resilience, and ecological sustainability. They find resonance with other scholarship as well. In *Depletion and Abundance*, Sharon Astyk suggests a new "home front" and a "domestic economy" tied into informal community networks that can respond to the triple threats of economic col-lapse, peak oil, and climate change. In *A Nation of Farmers*, she and Aaron Newton deliver an ambitious appeal for 100 million new farmers in the United States, dis-persed across urban, suburban, and rural areas. Bill McKibben focuses on this new economy in his book, *Eaarth*. Warning that climate chaos will transform the planet, he points out that society must adjust its habits. Urging an increase in suburban farming, he reports that American suburbs might be able to supply about 50 percent of their own food.[49]

The new *Plentitude* model has already gained momentum, as evidenced by thriving farmers markets, a "food-not-lawns movement" sweeping urban and suburban neighborhoods, and a renaissance in home gardening, beekeeping, chicken raising, home food preservation, composting, breadmaking, seed saving, fix-it-yourself approaches, cooking from scratch, and a host of other antique skills long suppressed by the global market. Books describe a booming urban homestead movement that brings self-sufficiency, monetary savings, and personal satisfaction to city dwellers.[50]

Providing a sensible pathway out of the tangled jungle of marketing, consumption, packaging, and global transport of products, the *Plentitude* model of consumption finds powerful alignment with Nature's Trust. It entices citizens to meet many of their basic needs in a way that embraces generational fiduciary duties. As Sharon Astyk describes, investing in the domestic economy allows citizens to live life "as though we hold the world – and our particular piece of it – in trust for future generations." But most intriguingly, the *Plentitude* system of self-provisioning seems to fill a happiness niche that the current economy leaves void. As Schor describes:

> Throughout the country and across the globe, millions are already following the path of plentitude – whatever they call it – creating a twenty-first century economy that has the potential to restore the earth.... [P]lentitude is not thriving only because it is fiscally intelligent. It is also growing because it repairs our fractured lives, heals our souls, and can make us truly wealthy in ways that have little to do with money and consumption. And as it does, it begins to build, step by step, a better way of human being. In the process, it promises to restore the bounty and beauty of our miraculous planet and all its inhabitants.[51]

TAMING THE BEAST: A CORPORATE TRUST RESPONSIBILITY

The modern mega-corporation represents a last failure of the industrial economy. While corporations have existed in some form or another since the birth of the United States, they have never reigned so powerfully over every aspect of human existence. Early American leaders worried greatly about unfettered corporate power. Thomas Jefferson said in 1816: "I hope we shall crush in its birth the aristocracy of our moneyed corporations which dare already to challenge our government to a trial by strength, and bid defiance to the laws of our country." Abraham Lincoln famously admonished, "[C]orporations have been enthroned.... an era of corruption in high places will follow ... until all wealth is aggregated in a few hands and the Republic is destroyed." Today, a growing number of commentators and citizens realize the destructive potential of the modern mega-corporation – and its utter lack of accountability. A robust body of literature describes how multinational corporations destroy priceless natural resources, eradicate indigenous communities, and suppress democracy in nations throughout the world. As James Speth points out, "[I]n a world where the environment is in as much trouble as today's and corporations are such a dominant force, something major must be done."[52]

The corporation embodies a crucial feature that can make it a menace to society: immunity from legal liability for damage it causes beyond the value of corporate assets. When the harm wrought by a corporation exceeds its corporate assets, victims may go uncompensated. As Ambrose Bierce wrote more than 100 years ago, the corporation amounts to "[a]n ingenious device for obtaining individual profit without individual responsibility." David Korten explains in his book, *When Corporations Rule the World*:

> [The corporation] allows virtually unlimited concentration of power with minimal public accountability or legal liability. Actual shareholders, the real owners, rarely have any role in corporate affairs and bear no personal liability beyond the value of their investments. Directors and officers are protected from financial liability for acts of negligence or commission by the corporation's massive legal resources and company paid insurance policies. The same criminal act that would result in a stiff prison sentence, or even execution, if committed by an individual, brings a corporation only a fine – usually inconsequential in relation to corporate assets and likely less than what it gained by committing the infraction. The prosecution of corporate executives for illegal corporate acts is extremely rare.[53]

If all corporations had binding procedures that guided them in a socially and environmentally responsible manner, perhaps this legal immunity might not be worrisome. But corporate decision making remains ethically barren, as its sole aim is maximizing profits for the shareholders. This pressures managers to externalize as much environmental damage as possible, placing the costs on the public or innocent victims. As Lovins and Cohen put it, "[E]cosystem services ... are not presently on any company or country's balance sheet." It should come as no surprise, then, when corporate decisions to skip costly safeguards result in massive environmental destruction and public harm; corporations are financially programmed toward risky behavior that raises their profit margins, hideous as the consequences may prove to a vulnerable public. As Joel Bakan explains in *The Corporation*, "Only pragmatic concern for its own interests and the laws of the land constrain the corporation's predatory instincts, and often that is not enough to stop it from destroying lives, damaging communities, and endangering the planet as a whole." He concludes that the corporation has become a "profoundly dangerous institution." One might reasonably surmise that extraordinarily hazardous activities, such as nuclear power generation and oil drilling, should not fall within the corporate grasp, period.[54]

And yet, across the globe, a corporate iron fist tightens its stranglehold on human and natural communities. Five powerful forces work in unison. First, corporations now control enormous global capital. As Speth reports, the 1,000 largest corporations now produce 80 percent of the world's output. These corporations have gargantuan economic prowess. ExxonMobil, for example, ranks larger in economic capacity than 180 individual countries in the world. Ford Motor Company's economy outranks that of South Africa, and Toyota grosses more than Norway. Wal-Mart's annual revenue exceeds the individual GDP of 161 different countries. This corporate capitalism has engendered extreme economic dependence, as many of the world's citizens now find themselves reliant on corporations for meeting their most basic needs. William Greider concludes: "People and communities, even nations, find themselves losing control over their own destinies, ensnared by the revolutionary demands of commerce."[55]

Second, the corporations now exert strong influence over the public mindset and civic ideology. On the cultural level, they push consumptive lifestyle addictions by bombarding citizens with manipulative advertising; the average American child receives 3,000 advertisements per day. On the political level, corporations promote a self-serving agenda that advances unregulated markets. Corporations also now own much of the media, a factor that risks subordinating a truth-seeking mission to corporate agendas.[56]

A third force exists in corporate control of lethal technology. In the days of Jefferson and Lincoln, even the most menacing corporations had limited reach and impact. Today, however, corporations deploy technology that can threaten entire planetary systems. Large agribusinesses push genetic modification of seeds that experts warn could wipe out a global food supply. The nuclear industry creates radioactive waste that can disperse across a hemisphere and last in deadly form for thousands of years. Fossil fuel companies drive greenhouse gas emissions that imperil Earth's climate system. Bill McKibben calculates that these corporations have an amount of reserves (fossil fuels that lie below ground but remain economically "above ground") that would pollute the atmosphere with *five times* the amount of carbon dioxide capable of causing a disastrous 2°C heating. He writes: "[T]his industry, and this industry alone, holds the power to change the physics and chemistry of our planet, and they're planning to use it."[57]

Fourth, corporations now control much of government. As Perkins describes, "[T]here is no separation between the people who run our biggest businesses and those in charge of our government." Speth surmises that today's corporations "are not merely the dominant economic actors, they are the dominant political actors as well." Ted Nace calls them "gangs of America." Corporate enmeshment with political power occurs through lobbying, campaign contributions, and political paybacks resulting in appointments of industry loyalists to top agency positions. Bearing the fangs of both Congress and the executive, a new corporate oligarchy – a "corporatocracy," as Perkins calls it – defies the constitutional arrangement of power devised by the Founding Fathers (corporations are mentioned nowhere in the U.S. Constitution). Greider concludes that "[t]his new institutional reality is the centerpiece in the breakdown of contemporary democracy."[58]

Multinational corporations wield a fifth aspect of power when they jump sovereign boundaries. The "corporate globalists," as some call them, operate in multiple countries and bear no particular allegiance to any country or any people. They escape legal accountability with frightening agility. Richard J. Barnet and John Cavanagh describe the problem in *Global Dreams*:

> [Modern corporations] have the technological means and strategic vision to burst old limits – of time, space, national boundaries, language, custom, and ideology. By acquiring earth-spanning technologies, by developing products that can be produced anywhere and sold everywhere, by spreading credit around the world, and by connecting global channels of communication that can penetrate any village or neighborhood, these institutions we normally think of as economic rather than political, private rather than public, are becoming the world empires of the twenty-first century.[59]

One landmark report describes a "power shift of stunning proportions ... away from national, state, and local governments and communities toward unprecedented centralization of power for global corporations, bankers, and global bureaucracies." Korten describes this global corporate aggregation of power as "the most rapid and sweeping institutional transformation in human history." Occurring primarily over the past two decades, he explains, "[i]t is a conscious and intentional transformation in search of a new world economic order in which business has no nationality and knows no borders. It is driven by global dreams of vast corporate empires, compliant governments, a globalized consumer monoculture, and a universal ideological commitment to corporate libertarianism." Set loose from their corporate boardrooms, huge multinationals now prowl as top predators across the planet. They devour the natural resource base of countless communities, leaving local authorities to throw their regulations at a pile of waste. Warning that corporate globalism threatens to swallow traditional sovereignty, Greider asserts: "These great changes sweep over the affairs of mere governments and destabilize the established political orders in both advanced and primitive societies."[60]

Corporations exist indefinitely. Never "rendered equal by the grave," Korten explains, corporations continue to amass power without any concomitant responsibility to the public or the planet. Their aggregated power – exerted through political dominion, economic capital, technological capability, social manipulation, and human exploitation – never confronts a point of "that's enough." As a result, the transnational corporate monarchies of today's world hulk indescribably larger than the nineteenth-century menaces that triggered grave warnings from Thomas Jefferson and Abraham Lincoln. As Speth rightly urges, "[T]he corporation must be the main object of transformative change."[61]

Fortunately, economic activity does not depend exclusively on the for-profit corporate model. Many other business structures, such as nonprofit corporations, partnerships, sole proprietorships, employee-owned businesses, and cooperatives, can carry a new economic vision forward. The nonprofit corporate model in particular may prove most promising to protect societal interests in endeavors that deal with survival resources (such as water delivery) or that create transition in energy systems (from fossil fuel/nuclear to renewable).

The real question becomes how to rein in the huge corporations. Beyond aggressive criminal prosecution and prison sentences for corporate presidents and high officers who violate laws, an institutional approach geared toward the corporation itself may include several strategies. A tame-the-beast approach finds reflection in a growing "corporate social responsibility" movement. It aims to persuade corporations to act responsibly by emphasizing the sheer profitability of meeting a triple "bottom line" that integrates profits, social ethics, and environmental stewardship, as Lovins and Cohen point out. Citizens can advance this initiative by mounting public relations campaigns against wrongdoer corporations. Nevertheless, this approach still concedes power to corporations by placing all reliance on their internal decision making. Some corporations, especially those holding massive investments in lethal or destructive enterprises – such as the nuclear industry, the mining industry, the chemical industry, and the weapons industry – may never become responsible because doing so might mean scaling back or eliminating their core pursuit. For those, termination of corporate status (discussed later) and restructuring into a different business form may be the only solution suited to the true problem.[62]

Another approach involves starving the beast. David Korten advocates redirecting market activity to local businesses to effectuate a transference of wealth from Wall Street to Main Street. As he puts it, "Starve the capitalist economy, nurture the mindful market."[63] Surely the burgeoning interest in farmers' markets and local food production presents a significant step in this direction. But a broader frame becomes necessary in order to restrain a corporate beast that can neither be tamed nor starved into serving the greater public good.

A fence-the-beast approach seeks to limit corporate activities and property ownership. Several towns in the United States have already passed community rights ordinances constraining the power of corporations. Spearheaded by the Community Legal Defense Fund, these towns assert local sovereignty to ban dangerous activities such as natural gas drilling methods (called fracking) that can cause severe water contamination. At least one state court (in New York) has upheld local authority to enact such a ban. While the strategy still remains untested in other courts, it has proved successful in coalescing community opposition to hazardous corporate enterprise.[64]

The most far-reaching approach remains revoking corporate charters. This strategy begins with a simple, irrefutable premise: corporations remain creatures of the state. As Lawrence Friedman explains, "The life of a corporation begins with a charter; and it ends if and when the charter runs out or is done away with." The corporate charter had its genesis in a state goal of promoting the public interest. Because the corporate form of enterprise could accomplish infrastructure and society-building tasks, the states chartered corporations to serve those ends. Both public need and service to society resided at the core of this powerful structure, so a liability shield extended to corporations to induce risk-free investment. But the rationale behind this corporate advantage falls away with today's malfeasant corporations. Speth notes that most states allow charter revocation where the corporation has committed gross violations against the public interest. He asserts: "Making this threat alive and real could have very salutary effects."[65]

In the early days, the state maintained tight supervision over the corporations it formed, understanding that corporate power was susceptible to abuse. There existed few corporations, and charters stood restrictive. The state limited the life spans of some corporations, restricted the property ownership of others, prohibited some from expanding, and set boundaries on limited liability. The state regularly pulled corporate charters for wrongdoing or failure to carry out duties. Charter revocation, Ted Nace notes, became "a death penalty for errant or scofflaw corporations." Over time, however, corporations began to dig their political claws into the state legislatures, and the restrictive charter system gave way to an automatic chartering system called "general incorporation." Corporate laws became increasingly lax and ever less attentive to the public interest. Eventually, the Supreme Court conferred "personhood" status to the corporations granting them some of the same rights held by individuals (absurd as the proposition remains). Nevertheless, as a basic matter, the corporate charter exists entirely as state-dependent and ultimately subject to the people's assertion of sovereignty. States still regularly suspend charters for failure to pay taxes and retain authority to draft future charters in restrictive ways that protect their citizens. (Perhaps eventually states may allow only nonprofit forms of those corporations that operate in crucial public realms).[66]

Revoking the corporate charter – that is, dismantling the corporation – may be the only way to deal with corporations (such as the fossil fuel industry) engaged in full-throttle pursuits that destroy the planet's life systems. As Naomi Klein asserts with respect to the fossil fuel industry, "wrecking the planet is their business model. It's what they do." Bill McKibben backs up the point with stark math, pointing out that fossil fuel corporations would have to relinquish $20 trillion in oil and coal reserves in order to leave underground the amount of fossil fuel energy sources that scientists deem necessary to protect the planet's climate system. The choice for society, then, has come into frightening focus: allow oil and coal companies to continue to reap huge profits, or phase out fossil fuels in order to maintain a functional climate necessary for human survival. Having it both ways has become impossible, as these corporations will fiercely resist a leave-it-underground policy. McKibben describes this sector as a "rogue industry, reckless like no other force on Earth." Quite plainly, the destructive force of their enterprise calls into question the continued legitimacy of their government-issued charters. Accomplishing charter revocations for huge multinational corporations that hold more political and economic power than many nations will surely push the frontiers of corporate law, but just as certain, the prospect of revocation remains achievable if only because the people, through their governments, created the fiction of corporations by chartering them in the first place.[67]

But for other corporations with less damaging pursuits, emphasis on government's trust responsibility in the chartering process may open new possibilities for corporate reform, at least when concerning natural resources. As prior chapters have made clear, the state remains bound by a sovereign fiduciary obligation to protect ecological assets for future generations. When the state enables a corporation through charter, this duty to the people necessarily flows through the charter as a fiduciary limit, an inherent encumbrance, to constrain the acts of the corporation. It would be difficult to imagine otherwise, as the state cannot abrogate its trust responsibility to the people. It can give no more power to a corporation – a creature of the state – than it, itself, gained from the people. It thus becomes possible to envision the public trust as an embedded limitation on the power of corporations to destroy public resources. Out of this concept arises a transformational characterization: the fiduciary corporation.

Of course, few of today's corporate captains or political leaders would willingly acknowledge an internal fiduciary limitation held by corporations toward the public, but its recognition may be crucial in order to change the frame of environmental law. Speth asserts the necessity of eliminating the imperative that drives corporations to "pursue [their] own self-interest and to give primacy to maximizing shareholder wealth." Revealing the corporation as a state-creature born within the cradle of sovereign fiduciary responsibility suggests an internal obligation (already present but unrecognized within all corporations) to protect natural resources for future generations. Activating this fiduciary duty would change the decision-making equation to incorporate the environmental responsibility that corporations have been content to ignore in their pursuit of profit. Given the right change-agents, such an old-but-new conception of corporate duty may come alive in shareholder meetings, corporate boardrooms, attorney general's offices, and ultimately, courts of law.[68]

But a surge in public sentiment undoubtedly remains crucial for the scale of change necessary. History runs rife with outbursts against corporations for their harms to the public. In the early nineteenth century, as Lawrence Friedman recounts, "People hated and distrusted corporations." If the past held such populist revolutions, the future may one day tell of a global uprising against multinationals. From the plundered forests of the Amazon, to the polluted waters of Manila Bay, to the hydro-fracked Pennsylvania hamlets, to the smog-choked cities of China, to the Mississippi cancer alleys, and to the radioactive villages in Japan, insurgency now rises against despotic corporations. Greider asserts that corporate oppression now steadily creates "the predicate for its own collapse" and will inevitably give way to a new "global humanism." But in order to address capitalism's "repetitive pathologies," he says, society needs a system that "genuinely merges the market with democracy." The public trust can respond to this appeal by drawing the contours of a *fiduciary corporation* that delegitimizes business decisions made in defiance of community property rights.[69]

Embedded in the core of democracy, the public trust embraces the expectation of natural abundance that guides people in judging responsible economic behavior from wrongful and abusive exploits. The trust calls for communities to assert their inherent sovereignty over corporations, not the other way around. It stands unifying in the revolutionary sense, presenting a concept capable of transcending sovereign boundaries with equal agility to that displayed by mega-corporations. In its planetary call, Nature's Trust demands sustaining natural capital at a level necessary for supporting economic well-being through the ages. But along with its economic content, Nature's Trust must offer a new conception of responsible property ownership, a matter taken up in the next chapter.

14

The Public Trust and Private Property Rights

Natural disasters have a way of trivializing property "ownership." As when a mile-wide tornado vacuums up a town. An entire town. Or when furnace-hot winds blow a canyon wildfire into a subdivision, or torrential rains swell a river over its banks, or a mudslide buries a neighborhood. Within minutes or hours, homes can turn into piles of toothpicks, or ashes, or debris, or wash away altogether. No, we don't really "own" property. It owns us.

In his eye-opening book, *Eaarth*, Bill McKibben identifies what grows more apparent, disaster by disaster: what were once so-called "freak events" now come at us with horrific regularity. Climate change has fundamentally altered our planet. As McKibben puts it, "We have traveled to a new planet, propelled on a burst of carbon dioxide." He says we might as well call this new planet "Eaarth" (sounds like a groaning Earth).[1] He suggests what should seem obvious by now but still escapes the human psyche: we need new habits for this planet. We need to hunker down, batten down the hatches, pull out the sandbags, fill up the water jugs, hose off the roof. And as this chapter points out, we need to change our conception of property law as well.

Why? Because, in comparison to the familiar old planet, this new Eaarth has rather harsh operating rules. Rules that will surely disrupt many of the amenities that industrialized society takes for granted. The Western lifestyle pampers beyond the normal zone of human need: seat warmers, electric toothbrushes, three-car garages, remote controls, ready-to-eat shrink-wrapped boiled eggs – you name it. McKibben's punch-in-the-gut wake-up call strongly suggests that we need to refocus on our fundamental needs. We need to remake society to provide resilience while we still have the chance. He writes: "[I]nstead of trying to fly the plane higher when the engines start to fail, or just letting it crash into the nearest block of apartments, we might start looking around for a smooth stretch of river to put it down in." Rather than adamantly denying the crisis on one hand, or grimly awaiting collapse on the other, he offers this possibility: "*[W]e might choose instead to try to manage our descent.*"[2]

This book began with a simple question: How will legal institutions respond to radically new environmental conditions? Will they promote survival or perpetuate the same policies that have brought the world to the edge of collapse? The question puts property law on trial. If the goal, as McKibben suggests, should be a managed descent from dangerously high altitudes, society must rethink property law, not just environmental law, because property law determines who has access to land, water, minerals, and other natural assets (society's landing strips, in effect). Environmental law, the focus of prior chapters, regulates pollution and resource destruction without regard to *who* owns the property. The industrial age launched flight in a time of seemingly illimitable resources, and past property allocations assumed stable abundance. But now Nature redraws the maps, making far fewer resources available to meet the needs of far more people.

This chapter explores private property rights on our changing planet. It offers the public trust as a principle to guide a managed "descent" – robustly affirming the stoutest sticks in the bundle of private property ownership while at the same time recalibrating many ownership responsibilities to the realities we face. The alternative, as landowners may soon realize, portends squatters, vandals, and ecological eviction. Rather than being anti–property law, the public trust stands as a *fundamental doctrine* of property law. The doctrine sets boundaries on what lands and resources can be privatized and secures a realm of public property rights necessary to sustain society's societal well-being and survival. Professor Michael Blumm describes the trust as a "vehicle for mediating between public and private rights" in the environmental context.[3]

The delineation between private and public property remains one of the most critical decisions society can make. Private control submits land and resources to the prerogatives of a private owner, who will often act selfishly. The U.S. Supreme Court long ago recognized that some resources stand so vital to society that they should not be put under private control. In *Illinois Central Railroad v. Illinois* (a case discussed throughout this book), the Court held that the shorefront of Lake Michigan remained off limits to privatization. Because the shoreline belonged in public trust to the citizens, the state legislature had no power to convey complete ownership of it to a private railroad corporation.[4]

A well-balanced society should harmonize private property rights with public property rights, as both serve crucial aspects of civic need. Private property rights establish a realm of near-exclusive privacy for the individual, both from society at large and from the government. Such private ownership creates social enrichment and stability, provides a base for economic activity, and secures a place for friendship and domestic life. Countries bereft of secure private property rights tend to be repressive, authoritarian, and unstable. Even as the law of property will change in significant ways, the core protections of private property must remain steadfast.

But while private property rights underpin individual liberty, they are not the sole foundation of it. Public property rights stand equally important, for they secure the life sources for all citizens: the air, water, oceans, wildlife, fish, forests, vegetation, and soils. Without an abundance of such natural wealth, there can be no social stability, and thus no individual liberty, for citizens struggling to survive can fall prey to tyrants. The full synergy between public and private property rights, rather than the dominance of one over the other, nourishes liberty and democracy.

Yet today across the globe, neoliberal, pro-market ideologies flaunt the public trust by promoting land and water grabs – privatizations that place control of life-sustaining resources in the hands of a very few. Corporations and powerful moneyed interests have commandeered the whole notion of property rights to their advantage, steering core principles far from their original premises. They even assert private property rights as a shield against regulation enacted to protect the common good, using constitutional law as a dangerous weapon for profiteering. As the sphere of public control shrinks, citizens stand to lose their right of self-determination.[5]

This chapter focuses on the interaction of private and public property rights in U.S. law, a legal system that presents a dramatic theatre for opposing doctrinal viewpoints. In recent years, neoliberal corruptions of U.S. property law have provoked land practices so destructive as to push ecosystems to collapse. But private ownership operating within a *public trust framework* impels long-term ecological protection. The public trust reanimates ancient law, protecting vital resources against privatization and preserving the state's right to regulate those resources that have been privatized. Its principles originate in the preindustrial era, at a time when survival did not depend on corporate-issued paychecks but instead depended directly on the wealth provided by Nature's assets. On a planet in the throes of resource collapse, these principles must again guide humans as they face harsh ecological conditions.

Repurposing modern property law to revive public rights presents significant questions. This chapter focuses on two in particular. First, what must be held in public ownership? Second, within the sphere of private property ownership, what responsibilities come with title? Only by confronting these questions can public and private ownership return to a healthy alignment. As a predicate to that discussion, this chapter first explores the fundamental nature of property. It then describes two competing conceptions of land profoundly shaping modern views of property rights – only one of which points to a safe ecological future.

THE BARGAIN

Several concepts mark the boundaries of property law. First, property is not God-given. Property remains a state-created legal institution – nothing more, nothing less. Despite the libertarian view that imagines a burly set of rights flowing to the individual without state involvement, in fact, private property becomes possible *only with* the backing of the state. As John Locke said, "The reason why men enter into society is the preservation of their property." Absent government involvement, no "private" property exists, for what makes it "private" in the first place is a system of law that prevents trespassing, without which interlopers could invade each day with impunity.[6]

Second, Americans hold two distinct sets of property rights, although libertarian rhetoric largely ignores one. The first set consists of the familiar private property rights that landowners enjoy, including powers of use, control, and conveyance of rights to others. These merge with a zone of individual privacy. Of course, not all people have such rights, as not all own property. The other set of rights – vested in all citizens equally – consists of shared ownership in public assets. As explained in prior chapters, such public ownership positions every citizen in a relationship with his or her government as beneficiary of a trust. These public ownership rights redoubtably stand as important as private ownership rights – perhaps much more so. An individual or entity, no matter how wealthy, could never accumulate privately that natural wealth accruing to all citizens in common. And too, the ecological assets of the public domain provide incalculable support to human survival.

As a third principle, the institution of private property aims to serve societal ends. It cannot be otherwise, because the system was promulgated by a government of the people. As Jean Jacques Rousseau proclaimed centuries ago in *The Social Contract*, "[T]he right which each individual has over his own estate is always subordinate to the right which the community has over all; without this, there would be neither stability in the social tie, nor any real force in the exercise of Sovereignty." As agent of the people, government must strike a balance between public and private rights to protect both the public interest and individual liberties. While society must safeguard individual ownership, the institution of private property cannot be a handmaiden of selfish exploit. The New Jersey Supreme Court underscored the point in a landmark case when it said, "Property rights serve human values. They are recognized to that end, and are limited by it." Many of today's profiteers invoke private property rights to decimate natural systems and drain the commonwealth of its most valuable assets. This suggests a mutant form of property law dangerously out of balance with society's needs.[7]

Fourth, property law is not set in stone. It adapts to change. For example, some forms of property, such as slavery, rot as abominations no longer recognized. New forms of property, such as patents on seeds, have recently come into being (sometimes for the worse). As Professor Richard Powell, a well-known property law scholar, once observed, "[T]ime marches on towards new adjustments between individualism and the social interests." Our present legal view of property rights grew in a brief time span during an era of abundant resources, an era now fading fast. As the New

Jersey Supreme Court explained, "'[A]n owner must expect to find the absoluteness of his property rights curtailed by the organs of society.... The necessity for such curtailments is greater in a modern industrialized and urbanized society than it was in the relatively simple American society of fifty, 100, or 200 years ago.'" In other words, Nature's assailants must adjust their reasonable expectations to a new reality.[8]

Fifth, a long-standing maxim of common law holds that "one should so use his property as not to injure the rights of others." As the U.S. Supreme Court declared in 1934, "[N]either property rights nor contract rights are absolute; for government cannot exist if the citizen may at will use his property to the detriment of his fellows." While it is often said that "a man's home is his castle," the old adage trudges as an overstatement. True, the personal privacy zone associated with property ownership sequesters nearly inviolate expectations, and this should remain so. But it has never been true that a property owner may use land virtually any way he or she pleases without being subject to higher public authority. The fact remains that property ownership exists not as a one-way street; instead it creates a *relationship* with the state that comes with obligations. As one property law text explains, "Property rights are not absolute.... [O]wners have obligations as well as rights."[9]

Sixth (and flowing directly from the preceding), private property has always been subject to government regulation on behalf of the public. As the Supreme Court said in 1934, "Equally fundamental with the private right is that of the public to regulate it in the common interest." Some present-day libertarians bristle against regulation. But their conception of property wanders far afield from established understandings, as it focuses on *rights* while often ignoring *responsibilities*. Rights and responsibilities form the two sides of the same ownership coin. A landowner would have little enjoyment of property if a neighbor could use property in ways that inflicted harm across the fence. A textbook explanation provides: "To give one person an absolute legal entitlement would mean that others could not exercise similar entitlements." Stated another way, one property owner's *right* to be free from substantial harm derives from the *responsibility* of the other property owner to refrain from imposing such harm, and vice versa. Reflecting those mutual duties, regulations give rise to an obvious reciprocity of advantage to all property owners.[10]

Finally, the adjustment between property use and responsibility to the commonwealth plays out awkwardly in the realm of takings law, deriving from the Fifth Amendment of the U.S. Constitution which states: "nor shall private property be taken for public use without just compensation." The amendment has engendered a tangled body of judicial decisions, because the clause itself begs the question: Exactly what is the "property" that cannot be taken without compensation? The public trust doctrine shapes a response. By restricting what can be privatized by government and also delineating the rights, responsibilities, and primordial easements embedded in private property, the doctrine largely defines what can be considered "property" that, if taken, affords a right of compensation. As the discussion that follows elaborates, modern courts have found some private property encumbered by a reserved trust easement or servitude held by the people through their government. In other words, the private property owner did not acquire the full "bundle" of rights when the government first conveyed title. As the Ninth Circuit explained in a case involving beachfront property, "The 'doctrine reserves a public property interest, the *jus publicum*, in tidelands and the waters flowing over them, despite the sale of these lands into private ownership.'" It follows that the Fifth Amendment provides no compensation when government steps in to limit landowner activities that interfere with a right the public has held all along. As Professor Blumm concludes, existing public trust rights can form "an absolute defense to any takings claim."[11]

LAND AS COMMONWEALTH OR COMMODITY?

While these broad contours of property law remain steadfast, cultural views toward land have shifted dramatically from America's early years to the present. Prior chapters explored the modern ascendancy of global industrialism and its toppling of cultural and economic understandings that had governed society for many ages. Just as mass commercialization and convenience-marketing shoved aside a broad social ethic against waste and obliterated the cultural emphasis on self-sufficiency, so did modernization trigger a titanic shift in societal attitudes toward land. Land became seen as a market commodity. Property ownership, previously engaged to promote community aims, morphed into a sharply individualistic enterprise which, when profit-driven, could turn ruthless toward the community.

In today's property law arena, the vestiges of human land tradition compete with consumer lifestyles. One orientation views land as part of a greater commonwealth, whereas the other views land as a commodity available for exploit. The ramifications of these competing attitudes carry great consequence for ecological health. As Aldo Leopold famously said, "We abuse land because we regard it as a commodity belonging to us. When we see land as a community to which we belong, we may begin to use it with love and respect."[12] To survive new ecological conditions, society must reclaim a view of property ownership that supports, rather than undermines, the community.

The discussion that follows describes the opposing "commonwealth" and "commodity" views of land. Several aspects of the commonwealth approach gain expression in the writings of Aldo Leopold and Wendell Berry. Some also find reflection in native traditions as well as in classical American republicanism, which, as Professor Myrl Duncan writes, "emphasized civic virtue and the good of the community at large." The commodity model, on the other hand, gains strong expression in modern libertarianism, which voices the interest of the individual over the community and promotes an extreme view of free-market supremacy. Notions of personal liberty (associated with land ownership) form a strong thought tradition in both frames. But as the following discussion elaborates, the commodity frame uses liberty aspirations to peddle market dependency that perpetuates economic oppression. The commonwealth frame invokes liberty passions to advance self-sufficiency and resist corporate totalitarianism in the daily life of citizens. As a later discussion explains, only the commonwealth frame reflects the public trust doctrine's core populist concern of avoiding state/market hegemony over land and resources.[13]

A Commonwealth View of Property

A commonwealth frame positions individual land ownership within the broader context of the social, ecological, and generational community. Several features flow from this. First, the commonwealth view values natural land uses that provide benefit to the owner while maintaining ecological balance. Wendell Berry puts it well when he says that the use must be suited to the "nature of the place." In early America, people used land chiefly for food production. Subsistence use ranked so high that many thought it a natural birthright of citizens to own farm property. This productive use of land enabled self-sufficiency at a time when pioneers struggled for survival. During the two world wars, a strong subsistence interest again surged through American culture, this time tied to war patriotism. Across the country, families planted Victory Gardens in their yards so as to free up the commercial food supply for the military. Today, the importance of subsistence from land appears again as a modern food crisis consigns a growing number of Americans to hunger, including a quarter of the children in the United States. Wendell Berry ties subsistence use of land to democracy itself, stating:

> If many people do not own the usable property, then they must submit to the few who do own it. They cannot eat or be sheltered or clothed except in submission. They will find themselves entirely dependent on money; they will find costs always higher, and money always harder to get. To renounce the principle of democratic property, which is the only basis of democratic liberty, in exchange for … the economics of the so-called free market is a tragic folly.[14]

Second, the commonwealth frame supports regulation of individual parcels to protect the broad interests of the community as a whole. This aspect also emerges from early U.S. history. Professor Eric Freyfogle reports that colonial America experienced extensive land-use regulation. Laws not only constrained harmful activities but also imposed "affirmative duties" on private landowners to promote social aims. The community's needs permeated ownership of private land – "Everywhere, town leaders asserted the community's interest in private land-use decisions, just as communities in England had done since time immemorial." Characteristically, the Massachusetts Supreme Judicial Court declared in 1851: "All property in this commonwealth ... is derived directly or indirectly from the government, and held subject to those general regulations, which are necessary to the common good and general welfare." Americans of this era generally did not view property regulation as a threat to personal liberty. As Freyfogle describes, "[I]t was *collective* liberty that was the primary issue of the day: It was the power of the colonists as a people to govern themselves without interference, not the rights of individuals as such to resist constraint." Even amid robust property regulation, land liberty flourished in multiple intrinsic ways: in the possession and quiet enjoyment of property; in the nearly sacrosanct realm of privacy within property boundaries; in the economic independence gained through subsistence use of land; in the security of title from arbitrary government confiscation; and in the domestic use of land on which a family legacy could accrue over the generations. Rights to destroy the landscape did not enter into the liberty equation back then.[15]

As a third feature, the commonwealth frame situates individual parcels within the broader ecological fabric that transcends human-drawn boundaries. As Aldo Leopold described in his classic book, *A Sand County Almanac*, "[Land] is a fountain of energy flowing through a circuit of soils, plants, and animals.... [I]t is a sustained circuit, like a slowly augmented revolving fund of life." Placing supreme importance on ecosystems that support all of society, this frame recognizes universal ecological stewardship responsibilities as part of property ownership. Leopold declared: "A thing is right when it tends to preserve the integrity, stability, and beauty of the biotic community. It is wrong when it tends otherwise." To preserve some parts of the circuit and not others, he concluded, defies basic ecological principles and invites breakdown.[16]

Fourth, the commonwealth frame protects generational interests. It conceives of each present owner as, basically, a "tenant for life" – that is, one entitled to possession and fruits of the land but not privileged to damage or deplete the property's natural assets at the expense of future generations. The concept runs analogous to the standard expectation that renters leave leased property in the same condition in which they found it. This land use duty is conceived as arising from the mortal limits of property ownership. Time, the loyal deputy of Nature, effectively creates successive life-tenancies in land, thus reserving ownership rights and expectations to future generations over the course of perpetuity. In the commonwealth view, these future generations have an equal right to the land as their just inheritance in the natural order of the world. A well-known native proverb, "We do not inherit the earth from our ancestors; we borrow it from our children," reflects this principle. The approach also finds a rich basis in the political history of the United States. As Thomas Jefferson asserted in his letter to John Taylor: "[E]very generation coming equally, by the laws of the Creator of the world [is entitled] to the free possession of the earth He made for their subsistence, unencumbered by their predecessors, who, like them, were but tenants for life." In a letter to James Madison, he wrote that no person by natural right could "eat up the usufruct of the lands for several generations to come," because "then the lands would belong to the dead, and not to the living." Jefferson famously declared: *"[T]he earth belongs in usufruct to the living;* [and] the dead have neither powers nor rights over it."[17]

The life-tenancy construct invokes a strong prohibition on waste, discussed in earlier chapters. John Locke (to which many attribute American property law concepts) expressed this view by saying, "Nothing was made by God for man to spoil or destroy." The political philosopher Edmund Burke echoed it as well when he asserted, "temporary possessors and life-renters [of a society] ... should not think it amongst their rights to ... commit waste on the inheritance." Early colonial property law enforced anti-waste duties to the next generation. People commonly owned property as "fee tail," which organized hereditary succession of land along the bloodline of a family. This type of estate created successive life estates in lineal descendants and thereby prohibited the present family owner from committing waste that would diminish the rightful inheritance of future generations. Although this form of ownership was later abolished in most states because of its monarchy-like insinuations, the no-waste rule remains a standard trait of life-estates and trusts.[18]

A fifth feature of the commonwealth frame recognizes emotional and spiritual attachment to land, both of which reinforce an ethical duty to protect ecology. While U.S. property law now largely ignores sentimental bonds to property, Justice Oliver Wendell Holmes gave the matter poetic force when he declared: "[M]an, like a tree in a cleft of a rock, gradually shapes his roots to his surroundings, and when the roots have grown to a certain size, cannot be displaced without cutting at his life." Aldo Leopold believed that strong ties of "love, respect, and admiration for land" were requisite for kindling a widespread ethic toward land. Lamenting that Western society lacked such a land ethic, he hoped that it would evolve as society matured, just as social ethics had come to reject property rights to enslaved human beings. Traditional native property regimes, rooted for many hundreds or thousands of years in the same landscape, provide the most poignant examples of this land ethic. Professor Rebecca Tsosie describes the indigenous view that humans and Nature unify as "one ordered, balanced, and living whole." A strong land ethic now finds legal formalization in countries such as Ecuador and Bolivia, both of which have passed constitutional amendments recognizing the rights of Nature to exist. This growing "rights of Nature" movement confronts the dominant Western attitude that views mutilation of landscapes as normal, even desirable.[19]

Finally, the land-as-commonwealth frame rejects the outright commodification of land in the marketplace and questions as artificial and potentially destructive the market value assigned to land – a value that can inflate rapidly and then suddenly implode. This frame instead focuses on the *inherent and enduring* value of land, particularly its role in serving families, neighborhoods, and communities. Similarly, while the commodity frame promotes liquidity of land, the commonwealth frame recognizes the tangible necessity of human "staying power" on land to allow the kind of human-nature relationships that naturally kindle land stewardship. Although modern-day culture normalizes market predation of land, there have been strong aversions to it in traditional native culture. The Northwest Indian Prophet Smohalla once said: "Those who cut up the lands or sign papers for lands will be defrauded of their rights and will be punished by God's anger." Today across the United States, an anti-commodification trend now finds reflection in a growing number of voluntary conservation easements entered into between willing property owners and local land trusts. Designed to protect lands in perpetuity, these easements limit harmful activities on land and operate to shield land from destructive market forces. In the United Kingdom, innovative land-holding arrangements called "community land trusts" remove entire blocks of land from the marketplace in order to provide long-term security to the local population.[20]

A Commodity View of Property

Despite the possibility of viewing land as coupled with commonwealth, unquestionably the dominant cultural frame in the modern United States depicts land as a commodity. Sliced and diced by surveyors, processed by developers, and packaged by real estate brokers, land is put to market much like a fungible product with an overriding purpose to bring profit. Feature by feature, the commonwealth and commodity frames line up as opposites.

First, the commodity model ignores the natural productive capacity of land. Land undergoes intensive processing that destroys its potentiality for both food and ecosystems – it is drained, cleared, bulldozed, graded, paved, replanted, chemical-sprayed, and machine-groomed. In the suburbs, developers casually eradicate whole habitats and communities of species, swapping them out for manicured landscapes to adorn tract homes and McMansions. Rather than provide ground for food cultivation, residential yard space today announces conformity with neighborhood conventions. As homeowners spend profuse amounts of time and energy indulging a national grooming fetish rather than raising food, Wendell Berry warns:

> We have an unprecedentedly large urban population that has no land to grow food on, no knowledge of how to grow it, and less and less knowledge of what to do with it after it is grown. That this population can continue to eat through shortage, strike, embargo, riot, depression, war – or any of the other large-scale afflictions that societies have always been heir to and that industrial societies are uniquely vulnerable to – is not a certainty or even a faith; it is a superstition.

These modern land practices have evicted from American memory an original core liberty embodied in property rights – that of enjoying self-sufficiency on a plot of land that one owns. In fact, property ownership has flipped from supporting self-sufficiency to enticing extreme financial exposure, at least in cases where ownership tethers to high-interest mortgages.[21]

Second, the commodity frame promotes land use as a highly individualistic enterprise, one wholly detached from the needs of the community. Consequently, land use *regulation* becomes viewed as a threat to personal liberty. Ironically, however, some of the most audacious infringements on personal daily life remain overlooked because they come not from government but from developers. Private land use ordinances known as CC&Rs (Conditions, Covenants, and Restrictions) regulate subdivisions with oppressive rules aimed toward suburban idealism. Some control all manner of detail, including, for example, the color of homes, the type of landscaping, the location of parked cars, the length of time a garage door can be open, and even the width of outdoor flowerpots. They often ban clotheslines, vegetable gardens, home chicken coops, tree houses, and other remnants of independent householding. In urban America, it becomes hard to escape CC&Rs: more than 55 million Americans live in communities subject to such private government. Yet still, government land use regulation draws far more intense political opposition.[22]

Third, the commodity frame uses abstraction in the form of boundaries to excuse land parcels from obligations to the ecological community. The packaging of land with constructed lot lines means that the consumers (lot purchasers) rarely have to contemplate the natural systems constantly recruiting their lands into ecological service. As Professor Freyfogle points out, "At the boundary line, my responsibility ends, or so thinks the modern mind."[23] In reality, of course, there can be no ecological severance of land from its surrounding natural systems, lot lines notwithstanding. Boundary illusion perpetuated by the commodity frame encourages landowner irresponsibility wholly unsuited to the times.

Fourth, the land-as-commodity frame ignores any duty to the coming generations. Concern over the landscape that future generations will inherit – barren or abundant – rarely enters into real estate conversations. Rather than prohibit waste to the land, the commodity frame promotes the all-out conversion, depletion, and destruction of land wealth *on a daily basis*. It has prompted a modern land frenzy driving ecology into colossal deficit, leaving future generations with a punishing ecological mortgage. Just as Jefferson warned against, the land now belongs to the dead, not the living.[24]

Fifth, the commodity frame allows no explanatory space for emotional or spiritual attachment to the land or natural world – not surprisingly, because a frame that acknowledges such attachment could not at the same time sanction human ruin of Nature. Modern industrial culture suppresses emotional ties to land in several ways, not the least of which concerns mobility. Americans, on average, move every five years, undermining any "staying power" on land. Apart from this, as Richard Louv laments in his book, *Last Child in the Woods*, children no longer explore natural landscapes regularly and on their own adventurous terms. Glued to an assortment of electronics, incessantly hustled to indoor activities, and herded en masse to sports fields and basketball arenas, many children today know only a fabricated world that stirs no sentimental or spiritual call for Nature. Louv calls this Nature-Deficit Disorder.[25] Sadly too, uglification of the countryside by developers obliterates countless opportunities for natural interaction between children and their ecology.

Finally, the commodity frame treats land largely as a fungible product, tossing it onto the owner's pile of other financial accumulations such as stocks, bonds, and annuities. As Professor Margaret Jane Radin explains, an object becomes *fungible* if "it is perfectly replaceable with money," and remains *personal* if "it has become bound up with the personhood of the holder and is no longer commensurate with money."[26] The distinction provides insights to the commodity frame, which looks to market price as the sole measure of land value. Calibrating to financial indicators such as comparable home sales and interest rates, property values fluctuate in a market over which the owner has no control. The abstraction overlooks the tangible, steadfast ecological value of land to the individual and community: the quality of its soils, the purity of its water, the abundance of its habitat, the aesthetics of its open space, its capacity for food and fiber production, and so forth. Operating in a wholly contrived realm, market prices climb and drop precipitously even when the actual character of the land remains unchanged. Such artificial valuation destabilizes property ownership and land use.

Libertarians advance this commodity view most overtly by challenging regulations designed to protect society and ecology. When such regulations decrease the market value of property, they demand Fifth Amendment compensation, claiming a "taking" of private property. As Professor Michael Blumm points out, the view reflects a "fixation" on the Fifth Amendment as the "sine qua non of property." The commodity view of land now dominates Supreme Court jurisprudence. For example, focusing not on ecological or natural value, but solely on market value, the *Lucas* case declared an unconstitutional "taking" of private property where a regulation deprives the owner of all economically viable use. Within this legal framework, historic American ideals of property ownership have mutated into a rather debauched form of "liberty" – market freedom to despoil the commonwealth for profit.[27]

The Boundaries of Worthless Deeds

Clearly humanity will have to rethink this dominant commodity property frame in order to survive on a ravaged planet Eaarth. Private land comprises nearly two-thirds of the land base in the United States. Excusing these owners from ecological obligation drives natural systems to collapse – exactly what is happening now. As Ralph Waldo Emerson said long ago, "As long as our civilization is essentially one of property, of fences, of exclusiveness, it will be mocked by delusions."[28]

Yet the commodity frame remains hard to dislodge because it (falsely) projects an image of providing more protection of private property rights – and therefore, seemingly providing more individual liberty – than does the commonwealth frame. But liberty to destroy land with impunity runs deceptive; in the end, it will trigger conditions that shackle individual freedom, threaten personal security, and impair property rights all at once. A hard reality remains: all property enjoyment depends on high-functioning natural infrastructure, now vandalized behind the banner of private property rights. Ignoring this reality leads to exacerbated floods, fires, droughts, crop losses, insect infestations, hurricanes, landslides, and heat waves. All make for worthless deeds.

Climate crisis becomes the ultimate agent of land condemnation. Like a surveyor redrawing the maps of habitable land, rising sea levels portend nearly inconceivable losses of coastal property. Already, drowning island nations and many oceanfront communities worldwide are exploring relocation. And when climate-caused natural disasters such as hurricanes and prolonged drought occur, human refugees desperately search for survival resources. Ensuing chaos and riots toss title to the invaders, and personal liberty suffers (Hurricane Katrina, for instance, brought the equivalent of a police state to New Orleans).[29]

Nature will determine new necessities on planet Eaarth, and property law must either respond or become the overseer of human oppression. In history, American property law shunned a commodity frame in order to advance human rights, culminating with the abolishment of slavery. The great challenge ahead lies in transforming property law so as to bring ecological obligation squarely within the boundaries of individual ownership. As Professor Freyfogle notes, today's lawmaking task should not be to allocate resources, for that has been done, but rather "to reconfigure what it means to own" so that society does not plunge beyond the limits of sustainability.[30]

One might justifiably ask why we need a reconception of property when there already exists a plethora of land use regulations designed to protect wetlands, species, trees, and other resources on private property. It is because such protections are constantly undermined by the commodity frame of property, which repeatedly sets up a highly charged political context *at the point of regulation*. Treating land as a fungible good, this frame puts all of the emphasis on market profits impacted by any regulatory decision. When the quantifiable economic harm juxtaposes against environmental harm, the natural destruction often seems incremental and speculative, certainly not enough to justify blocking a lucrative development. Cumulative factors create a reoccurring quandary: to solve an environmental problem, one must focus on even the small actions (because they all add up), yet doing so causes intense landowner resentment as the individual sacrifice seems way out of proportion to the amount of public harm avoided.

In face of this, land use officials routinely cave in to development pressure. Professor Dale Goble describes a "Tragedy of Fragmentation," explaining, "boundaries produce fragmentation, and fragmentation, in turn, fosters myopic decisions; these small decisions, however, eventually aggregate to produce a large decision that is never directly made." As an example, he points to the destruction of 50 percent of the wetlands along the coasts of Connecticut and Massachusetts in merely two decades. It was not as if any agencies looked seriously at the consequence of wiping out half of all the wetlands and decided that was a good idea – they surely would not have – but hundreds of isolated regulatory decisions on small tracts of land delivered the same result. In the end, this wetland eradication threatens the enjoyment of private property because it removes protective natural buffers against storm damage.[31]

The commonwealth frame urges a new cultural understanding of property obligation, one that views natural infrastructure protection as an inherent responsibility of parcel ownership, akin to property taxes. Most property owners understand well that taxes enable government to build infrastructure such as roads, sewer systems, water systems, and drainage systems, without which their land would be next to economically worthless. And yet the same landowners would fill wetlands even though doing so increases the risk of flood to their neighborhood. Changing the frame to emphasize community *natural* infrastructure normalizes the burden of any landowner to protect a portion, however small, of the system as a whole.[32]

The public trust doctrine fits easily within this land-as-commonwealth cultural frame. It eschews human-made boundaries as the determinative source of owner responsibility, instead weaving ecological duty into private ownership. As many scholars now recognize, the public trust doctrine presents a balanced accommodation between the public and private spheres of property ownership, one necessary to advance the interests of society.[33] The next two sections explore two key aspects of the doctrine: (1) limits on the privatization of property; and (2) infusion of ecological obligation into private title.

PUBLIC TRUST PROPERTY AND RESTRAINTS ON PRIVATIZATION

Legislative conveyance of private title must comply with the public trust duty, as the U.S. Supreme Court long ago made clear in *Illinois Central*. Some resources stand so crucial to societal well-being that they cannot be privatized at all, for doing so would place them in the hands of private parties who would exploit them at peril to society. When considering the supreme public importance of Lake Michigan's shoreline, the Court emphasized, "The control of the state for the purposes of the trust can never be lost." But as Chapter 8 explained, the Court's test allows privatization of public trust assets where: (1) the grant serves trust purposes, "promoting the interests of the public"; and (2) the grant does not *substantially impair* the public interest in the lands and waters remaining. Modern courts have followed this two-pronged test and have even added to the restrictions. In *Lake Michigan Federation v. U.S. Army Corps of Engineers*, the federal district court of Illinois found the public trust violated when the "primary purpose" of a legislative grant of trust property aims to benefit a private interest. The court overturned a legislative grant of shoreline to Loyola University, stating, "What we have here is a transparent giveaway of public property to a private entity. The lakebed of Lake Michigan is held in trust for and belongs to the citizenry of the state."[34]

The test readily applies to lands and resources presently held in public ownership, providing a check against conveyance to private parties. But, what about resources that have already been granted in violation of the test? That, in fact, was the circumstance underlying *Illinois Central*. Finding that privatization of the shoreline would compromise the ability of future legislatures to safeguard the public's interest, the Court declared: "The legislature could not give away nor sell the discretion of its successors in respect to matters, the government of which, from the very nature of things, must vary with varying circumstances." The Court consequently found the grant voidable – retroactively – and held that the attorney general could take back the land on behalf of the people. Such action would not amount to an act of condemnation, which requires compensation for private property rights taken by government, because the railroad never gained proper title in the first place. As the Court declared: "Any grant of the kind is necessarily revocable, and the exercise of the trust by which the property was held by the state can be resumed at any time.... [T]he power to resume the trust whenever the state judges best is, we think, incontrovertible."[35]

Modernizing this approach, some courts have reconceptualized the nature of private title acquired in trust lands, describing such title as conditional in the first place. As Professor Blumm explains, two courts have authorized states to take back shoreline property originally conveyed to private parties in the nineteenth century when the private owners changed the land use in ways that deviated markedly from the grant purpose. One case, *Vermont v. Central Vermont Railway*, involved shoreline along Lake Champlain granted by the legislature in 1827 to private owners for the purpose of building wharves and filling tidelands. In 1849, a railroad company acquired the land and (more than a century later, in the late 1980s) sought to convey the property to a real estate developer. The state of Vermont sued to block the sale, challenging the company's title on public trust grounds. Finding a public trust over the shore lands, the Vermont Supreme Court construed the private title as limited. Explaining that the public's unique interest in trust property "transcends the ordinary rules of property law," the court classified the private title as fee simple subject to a "condition subsequent." The term describes a venerable estate of property law that basically amounts to a conditional grant of property allowing the *grantor* to take back the property if ever the owner (or successor) violates the original condition. Finding that the Vermont legislature could grant trust land only to promote public purposes (per the *Illinois Central* test), the court concluded that the shore land was held "subject to the condition subsequent" that the lands continue to be used for such purposes.[36]

To put it another way, this construction seemingly subjects the original owner (grantee) and all subsequent owners to ongoing compliance with the *Illinois Central* test. When the condition becomes broken – because the property use fails to advance a trust purpose – the legislature may justifiably revoke the grant without compensation. It could not be otherwise, because the legislature never had power in the first place to abdicate complete control over the people's trust assets. If the owner wants to change the public use for which the property was originally granted (without permission of the legislature), the state trustee may exercise the public's "right of reentry" – a right reserved from the original grant – and take back the land. As Blumm reports, the Supreme Judicial Court of Massachusetts followed this approach when construing nineteenth-century grants of title for wharfs in Boston Harbor. Calling the grants "fee[s] simple ... subject to the condition subsequent," the court found the private title subject to forfeiture when the owner tried to develop the lands for condominiums.[37]

This characterization confronts the problem of changing circumstances using an established estate familiar in property law. By interpreting the acquired private title as *conditional title* that allows revocation if the use turns hostile to the public at a future point in time, the test offers built-in protection for future generations whose circumstances cannot be foreseen at the time of the original grant but whose fundamental interest in survival and basic well-being remains constant through passing time. The approach will surely prove crucial in a world of collapsing ecosystems as privatized trust lands and resources become essential to society's survival.

While revocation of title without compensation may be used rarely today, Professor Myrl Duncan notes its prevalence in the colonial era, reporting that legislatures regularly appropriated land for road building. Since then, society has struck a more protective stance toward private property rights, and the condemnation of roads is surely (and justifiably) compensable. But ultimately, underlying the Fifth Amendment takings clause are the reasonable expectations of the landowner, and these will change as society's circumstances change. Trust property that critically impacts society carries special significance. Uses that either inappropriately limit public benefit in the property or harm the remaining assets in the trust remain rarely justified by the reasonable expectations of the landowner. As courts emphasize: "[P]arties acquiring rights in trust property generally hold those rights subject to the trust, and can assert no vested right to use those rights in a manner harmful to the trust."[38]

Moreover, courts have made clear that public rights in trust property can rest dormant through successive private owners of land, to be revived by the sovereign when needed to protect public needs. As one court said, "That generations of trustees have slept on public rights does not foreclose their successors from awakening." And as the Vermont court explained, "The state acts as administrator of the public trust and has a continuing power that 'extends to the revocation of previously granted rights or to the enforcement of the trust against lands long thought free of the trust.'" The owner can maintain his or her security of title simply by adhering to uses consistent with the public trust.[39]

Of course, the class of lands and resources subject to revocation must be limited, as a broad scope would eviscerate the Fifth Amendment's takings clause. The Massachusetts and Vermont courts justified revocation of shore lands by noting the "peculiar nature" or "special nature" of such land in light of the public demand for tidelands (for navigation, commerce, fishing, recreation, and conservation). The vast majority of private parcels escape this "special nature" classification because they carry low ecological or other value for the public. In *Illinois Central*, the Supreme Court made clear that such nonexceptional property could be privatized free of the trust. However, the Court also alluded that the realm of trust property was not rigidly confined to shorelines but included other property of a *special character*, stating, "So with trusts connected with public property, or property of a special character, like lands under navigable waters; they cannot be placed entirely beyond the direction and control of the state."[40]

Property of a special character undoubtedly encompasses some lands and resources reaching beyond the traditional streambeds. In a climate-stricken world, scarcity puts a premium on nearly all natural assets, and "special character" lands and resources will surely prove to be an expanding sphere. While quiet enjoyment or reasonable use of crucial lands or resources should not trigger revocation, practices that threaten society by contravening the two-pronged *Illinois* test – either by (1) restricting the public's use of a vital resource or (2) polluting or destroying ("substantially impairing") remaining trust resources – violate the inherent condition attached to original title. The following discussion draws on this test to suggest two broad categories of revocation.

Crucial Resource Revocations

The first prong of the *Illinois Central* test sets a limit on privatization by allowing only conveyances of trust resources that further trust purposes. But some acts of privatization, as a per se matter, run antithetical to trust purposes because they allow private parties to monopolize crucial life sources, which would deprive citizens of access to meet their most paramount needs. As Professor Blumm observes, "The doctrine's central purpose may be to serve as a vehicle to avoid monopolization of resources with important public values."[41] Two trust assets, though not exclusive, fit obviously into the "life source" category: water and seeds. In today's world, both remain subject to dangerous control by global corporations. As illustrated later in the chapter, the public trust will not intrude into benign usufruct possession but should intervene when possessors attempt harmful domination and control of the asset.

Waters. Inherently a public good, water remains essential to life itself, yet scarcity looms on many fronts. Increasingly, various parts of the United States have faced severe water shortages, threatening dry faucets in a matter of days or weeks as a result of prolonged drought caused by global heating. Many countries elsewhere regularly experience water scarcity that endangers survival. Yet even as scarcity intensifies the public need for water, policy leaders trend toward privatizing this life source. Increasingly, governments treat water "solely as a consumer commodity," as Professor Craig Arnold observes. In countries around the world, local governments now confer bottling rights to local water supplies, placing the survival of their own citizens in the hands of corporations that operate bereft of any moral sensibility. Water policy experts Maude Barlow and Tony Clarke warn of an emerging "water elite that will determine the world's water future in its own interest." They note: "In such a scenario, water will go to those who can afford it and not to those who need it." In South Africa, privatization led to water apartheid, as private companies cut supplies to millions of residents. And across the globe, a bulk transport water industry has established itself. In Alaska, a company has gained rights to suck 12 billion gallons of water per year from Blue Lake (located 6 miles east of Sitka) for shipment to India – doubtless only the beginning of similar ventures. Corporate hegemony over this life source portends danger for all citizens.[42]

In *Illinois Central*, the Supreme Court declared government's trust duty to "preserve such waters for the use of the public." Other cases too have long recognized the limits of privatizing water. In 1821, the New Jersey Supreme Court stated that a "transient usufructuary possession, only, can be had" in the resource. California's *Mono Lake* decision squarely defined water as a public trust asset, and the Supreme Court of Hawaii has conferred public trust status on groundwater, recognizing the integral connectivity of the hydrologic cycle. Other countries such as South Africa and Kenya now have constitutional provisions establishing a public trust over water. Maude Barlow describes a rising global water justice movement pressing for such constitutional protection in countries throughout the world. Here, as in the context of other crucial life sources, the public trust forms a vector of essential human rights advocacy.[43]

Courts should invoke the trust over water resources not only to prevent privatization of water in the first place but also to revoke private rights previously granted where such privatization impairs necessary public access and use. This revocation authority finds clear affirmation in the U.S. *Mono Lake* case, where the California Supreme Court underscored the duty of "*continuing supervision* over the taking and use of the appropriated water." Emphasizing that water appropriators "can claim no vested right" to water, the court declared that "the continuing power of the state as administrator of the public trust ... extends to the revocation of previously granted rights." The court also underscored the sovereign's power to adjust to new circumstances (which will prove increasingly important in the context of climate change), declaring: "[T]he state is not confined by past allocation decisions which may be incorrect in light of current knowledge or inconsistent with current needs." The Supreme Court of Hawaii likewise embraced this reasoning in its leading water trust case. Now firmly established in the water context, the same fountain of authority to resist privatization and to revoke permits should extend to other life sources, such as seeds.[44]

Seed Patents. Seed patents represent one of the most alarming efforts to date to privatize a natural resource long thought common to all. For thousands of years since the beginning of the agricultural era, generations of farmers have cultivated crops by collecting and storing seeds. As Professor Keith Aoki wrote in an extensive article on the future of food, even though crop seeds largely result from human-directed selective breeding, they remain, inherently, "natural resources." Until the 1970s, as Aoki explained, most nations considered plant resources as part of biodiversity, treated by law as the "common heritage of humankind."[45] The classification implicitly recognizes a public trust over seeds.

Over the last three decades, advances in molecular biology have allowed corporations to deviate from traditional seed selection practices by developing genetically modified seed. Such "transgenic" seed, as it is called, arrives (in effect) sterile, incapable of producing seeds for another generation of plants. Use of transgenic seed forces farmers into a pattern of continual purchase; they lose the means of self-sufficiency formerly gained from their own collection of seeds. Intellectual property law has responded to this corporate scheme by allowing patents on transgenic seed, creating private rights not formerly recognized. In other words, the seed supply – a life source previously treated as part of the commonwealth of humankind – now comes subject to privatization.[46]

These events have concentrated a dangerous amount of power in corporate hands. Four companies now control more than half of the global proprietary (e.g., brand-name) seed market. In the United States alone, for example, Monsanto Company's patented seeds allegedly grow on about 90% of all soybean farms in the country. The concentration of seeds in a small number of corporate hands is associated with declining rates of saving and replanting seeds, as well as reduced seed diversity.[47]

As if these effects of corporate control were not enough, transgenic seed growing on one field can contaminate other fields through natural pollen drift (and other means), defeating sustainable practices adhered to by non-transgenic farmers. Quite nefariously, those farmers who involuntarily and unwittingly raise commercial crops from the trespassing patented seed find themselves not only victims of industrial seed pollution but also fear (despite corporate assurances to the contrary) being subject to lawsuits for infringing on the private property rights conjured by corporations in the form of seed patents. A more perverse application of property principles would be hard to imagine. Moreover, according to a number of farm organizations, transgenic seed will not only contaminate organic seed but will eventually *overcome* it, making coexistence between transgenic seed and organic seed impossible.[48]

When aggressive corporations monopolize and usurp the localized, democratic means of providing a food source, they create the prospect of "food fascism," warns Dr. Vandana Shiva, a world-renown food activist from India.[49] The patent represents a conveyance of private property rights in a trust asset (seeds) long deemed part of the "common heritage of humankind." In issuing seed patents, government must adhere to fiduciary duties established by the *Illinois Central* case. Government can only allow privatization of such crucial resources where doing so promotes public use of the asset. In the case of transgenic seed, privatization not only restricts public access to particular seeds but also threatens to terminate public access to a natural seed supply altogether, allowing the very monopolization that the *Illinois Central* test aims to prevent. The seed patent begs revocation under the trust where a corporation deploys it as a legal weapon to divest citizens of the means of creating their own food supply using time-honored traditional methods. In both the water and seed contexts, the power of revocation remains a necessary legal tool to correct past privatizations that now threaten basic human rights of freely accessing Nature's life sources.

Public Hazard Revocations

The discussion in the preceding section focused on *beneficial* resources privatized in violation of the first prong of the *Illinois Central* alienation test. In a very different set of circumstances, privatization allows industrial practices that "substantially impair" the remaining assets in Nature's Trust, contravening the second prong of the *Illinois Central* test. The fossil fuel and hard-rock mining sectors provide examples of industries failing this test time and again as they deploy equipment and processes that wreak devastation across ecosystems, landscapes, and the planet's circulatory and biological systems. This brief discussion suggests that such industries, never before held accountable under the public trust doctrine, are using private resource rights that remain subject to revocation by government trustees.

Mining companies in the United States receive the right to mine hard-rock minerals on federal public lands through "unpatented" mining claims, which are considered private property rights. Some corporations gain land patents, or deeds, to the land as well. When Congress first created unpatented mining claims, it gave no consideration to the *Illinois Central* tests. Early mining claims did not generally cause large-scale damage, simply because the technology was rudimentary. But the old prospectors' crude pick-axes and sluice boxes slipped as relics into history, replaced by highly destructive processes such as toxic cyanide heap leaching and strip mining. Mining has polluted at least 26,000 kilometers of rivers in the U.S. West alone.[50]

Oil, natural gas, and coal development projects generally gain authorization through leases, which are forms of privatization (either directly granted by government or recognized and enforced by government). Such leases fail the "substantial impairment" test, by allowing uses that destroy waters, wildlife, and landscapes. The 2010 BP oil spill, for example, sent an estimated 185 million gallons of oil into the Gulf of Mexico. A 2011 Exxon spill released 42,000 gallons of crude oil into the pristine Yellowstone River of Montana. Modern coal-mining methods obliterate entire mountaintops, destroy forests and the countless species living in them, and flush toxins into the watersheds below. Natural gas development can poison wells and aquifers through hydraulic fracturing methods (fracking). Beyond this, the development of oil, gas, and coal create greenhouse gas emissions that pose a mounting and unacceptable threat to life on the planet, as prior chapters have explained. While the fossil fuel and mining sectors do not stand alone in their ability to inflict colossal devastation, they serve as prime examples of privatization that fails the "substantial impairment" test.[51]

Professor John Davidson proposes a "public hazards doctrine" to capture the substantial impairment type of trust violation, as explained in Chapter 7. He notes the need to maintain sovereign control over "critically hazardous resources" as a parallel to the trust's protection of beneficial resources for the public.[52] Similar to the conveyance of water rights and seed patents, fossil fuel leases and unpatented mining claims (and other forms of privatization that promote development of hazard resources) should remain subject to the "continuing supervision" of the state. Where the exercise of such private rights in trust resources substantially impairs the remaining assets in the people's trust, such rights warrant revocation without compensation. A "public hazard" doctrine represents a necessary and inevitable progression of the two-part test announced by the Supreme Court long ago.

"THE EARTH BELONGS IN USUFRUCT TO THE LIVING": TRUST EASEMENTS AND SERVITUDES ON PRIVATE PROPERTY

Whereas the previous section explored sovereign authority to revoke private title, this section illuminates public ecological rights in privately held property. Most titles cannot be revoked without compensation, but regardless, public rights operate (alongside private rights) in the bundle of entitlements attached to the land. In limited circumstances already recognized by courts, the trust provides public access to private land such as tidelands and upland beaches. Using the same rationale, Nature's Trust advances a commonwealth vision of land by restoring ecological duty in private title.

Property ownership thrusts a citizen into a *relationship* with the broader community, because the property owner controls resources needed by society. As Professor Blumm explains, several public trust cases articulate a "conceptual severance" of title into private rights and public rights, both of which operate concurrently within the same boundaries.[53] In these cases (most of which involve privately owned land along shorelines), courts characterize title as a combination of *jus publicum* (the public ownership interest) and *jus privatum* (the private ownership interest). Combined, they make up the full bundle of property rights in the land.

The *jus privatum* (revocable or otherwise) secures the classic rights that private property owners enjoy, including: (1) the right to possess and use property; (2) the right to exclude others (although, as to shoreline property, this right remains limited); (3) the power to transfer the property to another; and (4) the right of legal recourse if someone damages the property or infringes upon quiet enjoyment.[54] The *jus publicum* (coexisting with these private rights) consists of public rights that may have the character of an *easement* or a *servitude*, or both. An *easement* (found usually on beach or other waterfront property) protects the public's preexisting right of access to trust resources. A *servitude* safeguards ecology for the public by limiting the private owner's ability to destroy the land. As noted earlier, these public property rights do not give rise to constitutional takings because they remain antecedent, reserved rights – originating before government granted any private interests in the land. The discussion that follows explores these two applications of *jus publicum*.

The Public Trust Easement

In the case of an *easement*, the public retains access over private property to enjoy a public trust resource. Most jurisdictions recognize a reserved public right of access along navigable waters beneath the high water mark, regardless of private ownership. Courts in some states, most notably Oregon and New Jersey, have also found a public easement extending upland on the dry sand portion of the beach. Justifying this public access on the basis of practical need, the New Jersey Supreme Court stated: "Reasonable enjoyment of the foreshore and the sea cannot be realized unless some enjoyment of the dry sand area is also allowed." As Professor Blumm and Lucus Ritchie report, courts in several other states have created public recreational easements over beach property.[55]

The public trust easement nevertheless applies to an exceedingly narrow set of private lands – those enclosing traditional public trust resources that provide beneficial uses such as fishing, hunting, navigation, and recreation. Because the public right of access directly interferes with the private right to exclude – one of the classic rights in the private ownership bundle – courts have invoked it sparingly, and rightly so. As Professor Blumm explains, courts aim toward an "accommodation," balancing both public and private rights. The most detailed application of the accommodation test was formulated by the New Jersey Supreme Court in *Matthews v. Bay Head Improvement Association.* The court held that public easements to access privately owned dry sand beaches must arise when "reasonably necessary," as determined by: (1) the nature and extent of public demand for the beaches; (2) the extent and availability of nearby public beaches for alternative access; (3) the owner's use of his or her beach; and (4) the location of the dry sand area in relation to the foreshore.[56]

Without a doubt, public trust easements traverse accreting doctrinal sands. As the *Matthews* court emphasized, the public trust cannot be "'fixed or static'" but rather must "'be molded and extended to meet changing conditions and needs of the public it was created to benefit.'" It noted in particular that increased population pressure on the beaches will necessitate more access. But in the future, other requirements, such as the need to access food and water sources, may have crucial bearing as well. In deciding where these *jus publicum* easements should land, courts should look first to corporate-owned and association-owned property rather than to lots owned by individuals or families, for the obvious reason that the latter protect personal privacy interests. By contrast, businesses and associations have always been limited in their power to exclude the public.[57]

The Public Trust Servitude

The public trust *servitude* instills ecological obligation into private ownership. It contrasts with the current boundary-based approach to private ownership, which largely fences off duty to the broader ecosystem. Private boundaries have always proved dysfunctional in the ecological sense. As Professor Eric Freyfogle explains, "The public has a legitimate interest in how *all* lands are used. No land use takes place in isolation."[58]

Property law has long recognized that some public ownership interests transcend private lot lines. For example, the public owns the sky overhead. The public owns

the birds that land in the backyard and the deer that pass through. A stream travers-
ing a private parcel remains subject to allocation by government (although Eastern
water laws do give riparian landowners advantage). It has always been the case that
property owners may not take or damage these public resources without license
from the government, which acts on behalf of the people. The recognition of public
rights within private lot lines must now extend to ecological protection.[59]

The public trust servitude limits damaging uses of property that would "substantially impair" public trust assets. The servitude already manifests in several cases
prohibiting owners of shoreline property from filling tidelands in a way that would
interfere with public trust purposes. While such cases tend to anchor the servitude
at the shoreline, climate crisis will surely force a stretch of this servitude to protect
more of the "ordinary nature" existing across private lands. Natural systems cannot
be sustained at a high level of function without infusing obligation into the entire
ecological *res* of Nature's Trust.[60]

In 1972, the Wisconsin Supreme Court steered the public trust in this direction
by formulating the "natural use" doctrine. In *Just v. Marinette County*, private landowners challenged a wetlands regulation as a Fifth Amendment taking of their private property. Rejecting their position, the court held that the regulation carried out
the state's "active public trust duty" to eradicate pollution. It declared an organic
landowner obligation to protect natural systems on private property, explaining:

> An owner of land has no absolute and unlimited right to change the *essential nat-
> ural character* of his land so as [to] use it for a purpose for which it was unsuited in
> its natural state and which injures the rights of others.... This is not a case where an
> owner is prevented from using his land for natural and indigenous uses. The uses
> consistent with the nature of the land are allowed.

Finding no property right to change the "natural character" of land, the *Just* rule
upholds the reasonable expectations of a landowner, but only so far as consistent
with nature's own zoning laws. Professor Blumm reports judicial acceptance of the
"natural use" rule in several states.[61]

It remains to be seen whether courts and lawmakers will find the *jus publicum* servitude applicable to all private property or to just a limited category of property that
displays riparian characteristics. In that regard, property law sits at a critical juncture.
The precedent began at water's edge in cases involving shoreline, and some courts
have been reluctant to take it beyond those areas. Their hesitancy seemingly arises
out of an entrenched property law tradition that emphasizes "constituent parts rather
than the whole," as Professor Myrl Duncan describes. The modern servitude surely
must extend beyond narrow categories to be fully effective, because ecology con-
nects all land, water, air, species, and habitat. The *Just* court, for example, emphasized the role of wetlands as "a necessary part of the ecological creation."[62]

As Professor Duncan surmises, the "old order" of property law, with its "atomistic rather than interconnected" worldview, will collapse when faced with imperatives identified by conservation biology.[63] As primitive understandings yield to a more advanced and holistic recognition of ecology, property law will inevitably reshape itself to recalibrate the balance of private property rights and public property rights. To achieve consistency with Nature's own laws, property law must move beyond splintered resource categories to expansively protect all natural assets that remain crucial to ecosystem functioning, *wherever located*. In a world of climate unrest, some properties that once had no obvious importance to society will undoubtedly (and perhaps rapidly) gain value as habitats shift, water sources dry up, human populations migrate, and new conditions arise.

Professor William Rodgers has expressed the plausibility of a "universal 'good husbandry'" duty on the part of landowners arising from the public trust. To this end, we should think of the *jus publicum* servitude as extending across all "private" property, with the scope and importance of such servitude shrinking or expanding according to public needs. The servitude represents the public's retained ownership interest in the ecological assets on private land, recognized by the U.S. Supreme Court when it declared in 1907: "[T]he State has an interest independent of and behind the titles of its citizens, in all the earth and air within its domain." As Professors Sally Fairfax and Leigh Raymond explain, "No matter how clear the deed ... that ostensibly gave the private landowner dominion over a piece of land, that title is always subject to underlying limits of public rights."[64]

A servitude recognizing the public trust interest in land aligns with the commonwealth frame discussed earlier that views property owners as life tenants with duties to coming generations. Invoking classic property law terminology, future generations may be classified as "remaindermen" – those who stand to inherit when the present life-estate ends. The relationship between present and future generations becomes one of a trust in itself, for under textbook property law, "A life tenant is considered in law to be a trustee or quasi-trustee" for the remaindermen and occupies a "fiduciary relation" toward these remaindermen. By characterizing present landowners as individual trustees in their own right with duties to remainder generations, the life-tenancy construct instills lasting ecological obligation into private land title. As one case explains, "[It] is the duty of a life tenant to ... preserve the property and to prevent decay or waste." Justice Christopher Weeramantry, former judge on the International Court of Justice, gave credence to the construct when he wrote in an opinion, "[L]and is never the subject of human ownership, but is only held in trust, with all the connotations that follow of due care, wise management, and custody for future generations." The Supreme Court of India has similarly implied an individual trust-like duty on every landowner. Moreover, the idea has at last made its way into U.S. property law circles, with one leading textbook offering the possibility that "present generations are life tenants of the earth's resources and future generations hold remainder interests."[65]

Acknowledging community and generational ecological property rights across privately owned land in the form of a reserved trust servitude would fundamentally advance the "natural use" doctrine announced by the *Just* court. This, in turn, would enhance protection of all private property rights, because the servitude legally secures the natural infrastructure on which those property rights irrefutably depend. However, those who espouse the land-as-commodity frame will oppose any such expansion of the public trust, because it questions any private owner's "right" to destroy natural resources. In their view, land is worth money, and an owner's most prized property right remains the right to profit from "development" (often destruction) of land. And what would this portend for regulatory takings? In an extreme libertarian view, the developer should be compensated when forced to refrain from any damaging activity.

Some commentators express concern that an expansive trust doctrine would greatly restrict the realm of regulatory takings (the environmental sort, at least). In fact, this horse has already left the barn. As Professor Blumm notes, the Supreme Court in *Lucas v. South Carolina Coastal Council* recognized the public trust as one of the "background principles" of property law that can defeat takings claims. The Court made clear that there can be no regulatory taking of private property if a "logically antecedent inquiry" shows that the landowner's proposed use was "not part of his title to begin with." Subsequent cases have expressly held that public trust rights on private land remain antecedent and reserved in their character and therefore do not give rise to takings claims (though the interpretive scope of such public trust rights remains in flux).[66]

Narrowing the realm of regulatory takings may be a step long overdue. The doctrine has been fraught with conceptual difficulty and contrived interpretations since its inception. Historically, landowners received no compensation for regulation that reduced land values. The troubled principle made its awkward debut in 1922 in a case called *Pennsylvania Coal Company v. Mahon*, when Justice Holmes famously said, "while property may be regulated to a certain extent, if regulation goes *too far* it will be recognized as a taking." The Supreme Court has found itself on a slippery slope ever since, struggling to define exactly what "too far" means in a world of fast-collapsing resources. As Justice Holmes himself emphasized in *Mahon*, most regulation will not trigger compensation because "[g]overnment hardly could go on" if it had to pay every owner for diminishment in property value.[67]

The basic problem afflicting regulatory takings law has to do with the characterization of destructive intent as a *property right*. Property has always been regulated for the benefit of society, and landowners have never been able to do whatever they please on their property. By protecting ecology on private property, the trust doctrine does nothing to deprive the landowner of the classic property rights encompassed in *jus privatum*, as explained earlier in the chapter. Even under an expansive trust doctrine, public and private uses may co-exist.[68]

Regulatory takings doctrine has never fully explained how "property" can be taken when the property *uses* are merely regulated. If property were in fact "taken," the government would hold a property right after paying compensation. But, unlike a physical condemnation case where the government gains title to land in exchange for compensation, the government gains *nothing* in a regulatory takings case. In fact, even after a successful takings case (where the landowner receives compensation for decreased land value), the offending regulation can be lifted off the books – a prospect not at all unusual given erratic swings in politics. With the regulation removed, the land value would rise again, and the owner who pocketed compensation for the burden of past regulation would enjoy a windfall at taxpayer expense. Relying on conjured property "rights," the environmental regulatory takings cases have taken shape around a hollow core.

In the end, property law seeks to balance society's reasonable expectations against the reasonable expectations of private property owners. The rise of industrialization and neo-market ideologies engendered a commodity frame that all but erased one side of the equation – the *community's* reasonable expectations in how private land can be used. And on the landowner side, the frame redefined reasonable expectations to reflect solely market development potential as property came to be valued for its price tag rather than for its intrinsic worth. This reductionist approach toppled the age-old balance between public and private reasonable expectations. Applied transformatively, the public trust doctrine would recognize a *jus publicum servitude* on private lands, thereby restoring the balance of property law to protect *both* commonwealth expectations in ecology and personal liberty in property. As Professor Sax long ago recognized, the public trust remains the penultimate guardian of reasonable expectations, acting as a legal stronghold against destabilizing forces that bring on crisis and collapse – and with them, Nature's own land condemnations.[69]

THE FUTURE OF PROPERTY

This chapter began with an observation: if modern industrialized society hopes to adapt to strikingly harsh planetary conditions, it needs to firm up property law. Doing so does not necessarily mean inventing new concepts; rather it can mean reviving old ones. Long after market extremists drove old understandings off the rails, the public trust doctrine now stands poised to bring property law back into equilibrium. But how, in this industrialized world dominated by a commodity view of land, can private property rights adherents resurrect the sustaining principles of public trust law? One obvious way involves reforming statutes, land use codes, and doctrines.

But also, a compatible approach tills those very land practices that announce the commonwealth frame. Property law, for better or worse, follows cultural norms. This alone proves empowering, for it means that landowners can provide an impetus for property law reform by managing their lands from a reclaimed commonwealth perspective.

Such assertions of commonwealth thinking now appear across the United States. Community gardens, inner-city farms, and urban homesteads increasingly proliferate in broad revival of the human instinct to draw sustenance from the land. Ambitious calls for home food production come from every corner of the United States. A food-not-lawns movement slowly but steadily sprouts in the grassroots of suburbia. A burgeoning interest in habitat gardens, organic pest control, and natural storm water systems all reflect growing ecological awareness among the landowner classes. More than 1,700 land trusts now work with private landowners to enter into conservation easements designed to secure an ecological legacy for future generations. An impressive array of community tree-planting programs across the world set a heroic aim to draw down atmospheric carbon dioxide to help stabilize climate. These all illuminate the beginnings of a cultural shift back from land-as-commodity to land-as-commonwealth.[70]

It will take enormous numbers of citizens to grow these seeds of change into a land revolution so strong that it displaces the market-driven system of land exploitation. But if citizens across the industrialized world begin to act in ways that honor ecology, community, and future generations – while asserting their original public trust rights as beneficiaries of Nature's Trust – they will, in effect, become the living manifestations of the land ethic that Aldo Leopold urged. Those who truly cherish private property rights will find their calling in this land-as-commonwealth frame, as they will come to learn that their liberty and quiet enjoyment of land depends, first and foremost, on Earth's life-sustaining ecological endowment.

The New World: A Planetary Trust

The last time we saw anything like this was never.... I don't know how to say it any clearer than that it is the largest threat to human life our state has experienced in anyone's lifetime.

Connecticut Governor Dannel Malloy, remarks in response to Hurricane
Sandy's approach, October 28, 2012[1]

As climate vengeance strikes communities with greater frequency and horrifying intensity, citizens across the planet now bear witness to the lethal consequences of humanity's industrialized path. Yet environmental law, society's major instrument to impart ecological responsibility, does little to bring human actions into compliance with Nature's laws – the laws that really count. In fact, environmental regulation hastens this course of disaster. This book began by explaining how that could possibly be.

Arising primarily from statutes passed in the 1970s, the field of environmental law stands as a failed legal experiment. The administrative state vests agencies with breathtaking power that came justified by one simple assumption: officials will deploy public resources and invoke their technical expertise *on behalf of the public interest*. Instead, too many environmental agencies today use their power to carry out profit agendas set by corporations and singular interests. As Part I of this book explained, environmental agencies have fallen captive to the industries they regulate. Consequently, they use the laws' permit provisions to legalize the very damage the statutes were designed to prevent. Nearly across the board, environmental statutory processes do not prohibit harm: they permit it.

The problem lies not in the statutes themselves but in the frame governing environmental law. As a political frame, it continually bends agencies into serving those parties holding the most political power, which in today's world often means corporations rather than the general public. In many U.S. agencies, decisions flow from what the politics will allow, not what the statutes say. High-ranking political operatives use their discretion to favor the industries they continue to serve from inside the agency. Staff scientists and permit writers operating within highly charged political cultures suffer varying degrees of pressure to fall in line with the agency's political agenda. These pressures remain obscured from the public, taking place in procedural fortresses made nearly impenetrable by their sheer complexity.

In a three-branch system of government, courts and legislatures should provide meaningful checks and balances to rein in the executive branch and its agencies. But Congress, more susceptible to corporate influence than ever before, deadlocks over environmental policy. Its minimal involvement typically consists of appropriations riders passed to legalize industry behavior that would otherwise violate statutory mandates. Courts, while positioned to force agency compliance with statutory mandates, play a weak role because of a deference doctrine, which accords agency technical decisions a presumption of validity. Absent effective oversight by the other two branches of government, a dangerous amount of power accumulates in the executive branch, both on the federal and state levels. While legal structures vary considerably among different nations, the untrammeled power of agencies, wherever located, can create an administrative tyranny over Nature and a menace to environmental democracy.

Society stands at a crucial moment in time. Actions taken now and in the next few years will determine how well humanity will survive on the planet. Warnings of tipping points, irreversible losses, and unpredictable cataclysmic planetary change now pour from the scientific community in growing torrents of alarm.[2] Increasingly, the science makes clear that this moment can be revolutionary, or it can be suicidal. Guiding humanity to a safe ecological path before crossing irrevocable thresholds becomes the most urgent call on Earth.

Humanity cannot hope for a livable planet if government agencies continue to license industries to pollute and destroy the remaining natural resources. Environmental law becomes profoundly relevant to the daily life and future well-being of every citizen alive today. In words that now reverberate truth in nearly every nation, Ansel Adams once said: "It is horrifying that we have to fight our own government to save the environment."[3] Citizens living in all parts of the world stand on common ground as never before, in both their challenge and mission.

This book has developed a paradigm called Nature's Trust to reconstitute environmental law in countries throughout the world. It calls forth an ancient duty embodied in the public trust doctrine, a legal principle that has flowed through countless forms of government through the ages. At its core, the doctrine declares public property rights originally and inherently reserved through the peoples' social contract with their sovereign governments. The trust remains an attribute of sovereignty that cannot be alienated by any legislature. This principle designates government as trustee of crucial natural resources and obligates it to act in a fiduciary capacity to protect such assets for the beneficiaries of the trust, which include both present and future generations of citizens. Unlike the permissive bent of administrative discretion under statutory law, the public trust imposes a strict duty to protect the people's commonwealth. At a time when government actions worldwide threaten to rob today's youth of an ecologically secure future, the trust breathes legal rights into the aspiration of intergenerational equity.

While the public trust has long offered a theoretical ideal for environmental law, until now it has lacked the precision necessary to apply it to a broad realm of practical conflicts arising before modern legislatures and agencies. This book sought to illuminate a fiduciary path by setting forth the substantive and procedural obligations incumbent on government entities as trustees of public resources. They must protect the trust, not allow waste, maximize the societal value of trust assets, restore assets where they have been damaged, and recoup monetary damages from third parties that have injured the assets. Further, a legislature must not alienate public trust assets where doing so would not serve public trust purposes, or would substantially impair the ecological wealth remaining in the trust. These are active duties, leaving no room for idle management. Government's failure to protect the planet's climate system on which all life depends amounts to the most dangerous perversion of this fiduciary responsibility.

In terms of procedural duties, the trust dismantles the political frame that warps bureaucratic decision making. Agency trustees hold an unwavering duty of undivided loyalty to the public (both present and future generations) and must abide by the highest "punctilio" of fiduciary care.[4] Those who allow the destruction of natural resources to advance singular and corporate interests, or to serve their own political or bureaucratic interests, act in violation of their duty. In addition, the trust model requires that agencies act in good faith, with reasonable skill, and with due caution for protecting vital assets. These duties re-posture scientific uncertainty and lay the legal ground for a precautionary approach. Rather than providing a ready excuse *not to* regulate industry behavior, scientific uncertainty compels agencies to disallow pollution, resource destruction, chemical introduction, and genetic modification unless and until conclusive proof exists that such practices will not pose harm. This reversal becomes precisely what is needed in a world in which agency safety reviews cannot hope to keep pace with industry's experimentation.

As a property concept, Nature's Trust applies to any level, from local to global. Not reliant on legislative enactments, it stands as the only organic, holistic approach to defining government obligation. It characterizes all sovereigns – nations, states, and tribes – as co-tenant trustees of shared trans-boundary assets, joined together in a property-based framework of corollary and mutual responsibilities. Their reciprocal obligations include the duty to protect and guard against waste to the common asset. Extrapolated to a planetary level, the trust offers a model for global responsibility at a time when international law wholly fails to address the world's most urgent environmental crises.⁵ The approach has spawned a legal campaign known as Atmospheric Trust Litigation brought on behalf of children and youth of the world. The litigation (discussed in Chapter 10) seeks to force governments to control carbon pollution in accordance with scientific prescriptions before indolent officials draw the shades on the last window of opportunity to prevent climate catastrophe.

Any trust relies on strong judicial enforcement of fiduciary duties. Without a robust judiciary, there exists no trust – only tyranny. This book devoted a chapter to judicial enforcement, outlining steps that judges could take immediately, within their realm of authority and judicial tradition, to restore integrity to environmental law and enforce the property rights of citizen beneficiaries. It argued for judicial review of legislative action under fiduciary standards of loyalty to the public. It underscored the need for judicial remedies to address the institutional dysfunction of agencies in their management of resources. When faced with long-standing agency incompetence, corruption, and dereliction of duty, courts prove effective only by intervening (either temporarily or for protracted periods) directly into the agency's processes. Chapter 11 also detailed the elements of structural injunctions and described institutional remedies that could promote effective judicial supervision. While these types of remedies have ample precedent and remain well within the realm of equitable authority, courts have not yet used them widely in environmental law.

Today's judges retain all of the tools necessary to enforce public trust obligations. But enforcement requires courage and a change of judicial mindset, an awakening by judges to the ecological urgencies of today's world, and an appreciation of their branch's crucial role in government's balance of power. The world needs extraordinary jurists across the globe who, in solidarity with great legal minds that came before them, will rise to their constitutional duties and enforce the rights of the people as beneficiaries of Nature's Trust.

A legal paradigm gains vitality from the shared values of the community and, more fundamentally, from the long-standing expectations of humanity. To a great extent, environmental law has come unmoored from these intuitive anchors. Public trust principles aim to protect future generations, secure natural commonwealth for the public, promote the highest, non-wasteful uses of resources, and uphold the right of Nature to exist and flourish. Tapping a wellspring of human understanding that remains instinctive, passion-bound, and deeply shared among citizens of distant cultures, Nature's Trust can evoke a moral language to access strong human sensibilities. The same trust principles that flow through a judge's pen can be preached from a pulpit or spoken as the last words from a grandmother to her grandchildren anywhere in the world – because the trust encompasses a moral covenant that transcends all governments, cultures, and peoples on Earth.

As Part II of this book explained, the basic components of a trust paradigm already exist in the law. The framework stands ready for citizens to activate in nations having governments that gain power from the people. But in some countries (including the United States), serious institutional problems fester within democracy. Without fundamental change to eliminate corporate influence in politics, industry groups will continue to thwart environmental progress. Campaign finance reform represents one of the weightiest *environmental* priorities of our day.

Other forces beyond politics also carry great influence and weight in organizing human behavior. The traditions, institutions, and habits of industrial society devour natural resources at break-neck pace, and a trust paradigm will accomplish little if root behaviors persist. As Burns H. Weston and David Bollier write in *Green Governance*, "The mythological vision of human progress through ubiquitous market activity simply cannot be fulfilled; it demands more than Nature can deliver and inflicts too much social inequity and disruption in the process."[6]

Simply put, environmental law cannot protect the ecological integrity of those societies afflicted with an economic disease that devours the resources necessary for their own existence and perpetuation. As James Speth has written, we must confront today's predatory capitalism, which has unleashed many caustic forces against environmental law and society as a whole. These include: (1) a profit-based system that ignores ecological costs; (2) a dangerous dependence on fossil fuels; (3) a compulsion toward unlimited economic growth; (4) a poorly designed system of production that creates waste and pollution; (5) a culture of overconsumption; and (6) ruling corporate powers capable of inflicting staggering ecological damage. These problems characterize the modern industrial state both in its stage of modern fruition and in its developing-world ambition, each pushing Earth toward the same demise. Fortunately, many inspirational, practical, transformational proposals now exist for societal change in business, politics, lifestyle, and culture. Nature's Trust synergizes with, and draws strength from, a quiet renaissance now sweeping the world.

Leading thinkers now envision an economy that can harmonize with Nature's own laws, one that would undertake the epochal task of rebuilding natural wealth by restoring damaged ecosystems. This new economy would reconstitute sustainable and productive work that advances, rather than undermines, community goals. It would transform the energy infrastructure from fossil fuels to renewable sources. It would install resilient adaptation systems to protect human communities from extremes brought on by climate change and resource scarcity. A magnificent transference of power from Wall Street to Main Street (as David Korten puts it) would relocalize community economies to meet as many human needs as possible on a local basis. Industry would redesign and retrofit manufacturing processes with an aim toward zero waste and no pollution. Revived, time-tested values of self-sufficiency, thrift, and simplicity would inspire personal responsibility (for the first time in generations) for growing and preserving part of the household food supply. This economic vision vests power in the people. Corporations, having no *actual personhood*, would be rightly recognized as legal entities created by state-issued charters, bound by the same public fiduciary responsibilities as the governments that created them.

This book also addressed the interaction of property law and environmental law, offering ways to realign the expectations of land ownership in accordance with new ecological realities. The public trust exalts and protects the personal liberty and security associated with private property ownership; at the same time, it situates such ownership in balance with the needs of the community – both present and future generations. The trust effectuates those commonwealth understandings between society and property owners that remain necessary to protect vital ecology, without which even the most jealously guarded property rights will disintegrate into worthless deeds. The Nature's Trust paradigm affirms the right of the people, through their government, to revoke title (without compensation) to (1) *survival resources* needed by the public that become monopolized by corporations; and (2) *hazard resources* subject to forms of corporate exploit that substantially impair remaining trust resources and ecology. The framework also clarifies the people's retained property rights on private land as exercised through a trust servitude (to protect ecology) and, in rare cases, through a reserved easement (to access resources).

PLANETARY PATRIOTISM

While the fundamental legal components of Nature's Trust already exist, justice has never proved self-executing. Throughout history, governments have served a powerful few at the expense of the majority until oppression grew so intolerable that citizens would submit to it no longer. At pivotal times, citizens have united in revolutionary force to redirect power toward higher ideals and core human rights. Citizenship remains the lifeblood of any democracy.[7]

Today, global environmental damage rises intolerably. The fossil fuel and nuclear industries now possess the capability of destroying planetary systems necessary for life on Earth to exist and thrive, and they have made governments worldwide their partners in a dangerous chase of profit. Fossil fuel corporations remain bent on burning all of the petroleum and coal in their proven reserves. As author Bill McKibben makes clear, the carbon emissions from this would be enough – five times over – to heat the planet to a level that leading scientists warn will trigger catastrophic and irreversible climate change. McKibben calls the fossil fuel industry "Public Enemy Number One to the survival of our planetary civilization."[8]

These global multinational corporations gain license under existing environmental law. When one company's tar sand development proposal finds fervent political support among a multitude of U.S. and Canadian governmental officials and agencies – even though the resulting carbon emissions could amount to "game over for the planet" (as a prominent climate scientist warns) – citizens should recognize something deeply, terrifyingly wrong with their government.[9]

Global citizens waking up to the prospect of runaway climate change must act on their human impulse to demand accountability from officials before it is too late. Corrupted climate policy has already provoked waves of citizen protests in cities across the world. In October, 2009, 5,200 citizen demonstrations in 181 countries galvanized around a target to limit atmospheric carbon dioxide to 350 parts per million, the maximum amount of pollution that represents a safety zone for the planet, according to several leading climate scientists. As organizer Bill McKibben described, "People around the world who speak four or five hundred different languages ... were all saying the same thing – 350 means survival for us...." In May 2011, youth marched in twenty-five countries worldwide to show support for the Atmospheric Trust Litigation cases aimed at forcing carbon reduction toward the goal of 350 ppm. A remarkable global coalescence continues to surge as citizens worldwide recognize their universal peril.[10]

In his book, *Blessed Unrest*, Paul Hawken reports tens of millions of people in grassroots organizations across the planet advocating for environmental health, social justice, and indigenous rights. Rising ubiquitously as a movement, he says, "It is taking shape in schoolrooms, farms, jungles, villages, companies, deserts, fisheries, slums [and even] fancy New York hotels." Bursting conventional organizational models, this movement confronts common state/market forces bearing down on people of all nationalities and suggests a solidarity among citizens never before seen on Earth. Hawken asks, could this be "an instinctive, collective response" to a common threat?[11]

Such far-flung and irrepressible flares of activism ignite as a new form of patriotism: *planetary patriotism*. The heart of patriotism lies in righteous defense of community values, family security, individual dignity, and collective expectations. As Eric Lieu and Nick Hanauer assert in *The True Patriot*, "True love of country is giving ourselves to a cause and a purpose larger than ourselves."[12] Patriotism defends the territory and resources that support survival – and the public and private property rights anchoring the community. In the past, nearly all patriotism aligned strictly with national borders. But today's planetary patriotism defies borders. Asserting natural rights that have pulsed through humanity since time immemorial, planetary patriotism grows every bit as incensed, undaunted, expectant, and revolutionary as other acts of patriotism, but with a marked difference: it does not defend the nation-state, for the nation-state has turned its environmental power against its own people.

This form of patriotism does not answer to any government, does not find its backing from any military, and does not draw its power from the barrel of a machine gun. Planting stakes in common ground across sovereign borders, planetary patriotism materializes from citizens uniting together as humanity in concerted, urgent defense of life on Earth. As Hawken says, "It is a massive enterprise undertaken by ordinary citizens everywhere, not by self-appointed governments or oligarchies."[13] These citizens act in every venue of society – in courtrooms, classrooms, boardrooms, factories, hospitals, clubhouses, penthouses, press rooms, slums, and in the streets – across all reaches of the globe.

SAFEGUARDING THE SURVIVAL TRUST: CLIMATE VICTORY SPEAKERS

Planetary patriots must recognize climate crisis as the paramount emergency in defending Earth's survival systems. Business-as-usual pollution threatens to bring 11°F planetary heating *by the end of the century*, yielding temperatures that would sear New York City with heat typical of a Middle Eastern country. This unimaginable scenario – one that McKibben describes as "a planet straight out of science fiction" – leaves grave doubt as to whether children born today could survive the environmental chaos set to call later in their life spans. Only a massive global effort surpassing the scale of World War II carries hope of stabilizing climate before Nature crosses a point of no return. To avert climate catastrophe, leading climate scientists call for an *annual* 6 percent emissions reduction on a global level *beginning in 2013*. Pushing a still-rising trajectory of emissions into steep decline across the world requires all of the resources governments can amass to create new energy, transportation, and food systems geared towards ultimately achieving a zero-carbon society. The effort requires mobilizing citizens towards personal carbon reduction as well.[14]

Despite the enormity of this challenge, the world holds tremendous capacity to mount an all-out atmospheric defense effort. The chief limiting force lies in the human imagination of what remains possible. As Lester Brown recounts in his book, *Mobilizing to Save Civilization*, World War II serves as a reminder of how fast society can react to urgent threats. With stunning speed, all sectors of American society re-geared to support the war effort. For three years, the auto industry stopped making cars and produced defense vehicles. A toy company made compasses; a corset manufacturer made grenade belts. The financial world sold war bonds. States lowered their speed limits to conserve gas. Communities planted victory gardens to grow food locally so that the commercial food supplies could be sent to the troops. Children collected recyclable materials. Families made do with the bare minimum.[15]

In sweeping patriotic defense, no one stands at the sidelines. People across all walks of life lend every skill they have to the effort – and they take initiative. Drawn to a greater cause, average citizens transform overnight into heroes. And truly great leaders inspire great action. As President Franklin Delano Roosevelt proclaimed to America at the outset of World War II: "*Let no man say it cannot be done....* Speed will save lives; speed will save this Nation which is in peril; speed will save ... our civilization."[16] Today's planetary patriotism summons the very same courage and determination that emboldened our forebears who fought for their children's lives and futures – because in a very real sense, these stand in jeopardy once again.

America's massive World War II mobilization came catalyzed by average citizens. Nationally, 100,000 Victory Speakers stepped forward to galvanize their local communities in support of the war effort. These citizen volunteers dedicated themselves to making short speeches regularly, in multiple forums, in order to convey the nature of the threat, the need for citizen support, and the need for conservation at home. Victory Speakers were the "trusted and familiar voices" in the community – such as the bankers, carpenters, mothers, and schoolteachers – who, at the grassroots level, jolted people from the distractions of their daily lives and alerted them to a foreboding threat that endangered the fundamental liberties of their society. The war effort, which required the support of every citizen, would not have succeeded without these catalysts.[17]

Today's ecological crisis requires a global mobilization far exceeding World War II. Society needs Victory Speakers *in every nation* who can engage four challenges: (1) wake up their fellow citizens to climate crisis and other ecological threats; (2) inspire citizens to force government leadership in response; (3) model personal low-carbon lifestyle change; and (4) seed communities with relocalization initiatives. These are addressed in the sections that follow.

Waking Up to a New Reality

The remarkable Victory Speakers of yesterday accomplished a *frame change*, an awakening so powerful that it swept all of society into the war effort. They invoked a new understanding of the reality in which people lived. This understanding arrived as an "inconvenient truth" because it required a swift and all-encompassing response from people whose lives were not immediately affected.

The climate mobilization of today needs a similar wake-up call, particularly in the United States. As commentator David Roberts reports, about 75 percent of the American public sits as a "mushy middle" on climate – they have little engagement in the issue and have no strong feelings. These citizens still assume that they live in a world of abundant and unlimited resources, even while ecology collapses around them. Climate change information reaches the public in the form of disaster headlines from around the globe or in scientific reports that lack accessible language; the situation often provokes confusion, distraction, and even denial. Summarizing a recent study in *Nature Climate Change*, Roberts notes that citizens can be moved to take action when extreme weather events and other global warming indicators come interpreted by people they trust. The mushy middle seeks guidance not from scientists, reporters, or activists, but from "more familiar, proximate sources of authority and trust." In other words, jolting the majority out of its slumber and calling it to action in face of climate threat can only be accomplished through the efforts of *ordinary people*, the Victory Speakers of today's crisis. As Roberts urges, "The climate communication effort must prioritize seeding local communities with those kinds of communicators."[18]

Igniting Citizenship and Inspiring Leadership

Climate Victory Speakers confront a profound hurdle not experienced by their wartime predecessors. In World War II, the U.S. government acted with urgency to protect its citizens. In today's world, the requisite frame change concerns *government itself* as the U.S. government (along with other nations) sits idle in response to the greatest threat humanity has ever faced. Scores of officials in countries throughout the world have allied with fossil fuel corporations – the "enemy" as McKibben deliberately uses the term – corporations that hold both the profit motive and the ability to emit pollution capable of destroying Earth's balanced climate system.

Modern Victory Speakers must reignite society's most basic expectation of government, that is, requiring officials to act out of loyalty to citizens. If Abraham Lincoln's famous statement still holds true that "[p]ublic sentiment is everything," citizens must announce an instruction so compelling and a moral duty so stirring that it will inspire government officials to break though political barriers to regulate the most powerful corporations and private profiteers on the planet.[19]

Climate will not stabilize unless government workers themselves emerge as change agents – inside courts, agencies, state and federal legislatures, provincial bodies, city councils, school boards, soil districts, water agencies, and all other forums holding authority. Those sitting within federal and state environmental agencies bear the greatest moral weight, for their position during a time of tipping points carries consequences for the survival and welfare of human beings. Unlike many who stayed quiet and passive in the George W. Bush administration, or who retired all too quietly when they became shocked at the internal corruption, today's climate predicament requires people *on the inside* to take bold action to transform the system, not withdraw from it. It will take immense personal courage to do so, but true leaders will find themselves duty-bound to a higher calling that sounds from this planetary emergency.

Transformative societal change rarely happens, however, without strong pressure also arising from outside government institutions. Changing the frame often means turning civic energy away from the processes fixed in place by the old frame. As Professor Francis Fox Piven, a scholar of social movements, writes, "[A] movement must use its distinctive repertoire of drama and disturbance, of crowds and marches and banners and chants, to raise the issues that are being papered over by normal politics, for the obvious reason that normal politics is inevitably dominated by money and propaganda." When an environmental regulatory agency or a legislature becomes fully captive to industry, avenues of paper democracy (such as letters to Congressmen and comments on proposed agency rule-makings) lose much of their former effectiveness. Piven attributes history-changing movements partly to their exertion of the "kind of power that results from refusing co-operation in the routines that institutionalized social life requires." She elaborates: "That is the power that workers wield when they walk off the job, or that students muster when they refuse to go to class, or that tenants have when [they] refuse to pay the rent, or that urban crowds exert when they block streets and highways."[20]

Peaceful public demonstration remains one of the most highly cherished and fundamental forms of expression. It stays effective precisely because it puts faces on the issue and puts the issue in the faces of elected officials. When conventional processes of citizen democracy become rigged and ineffectual, citizens inevitably turn to street democracy through public protest. Throughout history, major movements have gained unstoppable momentum at this stage. Mahatma Gandhi's famous salt march to the sea, for example, epitomized the populist assertion of public trust rights through civil disobedience. The British government had essentially alienated an asset in the public trust corpus by imposing a heavy tax on salt to benefit corporate interests, thereby preventing the commoners in India from collecting a resource vital for their needs. A nonviolent march led by Gandhi proclaiming public rights to salt grew into a cause joined by thousands. The masses of arrested people ultimately overwhelmed the jails and forced the British government to concede the people's ancient right.[21]

Today, the environmental movement shows clear signs of shifting out of the political frame as climate protests mount worldwide. In the largest climate protest in U.S. history, more than 35,000 citizens marched in the streets of Washington, D.C. on February 17, 2013 to condemn the proposed Keystone XL Pipeline project. Global protests also rise over predatory capitalism and government corruption, both systemic forces behind environmental eradication. The 2011 Occupy protests occurring throughout the United States and other countries took the torch to some of industrial society's "deep institutional lacunae and inconsistencies," as Piven notes. Weston and Bollier observe: "What united the wildly diverse [Occupy] protesters is precisely the conviction that *the system itself is the problem.*" These sweeping insurrections stand poised to force transformative societal change.[22]

To save the planet, an idea must catch this current of social change and spread virally across the globe through all possible forums, both within and outside of existing legal processes. Nature is not a commodity; it comprises a trust endowment to support the survival of present and future generations, and government remains duty-bound to protect and restore it. The public trust embraces an idea whose time, once again, has come.[23]

Modeling Individual Lifestyle Change

Like World War II, the necessary frame change must extend to the individual level. It will do little good to insist on fiduciary performance by government in protecting climate and ecology if adults continue to overconsume resources and devour the assets of their children's natural trust. As Chapter 12 surmised, the trust frame highlights moral values that have guided sustainable societies since time immemorial. Today's Victory Speakers face the crucial task of bringing this frame to a personal level and modeling deep individual lifestyle change.

The universal conservation that marked the World War II effort responded to a fundamental moral call. Once Victory Speakers conveyed to their fellow citizens the need for sending as much food and goods as possible from the home front to the troops, Americans came to understand clearly that the lives of fighting soldiers hinged on daily conservation practices back home. Any waste on the home front became a direct affront to the families that had sent their sons into war. Government posters announced a conservation and home food production campaign with slogans such as "Food is a Weapon; Don't Waste It," "Do With Less So They'll Have Enough," "Can All You Can: It's a Real War Job!" "Your Victory Garden Counts More than Ever!"[24] High-spirited patriotism amplified the call for conservation.

Today's Climate Victory Speakers must once again thrust these moral questions surrounding consumption and waste to the forefront. Just as in times past, the destiny of children and young people hinges, quite profoundly, on lifestyle choices made by adults living today. Describing "the anguish of standing behind a child, looking with her at the road ahead," author Barbara Kingsolver writes: "The truth is so horrific: we are marching ourselves to the maw of our own extinction." But while the moral implications of overconsumption cry out to the future, they remain silenced by a society that takes an altogether demoralized stance toward pollution, materialism, waste, and sheer greed. No longer can personal sacrifices and hard choices be deferred to the future. As Kingsolver says, "When my teenager worries that her generation won't be able to fix this problem, I have to admit to her that it won't be up to her generation. It's up to mine. This is a now-or-never kind of project."[25]

Victory Speakers stand positioned to model old-but-new low-carbon lifestyles that infuse these moral imperatives with practical possibility. In World War II, Victory Speakers taught families how to grow their own food, can and preserve foods, and cook efficiently, among other skills. Victory Speakers lived the changes they urged others to adopt, giving powerful example to Gandhi's famous observation that personal change can help activate social transformation. Today's industrialized society needs the same kind of citizen catalysts to blaze a path away from over-consumption.

Global Relocalization

Finally, today's Victory Speakers inherit the role of leading their fellow citizens in an effort to adapt social and market structures to current imperatives. Climate defense requires a monumental project to "power down" as part of a transition away from fossil fuels (and for developing nations, the project entails steering clear of a fossil-fuel growth trajectory). A movement called *relocalization* presents the best strategy for meeting the 6 percent annual carbon reduction trajectory for climate recovery. It also offers the most practical framework for confronting new ecological realities, through adaptive system change aimed to enhance community resilience and self-sufficiency.[26]

Relocalization seeks to disengage communities from high-carbon global economic dependency, striving instead to build sustainability and self-sufficiency at the local level. Born from an awakening as to the inexorable limits of today's global society, this undertaking promotes place-based resilience. As Raymond De Young and Thomas Princen explain in *The Localization Reader*, "Localization is a process of social change pointing towards localities. Its primary concern is how to adapt institutions and behaviors to live within the limits of natural systems." Across the world, an increasing number of "transition towns" self-identify as communities fully engaged in a "downshift" from the state of overconsumption to sustainable and adaptive living.[27]

Rescaling both production and consumption to the community level, the relocalization effort entails reconfiguring local institutions, economies, and societal structures to provide food, energy, housing, clothing, and transportation through proximate resources as much as possible. Initiatives include, for example, community gardens, local farms, community renewable energy projects, micro-manufacturing enterprises, recommissioned infrastructure for food processing (such as mills and silos), increased public transportation, car-sharing programs, walkable cities, and endless other possibilities. This task brings together entire communities in a common undertaking. As David Orr urges in response to climate crisis, "This is 'all hands on deck' time."[28]

Rob Hopkins, a founder of this movement, points out that relocalization does not amount to "an isolationist process of turning our backs on the global community." To the contrary, it answers needs of local communities in every part of the globe. Hopkins describes relocalization as "communities and nations meeting each other not from a place of mutual dependency, but of increased resilience." Localization does not envision a severance of all trade. International trade remains inevitable, but a growing amount of goods to meet "core needs" will be locally sourced, and the average miles that commodities travel will decline. As Hopkins notes, "There is a far stronger case for importing computers and electronics than apples and chicken."[29]

The relocalization strategy intentionally rejects many harmful dynamics underlying the unsustainable global economy, such as the concentration of economic power in multinational corporations having little or no connection with, or allegiance to, the local community. By shifting society's economic pursuits and power back to the local level, the relocalization strategy incubates many of the forward-looking economic ideas asserted in Chapter 13.

Relocalization creates a path of reconciliation between trust values and daily living. For many, professing environmental values remains much easier than *living* environmental values. The relocalization movement, like wartime mobilization, contextualizes personal behavior in community aims, transforming it from an insignificant drop in the bucket to part of a great undertaking. The act of eating locally becomes an intensely patriotic act.

Localization also envisions opportunities for political innovation by transferring much (though not all) power to the local level and creating "widely distributed leadership and authority." The need for democracy's rebirth within the cradle of localized institutions could not be clearer today as national parties deadlock over anachronistic paradigms, leaving serious problems to worsen in a vacuum of governance. As Eric Liu and Nick Hanauer describe U.S. politics in their book, *Gardens of Democracy*, "Our politics has become an over-rehearsed, over-ritualized, piece of stage combat" between two antiquated ideologies typified by the left and the right. Political rearrangement, in their view, becomes inevitable.[30]

The task of creating new political processes and institutions at the local level requires legal paradigms that rescale to this level. Nature's Trust provides three crucial dimensions to this effort. First, it provides tangible legal principles to guide local decision makers in environmental management and sustainable resource use. The fiduciary standards of protection, no waste, and maximization of societal value, for example, can offer beacons of duty for relocalized decision making.

Second, trust principles provide legal levers by which local communities may assert ecological rights against federal and state environmental agencies (which still hold permitting power under environmental law). Without some legal check, the national environmental decision makers will continue to allow corporations to exploit localities as their resource colonies. Chapter 10 discussed the trust relationships between state and federal governments as co-trustees of shared assets.

Finally, Nature's Trust provides a framework by which local trustees can assess and quantify their global obligations to planetary assets such as the atmosphere. Scaling up and down to match the scope of the ecosystem, a Nature's Trust approach can clarify fiduciary duties toward planetary assets in no less measure than it can duties toward a local wetland. As Chapter 10 suggested, jurisdictions in the United States, for example, bear a fiduciary duty of protecting the atmospheric trust by reducing carbon dioxide emissions by at least 6 percent annually. Without this ability to translate global duties into local responsibilities, the relocalization effort could slip into parochialism and ignore the most important ecological assets of all – the planetary life systems supporting all humanity.

HUMANITY'S QUEST

Terry Tempest Williams writes: "The eyes of the future are looking back at us and they are praying for us to see beyond our own lifetime."[31] Climate crisis calls forth the basic parental responsibility to secure a safe future for our collective children. Human beings have always had the instinct to protect their young. Urgent, singular dangers to children tend to provoke immediate and heroic responses, even from strangers. But reacting to universal climate change and environmental collapse is not as clear as, say, grabbing a toddler before she runs into a busy street or falls into a swift river. The sheer enormity of the challenge can make one feel as if personal actions rank insignificant, even infinitesimal. Looming climate tipping points cause some to think the task impossible.

But understanding a tipping point of a human kind can induce individual action. In his book, *The Tipping Point*, Malcomb Gladwell explains how societal change can advance more rapidly than can be imagined once it reaches a cultural tipping point. Blowing apart conventional ideas of incremental progress, Gladwell explains that society follows "the rules of epidemics" in the pace of social transformation. Some movements seem to take off with astonishing speed simply as a result of actions taken by relatively few citizens. Like epidemics, such social change seems propelled by contagious infection, spreading through society and communities "just like viruses do."[32]

The point is that just a handful of citizens can start a monumental transformation that occurs with awesome speed. Paul Revere's famous midnight ride to Lexington, Virginia, as Gladwell points out, represents a "word-of-mouth epidemic." After learning on April 18, 1775 that the British would make a major move to suppress colonial leaders the next day, Revere jumped on a horse at 10:00 PM with a call to arms: *The British are coming! Spread the word!* By midnight, this legendary hero had triggered the tipping point for revolutionary action. Gladwell recounts: "Church bells started ringing. Drums started beating. The news spread like a virus as those informed by Paul Revere sent out riders of their own, until alarms were going off throughout the entire region." From this 13-mile ride came the American Revolution. Such groundswells and rapid transitions punctuate history. The fall of the Berlin Wall, the World War II mobilization, and the Arab Spring all resulted from viral spread of ideas. The last instruction in a message intended to mobilize society must be "pass it on."[33]

Presenting what he calls the "law of the few," Gladwell asserts that social epidemics commence and spread through the efforts of a "handful of exceptional people." These Paul Reveres of society convey contagious ideas that spread wildly and change the course of history. The impact of these individuals cannot be explained by the amount of time they devote or by the amount of money they spend on a cause. As Gladwell says, "To appreciate the power of epidemics, we have to abandon this expectation about proportionality." The view offers rational payback to citizens who engage a monumental problem such as climate change. Gladwell tells us: "Look at the world around you. It may seem like an immovable, implacable place. It is not. With the slightest push – in just the right place – it can be tipped." We live today at a time in which "the unexpected becomes expected, [and] where radical change is more than possibility. It is a certainty."[34]

HUMANITY'S RESOLVE

Humanity's quest has always been fueled by perseverance. Paul Hawken says, "If you look at the science about what is happening on earth and aren't pessimistic, you don't understand the data. But if you meet the people who are working to restore this earth and the lives of the poor, and you aren't optimistic, you haven't got a pulse." A person with purpose and resolve will not insist on the precise calculus of causation to know his or her role, but will leave much to the mystery of chance, following a deep confidence that innumerable other individuals act and sacrifice out of a similar conviction – one that comes from the common love of children and a reverence for life. Hawken writes that inspiration lies in humanity's persistent and undaunted willingness "to restore, redress, reform, rebuild, recover, reimagine, and reconsider."[35]

Our actions in these next few years will determine the future for our children, their children, and innumerable generations to come. We, the living generation, once had a dependent position in the great wheel of life – not yet born, but with primal expectations nonetheless vested in the hearts of our ancestors, our interests clearly at stake in their decisions. Rather than living life according to Jefferson's great rule that all generations come equally, a generational power now reins in tyranny over the planet and its people. It is a power held in fortune and corruption, exercised through laws at every level that allow the devastation of society's survival resources: the air, the oceans, the forests, the fisheries, the wildlife, the rivers, the aquifers, and the lands.

Humanity's timeless covenant running through the generations finds its highest legal expression in the principled essence of the public trust. We must wake it, teach it, preach it, plant it, enforce it, write it, till it, build it, and all live it now. This fleeting time on Earth calls forth all cultures, peoples, and nations across the world to carry out the sacred promise that has sustained civilization since the dawn of time. Together we hold not the *power* of life, but the *trust* of life.

Notes

References in the book are generally consolidated into endnotes appearing at the end of the paragraph.

PREFACE

1 Mary Christina Wood, Fishtrap Writers' Conference, Wallowa, Oregon, 2005
2 For background on causes of salmon mortality, *see* Mary Christina Wood, *The Tribal Property Right to Wildlife Capital (Part I): Applying Principles of Sovereignty to Protect Imperiled Wildlife Populations*, 37 IDAHO L. REV. 1, 44 (2000). The discussion of salmon management in this Preface refers to all of the species that collectively inhabit the Columbia River Basin, not just chum salmon.
3 For quoted source, *see* Mary Christina Wood, *The Politics of Abundance: Toward a Future of Tribal-State Relations*, 83 OR. L. REV. 1331, 1337 (2004) (quoting NMFS).
4 For a description of the 1994 salmon collapse, *see id.* at 1340.
5 For quoted source, *see* JAMES GUSTAVE SPETH, THE BRIDGE AT THE EDGE OF THE WORLD: CAPITALISM, THE ENVIRONMENT, AND CROSSING FROM CRISIS TO SUSTAINABILITY x (Yale U. Press 2008).
6 *See* Wood, *Politics of Abundance, supra* note 3, at 2. Granted, the Indian population in the basin was a fraction of the present population, but the point remains that the native demand for fish was so great as to necessitate a policy of restraint to prevent the runs from diminishing over time.
7 SPETH, *supra* note 5, at xiii–xiv.

INTRODUCTION: "YOU CAN'T NEGOTIATE WITH A BEETLE"

1 For quoted statements, *see* Oren Lyons, *The Ice Is Melting*, TWENTY-FOURTH ANNUAL E. F. SCHUMACHER LECTURES (New Economics Institute Oct. 2004); Tim Knauss, *Onondaga Faithkeeper Oren Lyons Speaks Out on the Environment: "Business as Usual Is Over,"* POST-STANDARD (Feb. 9, 2008).
2 For an overall description of the environmental crisis, *see* BILL MCKIBBEN, EAARTH: MAKING A LIFE ON A TOUGH NEW PLANET 3–6 (Times Books 2010); *see also* CRAIG COLLINS, TOXIC LOOPHOLES: FAILURES AND FUTURE PROSPECTS FOR ENVIRONMENTAL LAW 238 (Cambridge U. Press 2010). For reporting on oceans, *see* Randolph E. Schmid, *Ocean Dead Zones Become a Worldwide Problem*, BOSTON GLOBE (Aug. 14, 2008); Kenneth R. Weiss, *A Primeval Tide of Toxins*, L.A. TIMES (July 30, 2006); Kenneth R. Weiss, *Dark Tides, Ill Winds*, L.A. TIMES (Aug. 1, 2006); Kenneth R. Weiss, *Dead Zones Off Oregon and Washington Likely Tied to Global Warming, Study Says*, L.A. TIMES (Feb. 15, 2008).

3 *See* Kenneth R. Weiss, *Plague of Plastic Chokes the Seas*, L.A. TIMES (Aug. 2, 2006).

4 For background on ocean fisheries health, *see* MICHAEL W. BECK *ET AL.*, SHELLFISH REEFS AT RISK: A GLOBAL ANALYSIS OF PROBLEMS AND SOLUTIONS 11 (The Nature Conservancy 2009); Weiss, *Primeval Tide, supra* note 2; Boris Worm *et al.*, *Impacts of Biodiversity Loss on Ocean Ecosystem Services*, 314 SCI. 787, 790 (2006) (projecting "the global collapse of all taxa currently fished by the mid-21st century" based on current trends).

5 For quoted source, *see* Roger Highfield, *Greenhouse Gases are Turning Oceans Acidic*, THE TELEGRAPH (May 23, 2008). For additional background, *see* JAMES GUSTAVE SPETH, THE BRIDGE AT THE EDGE OF THE WORLD: CAPITALISM, THE ENVIRONMENT, AND CROSSING FROM CRISIS TO SUSTAINABILITY 1 (Yale U. Press 2008); Charlotte Amalie, *Time Bomb Ticking for Coral Reefs?* MSNBC (Oct. 27, 2006).

6 Weiss, *Primeval Tide, supra* note 2.

7 For quoted source, *see* ELIZABETH KOLBERT, FIELD NOTES FROM A CATASTROPHE: MAN, NATURE, AND CLIMATE CHANGE 189 (Bloomsbury 2006).

8 For quoted sources, *see* SPETH, *supra* note 5, at 1–2, 5, 8, 237; JARED DIAMOND, COLLAPSE: HOW SOCIETIES CHOOSE TO FAIL OR SUCCEED 6–7, 498 (Penguin Books 2005) (emphasis added). For referenced source, *see* MCKIBBEN, EAARTH, *supra* note 2, at 1–3. For a sampling of collapse scholarship, *see* MARK LYNAS, SIX DEGREES: OUR FUTURE ON A HOTTER PLANET (Nat'l Geographic Society 2008); DAVID SPRATT & PHILIP SUTTON, CLIMATE CODE RED: THE CASE FOR EMERGENCY ACTION (Scribe Pub. 2008).

9 THE 11TH HOUR, MOTION PICTURE (Warner Brothers 2007).

10 *See* CAESAR FLAVIUS JUSTINIAN, THE INSTITUTES OF JUSTINIAN WITH ENGLISH INTRODUCTION, TRANSLATION, AND NOTES (Thomas Collett Sandars trans., William S. Hein & Co. 1984).

11 DIAMOND, *supra* note 8, at 23.

12 Richard J. Lazarus, *Environmental Law after Katrina: Reforming Environmental Law by Reforming Environmental Lawmaking*, 81 TULANE L. REV. 1, 22 (2007).

13 For a compilation of many federal environmental statutes, *see* SELECTED ENVIRONMENTAL LAW STATUTES (West 2011–12).

14 For quoted source, *see* James Hansen, *Why We Can't Wait*, THE NATION (May 7, 2007) ("If we do follow that [BAU] path, even for another ten years, it guarantees that we will have dramatic climate changes that produce what I would call a different planet."). For climate science, *see* James Hansen *et al.*, *Climate Change and Trace Gases*, 365 PHIL. TRANS. R. SOC'Y 1925, 1939 (July 15, 2007).

15 *See* Mass. v. EPA, 549 U.S. 497, 510 (2007) (describing petition).

16 For an explanation of ecosystem damage, *see generally* REED F. NOSS *ET AL.*, USGS, ENDANGERED ECOSYSTEMS OF THE UNITED STATES: A PRELIMINARY ASSESSMENT OF LOSS AND DEGRADATION app. A (1995).

17 For quoted source, *see* SPETH, *supra* note 5, at 1. For referenced source, *see* IUCN, 2008 IUCN RED LIST OF THREATENED SPECIES tbl. 1 (2008) (using percentage derived from 44,838 species assessed).

18 *See* WWF, LIVING PLANET REPORT 2008, at 3 (Chris Hails ed., 2008); SPETH, *supra* note 5, at 1; The Worldwatch Inst., VITAL SIGNS 2002, 104 (2002); MILLENNIUM ECOSYSTEM ASSESSMENT, ECOSYSTEMS AND HUMAN WELL-BEING: GENERAL SYNTHESIS, at viii, 6 (José Sarukhán & Anne Whyte, eds., 2005).

19 *See* William B. Meyer, *Present Land Use and Land Cover in the U.S.A.*, CONSEQUENCES: THE NATURE AND IMPLICATIONS OF ENVIRONMENTAL CHANGE 24–33 (1995); COUNCIL ON ENVTL. QUALITY: 21ST ANNUAL REPORT 137 (1990); EPA, TOXICS RELEASE INVENTORY REPORTING YEAR 2007 PUBLIC DATA RELEASE: SUMMARY OF KEY FINDINGS 1 (2007); THEO

COLBORN ET AL., OUR STOLEN FUTURE (Penguin Group 1997); ANNE PLATT MCGINN, WORLDWATCH PAPER #153: WHY POISON OURSELVES? A PRECAUTIONARY APPROACH TO SYNTHETIC CHEMICALS (World Watch Institute 2000); EPA, NAT'L WATER QUALITY INVTRY: RPT. TO CONGRESS, 2004 RPT'ING CYCLE: FINDINGS 9, 13 (2009); BARBARA C. SCUDDER ET AL., U.S. GEOLOGICAL SURV., SCI. INVESTIGATIONS RPT. 2009–5109, MERCURY IN FISH, BED SEDIMENT, AND WATER FROM STREAMS ACROSS THE UNITED STATES, 1998–2005, at 3 (2009).

20 For quoted source, *see* SPETH, *supra* note 5, at 78 (quoting Richard Andrews). *See also* WWF, LIVING PLANET REPORT 2000, at 1 (Jonathan Loh, ed., 2000); PAUL HAWKEN ET AL., NATURAL CAPITALISM: CREATING THE NEXT INDUSTRIAL REVOLUTION 4 (Little, Brown & Co. 1999).

21 *See* Mary Christina Wood, *"You Can't Negotiate with a Beetle:" Environmental Law for a New Ecological Age*, 50 NAT. RESOURCES J. 167, 192 (2010).

22 *See* ROBERT F. KENNEDY JR., CRIMES AGAINST NATURE: HOW GEORGE W. BUSH & HIS CORPORATE PALS ARE PLUNDERING THE COUNTRY & HIJACKING OUR DEMOCRACY 32–33 (Harper Collins 2004); DAVID SCHOENBROD, POWER WITHOUT RESPONSIBILITY: HOW CONGRESS ABUSES THE PEOPLE THROUGH DELEGATION (Yale U. Press 1993); DAVID MICHAELS, DOUBT IS THEIR PRODUCT: HOW INDUSTRY'S ASSAULT ON SCIENCE THREATENS YOUR HEALTH (Oxford U. Press 2008); COLLINS, *supra* note 2, at 3.

23 *See, e.g.*, *Mt. Graham Red Squirrel v. Espy*, 986 F.2d 1568, 1576 (9th Cir. 1993); *Marsh v. Or. Nat. Resources Council*, 490 U.S. 360, 378 (1989); *Chevron U.S.A., Inc. v. Nat. Resources Def. Council*, 467 U.S. 837, 843–844 (1984). *See also* RONALD A. CASS ET AL., ADMINISTRATIVE LAW: CASES AND MATERIALS 216–17 (Little, Brown & Co. 2d ed. 1994).

24 For quoted sources, *see* Hansen *et al.*, *Climate Change*, *supra* note 14, at 1949 ("imminent peril"); Jim Hansen, *The Threat to the Planet*, N.Y. REV. (July 13, 2006) ("transform the planet"). For discussion of projected harm from climate change, *see* Steve Connor, *The Earth Today Stands in Imminent Peril*, THE INDEPENDENT (June 19, 2007); GLOBAL HUMANITARIAN F., THE ANATOMY OF A SILENT CRISIS 9 (2009); Geoffrey Lean, *A World Dying, But Can We Unite to Save It?* THE INDEPENDENT (Nov. 18, 2007); SPRATT & SUTTON, *supra* note 8, at 87–88, 90, 101–02; U.S. GLOBAL CHANGE RESEARCH PROGRAM, GLOBAL CLIMATE CHANGE IMPACTS IN THE UNITED STATES (Thomas Karl *et al.*, eds., Cambridge U. Press 2009); James Hansen, *Huge Sea Level Rises Are Coming – Unless We Act Now*, NEW SCIENTIST (July 25, 2007); KURT M. CAMPBELL ET AL., THE AGE OF CONSEQUENCES: THE FOREIGN POLICY AND NATIONAL SECURITY IMPLICATIONS OF GLOBAL CLIMATE CHANGE 8 (Sharon Burke *et al.*, eds., 2007); Nigel Morris, *Climate Change Could Force One Billion from Their Homes by 2050*, THE INDEPENDENT (Apr. 29, 2008); LYNAS, *supra* note 8, at 180–81; SPETH, *supra* note 5, at 25.

25 For quoted source, *see* Hansen *et al.*, *Climate Change*, *supra* note 14, at 1925 (emphasis added). For explanation of tipping points, *see* FRED PEARCE, WITH SPEED AND VIOLENCE: WHY SCIENTISTS FEAR TIPPING POINTS IN CLIMATE CHANGE 74, 238–39 (Beacon Press 2007); *Ctr. for Biological Diversity v. Nat'l Highway Traffic Safety Admin.*, 508 F.3d 508, 523 (9th Cir. 2007) (noting, "Several studies also show that climate change may be non-linear, meaning that there are positive feedback mechanisms that may push global warming past a dangerous threshold [the 'tipping point']."); James E. Hansen, *Dangerous Human-Made Interference with Climate: Hearing on "Dangerous Global Warming" Before the U.S. House of Representatives Select Committee on Energy Independence and Global Warming*, 110th Cong. 5 (2007) (testimony) ("In the past few years it has become clear that the Earth is close to dangerous climate change, to tipping points of the system with the potential for irreversible deleterious effects."); Seth Borenstein, *Thawing Permafrost Vents Gases to Worsen Warming*, ASSOCIATED PRESS (Nov. 30, 2011); Hansen *et al.*, *Climate Change*, *supra* note 14, at 1 (abstract) ("A climate forcing

that 'flips' the albedo of a sufficient portion of an ice sheet can spark a cataclysm."); U.S. GLOBAL CHANGE, *supra* note 24, at 17.

26 For current levels of CO_2 in the atmosphere, *see* National Oceanic and Atmospheric Administration, *Recent Mauna Loa CO2*, EARTH SYSTEM RESEARCH LABORATORY, http://www.esrl.noaa.gov/gmd/ccgg/trends/; *see also* Geoffrey Mohan, *Carbon Dioxide Levels in Atmosphere Pass 400 Milestone, Again*, L.A. TIMES (May 20, 2013) (reporting levels of 400 parts per million). For historical comparison and future projection, *see* Brief for Dr. James Hansen as *Amicus Curiae* Supporting Petitioners, *Alec L. et al. v. Lisa Jackson et al.*, Case No. 3:11-cv-02203 EMC (N. D. Cal. 2011) at 6, 16 ("The CO_2 concentration is now to a level not seen on Earth for at least 3 million years.") (also noting 2°C in the pipeline, which equates to 3.6°F), http://ourchildrenstrust.org/page/51/federal-lawsuit (follow link to read *James Hansen's Amicus Brief*). For additional explanation, *see* PEARCE, *supra* note 25, at 238–39; SPRATT & SUTTON, *supra* note 8, at 222–33; James Hansen *et al.*, *Target Atmospheric CO2: Where Should Humanity Aim?* 2 OPEN ATMOSPHERIC SCI. J. 217, 221 (Nov. 2008); *Hansen Testimony, supra* note 25, at 12 (warning, "[I]gnoring the climate problem at this time, for even another decade, would serve to lock in future catastrophic climatic change and impacts that will unfold during the remainder of this century and beyond."); INTERGOVERNMENTAL PANEL ON CLIMATE CHANGE, CLIMATE CHANGE 2007: SYNTHESIS REPORT 31–33, 45, 48–53 (2007); U.S. GLOBAL CHANGE, *supra* note 24; ADVANCING THE SCIENCE OF CLIMATE CHANGE 28, 40–41 (Nat'l Academic Press 2010).

27 THOMAS L. FRIEDMAN, HOT, FLAT, AND CROWDED: WHY WE NEED A GREEN REVOLUTION AND HOW IT CAN RENEW AMERICA 44 (Farrar, Straus and Giroux 2008)(citing the scientific society, Sigma XI). For the prescription to cut carbon emissions 6% a year, *see* James Hansen *et. al.*, *Scientific Case for Avoiding Dangerous Climate Change to Protect Young People and Nature*, CORNELL U. LIBRARY, arXiv:1110.1365v3 (Mar. 2012), http://arxiv.org/abs/1110.1365. The prescription is designed to return Earth's energy balance by lowering atmospheric carbon to 350 parts per million (ppm). *See also* Hansen *et al.*, *Target, supra* note 26, at 217 ("If humanity wishes to preserve a planet similar to that on which civilization developed and to which life on Earth is adapted, paleoclimate evidence and ongoing climate change suggest that CO_2 will need to be reduced from its current 385 ppm to at most 350 ppm.... If the present overshoot of this target CO_2 is not brief, there is a possibility of seeding irreversible catastrophic effects.").

28 The scientific climate prescription contains a measure for drawdown of 100 gigatons of carbon through natural forest restoration and soil sequestration. *See* Hansen *et al.*, *Scientific Case*, *supra* note 27.

29 SPETH, *supra* note 5, at 236–37.

30 For quoted sources, *see* Alex Steffen, WORLD CHANGING ("facing two futures"), http://www.worldchanging.com/bios/alex.html; SPETH, *supra* note 5, at xiv; Alex Steffen, *The Real Green Heretics*, WORLD CHANGING (May 28, 2008) ("we argue paper or plastic") (emphasis in original), http://www.worldchanging.com/archives/008064.html.

31 There were 1,443 air permits pending and 1,189 water permits pending. These included ones open for notice and comment.

32 DIAMOND, *supra* note 8, at 498.

33 *See, e.g., Ariz. Ctr. for Law in the Pub. Interest v. Hassell*, 837 P.2d 158, 169 (Ariz. Ct. App. 1991) ("The beneficiaries of the public trust are not just present generations but those to come.").

34 For quoted source, *see Geer v. Connecticut*, 161 U.S. 519, 534 (1896); *see also* GEORGE G. BOGERT *ET AL.*, BOGERT TRUSTS AND TRUSTEES § 582 (West rev. 2nd ed. 1980) ("The trustee has a duty to protect the trust property against damage or destruction."); RESTATEMENT (SECOND) OF TRUSTS § 176 (1959) ("The trustee is under a duty to the beneficiary to use reasonable care and skill to preserve the trust property.").

35 For quoted source, *see* Joseph L. Sax, *The Public Trust Doctrine in Natural Resource Law: Effective Judicial Intervention*, 68 MICH. L. REV. 471, 484 (1970). For characterization of the public trust as a natural right, *see* JOHN CRONIN & ROBERT F. KENNEDY, JR., THE RIVERKEEPERS 141 (Touchstone 1999) ("[P]ublic trust rights are said to derive from 'natural' or God-given law. They cannot be extinguished.").

36 *Ill. Cent. R.R. Co. v. Ill.*, 146 U.S. 387, 455 (1892) (emphasis added) (noting, however, that parcels can be alienated "when parcels can be disposed of without detriment to the public interest in the lands and waters remaining").

37 *Geer*, 161 U.S. at 529. *See also Lake Mich. Fed'n v. U.S. Army Corps of Eng'rs*, 742 F. Supp. 441, 445 (N.D. Ill. 1990) ("[T]he public trust is violated when the primary purpose of a legislative grant is to benefit a private interest.").

38 The English Magna Carta, often cited as a source of the public trust doctrine, forced the British monarchy to open access to resources such as navigable waterways. For discussion, *see* CRONIN & KENNEDY, *supra* note 35, at 139–42; *see also* PETER LINEBAUGH, THE MAGNA CARTA MANIFESTO: LIBERTIES AND COMMONS FOR ALL (U. Cal. Press 2008). The Salt March was in response to Britain's heavy tax and monopoly on salt. Cast in public trust terms, the British government fully alienated an element of the public trust corpus to private interests. Gandhi's nonviolent march to the sea for the purpose of collecting salt drew so many people that the jails overflowed with those arrested, and the British had to change the law. For a summary, *see* Vinay Lal, *Dandi: Salt March*, INDIA AND ITS NEIGHBORS, http://www.sscnet.ucla.edu/southasia/History/Gandhi/Dandi.html.

1. "YOU ARE DOING A GREAT JOB"

1 Press Release, Nat'l Press Club, *An Urgent Call to Action: Scientists and Evangelicals Unite to Protect Creation* (Jan. 17, 2007) (emphasis added).

2 For the authority to regulate, *see* Clean Air Act § 202, 42 U.S.C. § 7401 (2012); Mass. v. EPA, 549 U.S. 497, 528, 533 (2007) (quoting the CAA § 202(a)(1)) (emphasis added); *see also Regulating Greenhouse Gas Emissions Under the Clean Air Act*, 73 Fed. Reg. at 44,355 ("[I]t has become clear that if EPA were to regulate greenhouse gas emissions from motor vehicles under the Clean Air Act, then regulation of [other sources] could also be triggered.").

3 For quoted sources, *see* VERNER E. SUOMI ET AL., CARBON DIOXIDE AND CLIMATE: A SCIENTIFIC ASSESSMENT at viii (Nat'l Acad. of Sciences 1979); George Monbiot, *The Planet Is Now So Vandalised That Only Total Energy Renewal Can Save Us*, THE GUARDIAN (Nov. 28, 2008). For referenced source, *see* Nat'l Climate Program Act, Pub. L. No. 95–367, 92 Stat. 601 (1978) (codified at 15 U.S.C. §§ 2901–2908). *See also* Global Climate Protection Act of 1987, Pub. L. No. 100–204, §§ 1101–1106, 101 Stat. 1407 (1987) (declaring an urgency to act "*in time to protect the climate*") (emphasis added).

4 *See Greenhouse Effect and Global Climate Change: Hearing Before the Sen. Comm. on Energy and Nat. Resources*, 100th Cong. 51–54 (1988) (statement of Dr. James Hansen, Director, NASA Goddard Inst. for Space Studies).

5 *See* AL GORE, AN INCONVENIENT TRUTH: THE PLANETARY EMERGENCY OF GLOBAL WARMING AND WHAT WE CAN DO ABOUT IT 38–41 (2006); *see also* Mass. v. EPA, 549 U.S. at 507.

6 For reporting on the summer of 1988, *see* Liane Hansen & Laura Krantz, *Remembering the 1988 Yellowstone Fires*, NAT'L PUBLIC RADIO (Aug. 31, 2008); Ronald Smothers, *Drought Brings Mississippi Traffic to Slow Crawl*, N.Y. TIMES (June 18, 1988); Keith Schneider, *Drought Disaster Covers 40% of Nation's Counties*, N.Y. TIMES (June 23, 1988); Ralph M. Chite,

Emergency Funding for Agriculture: A Brief History of Congressional Action, 1988-June 1999 (July 19, 1999).

7   Ben Block, *A Look Back At James Hansen's Seminal Testimony On Climate, Part Two*, GRIST (June 18, 2008) (quoting Hansen) (emphasis added).

8   For Hansen's later description of the political interference, *see Political Interference with Government Climate Change Science: Hearing Before the House. Comm. on Oversight and Gov't Reform*, 104th Cong. 3 (Mar. 19, 2007) (statement of James E. Hansen); *see also* HOUSE COMM. ON OVERSIGHT AND GOV'T REFORM, 110TH CONG., RPT. ON POLITICAL INTERFERENCE WITH CLIMATE CHANGE SCIENCE UNDER THE BUSH ADMINISTRATION at i (Dec. 18, 2007).

9   For quoted source, *see* ROBERT F. KENNEDY, JR., CRIMES AGAINST NATURE: HOW GEORGE W. BUSH AND HIS CORPORATE PALS ARE PLUNDERING THE COUNTRY AND HIJACKING OUR DEMOCRACY 96 (HarperCollins 2004); *see also* JEFF GOODELL, BIG COAL: THE DIRTY SECRET BEHIND AMERICA'S ENERGY FUTURE 186–87 (Houghton Mifflin 2007).

10   For quoted source, *see* KENNEDY, CRIMES AGAINST NATURE, *supra* note 9, at 96. *See also* Anne C. Mulkern, *Watchdogs or Lap Dogs? When Advocates Become Regulators*, DENVER POST (May 24, 2004).

11   For quoted treaty, *see* U.N. Framework Convention on Climate Change art. 2, May 9, 1992, Sen. Treaty Doc. No. 102–38, 1771 U.N.T.S. 107.

12   For reporting on Bush's campaign promise, *see* Andrew C. Revkin, *Despite Opposition in Party, Bush to Seek Emissions Cuts*, N.Y. TIMES (Mar. 10, 2001).

13   *See* Mass. v. EPA, 549 U.S. at 510 (summarizing petition and procedural background). *See also* Control of Emissions from New and In-use Highway Vehicles and Engines, 66 Fed. Reg. 7,486 (Jan. 23, 2001) (requesting public comment on petition to regulate auto emissions under the CAA).

14   For quoted source, *see* Revkin, *Despite Opposition*, *supra* note 12 (statement of Ebell). For description of the Whitman statement, *see* GOODELL, *supra* note 9, at 192. For background on Haley Barbour and his letter, *see* Robert F. Kennedy Jr., *For They That Sow the Wind Shall Reap the Whirlwind*, HUFFINGTON POST (Aug. 29, 2005). For a description of ties between ExxonMobil and the Competitive Enterprise Institute, *see* Steven Mufson, *Exxon Mobil Warming Up to Global Climate Issue*, WASH. POST (Feb. 10, 2007). *See also Exxon Blinks in the Global Warming Debate*, CNNMONEY (Sept. 20, 2006).

15   Josh Nelson, *Will the GOP Nominate a Climate Change Denier in 2012?* HUFFINGTON POST (Nov. 18, 2009) (quoting Haley memo). *See also, generally*, JONAS MECKLING, CARBON COALITIONS: BUSINESS, CLIMATE POLITICS, AND THE RISE OF EMISSIONS TRADING (MIT Press 2011).

16   For quoted source, *see* U.S. Dept. of Energy, *Response to Several FOIA* (Freedom of Information Act) *Requests* (Kemp Letter available as pdf), energy.gov/sites/prod/files/maprod/documents/nepdg_12501_12750.pdf. For the Bush turnaround on climate dioxide regulation, *see* Judy Pasternak, *Bush's Energy Plan Bares Industry Clout*, L.A. TIMES (Aug. 26, 2001); Christopher Drew & Richard A. Oppel, *AIR WAR–Remaking Energy Policy; How Power Lobby Won Battle of Pollution Control at EPA.*, N.Y. TIMES (Mar. 6, 2004); GOODELL, *supra* note 9, at 191–201.

17   For quoted source and additional background, *see* KENNEDY, CRIMES AGAINST NATURE, *supra* note 9, at 98–99, 102–05, 111. For background on the energy task force and its plan, *see* GOODELL, *supra* note 9, at 201.

18   *See* Control of Emissions from New Highway Vehicles and Engines, 68 Fed. Reg. 52,922–32 (Sept. 8, 2003) (EPA's review of the public comments and denial of the petition to regulate certain GHG emissions from new automobiles under the CAA).

19   For quoted source, *see* Letter from John Bridgeland, Deputy Assistant to the President for Domestic Policy, and Gary Edson, Deputy Assistant to the President for International

Economic Affairs to Dr. Bruce Alberts, President, National Academy of Sciences (May 11, 2001); Committee on the Science of Climate Change, National Research Council, Climate Change: An Analysis of Some Key Questions 1 (2001) (emphasis added); *see also* Mass. v. EPA, 549 U.S. at 511 (citing NRC report at 1). For a description of the White House's climate deception, *see* Tim Dickinson, *Six Years of Deceit: Inside the Bush Administration's Secret Campaign to Deny Global Warming and Let Polluters Shape America's Climate Policy*, Rolling Stone (Jun. 28, 2007) (asserting that the White House executed an "industry-formulated disinformation campaign designed to actively mislead the American public on global warming and to forestall limits on climate polluters").

20 Political Interference Rpt., *supra* note 8, at i (emphasis added) (also documenting instances of political interference and censorship).

21 For quoted sources, *see* Ross Gelbspan, The Heat is On: The Climate Crisis, the Cover-up, the Prescription 9 (Perseus Books 1998); Political Interference Rpt., *supra* note 8, at 16, 17 (quoting API internal memo); *see also* Ross Gelbspan, Boiling Point: How Politicians, Big Oil and Coal, Journalists, and Activists Have Fueled a Climate Crisis – and What We Can Do to Avert Disaster 263 (Basic Books 2004). For reporting on fossil fuel company profits, *see* Bill McKibben, *Global Warming's Terrifying New Math*, Rolling Stone (July 19, 2012).

22 For quoted source, *see* Andrew C. Revkin, *Bush Aide Softened Greenhouse Gas Links to Global Warming*, N.Y. Times (June 8, 2005).

23 For quoted sources, *see* Ross Gelbspan, *Snowed*, Mother Jones (May/June 2005) ("reposition global warming") (quoting internal strategy documents); Gore, An Inconvenient Truth, *supra* note 5, at 256; Andrew C. Revkin, *Industry Ignored Its Scientists on Climate*, N.Y. Times (Apr. 23, 2009) (quoting Monbiot). For referenced source, *see* Union of Concerned Scientists, *Smoke, Mirrors, and Hot Air: How ExxonMobil Uses Big Tobacco's Tactics to Manufacture Uncertainty on Climate Science* 29 (2007). For additional discussion on industry strategy, *see* Political Interference Rpt., *supra* note 8, at ii.

24 For quoted source, *see* UCS, *Smoke, Mirrors*, *supra* note 23, at 1. For further description of the industry's climate skeptics, *see* Goodell, *supra* note 9, at 181; Seth Shulman, Undermining Science: Suppression and Distortion in the Bush Administration 24 (U. of Cal. Press 2008).

25 For quoted sources, *see* Ross Gelbspan, The Heat Is On, *supra* note 21, at 9; Chris Mooney, The Republican War on Science 80 (Basic Books 2005) (quoting the editor-in-chief of *Science*, Donald Kennedy); Revkin, *Industry Ignored*, *supra* note 23 (emphasis added) (quoting 1995 industry document); *see also* Juliet Eilperin, *Industries Buried Internal Findings: Climate Wording Cut From Public Report*, Wash. Post (Apr. 25, 2009).

26 For quoted sources, *see* UCS, *Smoke, Mirrors*, *supra* note 23, at 2; Political Interference Rpt., *supra* note 8, at 17, 33 (stating also, "The White House ... sought to minimize the significance and certainty of climate change by *extensively editing* government climate reports") (emphasis added). For description of Cooney's role, *see* Dickinson, *supra* note 19 ("Now, with Cooney in the White House, the industry had its own anti-climate man running the disinformation campaign.").

27 For a full exposé on CEI's response to the *U.S. Climate Action Report*, *see* Dickinson, *supra* note 19; UCS, *Smoke, Mirrors*, *supra* note 23, at 21–22; Shulman, *supra* note 24, at 22. Ebell's e-mail came to light in 2003 as a result of a Freedom of Information Act request by Greenpeace.

28 For the quoted Ebell e-mail, *see* UCS, *Smoke, Mirrors*, *supra* note 23, app. C, at 57 (emphasis added). For discussion, *see* Dickinson, *supra* note 19; Greenpeace Int'l, *Greenpeace Obtains Smoking-Gun Memo: White House/Exxon Link*, Greenpeace (Sept. 9, 2003),

http://www.greenpeace.org/international/news/investigation-of-exxon-front-g; SHULMAN, *supra* note 24, at 24–25.

29 For quoted sources, *see* Andrew C. Revkin, *U.S. Report Turns Focus to Greenhouse Gases*, N.Y. TIMES (Aug. 26, 2004) (quoting President Bush); POLITICAL INTERFERENCE RPT., *supra* note 8, at 16; Dickinson, *supra* note 19 (quoting Cooney's draft letter and reporting on the administration's – and specifically Cooney's – response to the Climate Action Report).

30 For a source quoting O'Keefe and providing a full exposé of the incident, *see* Dickinson, *supra* note 19. At the time of the letter, O'Keefe was associated with the George C. Marshall Institute. As Dickinson interpreted the handwritten postscript from O'Keefe, it was a "pat on the back" for Cooney from his old boss. *Id.* O'Keefe's original letter to the White House Chief of Staff, Andrew Card, carried a formal tone, seemingly indicating that the informal postscript was added into the faxed version to Cooney. But even if it was in the original and directed to Card, the postscript would have carried the same implications as to government-industry intimacy. The fax to Cooney was obtained through a Freedom of Information Act request by Greenpeace, but the original letter to Card was not available, so it remains uncertain at what stage the postscript was added. The O'Keefe letter is described in Decl. of Rick S. Piltz in Support of Memo of *Amici Curiae* John F. Kerry and Jay Inslee at 17, par. 36–37, Center for Biological Diversity v. Brennon, No. C06–7062 (SBA) (N. D. Cal., Feb. 7, 2007) (attaching O'Keefe letter as Exhibit I), http://www.biologicaldiversity.org/programs/climate_law_institute/fighting_climate_science_suppression/enforcing_national_assessment_of_climate_change/pdfs/Piltz-Declaration.pdf.

31 For quoted sources, *see* POLITICAL INTERFERENCE RPT., *supra* note 8, at 18–19; Dickinson, *supra* note 19.

32 For quoted source and background, *see* POLITICAL INTERFERENCE RPT., *supra* note 8, at 22 (quoting Mar. 4, 2003 e-mail).

33 For quoted sources, *see* Dickinson, *supra* note 19; POLITICAL INTERFERENCE RPT., *supra* note 8, at 21–25.

34 For quoted sources and a full account of the EPA response to White House edits, *see* POLITICAL INTERFERENCE RPT., *supra* note 8, at 21–25. For reporting, *see* Duncan Campbell, *White House Cuts Global Warming from Report*, THE GUARDIAN (June 20, 2003); *Climate Change Research Distorted and Suppressed*, UNION OF CONCERNED SCIENTISTS (June 30, 2005); *EPA's Whitman Submits Resignation Letter*, CNN (May 21, 2003).

35 For mortality statistics during the European heat wave, *see* WORLD HEALTH ORGANIZATION, IMPROVING PUBLIC HEALTH RESPONSES TO EXTREME WEATHER/HEAT-WAVES–EUROHEAT, MEETING RPT. 6 (2007). For the relationship between heat waves and global warming, *see Heatwaves are Proof of Global Warming, Says NASA Scientist*, INDEP. (Aug. 5, 2012).

36 For reporting on the aftermath of the European heat wave, *see* Amelia Gentleman, *400 Victims of Heatwave Unclaimed*, THE GUARDIAN (Aug. 25, 2003). For EPA's denial, *see* Control of Emissions from New Highway Vehicles and Engines, 68 Fed. Reg. 52,922–02 (Sept. 8, 2003). For the U.S. share of global emissions at the time, *see* GORE, AN INCONVENIENT TRUTH, *supra* note 5, at 250.

37 For reporting on Connaughton's role, *see* POLITICAL INTERFERENCE RPT., *supra* note 8, at 29. Some of Connaughton's involvement was in late June, just before Whitman's resignation was effective, but other rounds of editing came after she left. Whitman's resignation became effective June 27, 2003. *EPA Chief Christine Whitman Steps Down*, PBS ONLINE NEWSHOUR (May 21, 2003).

38 For the quoted source and reporting on the CEQ edits, *see* POLITICAL INTERFERENCE RPT., *supra* note 8, at 28–29, 31. For the EPA rule, *see* Control of Emissions from New Highway Vehicles and Engines, 68 Fed. Reg. at 52,930.

39 For the quoted EPA rule, *see* 68 Fed. Reg. at 52,930. For quoted CEQ edits and reporting on EPA's initial draft of the petition denial and subsequent edits, *see* POLITICAL INTERFERENCE RPT., *supra* note 8, at 30–31. For quoted *amicus* brief, *see* Brief of *Amici Curiae* Climate Scientists David Battisti *et al.* in Support of Petitioners at 21, 22, Mass. v. EPA, 549 U.S. 497 (2006) (emphasis added), http://docs.nrdc.org/globalWarming/files/glo_06083101G.pdf.

40 For quoted source, *see Mass. v. EPA*, 549 U.S. at 510 (quoting 1998 legal opinion). On the same day EPA issued the petition denial, it issued a new legal opinion, called the Fabricant Memo. That memo, issued by Robert E. Fabricant, EPA's General Counsel, overturned the earlier legal opinion and concluded that EPA did not have authority to regulate greenhouse gases under the Clean Air Act. *See* POLITICAL INTERFERENCE RPT., *supra* note 8, at 28–29. For EPA's legal reasoning behind its decision not to regulate, *see* Control of Emissions from New Highway Vehicles and Engines, 68 Fed. Reg. at 52,927–29; *Mass. v. EPA*, 549 U.S. at 512–13. For reporting on Jeffrey Holmstead, *see* Mulkern, *supra* note 10.

41 For a summary of the states' position challenging EPA's denial, *see Mass. v. EPA*, 549 U.S. at 505 n.2; Final Brief for the Petitioners in Consolidated Cases at 2–3, Mass. v. EPA, 433 F.3d 66 (C.A.D.C. 2005) (Nos. 03–1361), 2005 WL 257460, *rev'd* 549 U.S. 497 (2007). For commentary on Barbour, *see* Kennedy, *For They That Sow*, *supra* note 14.

42 For quoted source, *see* Geoffrey Lean, *Global Warming Approaching Point of No Return, Warns Leading Climate Expert*, INDEP. (Jan. 23, 2005) (quoting Pachauri).

43 For quoted sources, *see* Revkin, *Bush Aide Softened*, *supra* note 22 ("an air of doubt"); Andrew C. Revkin, *Ex-Bush Aide Who Edited Climate Reports to Join ExxonMobil*, N.Y. TIMES (June 15, 2005) ("great job"). *See also* Andrew C. Revkin, *Editor of Climate Reports Resigns*, N.Y. TIMES (June 10, 2005). Rick Piltz, a senior researcher with the Climate Change Science Program (the agency that produced reports that Cooney edited) resigned on March 2, 2005. On June 1, Piltz sent a devastating fourteen-page letter to agency principals summarizing Cooney's intervention with scientific processes.

44 For the quoted D.C. court opinion, *see* Mass. v. EPA, 415 F.3d. 50, 57 (D.C. Cir. 2005). For the referenced Congressional investigation, *see* POLITICAL INTERFERENCE RPT., *supra* note 8, at 27–31.

45 For quoted source, *see Mass. v. EPA*, 549 U.S. at 522 n.18 (emphasis added) (describing and quoting Declaration of Michael MacCracken, Former Executive Director of U.S. Global Change Research Program). For reported damage from Hurricane Katrina, *see* U.S. DEP'T OF COM. & NAT'L OCEANIC & ATMOSPHERIC ADMIN., SERV. ASSESSMENT: HURRICANE KATRINA, AUG. 23–31, 2005 (June 2006). For the 2005 hurricane count, *see* Nat'l Oceanic & Atmospheric Admin. (NOAA), *State of the Climate, Hurricanes & Tropical Storms, Annual 2005*, NOAA NAT'L CLIMATIC DATA CTR. (Dec. 2005).

46 For quoted source, *see* Jim Hansen, *Climate Change: On the Edge*, INDEP. (Feb. 17, 2006).

47 For quoted sources, *see* INTERGOVERNMENTAL PANEL ON CLIMATE CHANGE, CLIMATE CHANGE 2007: SYNTHESIS REPORT: SUMMARY FOR POLICYMAKERS 2 (2007) (emphasis added); *see also* Press Release, *United Nations Environment Programme, Evidence of Human-Caused Global Warming "Unequivocal," says IPCC* (Feb. 2, 2007); *Mass. v. EPA*, 549 U.S. at 513 (quoting petition denial); Control of Emissions From New Highway Vehicles and Engines, 68 Fed. Reg. at 52,930. For reporting on the American Enterprise Institute award, *see* Ian Sample, *Scientists Offered Cash to Dispute Climate Study*, THE GUARDIAN (Feb. 1, 2007).

48 For quoted case, *see Mass. v. EPA*, 549 U.S. at 504–05, 528–30 & n. 29.

49 For quoted case, *see id.* at 532–33.

50 For quoted source, *see* Hansen, *Political Interference Testimony, supra* note 8, at 4, 8, 10 (emphasis added). For referenced Congressional report and proceedings, *see* POLITICAL INTERFERENCE RPT., *supra* note 8, at i, 4 (noting that the investigation had been ongoing for sixteen months). One hearing was held in January and one in March; *see Committee Holds Hearing on Political Influence on Government Climate Change Scientists*, COMM. ON OVERSIGHT & GOV'T REFORM. For reporting on Hansen's 2006 testimony on political interference, *see* Andrew C. Revkin, *Climate Expert Says NASA Tried to Silence Him*, N.Y. TIMES (Jan. 26, 2006). For the Union of Concerned Scientists' statement, *see* UNION OF CONCERNED SCIENTISTS, *The A to Z Guide to Political Interference in Science*.

51 For quoted case, *see Mass. v. EPA*, 549 U.S. at 535. For the remanded case, *see Mass. v. EPA*, 249 F. App'x 829, 829 (D.C. Cir. 2007).

52 *Dangerous Human-Made Interference with Climate: Testimony of James E. Hansen to Select Committee on Energy Independence and Global Warming, U.S. House of Representatives*, at 3, 17–18 (Apr. 26, 2007).

53 For an account of proposed coal-fired plants, *see* NAT'L ENERGY TECH. LAB., TRACKING NEW COAL-FIRED POWER PLANTS: COAL'S RESURGENCE IN ELECTRIC POWER GENERATION (May 1, 2007).

54 For a description of melting, *see* Al Gore, Op-Ed., *Moving Beyond Kyoto*, N.Y. TIMES (July 1, 2007); Thomas Homer-Dixon, Op-Ed., *A Swiftly Melting Planet*, N.Y. TIMES (Oct. 4, 2007).

55 James Hansen *et al.*, *Climate Change and Trace Gases*, 365 PHIL. TRANS. R. SOC'Y. 1925, 1939 (July 15, 2007) (emphasis added).

56 For explanation of 450 ppm, *see Understanding 350: FAQs (Frequently Asked Questions)*, 350.ORG (response to "[a]nd what about all the other targets people are aiming for?"), http://www.350.org/en/node/48. For Hansen's testimony using the 450 ppm target, *see* Hansen, *Dangerous Interference Testimony, supra* note 52, at 17.

57 Gore, *Moving Beyond Kyoto, supra* note 54.

58 For quoted source, *see* Seth Borenstein, *"The Arctic is Screaming"–Summer Sea Ice Could Be Gone in Five Years*, SEATTLE TIMES (Dec. 11, 2007) (emphasis added). *See also* Alister Doyle, *Artic Thaw May be at "Tipping Point,"* REUTERS (Sept. 28, 2007).

59 For quoted source, *see* Michael Milstein, *Greenland Ice Melt Shocks Scientists*, THE OREGONIAN (Sept. 9, 2007). For effects of sea level rise, *see* Thomas Wagner, *Millions at Risk from Rising Sea Levels*, USA TODAY (Mar. 29, 2007); Nell Greenfieldboyce, *Study: 634 Million People at Risk from Rising Seas*, NPR (Mar. 28, 2007).

60 For quoted source, *see* Seth Borenstein, *Scientists Hopeful Despite Climate Signs*, WASH. POST (Sept. 23, 2007); *see also* Tracy L. Barnett, *James Hansen Embodies the "Never-Give-Up Fighting Spirit,"* HUFFINGTON POST (Dec. 9, 2009).

61 For an account of the Kingsnorth action, *see* Geraldine Bedell, *Why Six Britons Went to Eco War*, THE GUARDIAN (May 30, 2009).

62 For quoted source, *see* Letter from Roderick L. Bremby, Secretary of the Kan. Dept. of Health and Envtl., to Mr. Wayne Penrod, Senior Manager of Sunflower Electric Power Corp. (Oct. 18, 2007) (emphasis added), *in* Protestant's Response, Ex. 7, In the Matter of Basin Elec. Power Co. (No. 07–2801), at 89, http://deq.state.wy.us/eqc/orders/Air%20Closed%20Cases/07–2801%20 Dry%20Fork%20Station/Protestants'%20EXHIBITS%201–7.pdf. For explanation of subsequent legislative action, *see* Robert L. Glicksman, *Coal-Fired Power Plants, Greenhouse Gases, and State Statutory Substantial Endangerment Provisions: Climate Change Comes to Kansas*, 56 KAN. L. REV. 517, 518, 565–67 (2008). For general reporting on the Kansas permit denial, *see* Matthew L. Wald, *Citing Global Warming, Kansas Denies Plant Permit*, N.Y. TIMES (Oct. 20, 2007); Steven Mufson, *Power Plant Rejected Over Carbon Dioxide for First Time*, WASH. POST A1 (Oct. 19, 2007).

63 For quoted source, *see* POLITICAL INTERFERENCE RPT., *supra* note 8, at 12 (quoting D. Gerberding); *see also* Andrew C. Revkin, *White House Cuts to Climate Testimony Raise Questions*, N.Y. TIMES (Oct. 25, 2007).

64 For the back-story on Dr. Gerberding's testimony, *see* POLITICAL INTERFERENCE RPT., *supra* note 8, at 12; H. Josef Hebert, *Cheney Wanted Cuts in Climate Change Testimony*, USA TODAY (July 8, 2008) (also reporting the White House's official explanation for the deletions). According to Burnett, Cheney's office and the White House Council on Environmental Quality worried that testimony by key health officials about global warming's consequences on public health or the environment could make it more difficult to avoid regulating carbon dioxide and other greenhouse gases. Hebert, *supra*.

65 For Hansen's testimony, *see Direct Testimony of James Hansen*, In re Interstate Power and Light Company (Iowa Utils. Bd., 2007) (No. GCU-07-1). For an account of Hansen's out-reach efforts, *see* Lisa Sorg, *James Hansen Won't Be Quiet: NASA Scientist Calls for 10-year Moratorium on Coal-Fired Power Plants*, INDYWEEK (Dec. 5, 2007).

66 For quoted source, *see* Hansen Testimony, *Interstate Power*, *supra* note 65, at 3.

67 For quoted source, *see id.* at 3 (emphasis added). Hansen was referring to plants that do not sequester carbon dioxide. While technology to achieve carbon sequestration from coal-fired plants remains a theoretical possibility, it has not reached a stage of general feasibility, and many doubt that it ever will.

68 For referenced source, *see* IPCC SYNTHESIS RPT., *supra* note 47, at 30, 50–52, 69. For background reporting, *see* Elisabeth Rosenthal, *U.N. Report Describes Risks of Inaction on Climate Change*, N.Y. TIMES (Nov. 17, 2007).

69 Rosenthal, *supra* note 68.

70 For quoted sources, *see* Rosenthal, *supra* note 68 (emphasis added to Pachauri's quote).

71 For quoted source and other references, *see* Joseph Romm, *Desperate Times, Desperate Scientists*, SALON (Dec. 12, 2007). For reference on global heating, *see* McKibben, *New Math*, *supra* note 21 (noting potentially 0.8°C heating in the pipeline as a result of existing atmospheric CO_2).

72 For quoted source, *see Q&A: Bali Conference "Very Much a Make or Break."* INTER PRESS SERV. (Nov. 24, 2007) (quoting Yvo de Boer, Exec. Sec'y of the U.N. Framework Conv. on Climate Change (UNFCCC)).

73 For quoted source, *see* Al Gore, *Nobel Lecture* (Dec. 10, 2007) (transcript).

74 For a summary of the AGU agenda, *see* American Geophysical Union, *Agenda, AGU Fall Meeting*, 10–14 December 2007.

75 Ross Gelbspan, *It's Too Late to Stop Climate Change, Argues Ross Gelbspan – So What Do We Do Now?* GRIST (Dec. 11, 2007) (later posting of earlier e-mail) (emphasis added).

76 For Bali reporting, *see* Andrew C. Revkin, *Bali Update: "Non-Paper" a Nonstarter for U.S.*, N.Y. TIMES DOT EARTH (Dec. 11, 2007); Thomas Fuller & Peter Gelling, *Deadlock Stymies Global Climate Talks*, N.Y. TIMES (Dec. 12, 2007); Charles J. Hanley, *U.S. Faces New Demands at Bali Talks*, USA TODAY (Dec. 12, 2007); Richard Lloyd Parry, *U.S. Rejects Climate Guidelines at Bali Conference*, THE TIMES (Dec. 13, 2007); Amanda Beck, *Carbon Cuts a Must to Halt Warming – U.S. Scientists*, REUTERS (Dec. 13, 2007); Thomas Fuller & Elizabeth Rosenthal, *Gore Joins Chorus Chiding U.S. at Climate Talks*, N.Y. TIMES (Dec. 14, 2007); Juliet Eilperin, *Europeans Raise Ante at Bali Climate Talks*, WASH. POST (Dec. 14, 2007); Thomas Fuller & Andrew C. Revkin, *U.S. Reversal Leads to Bali Climate Accord*, SEATTLE TIMES (Dec. 16, 2007).

77 For quoted source, *see* Bill McKibben, *Remember This: 350 Parts Per Million*, WASH. POST (Dec. 28, 2007). For background and description of Hansen presentation, *see NASA at 2007 Fall American Geophysical Union Meeting: Scientific Presentations*, NASA (Dec. 10, 2007);

Rajendra Pachauri Endorses 350 ppm, Not As IPCC Chair But "as a Human Being," THINK PROGRESS (Aug. 25, 2009), http://thinkprogress.org/climate/2009/08/25/204549/ipcc-chair-rajendra-pachauri-350-ppm-bill-mckibben/; Mason Inman, *Global Warming "Tipping Points" Reached, Scientist Says,* Nat'l Geographic News (Dec. 14, 2007); DAVID SPRATT & PHILLIP SUTTON, CLIMATE CODE RED: THE CASE FOR A SUSTAINABILITY EMERGENCY 27 (Scribe Pub. 2008).

78 Al Gore, *Address to the International Summit on Climate Change in Bali* (Dec. 13, 2007); *see also* Catherine Brahic, *Al Gore Tells Bali the Inconvenient Truth on U.S.,* NEW SCIENTIST ENVT. (Dec. 13, 2007).

79 For reporting on Gore's appearance, *see* Richard Harris & Robert Siegel, *Gore Condemns U.S. Stance at Climate Talks,* NPR's ALL THINGS CONSIDERED (Dec. 13, 2007).

80 For summary of Bali outcome, *see* Juliette Jowit, Caroline Davies & David Adam, *Late-Night Drama Pushes U.S. into Climate Deal,* THE GUARDIAN (Dec. 16, 2007).

81 For reporting on the suppressed endangerment finding, *see* Dina Cappiello, *EPA Chief Won't Explain Climate Choices,* HUFFINGTON POST (July 24, 2008); Juliet Eilperin, *EPA E-Mail Concluded Global Warming Endangers Public Health, Senator Says,* WASH. POST A19 (July 25, 2008); John Shiffman & John Sullivan, *An Eroding Mission at EPA,* PHILADELPHIA INQUIRER (Dec. 2, 2008); Felicity Barringer, *White House Refused to Open Pollutants E-Mail,* N.Y. TIMES (June 25, 2008); Jim Tankersley & Alexander C. Hart, *Bush-Era EPA Document on Climate Change Released,* L.A. TIMES (Oct. 14, 2009); *see also* Juliet Eilperin & R. Jeffrey Smith, *EPA Won't Act on Emissions This Year,* WASH. POST A1 (July 11, 2008).

82 *See Jason Burnett, Bush Official Who Just Resigned, to Aid Obama,* HUFFINGTON POST (July 6, 2008); Erica Werner, *Ex-EPA Official Critical on Climate Change,* HUFFINGTON POST (June 5, 2008); Cappiello, *supra* note 81.

83 Letter from Stephen P. Johnson, Administrator, U.S. EPA, to President George W. Bush (Jan. 31, 2008); *see also* David Doniger, *Bush's Johnson Stood up for Climate,* GRIST (Feb. 10, 2011).

84 For quoted source, *see* Ian Talley & Siobhan Hughes, *White House Blocks EPA Emissions Draft,* WALL ST. J. (June 30, 2008). *See also* Press Release, House Select Committee on Energy Independence and Global Warming, *Markey: On Global Warming Decision, White House Hacks Slash While Planet Burns* (July 11, 2008) (detailing progression of drafts of rule-making).

85 For quoted sources, *see* David A. Fahrenthold & Juliet Eilperin, *Warming is Major Threat to Humans, EPA Warns,* WASH. POST A01 (July 18, 2008) ("emphasize the complexity") (quoting Jason Burnett, describing the Administration's directive to EPA); Eilperin & Smith, *supra* note 81 ("To defer compliance"). For the Advance Notice, *see* Regulating Greenhouse Gas Emissions Under the Clean Air Act, 73 Fed. Reg. 44,354–01 (July 30, 2008). For EPA's stance regarding regulation, *see* Preface, Regulating Greenhouse Gas Emissions from the Clean Air Act, *supra* at 44,355.

86 For referenced and quoted report, *see* U.S. CLIMATE CHANGE SCIENCE PROGRAM, ANALYSES OF THE EFFECTS OF GLOBAL CHANGE ON HUMAN HEALTH AND WELFARE AND HUMAN SYSTEMS (Sept. 2008); *See also* Press Release, Environmental Protection Agency, EPA Releases Report on Climate Change and Health (July 17, 2008). For reporting and commentary on the Desert Rock plant and Holmstead, *see* Nellis Kennedy & Winona LaDuke, *Opportunity Knocks But It's Not Desert Rock,* NAVAJO TIMES (June 18, 2009); Ana Unruh Cohen, *Holmstead Resigns,* GRIST (July 20, 2005); Ted Holteen, *N.M. Tries to Stop Desert Rock Permit,* DURANGO HERALD (July 11, 2008). In April 2009, the Obama administration pulled the permit. According to one report, "EPA found that the permitting process was issued prematurely, before complete analysis could be conducted...." Marjorie Childress, *EPA Pulls the Plug on Desert Rock Coal-Fired Power Plant,* N.M. INDEP. (Apr. 28, 2009).

87 For quoted source, *see* Michael Wolkind, *How We Won Acquittal of Kingsnorth Six*, THE GUARDIAN (May 31, 2009).

88 For reporting on the trial, *see* John Vidal, *Not Guilty: The Greenpeace Activists Who Used Climate Change as a Legal Defence*, THE GUARDIAN (Sept. 11, 2008).

89 For quoted source, *see id*; *see also* Wolkind, *supra* note 87.

90 For quoted source, *see* Paul Vitello, *Gore's Call to Action*, N. Y. TIMES: THE CAUCUS (Sept. 24, 2008). Gore's appeal was confined to plants that did not use carbon capture and storage technology. *See* Matthew Knight, *Gore Calls for Coal Plant Protests*, CNN (Sept. 25, 2008). For reporting on Australia actions, *see* 25 Arrested at NSW Power Station Protest, SYDNEY MORNING HERALD (Nov. 1, 2008) (the Bayswater Power Station); *Protesters Chained to Collie Power Conveyor*, W. AUSTRALIAN (Nov. 5, 2008); Protesters Target Hazelwood Power Station, ABC NEWS (Nov. 6, 2008); *Police Arrest Tarong Power Protesters*, ABC NEWS (Nov. 7, 2008); *Climate Activists Disrupt Australian Power Plant*, REUTERS (Nov. 10, 2008) (the Tarong Power Station).

91 For Bjerknes Lecture and abstract, *see* James Hansen, NASA Goddard Institute for Space Studies, Bjerknes Lecture at the American Geophysical Union Fall Meeting: Threat to the Planet: Dark and Bright Sides of Global Warming (Dec. 17, 2008). For the referenced paper, *see* James Hansen *et al.*, *Target Atmospheric CO2: Where Should Humanity Aim?* 2 OPEN ATMOSPHERIC SCI. J. 217 (Nov. 2008).

92 For reporting on the endangerment finding, *see* Aaron Wiener, *As Copenhagen Talks Open, EPA Issues Endangerment Finding*, WASH. INDEP. (Dec. 7, 2009); Dina Cappiello & H. Josef Hebert, *EPA Says Greenhouse Gases Endanger Human Health*, REAL CLEAR POLITICS (Dec. 8, 2009) ("The EPA and the White House have said regulations on greenhouse gases will not be imminent even after an endangerment finding, saying that the administration would prefer that Congress act to limit such pollution through an economy-wide cap on carbon dioxide and other greenhouse gases.").

93 For quoted source, *see* Geoffrey Lean, *Copenhagen: The Lessons We Are Being Forced to Learn*, THE TELEGRAPH (Dec. 12, 2009) (quoting the Group of 77's Lumumba Stanislaus Di-Aping). For additional reporting on Copenhagen, *see* Colin Freeman, *Copenhagen Climate Summit: 1,000 Anarchists Arrested*, THE TELEGRAPH (Dec., 12, 2009).

94 For quoted source, *see* Steve Connor, *Father of Climate Change: 2C Limit Is Not Enough*, INDEP. (Dec. 8, 2011) (quoting Jim Hansen at the 2011 United Nations Climate Change Conference in Durban, South Africa); *see also* McKibben, *Remember This*, *supra* note 77 (quoting Jim Hansen). For lobbying figures, *see* Dan Shapley, *Fossil Fuel Industry Outspending Clean Energy by Nearly 7 to 1*, THE DAILY GREEN (Aug. 31, 2009). For reporting on Obama's offer and other nations' pledges, *see* Suzanne Goldenberg, *Obama Offers Copenhagen Little Hope*, THE GUARDIAN (Dec. 18, 2009); John Heilprin, *U.N. Says Nations' Greenhouse Gas Pledges Too Little*, U.S. NEWS & WORLD RPT. (Feb. 1, 2010); Suzanne Goldenberg & Allegra Stratton, *Barack Obama's Speech Disappoints and Fuels Frustration at Copenhagen*, THE GUARDIAN (Dec. 18, 2009). The reductions Obama mentioned were 17%, but those were calibrated to a 2005 baseline, so they were inflated in comparison to the 1990 baseline that most other countries followed. The actual reduction in relation to 1990 baselines was only 3–4%. *Climate Pledges Made By Countries Before Summit*, SEATTLE TIMES (Dec. 7, 2009).

95 Pat Parenteau, Op., *Is the Durban Platform a Suicide Pact?* VTDIGGER.ORG (Dec. 20, 2011).

96 For temperature reporting, *see* Brad Lendon, *2012 Hottest Year on Record, Federal Agency Says*, CNN.COM (Sept. 18, 2012). Following the endangerment finding, EPA was required to regulate greenhouse gas emitters, but it did so in slow and incremental fashion. For background, *see* EPA, FACT SHEET: FINAL RULE–PREVENTION OF SIGNIFICANT DETERIORATION AND TITLE V OPERATING PERMIT GREENHOUSE GAS (GHG) TAILORING RULE STEP 3 AND

GHG PLANTWIDE APPLICABILITY LIMITS 1–2 (2012). For criticism of the Obama administration's climate policy during the president's first term, *see* Tim Ream, *Climate Crisis Worsens While We Wait for Action*, REGISTER-GUARD (Jan. 25, 2013).

97 For quoted source and explanation of the 6% reduction prescription, *see* Brief for Dr. James Hansen as *Amicus Curiae* Supporting Petitioners, Alec L. et al. v. Lisa Jackson et al., Case No. 3:11-cv-02203 EMC (N. D. Cal. 2011) (emphasis added), http://ourchildrenstrust.org/sites/default/files/Hansen%20Amicus%20.pdf. Atmospheric Trust Litigation is coordinated by the group, Our Children's Trust. The litigation documents and expert declarations are located at the group's Web site, http://ourchildrenstrust.org/. A list of experts and greater detail of the litigation is provided in Chapter 10.

98 Monbiot, *supra* note 3.

2. MODERN ENVIRONMENTAL LAW: THE GREAT LEGAL EXPERIMENT

1 *See* Noah Adams, *Virginia Strip-Mining Death Brings Reforms*, NPR (Feb. 7, 2005); Erik Reece, *Moving Mountains: The Battle for Justice Comes to the Coal Fields of Appalachia*, ORION (Jan.–Feb. 2006); Brandon Keim, *Blowing the Top Off Mountaintop Mining*, WIRED (Sept. 10, 2007).

2 ROBERT F. KENNEDY, JR., CRIMES AGAINST NATURE: HOW GEORGE W. BUSH & HIS CORPORATE PALS ARE PLUNDERING THE COUNTRY & HIJACKING OUR DEMOCRACY 115 (HarperCollins 2004).

3 For quoted source, *see* KENNEDY, *supra* note 2, at 114. For reporting on mountaintop removal, *see* John M. Broder, *Rule to Expand Mountaintop Coal Mining*, N.Y. TIMES (Aug. 23, 2007); Jeff Biggers, *The Coalfield Uprising*, THE NATION (Oct. 19, 2009); Rob Perks, *Mountaintop Mining in Virginia's Blue Ridge?* NAT. RESOURCES DEF. COUNCIL STAFF BLOG (Aug. 27, 2009).

4 For a history of coal mining in Appalachia, *see* JAMES S. LYON ET AL., MINERAL POLICY CTR., BURDEN OF GILT: THE LEGACY OF ENVIRONMENTAL DAMAGE FROM ABANDONED MINES, AND WHAT AMERICA SHOULD DO ABOUT IT 4 (June 1993).

5 For quoted source, *see* Laura Parker, *Mining Battle Marked by Peaks and Valleys*, USA TODAY (Apr. 19, 2007) (quoting attorney Joe Lovett). For descriptions of the mountaintop removal practice, *see* KENNEDY, *supra* note 2, at 115; Reece, *supra* note 1; Juliet Eilperin, *EPA to Scrutinize Permits for Mountaintop-Removal Mining*, WASH. POST (Mar. 25, 2009).

6 For reporting on protestors, *see* Reece, *supra* note 1 (picture dated May 31, 2005). For descriptions of environmental and health effects of coal mining, *see* Margaret A. Palmer *et al.*, *Mountaintop Mining Consequences*, 327 SCI. 148 (2010); Michael Hendryx & Melissa M. Ahern, *Mortality in Appalachian Coal Mining Regions: The Value of Statistical Life Lost*, PUB. HEALTH RPTS. 541 (2009); Ben Adducchio, *PA DEP: Mine Discharges Contributed to Dunkard Fish Kill*, W. VA. PUB. BROAD. (Oct. 16, 2009); KENNEDY, *supra* note 2, at 116; Reece, *supra* note 1.

7 For quoted source, *see* Jeff Biggers, *Breaking: EPA Clears Waterboarding Permits for Appalachia*, THE HUFFINGTON POST BLOG (May 15, 2009). The federal agencies involved in mountaintop removal are the President's Council on Environmental Quality (CEQ), the EPA, the U.S. Army Corps of Engineers, the Department of the Interior, and the Office of Surface Mining Reclamation and Enforcement. Multiple state agencies also have jurisdiction over mountaintop removal. For statistics on number of fills, *see* Reece, *supra* note 1. In January 2011, EPA issued its first veto of a mountaintop removal permit. *See* Jeff Biggers, *Breaking: EPA Vetoes Largest Mountaintop Removal Permit: New Era of Civility in the Coalfields?* THE HUFFINGTON POST BLOG (Jan. 13, 2011). The veto, however, was later overturned in court. *See* Mingo Logan Coal Co. v. U.S. EPA, 850 F. Supp. 2d 133 (D.D.C. 2012).

8 For referenced source, *see* KENNEDY, *supra* note 2, at 43. For statutory requirements, *see* Clean Water Act § 101, 33 U.S.C. § 1251(a)(1)(2006) ("[I]t is the national goal that the discharge of

pollutants into the navigable waters be eliminated by 1985."); Nat'l Forest Mgt. Act of 1976, 16 U.S.C. § 1600 (1976); Endangered Species Act of 1973, 16 U.S.C. § 1531 (1973); Jack Lewis, *The Birth of EPA*, EPA JOURNAL (Nov. 1985) (discussing original Clean Air Act requirements).

9 DEVRA DAVIS, WHEN SMOKE RAN LIKE WATER: TALES OF ENVIRONMENTAL DECEPTION AND THE BATTLE AGAINST POLLUTION 91, 97 (Basic Books 2002).

10 For referenced source, *see id.* at 94 (describing Ruckleshaus's observation). For quoted sources, *see* DAVID MICHAELS, DOUBT IS THEIR PRODUCT: HOW INDUSTRY'S ASSAULT ON SCIENCE THREATENS YOUR HEALTH 51, 100 (Oxford U. Press 2008); *see also* DAVIS, *supra* note 9, at 100; JAMES GUSTAVE SPETH, THE BRIDGE AT THE EDGE OF THE WORLD: CAPITALISM, THE ENVIRONMENT, AND CROSSING FROM CRISIS TO SUSTAINABILITY 78 (Yale U. Press 2008).

11 *Id.* at 83. For a brief discussion of the constitutional tripartite system, *see* 9 WEST'S ENCYCLOPEDIA OF AMERICAN LAW, SEPARATION OF POWERS 109–11 (Shirelle Phelps & Jeffrey Lehman eds., 2d ed. 2005).

12 CRAIG COLLINS, TOXIC LOOPHOLES: FAILURES AND FUTURE PROSPECTS FOR ENVIRONMENTAL LAW 2 (Cambridge U. Press 2010). For discussion of agency capture, *see generally* Richard B. Stewart, *The Reformation of American Administrative Law*, 88 HARV. L. REV. 1667 (1975); JAMES BUCHANAN & GORDON TULLOCK, THE CALCULUS OF CONSENT: LOGICAL FOUNDATIONS OF CONSTITUTIONAL DEMOCRACY (U. of Mich. Press 1965).

13 For an explanation of common law, *see* 3 WEST'S ENCYCLOPEDIA OF AMERICAN LAW, COMMON LAW 30–31 (Shirelle Phelps & Jeffrey Lehman eds., 2d ed. 2004).

14 For referenced sources, *see* Ill. Cent. R.R. Co. v. Ill., 146 U.S. 387, 455 (1892); Ga. v. Tenn. Copper Co., 206 U.S. 230, 237 (1907).

15 For discussion of nuisance and its relationship to modern environmental law, *see* 4 WEST'S ENCYCLOPEDIA OF AMERICAN LAW, ENVIRONMENTAL LAW 170 (Shirelle Phelps & Jeffrey Lehman eds., 2d ed. 2005); Christine Meisner Rosen, *"Knowing" Industrial Pollution: Nuisance Law and the Power of Tradition in a Time of Rapid Economic Change, 1840–1864*, 8 ENVTL. HISTORY 565 (2003); Alexandra B. Klass, *Common Law and Federalism in the Age of the Regulatory State*, 92 IOWA L. REV. 545, 547–49 (2007). For the elements of nuisance, *see* RESTATEMENT (SECOND) OF TORTS § 821D (1979).

16 For background on modern laws, *see* Robert V. Percival, *Separation of Powers, the Presidency, and the Environment*, 21 J. LAND RESOURCES & ENVTL. L. 25, 32, 35 (2001).

17 For general discussion of permitting process, *see, e.g.*, ROBERT V. PERCIVAL ET AL., ENVIRONMENTAL REGULATION: LAW, SCIENCE, AND POLICY 799 (2d ed., Aspen Publ's 1996).

18 For explanation of the nuisance test, *see* 4 WEST'S ENCYCLOPEDIA, *supra* note 15, at 170–71.

19 For quoted case, *see* Am. Mining Cong. v. U.S. Envtl. Prot. Agency, 824 F.2d 1177, 1189 (D.C. Cir. 1987) (referencing RCRA). For a statutory compilation, *see* SELECTED ENVIRONMENTAL LAW STATUTES: 2011–2012 EDUCATIONAL EDITION (Thomson West ed., 2012). For discussion of industry lobbying in EPA, *see, e.g.*, Robert Dreyfuss, *Toxic Cash: How Lobbyists Poisoned the EPA*, THE AMERICAN PROSPECT (Nov. 19, 2001); Sonya Lunder & Jane Houlihan, *EPA Axes Panel Chair at Request of Chemical Industry Lobbyists*, ENVTL. WORKING GRP. (Mar. 2008), http://www.ewg.org/reports/decaconflict.

20 For referenced source, *see* CHARLES F. WILKINSON, CROSSING THE NEXT MERIDIAN: LAND, WATER, AND THE FUTURE OF THE WEST 209 (Island Press 1992).

21 For jurisdictional background on Columbia River fisheries regulation and management, *see* Mary Christina Wood, *Fulfilling the Executive's Trust Responsibility Toward the Native Nations on Environmental Issues: A Partial Critique of the Clinton Administration's Promises and Performance*, 25 ENVTL. L. 733, 762–70 (1995).

22 Paul VanDevelder, *Saving the Columbia and Snake River Salmon*, L.A. TIMES (July 6, 2009).

23 Clean Water Act § 101, § 404, 33 U.S.C. § 1251(a), § 1344(a)(2006). For detailed analysis of several environmental programs, *see* COLLINS, *supra* note 12. For discussion of Clean Water Act

permitting as it applies to mountaintop removal in Appalachia, *see* Biggers, *EPA Vetoes, supra* note 7; Renee Schoof, *EPA Holds Up 79 Permits for Appalachian Surface Mines*, Phys.org (Sept. 15, 2009).

24 For discussion of regulatory loopholes, *see* Collins, *supra* note 12.

25 For quoted sources, *see* Collins, *supra* note 12, at 2; David Schoenbrod, Power without Responsibility: How Congress Abuses the People through Delegation 14, 59 (Yale U. Press 1993).

26 For discussion of discretion, *see id.* at 49.

27 For a description of forest ecosystems and their pressures, *see* Susan M. Stein et al., U.S. Dep't of Agric., Forest Serv., National Forests on the Edge: Development Pressures on America's National Forests and Grasslands 2 (2007). For an account of the Forest Service's liquidation policy, *see* Sierra Club v. Hardin, 325 F. Supp. 99, 122–24 (D. Alaska 1971); Paul W. Hirt, A Conspiracy of Optimism: Management of the National Forests since World War Two, at xliv (U. of Neb. Press 1994).

28 For referenced case, *see* W. Va. Div. of the Izaac Walton League of Am. v. Butz, 367 F. Supp. 422 (N.D. W. Va. 1973). For referenced statute, *see* Nat'l Forest Mgt. Act of 1976 § 6, 16 U.S.C. § 1604 (1976). For discussion of NFMA and its impetus, *see* Federico Cheever, *Four Failed Forest Standards: What We Can Learn from the History of the National Forest Management Act's Substantive Timber Management Provisions*, 77 Or. L. Rev. 601, 620 (1998); Charles F. Wilkinson, *The National Forest Management Act: The Twenty Years Behind, the Twenty Years Ahead*, 68 U. Colo. L. Rev. 659 (1997).

29 Cheever, *supra* note 28, at 606; *see also id.* at 644 (discussing discretion).

30 For quoted case, *see* Seattle Audubon Soc'y v. Evans, 771 F. Supp. 1081, 1089–90 (W.D. Wash.), *aff'd*, 952 F.2d 297 (9th Cir. 1991). For discussion of forest destruction under the NFMA, *see generally* U.S. Dep't of Agric., Sustaining the People's Lands: Recommendations for Stewardship of the National Forests and Grasslands into the Next Century (1999); Cheever, *supra* note 28.

31 For estimate of remaining old growth, *see* Seattle Audubon Soc'y v. Lyons, 871 F. Supp. 1291, 1301 (W.D. Wash. 1994).

32 For quoted source, *see* Oliver A. Houck, *The Endangered Species Act and Its Implementation by the U.S. Departments of Interior and Commerce*, 64 U. Colo. L. Rev. 277, 317 (1993); *see also* Daniel J. Rohlf, *Jeopardy Under the Endangered Species Act: Playing a Game Protected Species Can't Win*, 41 Washburn L.J. 114, 151 n.153 (2001); Collins, *supra* note 12, at 141. For statistics on wetlands permits, *see* Jeffrey A. Zinn & Claudia Copeland, CRS Issue Brief for Congress: Wetland Issues, at CRS-6 (2006).

33 For referenced statute, *see* Clean Water Act § 101, § 402, 33 U.S.C. § 1251(b), § 1342(b)(1)(B) (2006). For discussion of statutory requirements, *see* Mary Christina Wood, *EPA's Protection of Tribal Harvests: Braiding the Agency's Mission*, 34 Ecology L.Q. 175, 181 (2007). For reporting on permit violations and expired permits, *see Biggest U.S. Water Polluters Not Punished*, Envtl. News Serv. (May 28, 2001). For a summary of EPA's administrative policy for dealing with permits, *see NPDES Frequently Asked Questions*, U.S. Envtl. Prot. Agency, http://cfpub.epa.gov/npdes/allfaqs.cfm?program_id=0#80.

34 For quoted source, *see* Kennedy, *supra* note 2, at 126. For additional discussion of harm from coal-fired plants, *see Deadly Power Plants? Study Fuels Debate*, NBCNews.com (June 9, 2004); Davis, *supra* note 9, at 121; Michaels, *supra* note 10, at 177.

35 For reporting on 2011 mercury standard, *see* Neela Banerjee, *EPA Issues Strong Limits on Mercury Emissions from Smokestacks*, L.A. Times (Dec. 21, 2011); Neela Banerjee, *Obama Faces a Battle on Air Rules*, L.A. Times (Dec. 22, 2011). For discussion of harm from mercury, *see Mercury: Human Exposure*, U.S. Envtl. Prot. Agency (Feb. 7, 2012), http://www.epa.gov/mercury/exposure.htm.

36 U.S. GOV'T ACCOUNTABILITY OFFICE, CHEMICAL REGULATION: OBSERVATIONS ON IMPROVING THE TOXIC SUBSTANCES CONTROL ACT 4 (2009). For a description of the EPA chemical review process, *see* David Ewing Duncan, *Chemicals Within Us*, NAT'L GEOGRAPHIC.

37 For discussion of Atrazine, *see* Charles Duhigg, *Debating How Much Weed Killer Is Safe in Your Water Glass*, N.Y. TIMES, Aug. 22, 2009; Jennifer Beth Sass & Aaron Colangelo, *European Union Bans Atrazine, While the United States Negotiates Continued Use*, 12 INT'L J. OCCUPATIONAL & ENVTL. HEALTH 260 (2006); KENNEDY, *supra* note 2, at 91–92; MAE WU ET AL., NAT. RESOURCES DEF. COUNCIL, STILL POISONING THE WELL: ATRAZINE CONTINUES TO CONTAMINATE SURFACE WATER AND DRINKING WATER IN THE UNITED STATES (2010), http://www.nrdc.org/health/atrazine/files/atrazine10.pdf.

38 For quoted source, *see* Charles Duhigg, *Millions in U.S. Drink Dirty Water, Records Show*, N.Y. TIMES (Dec. 8, 2009).

39 For quoted source, *see* COLLINS, *supra* note 12, at 70. For quoted case, *see* McElmurray v. U.S. Dep't of Agric., 535 F. Supp. 2d 1318, 1333 (S.D. Ga. 2008). For additional reporting and analysis on harm from sewage sludge, *see* Caroline Snyder, *The Dirty Work of Promoting "Recycling" of America's Sewage Sludge*, 11 INT'L J. OCCUPATIONAL & ENVTL. HEALTH 415, 415 (2005), http://www.sludgefacts.org/IJOEH_1104_Snyder.pdf; John Heilprin & Kevin S. Vineys, *Did Pollutants Used as Fertilizer Kill Cattle?* NBCNEWS.COM (Mar. 6, 2008); Ellen Z. Harrison & Summer Rayne Oakes, *Investigation of Alleged Health Incidents Associated with Land Application of Sewage Sludges*, 12 NEW SOLUTIONS 387 (2002) (concluding "that surface-applied Class B sludges present the greatest risk and should be eliminated"); Josh Harkinson, *Sludge Happens*, MOTHER JONES (May/June 2009); COLLINS, *supra* note 12, at 71.

40 For quoted sources, *see* Rohlf, *supra* note 32, at 151 (the "Services" referenced by Rohlf are the U.S. Fish and Wildlife Serv. and the Nat'l Marine Fisheries Serv.); Nat'l Wildlife Fed'n v. Nat'l Marine Fisheries Serv., 481 F.3d 1224, 1239 (9th Cir. 2007); Houck, *supra* note 32, at 321.

41 For discussion of enforceability of NEPA promises, *see* Daniel R. Mandelker, NEPA Law and Litigation, Ch. 4, § VII, § 4:67, pp. 4–307 through 4–309 (2d. ed. West 2012). See also Ogunquit Village Corp. v. Davis, 553 F.2d 243, 245 (1st Cir. 1977).

42 For statistics on listed species, *see* U.S. FISH & WILDLIFE SERV., SPECIES REPORTS: DELISTING REPORT. For general analysis of the ESA, *see* Robert L. Fischman, *Predictions and Prescriptions for the Endangered Species Act*, 34 ENVTL. L. 451, 471 (2004). For an explanation of the jeopardy evaluation, *see* Mary Christina Wood, *Protecting the Wildlife Trust: A Reinterpretation of Section 7 of the Endangered Species Act*, 34 ENVTL. L. 605 (2004).

43 THEODOR SEUSS GEISEL, THE LORAX (Random House 1971).

44 For discussion of the fish consumption standard, *see* Wood, *Braiding*, *supra* note 33, at 186.

45 For referenced source, *see* MICHAELS, *supra* note 10. For an example of the administrative risk assessment approach, *see* U.S. ENVTL. PROT. AGENCY, METHODOLOGY FOR DERIVING AMBIENT WATER QUALITY CRITERIA FOR THE PROTECTION OF HUMAN HEALTH § 2.4 (2000). For analysis of EPA's approach, *see* NATIONAL RESEARCH COUNCIL, SCIENCE AND DECISIONS: ADVANCING RISK ASSESSMENT (2009), U.S. ENVTL. PROT. AGENCY, NAT'L ENVTL. JUSTICE ADVISORY COUNCIL, FISH CONSUMPTION AND ENVIRONMENTAL JUSTICE 58–61 (2002); Albert C. Lin, *The Unifying Role of Harm in Environmental Law*, 2006 WISC. L. REV. 897 (2006).

46 For referenced source, *see* Cornelia Dean, *Panel Seeks Changes in EPA. Reviews*, N.Y. TIMES (Dec. 4, 2008).

47 For cancer statistics, *see* NAT'L CANCER INST., SEER CANCER STATISTICS REVIEW 1973–1990 (Barry A. Miller *et al.* eds., 1993); AM. CANCER SOC'Y, *Cancer Facts & Figures 2009* 1 (2009).

48 *See* MICHAELS, *supra* note 10 at 97–109.

3. THE POLITICS OF DISCRETION

1 Oliver A. Houck, *On the Law of Biodiversity and Ecosystem Management*, 81 MINN. L. REV. 869, 928–29 (1997).

2 *Id.* at 928 & n.366. *See also* Osha Gray Davidson, *The Bush Legacy: An Assault on Public Protections*, OMB WATCH, 23 (2009). For a full account of captured agency behavior across the major U.S. federal pollution programs, *see* CRAIG COLLINS, TOXIC LOOPHOLES: FAILURES AND FUTURE PROSPECTS FOR ENVIRONMENTAL LAW (Cambridge U. Press 2010).

3 Whitman v. Am. Trucking Assoc., 531 U.S. 457, 474–75 (2001) (quoting Mistretta v. U.S., 488 U.S. 361, 416 (1989)); *see also* Charles H. Koch, Jr., 3 ADMIN. L. & PRAC. § 12.13 (2d ed. 1997).

4 For quoted source, *see* COLLINS, *supra* note 2; *see also* DEVRA DAVIS, WHEN SMOKE RAN LIKE WATER: TALES OF ENVIRONMENTAL DECEPTION AND THE BATTLE AGAINST POLLUTION (Basic Books 2002). For regulatory history of lead in gasoline, *see* Kevin Drum, *How Did Lead Get into Our Gasoline Anyway?* MOTHER JONES (Jan. 7, 2013).

5 For quoted sources, *see* DAVID SCHOENBROD, POWER WITHOUT RESPONSIBILITY: HOW CONGRESS ABUSES THE PEOPLE THROUGH DELEGATION 55–57 (Yale U. Press 1993); Oliver A. Houck, *The Endangered Species Act and Its Implementation by the U.S. Departments of Interior & Commerce*, 64 U. COLO. L. REV. 277, 326–27, 358 (1993). For general discussion of industry influence, *see* NAOMI ORESKES & ERIK M. CONWAY, MERCHANTS OF DOUBT: HOW A HANDFUL OF SCIENTISTS OBSCURED THE TRUTH ON ISSUES FROM TOBACCO SMOKE TO GLOBAL WARMING (Bloomsbury Press 2010).

6 *See* Clean Water Act 404(a), 33 U.S.C. § 1344 (2006). For materials discussing the scope of wetlands regulation and key terms under section 404, *see* William H. Rodgers, Jr., § 4:12. *Section 404 – Disposal of Dredged and Fill Material: Theory and Background; Navigable Waters; Judicial Review*, 2 ENVTL. L. § 4.12 (2012); Patrick Parenteau, *Anything Industry Wants: Environmental Policy under Bush II*, 14 DUKE ENVTL. L. & POL'Y F. 363, 380 (2004).

7 Parenteau, *supra* note 6, at 363. For further discussion of the Bush administration changes in policy, *see* ROBERT F. KENNEDY, JR., CRIMES AGAINST NATURE: HOW GEORGE W. BUSH AND HIS CORPORATE PALS ARE PLUNDERING THE COUNTRY AND HIJACKING OUR DEMOCRACY (HarperCollins 2004); SETH SHULMAN, UNDERMINING SCIENCE: SUPPRESSION AND DISTORTION IN THE BUSH ADMINISTRATION (U. of Cal. Press 2008); MARK BOWEN, CENSORING SCIENCE: INSIDE THE POLITICAL ATTACK ON DR. JAMES HANSEN AND THE TRUTH OF GLOBAL WARMING (Penguin Group 2008). For an empirical study of rule-making during political transitions, *see* Anne Joseph O'Connell, *Political Cycles of Rulemaking: An Empirical Portrait of the Modern Administrative State*, 94 VA. L. REV. 889, 891 (2008).

8 For a discussion of the mercury rules, *see* Robert F. Kennedy, Jr., *Keynote Address: We Must Take America Back*, 22 J. ENVTL. L. & LITIG. 201, 211 (2007); COLLINS, *supra* note 2, at 47. The Union of Concerned Scientists reports that the Bush mercury rule contained "no fewer than 12 paragraphs lifted, sometimes verbatim, from a legal document prepared by industry lawyers." Union of Concerned Scientists, *EPA Ignored Science When Regulating Power Plant Mercury Emissions* http://www.ucsusa.org/scientific_integrity/abuses_of_science/mercury-emissions. html. The Bush mercury rule was eventually overturned in court. *See* Robin Bravender, *Bush Rules on Toxic Mercury from Power Plants Overturned*, SCI. AM. (FEB. 23, 2009). In 2011, the Obama administration issued a new mercury rule. *See* Neela Banerjee, *Obama Faces a Battle on Air Rules*, L.A. TIMES (Dec. 22, 2011). For discussion of New Source Review Requirements affecting dinosaur plants, *see* Parenteau, *supra* note 6, at 373–75; COLLINS, *supra note 2*, at 42–48. For a discussion of rules on coal-fired plants near national parks, *see* Juliet Eilperin, *EPA Proposal Would Ease Clean-Air Rules for National Parks*, WASH. POST (NOV. 19, 2008).

9 For relevant forest laws, *see* 16 U.S.C. §§ 6515(a)-(c) (pre-decisional administrative review process); 16 U.S.C. § 6554(a) (categorical exclusion for certain logging and clear-cutting termed "applied silvicultural assessments"); 16 U.S.C. §§ 6514(a)-(c) (crippling action alternatives

analysis, the heart of NEPA). For analysis of Healthy Forest Initiative, *see* JAN G. LAITOS ET AL., NATURAL RESOURCES LAW 434–37 (Thompson West 2006). For the roadless rule, *see* 70 Fed. Reg. 25, 654 (May 13, 2005); *see also* Felicity Barringer, *Judge Voids Bush Policy on National Forest Roads,* N.Y. TIMES (Sept. 21, 2006). For discussion of changes to regional forest protection, *see* LAITOS ET AL., *supra*; *see also* Glen Martin, *Sierra Protection Plan Under Review; Bush May Loosen Logging Restrictions,* SAN FRAN. CHRON. (Feb. 4, 2003).

10 On the arsenic rule, *see* KENNEDY, *supra* note 7, at 53–56; Douglas Jehl, *E.P.A. to Abandon New Arsenic Limits for Water Supply,* N.Y. TIMES (Mar. 21, 2001). For a discussion of changes to wetlands regulation, *see* Parenteau, *supra* note 6, at 378–81. For a discussion of the fill rule, *see* KENNEDY, *supra* note 7, at 138. For the stream buffer rule, *see* 73 Fed. Reg. 75, 814 (Dec. 12, 2008). The stream buffer rule had a contorted history that still unfolds. *See* General Accountability Office, GAO-10-206, *Surface Coal Mining 2010,* p. 3, n. 5 (Jan. 2010).

11 For a discussion of the midnight regulations, *see* Christine A. Klein, *The Environmental Deficit: Applying Lessons from the Economic Recession,* 51 ARIZ. L. REV. 651, 663 n. 76, 680 (2009); Joaquin Sapien & Jesse Nankin, *Midnight Regulations,* PROPUBLICA (Nov. 18, 2008).

12 For a discussion of how the midnight rules fared after Bush left office, *see* Kathlyn Stone, *Obama Overturns Bush Midnight Rules on Science, Health Care,* DIGITAL J. (Mar. 5, 2009).

13 For the goal of water pollution programs, *see* Clean Water Act (CWA), 33 U.S.C.A. § 1251(a)(2) (West 2012) ("[I]t is the national goal that wherever attainable, an interim goal of water quality which provides for the protection and propagation of fish, shellfish, and wildlife and provides for recreation in and on the water be achieved by July 1, 1983."); *see also* Kan. Nat. Resource Council, Inc. v. Whitman, 255 F. Supp. 2d 1208 (D. Kan. 2003) (noting that the Clean Water Act "has a goal of achieving 'fishable/swimmable' waters ... wherever possible"). Generally an activity falls under the 402 program or the 404 program, but not both. *See* 40 C.F.R. § 122.3(b) (2008) (discharge of dredge or fill material subject to 404 permitting is excluded from 402 NPDES permitting).

14 For quoted source, *see* KENNEDY, *supra* note 7, at 138. For the "fill rule," *see* 67 Fed. Reg. 31,129 30 (May 9, 2002) (defining "fill material" to include "material placed in waters of the U.S. [that] has the effect of ... [c]hanging the bottom elevation of any portion of a water," and including "'placement of ... slurry, or tailings or similar mining-related materials'."). The effluent limitations weave through the statute. For a discussion, *see* Environmental Protection Agency, *Detailed Guidance: Improving EPA Review of Appalachian Surface Coal Mining Operations* 4–7 (Apr.1, 2010). The limitation for gold mines is found at New Source Performance Standards (NSPS), 40 C.F.R. § 440.104(b)(1). The EPA had developed an earlier limitation for gold and other mines back in 1975, at which point it became illegal to dump untreated mine tailings directly into the waters. *See* 40 Fed. Reg. 51,748 (Nov. 6, 1975). As to 404 permits, they do have to comply with standards called the 404(b)(1) guidelines, but those are far more amorphous and discretionary than numerical effluent limitations. For explanation, *see* EPA *Detailed Guidance, supra,* at 17–18. On their face, however, even the guidelines prohibit activity that would significantly degrade a waterway. *Id.* That requirement has long been ignored by the agencies in the case of mountaintop removal. And while another provision of the Clean Water Act (§ 401) gives states the power to stop federal permits by finding that they fail to meet state water quality standards, the state environmental agencies usually do not lift their regulatory hammer against politically favored industries. For a discussion of section 401, *see id.* at 4; 40 C.F.R. § 131.4(2012).

15 For referenced case and description of allowed mining waste, *see* Coeur Alaska, Inc. v. Southeast Alaska Conservation Council, 557 U.S. 261, 267, 271, 297 (2009) (Ginsberg, J., dissenting).

16 For quoted sources, *see* SEN. RPT. NO. 92–414, 7 (1971); *Coeur Alaska,* 557 U.S. at 302–03 (J. Ginsberg, dissenting) (emphasis added). The Clean Water Act sets forth its policy of pollution elimination in 33 U.S.C. § 1251(a)(1). The mine could have operated at another site using a

dry tailings disposal area that did not entail a water discharge (although that option would have been more costly). *See* Letter from Sierra Club *et al.* to President Barak Obama re: the Fill Rule 2 (July 17, 2009), seacc.org/mining/.../GreenGrouplettertoPresidentObama7172009.pdf.

17 For quoted source, *see* KENNEDY, *supra* note 7, at 117 (also reporting $20 million in campaign contributions to President Bush and other Republicans in 2000, and then another $21 million thereafter, by coal-mining companies and coal-burning utilities). For a discussion of the permitting context of mountaintop removal, *see* EPA *Detailed Guidance*, *supra* note 14, at 4. EPA guidance also indicates that discharges from sediment ponds and any "other stormwater discharges" require section 402 permits, but this clearly does not encompass the fill itself that piles into and destroys the streambeds. The stream buffer rule is altogether separate from the fill rule, and it derives from a different statute, The Surface Mining Control and Reclamation Act. The rule prohibits, with some exceptions, surface mining activities that would disturb land within 100 feet of a perennial or intermittent stream. 30 C.F.R § 816.57. The prohibition applies to mountaintop removal. However, the U.S. Department of Interior attempted to do away with this rule. *See* 73 Fed. Reg. 75, 814 (2008). The rule was challenged in Nat'l Parks Conserv. Ass'n v. Salazar, 660 F. Supp. 2d 3 (D.C. Cir. 2009). Subsequently, the parties settled the case pending release of a new rule, which, as of January 2013, had not yet been released. In the interim, the stream buffer rule remains in effect and provides a limitation to mountaintop removal by requiring, with some exceptions, that mining waste shall not be released within 100 feet of perennial or intermittent streams. However, this rule protects only "perennial or intermittent streams," so that mining waste, including overburden, can presumably be placed in other waters (lakes, ponds, etc.).

18 For quoted source, *see* KENNEDY, *supra* note 7, at 131, 138. For additional reporting, *see* Osha Gray Davidson, *The Ungreening of America: Dirty Secrets*, MOTHER JONES (Sept.–Oct. 2003); NPR, *Former Official Ordered to Prison in Abramoff Scandal* (June 27, 2007). For full background on the lawsuit that created pressure for a fill rule, *see* Mark Baller & Leor Joseph Pantilat, *Defenders of Appalachia: The Campaign to Eliminate Mountaintop Removal Coal Mining and the Role of Public Justice*, 37 ENVTL. L. 629, 644–45. The fill rule was issued as the district court was drafting its opinion in the pending litigation. Judge Haden found that the rule violated the Clean Water Act. *See id.* at 645–46; Kentuckians for the Commonwealth, Inc. v. Rivenburgh (Kentuckians I), 204 F. Supp. 2d 927, 946 (S.D. W.Va. 2002); Kentuckians for the Commonwealth, Inc. v. Rivenburgh, 206 F. Supp. 2d 782, 791 (S.D. W.Va. 2002) (summarizing earlier holding). On appeal, the Fourth Circuit overruled the district court judge and vacated the opinion. *See* Baller & Pantilat, *supra*, at 646. The fill rule, it should be noted, was originally proposed by the Clinton administration, which also favored mountaintop removal. The rule was never finalized, because of substantial public opposition. The Bush administration finalized the rule, but with substantial changes that gave leniency to industry. For a history, *see* Claudia Copeland, Cong. Research Serv., *Mountaintop Mining: Background on Current Controversies* 5–6 (Aug. 1, 2002).

19 For quoted source, *see* Lynne Peeples, *Water Pollution Regulations Underestimate Fish Consumption, Endangering Public Health*, HUFFINGTON POST (Nov. 17, 2011) (quoting Professor O'Neill). For the Clean Water Act standard, *see* CWA § 1251(a)(2). For human health criteria regarding fish consumption, *see* *Revised National Recommended Water Quality Criteria for the Protection of Human Health*, EPA (Dec. 2003). For fish consumption data, *see* EPA, *Estimated Per Capita Fish Consumption in the United States*, 4–6 (Aug. 2002). A typical six-ounce can of tuna contains one ounce of water or oil and five ounces of fish.

20 For quoted source, *see* Jeff Ruch, *Endangered Species Act Implementation: Science or Politics?: Oversight Hearing Before the House Natural Resources Committee*, 32–42 (2007) (testimony

of Jeff Ruch, Exec. Dir. of Publ. Employees for Envtl. Resp.), http://www.peer.org/assets/docs/doi/07_9_5_peer_testimony.pdf. For additional background on the Hall policy, *see* Union of Concerned Scientists, *Scientists Challenge Restrictions on Use of Genetic Studies for Endangered Species Review*, http://www.ucsusa.org/scientific_integrity/abuses_of_science/endangered-species-genetics.html.

21 For quoted source, *see* Holly Doremus, *Science Plays Defense: Natural Resource Management in the Bush Administration*, 32 ECOLOGY L.Q. 249, 267 (2005); *see also id.* at 261, 286–87 (explaining risk choice in regulatory decisions). For the ESA standard, *see* 16 U.S.C. § 1533(b)(1)(A). For a discussion of risk choice in toxics regulation, *see* Wendy E. Wagner, *The Science Charade in Toxic Risk Regulation*, 95 COLUM. L. REV. 1613 (1995).

22 For quoted source, *see* Office of the Inspector General, *Report of Investigation of Julie MacDonald, Deputy Assistant Secretary, Fish, Wildlife & Parks*, U.S. FISH & WILDLIFE SERV. 2, 5. For another investigation on MacDonald, *see* U.S. GOV'T ACCOUNTABILITY OFFICE, GAO-08-688T, Endangered Species Act Decision Making 1, 43 (2008). For the investigation into the northern spotted owl non-listing, *see* U.S. GEN. ACCOUNTING OFFICE, RPT. NO. GAO/RCED-89-79, Endangered Species: Spotted Owl Petition Evaluation Beset by Problems 1, 12 (1989) (reporting that the decision not to list the northern spotted owl was made partially because top U.S. Fish and Wildlife Officials "would not accept [such] a decision..." and stating, "These problems raise serious questions about whether FWS maintained its scientific objectivity during the spotted owl petition process.").

23 For quoted sources, *see Feds Won't Probe Biologist's Klamath Fish Kill Charges*, ASSOCIATED PRESS (Mar. 23, 2003) (reporting case in which the judge found evidence of "improper political pressure"); Pac. Coast Fed'n of Fishermen's Assocs. v. U.S. Bureau of Reclamation, 426 F.3d, 1082, 1094 (9th Cir. 2005). For reporting on the Klamath decision, *see* Jo Becker & Barton Gellman, *Leaving No Tracks*, WASH. POST at A01 (June 27, 2007); Don Thompson, *U.S. Won't Probe Whistle-Blower's Salmon Allegations*, REGISTER-GUARD at D4 (Mar. 25, 2003).

24 For quoted sources, *see* Associated Press, *Oil Brokers Sex Scandal May Affect Drilling Debate*, USA TODAY (Sept. 11, 2008); Derek Kravitz & Mary Pat Flaherty, *Report Says Oil Agency Ran Amok*, WASH. POST (Sept. 11, 2008).

25 PETER C. YEAGER, THE LIMITS OF LAW: THE PUBLIC REGULATION OF PRIVATE POLLUTION, 251 (Cambridge U. Press 1991).

26 COLLINS, *supra* note 2, at 3.

27 For quoted source, *see* COLLINS, *supra* note 2, at 64. For referenced source, *see* DAVID MICHAELS, DOUBT IS THEIR PRODUCT: HOW INDUSTRY'S ASSAULT ON SCIENCE THREATENS YOUR HEALTH 32 (Oxford U. Press 2008). For the practice of pre-announced inspections, *see* Environmental Protection Agency, Chapter 2, Inspection Procedures, NPDES Compliance Inspection Manual, EPA 305-X-04-001, at 2–6 (July 2004) ("EPA conducts both announced and unannounced inspections.... Each region uses different criteria to determine whether to announce inspections.").

28 For quoted source, *see* KENNEDY, *supra* note 7, at 106. For a full account of the NSR prosecutions, *see* Joel Mintz, *"Treading Water:" A Preliminary Assessment of EPA Enforcement During the Bush II Administration*, 34 ENVTL. L. RPT. 10912, 10917–19 (2004); Bruce Barcott, *Changing All the Rules*, N.Y. TIMES (Apr. 4, 2004).

29 Mintz, *supra* note 28, at 10917–18.

30 For quoted sources, *see* Mintz, *supra* note 28 ("prevent any enforcement case," quoting J. P. Suarez, EPA Assistant Administrator, Office of Enforcement and Compliance Assurance during 2002 and 2003); KENNEDY, *supra* note 7, at 106.

31 For quoted and referenced source, *see* COLLINS, *supra* note 2, at 38–39.

32   For quoted sources, *see* Richard Caplan, U.S. Public Interest Research Group Education Fund, *Permit to Pollute: How the Government's Lax Enforcement of the Clean Water Act is Poisoning Our Waters* 4 (Aug. 2002); Charles Duhigg, *Clean Water Laws Are Neglected, at a Cost in Suffering*, N.Y. TIMES (Sep. 13, 2009). Reporter Charles Duhigg's article was part of a series of investigative reports on water pollution. Other articles were Charles Duhigg, *Toxic Waters: Find Water Polluters Near You*, N.Y. TIMES; Charles Duhigg, *Millions in U.S. Drink Dirty Water, Records Show*, N.Y. TIMES (Dec. 8, 2009).

33   For referenced investigative report, *see* Duhigg, *Dirty Water*, *supra* note 32, at A1.

34   For quoted sources, *see* Duhigg, *Suffering*, *supra* note 32 ("pressured by industry friendly"); Duhigg, *Dirty Water*, *supra* note 32, at A1 ("The same people"). For referenced report, *see* Duhigg, *Suffering*, *supra* note 32.

35   For quoted source, *see* Duhigg, *Suffering*, *supra* note 32.

36   For quoted sources, *see* Steve Duin, *Measuring the Hot Air Quality at DEQ*, THE OREGONIAN (Aug. 31 2009) ("regulatory captivity"); Steve Duin, *That Fine Mess at Oregon's DEQ*, THE OREGONIAN (Sept. 6, 2007) ("emasculated, isolated, compromised disaster"); COLLINS, *supra* note 2, at 40. For additional reporting on Oregon's DEQ, *see* Ben Sherman, *Cutbacks, Low Morale, Cast Haze Over DEQ*, THE OREGONIAN (Feb. 10, 2008).

37   W. Va. Highlands Conservancy v. Norton, 161 F. Supp. 2d 676, 683–84 (S.D.W.V. 2001) (emphasis added).

38   For quoted source, *see* PEER Testimony, *supra* note 20, at 34–35; For analysis of the Reagan administration, *see* Brent Blackwelder, *Economic and Environmental Perspective on President Reagan on the Occasion of the 100th Anniversary of His Birth*, ENERGY BULLETIN (Feb. 21, 2011). For analysis of the Clinton administration's posture on ESA regulation, *see* PEER, *War of Attrition: Sabotage of the Endangered Species Act by the U.S. Department of Interior* (Dec. 1997), http://www.peer.org/assets/docs/whitepapers/1997_war_of_attrition.pdf. For analysis of the Obama smog rule, *see* Juliet Eilperin, *Obama Pulls Back Proposed Smog Standards in Victory for Business*, WASH. POST (Sept. 2, 2011).

39   Michael C. Blumm & William Warnock, *Roads Not Taken: EPA vs. Clean Water*, 33 ENVTL. L. 79, 80–81, 111 (2003).

40   MICHAELS, *supra* note 27, at 110, 120.

4. BEHIND THE GRAND FAÇADE

1   *See* NAOMI ORESKES & ERIK M. CONWAY, MERCHANTS OF DOUBT: HOW A HANDFUL OF SCIENTISTS OBSCURED THE TRUTH ON ISSUES FROM TOBACCO SMOKE TO GLOBAL WARMING (Bloomsbury Press 2010).

2   For more in-depth treatment of the industry tactics discussed in this chapter, *see generally id.*; JAMES HOGGAN, CLIMATE COVER-UP: THE CRUSADE TO DENY GLOBAL WARMING (Greystone Books 2009); DEVRA DAVIS, WHEN SMOKE RAN LIKE WATER: TALES OF ENVIRONMENTAL DECEPTION & THE BATTLE AGAINST POLLUTION (Basic Books 2002); ROBERT F. KENNEDY JR., CRIMES AGAINST NATURE: HOW GEORGE W. BUSH & HIS CORPORATE PALS ARE PLUNDERING THE COUNTRY & HIJACKING OUR DEMOCRACY (HarperCollins 2004); DAVID MICHAELS, DOUBT IS THEIR PRODUCT: HOW INDUSTRY'S ASSAULT ON SCIENCE THREATENS YOUR HEALTH (Oxford University Press 2008); RESCUING SCIENCE FROM POLITICS: REGULATION & THE DISTORTION OF SCIENTIFIC RESEARCH (Wendy Wagner & Rena Steinzor eds., Cambridge University Press 2006); SETH SHULMAN, UNDERMINING SCIENCE: SUPPRESSION AND DISTORTION IN THE BUSH ADMINISTRATION (University of California Press 2008).

3 Richard J. Lazarus, *Environmental Law after Katrina: Reforming Environmental Law by Reforming Environmental Lawmaking*, 81 TUL. L. REV. 1019, 1045 (2007). *See also* Holly Doremus, *Science Plays Defense: Natural Resource Management in the Bush Administration*, 32 ECOLOGY L.Q. 249, 287 (2005).

4 Robert F. Kennedy, Jr. & Christine Todd Whitman, *The Environment: A Debate*, OUTSIDE MAGAZINE (Nov. 1, 2004).

5 *See* Tim Dickinson, *The Secret Campaign of President Bush's Administration to Deny Global Warming*, ROLLING STONE (June 29, 2007). *See also* Press Release, Constellation Energy, *Constellation Energy Names James L. Connaughton Executive Vice President, Corporate Affairs, Public & Environmental Policy* (Feb. 23, 2009).

6 For quoted sources, see Matthew Daly, THE ASSOCIATED PRESS, *Nethercutt Joins Lobbying Firm* (Jan. 30, 2005) (discussing Griles as "go-to broker"); JOHN ANDERSON, FOLLOW THE MONEY: HOW GEORGE W. BUSH AND THE TEXAS REPUBLICANS HOG-TIED AMERICA 258 (Scribner, 2007) (quoting Inspector General's report). *See also* Anne C. Mulkern, *Watchdogs or Lap Dogs? When Advocates Become Regulators*, THE DENVER POST A1 (May 23, 2004); Elizabeth Shogren, *Interior's Deputy Cleared of Most Ethics Charges*, L.A. TIMES (Mar. 17, 2004); Dana Milbank, *Abramoff, Prison and a Crazy Little Thing Called Love*, WASH. POST (June 27, 2007).

7 For background on Holmstead, *see* Public Citizen Congress Watch, *EPA's Smoke Screen: How Congress Was Given False Information While Campaign Contributions & Political Connections Gutted a Key Clean Air Rule* (Oct. 2003). The EPA granted the permit in 2008. *See* Press Release, EPA, *EPA Issues Air Permit for Desert Rock Energy Facility* (July 31, 2008). Later, under the Obama administration, EPA withdrew the permit because it had not undergone proper procedural review. *See* Marjorie Childress, *EPA Pulls the Plug on Desert Rock Coal-Fired Power Plant*, THE N.M. INDEPENDENT (Apr. 28, 2009). For reporting on Norton, *see* Neil A. Lewis, *Justice Department Investigates Ex-Official's Ties to Shell*, N.Y. TIMES (Sept. 17, 2009). The Justice Department declined to file charges against Norton. An Office of Inspector General Report did not find conclusive evidence of legal violations, although it did find aberrations with respect to the way the Bureau of Land Management handled the leasing process. *See* Dan Berman, *Former Interior Secretary Gale Norton Won't Face Charges*, POLITICO (Dec. 10, 2010).

8 For background on the referenced George W. Bush political appointees, *see* KENNEDY, *supra* note 2, at 32, 98.

9 For quoted sources, *see* Bruce Barcott, *Changing All the Rules*, N.Y. TIMES (Apr. 4, 2004); KENNEDY, *supra* note 2, at 32. For additional perspective, *see* SHULMAN, *supra* note 2, at 68.

10 For a survey of industry-friendly regulatory changes pushed by political appointees in the George W. Bush administration, *see* KENNEDY, *supra* note 2, at 33, 126–27, 141.

11 The Mercury Rule was introduced as part of the "Clear Skies" initiative. Estimates at the time noted that "the Bush plan will allow 264 more tons of mercury emissions by 2018 than would the current regulatory approach." ZACHARY CORRIGAN, U.S. PUBLIC INTEREST RESEARCH GROUP EDUCATION FUND, FISHING FOR TROUBLE: HOW TOXIC MERCURY CONTAMINATES OUR WATERWAYS & THREATENS AND THREATENS RECREATIONAL FISHING 15 (2003). For discussion, *see* Eric Pianin, *Proposed Mercury Rules Bear Industry Mark*, WASH. POST A4 (Jan. 31, 2004); SHULMAN, *supra* note 2, at 68; KENNEDY *supra* note 2, at 119, 124–25; Robert F. Kennedy, Jr., *Keynote Address: We Must Take America Back*, 22 J. ENVTL. L. & LITIG. 201, 211 (2007).

12 For the referenced source, *see* 2004 *Scientist Statement on Restoring Scientific Integrity to Federal Policy Making*, UNION OF CONCERNED SCIENTISTS (Feb. 8, 2005). For further background on politicized science, *see generally* SHULMAN, *supra* note 2; MARK BOWEN, CENSORING

SCIENCE: INSIDE THE POLITICAL ATTACK ON DR. JAMES HANSEN & THE TRUTH OF GLOBAL WARMING (Penguin Group 2008); CHRIS MOONEY, THE REPUBLICAN WAR ON SCIENCE (Basic Books 2005). For developments within the Obama administration, *see A Progress Report on Scientific Integrity: The Road to Independent Science*, UNION OF CONCERNED SCIENTISTS (May 28, 2012).

13 For referenced source, *see Voices of Federal Climate Scientists*, UNION OF CONCERNED SCIENTISTS (Jan. 25, 2007). For a discussion on CEQ interference with global warming reports, *see* SHULMAN, *supra* note 2, at 19. For additional discussion of political interference, *see* BOWEN, *supra* note 12; MOONEY, *supra* note 12.

14 For referenced sources, *see Survey: U.S. Fish & Wildlife Service Scientists (2005)*, UNION OF CONCERNED SCIENTISTS (Feb. 9, 2005); *Summary of National Oceanic & Atmospheric Administration (NOAA) Fisheries Service Scientists Survey*, UNION OF CONCERNED SCIENTISTS (June 28, 2005); *Voices of EPA Scientists*, UNION OF CONCERNED SCIENTISTS (Apr. 23, 2008). For reporting on the Mercury Rule, *see* Felicity Barringer, *EPA Accused of a Predetermined Finding on Mercury*, N.Y. TIMES (Feb. 4, 2005).

15 For the UCS report, *see Freedom to Speak?* UNION OF CONCERNED SCIENTISTS (Aug. 27, 2009). For the NASA Inspector General report, *see* Investigative Summary Regarding Allegations that NASA Suppressed Climate Change Science & Denied Media Access to Dr. James E. Hansen, a NASA Scientist (June 2, 2008) (emphasis removed).

16 UCS, *Voices*, *supra* note 14.

17 For referenced and quoted sources, *see* UCS, *USFWS Survey*, *supra* note 14; UCS, *NOAA Survey*, *supra* note 14. Ian Urbina, *U.S. Said to Allow Drilling without Needed Permits*, N.Y. TIMES A1 (May 14, 2010).

18 For quoted and referenced sources, *see* SHULMAN, *supra* note 2, at xiii; *Voices of Federal Food Safety Scientists & Inspectors*, UNION OF CONCERNED SCIENTISTS 2 (2010) (also noting that 25% of respondents reported situations in which corporate interests forced the "withdrawal or significant modification" of an agency action designed to protect the public). For discussion of the Keystone Pipeline decision, *see* John M. Broder, *Keystone XL Pipeline Decision to Be Investigated*, N.Y. TIMES A14 (Nov. 7, 2011). The UCS maintains a scorecard of political interference within the Obama agencies. *See Mountain or Molehill? Analysis of Charges of Political Interference in Science against the Obama Administration*, UNION OF CONCERNED SCIENTISTS (Jan. 28, 2011).

19 For quoted source, *see* Jeff Ruch, *Endangered Species Act Implementation: Science or Politics?: Hearing Before the Comm. on Nat. Resources U.S. House of Rep.*, 110th Cong. 5 (2007) (testimony of Jeff Ruch, Exec. Dir. of Pub. Employees for Envtl. Responsibility). For the UCS survey results, *see* UCS, *USFWS Survey*, *supra* note 14.

20 For referenced case, *see* Garcetti v. Ceballos, 547 U.S. 410, 410 (2006). For referenced statute, *see* Whistleblower Protection Act, 5 U.S.C.A. § 2302 (2008). This statute protects a covered employee from a personnel action resulting from the disclosure of information reasonably believed by the covered employee to evidence "a violation of any law, rule or regulation, or . . . gross mismanagement, a gross waste of funds, an abuse of authority, or a substantial and specific danger to public health or safety." 5 U.S.C.A. § 2302(b)(8)(A)(i)-(ii). For discussion of whistle-blower protections, *see* Ruch, *Testimony*, *supra*, note 19.

21 For quoted sources, *see* Federico Cheever, *Four Failed Forest Standards: What We Can Learn from the History of the National Forest Management Act's Substantive Timber Management Provisions*, 77 OR. L. REV. 601, 704 (1998); Sierra Club v. Thomas, 105 F. 3d 248, 251 (6th Cir. 1997), *vacated*, 523 U.S. 726 (1998); Sierra Forest Legacy v. Rey, 577 F.3d 1015, 1026 (9th Cir. 2009) (Judge Noonan) (emphasis added). For discussion of Forest Service bias, *see* RANDAL O'TOOLE, REFORMING THE FOREST SERVICE 104–07 (Island Press 1988); Sara A. Clark,

Taking a Hard Look at Agency Science: Can the Courts Ever Succeed? 36 ECOLOGY L.Q. 317, 323 (2009).

22 For quoted sources, *see* Lazarus, *supra* note 3; Scott Learn, *Cutbacks, Low Morale Cast Haze Over DEQ*, THE OREGONIAN (Feb. 10, 2008) (quoting Rep. Dingfelder). For referenced surveys, *see* UCS, *NOAA Survey supra* note 14; UCS, *USFWS Survey, supra* note 14.

23 For discussion of conflicts in the water context, *see* HOLLY D. DOREMUS, WATER WAR IN THE KLAMATH BASIN: MACHO LAW, COMBAT BIOLOGY, & DIRTY POLITICS (Island Press 2008); Ann C. Juliano, *Conflicted Justice: The Department of Justice's Conflict of Interest in Representing Native American Tribes*, 37 GA. L. REV. 1307 (2003). The agencies with often opposing interests within the same basin are the Bureau of Reclamation, the U.S. Fish and Wildlife Service, the Bureau of Indian Affairs, and the National Marine Fisheries Service.

24 For quoted source, *see* Michael C. Blumm, Abstract, *The Bush Administration's Sweetheart Settlement Policy: A Trojan Horse Strategy for Advancing Commodity Production on Public Lands*, 34 ENVTL. L. RPT. 10397, 10399, 10406, 10412, 10417 (2004). For reporting, *see* Brian Dakss, *Lawsuits, Not Lawmakers, Make Policy*, CBS NEWS (Feb. 11, 2009); *New Anti-Environment Tack by Bush?* CBS NEWS (Apr. 20, 2003).

25 For quoted source, *see* DAVIS, *supra* note 2, at 107–08. For referenced statute, *see* Paperwork Reduction Act of 1980, 44 U.S.C.A § 3504 (a)(1)(A)(2002).

26 For quoted sources, *see* Interference at the EPA: Science & Politics at the U.S. Environmental Protection Agency, *summary*, UNION OF CONCERNED SCIENTISTS (Apr. 2008); KENNEDY, *supra* note 2, at 59. For referenced statute, *see* Administrative Procedure Act, 5 U.S.C. § 552(b) (2009). For an explanation of internal decision making, *see Notice-and-Comment Rulemaking*, OMB WATCH (Oct. 3, 2007) (flowchart outlining the complicated nature of OMB decision making not subject to APA notice-and-comment requirements), http://www.ombwatch.org/node/3467; Curtis W. Copeland, *The Role of the Office of Information and Regulatory Affairs in Federal Rulemaking*, 33 FORDHAM URB. L.J. 1257, 1281 (2006).

27 For quoted source, *see* KENNEDY, *supra* note 2, at 75. For referenced source, *see Scientific Integrity Recommendations for the Office of Information and Regulatory Affairs*, UNION OF CONCERNED SCIENTISTS, 1 (2009). For general discussion of OIRA, *see* KENNEDY, *supra* note 2, at 59–75; U.S. GOV'T ACCOUNTABILITY OFFICE, GAO-03-929, RULEMAKING: OMB's ROLE IN REVIEWS OF AGENCIES' DRAFT RULES & THE TRANSPARENCY OF THOSE REVIEWS (2003); Osha Gray Davidson, *The Bush Legacy: An Assault on Public Protections*, OMB WATCH 28 (2009), http://www.ombwatch.org/files/bushlegacy.pdf; Regulatory Review, 74 FED. REG. 5977 (Jan. 30, 2009).

28 For quoted source, *see* Davidson, *supra* note 27, at 28. For referenced sources and additional discussion, *see* Copeland, *supra* note 26, at 1261–62, 1267; Exec. Order No. 12,291, 46 Fed. Reg. 13193 (Feb. 17, 1981); Exec. Order No. 12,866, 58 Fed. Reg. 51735, 51743 (Sept. 30, 1993); Exec. Order No. 13,422, 72 Fed. Reg. 2763, 2763 (Jan, 18, 2007)(revoked).

29 For quoted source, *see* MICHAELS, *supra* note 2, at 80, 179. For referenced statute, *see* Data Quality Act, Consolidated Appropriations – FY 2001, Appendix C, Pub. L. No. 106–554, § 515(b)(2)(A), 114 Stat 2763, 2763A-154, (2000).

30 For quoted sources, *see* Davidson, *supra* note 27, at 27; KENNEDY, *supra* note 2, at 59. While the OIRA does have some scientists, the Union of Concerned Scientists notes that the staff is not nearly adequate to engage in full review of the science behind the broad spectrum of agency decisions. *See* UCS, *Scientific Integrity, supra,* note 27. For additional analysis, *see CPR's Eye on OIRA*, CENTER FOR PROGRESSIVE REFORM (2008); Rena Steinzor, Michael Patoka & James Goodwin, *Behind Closed Doors at the White House: How Politics Trumps Protection of Public Health, Worker Safety and the Environment*, CENTER FOR PROGRESSIVE REFORM (Nov. 2011).

31 For quoted sources, *see* Wagner & Steinzor, *supra* note 2, at 4; MICHAELS, *supra* note 2, at x. For referenced source, *see* ORESKES & CONWAY, *supra* note 1. This rich genre of literature includes WHEN SMOKE RAN LIKE WATER: TALES OF ENVIRONMENTAL DECEPTION & THE BATTLE AGAINST POLLUTION, *see* DAVIS, *supra* note 2.

32 For a discussion and case studies of regulatory delay caused by uncertainty, *see id.* at xix ("The absence of evidence of harm – even when no effort has been made to gather such evidence – becomes grounds for inaction.").

33 For quoted sources, *see* MICHAELS, *supra* note 2, at x (reporting cigarette company memo); HOGGAN, *supra* note 2, at 1, 62–67 (quoting and discussing Luntz document) (emphasis in original Luntz memo). For further discussion of industry uncertainty tactics, *see* MICHAELS, *supra* note 2, at 56; Patrick Parenteau, *Anything Industry Wants: Environmental Policy under Bush II*, 14 DUKE ENVTL. L. & POL'Y F. 363, 401–05 (2004).

34 For quoted sources, *see* Dana Milbank, *Washington Sketch: A Hostile Climate for Sen. Inhofe the Warming Skeptic*, WASH. POST (Oct. 28, 2009).

35 For quoted sources, *see* MICHAELS, *supra* note 2, at 56; DAVIS, *supra* note 2, at 126–33. For recent reporting on the history of lead in gasoline and the industry's efforts to obstruct regulation, *see* Kevin Drum, *How Did Lead Get Into Our Gasoline Anyway?* MOTHER JONES (Jan. 7, 2013).

36 For quoted source, *see* Jeff Ruch, *Chemical Industry Is Now EPA's Main Research Partner*, PUBLIC EMPLOYEES FOR ENVIRONMENTAL RESPONSIBILITY (PEER) (Oct. 5, 2005). For the Government Accountability Office warning, *see* U.S. GOV'T ACCOUNTABILITY OFFICE, GAO-05-191, FEDERAL RESEARCH: NIH & EPA NEED TO IMPROVE CONFLICT OF INTEREST REVIEWS FOR RESEARCH ARRANGEMENTS WITH PRIVATE SECTOR ENTITIES (2005). For referenced source, *see* Alan C. Miller & Tom Hamburger, *EPA Relied on Industry for Plywood Plant Pollution Rule*, L.A. TIMES (May 21, 2004). For additional discussion, *see* Davidson, *supra* note 27, at 17; SHULMAN, *supra* note 2, at 75.

37 For quoted source, *see* MICHAELS, *supra* note 2, at 53. For additional discussion, *see* Wagner & Steinzor, *supra* note 2, at 2–3.

38 For quoted sources, *see* ORESKES & CONWAY, *supra* note 1, at 9; MICHAELS, *supra* note 2, at 57–58. For further discussion, *see* Thomas O. McGarity, J.D., *Defending Clean Science from Dirty Attacks by Special Interests*, in Wagner & Steinzor, *supra* note 2, at 24.

39 For quoted source, *see* Wagner & Steinzor, *supra* note 2, at 1, 29–33.

40 MICHAELS, *supra* note 2, at 60.

41 For quoted source, *see* ROSS GELBSPAN, BOILING POINT: HOW POLITICIANS, BIG OIL AND COAL, JOURNALISTS, AND ACTIVISTS HAVE FUELED THE CLIMATE CRISIS – AND WHAT WE CAN DO TO AVERT DISASTER 52, 61, 68–74 (Basic Books 2004). *See also* Naomi Oreskes, *The Scientific Consensus on Climate Change*, 306 SCI. 1686 (2004). Oil companies have been charged with conspiracy in disseminating climate disinformation in at least one lawsuit. *See* Comer v. Murphy Oil USA, 585 F.3d 855 (5th Cir. 2009). The conspiracy claims were dismissed for lack of standing, refiled in 2011, and dismissed again for the same reasons by a Mississippi federal district court judge on March 20, 2012. *See* Kristin Lands, *Comer v. Murphy Oil USA, Inc. Dismissed by Mississippi Federal Court*, CLIMATE CHANGE INSIGHTS (Apr. 3, 2012).

42 Doremus, *Science Plays Defense*, *supra* note 3, at 254–55.

43 For quoted sources, *see* Wendy E. Wagner, *The Science Charade in Toxic Risk Regulation*, 95 COLUM. L. REV. 1613, 1617 (1995); Doremus, *Science Plays Defense*, *supra* note 3, at 253, 256.

44 *See, e.g.*, *Air Quality Acronyms and Common Abbreviations*, PENNSYLVANIA DEPARTMENT OF ENVIRONMENTAL PROTECTION, http://www.dep.state.pa.us/dep/deputate/airwaste/aq/misc/acronyms.pdf; *Commonly Used Acronyms List*, EPA, http://yosemite.epa.gov/osw%5Crcra.nsf/How+To+Use#acronyms.

45 For quoted sources, *see* SHULMAN, *supra* note 2, at xx (noting also, "Taken together, the stories ... expose a calculated strategy by the administration to mislead the public."); *see also id.* at 68, 76; Christine A. Klein, *The Environmental Deficit: Applying Lessons From the Economic Recession*, 51 ARIZ. L. REV. 651, 663–64 (2009).

46 Oliver A. Houck, *Damage Control: A Field Guide to Important Euphemisms in Environmental Law*, 15 TUL. ENVTL. L.J. 129, 129 (2001). For general discussion of Forest Service, *see, e.g.*, Susan Gallagher, *Foresters Tout Better Clear-Cuts*, L.A. TIMES (Mar. 1, 1998) (reporting critic's view that Forest Service has tried to greenwash clear-cuts with buzzwords).

5. THE ADMINISTRATIVE TYRANNY OVER NATURE

1 District Judge Urbina issued a temporary restraining order blocking the BLM from leasing the seventy-seven parcels in question, finding that the Environmental Impact Statement (EIS) was inadequate. So. Utah Wilderness Alliance v. Allred, Case No. 1:08-CV-02187-RMU (D. D.C., filed Dec. 2008). The Department of the Interior subsequently canceled the leases on the land. Leslie Kaufman, *Drilling Leases Scrapped in Utah*, N.Y. TIMES (Feb. 5, 2009). DeChristopher and his supporters raised $81,000 to make a down payment on the leases, but the money was rejected by the BLM. *See* Abe Streep, *The Trials of Bidder 70*, OUTSIDE (Oct. 27, 2011).

2 AL GORE, THE ASSAULT ON REASON 73–74 (Penguin Group 2007).

3 For quoted sources, *see* Bruce A. Ackerman, *The Storrs Lectures: Discovering the Constitution*, 93 YALE L.J. 1013, 1028 (1984); Sandra Beth Zellmer, *Sacrificing Legislative Integrity at the Altar of Appropriations Riders: A Constitutional Crisis*, 21 HARV. ENVTL. L. REV. 457, 522 (1997).

4 CHARLIE SAVAGE, TAKEOVER: THE RETURN OF THE IMPERIAL PRESIDENCY AND THE SUBVERSION OF AMERICAN DEMOCRACY 350 (Little, Brown & Co. 2007) (original emphasis removed). *See also id.* at 329–30.

5 For quoted sources, *see* GORE, *supra* note 2, at 245 (quoting Lincoln); *id.* at 245, 246, 249, 255.

6 For quoted sources, *see* Richard J. Lazarus, *Congressional Descent: The Demise of Deliberative Democracy in Environmental Law*, 94 GEO. L.J. 619, 621–22 (2006) GORE, *supra* note 2, at 235–36, 239.

7 Lazarus, *Congressional Descent*, *supra* note 6, at 632.

8 Richard J. Lazarus, *Environmental Law after Katrina: Reforming Environmental Law by Reforming Environmental Lawmaking*, 81 TULANE L. REV. 1019, 1053 (2007).

9 For additional discussion of riders, *see* Zellmer, *supra* note 3, at 458 (warning that the repeated abuse of environmental appropriation riders creates a serious constitutional crisis).

10 For description of individual riders, *see* Lazarus, *Congressional Descent*, *supra* note 6, at 642–45.

11 *See Emergency Supplemental Appropriations for Additional Disaster Assistance, for Anti-Terrorism Initiatives, for Assistance in the Recovery from the Tragedy that Occurred at Oklahoma City, and Rescissions Act*, 1995, Pub. L. No. 104–19, 109 Stat. 194. For discussion, *see* Zellmer, *supra* note 3, at 465–66.

12 For quoted source, *see* Lazarus, *Congressional Descent*, *supra* note 6, at 646. For background on Sen. Craig and the FPC rider, *see* Blaine Harden, *Zeroing Out the Messenger*, WASH. POST A21 (Nov. 30, 2005). The Ninth Circuit Court of Appeals later invalidated the FPC rider. Nw. Envtl. Def. Ctr. v. Bonneville Power Admin., 477 F.3d 668 (2007).

13 For discussion, *see* Robert V. Percival, *Regulatory Evolution and the Future of Environmental Policy*, 1997 U. CHICAGO LEGAL FORUM 159, 160 (1997).

14 For quoted sources, *see* Lazarus, *Congressional Descent*, *supra* note 6, at 632; GORE, *supra* note 2, at 77; *see also id.* at 236 ("It is the pitiful state of our legislative branch that primarily explains the failure of our vaunted system of checks and balances to prevent the dangerous overreach by

our executive branch, which now threatens a radical transformation of the American system."). For referenced case, *see* Citizens United v. Fed. Election Comm'n, 130 S.Ct. 876 (2010).

15 Roscoe Pound, Justice According to Law 73 (Yale U. Press 1951).

16 *Id.* at 81–84 (emphasis added).

17 For analysis of the standing doctrine, *see* Robert Meltz, *The Pendulum Swings Back: Standing Doctrine after* Friends of the Earth v. Laidlaw, UNT Digital Library (Mar. 14, 2000).

18 Lisa Kloppenberg, Playing it Safe: How the Supreme Court Sidesteps Hard Cases and Stunts the Development of Law 39–43, 46, 66 (N.Y.U. Press 2001).

19 For referenced case establishing rule-making deference, *see* Chevron, U.S.A., Inc. v. Nat. Resources Def. Council, Inc., 467 U.S. 837, 844 (1984).

20 Ronald A. Cass *et al.*, Administrative Law: Cases and Materials 216–17 (Little, Brown & Co. 2d ed. 1994). For cases according technical deference, *see* Marsh v. Or. Nat. Resources Council, 490 U.S. 360, 378 (1989); Baltimore Gas and Elec. Co. v. Nat. Resources Def. Council, 462 U.S. 87, 103 (1983).

21 For the judicial approach to evaluating evidence for admission in nonadministrative cases, *see* Daubert v. Merrell Dow Pharmaceuticals, Inc., 509 U.S. 579 (1993).

22 Sierra Club v. Thomas, 105 F.3d 248, 250 (1997) (decision vacated by the Supreme Court for lack of ripeness in Ohio Forestry Ass'n, Inc. v. Sierra Club, 523 U.S. 726 (1998)). *See also* Sierra Club v. Espy, 822 F. Supp. 356, 370 (1993) (*overruled by* Sierra Club v. Espy, 18 F.3d 1202 (1994)).

23 The Columbia River litigation involving salmon listed under the Endangered Species Act represents this kind of protracted litigation. For analysis, *see* Mary Christina Wood, *Restoring the Abundant Trust: Litigation in Pacific Northwest Salmon Recovery*, 36 ELR News & Analysis 10,163 (2006).

24 For an example of meaningful oversight of a remand process, *see* Nat'l Wildlife Fed. v. Nat'l Marine Fisheries Serv., 2005 WL 1398223 at 5 (D. Or 2005) (imposing substantive protections for imperiled fish by ordering "spill" of water over the dams to assist salmon migration during the protracted remand period). For background, *see* Katherine Warren Lewis, *"Running the River" to Change the Status Quo: Using the Endangered Species Act to Advocate for Dam Removal in National Wildlife Federation v. National Marine Fisheries Service*, 26 J. Land Res. & Envtl. L. 195, 201–02 (2005).

25 *See generally* Jeffrey Rudd, *The Evolution of the Legal Process School's "Institutional Competence" Theme: Unintended Consequences for Environmental Law*, 33 Ecology L.Q. 1045 (2006).

26 For referenced statutes, *see* Administrative Procedures Act, 5 U.S.C.A. § 553(b)(West 2012); National Environmental Policy Act of 1969, 42 U.S.C.A. §4332(2)(c)(West 2012).

27 Paul Loeb, *Time to be a Citizen*, Experience L!fe (July-Aug. 2003), http://experiencelife. com/article/time-to-be-a-citizen. *See also* Paul Loeb, *Time to be a Citizen, in* John de Graaf, Take Back Your Time: Fighting Overwork and Time Poverty in America 67 (Berrett-Koehler Publ's 2003).

28 David Schoenbrod, Power Without Responsibility: How Congress Abuses the People Through Delegation 60 (Yale U. Press 1993).

29 For the Bush ESA regulation, *see* Interagency Cooperation Under the Endangered Species Act, 73 Fed. Reg. 47,868 (proposed Aug. 15, 2008) (codified at 50 C.F.R. pt. 402); Dina Cappiello, *Rush to Read 200,000 Comments on Species Act*, San Fran. Chronicle A4 (Oct. 22, 2008). President Obama overrode the rule in March of 2009. *See* Jim Tankersley, *Obama Boosts Endangered Species Protection*, L.A. Times (Mar. 4, 2009).

30 Ross Gelbspan, Boiling Point: How Politicians, Big Oil and Coal, Journalists, and Activists Have Fueled the Climate Crisis—and What We Can Do to Avert Disaster 132 (Basic Books 2004).

31 *Id.* at 128, 146.
32 *Id.* at 146.
33 Michael Shellenberger & Ted Nordhaus, *The Death of Environmentalism: Global Warming Politics in a Post-Environmental World* 6–7 (2004).
34 National Environmental Policy Act of 1969, 42 U.S.C.A. § 4331(b) (West 2012) (emphasis added).
35 For quoted source, *see* Elisabeth Rosenthal & Dan Frosch, *Pipeline Review Is Faced With Question of Conflict,* N.Y. TIMES A11 (Oct. 8, 2011) (quoting Prof. Echeverria).
36 For referenced investigation, *see* Office of Inspector General, *Special Review of the Keystone XL Pipeline Permit Process,* Report No. AUD/SI-12–28 at 10–12 (Feb. 2012). For reporting on Keystone decision and its NEPA process and citizen protests, *see* John M. Broder & Dan Frosch, *Watchdog Clears State Department of Impropriety in Review of Pipeline Project,* N.Y. TIMES A16 (Feb. 10, 2012); Rosenthal & Frosch, *supra* note 35; Jane Mayer, *Taking it to the Streets,* THE NEW YORKER (Nov. 28, 2011); John M. Broder, *Keystone XL Pipeline Decision to Be Investigated,* N.Y. TIMES A14 (Nov. 8, 2011).
37 For referenced and quoted case, *see* Vt. Yankee Nuclear Power Corp. v. Nat. Resources Def. Council, 435 U.S. 519, 558 (1978); *see also* Paul S. Weiland, *Amending the National Environmental Policy Act: Federal Environmental Protection in the Twenty-First Century,* 12 J. LAND USE & ENVTL. L. 275 (1997). For quoted source, *see* William H. Rodgers, Jr., *NEPA at Twenty: Mimicry & Recruitment in Environmental Law,* 20 ENVTL. L. 485, 493–95 (1990). *See also* Thomas France, *NEPA–The Next Twenty Years,* 25 Land & Water L. Rev. 133, 134 (1990).
38 Michael M'Gonigle, *Green Legal Theory: A New Approach to the Concept of Environmental Law,* 4 Ökologisches-Wirtschaften 34, 35 (2008), http://www.oekologisches-wirtschaften.de/index.php/oew/article/view/594/594.
39 Michael M'Gonigle, *The Elephants of Doom in Copenhagen,* THE TYEE (Dec. 8, 2009), http://thetyee.ca/Opinion/2009/12/08/ElephantsOfDoom/ (emphasis added).
40 Oliver Houck, *Sisyphus on a Roll: Society Faces the High Price of Capitalism,* 25 THE ENVTL. FORUM 6, 7 (Nov/Dec 2008).
41 M'Gonigle, *Green Legal Theory, supra* note 38, at 38.

6. THE INALIENABLE ATTRIBUTE OF SOVEREIGNTY

1 Geer v. Conn., 161 U.S. 519, 534 (1896).
2 Joseph L. Sax, *The Public Trust Doctrine in Natural Resource Law: Effective Judicial Intervention,* 68 MICH. L. REV. 471, 484 (1970).
3 For quoted sources, *see* Gerald Torres, *The Public Trust: The Law's DNA,* Keynote Address at the University of Oregon School of Law (Feb. 23, 2012); Charles F. Wilkinson, *The Headwaters of the Public Trust: Some Thoughts on the Source and Scope of the Traditional Doctrine,* 19 ENVTL. L. 425, 431 (1989); *Geer,* 161 U.S. at 526. Legal scholars describe the public trust as "one of the oldest principles known to civilized government." Atmospheric Trust Litigation Brief for *Amicus Curiae* Law Professors at 6, Alec L. v. Jackson (No. 3:11-cv-02203 EMC) (N.D. Cal. 2011) [hereinafter ATL Brief] (the author was among those scholars on the brief), http://ourchildrens-strust.org/page/51/federal-lawsuit; *see also* U.S. v. 1.58 Acres of Land, 523 F. Supp. 120, 122–23 (D. Mass. 1981) ("Historically, no developed western civilization has recognized absolute rights of private ownership in [submerged lands]. . . . Though private ownership was permitted in the Dark Ages, neither Roman law nor the English common law as it developed after the signing of the Magna Charta would permit it.") For a survey of the public trust in other countries, *see* Michael C. Blumm & Rachel D. Guthrie, *Internationalizing the Public Trust Doctrine:*

Natural Law and Constitutional and Statutory Approaches to Fulfilling the Saxion Vision, 45 UC DAVIS L. REV. 741 (2012).

4 For quoted sources, *see* THE INSTITUTES OF JUSTINIAN § 1.2.1 ("natural reason appoints") (stating also that natural law "obtains equally among all nations, because all nations make use of it."); PETER G. BROWN, RESTORING THE PUBLIC TRUST: A FRESH VISION FOR PROGRESSIVE GOVERNMENT IN AMERICA 78 (Beacon Press 1994); JOHN LOCKE, SECOND TREATISE OF CIVIL GOVERNMENT, Chapter XIII, § 149 (1689); Oposa v. Factoran, G.R. No. 101083 (S.C., July 30, 1993) (Phil.), *reprinted (excerpt) in* JAN G. LAITOS *ET AL.*, NATURAL RESOURCES LAW 441–44 (Thompson West 2006) (emphasis added). For other expressions of the public trust as natural law, *see* Arnold v. Mundy, 6 N.J.L. 1, 11 (N.J. 1821) (locating the trust in the "law of nature, which is the only true foundation of all the social rights"); Ill. Cent. R.R Co. v. Ill., 146 U.S. 387, 456 (1892) (a state legislature "cannot, consistently with the principles of the law of nature and the constitution of a well-ordered society, make a direct and absolute grant of the waters of the state, divesting all the citizens of their common right."); *Geer*, 161 U.S. at 523 (citing J. INST. § 2.1.12); Matthews v. Bay Head Improvement Ass'n, 471 A.2d 355, 360–61 (N. J. 1984) (citing J. INST. § 2.1.1, 5); Idaho v. Coeur d'Alene Tribe, 521 U.S. 261, 284 (1997) ("[W]aters uniquely implicate sovereign interests. The principle arises from ancient doctrines") (citing J. INST. § 2.1.2).

5 For quoted sources, *see* J. INST. § 2.1.1; *Geer*, 161 U.S. at 529 (involving wildlife); *Ill. Cent. R.R. Co.*, 146 U.S. at 456 (citing *Arnold v. Mundy*, 6 N.J.L. at 78).

6 *See, e.g. In re*: Water Use Permit Applications, 9 P.3d 409, 451–55 (2000) [hereinafter *Waiāhole Ditch*] (quoting Ariz. Cent. for Law in Pub. Interest v. Hassell, 837 P.2d 158, 168–69 (Ariz. Ct. App. 1991)) (noting that the state has a duty to protect the water resources for present and future generations). As Professor John Davidson points out, the trust carries both *inter*-generational and *intra*-generational protection. *See* John Davidson, *Taking Posterity Seriously: Intergenerational Justice*, Climate Legacy Initiative Research Forum of Vt. L. School (Jan. 2008), http://vlscli.wordpress.com/2008/01/28/taking-posterity-seriously-intergenerationaljustice/.

7 Ga. v. Tenn. Copper Co., 206 U.S. 230, 237 (1907); *see also Ill. Cent. R.R. Co.*, 146 U.S. at 453–54 (stating: "So with trusts connected with public property, or property of a special character, like lands under navigable waters; they cannot be placed entirely beyond the direction and control of the state.").

8 For quoted sources, *see Geer*, 161 U.S. at 529 (emphasis added); JEAN JACQUES ROUSSEAU, THE SOCIAL CONTRACT 31–32 (translated by G. D. H. Cole) (Cosimo, Inc. 2008) (reprint). For additional authority emphasizing the public purpose of the trust, *see* Lake Mich. Fed'n v. U.S. Army Corps of Eng'rs, 742 F. Supp. 441, 445 (N.D. Ill. 1990) ("[T]he public trust is violated when the primary purpose of a legislative grant is to benefit a private interest.").

9 For an expression of property rights accruing to nations, *see* Arnold v. Mundy, 6 N.J.L. 1 (1821) ("Everything susceptible of property is considered as belonging to the nation that possesses the country, and as forming the entire mass of its wealth."). Courts have distinguished between the police power and trust authority in the natural resources law context. *See* Kleppe v. N.M., 426 U.S. 529, 541 (1976).

10 Paul Finn, *A Sovereign People, A Public Trust*, in ESSAYS ON LAW AND GOVERNMENT, VOL. 1, 10–11 (Paul Finn ed., 1995). *See also* Owsichek v. Alaska, 763 P.2d 488, 493 (Alaska 1988) (noting that the public trust prevents monopolistic use of resources and stating, "'[I]n the American system of government with its concept of popular sovereignty this title [to wildlife] is reserved to the people or the state on behalf of the people.'") (citation omitted).

11 BROWN, *supra* note 4, at 70 (quoting JOHN LOCKE, SECOND TREATISE OF CIVIL GOVERNMENT ch. IX, § 131 (1821)). Locke repeatedly described government as held to a "fiduciary trust," a

term Brown notes "was part of the general vocabulary of Locke's contemporaries as the notion of popular sovereignty gained favor." *Id.* Notably too, the Federalist Papers that sketched the design of American government made abundant reference to the "public trust." *See, e.g.,* THE FEDERALIST No. 63, 65, 70. For a case describing the trust as a constraint on government, *see* State v. Sorensen, 436 N.W.2d 358, 361 (1989) (noting that the public trust "has been described by one of our cases as a burden, rather than a benefit").

12 For quoted source, *see* BROWN, *supra* note 4, at 70, 91.

13 President Abraham Lincoln, Gettysburg Address (1863); *see also* Center for Biological Diversity v. FPL Group, Inc., 83 Cal. Rptr. 3d 588, 598 n.14 (Cal. Ct. App. 2008) (noting sovereign trust duty "owing to the people" (internal citation omitted)).

14 For quoted sources, *see* 1.58 *Acres of Land*, 523 F. Supp. at 124 ("the trust is of such a nature"); Torres, *supra* note 3; *Ill. Cent. R.R. Co*, 146 U.S. at 453, 460. For other expressions of the trust as an attribute of sovereignty, *see Geer*, 161 U.S. at 604 (referring to "attribute of government"); *Waiāhole Ditch*, 9 P.3d at 443 (same); Parks v. Cooper, 676 N.W.2d 823, 837 (S. D. 2004) ("History and precedent have established the public trust as an inherent attribute of sovereign authority.... The doctrine exists independent of any statute."); Tex. v. Bartee, 894 S.W.2d 34, 41 (Tex. Ct. App. 1994) ("attribute of government"); Karl S. Coplan, *Public Trust Limits on Greenhouse Gas Trading Schemes: A Sustainable Middle Ground?* 35 COLUM. J. ENVTL. L. 287, 311 (2010) ("Public trust principles have been described as an essential attribute of sovereignty across cultures and across millennia.").

15 For referenced author, *see* John Davidson, *Taking Posterity Seriously: Intergenerational Justice, supra* note 6. For quoted sources, *see* U.S. CONST. preamble; EDMUND BURKE, REFLECTIONS ON THE REVOLUTION IN FRANCE 82 (as quoted in BROWN, *supra* note 4, at 67); Reliance Nat. Resources Ltd. v. Reliance Indus. Ltd., 7 S.C.C. (India 2010), C.A. Nos.428–4281/2010 at ¶94, http://indiankanoon.org/doc/1070490/.

16 For Jefferson's correspondence, *see* Letter from Thomas Jefferson to John Taylor (May 28, 1816), *in* SOCIAL AND POLITICAL PHILOSOPHY: READINGS FROM PLATO TO GANDHI 251, 252 (John Somerville & Ronald E. Santoni eds., 1963); Letter from Thomas Jefferson to James Madison (Sept. 6, 1789), *id.* at 261–63 (emphasis added). For the definition of "usufruct," *see* BLACK'S LAW DICTIONARY 1542 (7th ed. 2000).

17 For quoted sources, *see* Douglas L. Grant, *Underpinnings of the Public Trust Doctrine: Lessons from Illinois Central Railroad*, 33 ARIZ. ST. L.J. 849, 856–57 (citing Home Bldg. & Loan Ass'n v. Blaisdell, 290 U.S. 398, 435 (1934)) ("[T]he reservation of essential attributes of sovereign power is ... read into [a legislature's] contracts as a postulate of the legal order."); Newton v. Commissioners, 100 U.S. 548, 559 (1879).

18 *Ill. Cent. R.R. Co.*, 146 U.S. at 453, 455, 458, 460 (quoting People v. N.Y. & Staten Island Ferry Co., 68 N.Y. 71, 77 (1877) (emphasis added).

19 For quoted sources, *see* City of New Orleans v. Bd. of Comm'rs of Orleans Levee Dist., 640 So. 2d 237, 249 (1994) ("Because the police power") (emphasis added) (also stating, "The principle of constitutional law that a state cannot surrender, abdicate, or abridge its police power has been recognized without exception by the state and federal courts."); *Oposa, supra* note 4 (emphasis added). For additional description of the police power, *see* Reesman v. State, 445 P.2d 1004, 1007 (Wash. 1968) ("[The] [p]olice power is an attribute of sovereignty, an essential element of the power to govern, and a function that cannot be surrendered. It exists without express declaration....." (quoting Shea v. Olson, 53 P.2d 615, 619 (Wash. 1936)). If one seeks a constitutional provision within which to locate the public trust (through the reserved powers doctrine), Professor Grant's analysis suggests that one need look no farther than the most basic legislative enabling clauses of the federal and state constitutions. These clauses restrict legislative terms to a limited number of years, so that one sitting legislative body cannot snatch the

power of perpetual office; the clauses allocate and limit power "temporally within the legislative branch." Grant, *supra* note 17, at 872.

20 Hawaii's first judicial pronouncement of the trust was in McBryde Sugar Co. Ltd. v. Robinson, 504 P.2d 1330, 1338–39 (Haw. 1973). The trust is codified in Haw. Const. art. XI, § 1. For quoted case, *see Waiāhole Ditch*, 9 P.3d at 142–43. For discussion of the public trust in state constitutions, *see* Matthew T. Kirsch, *Upholding the Public Trust in State Constitutions*, 46 Duke L.J. 1169, 1178–86 (1997). For discussion of the trust as embodied in the statutes and constitutions of other nations, *see* Blumm & Guthrie, *supra* note 3.

21 For quoted sources, *see* James L. Huffman, *Speaking of Inconvenient Truths–A History of the Public Trust Doctrine*, 18 Duke Envtl. L. & Pol'y F. 1, 101 (2007); ATL Brief, *supra* note 3, at 7. For a response to Professor Huffman, *see* Hope M. Babcock, *The Public Trust Doctrine: What a Tall Tale They Tell*, 61 S.C. L. Rev. 393 (2009).

22 PLL Mont., LLC v. Mont., 132 S. Ct. 1215, 1235 (2012) (stating, "the public trust doctrine remains a matter of state law...."). The statement amounts to dictum, as the case involved no issue of a federal trust. (Dictum is extraneous language in an opinion not crucial to the holding.) For another case referring, in dictum, to the trust as a state doctrine, *see* District of Columbia v. Air Fla., Inc., 750 F.2d 1077, 1082–83 (D. C. Cir. 1984) ("[T]he public trust doctrine has developed almost exclusively as a matter of state law."). In federal atmospheric trust litigation, the district court judge dismissed any federal trust obligation based on *PLL Mont., LLC v. Mont. See* Alec L. v. Jackson, Civ. 1:11-cv-02235, 863 F. Supp. 2d 11, 15 (D. D.C. May 31, 2012). The case is on appeal. Other cases have recognized a federal public trust. *See* Zygmunt J.B. Plater et al., Environmental Law and Policy: Nature, law, and Society 1103 (3rd ed. 2004) ("In several cases, courts have asserted that the federal government is equally accountable and restricted under the terms of the public trust doctrine....").

23 National Environmental Policy Act (NEPA), 42 U.S.C.A. § 4331(b)(1)(2012). Many other statutes impose a duty on federal agencies to act as trustees in seeking compensation for damage to public assets. *See, e.g.,* Comprehensive Envtl. Response, Compensation, & Liability Act (CERCLA), 42 U.S.C. § 9607(f)(1)(2004); Oil Pollution Act of 1990 (OPA), 33 U.S.C. § 2706(b)(2) (2004); Clean Water Act (CWA), 33 U.S.C.A. § 1319 and §1321(b)(2)(A) (2012); Marine Protection, Research and Sanctuaries Act (MPRSA), 16 U.S.C.A. § 1437 (2012).

24 For quoted source, *see* Mary Turnipseed *et al.*, *The Silver Anniversary of the United States' Exclusive Economic Zone: Twenty-Five Years of Ocean Use and Abuse, and the Possibility of a Blue Water Public Trust Doctrine*, 36 Ecol. L. Q. 1, 45 (2009); *see also* ATL Brief, supra note 3, at 6, 18–21. The *Illinois Central* decision expressed the navigation servitude when it declared that the states' trust ownership of submerged lands was "subject always to the paramount right of congress to control their navigation so far as may be necessary for the regulation of commerce with foreign nations and among the states." *Ill. Central R.R. Co.*, 146 U.S. at 435. Professor Zygmunt Plater and his co-authors explain the federal trusteeship in their leading textbook on environmental law. Plater et al., *supra* note 22, at 1103 ("Since [t]he federal government is a creature of the states by delegation through the Act of Union and the federal Constitution ... the federal government is therefore exercising delegated powers ... [and] cannot have greater rights and fewer limitations than the entities that created it."). Notably too, the original trusteeship inherited by the American states was quintessentially *national* in character, deriving from the English Crown. *See* Utah Div. of State Lands v. U.S., 482 U.S. 193, 196 (1987) (explaining that when the 13 Colonies became independent from Great Britain, they claimed title to the streambeds as "the sovereign successors to the English Crown").

25 *1.58 Acres of Land*, 523 F. Supp. at 120–21, 123–5 (emphasis added). In that case, the federal government sought to condemn waterfront property for a public use. The State of Massachusetts opposed the condemnation on the grounds that it could "vitiate the perpetual public trust"

held by the state. The court found the trust equally applicable to the federal government. For other cases supporting a federal trust obligation in natural resources management, *see, e.g.*, Complaint of Steuart Transp. Co., 495 F. Supp. 38, 40 (E.D. Va. 1980) (allowing federal government to recover damages for destroyed migratory waterfowl under common law public trust theory); Palila v. Haw. Dept. of Land and Nat. Resources, 471 F. Supp. 985, 992 (D. Haw. 1979) (implying a federal property interest in wildlife populations); N.Y. v. DeLyser, 759 F. Supp. 982, 990 (W.D.N.Y. 1991) (finding no federal jurisdiction over state public trust claim but affirming federal commerce and navigation interest in submerged lands).

26 For quoted cases, *see* Light v. U.S., 220 U.S. 523, 537 (1911) (quoting in part U.S. v. Trinidad Coal & Coking Co., 137 U.S. 160 (1890)); *Trinidad Coal*, 137 U.S. at 170 (also finding that the public lands "[are] held in trust for all the people"). *See also* Camfield v. U.S., 167 U.S. 518, 524 (1897) ("[I]t would be recreant to its duties as trustee for the people of the United States to permit any individual or private corporation to monopolize them for private gain.").

27 Ala. v. Tex., 347 U.S. 272, 277–82 (1954) (emphasis added).

28 For the Supremacy Clause, *see* U.S. CONST. art. VI, cl. 2. For cited case, *see* 1.58 *Acres of Land*, 523 F. Supp. at 123–125.

29 For the traditional law of the Navajo Nation, *see* THE FUNDAMENTAL LAWS OF THE DINÉ, http://www.navajocourts.org/dine.htm. For principles of federal Indian law expressing original and inherent sovereignty, *see* Worchester v. Ga., 31 U.S. 515, 561–62 (1832).

30 For discussion of tribal salmon management, *see* Mary Christina Wood, *The Tribal Property Right To Wildlife Capital (Part I): Applying Principles Of Sovereignty To Protect Imperiled Wildlife Populations*, 37 IDAHO L. REV. 1, 2 (2000). For discussion of modern tribal management principles, *see* Mary Christina Wood & Zachary Welcker, *Tribes As Trustees Again (Part I): The Emerging Tribal Role In The Conservation Trust Movement*, 32 HARV. ENVTL. L. REV. 373, 385–86 (2008). For discussion of both historical and modern environmental practices on Indian lands, *see generally* JOSEPH M. PETULLA, AMERICAN ENVIRONMENTAL HISTORY: THE EXPLOITATION AND CONSERVATION OF NATURAL RESOURCES (Boyd & Fraser Pub. Co. 1977); Ward Churchill & Winona LaDuke, *Native America: The Political Economy of Radioactive Colonialism*, 13 THE JOURNAL OF ETHNIC STUDIES (Fall 1985).

31 For a case asserting the co-trustee relationship, *see* Coeur d'Alene Tribe v. Asarco Inc., 280 F. Supp. 2d 1094, 1114–15 (D. Idaho, 2003), *modified in part*, U.S. v. Asarco, Inc., 471 F. Supp. 2d 1063, 1068–69 (D. Idaho 2005) (recognizing the Coeur d'Alene Tribe as the co-trustee of Lake Coeur d'Alene for purposes of CERCLA).

32 For quoted source, *see* Seminole Nation v. U.S., 316 U.S. 286, 297 (1942). For discussion of the federal Indian trust responsibility, *see* Mary Christina Wood, *Indian Land And The Promise Of Native Sovereignty: The Trust Doctrine Revisited*, 1994 UTAH L. REV. 1471, 1477–80 (1994); Mary Christina Wood, *The Indian Trust Responsibility: Protecting Tribal Lands And Resources Through Claims Of Injunctive Relief Against Federal Agencies*, 39 TULSA L. REV. 355 (2003). *See also* Dept. of Int. v. Klamath Water Users Protective Ass'n, 532 U.S. 1, 11 (2001) (stating that the Indian trust "has been compared to one existing under a common law trust, with the United States as trustee, the Indian tribes or individuals as beneficiaries, and the property and natural resources managed by the United States as the trust corpus"). For a case construing a treaty right to environmental protection, *see* U.S. v. Wash., 2007 WL 2437166, 10 (W.D. Wash. 2007). For discussion of tribal treaty rights deriving from co-ownership of the fishery, *see* Mary Christina Wood, *The Tribal Property Right To Wildlife Capital (Part I)*, *supra* note 30, at 2. For discussion of the modern tribal conservation trust movement, *see* MARY BETH R. MIDDLETON, TRUST IN THE LAND: NEW DIRECTIONS IN TRIBAL CONSERVATION (U. Ariz. Press 2011); Wood & Welcker, *supra* note 30. For the tribal role in setting pollution standards

off the reservation, *see* Edmund J. Goodman, *Indian Tribal Sovereignty and Water Resources: Watersheds, Ecosystems and Tribal Co-Management*, 20 J. Land Resources And Envtl. L. 185 (2000).

33 For quoted source, *see* Wood & Welcker, *supra* note 30, at 373 (quoting Rennard Strickland). For discussion of environmental damage in Indian Country, *see* Wood, *Trust Doctrine Revisited*, *supra* note 32.

34 For quoted case, *see* City of Milwaukee v. State, 214 N.W. 820, 830 (Wisc. 1927). For the legislative trust role, *see* Appleby v. N.Y., 271 U.S. 364, 383 (1926) (citing *People v. N.Y. & Staten Island Ferry Co.*, 68 N.Y. 71, 77–78 (1877)) (recognizing the state legislature's constitutionally-granted trusteeship, subject to Congress); *Geer*, 161 U.S. at 526 ("[T]he power ... is to be exercised, like all other powers of government, as a trust for the benefit of the people, and not as a prerogative for the advantage of the government as distinct from the people."). For a trustee's delegation authority and limits, *see* Restatement (Second) of Trusts: Duty Not To Delegate § 171 (1959) ("Although a trustee cannot properly delegate the administration of the trust, he can in administering the trust properly delegate the performance of certain kinds of acts."); George G. Bogert et al., Bogert Trusts and Trustees § 611 and § 555 (West rev. 2d ed. 1980); *Ill. Cent. R.R. Co.*, 146 U.S. at 453–54 ("In the administration of government the use of such powers may for a limited period be delegated to a municipality or other body, but there always remains with the state the right to revoke those powers and exercise them in a more direct manner, and one more conformable to its wishes. So with trusts connected with public property, or property of a special character, like lands under navigable waters; they cannot be placed entirely beyond the direction and control of the state."); *see also* Muench v. Pub. Serv. Comm'n, 55 N.W.2d 40, 46 (Wis. 1952). For a trustee's general duty of management, *see* Bogert Trusts 2d, *supra*, §541; Restatement (Third) of Trusts: Duty of Prudence § 77 (2007); Restatement (Second) of Trusts: Duty To Exercise Reasonable Care And Skill § 174 (1959). For the trustee's duty of loyalty, *see* Restatement (Third) of Trusts: Powers And Duties of Trustees § 70 (2007).

35 For quoted cases, *see* Lake Mich. Fed'n, 742 F. Supp. at 446 ("The very purpose"); Ariz. Ctr. for Law in the Pub. Interest v. Hassell, 837 P.2d 158, 169 (Ariz. Ct. App. 1991) ("The check and balance"). For cited source, *see* Joseph L. Sax, *Liberating the Public Trust From Its Historical Shackles*, 14 UC Davis L. Rev. 185, 188 (1980). For further discussion of the judicial role enforcing the trust, *see* Harrison C. Dunning, *The Public Trust: A Fundamental Doctrine of American Property Law*, 19 Envtl. L. 515, 515–25 (1989); Grant, *supra* note 17, at 849–50.

36 Brown, *supra* note 4, at 69.

7. THE ECOLOGICAL *RES*

1 Maude Barlow, Blue Covenant: The Global Water Crisis and the Coming Battle for the Right to Water 91 (New Press 2007).

2 Reliance Nat. Resources Ltd. v. Reliance Indus. Ltd., 7 S.C.C. 129 pt. I, ¶ 11 (India 2010), http://www.indiankanoon.org/doc/1070490.

3 *See* J.B. Ruhl & James Salzman, *Ecosystem Services and the Public Trust Doctrine: Working Change from Within*, 15 S.E. Envtl. L.J. 223, 230 (2006).

4 For quoted sources, *see* Ill. Cent. R.R. Co. v. Ill., 146 U.S. 387, 452 (1892) ("It is a title held in trust for the people of the State, that they may enjoy the navigation of the waters, carry on commerce over them, and have liberty of fishing therein, freed from the obstruction or interference of private parties."); *see also id.* at 455 ("It would not be listened to that the control and management of the harbor of that great city – *a subject of concern to the whole people of the*

state – should thus be placed elsewhere than in the state itself.") (emphasis added); Charles F. Wilkinson, *The Public Trust Doctrine in Public Lands Law*, 14 UC DAVIS L. REV. 269, 315 (1980).

5 DAVID C. SLADE, THE PUBLIC TRUST DOCTRINE IN MOTION at x (PTDIM, LLC 2009) (quoting Letter from Thomas Jefferson to Samuel Kercheval (July 12, 1816)).

6 Raleigh Avenue Beach Ass'n v. Atlantis Beach Club, Inc., 879 A.2d 112, 121 (N.J. 2005) (quoting Matthews v. Bay Head Improvement Ass'n, 471 A.2d 355, 365 (N.J. 1984)); *see also In re* Water Use Permit Applications, 9 P.3d 409, 447 (Haw. 2000) [hereinafter *Waiāhole Ditch*] ("Whatever practices the ancients may have observed in their time, therefore, we must conclude that the reserved trust encompasses any usage developed in ours."); Marks v. Whitney, 491 P.2d 374, 380 (Cal. 1971) ("In administering the trust the state is not burdened with an outmoded classification favoring one mode of utilization over another.").

7 For a discussion of constitutive common law, *see* Evan Fox-Decent, *Democratizing Common Law Constitutionalism*, 55 McGILL L.J. 511, 524 (2010) (discussing common law "constitutionalism"). The body of federal Indian law represents a similar species of law, imbued with principles defining the very nature of, and obligations surrounding, the sovereign relationships.

8 *In re* Hood River, 227 P. 1065, 1086–87 (Or. 1924).

9 For quoted sources, *see Waiāhole Ditch*, 9 P.3d at 448; *Matthews*, 471 A.2d at 363 (quoting N.J. Sports & Exposition Auth. v. McCrane, 292 A.2d 580, 598 (N.J. Super. Ct. Law Div. 1971)). *See also* Arnold L. Lum, *How Goes the Public Trust Doctrine: Is the Common Law Shaping Environmental Policy?* 18 NAT. RESOURCES & ENV'T 73 (2003). For additional cases extending the geographical scope of the doctrine, *see*, *e.g.*, Nat'l Audubon Soc'y v. Super. Ct., 658 P.2d 709, 719–22 (Cal. 1983) (non-navigable tributaries); Baxley v. State, 958 P.2d 422, 434 (Alaska 1998) (wildlife); *Matthews*, 471 A.2d at 358 (dry sand area); Robinson v. Ariyoshi, 658 P.2d 287, 310 (Haw. 1982) (groundwater); Just v. Marinette Cnty., 56 Wis.2d 7, 18–20 (Wis. 1972) (wetlands); Big Sur Properties v. Mott, 62 Cal. App. 3d 99 (Cal. App. 1976) (park).

10 For a discussion of the traditional approach, *see* Richard J. Lazarus, *Changing Conceptions of Property and Sovereignty in Natural Resources: Questioning the Public Trust Doctrine*, 71 IOWA L. REV. 631, 710–11 (1986); *see also*, Ruhl & Salzman, *supra* note 3, at 229; Opinion of the Justices, 313 N.E.2d 561 (Mass. 1974); Bell v. Town of Wells, 557 A.2d 168 (Me. 1989); SLADE, *supra* note 5, at 29–31 (discussing Maine law).

11 For quoted source, *see Ill. Cent. R.R. Co.*, 146 U.S. at 454 (emphasis added). *See also* Orion v. Washington, 47 P.2d 1062, 1073 (Wash. 1987) ("The trust's relationship to navigable waters and shorelands resulted not from a limitation, but rather from a recognition of where the public need lay.") (citation omitted).

12 *See e.g.*, James L. Huffman, *A Fish out of Water: The Public Trust Doctrine in a Constitutional Democracy*, 19 ENVTL. L. 527 (1989).

13 For quoted source, *see* Gerald Torres, *The Public Trust: The Law's DNA*, Keynote Address at the University of Oregon School of Law (Feb. 23, 2012). For referenced source, *see* Michael C. Blumm, *The Public Trust Doctrine and Private Property: The Accommodation Principle*, 27 PACE ENVTL. L. REV. 649 (2010).

14 Reed F. Noss, *Some Principles of Conservation Biology, as They Apply to Environmental Law*, 69 CHI.-KENT L. REV. 893, 894, 905 (1994).

15 Geer v. Conn., 161 U.S. 519 (1896). While part of the *Geer* opinion dealing with the commerce clause was later overruled by Hughes v. Okla., 441 U.S. 322 (1979), the trust portion remained intact. *See* Mary Christina Wood, *The Tribal Property Right to Wildlife Capital (Part I): Applying Principles of Sovereignty to Protect Imperiled Wildlife Populations*, 37 IDAHO L. REV. 1, 60–63 (2000), and sources cited therein.

16 Phillips Petroleum Co. v. Miss., 484 U.S. 469, 475 (1988).

17 For referenced case, *see Waiāhole Ditch*, 9 P.3d at 447–48 (finding groundwater a trust asset). For a sampling of other water cases, *see In re* Appeal of Town of Nottingham, 904 A.2d 582 (N.H. 2006) (not extending trust to groundwater); Mich. Citizens for Water Conservation v. Nestle Waters N. Am., Inc., 709 N.W.2d 174 (Mich. Ct. App. 2006) (same); R. D. Merrill v. Pollution Control Hearings Bd., 969 P.2d 458 (Wash. 1999) (same); *see also* SLADE, *supra* note 5, at 10–14 (discussing cases that exclude groundwater).

18 Arnold v. Mundy, 6. N.J.L. 1, 54 (N.J. 1821).

19 *Ecosystem Services*, ECOLOGICAL SOC'Y OF AM. 1 (Summer 2000) (emphasis added).

20 Noss, *supra* note 14, at 893.

21 Robert B. Keiter, *Conservation Biology and the Law: Assessing the Challenges Ahead*, 69 CHI.-KENT L. REV. 911, 911 (1994).

22 For quoted cases, *see Waiāhole Ditch*, 9 P.3d at 445, 447, 458; *Marks*, 491 P.2d at 380.

23 For quoted cases, *see Just*, 56 Wis.2d at 16–17 (emphasis added); Oposa v. Factoran, G.R. No. 101083 (S.C., July 30, 1993) (Phil.), *reprinted (excerpt) in* JAN G. LAITOS ET AL., NATURAL RESOURCES LAW 441–44 (Thompson West 2006).

24 ALDO LEOPOLD, ROUND RIVER 145–46, 162 (Oxford U. Press 1993).

25 For quoted sources, *see* NAT'L RESEARCH COUNCIL, VALUING ECOSYSTEM SERVICES: TOWARD BETTER ENVIRONMENTAL DECISION-MAKING 17 (Nat'l Acads. Press 2005) ("the myriad life") (emphasis added) (citations omitted); Noss, *supra* note 14, at 906. For referenced sources, *see* MILLENNIUM ECOSYSTEM ASSESSMENT, ECOSYSTEMS AND HUMAN WELL-BEING: SYNTHESIS (2005); Robert Costanza et al., *The Value of the World's Ecosystem Services and Natural Capital*, 387 NATURE 253, 253–54 (1997) ($30 trillion annual value). For additional analysis of ecosystem services, *see* NATURE'S SERVICES: SOCIETAL DEPENDENCE ON NATURAL ECOSYSTEMS (Gretchen Daily ed., Island Press 1997). For examples of ecosystem services saving costs, *see Projected Environmental Benefits of Community Tree Planting: A Multi-Site Model Urban Forest Project in Atlanta*, AM. FORESTS 2 (Oct. 2002); Eddie Nickens, *A Watershed Paradox – New York City's Water Quality Protection Efforts*, AM. FORESTS (Winter 1998).

26 Ruhl & Salzman, *supra* note 3, at 232–38 ("[W]e propose integrating natural capital and ecosystem services within the public trust doctrine's utilitarian core to make it more ecological on its surface."). But interestingly, the article argues for recognizing ecosystem services without expanding the traditional footprint of the public trust – that is, beyond the streambeds. In other words, it promotes an expanded conception of the trust *interest*, but not the trust *res*.

27 Professor John Davidson, *Remarks at the University of Oregon School of Law Public Interest Environmental Law Conference*, Panel on Public Trust and Atmospheric Trust Litigation (Mar. 3, 2012).

28 For the full scope of environmental law emanating from the police power, *see generally* WILLIAM H. RODGERS, ENVIRONMENTAL LAW, 2D (West Publishing, 1994).

29 For quoted and referenced cases, *see* Bonser-Laine et al. v. Tex. Comm'n on Envtl. Quality, Cause No. D-1-GN-11-002194 (Tex. 201st Jud. Civ. Dist. Ct. Aug. 2, 2012), http://ourchildrenstrust.org/sites/default/files/TexasFinalJudgment.pdf; Order Granting in Part and Denying in Part Defendant's Motion to Dismiss Plaintiffs' Amended Complaint, Sanders-Reed et al. v. Martinez, No. D-101-CV-2011-01514 (N.M. 1st Jud. Dist. Ct. July 14, 2012), http://ourchildrenstrust.org/sites/default/files/Order%20Denying%20Motion%20to%20Dismiss.pdf; *see also* David Morris, *Texas Judge Rules the Sky Belongs to Us All*, HUFFINGTON POST (July 26, 2012). For other referenced laws and case, *see* Comprehensive Environmental Response, Compensation, and Liability Act, 42 U.S.C. §§ 9601–9675, 9601(16)(2012) (definition of "natural resources"); *see also id.* at § 9607(f)(1) (natural resources liability); HAW. CONST. art. XI, § 1; PA. CONST. art. I, § 27 (stating also, "The people have a right to clean air, pure water, and to the preservation of the natural, scenic, historic and esthetic values of the environment."); Community

Legal Defense Fund (rights of nature ordinances), http://celdf.org/article.php?id=410; CONST. OF THE REP. OF ECUADOR, Title II, ch. 7, art. 71 (2008), http://pdba.georgetown.edu/ Constitutions/Ecuador/english08.html; John Vidal, *Bolivia Enshrines Natural World's Rights with Equal Status for Mother Earth*, THE GUARDIAN (Apr. 10, 2011); *Reliance Nat. Resources Ltd.*, 7 S.C.C. 106, ¶ 84 (India) (Sathasivam, J., dissenting); Michael C. Blumm & Rachel D. Guthrie, *Internationalizing the Public Trust Doctrine: Natural Law and Constitutional and Statutory Approaches to Fulfilling the Saxion Vision*, 45 UC DAVIS L. R. 741 (2012).

30 *Ill. Cent. R.R. Co.*, 146 U.S. at 460 (emphasis added).

31 For quoted sources, *see* LEOPOLD, *supra* note 24, at 146, 159; Sierra Club v. Morton, 405 U.S. 727, 750 (1972) (quoting CONSERVE – WATER, LAND AND LIFE 4 (Nov. 1971)).

32 For quoted sources, *see* Noss, *supra* note 14, at 898 (quoting in part Frank Egler); LEOPOLD, *supra* note 24, at 146–47; *see also* DEFENDERS OF WILDLIFE, KEEPING EVERY COG AND WHEEL: REFORMING AND IMPROVING THE NATIONAL WILDLIFE REFUGE SYSTEM (2008).

33 For referenced and quoted report, *see* U.S. GLOBAL CHANGE RESEARCH PROGRAM, GLOBAL CLIMATE CHANGE IMPACTS IN THE UNITED STATES 9, 11, 28–29 (Thomas Karl *et al.*, eds. Cambridge U. Press 2009). For quoted source, *see* Ross Gelbspan, Boiling Point: How Politicians, Big Oil and Coal, Journalists, and Activists Have Fueled the Climate Crisis – and What We Can Do to Avert Disaster 1 (Basic Books 2004). For additional climate projections, *see* James Hansen *et al.*, *Global Warming in the Twenty-First Century: An Alternative Scenario*, 97 PNAS 9875 (2000); Andrew C. Revkin, *"Averting Our Eyes": James Hansen's New Call for Climate Action*, N.Y. TIMES (Nov. 28, 2007).

34 For quoted report, *see* KURT M. CAMPBELL ET AL., THE AGE OF CONSEQUENCES: THE FOREIGN POLICY AND NATIONAL SECURITY IMPLICATIONS OF GLOBAL CLIMATE CHANGE 5–7 (Sharon Burke *et al.* eds., Center for a New American Security 2007) (emphasis added) (also stating, "[G]lobal warming poses not only environmental hazards but profound risks to planetary peace and stability as well."), http://csis.org/files/media/csis/pubs/071105_ageofconsequences.pdf; *see also id.* at 7 (stating that if the world experiences 5.6°C heating by 2100 (a possibility within the projections of the UN climate scientists): "This catastrophic scenario would pose almost inconceivable challenges as human society struggled to adapt. It is by far the most difficult future to visualize without straining credulity."). For quoted case, *see Oposa*, *supra* note 23. For a summary of the 2007 UN climate report by the IPCC, *see* Catherine Brahic, *Blame for Global Warming Placed Firmly on Humankind*, NEWSCIENTIST (Feb. 2, 2007) ("The IPCC report says the rise in global temperatures could be as high as 6.4°C by 2100."). For a description of climate-induced mass human migration, *see* Stefan Lovgren, *Climate Change Creating Millions of "Eco Refugees," UN Warns*, NAT'L GEOGRAPHIC NEWS (Nov. 18, 2005).

35 Joseph L. Sax, *Liberating the Public Trust Doctrine from Its Historical Shackles*, 14 UC DAVIS L. REV. 185–88, 193 (1980).

36 For quoted cases and sources, *see Marks*, 491 P.2d at 380 ("The public uses to which tidelands are subject are sufficiently flexible to encompass changing public needs."); *Matthews*, 471 A.2d at 362 (dry sand beaches) (quoting *McCrane*, 292 A.2d at 598); *Just*, 56 Wis. 2d at 16; Torres, *Public Trust*, *supra* note 13.

37 For quoted case, *see* New Jersey v. New York, 283 U.S. 336, 342 (1931). For importance of groundwater, *see* Yee Huang, *Protecting the Invisible: The Public Trust Doctrine and Groundwater*, CTR. FOR PROGRESSIVE REFORM (July 24, 2009), http://www.progressivereform.org/CPRBlog.cfm?idBlog=897E966E-C8F9-131C-E12ABAA7E9BF8A60. For an overall description of ecosystem services, *see* MILLENNIUM ECOSYSTEM ASSESSMENT, GLOBAL ASSESSMENT REPORTS (2005). For a discussion of South Africa's treatment of water under the public trust, *see* David Takacs, *The Public Trust Doctrine, Environmental Human Rights, and*

the Future of Private Property, 16 N.Y.U. ENVTL. L.J. 711, 740–47 (2008). For the value of soil in carbon sequestration, *see* Rattan Lal, *Soil Carbon Sequestration Impacts on Global Climate Change and Food Security*, 304 SCI. 1623, 1625–26 (2004).

38 For quoted cases, *see Waiāhole Ditch*, 9 P.3d at 500–01; *Oposa, supra* note 23 (noting that, in a mere twenty-five years, the forest cover had plummeted from 53% of the land mass to 2.8%); *Reliance Nat. Resources Ltd.*, 7 S.C.C. 188, pt. V, ¶ 135, pt. IV, ¶ 77 (India) ("[M]arkets, with their emphasis on current consumption and short run profits, may lead to faster depletion, and consequently necessitate a far greater and indeed a primary role for the State."). For mention of this factor, *see* Harrison C. Dunning, *The Public Trust: A Fundamental Doctrine of American Property Law*, 19 ENVTL. L. 515, 522 (1989) (noting that "[n]avigable bays, lakes, and rivers share, in addition to scarcity, a natural suitability for common use").

39 For quoted source, *see* TERRY GLAVIN, THE SIXTH EXTINCTION: JOURNEYS AMONG THE LOST AND LEFT BEHIND 35 (Thomas Dunne Books 2007). For additional discussion of dwindling natural resources, *see* IPCC, SUMMARY FOR POLICYMAKERS 11 (2007) ("[a]pproximately 20–30% of plant and animal species assessed so far are likely to be at increased risk of extinction if increases in global average temperature exceed 1.5–2.5°C"), http://www.ipcc.ch/pdf/assessment-report/ar4/wg2/ar4-wg2-spm.pdf; RICHARD HEINBERG, PEAK EVERYTHING: WAKING UP TO THE CENTURY OF DECLINES (New Soc'y Publ's 2007); CHARLES L. BOLSINGER & KAREN L. WADDELL, U.S. DEP'T OF AGRIC., AREA OF OLD-GROWTH FORESTS IN CALIFORNIA, OREGON, AND WASHINGTON 2 (1993) (only about 10% of the ancient, old-growth forests remain in the Pacific Northwest); THOMAS DAHL, U.S. FISH & WILDLIFE SERV., STATUS AND TRENDS OF WETLANDS IN THE CONTERMINOUS UNITED STATES 1998 TO 2004 57 (2006); BIOLOGICAL RES. DIV., U.S. GEOLOGICAL SURVEY, STATUS AND TRENDS OF THE NATION'S BIOLOGICAL RESOURCES: GRASSLANDS 465 (1998); *Experts Warn of Severe Water Shortages by 2080*, MSNBC (Nov. 18 2008).

40 For quoted case, *see* Stevens v. City of Cannon Beach, 317 Or. 131, 138–9 (1993) (quoting State *ex rel.* Thornton v. Hay, 254 Or. 584, 596 (1969)).

41 For quoted sources, *see* Dunning, *supra* note 38, at 523; *Nat'l Audubon Soc'y*, 658 P.2d at 724; *Matthews*, 471 A.2d at 364; Mineral Cnty. v. Nev. Dep't of Conservation & Nat. Resources, 117 Nev. 235, 248 (2001).

42 For quoted sources, *see New Jersey v. New York*, 283 U.S. at 342; *Nat'l Audubon Soc'y*, 658 P.2d at 712; Wilkinson, *supra* note 4, *at* 315.

43 For quoted sources, *see* J. INST. 2.1.1 (Roman law); *Geer*, 161 U.S. at 525 ("[t]hese things are those which the jurisconsults called '*res communes.*'. . . [T]he air, the water which runs in the rivers, the sea, and its shores . . . [and] wild animals" (internal quotations omitted)); *Ill. Cent. R.R. Co.*, 146 U.S. at 453; *Wis. v. Ill.*, 278 U.S. 367, 408 (1929) (noting rivers as highways); *Stevens*, 317 Or. at 138 (citing *Thornton*, 254 Or. at 588–89). *See also generally* Dunning, *supra* note 38, at 515–25 (noting navigable bays, lakes, and rivers share the feature of suitability for common use); Gerald Torres, *Who Owns the Sky?* 18 PACE ENVTL. L. REV. 227, 241–42 (2001).

44 For quoted and referenced sources, *see Matthews*, 471 A.2d at 365 (citations omitted); *Nat'l Audubon Soc'y*, 658 P.2d at 719–21.

45 For general discussion of the commons, *see* David Bollier, *The Growth of the Commons Paradigm*, UNDERSTANDING KNOWLEDGE AS A COMMONS: FROM THEORY TO PRACTICE 27 (Charlotte Hess & Elinor Ostromed eds., 1st ed., MIT Press 2006).

46 For quoted sources, *see* Garrett Hardin, *The Tragedy of the Commons*, 162 SCI. 1243 (1968); Bollier, *supra* note 45, at 28, 33.

47 For quoted source, *see* BURNS H. WESTON & DAVID BOLLIER, GREEN GOVERNANCE: ECOLOGICAL SURVIVAL, HUMAN RIGHTS, AND THE LAW OF THE COMMONS 3 & n.1, 21,

125 (Cambridge U. Press 2013); *see also The State of the Commons: A Report to Owners from Tomales Bay Institute* 3 (2003).

48 WESTON & BOLLIER, *supra* note 47, at 104, 106, 241.

49 *Id.* at 240–41, 245.

50 Bollier, *supra* note 45, at 33–34.

51 For one argument that the trust should include cultural heritage, *see, e.g.,* Edith Brown Weiss, *The Planetary Trust: Conservation and Intergenerational Equity,* 11 ECOLOGY L.Q. 495, 502 (1984).

52 For quoted sources, *see Sierra Club,* 405 U.S. at 750 n. 8; J. INST 2.1.7, 2.1.1.

8. FIDUCIARY STANDARDS OF PROTECTION AND RESTORATION

1 *See* Chris Ariens, *CNN's Look at "Toxic America,"* TVNEWSER (May 31, 2010).

2 GEORGE LAKOFF, DON'T THINK OF AN ELEPHANT!: KNOW YOUR VALUES AND FRAME THE DEBATE: THE ESSENTIAL GUIDE FOR PROGRESSIVES at xv (Chelsea Green Publ'g 2004).

3 For quoted source, *see* GEORGE G. BOGERT ET AL., BOGERT TRUSTS AND TRUSTEES § 582, at 346 (West rev. 2d ed. 1980) [hereinafter BOGERT TRUSTS 2d]. For additional authority, *see* RESTATEMENT (SECOND) OF TRUSTS § 176 (1959) ("The trustee is under a duty to the beneficiary to use reasonable care and skill to preserve the trust property."); 76 AM. JUR. 2D TRUSTS § 404 (2012) ("A trustee has the right and the duty to safeguard, preserve, or protect the trust assets and the safety of the principal." (citations omitted)); GEORGE T. BOGERT, TRUSTS § 99 (West 6th ed. 1987) [hereinafter BOGERT TRUSTS 6th] ("The trustee has a duty to take whatever steps are necessary ... to protect and preserve the trust property from loss or damage." (citation omitted)). For a sampling of cases expressing the duty, *see* Geer v. Conn., 161 U.S. 519, 534 (1896) ("[I]t is the duty of the legislature to enact such laws as will best preserve the subject of the trust, and secure its beneficial use in the future to the people of the state."); Nat'l Audubon Soc'y v. Super. Court of Alpine County, 658 P.2d 709, 724 (Cal. 1983) [hereinafter *Mono Lake*], *cert. denied sub nom,* City of L.A. Dep't of Water & Power v. Nat'l Audubon Soc'y, 464 U.S. 977 (1983); *In re* Water Use Permit Applications, 9 P.3d 409, 451–53 (Haw. 2000) [hereinafter *Waiāhole Ditch*] ("substantial impairment" standard). For a case relying on an expert's judgment of fiduciary care, *see In re* Estate of Rowe, 712 N.Y.S.2d 662, 665–66 (N.Y. App. Div. 2000) (testimony as to propriety of a particular stock investment by trustee).

4 For quoted sources, *see* U.S. v. White Mt. Apache Tribe, 537 U.S. 465, 475 (2002) ("fall into ruin on his watch"); BOGERT TRUSTS 6th, *supra* note 3, at § 107. For additional sources and cases, *see* 76 AM. JUR. 2D TRUSTS, § 606 (noting that it is within the "power, and a duty of the trustee, to institute actions ... for the protection of the trust estate"); State v. City of Bowling Green, 313 N.E.2d 409, 411 (Ohio 1974); *Mono Lake* 658 P.2d at 728 (noting "affirmative duty" imposed by the trust of "continuing supervision" over the assets); Lytle v. Payette–Or. Slope Irr. Dist., 152 P.2d 934, 939 (1944) (trustee breached the active duty of protection by failing to control an aggressive noxious weed on farm property); *see also* Moore v. Philips 627 P.2d 831, 834 (Kan. App. 1981) ("The owner of a reversion or remainder in fee has a number of remedies available to him against a life tenant who commits waste. He may recover compensatory damages for the injuries sustained.").

5 For quoted sources, *see* Burns H. Weston & Tracy Bach, *Recalibrating the Law of Humans with the Laws of Nature: Climate Change, Human Rights, and Intergenerational Justice,* CLIMATE LEGACY INITIATIVE 60 (2009), http://www.vermontlaw.edu/Documents/CLI%20Policy%20 Paper/CLI_Policy_Paper.pdf; Ian Urbina, *Despite Moratorium, Drilling Projects Move Ahead,* N.Y. TIMES (May 23, 2010). Governmental climate policies worldwide are widely criticized

as inadequate. Carbon reduction targets brought by nations to the Copenhagen Climate Conference in 2007, for example, were called a "disaster track" by climatologist Dr. James Hansen, who said as they would heat the planet well beyond any safe zone. *See* Suzanna Goldberg, *Copenhagen Climate Change Talks Must Fail, Says Top Scientist,* THE GUARDIAN (Dec. 2, 2009); *see also* Brief for Dr. James Hansen as *Amicus Curiae* Supporting Petitioners, Alec L. *et al.* v. Lisa Jackson *et al.,* Case No. 3:11-cv-02203 EMC (N. D. Cal. 2011), http://ourchildrenstrust.org/sites/default/files/Hansen%20Amicus%20.pdf.

6　*Waiāhole Ditch,* 9 P.3d at 455; *see also* District of Columbia v. Air Fla., Inc., 750 F.2d 1077, 1083 (D. C. Cir. 1984) (noting that the public trust "has evolved … into a source of positive state duties"); City of Milwaukee v. State, 214 N.W. 820, 830 (Wis. 1927) ("The trust reposed in the state is not a passive trust; it is governmental, active, and administrative … [and] requires the lawmaking body to act in all cases where action is necessary, not only to preserve the trust, but to promote it.").

7　Edith Brown Weiss, *The Planetary Trust: Conservation and Intergenerational Equity,* 11 ECOLOGY L.Q. 495 (1984); *see also Waiāhole Ditch,* 9 P.3d at 455; *Geer,* 161 U.S. at 534 (government must "preserve the subject of the trust and secure its beneficial use in the future to the people of the state").

8　RESTATEMENT (SECOND) OF TRUSTS § 365 (1959) (noting that a charitable trust can continue indefinitely where the income is paid to beneficiaries).

9　For the primary source on natural capital, *see* PAUL HAWKEN ET AL., NATURAL CAPITALISM: CREATING THE NEXT INDUSTRIAL REVOLUTION (Little, Brown & Co. 1999).

10　For a discussion of natural capital and salmon management, *see* Mary Christina Wood, *The Tribal Right to Wildlife Capital (Part I): Applying Principles of Sovereignty to Protect Imperiled Wildlife Populations,* 37 IDAHO L. REV. 1, 8–10 (2000).

11　For quoted sources, *see* THOMPSON ON REAL PROPERTY, SECOND THOMAS EDITION § 70.05(b) (David A. Thomas, ed. Michie 2005) ("consumption of things"); Melms v. Pabst Brewing Co., 79 N.W. 738, 739–40 (Wis. 1899) ("permanent injury to it"). *See also* Minneapolis Trust Co. v. Isedore Verhulst, 74 Ill. App. 350, 355 (Ill. Ct. App. 1897); RESTATEMENT (SECOND) OF TRUSTS § 365 (1959); Vaden v. Vaden, 38 Tenn. 444, 451 (Tenn. 1858) ("[The life tenant] may use it, and make all the profit on it he can, with due regard to its safety and protection.").

12　*Waihole Ditch,* 9 P.3d at 455 ("irreplaceable res"); Oposa v. Factoran, G.R. No. 101083 (S.C., July 30, 1993) (Phil.), *reprinted (excerpt) in* JAN G. LAITOS ET AL., NATURAL RESOURCES LAW 441–44 (Thompson West 2006). Courts have noted the duty against waste in the context of fisheries shared between state and tribal sovereigns. *See* Puget Sound Gillnetters Ass'n v. U.S. Dist. Court, 573 F.2d 1123 (9th Cir. 1978). *See also* U.S. v. White Mt. Apache Tribe, 537 U.S. 465, 475 (2003) (waste in Indian trust context). For a description of the life tenant as a trustee for the remainderman, *see Vaden,* 38 Tenn. at 451.

13　For quoted case, *see* Melms v. Pabst Brewing Co., 79 N.W. 738, 739 (Wis. 1899). *See also* THOMPSON, *supra* note 11, at § 70.07(k).

14　For referenced statutes, *see* National Environmental Policy Act, 42 U.S.C. § 4331; Federal Water Pollution Control Act, 33 U.S.C. §§ 1251(a) (Clean Water Act); National Forest Management Act of 1976, 16 U.S.C. § 1601(d)(1); Federal Land Policy and Management Act, 43 U.S.C. § 1701; Marine Mammal Protection Act, 16 U.S.C. § 1361(2), 1801(b)(4).

15　*See Waiāhole Ditch,* 9 P.3d at 440; *Mono Lake,* 658 P.2d at 728.

16　For quoted source, *see* Jim Hansen, *The Threat to the Planet,* N.Y. REV. (July 13, 2006). For dead rivers, *see* Ernest Atencio, *The Mine That Turned the Red River Blue,* HIGH COUNTRY NEWS (Aug. 28, 2000).

17　For quoted sources, *see* JAMES HANSEN, STORMS OF MY GRANDCHILDREN: THE TRUTH ABOUT THE COMING CLIMATE CATASTROPHE AND OUR LAST CHANCE TO SAVE HUMANITY 260, 269 (Bloomsbury USA 2009); THOMAS L. FREIDMAN, HOT, FLAT, AND CROWDED: WHY WE NEED A GREEN REVOLUTION – AND HOW IT CAN RENEW AMERICA 38 (Farrar, Straus

& Giroux 2008). For additional analysis on the climate danger of burning oil reserves, *see* Bill McKibben, *Global Warming's Terrifying New Math*, ROLLING STONE (July 19, 2012). For a discussion of peak oil, *see* ROB HOPKINS, THE TRANSITION HANDBOOK: FROM OIL DEPENDENCY TO LOCAL RESILIENCE 23 (Chelsea Green Publ'g 2008).

18 For quoted case, *see* Reliance Nat. Resources Ltd. v. Reliance Indus. Ltd. (India 2010) C.A. Nos.428–4281/2010 par. 79, 99, http://indiankanoon.org/doc/1070490/; *see also id.* at par. 94 (urging a "clear policy statement of conservation, which takes into account total domestic availability, the requisite balancing of current needs with those of future generations, and also India's security requirements"). On the Obama policy, *see* John Broder and Clifford Krauss, *Deepwater Oil Drilling Back in Biz*, THE N.Y. TIMES (Mar. 12, 2012).

19 For referenced source, *see* Edith Brown Weiss, *In Fairness to Future Generations and Sustainable Development*, 8 AM. U.J. INT'L. & POL'Y. 19, 26 (1992). *See also* BOGERT TRUSTS 6th, *supra* note 3, at § 122 (discussing private trust law arrangements for a sale of mineral resources).

20 For quoted source, *see* Weiss, *The Planetary Trust, supra* note 7, at 529. For an example of drought-induced water rationing, *see* Kelly Zito, *A Taste of Future Water Rationing: Bolinas, California Only Allowed 150 Gallons per Day per Customer or YOUR Water Shut Off*, SAN FRAN. CHRONICLE (FEB. 4, 2009).

21 For quoted source, *see* RICHARD M. PIOUS & CHRISTOPHER H. PYLE, THE PRESIDENT, CONGRESS, AND THE CONSTITUTION: POWER AND LEGITIMACY IN AMERICAN POLITICS 100 (The Free Press 1984). *See also* U.S. v. Midwest Oil Co., 236 U.S. 459, 474 (1915). For a discussion of World War II rationing, *see* *World War II Rationing on the U.S. Homefront*, http://www.ameshistoricalsociety.org/exhibits/events/rationing.htm.

22 For quoted source, *see* *Waiāhole Ditch*, 9 P.3d at 451.

23 For quoted sources, *see* THOMPSON, *supra* note 11; The World Charter for Nature, *adopted* by the U.N. General Assembly, Nov. 9, 1982, G.A. Res. 37/7, 37 U.N. GAOR Supp. (no. 51) at 17–18, U.N. Doc. A/37/51 (1982).

24 For referenced source, *see* Weiss, *The Planetary Trust, supra* note 7, at 513. For other sources, *see* *Bycatch*, GREENPEACE, http://www.greenpeace.org/international/en/campaigns/oceans/bycatch/; LAITOS ET AL., *supra* note 12, at 575.

25 For statement of rule against waste in water context, *see e.g.* *Waiāhole Ditch*, 9 P.3d at 47.

26 For sources on wind and coal uses of Appalachia mountains, *see e.g.*, *Coal River Mountain Watch: Coal River Wind*, http://crmw.net/projects/save-coal-river-mountain.php; Vicki Smith, *Coal v. Wind: Energy Fight Rages in W. Va.*, USA TODAY (Oct. 24, 2008); Brandon Keim, *Blowing the Top Off Mountaintop Mining*, WIRED (Sept. 10, 2007); *Hallowed Ground: From Cook Mountain to Blair Mountain and Beyond*, APPALACHIAN VOICES (May 25, 2011), http://appvoices.org/2011/05/25/hallowed-ground-from-cook-mountain-to-blair-mountain-and-beyond/.

27 For quoted source, *see* *Waiāhole Ditch*, 9 P.3d at 451; *id.* at 427 ("rigorous and affirmative" public interest review).

28 For quoted source, *see* *Waiāhole Ditch*, 9 P.3d at 449, 451–52. *See also*, City of Clifton v. Passaic Valley Water Comm'n, 539 A.2d 760, 765 (N.J. Super. Ct. Law Div. 1987) (holding that the public trust "applies with equal impact upon the control of drinking water reserves"); *see also* IDAHO CONST. art. XV §§ 3 & 5.

29 Clean Water Act, 33 U.S.C. § 1251(a)(2).

30 CRAIG COLLINS, TOXIC LOOPHOLES: FAILURES AND FUTURE PROSPECTS FOR ENVIRONMENTAL LAW 236–37 (CAMBRIDGE U. PRESS 2010). For a proposal to phase out pollution and toxic waste, *see* WILLIAM MCDONOUGH & MICHAEL BRAUNGART, CRADLE TO CRADLE: REMAKING THE WAY WE MAKE THINGS (N. Point Press 2002).

31 For quoted source, *see* Joel A. Tickner, *Why Risk Assessment Is Not Enough to Protect Health: Rationale for a Precautionary Approach to Science and Policy*, in RISK ASSESSMENT FOR ENVIRONMENTAL HEALTH at 431 (Mark Robson & William Toscano, eds. 2007).

32 For quoted sources, *see* WASH. DEP'T OF ECOLOGY, *What Are Persistent, Bioaccumulative Toxics (PBTs)*, http://www.ecy.wa.gov/programs/swfa/pbt/; Carol Dansereau *et al.*, *Visualizing Zero: Eliminating Persistent Pollution in Washington State* 5, WASH. TOXICS COALITION (2000), http://watoxics.org/files/visualizing-zero.

33 For quoted cases, *see Geer*, 161 U.S. at 529; *Waiāhole Ditch*, 9 P.3d at 450.

34 *Mono Lake*, 658 P.2d at 723–24.

35 *Waiāhole Ditch*, 9 P.3d at 449, 454 (emphasis added).

36 For quoted source, *see Waiāhole Ditch*, 9 P.3d at 453. For additional water trust cases expressing revocation authority, *see Mono Lake*, 658 P.2d at 723–24; Kootenai Envtl. Alliance v. Panhandle Yacht Club, 671 P.2d 1085, 1094 (Idaho 1983).

37 For quoted and referenced sources, *see* CLEAN WATER ACT, 33 U.S.C. § 1251(A)(1); SEN. RPT. NO. 92–414, 92 CONG., 1ST SESS. 41 (1971), *reprinted in* 2 ENVTL. POLICY DIV., CONG. REF. SERV., A LEGISLATIVE HISTORY OF THE WATER POLLUTION CONTROL ACT AMENDMENTS OF 1972, AT 1460 (Sen. Pub. Works Comm. Print 1973); 1972 U.S.C.C.A.N. 3668, 3709; *see also* Just v. Marinette County, 201 N.W.2d 761, 768 (Wis. 1972) ("The state of Wisconsin under the trust doctrine has a duty to eradicate the present pollution and to prevent further pollution in its navigable waters."). Permits issued under the Clean Water Act last only five years, but they are administratively extended. 33 U.S.C. § 1342(b)(1)(B). Most permits provide for cancellation in face of public harm. For public harm caused by permitted water pollution and agency practice, *see Toxic Waters, A Series About the Worsening Pollution in American Waters and Regulators' Response*, N.Y. TIMES (series beginning Aug. 22 2009).

38 For the public lands retention policy, *see* GEORGE CAMERON COGGINS, CHARLES F. WILKINSON & JOHN D. LESHY, FEDERAL PUBLIC LAND AND RESOURCES LAW 2 (Foundation Press 6th ed. 2007).

39 *Oposa, supra* note 12.

40 For restoration duty in private trust context, *see* RESTATEMENT (SECOND) OF TRUSTS § 205(a),(c)(1959). For restoration duty expressed in environmental statutes, *see* Endangered Species Act, 16 U.S.C. § 1531 *et seq.* Clean Water Act, 33 U.S.C. §§ 1251 *et seq*; Comprehensive Environmental Response, Cleanup, Liability Act (CERCLA), 42 U.S.C. § 9601 *et seq*; Resource Conservation Recovery Act, 42 U.S.C. § 6901 *et seq.*

41 *See* State v. Public Serv. Comm'n, 81 N.W.2d 71, 74 (Wis. 1957) (weighing public needs in administration of trust and noting, "'There must be a realistic and sane legal approach to this problem, namely a balancing of public need and convenience, against [traditional trust purposes,]'"); *Waiāhole Ditch*, 9 P.3d at 409, 422 (expressing government duty to protect public trust uses "'whenever feasible'") (citation omitted).

42 For a description of New York City design, *see* Bob Doppelt, *We Can Use Climate Change as an Opportunity to Create*, REGISTER-GUARD A9 (Feb. 3, 2010); *see also* Jane Margolies, *Rising Currents*, CHANGE OBSERVER (Jan. 14, 2010), http://changeobserver.designobserver.com/entry.html?entry=12477. For sea level rise, *see* James E. Hansen & Makiki Sato, *Paleoclimate Implications for Human-Made Climate Change* 20, NASA GODDARD INST. FOR SPACE STUDIES AND COLUMBIA U. EARTH INST. ("[W]e assert that multi-meter sea level rise on the century time scale are not only possible, but almost dead certain.").

43 F. STUART CHAPIN, III ET AL., PRINCIPLES OF ECOSYSTEM STEWARDSHIP, RESILIENCE-BASED NAT. RESOURCE MGT. IN A CHANGING WORLD 5–6 (F. Stuart Chapin III *et al.*, eds. Springer Science-Business Media 2009) (emphasis in original).

44 Brief for Dr. James Hansen as *Amicus Curiae* Supporting Petitioners, Alec L. *et al.* v. Lisa Jackson *et al.*, Case No. 3:11-cv-02203 EMC (N. D. Cal. 2011) at 5, http://ourchildrenstrust.org/page/51/federal-lawsuit; *see also id.* at 8 (stating, "Unless arrested by effective action, climate change will produce calamitous consequences for humanity and nature alike, as tipping points are reached and points of no return are crossed."). For the climate prescription, *see* James

Hansen *et. al., Scientific Case for Avoiding Dangerous Climate Change to Protect Young People and Nature*, CORNELL U. LIBRARY, arXiv:1110.1365v3 (Mar. 2012), http://arxiv.org/abs/1110.1365. This prescription expresses the fiduciary obligation that forms the basis of Atmospheric Trust Litigation suits and petitions across the United States.

45 For a discussion of the trustee's duty to recoup damages, *see* RESTATEMENT (SECOND) OF TRUSTS § 177 (1959) ("The trustee is under a duty to the beneficiary to take reasonable steps to realize on claims which he holds in trust."). For application to the public trust context, *see* Md. Dep't of Nat. Resources v. Amerada Hess Corp., 350 F. Supp. 1060, 1067 (D. Md. 1972) (holding that the state had a right to maintain common-law action for pollution of waters based on the public trust doctrine in the absence of state legislation); State Dep't of Envtl. Prot. v. Jersey Cent. Power & Light Co., 336 A.2d 750, 758–59 (N.J. Super. Ct. App. Div. 1975) (finding a duty to seek damages for harm to natural resources held in public trust), *rev'd on other grounds*, 351 A.2d 337 (N.J. 1976); State v. City of Bowling Green, 313 N.E.2d 409, 411 (Ohio 1974) (noting public trustees' "*obligation* ... to recoup the public's loss occasioned by ... damage [to] such property") (emphasis added); Wash. Dep't of Fisheries v. Gillette, 621 P.2d 764, 767 (Wash. Ct. App. 1980) (noting right and "fiduciary obligation of any trustee to seek damages for injury to the object of its trust"). For statutes providing for NRDs, *see* CERCLA, 42 U.S.C. §§ 9601–9675, § 9607(f)(1)(2000); Oil Pollution Act of 1990, 33 U.S.C. §§ 2701–2761 (2000); 33 U.S.C. § 2706 (2000); Federal Water Pollution Control Act, 33 U.S.C. § 1321(f)(4). For a listing of NRD actions, *see* U.S. General Accounting Office, *SUPERFUND: Status of Selected Federal Natural Resource Damage Settlements*, (Nov. 1996).

46 For quoted source, *see* BOGERT TRUSTS 6th, *supra* note 3, at § 166; *see also* BOGERT TRUSTS 2d, *supra* note 3, at § 871.

47 For an example of permit shield provision, *see* 42 U.S.C. § 9607(f)(1). For Canada's approach, *see* Canadian Environmental Protection Act, 1999 (S.C. 1999, c. 33).

48 For a discussion of the permit shield, *see* Piney Run Preservation Ass'n v. County Comm'rs of Carroll County, 268 F.3d 255, 269 (Md. 2001). For a provision allowing tribal suit if the permit was issued in contravention of the trust obligation, *see* 42 U.S.C. § 9607(f)(1)(2000).

49 Ill. Cent. R.R. Co. v. Ill., 146 U.S. 387, 453 (1892) (stating also, "The control of the state for the purposes of the trust can never be lost, except as to such parcels as are used in promoting the interests of the public therein, or can be disposed of without any substantial impairment of the public interest in the lands and waters remaining.").

50 Lake Mich. Fed'n v. U.S. Army Corp. of Eng'rs, 742 F. Supp. 441, 445 (N.D. Ill. 1990) (over-turning a grant by the Illinois State Legislature to Loyola University (a private nonprofit insti-tution) because it was made for the "primary purpose" of benefitting Loyola University, not the public). For additional cases, *see Kootenai Envtl. Alliance*, 671 P.2d at 1089 ("a two part test emerges to determine the validity of the grant of public trust property. One, is the grant in aid of navigation, commerce, or other trust purposes, and two, does it substantially impair the public interest in the lands and waters remaining?"); Wis. v. Public Serv. Comm'n, 81 N.W.2d 71, 74 (Wis. 1957) ("Certainly the trust doctrine would prevent the state from making any substantial grant of a lake bed for a purely private purpose.").

9. FROM BUREAUCRATS TO TRUSTEES

1 Meinhard v. Salmon, 164 N.E. 545, 546 (Ct. App. N.Y. 1928).

2 *Id. See also* DOUGLAS LAYCOCK, MODERN AMERICAN REMEDIES 593 (3d ed. 2002) ("A trustee is constantly subject to the temptation to use trust assets for his own benefit. The equity courts developed strict rules of fiduciary duty to combat that temptation.").

3 For quoted sources, *see* B. L. RAYNER, LIFE OF THOMAS JEFFERSON, WITH SELECTIONS FROM THE MOST VALUABLE PORTIONS OF HIS VOLUMINOUS AND UNRIVALED PRIVATE

CORRESPONDENCE 356 (Boston, Lilly, Wait, Colman, & Holden, 1834) ("When a man assumes a public trust"); PETER G. BROWN, RESTORING THE PUBLIC TRUST: A FRESH VISION FOR PROGRESSIVE GOVERNMENT IN AMERICA 79 (Beacon Press 1994). *See also* ROSCOE POUND AND THEODORE F. T. PLUCKNETT, READINGS ON THE HISTORY AND SYSTEM OF THE COMMON LAW 624 (Lawyers Coop. Publ'g Co. 3d ed. 1927) (quoting BRUCE WYMAN, THE SPECIAL LAW GOVERNING PUBLIC SERVICE CORPORATIONS § 331 (1911)) (describing duties of public service). For cases involving private citizens attempting to hold the government accountable for violating its public trust fiduciary duties, *see e.g.,* Nat'l Audubon Soc'y v. Sup. Ct., 658 P.2d 709 (Cal. 1983); In re Water Use Permit Applications 9 P.3d 409 (Haw. 2000)[hereinafter *Waiāhole Ditch*]; Gerwitz v. Long Beach, 330 N.Y.S.2d 495 (Sup. Ct. 1972).

4 For quoted sources, *see* Meinhard, 164 N.E. at 546 (J. Cardozo); GEORGE T. BOGERT, TRUSTS § 95, at 341–47 (West 6th ed. 1987) (also explaining that trust law "is principally desirous of procuring a result which will keep all trustees out of temptation...."); Karen E. Boxx, *Of Punctilios and Paybacks: The Duty of Loyalty Under the Uniform Trust Code,* 67 MO. L. REV. 279, 279–80 (2002) (emphasis added) (footnotes omitted). For additional discussion, *see* 76 AM. JUR. 2D *Trusts* § 350 (2005).

5 Geer v. Conn. 161 U.S. 519, 529 (1896). *See also* Joseph L. Sax, *The Public Trust Doctrine in Natural Resource Law: Effective Judicial Intervention,* 68 MICH. L. REV. 471, 490 (1970) (observing: "[A] court will look with considerable skepticism upon *any* governmental conduct which is calculated ... to subject public uses to the self-interest of private parties.").

6 For quoted sources, *see* Gerald Torres, *Who Owns the Sky?* 18 PACE ENVTL. L. REV. 227, 239 (2001); *Oil Brokers Sex Scandal May Affect Drilling Debate,* USA TODAY (Sept. 11, 2008) (quoting Office of Inspector General).

7 BOGERT TRUSTS 6th, *supra* note 4, at 341.

8 For quoted source, *see* BROWN, *supra* note 3, at 131. For referenced source, *see* Citizens United v. FEC, 130 S. Ct. 876, 913 (2010). As the dissent noted, it is "next to impossible" to prove that, in a given instance, a specific vote was exchanged for a specific campaign contribution. *Id.* at 965.

9 For quoted case, *see* Caperton v. A.T. Massey Coal Co., Inc., 556 U.S. 868, 872–88 (2009) (also asking whether "a person with a personal stake in a particular case had a significant and disproportionate influence in placing the judge on the case by raising funds or directing the judge's election campaign when the case was pending or imminent"). For the general judicial impropriety standard, *see id.* at 888–89. This standard has been adopted by the American Bar Association and nearly every state. For scholarship suggesting applying the duty of loyalty to members of Congress engaged in redistricting for purposes of election laws, *see* D. Theodore Rave, *Politicians as Fiduciaries,* 126 HARV. L. REV. 671 (2013).

10 For referenced sources, *see* Gerald Torres, *The Public Trust: The Law's DNA,* Keynote Address at the University of Oregon School of Law (Feb. 23, 2012); Sax, *The Public Trust Doctrine, supra* note 5, at 471.

11 For referenced and quoted regulation, *see* 5 C.F.R. § 2635.101(a)(2011); *id.* at § 2635 (Standards of Ethical Conduct for Employees of the Executive Branch); 5 U.S.C. § 3331 (Oath of Office). For other quoted source, *see* BOGERT TRUSTS 6th, *supra* note 4, at 343 (*"out of temptation"*) (emphasis added).

12 For background on the MMS and BP oil spill, *see* Russell Gold, Ben Casselman & Guy Chazan, *Leaking Oil Well Lacked Safeguard Device,* WALL ST. J. (Apr. 28, 2010); Juliet Eilperin, *U.S. Exempted BP's Gulf of Mexico Drilling From Environmental Impact Study,* WASH. POST (May 5, 2010); John M. Broder, *U.S. to Split Up Agency Policing the Oil Industry,* N.Y. TIMES (May 11, 2010); Juliet Eilperin & Ed O'Keefe, *Offshore Drilling Agency to Undergo Radical Overhaul,*

Salazar Announces, WASH. POST (May 12, 2010). For background on the Forest Service conflict of interest, *see* Chapter 4, supra.

13 CRAIG COLLINS, TOXIC LOOPHOLES: FAILURES AND FUTURE PROSPECTS FOR ENVIRONMENTAL LAW 235–36 (Cambridge U. Press 2010).

14 18 U.S.C. § 207(d)(2012).

15 BOGERT TRUSTS 6th, *supra* note 4, at § 167 613; *see also id.* at 558–66.

16 LOUIS D. BRANDEIS, OTHER PEOPLE'S MONEY – AND HOW THE BANKERS USE IT 92 (1914).

17 For a discussion of whistle-blower protections, *see* Henry Kelly *et al.*, *Flying Blind: The Rise, Fall, and Possible Resurrection of Science Policy Advice in the United States*, FED'N OF AM. SCIENTISTS 56 (2004). For a description of agency suppression of scientists, *see* Public Employees for Environmental Responsibility, *Endangered Species Act Implementation: Science or Politics?: Hearing Before the House Nat. Resources Comm.* (May 9, 2007) (testimony of Jeff Ruch, Executive Director), http://www.peer.org/assets/docs/doi/07_9_5_peer_testimony.pdf.

18 For referenced litigation, *see* Mass. v. EPA., 549 U.S. 497 (2007).

19 BOGERT TRUSTS 6th, *supra* note 4, at § 92, 328.

20 *Id.* at 328–30.

21 For quoted sources, *see id.* at 328–32 ("A co-trustee owes"); Crane v. Hearn, 26 N.J. Eq. 378, 381 (N.J. Ch. 1875) ("It is the duty").

22 For quoted case, *see* Costello v. Costello, 209 N.Y. 252, 261 (1913). *See also* RESTATEMENT (THIRD) OF TRUSTS: DUTY OF PRUDENCE § 77(2),(3)(2007); BOGERT TRUSTS 6th, *supra* note 4, at § 93, 334.

23 For reporting on regulation of oil drilling in the Gulf, *see* Eilperin, *supra* note 12.

24 *Federal Science and the Public Good: Securing the Integrity of Science in Policy Making*, UNION OF CONCERNED SCIENTISTS iii (2008). *See also Political Interference With Climate Change Science Under the Bush Admin.*, H.R. COMM. ON OVERSIGHT & GOV'T REFORM, 110th Cong., 33 (2007).

25 For a sampling of reform proposals, *see* UCS, *Federal Science, supra* note 24; Merrill Goozner & Corrie Maudlin, *Ensuring Independence and Objectivity at the National Academies*, CENTER FOR SCIENCE IN THE PUBLIC INTEREST (2006); Kelly *et al.*, *supra* note 17, at 2–4; *Scientific Integrity Recommendations for the Obama Administration*, UNION OF CONCERNED SCIENTISTS (Jul. 27, 2009); Dylan Blaylock, *GAP Submits Comments on Obama's Scientific Integrity Policy*, GOVERNMENT ACCOUNTABILITY PROJECT (May 23, 2009); *Letter to Office of Science & Technology Policy Re: Scientific Integrity in the Obama Administration*, CENTER FOR PROGRESSIVE REFORM (Apr. 3, 2009), http://www.progressivereform.org/articles/Holdren_CleanSci_Letter_040309.pdf. The Obama administration created a new emphasis on scientific integrity, but progress was criticized as slow and inadequate. *See Obama Administration a Year Behind on Scientific Integrity Plan*, UNION OF CONCERNED SCIENTISTS (Mar. 9, 2010).

26 *In re Hall*, 164 N.Y. 196, 199, 200 (1900); *see also* BOGERT TRUSTS 6th, *supra* note 4, at § 102, 366–67.

27 Joel A. Tickner, *Why Risk Assessment is Not Enough to Protect Health: Rationale for a Precautionary Approach to Science and Policy*, in RISK ASSESSMENT FOR ENVTL. HEALTH 423 (Mark G. Robson & William A. Toscano, eds., 2007); *see also id.* at 432 ("Reluctance to acknowledge uncertainty pushes agencies to use numbers as a façade to cover up what are often political decisions."); *id.* at 430 ("What is clear is that two different risk assessments, conducted on the same problem … will almost always come up with different answers."). For additional discussion, *see* COLLINS, *supra* note 13, at 236; *Toxic Ignorance: The Continuing Absence of Basic Health Testing for Top-Selling Chemicals in the U.S.*, ENVTL. DEF. FUND 7 (1997), http://www.edf.org/documents/243_toxicignorance.pdf.

28 For background on MMS's regulatory program, *see* Ian Urbina, *Despite Moratorium, Drilling Projects Move Ahead*, N.Y. TIMES A1 (May 24, 2010). According to the N.Y. *Times*, even after the BP well exploded, the agency doled out at least nineteen environmental waivers for drilling projects, in addition to at least seventeen permits for drilling. For criticism, *see* Mark Cherniak, *Oil Spill: Regulators & Citizens Missed Their Chance*, REGISTER-GUARD (May 12, 2010); Campbell Robertson & Clifford Krauss, *Gulf Spill is the Largest of Its Kind, Scientists Say*, N.Y. TIMES (Aug. 3, 2010). *See also* Complaint In Re: Oil Spill By the Oil Rig "Deepwater Horizon," Case 2:10-md-02179-CJB-SS, Par. 54, 63 (filed May 2, 2012, E. D. La.).

29 For quoted textbook, *see* CHRIS WOLD ET AL., CLIMATE CHANGE AND THE LAW 166 (2009). For quoted cases, *see* Ethyl Corp. v. EPA, 541 F.2d 1, 24–25 (D.C. Cir. 1976) (certiorari denied) (adopting precautionary approach); *Waiāhole Ditch*, P.3d at 466 n.59 and accompanying text; *see also id.* at 466–67 (quoting *Ethyl Corp*, 542 F.2d at 24–25 ("'Questions involving the environment are particularly prone to uncertainty.... [T]he statutes – and common sense – demand regulatory action to prevent harm, even if the regulator is less than certain that harm is otherwise inevitable.'").

30 For quoted sources, *see* Agne Sirinskiene, *The Status of Precautionary Principle: Moving Towards a Rule of Customary Law*, JURISPRUDENCE 2009, No. 4(118) 349, 360 (Mykolas Romeris U., Lithuania) (describing European law); CONST. OF THE REP. OF ECUADOR Tit. II, Ch. 7, Art. 4 (Oct. 20, 2008); *Rio Declaration on Environment and Development*, Principle 15, United Nations Conference on Environment and Development, Rio de Janeiro, Braz. (June 3–14, 1992). For additional discussion, *see* COLLINS, *supra* note 13, at 234–35.

31 For quoted sources, *see* U.N. Framework Convention on Climate Change, Art. 3 (Mar. 21, 1994); *The Copenhagen Diagnosis: Updating the World on the Latest Climate Science* at 7, UNSW Climate Change Research Centre (2009) (Executive Summary).

32 DAVID MICHAELS, DOUBT IS THEIR PRODUCT: HOW INDUSTRY'S ASSAULT ON SCIENCE THREATENS YOUR HEALTH at xi. (Oxford U. Press 2008). *See also* COLLINS, *supra* note 13, at 235.

33 *See* PRECAUTIONARY TOOLS FOR RESHAPING ENVIRONMENTAL POLICY (Nancy J. Myers & Carolyn Raffensperger, eds., Massachusetts Institute of Technology, 2006).

34 For quoted source, *see* Zuch v. Conn. Bank & Trust Co., Inc., 500 A.2d 565, 568 (Conn. App. Ct. 1985). For additional discussion of the accounting duty, *see* RESTATEMENT (THIRD) OF TRUSTS § 82(1)(2007); 76 AM. JUR. 2D *Trusts* § 371.

35 For examples of statutory reporting requirements, *see* Global Change Research Act of 1990, 15 U.S.C. §§ 2921–2961 (2006); Endangered Species Act, 16 U.S.C. §§ 1531–1544 (2006); 42 U.S.C. §§ 11001–110050 (2012); Emergency Planning and Community Right to Know Act, 42 U.S.C. § 11001 *et seq.* (1986).

36 For use of an accounting in the climate context, *see* Torres, *Who Owns the Sky? supra* note 6, at 547; Mary Christina Wood, *Atmospheric Trust Litigation, in* ADJUDICATING CLIMATE CHANGE: STATE, NATIONAL, AND INTERNATIONAL APPROACHES (William C. G. Burns & Hari M. Osofsky, eds., Cambridge University Press 2009).

37 For quoted case, *see* U.S. v. Midwest Oil Co., 236 U.S. 459, 474 (1915). For analysis of statutory boilerplate provisions, *see* Robert L. Glicksman, *Coal-Fired Power Plants, Greenhouse Gases, & State Statutory Substantial Endangerment Provisions: Climate Change Comes to Kansas*, 56 U. KAN. L. REV. 517, 565–95 (2008). Agencies have the power to revoke permits under the trust without providing compensation. *See* Ill. Cent. R.R. Co. v. Ill., 146 U.S. 387, 460 (1892) ("There can be no irrepealable contract in a conveyance of property by a grantor in disregard of a public trust, under which he was bound to hold and manage it."); Nat'l Audubon Soc'y v. Super. Ct., 658 P.2d 709, 723 (Cal. 1983); Kootenai Envtl. Alliance, Inc. v. Panhandle Yacht Club, Inc., 671 P.2d 1085, 1094 (Idaho 1983).

10. BEYOND BORDERS: SHARED ECOLOGY AND THE DUTIES
OF SOVEREIGN CO-TENANT TRUSTEES

1 *See* Mark Cohen *et al.*, *Modeling the Atmospheric Transport and Deposition of Mercury to the Great Lakes*, 95 ENVTL. RES. 247, 261 (2004); GREAT LAKES COMMISSION, EVALUATION OF TRANSPORT AND DEPOSITION OF MERCURY IN THE GREAT LAKES REGION (2010); GREGORY A. WETHERBEE *ET AL.*, FISSION PRODUCTS IN NATIONAL ATMOSPHERIC DEPOSITION PROGRAM – WET DEPOSITION SAMPLES PRIOR TO AND FOLLOWING THE FUKUSHIMA DAI-ICHI NUCLEAR POWER PLANT INCIDENT, MARCH 8–APRIL 5, 2011, U.S. GEOLOGICAL SURVEY OPEN-FILE RPT. 2011–1277 (2012).

2 For quoted sources, *see* SUSAN J. BUCK, THE GLOBAL COMMONS: AN INTRODUCTION 28 (Island Press 1998); Johan Rockström *et al.*, *Planetary Boundaries: Exploring the Safe Operating Space for Humanity*, 14 (2) ECOLOGY AND SOC'Y 32 (2009). WILLIAM BLACKSTONE, COMMENTARIES ON THE LAWS OF ENGLAND: BOOK THE FIRST 41 (Clarendon Press 1765).

3 Peter H. Sand, *Sovereignty Bounded: Public Trusteeship for Common Pool Resources*, 4 GLOBAL ENVTL. POL. 47, 57 (2004). For additional commentary, *see* Mary Turnipseed *et al.*, *Reinvigorating the Public Trust Doctrine: Expert Opinion on the Potential of a Public Trust Mandate in U.S. and International Environmental Law*, ENVT. MAG. Sep.–Oct. 2010, at 6, 12; Edith Brown Weiss, *The Planetary Trust: Conservation and Intergenerational Equity*, 11 ECOLOGY L. Q. 495 (1984).

4 *See* Suzanne Goldenberg *et al.*, *Leaked UN Report Shows Cuts Offered at Copenhagen Would Lead to 3C Rise*, THE GUARDIAN (Dec. 17, 2009). For additional discussion of perpetual failure in climate negotiations, *see Climate Change: Theatre of the Absurd*, THE ECONOMIST (Dec. 1, 2012).

5 For discussion of international climate stalemate, *see* Ronald Bailey, *Kicking the Can on Climate Change*, REASON (Mar. 2012); Alexander Ochs & Haibing Ma, *China Prepares to Steal United States' Thunder, May Launch Cap-and-Trade within Five Years*, WORLDWATCH INSTITUTE.

6 For quoted sources, *see* Mark Memmott, *Obama in Copenhagen; Climate Talks in Disarray; Urges "Action Over Inaction,"* THE TWO-WAY (Dec. 18, 2009); United Nations World Commission on Environment and Development, Our Common Future 271 (1987).

7 RICHARD J. BARNET & JOHN CAVANAGH, GLOBAL DREAMS: IMPERIAL CORPORATIONS AND THE NEW WORLD ORDER 422 (Touchstone 1995).

8 EDITH BROWN WEISS, IN FAIRNESS TO FUTURE GENERATIONS: INTERNATIONAL LAW, COMMON PATRIMONY, AND INTERGENERATIONAL EQUITY 45 (U.N. U. 1989); *see also* Weiss, *The Planetary Trust, supra* note 3.

9 For quoted sources, *see* Arnold v. Mundy, 6 N.J.L. 1, 71 (N. J. 1821) ("Everything susceptible"); Idaho *ex rel.* Evans v. Or., 462 U.S. 1017, 1031, n.1 (1983) (O'Connor, J., dissenting). *See also* Ga. v. Tenn. Copper Co., 206 U.S. 230, 237 (1907) ("[T]he state has an interest independent of and behind the titles of its citizens, in all the earth and air within its domain."). For cases finding shared property rights in fisheries or water, *see* Wash. v. Wash. State Commercial Passenger Fishing Vessel Ass'n, 443 U.S. 658, 676–79 (1979); Minn. v. Mille Lacs Band of Chippewa Indians, 526 U.S. 172, 204–05 (1999); Ariz. v. Cal., 373 U.S. 546, 600–01 (1963).

10 For quoted sources, *see* Ved P. Nanda & William K. Ris, Jr., *The Public Trust Doctrine: A Viable Approach to International Environmental Protection*, 5 ECOLOGY L. Q. 291, 306 (1976); Michael C. Blumm & Rachel D. Guthrie, *Internationalizing the Public Trust Doctrine: Natural Law and Constitutional and Statutory Approaches to Fulfilling the Saxion Vision*, 45 UC DAVIS L. REV. 741, 750 (2012). For examples of constitutional trust provisions in various countries, *see e.g.*, S. AFR. CONST., § 24 (1996); CONST. OF KENYA (2010); CONST. OF THE REPUBLIC OF ECUADOR, tit. 2, ch. 7, art. 71–74 (2008); CONST. OF UKRAINE, tit. I, art. 13

(1991); *see also* John Vidal, *Bolivia Enshrines Natural World's Rights with Equal Status for Mother Earth*, THE GUARDIAN (Apr. 10, 2011). For commentary on the doctrine's evolution in South Africa and other countries, *see* David Takacs, *The Public Trust Doctrine, Environmental Human Rights, and the Future of Private Property*, 16 N.Y.U. ENVTL. L.J. 711, 743 (2008). For judicial characterization of the trust as a covenant, *see* Alliance to Protect Nantucket Sound Inc. v. Energy Facilities Siting Bd., 932 N.E.2d 787, 816 (Mass. 2010) (Marshall, C.J., concurring and dissenting) ("The public trust doctrine stands as a covenant between the people of the Commonwealth and their government, a covenant to safeguard our tidelands for all generations for the use of the people.").

11   For quoted sources and referenced cases, *see* PATRICIA W. BIRNIE *ETAL.*, INTERNATIONAL LAW AND THE ENVIRONMENT 39 (Oxford U. Press 2009); Puget Sound Gillnetters Ass'n v. U.S. Dist. Court for W. Dist. of Wash., 573 F.2d 1123, 1126 (9th Cir. 1978) (holding that the treaty established something "analogous to a cotenancy [in fisheries], with the tribes as one cotenant and all citizens of the Territory (and later of the state) as the other."); U.S. v. Wash., 520 F.2d 676, 685–86, 690 (9th Cir. 1975) (applying co-tenancy construct, by analogy, to Indian fishing rights); U.S. v. 1.58 Acres of Land, 523 F. Supp. 120, 123 (D. Mass. 1981) (footnote omitted). For general discussion of co-tenancy, *see* BLACK'S LAW DICTIONARY 1603 (9th ed. 2009); JOSEPH WILLIAM SINGER, PROPERTY LAW: RULES, POLICIES, AND PRACTICES 664–65 (5th ed. 2010); 20 AM. JUR. 2D *Co-tenancy and Joint Ownership* § 1 (2012) (noting that a co-tenancy is "a tenancy under more than one distinct title, but with unity of possession."). The scholarly construct of sovereign co-tenancy originated in Mary Christina Wood, *Atmospheric Trust Litigation*, ADJUDICATING CLIMATE CHANGE: STATE, NATIONAL, AND INTERNATIONAL APPROACHES (William C.G. Burns & Hari M. Osofsky, eds., Cambridge U. Press 2009). For additional discussion, *see* Evan Fox-Decent, *From Fiduciary States to Joint Trusteeship of the Atmosphere: The Right to a Healthy Environment Through a Fiduciary Prism*, chapter in FIDUCIARY DUTY AND THE ATMOSPHERIC TRUST 263 (Ken Coghill, Charles Sampford, Tim Smith, eds, Ashgate Press 2012) (adopting the approach in the context of a human rights analysis of climate obligations and noting "the idea that states are essentially joint trustees of the earth's atmosphere").

12   For quoted sources, *see* GEORGE T. BOGERT, TRUSTS § 91 (West 6th ed. 1987) ("all must unite"); U.S. v. Wash., 520 F.2d at 685. For additional discussion of the co-tenant and co-trustee duty against waste, *see* BOGERT TRUSTS 6th, *supra*, § 92 ("It is the duty of one trustee to protect the trust estate from any misfeasance by his co-trustee.") (citation omitted); EARL P. HOPKINS, HANDBOOK ON THE LAW OF REAL PROPERTY § 214, at 342 (West 1896); WILLIAM F. WALSH, 2 COMMENTARIES ON THE LAW OF REAL PROPERTY § 131, at 69, 72 (M. Bender & Co. 1947); 76 AM. JUR. 2D *Trusts* §§ 331, 404 (2005) (footnote omitted) ("[T]he trustee must make the trust property productive, and must not suffer the estate to waste or diminish, or fall out of repair."); Lytle v. Payette-Or. Slope Irrigation Dist., 152 P.2d 934, 939 (Or. 1944) (describing waste as "'a spoil or destruction in ... corporeal hereditaments, to the [detriment of the one who has a] remainder or reversion'") (citation omitted); Dale E. Kremer, *The Inter Vivos Rights of Cotenants Inter Se*, 37 WASH. L. REV. 70 at 76 (1962).

13   Sand, *supra* note 3, at 57–58.

14   For quoted sources, *see* JUSTINIAN, THE INSTITUTES, 1.2.1, 2.1.1 (T. Sandars trans. 1st Am. Ed. 1876) ("By the law of nature these things are common to mankind–the air, running water, the sea, and consequently the shores of the sea."); Lord v. Steamship Co., 102 U.S. 541, 544 (1880) ("The Pacific ocean belongs"); Ala. v. Tex., 347 U.S. 272, 278 (1954) (Black, J., dissenting); U.N. Conv. on the Law of the Sea, Preamble, Dec. 10, 1982, 1833 U.N.T.S. 398; *id.* at Part XI,§ 3, art. 150, (b); U.N. Framework Conv. on Climate Change art. 2, 1771 U.N.T.S. 107, art. 3, ¶ 1, p. 4 (May 9, 1992) [hereinafter UNFCCC]. For commentary suggesting a planetary trust in oceans, *see generally* Mary Turnipseed *et al.*, *Using the Public Trust Doctrine to Achieve Ocean*

Stewardship, chapter in RULE OF LAW FOR NATURE (Christina Voight & Hans-Christian Bugge, eds, Cambridge University Press 2013); Gail Osherenko, *New Discourses on Ocean Governance: Understanding Property Rights and the Public Trust,* 21 J. ENVTL. L. & LITIG. 317 (2006); Mary Turnipseed *et al., The Silver Anniversary of the United States' Exclusive Economic Zone: Twenty-Five Years of Ocean Use and Abuse, and the Possibility of a Blue Water Public Trust Doctrine,* 36 ECOLOGY L.Q. 1 (2009). For discussion of an atmospheric trust, *see* Wood, ADJUDICATING CLIMATE CHANGE, *supra* note 11; Mary Christina Wood, *Atmospheric Trust Litigation across the World,* FIDUCIARY DUTY AND THE ATMOSPHERIC TRUST (Ken Coghill, Charles Sampford & Tim Smith, eds., Ashgate 2012); Gerald Torres, *Who Owns the Sky?* 18 PACE ENVTL. L. REV. 227 (2001).

15 For referenced sources, *see* Food and Agriculture Organization of the United Nations (FAO): International Treaty on Plant Genetic Resources for Food and Agriculture, 2400 U.N.T.S. 303, preamble, art. 1.1, art. 5.1a-f (Nov. 3, 2001); Convention on Biological Diversity, preamble, June 5, 1992, 1760 U.N.T.S. 79.

16 *See* UNESCO Convention for the Protection of the World Cultural and Natural Heritage, 16 Nov. 1972, Preamble, 1037 U.N.T.S. 151; World Heritage List, UNESCO WORLD HERITAGE CONV. The convention has been ratified by 190 parties.

17 For quoted source, *see Legality of the Threat or Use of Nuclear Weapons, Advisory Opinion,* 1996 I.C.J. 226, 455, 502 (July 8) (dissenting opinion of Justice Weeramantry). For referenced sources, *see* John Davidson, *Remarks at the University of Oregon School of Law Public Interest Environmental Law Conference,* Panel on Public Trust and Atmospheric Trust Litigation (Mar. 3, 2012); WEISS, IN FAIRNESS, *supra* note 8, at 70. For source on Fukushima, *see* Hiroko Tabuchi, *Japan Nuclear Plant May Be Worse Off Than Thought,* N.Y. TIMES (Mar. 29, 2012). For dangers of nuclear waste, *see* WILLIAM A. ALLEY & ROSEMARIE ALLEY, TOO HOT TO TOUCH: THE PROBLEM OF HIGH-LEVEL NUCLEAR WASTE (Cambridge Univ. Press 2012).

18 Sand, *supra* note 3, at 48.

19 There is a principle of international law preventing transboundary harm. However, the principle has not been applied with any sophistication to ecological harm arising from multifarious sources. For full discussion, *see* TRANSBOUNDARY HARM IN INTERNATIONAL LAW: LESSONS FROM THE TRAIL SMELTER ARBITRATION (Rebecca M. Bratspies & Russell A. Miller, eds., Cambridge U. Press, 2006).

20 *See* BOGERT TRUSTS 6th, *supra* note 12, at § 154 ("If the trustee is preparing to commit a breach of trust, the beneficiary need not sit idly by and wait until damage has been done. He may sue in a court of equity for an injunction against the wrongful act."); Marks v. Whitney, 491 P.2d 374, 381 (Cal. 1971) (private citizens have standing to sue under public trust, though a court may raise the issue on its own).

21 For quoted case, *see* U.S. v. Wash., 520 F.2d 676, 685 (9th Cir. 1975). For other sources on enforcement against waste, *see* 63C AM. JUR. 2D PROPERTY § 31; Chosar Corp. v. Owens, 370 S.E.2d 305, 307–08 (Va. 1988) (co-tenants found liable for waste); Anders v. Meredith, 1839 WL 525 (N.C. 1839). For materials discussing traditional native approach, *see* Burns H. Weston & Tracy Bach, *Recalibrating the Law of Humans with the Laws of Nature: Climate Change, Human Rights, and Intergenerational Justice,* Climate Legacy Initiative 31 (2009); REBECCA TSOSIE, WAR AND BORDER CROSSINGS: ETHICS WHEN CULTURES CLASH 271 (Peter A. French & Jason A. Short eds., 2005) ("sustainability was the natural result, if not the conscious goal, of deeply rooted environmental ethics and traditional land-based economies."); Robin Wall Kimmerer, *Weaving Traditional Ecological Knowledge into Biological Education: A Call to Action,* 52 BIOSCIENCE 432 (May 2002).

22 *See* Stephen C. Webster, *Chevron: "We're Not Paying" $27B fine for Ecuador Rain Forest Contamination,* CURRENT (July 20, 2009); *Ecuador Court Upholds $18bn Penalty against*

Chevron, THE GUARDIAN (Jan. 4, 2012). For reporting on aggregate wealth of multinational corporations, *see* Vincent Trivett, *25 US Mega Corporations: Where They Rank If They Were Countries,* BUSINESS INSIDER (June 27, 2011).

23 For quoted sources, *see* Susan Solomona *et al., Irreversible Climate Change Due to Carbon Dioxide Emissions,* 106 PROC. NAT'L ACAD. SCI. U.S. 1704, 1704 (Feb. 10, 2009) ("largely irreversible"); I. Allison *et al., The Copenhagen Diagnosis: Updating the World on the Latest Climate Science,* 49 U. OF NEW SOUTH WALES CLIMATE CHANGE RESEARCH CENTER (Nov. 2009) ("loc[k] in climate change"); Brief for James Hansen as *Amicus Curiae* supporting plaintiff at 6, Alec L. v. Jackson, No. 3:11-CV-02203, 5, 7 (N.D. Cal. Nov. 11, 2011) [hereinafter Hansen, *Amicus Brief*], http://ourchildrenstrust.org/page/51/federal-lawsuit. For additional discussion, *see* UNITED NATIONS ENVIRONMENT PROGRAMME, *Climate Change Science Compendium ii* (2009) (statement of Ban Ki-moon, Secretary-General of the United Nations: "[U]nless we act, we will see catastrophic consequences including rising sea levels, droughts and famine, and the loss of up to a third of the world's plant and animal species."); Johan Rockström, *et al., A Safe Operating Space for Humanity,* NATURE 461, 472–75 (Sept. 2009) (temperature increase of 6°C "would severely challenge the viability of contemporary human societies"); Patrick Parenteau, *Come Hell and High Water: Coping with the Unavoidable Consequences of Climate Disruption* 34 Vt. L. Rev. 957, 958–60 (2009) (citing reports and explaining unavoidable heating); James Hansen, *et al., Target Atmospheric CO2: Where Should Humanity Aim?* 2 OPEN ATMOSPHERIC SCI. J. 217 (Nov. 2008).

24 The approach known at Atmospheric Trust Litigation was originated in Wood, ADJUDICATING CLIMATE CHANGE, *supra* note 11.

25 For quoted source, *see* UNFCCC, *supra* note 14, art. 2; *see also id.,* art. 3 ¶ 3 ("Where there are threats of serious or irreversible damage [from climate change], lack of full scientific certainty should not be used as a reason for postponing such measures."). For the science underlying a 350 ppm target, *see* Hansen, *Amicus Brief, supra* note 23, at 7; Hansen *et al., Target, supra* note 23, at 217 ("If humanity wishes to preserve a planet similar to that on which civilization developed and to which life on Earth is adapted, paleoclimate evidence and ongoing climate change suggest that CO_2 will need to be reduced [to] at most 350 ppm."); Marlowe Hood, *UN Scientist Backs "350" Target for CO2 Reduction,* YAHOO! NEWS (Aug. 25, 2009).

26 For quoted source, *see* Paul Baer *et. al., A 350 ppm Emergency Pathway,* A Greenhouse Development Rights Brief, 4 (Nov. 2009) ("few if any peacetime precedents"). For the 350 trajectory of emissions reduction, *see* James Hansen *et. al., Scientific Case for Avoiding Dangerous Climate Change to Protect Young People, Future Generations, and Nature,* CORNELL U. LIBRARY, arXiv:1110.1365v3 (Mar. 2012); *see also* Hansen, *Amicus Brief, supra* note 23, at 5 (explaining trajectory as what is "minimally needed").

27 For quoted source, *see* I. Allison *et al., supra* note 23, at 51 ("drastically increases"); *see also Climate Change Science Compendium II,* UNITED NATIONS ENVIRONMENT PROGRAMME (2009) ("drastically increases"). For the 3.5% figure associated with a start date of 2005, *see* Hansen, *Amicus Brief, supra* note 23, at 14 (also warning that if reduction is delayed until 2020, the required rate would more than double to 15% each year); *see also* I. Allison *et. al., supra* note 23 at 51, fig. 22 (depicting different reduction trajectories based on start dates, but calibrating to the 2C goal rather than 1.5).

28 I. Allison *et. al., supra* note 23, at 7 (explaining near-zero emissions target).

29 For quoted sources, *see* Ry. Express Agency, Inc. v. People of N.Y., 336 U.S. 106, 110 (1949) ("[I]t is no requirement"); Mass. v. EPA, 549 U.S. 497, 525–26 (2007). *See also* NW. Envtl. Def. Ctr. v. Owens Corning Corp., 434 F. Supp. 2d 957, 968 (D. Or. 2006).

30 For quoted sources, *see* Dep't of Game of W.A. v. Puyallup Tribe, 414 U.S. 44, 49 (1973); UNFCCC, *supra* note 14, at art. 3, ¶ 4 (emphasis added). For discussion of the developing

nations' position, *see* Richard McGregor, *China Urges Rich Nations to Lead on Climate*, FIN. TIMES (June 4, 2007).

31 For quoted sources, *see* UNFCCC, *supra* note 14, at art. 3, ¶1; JOHN WILLARD, A TREATISE ON EQUITY JURISPRUDENCE 151 (1863). For a case discussing judicial approximation of justice, *see* U.S. v. Or., 913 F.2d 576, 580–81 (9th Cir. 1990).

32 For emissions information, *see* UNFCCC, *GHG Data from UNFCC*, http://unfccc.int/ghg_data/ghg_data_unfccc/items/4146.php; *Each Country's Share of CO2 Emissions*, UNION OF CONCERNED SCIENTISTS (using 2006 data from Energy Information Agency, Department of Energy). For CO_2 emissions per capita *see* UN, *Millennium Development Goal Data*, http://mdgs.un.org/unsd/mdg/Data.aspx (select "flat view," and then "carbon dioxide per capita").

33 For discussion of the atmospheric carbon budget concept, *see* R. A. Houghton, *Balancing the Global Carbon Budget*, 35 ANN. REV. EARTH & PLANETARY SCI. 313 (2007); Bill McKibben, *Global Warming's Terrifying New Math*, ROLLING STONE (July 19, 2012). For analogous prioritization of water use, *see* Adell Amos, *Freshwater Conservation: A Review of Oregon Water Law and Policy*, THE NATURE CONSERVANCY 50 (Aug. 2008) ("When water rights with the same priority date are in mutually exclusive conflict, domestic uses have preference over all others, and agricultural uses have preference over manufacturing uses."). For Britain's restriction on luxury carbon, *see* Elizabeth Rosenthal, *Britain Curbing Airport Growth to Aid Climate*, N. Y. TIMES (July 1, 2010).

34 For referenced source, *see* Paul Baer *et al.*, *Greenhouse Development Rights Framework: The Right to Development in a Climate Constrained World* 13–25 (Nov. 2008); *see also* Baer *et. al.*, *supra* note 26, at 16–9 (Executive Summary).

35 For a discussion of the judicial role in public trust enforcement, *see* Ariz. Ctr. for Law in the Pub. Interest v. Hassell, 837 P.2d 158, 169 (Ariz. Ct. App. 1991) ("The check and balance of judicial review provides a level of protection against improvident dissipation of an irreplaceable res."); Lake Mich. Fed'n v. U.S. Army Corps of Eng'rs, 742 F. Supp. 441, 446 (N. D. Ill. 1990) ("The very purpose of the public trust doctrine is to police the legislature's disposition of public lands. If courts were to rubber stamp legislative decisions … the doctrine would have no teeth. The legislature would have unfettered discretion to breach the public trust as long as it was able to articulate some gain to the public.").

36 For a discussion of principles in an ATL declaratory judgment, *see* Wood, FIDUCIARY DUTY *supra* note 14. For the ATL complaints and petitions, *see* Our Children's Trust, http://ourchildrenstrust.org/Legal; *Petitions*, http://ourchildrenstrust.org/US/StateAdministrativePetitions. For a case demonstrating ongoing jurisdiction in the natural resources context, *see, e.g.*, U.S. v. Wash., 384 F. Supp. 312, 346–47 (W.D. Wash. 1974) (treaty fishing rights litigation).

37 The initial ATL "hatch," coordinated by Our Children's Trust (OCT), consisted of a federal lawsuit, nine state law suits, thirty-nine petitions for state rule-making, and one notice of intent to sue, covering all but one state in the United States (delayed action in Massachusetts culminated with a filing of a petition on Nov. 1, 2012). These complaints and petitions are available on the OCT Web site, http://ourchildrenstrust.org/Legal. Media coverage is available at *Media Coverage* http://www.ourchildrenstrust.org/media. The prescription that these actions seek to enforce is discussed in the *amicus* brief of James Hansen in support of the litigation. *See* Hansen, *Amicus Brief*, *supra* note 23, at 2. The litigation drew supportive expert declarations from Paul R. Epstein, M.D. (human health); Ove Hoegh-Guldberg, Ph.D. (coral reefs/oceans); Sivan Kartha, Ph.D. (carbon math); Pushker Kharecha, Ph.D. (climate science and prescription); David Lobell, Ph.D. (agricultural impacts); Arjun Makhijani, Ph.D. (engineering and feasibility of reducing carbon emissions); Jonathan "Peck" Overpeck, Ph.D. (drought); Camille Parmesan, Ph.D. (species and extinction); Stephan Rahmstorf, Ph.D. (sea level);

Steven Running, Ph.D. (fire and forest ecosystems); James Gustave Speth, Ph.D. (government's ability to plan); Kevin Trenberth, Ph.D. (storm events); Lise Van Susteren, M.D. (psychological impacts). *See* declarations at http://ourchildrenstrust.org/page/91/expert-declarations.

38 The youth marches were organized by the nonprofit organization, Kids vs. Global Warming. *See MARCH with US*, iMATTER MARCH, http://www.imatteryouth.org/. For the short documentaries *see* http://ourchildrenstrust.org/trust-films. The documentaries were produced by WITNESS, http://www.witness.org/.

39 For quoted sources, *see* Joe Romm, *IEA: World on Pace for 11°F Warming, "Even School Children Know This Will Have Catastrophic Implications for All of Us*, THINK PROGRESS (Jan. 4, 2012) (Fatih Birol); Hansen, *Amicus Brief, supra* note 23, at 5, 7 (emphasis added). For sources on emissions and warming projections, *see* Joe Romm, *IEA: Global CO2 Emissions Hit New Record in 2011, Keeping World on Track for "Devastating" 11°F Warming By 2100*, THINK PRO-GRESS (May 25, 2012); *Update 2–Global CO2 Emissions Hit Record in 2011 led by China–IEA*, REUTERS (May 24, 2012).

11. NATURE'S JUSTICE: THE ROLE OF THE COURTS

1 Stix v. Commissioner, 152 F.2d 562, 563 (2d Cir. 1945). *See also* U.S. v. Mitchell, 463 U.S. 206, 226 (1983) (noting, in context of Indian trust doctrine, that a "fundamental incident" of the trust relationship is "the right of an injured beneficiary to sue the trustee for damages resulting from a breach of the trust").

2 OLIVER WENDELL HOLMES, JR., THE COMMON LAW 1 (Little, Brown, & Co. 1881). *See also In re* Hood River, 227 P. 1065, 1087, 1086 (Or. 1924) (stating that common law "precedents must yield to the reason of different or modified conditions," for "[i]f the common law should become ... crystallized ... it would cease to be the common law of history, and would be an inelastic and arbitrary code"). For justice and the law, *see* ROSCOE POUND, THE HISTORY AND SYSTEM OF THE COMMON LAW 2 (P.F. Collier & Son 1939) (stating, "the end of law is 'justice'").

3 For history of law, *see* MORTON J. HORWITZ, THE TRANSFORMATION OF AMERICAN LAW, 1870–1960: THE CRISIS OF LEGAL ORTHODOXY (Oxford U. Press 1992).

4 ROSCOE POUND, ADMINISTRATIVE LAW: ITS GROWTH, PROCEDURE, AND SIGNIFICANCE 28, 35 (U. Pitt. Press 1942) (stating also, "Control of an [omnipotent] administrative hierarchy, accountable only to an ultimate administrative head, will prove as effective a means of absolute government as was formerly control of an army," *id.* at 35–36.).

5 *See In re* Water Use Permit Applications, 9 P.3d 409, 455 (Haw. 2000) ("Just as private trustees are judicially accountable to their beneficiaries for dispositions of the res, so the legislative and executive branches are judicially accountable for the dispositions of the public trust.").

6 For quoted sources, *see* ROSCOE POUND, JUSTICE ACCORDING TO LAW 90 (YALE U. PRESS 1951) ("Not a little denunciation"); POUND, ADMINISTRATIVE LAW, *supra* note 4, at 44 ("constitutional legal polity"); Joseph L. Sax, *The Public Trust Doctrine in Natural Resource Law: Effective Judicial Intervention*, 68 MICH. L. REV. 471, 509, 559–60 (1970).

7 For quoted sources, *see* James L. Huffman, *Trusting the Public Interest to Judges: A Comment on the Public Trust Writings of Professors Sax, Wilkinson, Dunning and Johnson*, 63 DENV. U. L. REV. 565, 572 (1986); Sandra B. Zellmer, *The Devil, the Details, and the Dawn of the 21st Century Administrative State: Beyond the New Deal*, 32 ARIZ. ST. L.J. 941, 950 (2000). For a description of judicial election system, *see* Jed Handelsman Shugerman, *The Twist of Long Terms: Judicial Elections, Role Fidelity, and American Tort Law*, 98 GEO. L.J. 1349, 1351 (2010). For ethical rules binding the judiciary, *see* MODEL CODE OF JUDICIAL CONDUCT Canon 2 (2004).

8 Presbitero J. Velasco, Jr., *Manila Bay: A Daunting Challenge in Environmental Rehabilitation and Protection*, 11 OR. REV. INT'L L. 441, 452 (2009).

9 For application of private trust standards to public trustees, *see, e.g.*, Idaho Forest Indus., Inc. v. Hayden Lake Watershed Improvement Dist., 733 P.2d 733, 738 (Idaho 1987) (noting the administration of the "public trust is governed by the same principles applicable to the administration of trusts in general."); *see also* Osage Nation and/or Tribe of Indians of Okla. v. U.S., 66 Fed. Cl. 244, 247 (2005) ("The court ... sees no 'meaningful distinction between Indian trusts and private trusts.'"). For the requirement that courts have standards by which to review agency action, *see generally* Heckler v. Chaney, 470 U.S. 821, 828 (1985).

10 For quoted sources, *see* Sara A. Clark, *Taking a Hard Look at Agency Science: Can the Courts Ever Succeed?* 36 ECOLOGY L. Q. 317, 347 (2009); Wendy E. Wagner, *The Science Charade in Toxic Risk Regulation*, 95 COLUM. L. REV. 1613, 1665–66 (1995). For case law applying the deference doctrine to technical decisions, *see, e.g.*, Lands Council v. McNair, 537 F.3d 981 (9th Cir. 2008). For a case study of deference in the Columbia River salmon context, *see* Michael C. Blumm & Greg D. Corbin, *Salmon and the Endangered Species Act: Lessons from the Columbia Basin*, 74 WASH. L. REV. 519, 604 (1999).

11 For quoted sources, *see* POUND, ADMINISTRATIVE LAW, *supra* note 4, at 34 (emphasis added); *Mr. Justice Douglas*, TV Broad. (CBS REPORTS Sept. 6, 1972) (quoting Justice Douglas); Sierra Club v. Espy, 822 F. Supp. 356, 370 (1993), *rev'd on other grounds*, 38 F.3d 792 (5th Cir. 1994).

12 For quoted sources, *see* GEORGE G. BOGERT ET AL., TRUSTS AND TRUSTEES § 560 (West 3d ed. 2010) (describing deference in trust law); Carrier v. Carrier 123 N.E. 135, 138 (N.Y. 1919) (Justice Cardozo). At times, the judicial disposition toward agencies has been far more aggressive, marked by a "hard look" stance in the environmental realm. *See generally* William H. Rodgers, Jr., *Betty B. Fletcher: NEPA's Angel and Chief Editor of the Hard Look*, 40 ENVTL. L. RPT., NEWS & ANALYSIS 10268 (2010).

13 For quoted case, *see* Sierra Forest Legacy v. Rey, 526 F.3d 1228, 1236 (9th Cir. 2008) (Noonan, J., concurring). For a description of private trust law voiding decisions made in breach of the duty of loyalty, *see* BOGERT TRUSTS 3d, *supra* note 12, § 543; Piatt v. Longworth's Devisees, 27 Ohio St. 159, 195–96 (1875).

14 Daubert v. Merrell Dow Pharmaceuticals, Inc. *(Daubert II)*, 43 F.3d 1311, 1316 (9th Cir. 1995). *See also* Daubert v. Merrell Dow Pharmaceuticals, Inc., 509 U.S. 579 (1993) (requiring judicial assessment of scientific evidence). For materials on the judicial role and tools used in evaluating scientific evidence, *see* FED. JUDICIAL CTR., REFERENCE MANUAL ON SCIENTIFIC EVIDENCE 3, 5–7 (2d ed. 2000); *Science and Technology in Judicial Decision Making: Creating Opportunities and Meeting Challenges*, CARNEGIE COMM'N ON SCI., TECH., AND GOV'T 38–39 (1993).

15 For quoted sources, *see* Harrison C. Dunning, *The Public Trust: A Fundamental Doctrine of American Property Law*, 19 ENVTL. L. 515, 516, 523 (1989); Ill. Cent. R.R. Co. v. Ill., 146 U.S. 387, 453 (1892) (abridging the trust "has never been adjudged to be within the legislative power"). For referenced Arizona case law, *see* Ariz. Ctr. for Law in the Pub. Interest v. Hassell, 837 P.2d 158 (Ariz. Ct. App. 1991); Defenders of Wildlife v. Hull, 18 P.3d 722 (Ariz. Ct. App. 2001).

16 For quoted case, *see* Lake Mich. Fed'n, v. U.S. Army Corps of Eng'rs, 742 F. Supp. 441, 446 (N.D. Ill. 1990). For quoted source, *see* Sax, *supra* note 6, at 559. For an example of a judicial "check" approach, *see* Kootenai Envtl. Alliance, Inc. v. Panhandle Yacht Club, Inc., 671 P.2d 1085 (Idaho 1983) (discussing judicial deference to legislative action).

17 Marks v. Whitney, 491 P.2d 374, 381 (Cal. 1971).

18 Douglas L. Grant, *Underpinnings of the Public Trust Doctrine: Lessons from Illinois Central Railroad*, 33 ARIZ. ST. L.J. 849, 879–80 (2001). For duty of trustee to protect the trust assets from destruction, *see* BOGERT TRUSTS 3d, *supra* note 12, § 582.

19 McCleary v. State, 269 P.3d 227, 248 (Wash. 2012) (emphasis added).
20 For quoted sources, *see* CHARLES ALAN WRIGHT & ARTHUR R. MILLER, FEDERAL PRACTICE AND PROCEDURE § 2942 (2d ed. 1995); Linda Greenhouse, *A Voice From the Past*, N.Y. TIMES OPINIONATOR (June 1, 2011). For an example of a broad injunction in the desegregation context, *see* Swann v. Charlotte-Mecklenburg Bd. of Educ., 402 U.S. 1, 16 (1971) (injunctive remedy for schools that failed to integrate). For U.S. Supreme Court case law on injunctions, *see* Weinberger v. Romero-Barcelo, 456 U.S. 305, 312 (1982).
21 For literature on structural injunctions in institutional litigation, *see* Margaret G. Farrell, *The Function and Legitimacy of Special Masters: Administrative Agencies for the Courts*, 2 WIDENER L. SYMP. J. 235, 237 (1997) (remedy in complex litigation "is often prospective and affects large numbers of people as would a regulation or legislative rule"); Judith Resnik, *Managerial Judges*, 96 HARV. L. REV. 374, 424–25 (1982); Theodore Eisenberg & Stephen C. Yeazell, *The Ordinary and the Extraordinary in Institutional Litigation*, 93 HARV. L. REV. 465 (1980).
22 S. Burlington Cnty. N.A.A.C.P. v. Twp. of Mount Laurel, 336 A.2d 713 (N.J. 1975) (*Mount Laurel I*); S. Burlington Cnty. N.A.A.C.P. v. Twp. of Mount Laurel, 456 A.2d 390 (N.J. 1983) (*Mount Laurel II*).
23 *Mount Laurel I*, 336 A.2d at 727, 724, 734.
24 *Mount Laurel II*, 456 A.2d at 438, 490.
25 This litigation comprises many decisions and orders issued over the span of more than two decades. *See* Nat'l Wildlife Fed'n v. Nat'l Marine Fisheries Serv., No. CV 01–640-RE, 2005 WL 1278878, at *2–3 (D. Or. May 26, 2005); *id.* at *30–32 (Attachment 2, reviewing biological opinions and judicial treatment). For background, *see* Ken Olsen, *Salmon Justice*, HIGH COUNTRY NEWS (Jan. 22, 2007).
26 Nat'l Wildlife Fed'n v. Nat'l Marine Fisheries Serv., No. CV 01–640-RE, 2005 WL 2488447, at *3–6 (D. Or. Oct. 7, 2005). *See also* Olsen, *supra* note 25 (discussing litigation).
27 In this long-standing litigation, two class action suits, *Plata v. Schwarzenegger* and *Coleman v. Schwarzenegger*, were combined into the *Coleman* decision heard by a special federal panel. Coleman v. Schwarzenegger, No. CIV S-90–0520 LKK JFM P, 2009 WL 2430820, at *1 (E.D. Cal. & N.D. Cal. Aug 4, 2009). The dramatic climb in prison population that formed the crux of these cases began in the mid-1970s as a result of rigid sentencing laws and a wholesale failure in prisoner rehabilitation.
28 *Id.* at *7, *8 (summarizing preceding litigation, internal quotation marks omitted).
29 *Id.* at *10, *14–15 (summarizing preceding litigation, internal quotation marks omitted) (also quoting the district court's statement, "[T]he Court ... has no choice but to step in and fill the void."). The court in *Plata* appointed a Receiver, and the court in *Coleman* appointed a Special Master.
30 For quoted opinions, *see id.* at *1, *2, *3 (3-judge panel) (reassuring that the order is "narrowly tailored" and that it "extends no further than necessary to remedy those [constitutional] violations," *id.* at *2); Brown v. Plata, No. 09–1233, slip op. at 41, 48 (U.S. May, 23, 2011) (quoting Hutto v. Finney, 437 U.S. 678, 687 n.9 (1978)). For reporting on the prison release order, *see* Warren Richey, *Supreme Court: Can Judges Tell California to Release 40,000 Prisoners?* CHRISTIAN SCI. MONITOR (Nov. 30, 2010).
31 This litigation grew out of treaty promises dating back to the mid-1800s. The Washington case was handled by Judge Boldt, who issued the opinion, U.S. v. Wash., 384 F. Supp. 312 (W.D. Wash. 1974). The Oregon litigation was handled by Judge Belloni, who issued the opinion, Sohappy v. Smith, 302 F. Supp. 899 (D. Or. 1969).
32 CHARLES F. WILKINSON, MESSAGES FROM FRANK'S LANDING: A STORY OF SALMON, TREATIES, AND THE INDIAN WAY 38 (U. of Wash. Press 2000). For additional literature on the treaty rights, *see* FAY G. COHEN, TREATIES ON TRIAL: THE CONTINUING CONTROVERSY

OVER NORTHWEST INDIAN FISHING RIGHTS 187–92, 203–04 (U. of Wash. Press 1986); John Daniel, *Dance of Denial: Threats to Salmon in Columbia River Basin*, SIERRA 64, 70 (Mar.–Apr. 1993).

33 For quoted cases, *see* Wash. v. Wash. State Com. Passenger Fishing Vessel Ass'n, 443 U.S. 658, 660, 696 (1979) (quoting Puget Sound Gillnetters Ass'n v. U.S., 573 F.2d 1123, 1126 (9th Cir. 1978)) (stating also that the court may "issue detailed remedial orders as a substitute for state supervision." *Id.* at 695–96). For quoted commentary, *see* Fronda Woods, *Who's in Charge of Fishing?* 106 OR. HISTORICAL Q. 412, 432 (2005). For the original Boldt opinion (Wash.), *see U.S. v. Wash.*, 384 F. Supp. 312; *see also* U.S. v. Wash., 520 F.2d 676, 683–84 (9th Cir. 1975) (reviewing the Boldt opinion). For the Belloni opinion (Or.), *see Sohappy*, 302 F. Supp. at 910–11. For a description of the defiant state position in Washington, *see Puget Sound Gillnetters Ass'n*, 573 F.2d at 1128; Olsen, *supra* note 25 (describing tension from court rulings). For a discussion of the role of the court in managing the fisheries, *see U.S. v. Wash.*, 520 F.2d at 693 (Burns, J., concurring) ("[T]o affirm [the Boldt opinion] also involves ratification of the role of the district judge as a 'perpetual fishmaster.'"); U.S. v. Wash., 459 F. Supp. 1020 (W.D. Wash. 1978), *order aff'd*, 645 F.2d 749 (9th Cir. 1981); Michael C. Blumm & Brett M. Swift, *The Indian Treaty Piscary Profit and Habitat Protection in the Pacific Northwest: A Property Rights Approach*, 69 U. COLO. L. REV. 407, 456–57 (1998).

34 Seattle Sch. Dist. No. 1 of King Cnty. v. State, 585 P.2d 71, 85 (Wash. 1978); *McCleary*, 269 P.3d at 231–55.

35 *McCleary*, 269 P.3d at 246, 259 (quoting *Seattle Sch. Dist. No. 1 of King Cnty.*, 585 P.2d at 85) (citations omitted).

36 *McCleary*, 269 P.3d at 260–61.

37 Metro. Manila Dev. Auth. v. Concerned Residents of Manila Bay, G.R. No. 171947–48 (S.C., Dec. 18, 2008) (Phil.).

38 Velasco, *supra* note 8, at 442.

39 For quoted cases, *see* Oposa v. Factoran, G.R. No. 101083 (S.C., July 30, 1993) (Phil.), *reprinted (excerpt) in* JAN G. LAITOS ET AL., NATURAL RESOURCES LAW 441–44 (Thompson West 2006); *Metro. Manila Dev. Auth.*, G.R. No. 171947–48. *See also* Jay B. Rempillo, *SC Orders Executive Agencies to Clean-up Manila Bay*, SUP. CT. OF THE PHILIP. (Dec, 18, 2008).

40 For quoted cases, *see Coleman*, 2009 WL 2430820, at *79, *116 (prison case); *U.S. v. Wash.*, 384 F. Supp. at 346 (treaty case).

41 For referenced and quoted cases, *see* Coleman v. Schwarzenegger, No. CIV S-90-0520 LKK JFM P, 2010 WL 99000, at *1, *3 (E.D. Cal. & N.D. Cal. Jan. 12, 2010) (setting forth prison population benchmarks at: 167% in six months, 155% in twelve months, 147% in eighteen months, and 137.5% in twenty-four months); *Metro. Manila Dev. Auth.*, G.R. No. 171947–48.

42 Rule 42(b) of the Federal Rules of Civil Procedure allows courts to bifurcate issues into separate trials "[f]or convenience, to avoid prejudice, or to expedite and economize." FED. R. CIV. P. 42(b). The issues most typically bifurcated for trial are those of liability and relief. *See* G. Lee Garrett, Jr. & Anthony E. Diresta, *Strategies for Multi-Claim Litigation and Settlement Techniques*, 289 PLI/LIT 473, 508, 513 (1985). For the bifurcated approach in Indian treaty litigation, *see* U.S. v. Wash., 135 F.3d 618, 628 (9th Cir. 1998) (reviewing procedural history in the district court)

43 *Metro. Manila Dev. Auth.*, G.R. No. 171947–48. Specifically, the Supreme Court directed the Department of Education to "inculcate in the minds and hearts of students and, through them, their parents and friends, the importance of their duty toward achieving and maintaining a balanced and healthful ecosystem in the Manila Bay and the entire Philippine archipelago."

44 Velasco, *supra* note 8, at 448, 448–49 (emphasis added).

45 For quoted case, *see Metro. Manila Dev. Auth.*, G.R. No. 171947–48. For reporting on enforcement of the Manila Bay decision, *see SC Wants Concrete Plan for Manila Bay Cleanup*, ABS-CBNNEWS.COM (Mar. 4, 2011).

46 For cases discussed, *see Coleman*, 2010 WL 99000, at *1 (prison cases); Nat'l Wildlife Fed'n v. Nat'l Marine Fisheries Serv., 254 F. Supp. 2d 1196, 1215–16 (D. Or. 2003) (fisheries case).

47 For quoted case, *see Mount Laurel II*, 456 A.2d at 438–39, 454, 456.

48 *U.S. v. Wash.*, 459 F. Supp. at 1028, 1038, 1061. For discussion of the remedy, *see* Woods, *supra* note 33, at 432.

49 For the Oregon litigation and the CRFMP, *see* U.S. v. Or., 699 F. Supp. 1456, 1460 (D. Or. 1988); COLUMBIA RIVER FISH MANAGEMENT PLAN 48–57 (Oct. 7, 1988). For general discussion of consent decrees and settlement, *see* David L. Callies, *The Use of Consent Decrees in Settling Land Use and Environmental Disputes*, 21 STETSON L. REV. 871, 896–97 (1992); Melanie J. Rowland, *Bargaining For Life: Protecting Biodiversity Through Mediated Agreements*, 22 ENVTL. L. 503 (1992). For a discussion of tribal co-management resulting from treaty rights litigation, *see* Mary Christina Wood, *The Tribal Property Right to Wildlife Capital (Part I): Applying Principles of Sovereignty to Protect Imperiled Wildlife Populations*, 37 IDAHO L. REV. 1, 49–50 (2000); *Fall Fishery Blues*, COLUMBIA RIVER INTER-TRIBAL FISH COMMISSION, WANA CHINOOK TYMOO 18 (Winter 1999) (discussing co-management).

50 For the quoted case, *see Coleman*, 2009 WL 2430820, at *4 (and granting the receiver "all powers vested by law in the Secretary of the CDCR as they relate to the … California prison medical health care system," *id.* at *11). For a discussion of trustee removal in the private context, *see* BOGERT TRUSTS 3d, *supra* note 12, § 543.

51 *McCleary*, 269 P.3d at 247, 259, 261 (noting also that "'the legislature must … act within the confines of the judicial interpretation'") (citation omitted).

52 For reporting requirements, *see e.g.*, *Coleman*, 2010 WL 99000, at *3 (requiring the state to submit a report within fourteen days of each six-month benchmark deadline).

53 For quoted cases, *see Mount Laurel* II, 456 A.2d at 452; *Nat'l Wildlife Fed'n*, 2005 WL 2488447, at *3.

54 For reporting on retardant case contempt threats, *see* Matthew Daly, *Agriculture Chief's Priority: Avoid Jail*, USA TODAY (Feb. 23, 2008). For the Indian trust case, *see* Cobell v. Salazar, 573 F.3d 808 (D.C. Cir. 2009).

55 For quoted and referenced cases, *see Metro. Manila Dev. Auth.*, G.R. No. 171947–48; *McCleary*, 269 P.3d at 232 (citation omitted); *Coleman*, 2009 WL 2430820, at *105; Marbled Murrelet v. Babbitt, 918 F. Supp. 318, 322 (W.D. Wash. 1996) (USFWS case).

56 For quoted case, *see Coleman*, 2009 WL 2430820, at *7 (quoting *Plata* district court order) (citation omitted); *see also Coleman*, 2010 WL 99000, at *3. These two decisions are from the same three-judge special prison panel.

57 THE FEDERALIST NO. 78, at 438 (Alexander Hamilton).

58 In the federal Atmospheric Trust Litigation case described in Chapter 10, for example, Judge Robert L. Wilkins issued a summary order on May 31, 2012 dismissing the youth's lawsuit to force government action on climate. The task of carbon regulation, he found, was a matter best left to the federal agencies. The case was on appeal at the time of this writing. Alec L. v. Jackson, Civ. 1:11-cv-02235, 863 F. Supp. 2d 11, 17 (D. D.C. May 31, 2012), http://ourchildren-strust.org/page/51/federal-lawsuit. Courts inclined to dismiss common law claims tend to do so on the legal grounds of preemption, displacement, or political question doctrine. While beyond the scope of this chapter, much briefing argues the inapplicability of these defenses to atmospheric trust claims. For briefing, *see e.g.*, Memorandum in Opposition to Motion to Dismiss, *Alec L. v. Jackson*, No. 1:11-cv-2235, at 24–35 (D.D.C. Apr. 16, 2012), http://ourchildren-strust.org/page/51/federal-lawsuit (follow April 2012 link to "brief").

59 *McCleary*, 269 P.3d at 258, 259, 261, 262; *see also* Elizabeth Brown, *Distinguishing Public Nuisance and the Public Trust Doctrine: The Inapplicability of American Electric Power on Atmospheric Trust Litigation* (2012).

60 Idaho *ex rel.* Evans v. Or., 462 U.S. 1017, 1038 (1983) (O'Connor, J., dissenting).

61 Anthony D. Barnosky *et al.*, *Approaching a State Shift in Earth's Biosphere*, 486 NATURE 52, 52 (2012).

12. NATURE'S TRUST AND THE HEART OF HUMANITY

1 EDGAR BODENHEIMER *ET AL.*, AN INTRODUCTION TO THE ANGLO-AMERICAN LEGAL SYSTEM: READINGS AND CASES 3 (4th ed. 2004) (quoting Dworkin).

2 *See generally* Michael Shellenberger & Ted Nordhaus, *The Death of Environmentalism: Global Warming Politics in a Post-Environmental World* (2004).

3 For sources describing the environmental bombing of Appalachia, *see* Jeff Biggers, *The Coalfield Uprising*, THE NATION (Sept. 30, 2009) (describing "twice-daily, bone-rattling explosions and the quasi-apocalyptic storms of coal dust and fly rock" that cover residents' homes and gardens, and quoting one resident, "It's unreal. It's like we're living in a war zone."); Resolutions of Faith, Presbyterian Church, 217th General Assembly, Commissioners' Resolution (mountaintop removal has "forced families to live in fear for their lives and property or to abandon their family home place and leave a lifetime of memories"), http://ilove-mountains.org/resolutions.

4 President John F. Kennedy, Commencement Address at the American University in Washington (June 10, 1963).

5 For quoted source, *see* RENNARD STRICKLAND, TONTO'S REVENGE: REFLECTIONS ON AMERICAN INDIAN CULTURE AND POLICY 130 (U. of N.M. Press 1997). For a discussion of the manipulation of public sentiment by industry, *see* NAOMI ORESKES & ERIK. M. CONWAY, MERCHANTS OF DOUBT: HOW A HANDFUL OF SCIENTISTS OBSCURED THE TRUTH ON ISSUES FROM TOBACCO SMOKE TO GLOBAL WARMING (Bloomsbury Press 2010).

6 For the natural law origin of trust, *see* Arnold v. Mundy, 6 N.J.L. 1, 76–77 (N. J. 1821).

7 For quoted sources, *see* KATHLEEN DEAN MOORE & MICHAEL P. NELSON, MORAL GROUND: ETHICAL ACTION FOR A PLANET IN PERIL 40 (Trinity U. Press 2010); EDWARD O. WILSON, THE CREATION: AN APPEAL TO SAVE LIFE ON EARTH, 5 (W.W. Norton & Co. 2007); Burns H. Weston, *Climate Change and Intergenerational Justice: Foundational Reflections*, 9 VT. J. ENVTL. L. 375, 376 (2008).

8 EDMUND BURKE, REFLECTIONS ON THE REVOLUTION IN FRANCE 96 (Manchester U. Press 2006).

9 For quotes sources, *see* SUSAN DUNN, SOMETHING THAT WILL SURPRISE THE WORLD: THE ESSENTIAL WRITINGS OF THE FOUNDING FATHERS 284 (Basic Books 2006) (letter to Madison); SAUL K. PADOVER, THE WORLD OF THE FOUNDING FATHERS: BASIC IDEAS OF THE MEN THAT MADE AMERICA 285 (Gazelle Book Serv. Ltd. 1977) ("every generation coming equally").

10 Argument of the United States, *Fur Seal Arbitration* (U.S. v. Gr. Brit.), *reprinted in* 9 FUR SEAL ARBITRATION: PROCEEDINGS OF THE TRIBUNAL OF ARBITRATION (Gov't Printing Office 1895). *See also* Weston, *supra* note 7, at 417.

11 ZACHARY MICHAEL JACK, THE GREEN ROOSEVELT; THEODORE ROOSEVELT IN APPRECIATION OF WILDERNESS, WILDLIFE, AND WILD PLACES 291 (Cambria Press 2010).

12 DOUGLAS BRINKLEY, THE WILDERNESS WARRIOR: THEODORE ROOSEVELT AND THE CRUSADE FOR AMERICA at vi (HarperCollins Publ's 2009) (citing THEODORE ROOSEVELT, A BOOK-LOVER'S HOLIDAYS IN THE OPEN (1916)).

13 For quoted sources, *see* Colin Woodard, *In Greenland, an Interfaith Rally for Climate Change*, The Christian Science Monitor (Sept. 12, 2007); Pope Benedict XVI, *If You Want to Cultivate Peace, Protect Creation: Message of His Holiness for the Celebration of the World Day of Peace* (Jan. 1, 2010) ("*greater sense*"); Pope Benedict XVI, *Encyclical Letter* Caritas In Veritate *of the Supreme Pontiff Benedict XVI to the Bishops, Priests, and Deacons, Men and Women Religious, the Lay Faithful, and All People of Good Will on Integral Human Development in Charity and Truth* (July 7, 2009) ("*grave duty*"); *Proverbs* 13:22. The Pope has elaborated: "'We have inherited from past generations, and we have benefited from the work of our contemporaries; for this reason we have obligations towards all, and we cannot refuse to interest ourselves in those who will come after us, to enlarge the human family." Pope Benedict XVI, *Protect Creation, supra*. For general discussion on the religious assertion of duty to future generations, *see* Roger S. Gottlieb, A Greener Faith: Religious Environmentalism and Our Planet's Future 10 (Oxford U. Press 2006).

14 For quoted sources, *see* Edith Brown Weiss, In Fairness to Future Generations: International Law, Common Patrimony, and Intergenerational Equity 34, 293 (U.N. U. 1989); Moore & Nelson, *supra* note 7, at 41.

15 For quoted cases, *see* Alliance to Protect Nantucket Sound, Inc. v. Energy Facilities Siting Bd., 932 N.E. 2d 787, 816 (Mass. 2010) (Marshall, C.J., concurring and dissenting on other grounds) (emphasis added); Moss Point Lumber Co. v. Bd. of Supervisors of Harrison Cnty., 42 So. 290, 315 (Miss. 1906) (Whitfield, J., concurring). For cases expressing the trust duty to future generations, *see, e.g.*, Kelly v. 1250 Oceanside Partners, 140 P.3d 985 (Haw. 2006); Citizens for Responsible Wildlife Mgmt. v. State, 103 P.3d 203, 208 (Wash. Ct. App. Div. 2 2004); *see also* cases cited in Mary Christina Wood, *Advancing the Sovereign Trust of Government to Safeguard the Environment and Future Generations (Part I): Ecological Realism and the Need for a Paradigm Shift*, 39 Envtl. L. 43, 77 (2009).

16 For quoted sources, *see* John Edward Davidson, *The Public Trust and Atmospheric Trust Litigation Panel*, panel at the University of Oregon School of Law 30th Annual Public Interest Environmental Law Conference (Mar. 3, 2012); Ill. Cent. R.R. Co. v. Ill., 146 U.S. 387, 460 (1892); Lamprey v. Metcalf, 52 Minn. 181, 200 (Minn. 1893) (emphasis added); Moss Point Lumber Co., 42 So. at 315.

17 For native conceptions of property, *see generally* Thomas Hylland Eriksen, Globalization: The Key Concepts 147 (Berg 2007). For the contemporary commons movement, *see* Burns H. Weston & David Bollier, Green Governance: Ecological Survival, Human Rights, and the Law of the Commons 124–25 (Cambridge U. Press 2013).

18 For quoted sources, *see* Pope Benedict XVI, *Protect Creation, supra* note 13; *Creation Care for Pastors* (consortium of pastors and scientists), http://www.creationcareforpastors.com/; *Leviticus* 25:23 (Am. Stand. Version). *See also* Social Justice & Ecology Secretariat, *Healing a Broken World: Task Force on Ecology*, Promotio Iustitiae No. 106, 33 (2010) ("From a Judeo-Christian perspective, there is a 'covenant between human beings and the environment, which should mirror the creative love of God.' In other words, we assume an obligation that follows from faith to sustain creation and even enhance it.") (citation omitted); *Interfaith Power & Light: A Religious Response to Global Warming*, http://interfaithpowerandlight.org/about/mission-history/.

19 For the Biblical reference, *see Exodus* 20:15 (King James Version). For quoted source, *see* Ecumenical Patriarch Bartholomew I, *To Commit a Crime against the Natural World Is a Sin*, in Moore & Nelson, *supra* note 7, at 135.

20 Maude Barlow & Tony Clarke, *Who Owns the Water?* The Nation (Sept. 2, 2002) (emphasis added).

21 Winona LaDuke, *Redefining Progress: An Indigenous View of Industrialization and Consumption in North America, in* Tipping the Sacred Cow: The Best of LiP: Informed Revolt 192 (Brain Awehali ed., 1996–2007).

22 For quoted sources, *see* Gottlieb, *supra* note 13, at 23, 28 (see also 23–24, noting, "The sense of the earth as creation, the warning not to waste–these are *in the scriptures.*"); Pope Benedict XVI, *Protect Creation, supra* note 13 (omission of emphasis); Social Justice & Ecology Secretariat, *Healing a Broken World, supra* note 18, at 34; Justice Weeramantry, *Islam, the Environment and the Human Future,* Asian Tribune (July 7, 2007); Anupma Kaushik, *Mahatma Gandhi and Environment Protection,* The Gandhi Foundation (June 3, 2010) (quoting Gandhi).

23 For quoted sources, *see* U.S. Office of War Info. Div. of Pub. Inquiries, *Food Is a Weapon: Don't Waste It!: Buy Wisely – Cook Carefully – Eat It All: Follow the National Wartime Nutrition Program* (1943), http://digital.library.unt.edu/ark:/67531/metadc156/; Duke U. Libraries: Digital Collections, *Brief History of World War Two Advertising Campaigns, War Loans, and Bonds* ("consumers were deluged"). For sources describing World War II conservation practices, *see* Lester R. Brown, Plan B 3.0: Mobilizing to Save Civilization 279 (W.W. Norton & Co. 2008); World War II on the Home Front: Rationing (citing Ann Rosener, U.S. Office of War Information), http://www.learnnc.org/lp/editions/ww2-rationing/5945; Terrence H. Witkowski, *The American Consumer Home Front During World War II,* Advances in Consumer Research Vol. 25 (eds. Joseph W. Alba & J. Wesley Hutchinson, (1998)).

24 For referenced sources, *see* The Story of Stuff Project, http://www.storyofstuff.org/movies-all/story-of-stuff; John De Graaf et. al., Affluenza: The All-Consuming Epidemic (Berrett-Koehler Publ's 2001). For statistics on garbage, *see* Environmental Protection Agency, *Municipal Solid Waste* (2012), http://www.epa.gov/epawaste/nonhaz/municipal/index.htm.

25 For a discussion of the voluntary simplicity movement and lifestyle, *see* Mary Grigsby, Buying Time and Getting by: The Voluntary Simplicity Movement (St. U. of N.Y. 2004); Juliet B. Schor, The Overspent American: Why We Want What We Don't Need (Basic Books 1999); Thomas Princen, et. al., Confronting Consumption (MIT Press 2002); Sharon Astyk, Depletion and Abundance: Life on the New Home Front (New Soc'y Publ's 2008).

26 For quoted sources, *see* Aldo Leopold, A Sand County Almanac: With Essays on Conservation from Round River 237–63 (1986); Nahasdzáán dóó Yádiłhił Bitsąą dęę Beenahaz'áanii – Diné *Natural Law,* 1 N.N.C. § 205 (2002) (Navajo law), http://www.navajocourts.org/dine.htm; Gottlieb, *supra* note 13, at 42. For additional native expression, *see Members Projects: The Grandmothers' Circle,* http://www.wova-archive.org/mia/projects/kovelman.html.

27 For quoted and referenced sources, *see* Clare Kendall, *A New Law of Nature,* The Guardian (Sept. 24, 2008); Maude Barlow, *We Are Facing the Greatest Threat to Humanity: Only Fundamental Change Can Save Us,* The AlterNet (Oct. 15, 2010); Mari Margil, et. al., *Does Nature Have Rights? Transforming Grassroots Organizing to Protect People and the Planet* (2010) (discussing U.S. Rights of Nature initiatives), http://www.celdf.org/downloads/RightsofNatureReportWebENG%20DEC%202010.pdf; U.N. Gen. Assembly, World Charter for Nature (Oct. 28. 1982).

28 Sierra Club v. Morton, 405 U.S. 727, 742–43 (1972) (Douglas J., dissenting, citing Christopher D. Stone, Should Trees Have Standing? Law, Morality, and the Environment (3d. ed. 2010)).

29 For quoted sources, *see* Patricia Siemen, *Earth Jurisprudence: Toward Law in Nature's Balance,* 11 Barry L. Rev. 1, 2–3 (2008); Judith Koons, *Earth Jurisprudence,* 25 Pace Envtl. L. Rev. 263, 265, 339 (2008) (quoting Aldo Leopold, A Sand County Almanac). For additional sources

on Earth Jurisprudence, *History of CEJ*, CENTER FOR EARTH JURISPRUDENCE: MANY LAWS, ONE EARTH (2011), http://earthjuris.org/about/a-brief-history-of-cej/.

30 *See* Cormac Cullinan, *If Nature Had Rights*, ORION (Jan.–Feb. 2008); CORMAC CULLINAN, WILD LAW: A MANIFESTO FOR EARTH JUSTICE (Green Books 2003).

31 MOORE & NELSON, *supra* note 7, at xix.

32 Citizens United v. Federal Election Comm'n, 130 S. Ct. 876 (2010).

33 For a list of acronyms and their meanings, *see* Envtl. Protection Agency, *Terms & Acronyms* http://ofmpub.epa.gov/sor_internet/registry/termreg/home/overview/home.do. The acronyms stand for, respectively: Applicable or Relevant and Appropriate Requirement, Maximum Containment Level, National Emission Standard for Hazardous Air Pollutants, State Implementation Plan, Maximum Achievable Control Technology, Best Demonstrated Control Technology, and Best Available Control Technology.

34 D. Kapua'ala Sproat & Isaac H. Moriwake, chapter in CREATIVE COMMON LAW STRATEGIES FOR PROTECTING THE ENVIRONMENT 248, 280–81 (Clifford Rechtshaffen & Denise Antolini eds., Environmental Law Institute 2007). The Hawaii case is reported at *In re* Water Use Permit Application, 9 P.3d 409, 422 (Haw. 2000).

35 For quoted and referenced sources, *see* PETER G. BROWN, RESTORING THE PUBLIC TRUST: A FRESH VISION FOR PROGRESSIVE GOVERNMENT IN AMERICA 15–16, 49–50 (Beacon Press 1994); JOHN PERKINS, HOODWINKED 1 (Broadway Books 2009). For additional commentary, *see* Paul Krugman, *Conscience of a Liberal*, THE OPINION PAGES, N.Y. TIMES (Sept. 3, 2011).

36 For quoted source, *see* BROWN, *supra* note 35, at 17–18, 29, 142.

37 *Id.* at 7–12.

38 For quoted sources, *see id.* at 69; Reliance Nat. Resources Ltd. v. Reliance Indus. Ltd., C.A. No. 4273, 130–35 (India 2010) (J. B. Sudershan Reddy, majority opinion) (describing "predatory forms of capitalism" among extractive natural resource industries).

39 For quoted sources, *see* EDITH BROWN WEISS, IN FAIRNESS TO FUTURE GENERATIONS, *supra* note 14, at 45; BROWN, *supra* note 35, at 87; MOORE & NELSON, *supra* note 7, at xix ("greatest exercise"). *See also* Edith Brown Weiss, *Our Rights and Obligations to Future Generations for the Environment*, 84 AM. J. INT'L. L. 198, 200 (1990).

40 Craig Anthony Arnold, *Water Privatization Trends in the United States: Human Rights, National Security, and Public Stewardship*, 33 WM. & MARY ENVTL. L. & POL'Y REV. 785, 848–49 (2009).

41 For quoted cases, *see* Oposa v. Factoran, G.R. No. 101083 (S.C., July 30, 1993) (Phil.), *reprinted (excerpt) in* JAN G. LAITOS ET AL., NATURAL RESOURCES LAW 441–44 (Thompson West 2006); Fomento Resorts and Hotels Ltd. v. Minguel Martins (2009) 3 SCC 571 (India).

42 GOTTLIEB, *supra* note 13, at 7, 16.

43 For quoted sources, *see* GOTTLIEB, *supra* note 13, at 22, 31; SALLY G. BINGHAM, LOVE GOD, HEAL EARTH: 21 LEADING RELIGIOUS VOICES SPEAK OUT ON OUR SACRED DUTY TO PROTECT THE ENVIRONMENT at IX (St. Lynn's Press 1st ed. 2009).

44 For quoted source, *see* DAVID ORR, DOWN TO THE WIRE: CONFRONTING CLIMATE COLLAPSE 131–32 (Oxford U. Press 2009) (noting also that the "national brand of right-wing extremism is heavily infused with religious fundamentalism"). For reporting on religious leaders advocating environmental values, *see* 15 Green Religious Leaders, GRIST (July 25, 2007).

45 For quoted source, *see Amici Curiae* Memorandum in Support of Petition for Direct Review at 1, Svitak v. Wash., No. 87198–1 (Wash. 2012), http://ourchildrenstrust.org/state/Washington (follow link to June 2012 brief). For resolutions against mountaintop mining, *see* Resolutions of Faith, Presbyterian Church, 217th General Assembly, Commissioners' Resolution,

http://ilovemountains.org/resolutions. For a discussion of the Arctic protest, *see* GOTTLIEB, *supra* note 13, at 111–12.

46   For referenced sources, *see* WILSON, *supra* note 7; Jim Ball *et al.*, *An Urgent Call to Action: Scientists and Evangelicals Unite to Protect Creation* (Jan. 17, 2007), http://www.creationcare-forpastors.com/PDF_files/creationcarestatement.pdf.

47   GOTTLIEB *supra* note 13, at vii–viii, xx, 7, 11, 17.

48   For quoted sources, *see* BINGHAM, *supra* note 43, at viii; Pope Benedict XVI, *Protect Creation*, *supra* note 13 (emphasis added).

49   For quoted sources, *see* DONALD G. KAUFMAN & CECILIA M. FRANZ, BIOSPHERE 2000: PROTECTING OUR GLOBAL ENVIRONMENT 529 (3rd ed., Kendall Hunt Pub. Co. 2000) (Jewish prayer); Justice Weeramantry, *Islam, the Environment and the Human Future*, *supra* note 22. (headings omitted) (emphasis added); RICHARD C. FOLTZ ET AL., ISLAM AND ECOLOGY: A BESTOWED TRUST 127 (Center for the Study of World Religions, 2003); Hamid Mavani, Address at Islamic Cultural Center of Northern California, Temple Beth El, Berkeley, Cal. (Oct. 29, 2002) (transcript available at http://interfaithpowerandlight.org/wp-content/uploads/2010/01/sermon-dr-hamid-mavani.pdf). *See also* VINCENT J. CORNELL, VOICES OF ISLAM Vol. 1, 155 (Praeger Publ's, 2007) (describing the trust concept: "As the trustee of the natural world, human beings have certain duties and obligations"); Jim Motavalli *et al.*, *Stewards of the Earth: The Growing Religious Mission to Protect the Environment*, E MAGAZINE 24 (Oct. 31, 2002).

50   For quoted and referenced sources, *see* C. G. Weeramantry, *Buddhist Contribution to Environmental Protection*, ASIAN TRIBUNE (June 20, 2007); Dalai Lama, *An Ethical Approach to Environmental Protection* (June 5, 1986), http://www.dalailama.com/messages/environment/an-ethical-approach.

51   For referenced and quoted sources, *see* Klaus K. Klostermaier, A SURVEY OF HINDUISM 439 (St. U. of N.Y. Press, 3rd ed. 2007) (describing Gandhi's philosophy); *Judge Weeramantry Focuses on Hindu Contribution to Environment Protection*, ASIAN TRIBUNE (June 9, 2007) (abridged version of Justice Weeramantry's speech at World Future Council) (emphasis added).

13. USING EARTH'S INTEREST, NOT ITS PRINCIPAL

1   For quoted source, *see* Ben Rooney, *Drilling Ban to Cost Thousands of Jobs*, CNNMONEY.COM (June 4, 2010).

2   For quoted source, *see* Jason Brown, *Thousands Protest Drilling Moratorium at Rally*, ADVOCATE ACADIANA (July 21, 2010).

3   Naomi Klein, *Capitalism vs. The Climate*, THE NATION (Nov. 9, 2011) (stating also, "After years of recycling, carbon offsetting and light bulb changing, it is obvious that individual action will never be an adequate response to the climate crisis.").

4   L. HUNTER LOVINS & BOYD COHEN, CLIMATE CAPITALISM: CAPITALISM IN THE AGE OF CLIMATE CHANGE 5 (Hill & Wang 2011).

5   For quoted sources, *see* JULIET B. SCHOR, PLENITUDE: THE NEW ECONOMICS OF TRUE WEALTH 67–69 (Penguin Group 2010); JAMES GUSTAVE SPETH, THE BRIDGE AT THE EDGE OF THE WORLD: CAPITALISM, THE ENVIRONMENT, AND CROSSING FROM CRISIS TO SUSTAINABILITY at x (Yale U. Press 2008); BURNS H. WESTON & DAVID BOLLIER, GREEN GOVERNANCE: ECOLOGICAL SURVIVAL, HUMAN RIGHTS, AND THE LAW OF THE COMMONS 3, 23 (Cambridge U. Press 2013). For a description of natural capital, *see* Christopher L. Lant, J. B. Ruhl, & Steven E. Kraft, *The Tragedy of Ecosystem Services*, 58 BIOSCIENCE 969, 969 (Nov.

2008) ("[E]cosystems [are] a form of natural capital that yields a flow of ecosystem services per unit of time, similar to the way in which a fund of financial capital yields a flow of income or interest … [termed by some as] 'natural income.'"). The term "natural capital" was originally developed in PAUL HAWKEN ET AL., NATURAL CAPITALISM: CREATING THE NEXT INDUSTRIAL REVOLUTION 2 (Little, Brown & Co. 1999). For descriptions of resource consumption, *see* Ariel Schwartz, *In 20 Years, We Will Need a Second Earth*, FAST COMPANY (Oct. 13, 2010).

6   For quoted sources, *see* SCHOR, *supra* note 5, at 8–9; LOVINS & COHEN, *supra* note 4, at 273.

7   For quoted source, *see* SPETH, BRIDGE, *supra* note 5, at 65. For discussion of economic malaise, *see* SCHOR, *supra* note 5, at 7.

8   For quoted sources, *see* SPETH, BRIDGE, *supra* note 5, at 195; SCHOR, *supra* note 5,.

9   For quoted sources, *see* JOHN PERKINS, HOODWINKED 9 (Broadway Books 2009); SPETH, BRIDGE, *supra* note 5, at 189–90. For a discussion of conservative stereotyping of critics of capitalism, *see* Klein, *supra* note 3.

10 *Id.*

11 For quoted sources, *see* JOHN DE GRAAF & DAVID BATKER, WHAT'S THE ECONOMY FOR ANYWAY?: WHY IT'S TIME TO STOP CHASING GROWTH AND START PURSUING HAPPINESS 1 (Bloomsbury Press 2011); L. Hunter Lovins, *Reframing the Global Economy, Starting in Bhutan*, NATURAL CAPITALISM SOLUTIONS (May 15, 2012). For innovative ideas in order of mention, *see* WESTON & BOLLIER, *supra* note 5; SCHOR, *supra* note 5, at 1; LOVINS & COHEN, *supra* note 4; PETER G. BROWN & GEOFFREY GARVER, RIGHT RELATIONSHIP: BUILDING A WHOLE EARTH ECONOMY (Berrett-Koehler Publ's 2009); ROB HOPKINS, THE TRANSITION HANDBOOK: FROM OIL DEPENDENCY TO LOCAL RESILIENCE (Chelsea Green Publ'g Co. 2008); RICHARD HEINBERG, POWERDOWN: OPTIONS AND ACTIONS FOR A POST-CARBON WORLD (New Soc'y Publ's 2004); Sharon Astyk, *Imagining the Post-Industrial Economy*, ScienceBlogs Casaubon's Book (Nov. 10, 2011); DAVID C. KORTEN, THE GREAT TURNING: FROM EMPIRE TO EARTH COMMUNITY (Kumarian Press, Inc. & Berrett-Koehler Publ's, Inc. 2006); SHARON ASTYK, DEPLETION AND ABUNDANCE: LIFE ON THE NEW HOME FRONT (New Soc'y Publ's 2008).

12 For quoted sources, *see* HAWKEN ET AL., *supra* note 5, at 5; SCHOR, *supra* note 5, at 67–68.

13 For quoted sources, *see* LOVINS & COHEN, *supra* note 4, at 287–88, 277; DE GRAAF & BATKER, *supra* note 11, at 10–11; JOSEPH E. STIGLITZ ET AL., COMM'N ON THE MEASUREMENT OF ECON. PERFORMANCE & SOC. PROGRESS, *Report* 9, 12 (Sept. 14, 2009) ("steering a course"). For additional reporting, *see* *Sarkozy Adds to Calls for GDP Alternative*, WALL ST. J. (Sept. 14, 2009). As a matter of terminology, gross domestic product is roughly equivalent to gross national product. *Gross National Product – GNP*, INVESTOPEDIA.

14 For quoted and referenced sources, *see* SCHOR, *supra* note 5, at 18, 45; LOVINS & COHEN, *supra* note 4, at 277.

15 For a discussion of externalities, *see* LOVINS & COHEN, *supra* note 4, at 286.

16 For quoted source, *see* SCHOR, *supra* note 5, at 68. For a discussion of pollution costs from mining, *see* Jim Kuipers, *Putting a Price on Pollution*, MIN. POL'Y CTR. 2 (2003). For a discussion of costs from fossil fuels and climate change, *see* Matthew L. Wald, *Fossil Fuel's Hidden Cost Is in Billions, Study Says*, N.Y. TIMES (Oct. 19, 2009); Stephen Leahy, *Climate Change – US: Delay Now, Pay Dearly Later*, N. AM. INTER PRESS SERV. (Oct. 16, 2007).

17 For quoted source, *see* Geoffrey Lean, *Global Warming Approaching Point of No Return, Warns Leading Climate Expert*, INDEP. (Jan. 23, 2005) (quoting Dr. Pachauri). For referenced source, *see* HM TREASURY, *Stern Review on the Economics of Climate Change*, 2006 at vi (UK). For discussion of costs from Hurricaine Katrina, *see* SCHOR, *supra* note 5, at 15; *see also* Nina Chestney, *Many Climate Change Costs Seen Avoidable*, REUTERS (Sept. 14, 2009).

18 For quoted sources, *see* LOVINS & COHEN, *supra* note 4, at 19; SPETH, BRIDGE, *supra* note 5, at 100–02.

19 For reporting on destructive subsidies, *see* SPETH, BRIDGE, *supra* note 5, at 100 (2.5% of world's economy); SCHOR, *supra* note 5, at 75 (general discussion); LOVINS & COHEN, *supra* note 4, at 278 (fossil fuel sector subsidies, using estimates provided by the National Research Council); ENVTL. L. INST., ESTIMATING U.S. GOVERNMENT SUBSIDIES TO ENERGY SOURCES: 2002–2008 (2009) (reporting on fossil fuel and renewable energy subsidies); Teri Sforza, *Nuclear Risk "Socialized," Nuclear Profit "Privatized," Report Says*, ORANGE CNTY. REG. (Mar. 8, 2011) (nuclear subsidies); *Nuclear Power: Still Not Viable without Subsidies*, UNION OF CONCERNED SCIENTISTS (Feb. 15, 2011).

20 For quoted sources, *see* BILL MCKIBBEN, EAARTH: MAKING A LIFE ON A TOUGH NEW PLANET 65 (Times Books 2010); GRETCHEN C. DAILY, NATURE'S SERVICES: SOCIETAL DEPENDENCE ON NATURAL ECOSYSTEM 369 (Island Press 1997). For further discussion of costly but necessary infrastructure investment, *see* Klein, *supra* note 3. For a discussion of economic value of ecosystem services, *see* James Salzman, *Valuing Ecosystem Services*, 24 ECOLOGY L.Q. 887, 891 (1997) (noting the 1997 study estimating global value at $16–54 trillion a year, and comparing the figure to the global GNP of $18 trillion). For discussion of cost savings achieved through a shift to renewable energy, *see* LOVINS & COHEN, *supra* note 4, at 278; Alan Nogee *et al.*, Powerful Solutions: 7 Ways to Switch America to Renewable Electricity, UNION OF CONCERNED SCIENTISTS 7–8 (1999).

21 LOVINS & COHEN, *supra* note 4, at 150. For more on peak oil, *see* INT'L ENERGY AGENCY, WORLD ENERGY OUTLOOK 37 (2008).

22 LOVINS & COHEN, *supra* note 4, at 148, 150–151.

23 James Hansen *et al.*, *Climate Change and Trace Gases*, 365 PHIL. TRANS. R. SOC'Y 1925, 1939 (July 15 2007).

24 For referenced and quoted sources, *see* CNA, MIL. ADVISORY BD., POWERING AMERICA'S DEFENSE: ENERGY AND THE RISKS TO NATIONAL SECURITY at viii–ix, 7 (2009); CHRISTINE PARTHEMORE & JOHN NAGL, CTR. FOR A NEW AM. SECURITY (CNAS), FUELING THE FUTURE FORCE: PREPARING THE DEPARTMENT OF DEFENSE FOR A POST-PETROLEUM ERA 6 (2010). For referenced statistics on U.S. oil consumption, *see* Jonathan Fahey, *Throttling Back: Analysts Say Americans' Thirst for Gasoline is on a Long-Term Slide*, ASSOCIATED PRESS, REGISTER-GUARD B4 (Dec. 21, 2010).

25 For quoted sources, *see* THOMAS L. FRIEDMAN, HOT, FLAT, AND CROWDED: WHY WE NEED A GREEN REVOLUTION – AND HOW IT CAN RENEW AMERICA 80 (Straus & Giroux 2008). For referenced statistics, *see* CNAS REPORT, *supra* note 24, at 24–25; *see also* CNA, POWERING AMERICA'S DEFENSE, *supra*, note 24, at viii.

26 For quoted source, *see* CNA, POWERING AMERICA'S DEFENSE, *supra* note 24, at 7. For referenced source, *see* CNAS REPORT, *supra* note 24, at 6; *see also id.* at 3; ROXANA TIRON, $400 Per Gallon Gas to Drive Debate over Cost of War in Afghanistan, THE HILL (Oct. 15, 2009).

27 CNA, MIL. ADVISORY BD., NATIONAL SECURITY AND THE THREAT OF CLIMATE CHANGE 44–45 (2007). *See also* CNAS REPORT, *supra* note 24, at 8.

28 KURT M. CAMPBELL ET AL., THE AGE OF CONSEQUENCES: THE FOREIGN POLICY AND NATIONAL SECURITY IMPLICATIONS OF GLOBAL CLIMATE CHANGE 7 (Sharon Burke *et al.*, eds. 2007) (emphasis added). *See also* JOHN D. STEINBRUNER, CLIMATE AND SOCIAL STRESS: IMPLICATIONS FOR SECURITY ANALYSIS (The Nat'l Academies Press 2012).

29 For quoted and referenced sources, *see* CNA, POWERING AMERICA'S DEFENSE, *supra* note 24, at 1; CNAS REPORT, *supra* note 24, at 3–4; JAY INSLEE & BRACKEN HENDRICKS, APOLLO'S FIRE: IGNITING AMERICA'S CLEAN ENERGY ECONOMY 2–3 (Island Press 2008).

30 For referenced sources, *see* ARJUN MAKHIJANI, CARBON-FREE AND NUCLEAR-FREE: A ROADMAP FOR U.S. ENERGY POLICY 147 (RDR Books & IEER Press 2007); LESTER R. BROWN, PLAN B 4.0: MOBILIZING TO SAVE CIVILIZATION 254–55 (W.W. Norton & Co. 2009) (also

requiring reforestation and improved soil management to sequester carbon currently in the atmosphere); Todd Woody, *San Francisco Mayor Calls for City to Go 100% Renewable by 2020*, GRIST (Mar. 23, 2011); LOVINS & COHEN, *supra* note 4, at 163–66; SCHOR, *supra* note 5, at 175; INSLEE & HENDRICKS, *supra* note 29, at 17–19.

31 For quoted sources, *see* RICHARD HEINBERG, POST CARBON INST., SEARCHING FOR A MIRACLE: "NET ENERGY" LIMITS & THE FATE OF INDUSTRIAL SOCIETY 3, 7 (2009) ("no clear practical scenario"); RICHARD HEINBERG, THE PARTY'S OVER: OIL, WAR AND THE FATE OF INDUSTRIAL SOCIETIES (New Soc'y Publ's, 2003); RICHARD HEINBERG, POST CARBON INST., POST CARBON INSTITUTE MANIFESTO: THE TIME FOR CHANGE HAS COME 3 (2009) ("[W]e are living today"); Rob Hopkins, *Heinberg on "Resilient Communities: Paths for Powering Down,"* ENERGY BULL. (Mar. 31, 2008).

32 For quoted source, *see* RICHARD HEINBERG, POST CARBON INST., BEYOND THE LIMITS TO GROWTH 1 (2010). For referenced source, *see* DONELLA H. MEADOWS ET. AL., LIMITS TO GROWTH (Universe Books 1972).

33 CLIVE HAMILTON, GROWTH FETISH 3 (Pluto Press 2004).

34 For quoted sources, *see* HEINBERG, BEYOND THE LIMITS, *supra* note 32, at 1; Michael M'Gonigle, *Green Legal Theory*, ÖKOLOGISCHES WIRTSCHAFTEN 34 (Apr. 2008); James Gustave Speth, chapter in KATHLEEN DEAN MOORE & MICHAEL P. NELSON, MORAL GROUND: ETHICAL ACTION FOR A PLANET IN PERIL 8 (Trinity U. Press 2010).

35 For quoted sources, *see* DE GRAAF & BATKER, *supra* note 11, at 26; Speth, MORAL GROUND, *supra* note 34, at 7; LOVINS & COHEN, *supra* note 4, at 290–91; Nate Hagens, *Herman Daly: Towards A Steady-State Economy*, THE OIL DRUM (May 5, 2008) (quoting Herman Daly). For reference on planetary limits, *see* Johan Rockström *et al.*, *Planetary Boundaries: Exploring the Safe Operating Space for Humanity*, 14(2) ECOLOGY & SOC'Y 34 (2009).

36 SCHOR, *supra* note 5, at 168–71 (stating also, "There's not much in economic theory that actually requires growth.")

37 For quoted sources, *see* SPETH, BRIDGE, *supra* note 5, at 121; Hagens, *supra* note 35 (quoting Daly remarks, 2008). For referenced source, *see* HERMAN E. DALY, TOWARD A STEADY STATE ECONOMY (W.H. Freeman & Co. Ltd. 1973).

38 For a discussion of the measures, *see* HEINBERG, BEYOND THE LIMITS, *supra* note 32, at 3–6; SCHOR, *supra* note 5, at 16, 127, 130, 165, 175; SPETH, BRIDGE, *supra* note 5, at 120; Hagens, *supra* note 35; DE GRAAF & BATKER, *supra* note 11, at 7.

39 For referenced sources, *see* LOVINS & COHEN, *supra* note 4, at 6–8, 12–14, 284; Symposium, *Energy and the Economic Imperative: The Role of Efficiency in Creating a Robust Economy* (Apr. 26, 2010) (data on U.S. energy waste); Jonathan M. Cullen *et al.*, *Reducing Energy Demand: What are the Practical Limits?* 45 ENVTL. SCI. TECH. 1711, 1717 (2011) (data on reduced global energy demand becoming feasible through existing technology); *see also* Sarah Peach, *Current Technology Could Reduce Global Energy Demand by 85%*, CHEMICAL & ENGINEERING NEWS (Jan. 19, 2011).

40 For quoted sources, *see* SCHOR, *supra* note 5, at 87–89; WILLIAM MCDONOUGH & MICHAEL BRAUNGART, CRADLE TO CRADLE: REMAKING THE WAY WE MAKE THINGS 61–62 (North Point Press 2002). *See also* LOVINS & COHEN, *supra* note 4, at 284.

41 MCDONOUGH & BRAUNGART, *supra* note 40, at 56–58 (emphasis in the original).

42 For quoted sources, *see* MCDONOUGH & BRAUNGART, *supra* note 40, at 91, 104; LOVINS & COHEN, *supra* note 4, at 284–85. For examples and discussion of biomimicry, *see* ALEX STEFFEN, WORLD CHANGING: A USER'S GUIDE FOR THE 21st CENTURY 113 (Harry N. Abrams 2006); SCHOR, *supra* note 5, at 84–85.

43 For quoted source and discussion, *see* MCDONOUGH & BRAUNGART, *supra* note 40, at 24, 26–27, 43.

44 For quoted source, *see id.* at 60–61.

45 Photographer Christopher Jordan documents this waste in his dramatic photographic portrayal called *Running the Numbers: An American Self-Portrait*, http://www.chrisjordan.com/gallery/rtn/#about.

46 For quoted sources and discussion, *see* DE GRAAF & BATKER, *supra* note 11, at 30–33; SPETH, BRIDGE, *supra* note 5, at 156, 162. *See also* Klein, *supra* note 3 (urging an end to the "cult of shopping").

47 For quoted sources, *see* SCHOR, *supra* note 5, at 103–05 (also providing U.S. work statistics assuming a forty-hour work week); STEFANO BARTOLINI, MANIFESTO FOR HAPPINESS: SHIFTING SOCIETY FROM MONEY TO WELL-BEING 9–17 (emphasis in original).

48 SCHOR, *supra* note 5, at 101–03, 116.

49 For referenced and quoted sources, *see* DAVID C. KORTEN, AGENDA FOR A NEW ECONOMY: FROM PHANTOM WEALTH TO REAL WEALTH 141 (Berrett-Koehler Publ's 2009); ASTYK, DEPLETION AND ABUNDANCE, *supra* note 11; SHARON ASTYK & AARON NEWTON, A NATION OF FARMERS: DEFEATING THE FOOD CRISIS ON AMERICAN SOIL 10 (New Soc'y Publ's 2009); McKIBBEN, *supra* note 20, at 178–79. For a discussion of World War II domestic food production strategies, *see* David Becker, *Community Gardens Win the Food War*, FRIEND OF THE FARMER, http://friendofthefarmer.com/2011/05/community-gardens-and-food-wars/.

50 For a discussion of home provisioning (the need and the effort), *see* McKIBBEN, *supra* note 20, at 182; SCHOR, *supra* note 5, at 116. For resources on city homesteading, *see* CARLEEN MADIGAN, THE BACKYARD HOMESTEAD: PRODUCE ALL THE FOOD YOU NEED ON JUST A QUARTER ACRE! (Storey Publ'g 2009); NOVELLA CARPENTER, FARM CITY: THE EDUCATION OF AN URBAN FARMER (Penguin Books 2010); KELLY COYNE & ERIK KNUTZEN, THE URBAN HOMESTEAD: YOUR GUIDE TO SELF-SUFFICIENT LIVING IN THE HEART OF THE CITY (Process Media 2008); H.C. FLORES, FOOD NOT LAWNS: HOW TO TURN YOUR YARD INTO A GARDEN AND YOUR NEIGHBORHOOD INTO A COMMUNITY (Chelsea Green Publ'g 2006).

51 For quoted sources, *see* ASTYK, DEPLETION AND ABUNDANCE, *supra* note 11, at 18; SCHOR, *supra* note 5, at 183–84.

52 For quoted sources, *see Suggested Reading on Corporate Rights*, COMMUNITY ENVTL. LEGAL DEF. FUND 1–34 (quoting Jefferson), http://www.celdf.org/section.php?id=41; DAVID C. KORTEN, WHEN CORPORATIONS RULE THE WORLD 64 (Kumarian Press, Inc. 2001) (quoting Lincoln), as quoted in HARVEY WASSERMAN, AMERICA BORN & REBORN 89–90 (Collier Books 1983); SPETH, BRIDGE, *supra* note 5, at 165; For a discussion of corporate wrongdoing and ill effects of corporate capitalism, *see generally* KORTEN, WHEN CORPORATIONS RULE, *supra*; Klein, *supra* note 3.

53 For quoted sources, *see* AMBROSE BIERCE, THE DEVIL'S DICTIONARY, republished as AMBROSE, BIERCE, THE CYNIC'S WORD BOOK (Neale Publ'g Co. 1911); KORTEN, WHEN CORPORATIONS RULE, *supra* note 52, at 104. For a discussion of corporate protection against liability in the environmental context, *see* Hope M. Babcock, *Corporate Environmental Social Responsibility: Corporate "Greenwashing" or A Corporate Culture Game Changer?* 21 FORDHAM ENVTL. L. REV. 1 (2010).

54 For quoted sources, *see* LOVINS & COHEN, *supra* note 4, at 286; SPETH, BRIDGE, *supra* note 5, at 167–68, citing JOEL BAKAN, THE CORPORATION: THE PATHOLOGICAL PURSUIT OF PROFIT AND POWER 60–61 (Free Press 2004). For a discussion of the profit motive in the environmental context, *see* SPETH, BRIDGE, *supra* note 5, at 167. This profit maximization approach has long been thought of as a legal requirement, though more recent business law scholarship challenges that. *See* Judd F. Sneirson, *Doing Well by Doing Good: Leveraging Due Care for Better, More Socially Responsible Corporate Decisionmaking*, THE CORPORATE GOVERNANCE

L. Rev., vol 3, 438 (2007). For a position that corporate hazardous activity should be limited, _see_ Klein, _supra_ note 3 (suggesting reform to bar "outright dangerous and destructive behavior.").

55 For referenced and quoted sources, _see_ Speth, Bridge, _supra_ note 5, at 166, 170 (reporting also that there were only 7,000 multinationals in 1970; by 2007, there were at least 63,000, which collectively accounted for a quarter of gross world product); William Greider, One World, Ready or Not: The Manic Logic of Global Capitalism 12 (Simon & Schuster 1997). For information and statistics on individual corporate economies, _see_ Richard J. Barnet & John Cavanagh, Global Dreams: Imperial Corporations and the New World Order 14 (Simon & Schuster 1994); David L. Rainey, Sustainable Business Development: Inventing the Future through Strategy, Innovation, and Leadership 78 (Cambridge U. Press 2006); Michael Despines, _The Corporate Challenge_, Sustainable Thoughts (May 18, 2010); Sarah Anderson & John Cavanagh, _Top 200: The Rise of Global Corporate Power_, Global Policy Forum (2000); Vincent Trivett, _25 US Mega Corporations: Where They Rank If They Were Countries_, Business Insider (June 27, 2011).

56 For corporate advertising statistics, _see_ Am. Acad. of Pediatrics Com. on Commc's, _Children, Adolescents, and Advertising_, 118 Pediatrics No. 6 (Dec. 2006). For a discussion of corporate political agenda, _see generally_ William Greider, Who Will Tell the People : The Betrayal of American Democracy (Simon & Schuster 1992). For discussion of the corporate influence on media, _see_ Speth, Bridge, _supra_ note 5, at 168.

57 Bill McKibben, _Global Warming's Terrifying New Math_, Rolling Stone (July 19, 2012) (quoting James Hansen's statement that a 2-degree target is "a prescription for long-term disaster"). For dangers of genetic seed modification, _see_ Keith Aoki, Seed Wars: Controversies and Cases on Plant Genetic Resources and Intellectual Property 22 (Carolina Academic Press 2008).

58 For quoted sources, _see_ Perkins, _supra_ note 9, at 20–21; Speth, Bridge, _supra_ note 5, at 169; Ted Nace, Gangs of America: The Rise of Corporate Power and the Disabling of Democracy (Barrett-Koehler Publ's 2003); Greider, Who Will Tell The People, _supra_ note 56, at 331. _See also_ Korten, When Corporations Rule, _supra_ note 52, at 63–66. Speth reports corporate political action committee spending of $222 million in 2005. Speth, Bridge, _supra_ note 5, at 168–69.

59 For quoted sources, _see_ Speth, Bridge, _supra_ note 5, at 170–71 (describing "corporate globalists"); Barnet & Cavanagh, _supra_ note 55, at 14.

60 For quoted sources, _see_ Speth, Bridge, _supra_ note 5, at 171–72, _quoting_ John Cavanagh et al. Alternatives to Economic Globalization: A Better World Is Possible 18–19 (Berrett-Koehler Publ's 2002) (landmark report describing "power shift"); Korten, When Corporations Rule, _supra_ note 52, at 123; Greider, One World, _supra_ note 55, at 11. For additional discussion of predatory corporations, _see_ Perkins, _supra_ note 9.

61 For quoted sources, _see_ Korten, When Corporations Rule, _supra_ note 52, at 105; Speth, Bridge, _supra_ note 5, at 173.

62 For corporate responsibility and the triple bottom line, _see_ Lovins & Cohen, _supra_ note 4, at 9–10, 36–39. _See also_ Speth, Bridge, _supra_ note 5, at 174–78.

63 David C. Korten, The Post Corporate World: Life after Capitalism 262 (Barrett-Koehler Publ's 1999).

64 For a discussion of community action against fracking, _see_ Mari Margil, _Tackling Corporate Power, One Town at a Time_, Yes Magazine (Mar. 17, 2011). For an example of a town ordinance disallowing corporate mining activities, _see_ _Blaine Township Corporate Mining and Democratic Self-Government Ordinance_, http://www.celdf.org/article.php?id=427. For the state court ruling in New York holding that a town could ban drilling, _see_ Anschutz Exploration Corp. v. Town of Dryden, 35 Misc. 3d 450, 940 N.Y.S.2d 458 (Sup. Ct. 2012), _appeal filed_.

See also Dan Weissner, *New York Fracking Ban: Judge Rules Towns Can Prohibit Drilling*, HUFFINGTON POST (Feb. 21, 2012).

65 For quoted sources, *see* LAWRENCE FRIEDMAN, A HISTORY OF AMERICAN LAW 129–32 (3rd ed., Touchstone 2005); SPETH, BRIDGE, *supra* note 5, at 178–79. For works on revoking the corporate charter, *see* RICHARD L. GROSSMAN & FRANK T. ADAMS, TAKING CARE OF BUSINESS: CITIZENSHIP AND THE CHARTER OF INCORPORATION, preface (Charter Ink 1993); NACE, *supra* note 58, at 205 (noting that charter revocation "remains a legal option in every state"). For the history of corporations, *see* MICHAEL GROSSBERG & CHRISTOPHER L. TOMLINS, THE CAMBRIDGE HISTORY OF LAW IN AMERICA: VOLUME 1: *EARLY AMERICA* (1580–1815), 397–98 (Cambridge U. Press 2008); HERBERT HOVENKAMP, ENTERPRISE AND AMERICAN LAW: 1836–1937 56 (Harvard U. Press 1991); KERMIT L. HALL & PETER KARSTEN, THE MAGIC MIRROR: LAW IN AMERICAN HISTORY 96–97 (Oxford U. Press 2009).

66 For quoted source, *see* NACE, *supra* note 58, at 54. For a discussion of the public authority to create (and revoke) corporate charters, *see* HALL & KARSTEN, *supra* note 65, at 96. For historical restrictions on corporations, *see* NACE, *supra* note 58, at 53–55; FRIEDMAN, *supra* note 65, at 129–31; HOVENKAMP, *supra* note 65, at 57. For Supreme Court case law on corporate personhood, *see* Dartmouth College v. Woodward, 17 U.S. 518 (1819); Santa Clara v. S. Pac. R.R., 118 U.D. 394 (1886) (protecting corporations under the fourteenth amendment, as if they were natural persons).

67 For quoted and referenced sources, *see* MCKIBBEN, *New Math*, *supra* note 57 (quoting Klein, "wrecking the planet") ("rogue industry").

68 SPETH, BRIDGE, *supra* note 5, at 180.

69 For quoted sources, *see* FRIEDMAN, *supra* note 65, at 134; GREIDER, ONE WORLD, *supra* note 55, at 12, 469–70; *see also* SPETH, BRIDGE, *supra* note 5, at 180–82.

14. THE PUBLIC TRUST AND PRIVATE PROPERTY RIGHTS

1 BILL MCKIBBEN, EAARTH: MAKING A LIFE ON A TOUGH NEW PLANET 2–5, 45 (Times Books 2010).

2 *Id.* at 99 (emphasis in original).

3 *See* Michael C. Blumm, *The Public Trust Doctrine and Private Property: The Accommodation Principle*, 27 PACE ENVTL. L. REV. 649, 666 (2010).

4 Ill. Cent. R.R. Co. v. Ill., 146 U.S. 387 (1892).

5 For a discussion of neoliberal ideology and its effect on environmental policy, *see* M. Shamsul Haque, *The Fate of Sustainable Development under Neo-Liberal Regimes in Developing Countries*, 20 INT'L POL. SCI. REV. 197 (1999); MAUDE BARLOW, BLUE COVENANT: THE GLOBAL WATER CRISIS AND THE COMING BATTLE FOR THE RIGHT TO WATER (New Press 2008).

6 For quoted source, *see* JOHN LOCKE, LOCKE'S SECOND TREATISE OF CIVIL GOVERNMENT 77 (Lester DeKoster, ed., Wm. B. Eerdmans Pub. Co. 1978) (emphasis added). For a discussion of the private property bargain and government involvement, *see* ERIC T. FREYFOGLE, THE LAND WE SHARE: PRIVATE PROPERTY AND THE COMMON GOOD 206 (Island Press 2003) (noting, "At bottom, a landowner is a person who draws upon state power to protect a sphere of personal liberty in a way that curtails the liberties of everyone else."); Eric T. Freyfogle, *Goodbye to the Public-Private Divide*, 36 ENVTL. L. 7, 15 (2006) ("It is simply not the case that private rights exist apart from law ….").

7 For quoted sources, *see* JEAN-JACQUES ROUSSEAU, THE SOCIAL CONTRACT 21–22 (Oskar Piest ed., Hafner Publ'g Co. 1947); State v. Shack, 277 A.2d 369, 372 (N.J. 1971). *See also* Freyfogle,

Public-Private Divide, supra note 6, at 15 ("[P]roperty is legitimate only when the governing laws promote the common good. Property becomes illegitimate – even oppressive – when property rights allow owners to frustrate the common good.... Only secondarily is property an individual right.").

8 For quoted sources, *see* RICHARD R. POWELL & PATRICK J. ROHAN, POWELL ON REAL PROPERTY ¶ 746 (Matthew Bender, 1968); *Shack,* 277 A.2d at 373 (quoting RICHARD R. POWELL, THE LAW OF REAL PROPERTY, VOL. 5 ¶ 745 (P. Rohan rev. ed., 1970)).

9 For quoted sources, *see Shack,* 277 A.2d at 373 ("one should so use"); Nebbia v. N.Y., 291 U.S. 502, 523 (1934) ("[N]either property rights"); JOSEPH WILLIAM SINGER, PROPERTY LAW: RULES, POLICIES, AND PRACTICES at xliii (5th ed. Aspen Publishers 2010) (emphasis in original).

10 For quoted sources, *see Nebbia,* 291 U.S. at 523; SINGER, *supra* note 9, at xliii ("To give one"). For a discussion of the reciprocity of advantage in property regulation, *see* James M. McElfish, *Property Rights, Property Roots: Rediscovering the Basis for Legal Protection of the Environment,* 24 ENVTL. L. RPT. 10231, 10246 (1994); *see also* Dolan v. City of Tigard, 512 U.S. 374, 408–09 (1994); Lucas v. S.C. Coastal Council, 505 U.S. 1003, 1017–18 (1992); Penn. Cent. Transp. Co. v. City of N.Y., 438 U.S. 104, 140 (1978).

11 For quoted sources, *see* U.S. CONST. amend. V; Esplanade Prop. LLC v. City of Seattle, 307 F.3d 978, 985 (9th Cir. 2002) (emphasis added) (citation omitted); Michael C. Blumm & Lucus Ritchie, *Lucas's Unlikely Legacy: The Rise of Background Principles as Categorical Takings Defenses,* 29 HARV. ENVTL. L. REV. 321, 327 (2005). For commentary on the confusion arising from takings doctrine, *see* Rachel A. Rubin, *Taking the Courts: A Brief History of Takings Jurisprudence and the Relationship between State, Federal, and the United States Supreme Courts,* 35 HASTINGS CONST. L.Q. 897, 897 (2008). For decisions recognizing the public trust (and the closely related custom doctrine) as a defense to takings compensation claims, *see* Stevens v. City of Cannon Beach, 854 P.2d 449, 454–57 (Or. 1993) (finding that the doctrine of custom placed accessible dry sand beaches in Oregon in the public domain and encumbered privately held land, precluding takings claims for customary uses); Matthews v. Bay Head Improvement Ass'n, 471 A.2d 355, 364 (N.J. 1984) (finding no taking from public right to the use and enjoyment of submerged lands and incidental use of dry sand beaches); *Esplanade,* 307 F.3d at 984 ("the public trust doctrine burdened plaintiff's property," precluding a takings claim for shoreline development regulations).

12 ALDO LEOPOLD, A SAND COUNTY ALMANAC viii (Oxford U. Press 1989).

13 For quoted source, *see* Myrl L. Duncan, *Property as a Public Conversation, Not a Lockean Soliloquy: A Role for Intellectual and Legal History in Takings Analysis,* 26 ENVTL. L. 1095, 1137 (1996). *See also* Eric T. Freyfogle, *Property and Liberty,* 34 HARV. ENVTL. L. REV. 75, 101 (2010) (discussing the libertarian view of property rights).

14 For quoted source *see* WENDELL BERRY, BRINGING IT TO THE TABLE: ON FARMING AND FOOD 7, 34 (Counterpoint Press 2009). For a discussion of early subsistence use of land in America, *see* FREYFOGLE, THE LAND WE SHARE, *supra* note 6, at 53–55 (noting that Jefferson viewed property as a vital individual right because it could provide for subsistence living); PETER G. BROWN, RESTORING THE PUBLIC TRUST: A FRESH VISION FOR PROGRESSIVE GOVERNMENT IN AMERICA 219 (Beacon Press 1994). For a discussion of World War II subsistence use of land, *see* David Becker, *Community Gardens Win the Food Wars,* FRIEND OF THE FARMER (May 5, 2011), http://friendofthefarmer.com/2011/05/community-gardens-and-food-wars. For a discussion of modern hunger in the United States, *see* Kay Matthews, *Two Studies, Same Finding: Children in America Going Hungry,* DIGITAL J. (Nov. 17, 2009).

15 For quoted sources, *see* FREYFOGLE, THE LAND WE SHARE, *supra* note 6, at 51, 59, 62 (for general discussion of early property regulation, *see id.* at 52–63); Commonwealth v. Alger, 61 Mass. 53, 85 (1851).

16 For quoted sources, *see* LEOPOLD, SAND COUNTY ALMANAC, *supra* note 12, at 216 ("[Land] is a fountain"); *id.* at 224–25 ("A thing is right"); ALDO LEOPOLD, ROUND RIVER: FROM THE JOURNALS OF ALDO LEOPOLD 146–47 (Luna B. Leopold ed., Oxford U. Press 1953) ("If the land mechanism as a whole").

17 For quoted sources, *see* Karen E. MacDonald, *Sustaining the Environmental Rights of Children: An Exploratory Critique*, 18 FORDHAM ENVTL. L. REV. 1, 65 (2006) (quoting Native American proverb); *Letter from Thomas Jefferson to John Taylor (May 28, 1816)*, *in* SOCIAL AND POLITICAL PHILOSOPHY: READINGS FROM PLATO TO GANDHI 251, 252 (John Somerville & Ronald E. Santoni eds. Anchor Books, 1963); *Letter from Thomas Jefferson to James Madison (Sept. 6, 1789)*, *in* SOCIAL AND POLITICAL PHILOSOPHY, *supra*, at 261, 262 (internal quotation marks omitted) (emphasis in the original).

18 For quoted sources, *see* LOCKE, *supra* note 6, at 28; EDMUND BURKE, REFLECTIONS ON THE REVOLUTION IN FRANCE 192 (Penguin Books 1982). For a description of fee tail as successive life estates, *see* SINGER, supra note 9, at 513; *see also* Jeffery Evans Stake, *Evolution of Rules in a Common Law System: Differential Litigation of the Fee Tail and Other Perpetuities*, 32 FLA. ST. U. L. REV. 401, 411–12 (2005); John Davidson, *Taking Posterity Seriously: Intergenerational Justice*, VT. L. SCH.: CLIMATE LEGACY INITIATIVE (2008).

19 For quoted sources, *see* Tioga Coal Co. v. Supermarkets Gen. Corp., 546 A.2d 1, 5 (Pa. 1988) (quoting a letter written by Justice Holmes); LEOPOLD, SAND COUNTY ALMANAC, *supra* note 12, at 223–26; Rebecca Tsosie, *Tribal Environmental Policy in an Era of Self-Determination: The Role of Ethics, Economics, and Traditional Ecological Knowledge*, 21 VT. L. REV. 225, 279 (1996). For a discussion of the constitutional amendments of Ecuador and Bolivia, *see Bolivia and Ecuador Grant Equal Rights to Nature: Is "Wild Law" a Climate Solution?* NATION OF CHANGE (Nov. 21, 2011).

20 For quoted sources, *see* ALVIN M. JOSEPHY, JR., THE NEZ PERCE INDIANS AND THE OPENING OF THE NORTHWEST 435 (Yale U. Press 1997) (quoting Smohalla). For information on the United Kingdom's community land trusts, *see Community Land Trusts in a Nutshell*, NAT'L CLT NETWORK, http://www.wiltshirecommunitylandtrust.org.uk/files/27102011111013.pdf.

21 For quoted source, *see* BERRY, *supra* note 14, at 24. For additional discussion of the liberty values embodied in U.S. property rights, *see* Freyfogle, *Property and Liberty*, *supra* note 13; *id.* at 103 (discussing how eighteenth-century America's concept of liberty "chiefly meant an individual's right to acquire land for subsistence living on easy terms").

22 For various examples and discussion of CC&Rs, *see, e.g.,* DECLARATION OF COVENANTS, CONDITIONS, RESTRICTIONS AND EASEMENTS FOR MEADOW VISTA (Apr. 22 2004), http://www.meadowvistahoa.com/files/documents/ccrs.pdf; *Homeowners' Associations (HOAs) and CC&Rs*, NOLO; Claus von Zastrow, *"Last Child in the Woods:" Our Interview with Best Selling Author Richard Louv*, LEARNING FIRST ALLIANCE (Apr. 22, 2008); Patricia Salkin, *Feeding the Locavores, One Chicken at a Time: Regulating Backyard Chickens*, 34 ZONING AND PLAN. L. RPT. 1 (Mar. 2011); RICHARD LOUV, LAST CHILD IN THE WOODS: SAVING OUR CHILDREN FROM NATURE-DEFICIT DISORDER 27–29 (Algonquin Books 2005).

23 Eric T. Freyfogle, *The Construction of Ownership*, 1996 U. ILL. L. REV. 173, 175 (1996).

24 For a discussion of the libertarian frame and its rejection of duty to coming generations, *see* Freyfogle, *Property and Liberty*, *supra* note 13.

25 *See generally* LOUV, *supra* note 22.

26 Margaret Jane Radin, *Time, Possession, and Alienation*, 64 WASH. U. L.Q. 739, 748 n.26 (1986).

27 For quoted source, *see* Blumm, *Accommodation Principle*, *supra* note 3, at 653. For referenced Supreme Court case law on takings, *see* Lucas v. S.C. Coastal Council, 505 U.S. 1003, 1019 (1992) ("[W]hen the owner of real property has been called upon to sacrifice *all* economically

beneficial uses in the name of the common good, that is, to leave his property economically idle, he has suffered a taking.") (emphasis in original).

28　RALPH WALDO EMERSON, REPRESENTATIVE MEN 89 (CreateSpace 2012). For statistics on private property ownership, *see* RUBEN N. LUBOWSKI *ET AL.*, U.S. DEP'T OF AGRIC., MAJOR USES OF LAND IN THE UNITED STATES, 2002, at 35 (2006).

29　For commentary on climate refugees and forced migration, *see* Claire DeWitte, *At the Water's Edge: Legal Protections and Funding for a New Generation of Climate Change Refugees*, 16 OCEAN & COASTAL L.J. 211 (2010).

30　For quoted source, *see* ERIC T. FREYFOGLE, JUSTICE AND THE EARTH: IMAGES FOR OUR PLANETARY SURVIVAL 52 (1993); *see also* OLIVER WENDELL HOLMES, THE COMMON LAW 1 (Empire Books 2012) ("The life of the law has not been logic; it has been experience. The felt necessities of the time ... have had a good deal more to do than the syllogism in determining the rules by which men should be governed."). For scholarship urging a new focus on environmental responsibility in property ownership, *see* Craig Anthony Arnold, *The Reconstitution of Property: Property as a Web of Interests*, 26 HARV. ENVTL. L. REV. 281, 285, 333–64 (2002).

31　For quoted source, *see* Dale D. Goble, *The Property Clause: As if Biodiversity Mattered*, 75 U. COLO. L. REV. 1195, 1196 (2004).

32　For a discussion of natural infrastructure, *see* MARK A. BENEDICT & EDWARD T. MCMAHON, GREEN INFRASTRUCTURE: LINKING LANDSCAPES AND COMMUNITIES xvi (Island Press 2006).

33　For scholarship discussing the public trust's accommodation between public and private rights, *see generally* Blumm, *Accommodation Principle, supra* note 3; Duncan, *supra* note 13, at 1149–50.

34　For quoted cases, *see* Ill. Cent. R.R. Co. v. Ill., 146 U.S. 387, 453 (1892) ("The control of the state for the purposes of the trust can never be lost, except as to such parcels as are used in promoting the interests of the public therein, or can be disposed of without any substantial impairment of the public interest in the lands and waters remaining."); Lake Mich. Fed'n v. U.S. Army Corps of Eng'rs, 742 F. Supp. 441, 445, 447 (N.D. Ill. 1990); *see also In re* Water Use Permit Applications, 9 P.3d 409, 450 (Haw. 2000) [hereinafter *Waiāhole Ditch*] ("[W]hile the state water resources trust acknowledges that private use for 'economic development' may produce important public benefits and that such benefits must figure into any balancing of competing interests in water, it stops short of embracing private commercial use as a protected 'trust purpose.'").

35　*Ill. Cent. R.R. Co.*, 146 U.S. at 455, 460.

36　For quoted case, *see* State v. Central Vt. Ry. 571 A.2d 1128–30, 1135 (Vt. 1989) (CVR) (internal quotation and citation omitted) (noting ownership is "by the people in their character as sovereign in trust for public uses for which they are adapted"). The court found that the landowner, CVR, owned the lands "in fee simple impressed with the public trust doctrine." By this rationale, CVR was free to convey its land to any party so long as the land continues to be used for a public purpose. *See also* U.S. v. 1.58 Acres of Land, 523 F. Supp. 120, 123 (D. Mass. 1981) (noting, with respect to tidelands, "Though private ownership was permitted in the Dark Ages, neither Roman Law nor the English common law as it developed after the signing of the Magna Charta would permit it."). For commentary on CVR, *see* Blumm, *Accommodation Principle, supra* note 3, at 662.

37　For quoted case, *see* Boston Waterfront Dev. Corp. v. Commonwealth, 393 N.E.2d 356, 367 (Mass. 1979) (concluding that the wharf grants did not convey fee simple absolute title to the soil). For a discussion of *Boston Waterfront*, *see* Blumm, *Accommodation Principle, supra* note 3, at 662.

38　For quoted case, *see* CVR, 571 A.2d at 1132 (quoting Nat'l Audubon Soc'y v. Sup. Ct. of Alpine Cnty. 658 P.2d 709, 721 (Cal. 1983) (*Mono Lake*)). For referenced source, *see* Duncan, *supra* note 13, at 1136.

39 For quoted cases, *see* Az. Ctr. for Law in Public Interest v. Hassell, 837 P.2d 158, 171 (Ariz. Ct. App. 1991) ("slept on public rights"); CVR, 571 A.2d at 1136 (quoting *Mono Lake,* 658 P.2d at 723).

40 For quoted cases, *see* CVR, 571 A.2d at 1130 (quoting *1.58 Acres,* 523 F. Supp. at 122); *Boston Waterfront,* 393 N.E.2d at 367 (also describing "the public's property interest in shore property as "sui generis"); *Ill. Cent. R.R. Co.,* 146 U.S. at 454 (emphasis added) (stating also that title to Lake Michigan's lakebed "is a title different in character from that which the state holds in lands intended for sale.... [The lakebed] is a title held in trust for the people of the state." *Id.* at 452.).

41 Michael C. Blumm, *The Public Trust Doctrine – A Twenty-First Century Concept,* 16 HASTINGS W.-N.W. J. ENV. L. & POL'Y 105 (2010).

42 For quoted sources, *see* Craig Anthony Arnold, *Water Privatization Trends in the United States: Human Rights, National Security, and Public Stewardship,* 33 WM. & MARY ENVTL. L. & POL'Y REV. 785, 811 (2009). *See also* Maude Barlow & Tony Clarke, *Who Owns the Water?* THE NATION (Sept. 2, 2002). For reporting on prolonged drought, *see* Susannah Jacob, *A Small Town, Almost Waterless, Takes a Big Gamble,* N.Y. TIMES (Nov. 12, 2011). For reporting on South Africa water policy, *see* Netherlands Water Network, *The Water Sector in South Africa* (noting that, despite reform, privatization still results in cut-off of supplies to millions), http://www.waternetwork.co.za/water-sectors/sa-water-situation.html. For reporting on Alaska water appropriation from Blue Lake, *see* Lisa Song, *U.S. Company Plans to Ship Fresh Water from Alaska to India,* GUARDIAN ENVIRONMENT NETWORK (Sept. 6, 2010). For additional analysis of water privatization, *see* MAUDE BARLOW, BLUE COVENANT, *supra* note 5, at 164.

43 For quoted and referenced cases, *see Ill. Cent. R.R. Co.,* 146 U.S. at 453; Arnold v. Mundy, 6 N.J.L. 1, 71 (N.J. 1821); *Mono Lake,* 658 P.2d 709; *Waiāhole Ditch,* 9 P.3d at 447 (stating, "Water is no less an essential 'usufruct of lands' when found below, rather than above, the ground."). For referenced source, *see* BARLOW, *supra* note 5, at 164. For a discussion of South African water law, *see* David Takacs, *The Public Trust Doctrine, Environmental Human Rights, and the Future of Private Property,* 16 N.Y.U. ENVTL. L.J. 711, 743 (2008). Kenya's 2010 Constitution classifies as public "all rivers, lakes and other water bodies as defined by an Act of Parliament." CONSTITUTION, ch. 5, art. 62(1)(i)(2010) (Kenya). For treatment of water access as an essential human right, *see* Takacs, *supra,* at 728.

44 For quoted and referenced cases, *see Mono Lake,* 658 P.2d at 723, 728 (emphasis added); *Waiāhole Ditch,* 9 P.3d at 450. *See also* Kootenai Envtl. Alliance, Inc. v. Panhandle Yacht Club, Inc., 671 P.2d 1085, 1094 (Idaho 1983).

45 Keith Aoki, *Food Forethought: Intergenerational Equity and Global Food Supply – Past, Present, and Future,* 2011 WIS. L. REV. 399, 404, 422–23 (2011).

46 For a discussion of seed patents, *see* VANDANA SHIVA, EARTH DEMOCRACY: JUSTICE, SUSTAINABILITY, AND PEACE 149 (South End Press 2005); Aoki, *supra* note 45, at 430; Philip Howard, *Visualizing Consolidation in the Global Food Seed Industry: 1996–2008,* 1 SUSTAINABILITY 1266, 1268 (2009) (explaining that patents prohibit saving seeds and because it may not be economical and/or possible to enforce patents in certain areas, companies are developing transgenic seed incapable of self-reproducing using genetic use restriction technology - or, as some refer to it, Terminator Technology). *See also* Order Granting Def.'s Mot. to Dismiss, Organic Seed Growers & Trade Ass'n v. Monsanto Co., No. 11-cv-2163-NRB (S.D.N.Y. Feb. 24, 2012)(OSGATA) (explaining that the limited-use licenses required to use Monsanto's transgenic seeds authorize growers to use the seed only to grow a single crop).

47 For a discussion of the market share breakdown and the effect of seed concentration in corporate hands, *see* Howard, *supra* note 46, at 1270, 1266–67. For Monsanto's alleged share of the

seed market, *see* First Amended Complaint at 35, *OSGATA*, No. 11-cv-2163-NRB (June 1, 2011); *accord* Brief for Appellants at 25, *OSGATA*, No. 11-cv-2163-NRB (July 5, 2012) (Monsanto did not dispute the "over 85–90%" statistic).

48 For conclusions on pollen drift, *see* Order Granting Def.'s Mot. to Dismiss at 4, *OSGATA*, No. 11-cv-2163-NRB (Feb. 24, 2012) ("[S]ome unlicensed – and unintended – use of transgenic seeds is *inevitable*. Like any other seeds, transgenic seeds may contaminate non-transgenic crops through a variety of means....") (emphasis added). For arguments by farm organizations that transgenic seed will eventually overcome organic seed growing, *see* First Amended Complaint at 1, *OSGATA*, No. 11-cv-2163-NRB (June 1, 2011).

49 SHIVA, *supra* note 46, at 152.

50 Rights to mine are granted by the Mining Law of 1872, 30 U.S.C.A. § 22 (West 2011). For background, *see* JAN G. LAITOS ET AL., NATURAL RESOURCES LAW 288 (Thompson West 2002). For statistics on pollution from mining, *see id.* at 515.

51 For reporting on the BP spill, *see Gulf of Mexico Oil Spill (2010)*, N.Y. TIMES (Apr. 24, 2012). For reporting on the 2011 Exxon spill, *see* Dan Frosch & Janet Roberts, *Pipeline Spills Put Safeguards under Scrutiny*, N.Y. TIMES A1 (Sept. 9, 2011). For a discussion of coal mining, *see* Chapter 2. For damage from fracking, *see* David Beillo, *Hydraulic Fracturing for Natural Gas Pollutes Water Wells*, SCI. AM. (May 9, 2011). For discussion of atmospheric damage and climate disruption from fossil fuel emissions, *see* James Hansen *et al.*, *Climate Change and Trace Gases*, 365 PHIL. TRANS. R. SOC'Y 1925, 1939 (July 15 2007) (concluding that humanity "cannot release to the atmosphere all, or even most, fossil fuel CO_2" stored in the Earth; to do so "would guarantee dramatic climate change, yielding a different planet than the one on which civilization developed").

52 John Davidson, *Remarks at the University of Oregon 2012 Public Interest Environmental Law Conference*, Panel on Public Trust and Atmospheric Trust Litigation (Mar. 3, 2012).

53 *See* Blumm, *Accommodation Principle, supra* note 3, at 659.

54 For a discussion of the classic rights of property owners, *see* SINGER, *supra* note 9, at xliii.

55 For reserved right of access beneath high water mark, *see, e.g.*, Marks v. Whitney, 491 P.2d 374 (Cal. 1971). For quoted case, *see Matthews*, 471 A.2d at 365. For Oregon case law finding public access across dry sand beach, *see Stevens*, 854 P.2d at 453–54 (drawing on the ancient doctrine of custom, a close cousin of the public trust, to justify public access over all sandy beaches customarily used). For referenced article, *see* Blumm & Ritchie, *supra* note 11, at 350. Further cases recognizing public easements on ocean beaches are noted in Blumm, *Accommodation Principle, supra* note 3, at 665 n.71.

56 For quoted sources, *see* Blumm, *Accommodation Principle, supra* note 3, at 666; *Matthews*, 471 A.2d at 365. For a discussion of the traditional public trust easement below the high water mark to protect fishing, navigation, and other uses, *see* Esplanade Prop. LLC v. City of Seattle, 307 F.3d 978, 985 (9th Cir. 2002).

57 For quoted case, *see Matthews*, 471 A.2d at 365 (citation omitted); *see also id.* at 364 (population pressure); *id.* at 366 (noting the power of quasi-public organizations to exclude only when "reasonably and lawfully exercised in furtherance of the public welfare related to its public characteristics").

58 Freyfogle, *Public-Private Divide, supra* note 6, at 19 (emphasis added).

59 For cases recognizing public resource rights on private lands, *see* State v. Mallory, 83 S.W. 955, 959 (Ark. 1904) (wildlife); Schulte v. Warren, 75 N.E. 783, 786 (Ill. 1905) (same); City of Pasadena v. City of Alhambra, 207 P.2d 17, 28 (Cal. 1949) (groundwater) (internal citations omitted).

60 For a case applying substantial impairment test, *see Esplanade Prop.*, 307 F.3d at 985. For cases prohibiting fill of tidelands where it would interfere with trust purposes, *see id.*; *Marks*, 491 P.2d

374. For the importance of protecting "ordinary nature," *see* Holly Doremus, *Biodiversity and the Challenge of Saving the Ordinary*, 38 IDAHO L. REV. 325, 327 (2002).

61 For quoted case, *see* Just v. Marinette Cnty., 201 N.W.2d 761, 768 (Wis. 1972) (emphasis added). For referenced source, *see* Blumm & Ritchie, *supra* note 11, at 345 (reporting that states approving the *Just* rule include Florida, New Hampshire, South Dakota, South Carolina, Georgia, and New Jersey).

62 For quoted sources, *see* Duncan, *supra* note 13, at 1113; *Just*, 201 N.W.2d at 768.

63 Duncan, *supra* note 13, at 1113, 1130; *see also id.* at 1158–59.

64 For quoted sources, *see* William H. Rodgers, *Bringing People Back: Toward a Comprehensive Theory of Taking in Natural Resources Law*, 10 ECOLOGY L.Q. 205, 239 (1982); Ga. v. Tenn. Copper Co., 206 U.S. 230, 237 (1907); Leigh Raymond & Sally K. Fairfax, *The "Shift to Privatization" in Land Conservation: A Cautionary Essay*, 42 NAT. RESOURCES J. 599, 614 (2002).

65 For quoted sources, *see* Moore v. Phillips, 627 P.2d 831, 834 (Kan. Ct. App. 1981) ("A life tenant is considered") ("[It] is the duty"); Case Concerning the Gabčíkovo-Nagymaros Project (Hung. v. Slovk.), 1997 I.C.J. 7, 108 (Sept. 25, 1997) (separate opinion of Justice Weeramantry); Fomento Resorts & Hotels v. Minguel Martins, Civ. App. No. 4154 of 2000 (2009) (India) (stating also, "Today, every person exercising his or her right to use the air, water, or land and associated natural ecosystems has the obligation to secure for the rest of us the right to live or otherwise use that same resource or property for the long term and enjoyment by future generations."); EDWARD H. RABIN ET AL., FUNDAMENTALS OF MODERN PROPERTY LAW 256 (6th ed. Foundation Press 2011) (suggesting also that a life-tenant characterization might "prohibit current users of land and natural resources from destroying or impairing their essential character or long-term productivity").

66 For quoted sources, *see* Blumm & Ritchie, *supra* note 11, at 341–44; Lucas v. S.C. Coastal Council, 505 U.S. 1003, 1027 (1992) For commentary criticizing expansion of trust for its effect on takings doctrine, *see e.g.*, James L. Huffman, *Background Principles and the Rule of Law: Fifteen Years after Lucas*, 35 ECOLOGY L.Q.1, 12 (2008). For cases finding the trust (or custom doctrine) as a defense to regulatory takings claims, *see* Esplanade Prop. LLC v. City of Seattle, 307 F.3d 978, 984–87 (9th Cir. 2002); Matthews v. Bay Head Improvement Ass'n, 471 A.2d 355 (N.J. 1984); Stevens v. City of Cannon Beach, 854 P.2d 449, 456–57 (Or. 1993) (custom doctrine).

67 Penn. Coal Co. v. Mahon, 260 U.S. 393, 413–15 (1922) (emphasis added).

68 Blumm, *Accommodation Principle*, *supra* note 3, at 662.

69 Joseph L. Sax, *Liberating the Public Trust Doctrine from Its Historical Shackles*, 14 UC DAVIS L. REV. 185, 188–89 (1980).

70 For a call for home food production, *see* SHARON ASTYK & AARON NEWTON, A NATION OF FARMERS: DEFEATING THE FOOD CRISIS ON AMERICAN SOIL 10 (New Soc'y Publ's 2009) (calling for 100 million backyard farmers in the United States). For an endorsement of the food-not-lawn trend, *see* Mark Bittman, *Lawns Into Gardens*, N.Y. TIMES (Jan. 29, 2013). A Victory Garden movement gained support from First Lady Michelle Obama when she planted a garden on the White House South Lawn, reviving an effort by Eleanor Roosevelt, who planted the first White House victory garden. MICHELLE OBAMA, AMERICAN GROWN: THE STORY OF THE WHITE HOUSE KITCHEN GARDEN AND GARDENS ACROSS AMERICA (Crown Publ's 2012). For background on land trust movement, *see Land Trusts*, LAND TRUST ALLIANCE, http://www.landtrustalliance.org/land-trusts. For a tree-planting program in the United Kingdom (particularly in school locations) to offset carbon dioxide, *see* Carbon Footprint, UK Tree Planting, http://www.carbonfootprint.com/plantingtrees.html.

15. THE NEW WORLD: A PLANETARY TRUST

1 Amy Oliver _et al._, _Breaking News: Superstorm Sandy Finally Makes Landfall as Deadly Front Slams into East Coast with Millions Fearing the Worst_, MAIL ONLINE (Oct. 30, 2012) (quoting Gov. Malloy).

2 _See_ Stephanie Pappas, _Tipping Point? Earth Headed for Catastrophic Collapse, Researchers Warn_, YAHOO! NEWS (June 6, 2012).

3 Petition for Original Jurisdiction at 16, Barhaugh v. Mont., No. OP 11–0258 (Mont. May 4, 2011) (quoting Ansel Adams). _See also_ BURNS H. WESTON & DAVID BOLLIER, GREEN GOVERNANCE: ECOLOGICAL SURVIVAL, HUMAN RIGHTS, AND THE LAW OF THE COMMONS 262 (Cambridge U. Press 2013) ("The dysfunctionalities of existing systems of government and law cannot be denied, repressed, or finessed forever.").

4 Meinhard v. Salmon, 164 N.E. 545, 546 (N.Y. 1928) ("A trustee is held to something stricter than the morals of the market place. Not honesty alone, but the punctilio of an honor the most sensitive.") (opinion by Justice Benjamin Cardozo).

5 For commentary on failed international climate negotiations, _see Climate Change, Theatre of the Absurd_, THE ECONOMIST (Dec. 1, 2012).

6 WESTON & BOLLIER, _supra_ note 3, at 262 (stating also, "[T]he neoliberal project of ever-expanding consumption on a global scale [is a] utopian, totalistic dream.").

7 The concept of planetary patriotism was initially expressed in a speech, Mary Christina Wood, _Victory Speakers for Climate Crisis: Voicing Government's Obligation_, Feb. 17, 2008, Eugene, OR, http://law.uoregon.edu/assets/facultydocs/mwood/victoryclimate.pdf. For later essays and writings on the concept, _see Climate Patriotism_, ALEX STEFFAN, DEMOCRACY (Nov. 1, 2012), http://www.alexsteffen.com/2012/11/climate-patriotism; Robert Jensen, _The Call for Planetary Patriotism_, AL JAZEERA (Nov. 14, 2011) (interviewing historian Angus Wright), http://www.aljazeera.com/indepth/opinion/2011/11/201111410635906623.html.

8 For quoted source, _see_ Bill McKibben, _Global Warming's Terrifying New Math_, ROLLING STONE (July 19, 2012); _see also id._ (quoting James Hansen, "The target that has been talked about in international negotiations for two degrees of warming is actually a prescription for long-term disaster.").

9 For quoted source, _see_ Jane Mayer, _Taking It to the Streets_, NEW YORKER (Nov. 28, 2011) (quoting James Hansen).

10 For quoted source, _see Bill McKibben on International Climate Action Day_, GRISTV (Oct. 26, 2009), http://www.youtube.com/watch?v=p7v7HW-f6cs. For background on the October 2009 actions, _see Press Room_, 350.ORG, http://www.350.org/en/node/27; Joe Romm, _Bill McKibben's Wrap Up of the More Than 4300 (!) Demonstrations for 350 PPM Around the Planet_, THINK PROGRESS (Oct. 25, 2009) (quoting Bill McKibben's summary of reporters' conclusions). The marches supporting Atmospheric Trust Litigation, called the "iMatter Marches," were organized by the youth climate group, Kids v. Global Warming. _See_ KJ Antonia, _Kids v. the Government_, SLATE (May 5, 2011); _Kids vs. Global Warming Million Youth "iMatter" March" on Mother's Day: "Protect Planet for Our Future and Generations to Come,"_ WORLD CULTURE PICTORIAL (May 5, 2011); Joanna Zelman, _iMatter Marches Prove Younger Generation Is Ready To Fight Climate Change_, DESMOGBLOG.COM (May 19, 2011).

11 PAUL HAWKEN, BLESSED UNREST 3 (Viking 2007) (describing "coherent, organic, self-organized congregations involving tens of millions of people dedicated to change.").

12 ERIC LIU & NICK HANAUER, THE TRUE PATRIOT 41 (Sasquatch Books 2007) (stating, "Love of country cannot be a supersized version of individual narcism").

13 HAWKEN, BLESSED UNREST, _supra_ note 11, at 5.

14 For quoted source, *see* McKibben, *New Math, supra* note 8. For temperature consequences in major U.S. cities from projected BAU heating, see Deborah Zabarenko, *Climate Change, Labor Capacity Losses Examined by Government Scientists*, REUTERS (Feb. 24, 2013).

15 For referenced source, *see* LESTER BROWN, PLAN B 3.0: MOBILIZING TO SAVE CIVILIZATION 279–80 (W.W. Norton & Co. 2008); *see also* DORIS KEARNS GOODWIN, NO ORDINARY TIME: FRANKLIN AND ELEANOR ROOSEVELT: THE HOME FRONT IN WORLD WAR II (Simon & Schuster Paperbacks 1994).

16 President Franklin D. Roosevelt, State of the Union Message to Congress, Jan. 6, 1942 (emphasis added).

17 For background on World War II Victory Speakers, *see An Arsenal of Words: Victory Speakers Spread the Word*, LIFE ON THE HOME FRONT, http://arcweb.sos.state.or.us/pages/exhibits/ww2/life/speak.htm.

18 For quoted source, *see* David Roberts, *Severe Weather Can Change Minds–Some Minds, Anyway*, GRIST (Dec. 6, 2012) (emphasis in original) (stating also, "No amount of [climate] evidence, no clever slogan or term, can substitute for trust…. [T]he mushy middle *can* be moved by severe weather and the like – but not just anyone can move them.").

19 For quoted source, *see* Abraham Lincoln, *In the First Debate with Douglas*, Aug. 21, 1858, *in* THE WORLD'S FAMOUS ORATIONS (William Jennings Bryan ed., Bartleby.com 2003).

20 For quoted source, *see* Francis Fox Piven, *Occupy's Protest Is Not Over. It Has Barely Begun*, THE GUARDIAN (Sept. 17, 2012).

21 DENNIS DALTON, MAHATMA GANDHI: NONVIOLENT POWER IN ACTION 91–138 (Columbia U. Press 1993).

22 For quoted sources, *see* Piven, *supra* note 20; WESTON & BOLLIER, *supra* note 3, at 21 (emphasis in original). For reporting on the Keystone Pipeline demonstration, see Suzanne Goldenberg, *Keystone XL Protestors Pressure Obama on Climate Change Promise*, The Guardian (Feb. 17, 2013).

23 For discussion of ideas spreading virally, *see* Greg Craven, *My Vision*, http://www.gregcraven.org/index.php?option=com_content&view=article&id=13&Itemid=3&lang=en. For his book, *see* GREG CRAVEN, WHAT'S THE WORST THAT COULD HAPPEN? (Perigee Trade, 2009). The author is well-known for a climate YouTube video, *The Most Terrifying Video You Will Ever See*, describing a rational decision-making process in response to climate risk scenarios. The video went viral with 10.5 million views.

24 For poster images, *see* UNIFYING A NATION: WORLD WAR II POSTERS FROM THE NEW HAMPSHIRE STATE LIBRARY, http://www.nh.gov/nhsl/ww2/ww12.html.

25 For quoted source, *see* BARBARA KINGSOLVER, ANIMAL, VEGETABLE, MIRACLE 345–46 (Harper Perennial 2008).

26 The term "powerdown" is the title of a book by RICHARD HEINBERG, POWERDOWN: OPTIONS AND ACTIONS FOR A POST-CARBON WORLD (New Society Pub. 2004).

27 For quoted source, *see* THE LOCALIZATION READER: ADAPTING TO THE COMING DOWNSHIFT at xvii (Raymond De Young & Thomas Princen eds., MIT Press 2012). For additional resources describing "transition towns" and "downshifting," *see* Raymond De Young, THE LOCALIZATION PAPERS, http://www-personal.umich.edu/~rdeyoung; ROB HOPKINS, THE TRANSITION HANDBOOK: FROM OIL DEPENDENCY TO LOCAL RESILIENCE (Chelsea Green Pub. 2008).

28 For quoted source, *see* THE 11TH HOUR, MOTION PICTURE (Warner Brothers 2007).

29 For quoted source, *see* HOPKINS, *supra* note 27, at 69, 73.

30 For quoted sources, *see* Raymond De Young, *Definition*, THE LOCALIZATION PAPERS, *supra* note 27 ("widely distributed"); ERIC LIU & NICK HANAUER, THE GARDENS OF DEMOCRACY 6 (Sasquatch Books 2011).

31 TERRY TEMPEST WILLIAMS, RED: PASSION AND PATIENCE IN THE DESERT 229 (Vintage 2002).

32 For quoted source, see Malcolm GLADWELL, THE TIPPING POINT 7, 9 (LITTLE, BROWN & CO. 2000).

33 For quoted sources, *see id.* at 7, 30–32; Craven, *My Vision, supra* note 23.

34 For quoted source, *see* GLADWELL, *supra* note 32, at 11, 14, 19, 21, 259.

35 For quoted source, *see* Paul Hawken, *Commencement: Healing or Stealing?* Commencement Address, University of Portland (May 3, 2009), http://www.up.edu/commencement/default.aspx?cid=9456.

Index